MAO'S REVOLUTION AND THE
CHINESE POLITICAL CULTURE

MICHIGAN STUDIES ON CHINA

*Published for the Center for Chinese Studies
of the University of Michigan*

MICHIGAN STUDIES ON CHINA

THE RESEARCH ON WHICH THIS BOOK IS BASED WAS
SUPPORTED BY THE CENTER FOR CHINESE STUDIES
AT THE UNIVERSITY OF MICHIGAN.

MAO'S REVOLUTION
AND THE CHINESE
POLITICAL CULTURE

RICHARD H. SOLOMON

UNIVERSITY OF CALIFORNIA PRESS

BERKELEY, LOS ANGELES, LONDON

UNIVERSITY OF CALIFORNIA PRESS
BERKELEY AND LOS ANGELES, CALIFORNIA
UNIVERSITY OF CALIFORNIA PRESS, LTD.
LONDON, ENGLAND
Copyright © 1971 by
The Center for Chinese Studies
University of Michigan
First Paperback Edition 1972
Second Printing, 1974
ISBN: 0–520–02250–5
Library of Congress Catalog Card Number: 76–129606
Printed in the United States of America

FOR CAROL

Contents

PART III:
The Maoist Political Revolution

Preface

Over the centuries of Western contact with China there seem to have been as many "Chinas" in foreign eyes 'as there have been diverse motives for involvement in this universally intriguing society. Merchant and missionary, soldier and educator each filtered the reality of China and her people through the biases of his own cultural background, personal and professional interests, and the exigencies of the age in which he lived.

The present study of China and her twentieth century revolution was initiated in the hope that through the techniques of social science analysis—interviews using controlled sampling procedures and structured questioning, psychological projective tests, content analysis of published documents, and interpretation of data on the basis of social theory—it would be possible to come to some understanding of the Chinese revolution on Chinese terms. However, given the facts that China has not been open to direct observation, and that she has presented a constantly changing face to the foreign world over the past two decades, this has been no easy task.

The research and writing of this study consumed most of the decade of the 1960s, a time when China was undergoing domestic economic crisis and political upheaval. The resources and institutions which sustained the inquiry, however, were products of the threatening Cold War era of the 1950s for the United States. Throughout the years of this enterprise there has been an ever-present contrast between early assumptions and an evolving Chinese reality which has made it difficult to be assured that one's preconceptions were correct. This constant challenge has sustained the sense of relevance of a search for a core of meaning in the kaleidoscope of China's continuing social and political revolution.

When I began formal academic training in political science and Chinese area and language studies, in the late 1950s, the People's Republic was in the most heady days of the first decade of Party rule. The nation appeared to be cast in the Soviet mold: aggressive, totalitarian, and rapidly transforming itself into a major security problem for the United States. These were years when foreign observers asked themselves nervously whether the Chinese Communist leadership just might bring about a "Great Leap Forward" in economic development, and rapidly industrialize their agrarian society through the massed application of peasant labor power. And but for a few veiled indications of Sino-Soviet tension, visible only to specialists in propaganda analysis, the People's Republic of China appeared to be a durable member of the Soviet-dominated "Socialist Camp."

By the end of the 1960s, barely a decade later, there could not have been a more drastic change in China's image abroad. The Great Leap had generated an economic crisis which took half the decade to repair; and the once monolithic Chinese Communist Party appeared decimated by a premature succession crisis precipitated by conflict over the policies of aging Party Chairman Mao Tse-tung. In addition, the Sino-Soviet alliance seemed irreparably shattered, with the two giants of the Communist world squared off in a hostile confrontation that approached open warfare during 1969.

As China enters the 1970s, our subject appears to be going through yet another incarnation. A country which only two or three years ago seemed to be virtually in a state of civil war is apparently pulling itself together and rebuilding an authoritarian political order. The economic scars of the Cultural Revolution appear to be minimal. And a state which had totally isolated itself from the international community (China recalled all but one of its ambassadors during the Cultural Revolution) is now reasserting itself with an added confidence drawn from hydrogen weapons and a ballistic missile capability. Furthermore, China's claim to be the beacon of world revolution finds surprisingly strong echoes in political turmoil on university campuses around the world, where Chairman Mao is a symbolic leader for the most alienated of a generation of political activists.

In this study we have drawn upon three analytical approaches which provide a certain stability of perspective on our constantly changing subject. The basic assumption is that China's political gyrations reflect the process of nation-building, embodying social, economic, and political facets. It is assumed that in the transformation of a peasant society into an industrializing nation-state, China's political leadership will have to confront certain universal developmental problems. The most fundamental is the process of expanding popular political participation. In China's case, the peasantry, long passive in matters of politics, must be brought into active involvement with the many problems of social and economic modernization.

A second analytical assumption, which follows from this first problem, is that these new entrants into the political process will bring with them personal traits and a cultural inheritance from the prerevolutionary era. Popular attitudes, behavioral patterns, and emotional concerns which affect society's "political culture" will be carried over from the old society into the era of revolution, and will hinder efforts to promote social change.

In China's case, the adults active in political affairs during the first two decades of Communist Party rule were educated in a time when social change had not penetrated very deeply into the educational processes of the society. Many Party leaders were schooled before the fall of the Ch'ing Dynasty in 1911. Hence as the "revolutionary vanguard" seeks to promote a new mass culture in "proletarian" values and work styles, its efforts, to some degree, will be in conflict with the traditional cultural inheritance of the adult population. The political style of the revolutionary elite itself will show the influence of the prerevolutionary culture.

As this study progressed, it became apparent that some of the most intriguing aspects of Communist rule in China relate to the endurance of the traditional culture in the revolutionary era. As is elaborated in the second half of the analysis, the conception of the leadership process of Party Chairman Mao Tse-tung embodies a complex mixture of efforts to change part of China's traditional political culture and to draw upon other elements of the tradition in order to sustain political influence. Furthermore, much of the policy conflict among Party leaders during the Cultural Revolution of the late 1960s seems to relate to how much tolerance should be given to traditions which endure in the "work-style" (*tso-feng*) of Party cadres, or how much stress should be given to Mao's "revolutionary" conceptions of political leadership.

A third set of interpretive perspectives derives from the notion of political culture. It is assumed that a basic understanding of China's political culture is to be found through analysis of the society's socialization practices, the manner in which parents educate their children and teachers instruct their students to deal with the world they will know as adults. It is further assumed that the traditional political culture can be studied by means of analysis of the socialization experiences of adults reared in the last years of the imperial era; and that one measure of change is to be found in the contrast between the learning experiences of this older generation and that of younger generations of Chinese reared under Communist Party influence.

The enduring revolutionization of a society would seem to require a congruence between altered forms of social organization and the socialization experiences of those who live and work in the new society. If organizational changes are not supported by successful efforts to educate new values and patterns of behavior into the new leadership, tension will result. Efforts to reduce the conflict between personal need and organizational form will be resolved in favor of the individual's preferences. Again, as we shall stress later, research seemed to bear out this assumption about the critical importance of educational experiences in institutionalizing the revolution. Some of the most distinctive aspects of Chinese Communist political practice, the "thought reform" technique and "criticism–self-criticism" meetings, were designed to exert continuing pressure against the resurgence of traditional behavioral forms among Party cadres reared before "Liberation."

While these three analytical perspectives helped to provide certain foci for research activities and data interpretation, our initial interest was in trying to understand how Chinese themselves viewed their country's social and political revolution. Hence four years of formal study of Chinese political history, society, and language served as the basis for an interview project with members of three generations of adult Chinese. By means of these conversations, I sought to explore perceptions of their country's continuing revolution, their attitudes toward politics, and the learning experiences which underlay their social and political attitudes. This interview project is described in detail in the introductory chapter. Altogether more than ninety individuals participated, and the records revealed in rich detail attitudes and personal experiences which had found only limited expression in earlier classroom and social contacts.

As the interviewing proceeded, it became increasingly evident that the attitudes and experiences we were exploring had considerable inner coherence. They appeared to be integrated around several basic cultural assumptions concerning the nature of the individual, interpersonal relations, and the relation of the individual to society. The first two parts of this study explore this structured set of social attitudes—what we term the "dependency social orientation"— and the learning process by which it was inculcated in the generations of Chinese interviewed.

After completion of a major part of the project, I began to analyze a variety of published Chinese political materials. Some derived from the Confucian tradition, some were from the Nationalist period, but the majority were newspaper materials and documents of the Communist era. Particular emphasis was given to study of the leadership process of Communist Party Chairman Mao Tse-tung.

Two things became apparent in this documentary analysis. The social and political orientation of the Chinese we had interviewed very strongly reflected the values of the Confucian tradition—even where the individual had not been formally schooled in classical Confucian literature. Secondly, and of greater interest for the development of this study, it was found that Mao's conception of political leadership combined a complex reaction against many traditional values even as it drew upon those behavioral patterns and emotional concerns which he deemed essential in gaining popular support. The third part of the study explores this interrelationship between the traditional political culture and Mao's conception of leadership as it evolved over the years of struggle for power.

A first draft of this analysis was completed in the spring of 1966. At that time it was uncertain just how useful it would be to carry the study into areas of policy development in the years after the Party had come to power. The period of public criticism of the Party which followed the Hungarian upheaval of 1956, the so-called "Hundred Flowers Campaign," seemed to bear many marks of Mao's style of leadership, as did the "Great Leap Forward" of 1958–1960, a program for rapid economic development. Yet to the outside observer, the Party Chairman's influence on policy during nearly two decades of Party rule appeared to be but one element in a context of collective leadership.

This view of a basic consensus among the "Long March" generation of Party leaders, widely held among foreign observers of China, was shattered in the second half of 1966 by what Mao and his supporters termed a "Great Proletarian Cultural Revolution." Bitter differences among Party leaders, previously unimagined by most foreign observers, were brought into sharp focus by this crisis within the Party leadership over policy and personal political influence. The next three years of domestic political turmoil also saw the publication, primarily in China's "Red Guard" press, of previously secret documentary materials and speeches by high Party officials. This information added greatly to our understanding of policy disputes within the Party leadership and of the manner in which Mao Tse-tung sought to influence the course of China's social revolution.

It is rare in political science analysis to be able to conduct controlled experiments in which hypotheses about the leadership style of one man, or the inner dynamic of a political system, can be tested through the actual workings of the political process. In a completely fortuitous manner, the Cultural Revolution turned out to be just such a test of the interpretation of Mao's leadership style and its relation to aspects of China's political culture which we had drawn on the eve of the Cultural Revolution. Interviews with emigrés, reinterpretation of the field observations of earlier generations of anthropologists or sociologists, and analysis of published political documents, are but crude tools in the indirect study of a society and its politics. Hence we have relied heavily on documentary disclosures of the Cultural Revolution to substantiate interpretations developed earlier on the basis of limited and indirect information.

We had made certain inferences about the personality and style of Mao Tse-tung through analysis of highly selected and edited speeches and documentation of the pre-Liberation era. Publication of his previously unpublished speeches of the 1950s and 1960s delivered behind the closed doors of Party leadership conferences reveal in this man's direct and earthy language that many inferences had been correct. Furthermore, the details of a decade of increasingly serious dispute between Mao and other Party leaders over questions of national policy which were revealed during the Cultural Revolution make quite evident the manner in which Mao has projected his personal political style into policy formulations.

In both the form which the Cultural Revolution struggle took and the content of polemical attacks on various Party leaders, the events of the late 1960s help to confirm one of the basic assumptions behind this study: that of the endurance of the traditional culture in the revolutionary era as an impediment to efforts to promote rapid social change. Mao himself evidently saw the revolution as vulnerable to the resurgence of traditional patterns of behavior and social values as they endured in the personalities of the Chinese "masses" and individual Party leaders.

In what seems likely to be the last great political battle of his career, Mao appears determined to preserve his influence on the course of China's revolution by removing from power leaders opposed to his policies, and by attempting to institutionalize his "thought" in new organizations of political power. And he is looking for support mainly from a younger generation he hopes will grow to political maturity during the protracted conflict to preserve the momentum of social change.

The final section of this book, based on a year of documentary analysis and interviewing in Hong Kong in 1969, is an effort to detail Mao's attempt to institutionalize his impact on the Chinese revolution in the years after Liberation, against increasing resistance from other Party leaders.

In preparing this study for publication we became painfully aware of the length to which the presentation had grown. Earlier inclinations to publish the first three parts separately had been resisted largely because of our desire to explore in greater detail the relationship between Mao's personality and China's political life, and we were aware that the whole story had not been told. The Cultural Revolution enabled us to detail Mao's impact on the Chinese revolution, but the documentation which became available after 1966 has added considerable length to the study. We have decided to present the analysis in its current form despite its length for two reasons: First, the four parts comprise an integrated interpretation in which the first three parts establish the premises for Part Four. Second, the detailed political analysis in Part Four has not been developed by other authors thus far using Cultural Revolution documentation. Indeed, the detailed documentation throughout is presented in the spirit of drawing together important source material. Our basic concern, however, has been to provide firm evidence on the relationship between personality and politics.

Given the length of this study, we assume that many readers will have to approach the book selectively. Thus certain interpretive themes are repeated throughout the four parts of the analysis on the assumption that a limited amount of redundancy will assist the reader who does not have the time to follow the study through from beginning to end.

Acknowledgments

The errors and shortcomings of this study must be my personal responsibility. The research and analysis which preceded the writing, however, represent a collective effort, and I would be remiss if I did not indicate my indebtedness to the many colleagues and friends who provided assistance and insight.

I wish to express a particularly deep sense of gratitude to Professor Lucian W. Pye of the Massachusetts Institute of Technology, who first encouraged me to undertake the study of Chinese society and politics. He provided much of the intellectual stimulation behind this study; and his judicious combination of guidance and toleration of my research instincts enabled me to handle the data on their own terms. The interpretations developed here, however, rely heavily on his insights into the workings of China's political culture, as elaborated in his recent study, *The Spirit of Chinese Politics*.

Professor Alexander Eckstein gave much encouragement in his dual roles as friend and Director of the Center for Chinese Studies at the University of Michigan. Dr. Tsung-yi Lin, former Director of the Taipei Children's Mental Health Center and now Professor of Psychiatry at the University of Michigan, and his wife, Mei-chen, a social worker, both contributed substantially to the advancement of this project. They made research facilities and personnel available and then provided interpretive insights which reflect their years of professional experience.

Professor David C. McClelland of Harvard University gave particularly valuable guidance in the use and interpretation of the psychological projective tests employed during the interviews.

Several pages could be filled with the names of Chinese friends and colleagues in Taiwan, Hong Kong, and the United States who in numerous ways contributed to this study and to my understanding of their society, its customs, and the revolution. I particularly wish to express my gratitude to those who assisted in the period of field research. Chen Yüeh-hsiu, Ko Chü-yi, and Lin A-mei proved to be skillful interviewers. Wei Ju-lin and Chou Mei-jung assisted with transcription of interview records and data coding. Dr. Ko Yung-ho gave generously of his time and talents in training the interviewers in the administration of the psychological tests, and in developing coding procedures and interpretations.

Additional assistance in documentary research and data processing was provided by a number of my students. Jan Berris scoured the literature for independent observations of Chinese social life and customs and assisted in administering the research procedure used here to a sample of American students as a check on our interpretations. Ronald Suleski prepared the biographical sketches contained in Appendix V from the Chinese interview records. Mary Coombs and John Deegan worked on quantitative data preparation and processing, and Joan Lustbader, Lawrence Sullivan, and Catherine Winston provided additional assistance in documentary research.

As this study progressed I received valuable criticism and suggestions from numerous colleagues and teachers. Howard Rosenthal gave generously of his time and skills in matters of data processing and interpretation, as did Sam Popkin. I also wish to acknowledge help and criticism received from A. Doak Barnett, Parris Chang, Chang Chun-shu, Chu-yuan Cheng, Dr. Chien Ching-piao, Albert Feuerwerker, Edward Friedman, John Gittings, William E. Griffith, Melvin Gurtov, Charles Hucker, Talbott Huey, Dr. Hsu Chen-chin, Harold Isaacs, Ellis Joffe, Chalmers Johnson, Lau Yee-fui, Nathan Leites, Stanley Lubman, Roderick MacFarquhar, Donald J. Munro, Ithiel deSola Pool, Stuart Schram, Franz Schurmann, Richard Sorich, Tsao Pei-lung, Ezra Vogel, Wan Wei-ying, Allen S. Whiting, Col. William Whitson, Richard W. Wilson, the late Mary C. Wright, and Dr. Yeh Eng-kung.

Mrs. Janet Eckstein and Dr. Elizabeth K. Bauer did yeoman service in the final editing of the manuscript. And Mrs. Jacqueline Evans provided important assistance in her role as Executive Secretary of the University of Michigan Center for Chinese Studies.

Financial support for this study was provided by a number of institutions. The Foreign Area Fellowship Program supported a year of language and area studies, and the initial two-year period of field research. The Center for International Studies at M.I.T. assisted in the development of the TAT test materials. The Center for Chinese Studies at the University of Michigan supported a variety of research costs, and made it possible for me to take additional leave from teaching responsibilities in order to complete research and writing. A final year of research in Hong Kong was supported in part by grants from the Joint Committee on Contemporary China of the Social Science Research Council, and the National Science Foundation. The views and interpretations developed in this study, however, should not be attributed to any of these supporting institutions.

I also wish to express my thanks to the staff of the Universities Service Center of Hong Kong for providing research facilities and assistance, and two years of collegial atmosphere.

Finally, I wish to express filial gratitude to my own clan: to Harold and Alice Harris, and Ellen Solomon, for having generously supported so many years of study; and to my wife Carol, who in her capacities as teacher and social worker made possible many of the personal relationships which contributed so much to this study. Hopefully her forebearance during the years of research and writing has been rewarded by the many joys associated with this attempt to understand another people and their culture.

R.H.S.

Ann Arbor, Michigan
Summer, 1970

For many years we Communists have struggled for a cultural revolution as well as for a political and economic revolution, and our aim is to build a new society and a new state for the Chinese nation. That new society and new state will have not only a new politics and a new economy but a new culture.

MAO TSE-TUNG,
"On New Democracy" (1940)

The fact is, now we see that a revolution cannot change a nation—its tendencies and qualities and traits. . . . Only the form of power and of property [can be changed] but not the nation itself.

MILOVAN DJILAS (1968)*

* From "An Interview with Milovan Djilas," *The New York Times* (November 27, 1968), p. 10.

Worker striding past statue of Confucius
on the road to the Ming Tombs, suburbs of Peking.
René Burri, from Magnum.

Chapter 1

INTRODUCTION

This is a study of one of the twentieth century's most influential political leaders in his personal struggle to adapt the weighty cultural inheritance of a quarter of mankind to the political and economic challenges of a new era.

The career of Mao Tse-tung, from his early years as a student revolutionary in Hunan Province to his rise to leadership of the Chinese Communist Party and, after 1949, Chairmanship of the People's Republic, has been intimately related to the efforts of the Chinese people to transform their ancient society into a modern nation. This book explores Mao's gradual development of a new style of politics and social organization over three decades of power-conflict, followed by the struggle to institutionalize his concepts in post-Liberation China.

Most previous studies of China's efforts to enter the modern world have focused on the evolution of the country's historical institutions, on the ferment of new ideas and social values in a society which for thousands of years has had a highly developed intellectual tradition, and on efforts to transform a peasant society into an industrializing nation-state. Here we explore a different aspect of the story. It is our basic assumption that China's difficulties in responding to the changing world of the past century have been largely cultural and psychological in quality rather than institutional or economic. Mao Tse-tung began his political career in the period of cultural challenge of the late 1910s and early 1920s known as the "May Fourth" era. He is concluding his career with a "Great Proletarian Cultural Revolution," an astounding effort which began in the mid-1960s to confront once again what he and his Red Guard supporters called China's "four olds"—her traditional customs, habits, culture, and social thought.

Thus there is an important tension between Mao Tse-tung's personal conception of how China's political and social life should be, organized in the country's search for new greatness, and the endurance of old social attitudes and political habits of millions of Chinese who embody the legacy of China's past.

1

BASIC ISSUES IN CHINA'S POLITICAL CULTURE:
AMBIVALENCE TOWARD AUTHORITY AND
AVOIDANCE OF CONFLICT

The analytical perspective adopted in this study is exploration of
those Chinese social attitudes, emotional concerns, and moral
norms which influence political behavior—what has been termed
a society's "political culture." [1] This approach is an outgrowth of
earlier research which attempted to analyze differences in "national
character."

The underlying assumptions can be stated simply: Politics fundamentally involves the actions of individuals who decide how they
will behave in any given political situation—even if the pressures
of the social context establish clearly preferable alternatives. People are taught from early in life how to evaluate and respond to
"political" situations. Basic aspects of an individual's personality
include his attitudes toward those in positions of authority, and
toward the use of power, and his feelings about how to handle the
social conflict which is of the essence of politics.

Such attitudes are acquired within the family during childhood,
are reinforced and made more explicitly "political" as the individual matures and becomes a member of adult society, and are quite
stable over time. Finally, any given individual's attitudes, emotional concerns, and values concerning political behavior are not
unique. He will share certain aspects of his personality with others
in his society, for shared attitudes, emotions, and moral norms—
culture—are essential to coordinated social action.

We began our research by trying to identify the attitudes toward
politics, authority, and social conflict which are most meaningful
to people reared in the Chinese cultural tradition. First, we had to
identify the concepts and social values which Chinese associate
most closely with politics. From students of philosophy we learned
that social "harmony" and peace have long been considered basic

1. The concept of "political culture" was first suggested by Gabriel Almond in an article, "Comparative Political Systems," *Journal of Politics,* Vol.
XVIII, No. 3 (August 1956), pp. 391–409. This was an attempt to bring
together the systems-analysis approach to political analysis with earlier work
on the study of social and cultural systems, and "national character." More
elaborate discussions of this concept will be found in: Gabriel Almond and
Sidney Verba, *The Civic Culture: Political Attitudes and Democracy in Five
Nations* (Princeton: Princeton University Press, 1963), pp. 3–76; and Lucian Pye and Sidney Verba, *Political Culture and Political Development*
(Princeton: Princeton University Press, 1965), pp. 3–26, 512–560.

and enduring political values in the Confucian tradition.[2] However, these values have contrasted with the historical reality of periods of tranquillity and social order shattered by episodes of uncompromising political conflict and unrestrained violence. Historians of Chinese society have termed this alternating pattern of peace and conflict the "dynastic cycle." [3]

The foreign observer of China is continually struck by the many ways in which the Chinese social tradition emphasizes the love of peace and interpersonal harmony as social values. China's great cities bear such names as "Southern Peace" (Nanning), "Western Tranquillity" (Sian), and "Enduring Peace" (Yenan); and the country's first great revolutionary of the twentieth century, Sun Yat-sen, stressed that commitment to "the moral quality of peace" was a "special characteristic" of the Chinese people.[4] In contrast, however, one quickly discovers that one of the most enduring symbols of Chinese political life is that of the "Warring States," an ancient period of social fragmentation and violent struggle for power. More recently we have seen the incredible destructiveness of the nineteenth century peasant insurrection known as the "Kingdom of Heavenly Peace" (T'ai-p'ing T'ien-kuo), the struggle for power of the warlords of the 1920s, and the still unresolved civil war to control a capital once named "Northern Peace" (Peiping).

One senses in this contrast between the ideal and the reality issues of great emotional concern to the Chinese about the handling of aggressive emotions and interpersonal conflict. This is hardly to say, of course, that the Chinese are in any way unique in having difficulty coming to terms with the human capacity for aggression. Rather, it suggests that through the biases of culture and personality, questions of the handling of social conflict constitute a major area of tension in the Chinese political culture.

In a similar vein, the foreign observer is struck by the determination with which Mao Tse-tung, as leader of the Chinese Communist Party, has stressed the need for "struggle" and "class conflict" in China's search for social progress even decades after the basic consolidation of state power. This concern of Mao's that his people be repeatedly prodded to "struggle for progress" or to engage in

2. See Derk Bodde, "Harmony and Conflict in Chinese Philosophy," in Arthur F. Wright, ed., *Studies in Chinese Thought* (Chicago: University of Chicago Press, 1953), pp. 19–80.

3. *See,* for example, John T. Meskill, ed., *The Pattern of Chinese History: Cycles, Development, or Stagnation?* (Boston: Heath, 1965).

4. Cited from a 1927 work by Sun in Arthur F. Wright, "Struggle Versus Harmony: Symbols of Competing Values in Modern China," *World Politics,* Vol. VI, No. 1 (October 1953), pp. 31–44.

mutual criticism of "backward thinking," seems to imply that the Chinese people might otherwise rest content with ancient social norms and avoid the unpleasantness of interpersonal competition. Hence, in designing research procedures for this study we gave particular emphasis to exploring Chinese attitudes and experiences concerning matters of social conflict.

Another area of particular note to the foreign observer is the emphasis which the Confucian tradition has laid on deference to those in authority. In politics, questions of authority obviously predominate. Chinese for centuries have stressed "filial piety" as the basis of superior-subordinate relations. One senses in this concern with orderly dealings between superior and subordinate some relation to the concern with social conflict. Perhaps in the highly articulated stress on filial obedience and deferential service to those in authority, we hypothesized, there was more than the desire of the peasant family head to attain security in old age. There might also be a fear that those in subordinate positions might completely reject authority.

As will be detailed in following chapters, our interview data substantiate the view that there is a notable degree of ambivalence toward authority in the attitudes of those reared in the Chinese tradition: a paradoxical combination of the desire for a strong leader; yet a concomitant resentment against the demands of this powerful authority on the individual.

As psychologists and sociologists have stressed, culture and personality are both systemic in quality: They are not unrelated collections of ideas, or attitudes and emotions. They are both structured around certain unifying themes or assumptions.[5] One of the objectives of this study is to identify the basic assumptions of life and interpersonal relations which are reflected in the dominant values of the Chinese tradition and which structure personal attitudes.

The American cultural perspective, of course, places strong emphasis on the importance of the individual in society, on personal responsibility, and on self-realization. The Chinese emphasis on social interrelatedness, on the basic importance of group life, and on submission of the individual to collective interests, stands out as a fundamental cultural difference.[6] As we will detail, Chinese

5. On this point, see in particular the analysis by Talcott Parsons, "Social Structure and the Development of Personality: Freud's Contribution to the Integration of Psychology and Sociology," *Psychiatry,* Vol. XXI, No. 4 (September 1958), pp. 321–340.

6. For a discussion of these cultural differences on the basis of interview data derived from this study, see Richard H. Solomon, "Mao's Effort to Reintegrate the Chinese Polity: Problems of Conflict and Authority in Chinese Social Processes," in A. Doak Barnett, ed., *Chinese Communist Politics in Action* (Seattle: University of Washington Press, 1969), pp. 276–297.

criticism of individualism for its "selfishness," the demand of both family head and political leader that group needs take precedence over personal interests, and the use of collective forms of punishment, are all indications of a fundamental Chinese cultural assumption that social life is *interdependent*.

In this study we characterize the individual social orientation in the Chinese tradition as one of *dependency*. The notion of a dependency social orientation as the modal personality configuration[7] seems to bring together such major aspects of Chinese social action as the attitudes toward authority and conflict, and also establishes conceptual linkages between the system of personality and the larger cultural tradition.

There are many difficulties in attempting psychological research on a society like China, which at present is largely closed to direct observation. However, interviews with emigré Chinese confirm that some of the major political changes on the mainland promoted by Mao Tse-tung and the Chinese Communist Party are closely related to themes of personality and social attitude found throughout the Chinese cultural area. For example, one sees in the Chinese Communist use of isolation forms of political punishment (described in detail later) the manipulation of strong personality needs to be accepted by the group.

In later chapters of this study we stress the ways in which Mao Tse-tung's political style at once draws on aspects of the traditional Chinese political culture and also is in part an effort to reshape the traditional style of wielding authority. We see a confirmation of our interpretation of "the power of the word" in Mao's use of his "little red book" of quotations to assert his political influence. Similarly, in the Communists' emphasis on group life, there is a line of continuity with the traditional Chinese stress on subordination of the individual to the collective.

As points of contrast, whereas the Confucian political tradition inculcated fear of authority and popular political passivity before a literate elite, Mao Tse-tung has sought to "liberate" the masses from

7. It is with some reluctance that I use the term "modal personality," developed by Daniel J. Levenson and Alex Inkeles in their article, "National Character: The Study of Modal Personality and Socio-Cultural Systems" (in Gardner Lindzey, ed., *Handbook of Social Psychology* [Cambridge, Mass.: Addison-Wesley, 1954], pp. 997–1020). At first glance it seems to suggest that Chinese tend to be "all alike." Even in the small sample of Chinese interviewed for this study we see a rich variation in personality style which thoroughly eliminates any "all alike" interpretation. What our interview data do indicate, however, is that there is a range of social attitudes and emotional concerns common to this group, and shared patterns of behavior used in coping with interpersonal situations.

their anxiety in the face of authority and to bring them into active political participation. While the traditional culture stressed avoidance of social conflict and suppression of hostility and aggression, Mao has seen conflict as the basic process of social change, and hostility as the motivating force by which politically passive peasants will struggle to build themselves a new world.

In sum, this study stresses as the "dialectic" in China's national development not the conflict of classes but the tension between established patterns of culture and personality and the new values and behavioral norms which Mao Tse-tung sees as the basis for the reconstruction of the world's largest political and economic community.

THE STRUCTURE OF THIS STUDY

This book consists of four self-contained parts linked by interpretive themes: Part One explores the way in which Chinese traditionally educated their children, both informally within the family and through formal schooling. Part Two elaborates upon themes developed in Part One and describes the attitudes of adult Chinese concerning social life and politics. Part Three is an analysis of the development of Mao Tse-tung's political attitudes and style of action during the revolutionary struggle for power. Themes developed in the first two parts of the book are found to be closely related to the evolution of Mao's political style. Part Four is a detailed analysis of Mao's efforts after the attainment of national leadership in 1949 to institutionalize the style of political life which brought him, and the Chinese Communist Party, to power. This final section of the book is a study of the growing divergence between Mao's conception of the political process and that held by other leaders whom Mao in time came to see as burdened with traditional political attitudes. Together the four parts present a picture of the weight of China's cultural inheritance and of Mao's struggle against it, a struggle to preserve the meaning of his own life in the institutions of China's social revolution.

The manner in which hypotheses were formulated for this study and research procedures developed to test them parallels rather closely the progression of sections in this book. Our preliminary hypotheses were tested during a year of intensive interviewing of mainland-born Chinese in both Taiwan and Hong Kong.[8] Interpre-

8. For a formal statement of the hypotheses which structured this study, see Richard H. Solomon, *The Chinese Political Culture and Problems of Modernization* (Cambridge, Massachusetts: Center for International Studies, M.I.T., 1964).

tations were developed and refined during several years of teaching. The final section of the book dealing with recent political history was written three years after the preliminary form of the basic interpretation had been outlined.[9] It required a further year of interviewing and documentary research in Hong Kong, during which disclosures of the Cultural Revolution were incorporated into the study.

The four sections of the book draw on differing sources of data, and the analytical procedures employed vary according to the data used. In Part One we develop an interpretation of personality formation and its relationship to Chinese social values on the basis of interview recollections of childhood and descriptions of childrearing practices gathered from a sample of ninety-one mainland-born Chinese. The reliability of these interview data was tested against independent observations of Chinese family and village life by anthropologists and sociologists, and published autobiographies of native Chinese. From these data we develop the interpretation of the "dependency social orientation," inculcated into Chinese from childhood. Our assumption is that the learning of early life prepares a child to cope with the world he will inherit as an adult, and that the form and content of the educational experience reflects the social values and patterns of interpersonal relations of both parents and educators.

In Part Two we rely upon interview data to explore adult social and political attitudes. The fact that we find major continuities between childhood experiences and adult attitudes strengthens the interpretation that childhood learning is preparation for adult life, and that attitudes and behavioral patterns acquired early in life persist in adulthood.

In Part Three we develop an interpretation of Mao Tse-tung's political style on the basis of his formally published political writings in the years of struggle for power, and from historical studies of the Chinese Communist movement. Here again, we find important linkages between cultural themes analyzed in the first two parts of the book and Mao's political style.

In Part Four we analyze the development of conflict over policy and leadership technique within the Chinese Communist Party after 1949 on the basis of newspaper articles, formally edited speeches of Party leaders, and less formally published political documents and speeches by Mao Tse-tung which have come to light as a result

9. The draft interpretation which has been expanded into this study is the author's Ph.D. dissertation, *The Chinese Revolution and the Politics of Dependency: The Struggle for Change in a Traditional Political Culture* (Massachusetts Institute of Technology, 1966).

of the Cultural Revolution. Here our analytical approach combines more familiar techniques of documentary interpretation and personnel analysis with interpretation of the China mainland press in a manner that some have characterized as "Kremlinology" or "esoteric communication" analysis.[10]

In conclusion, we summarize the interplay between the traditional political culture and Mao Tse-tung's efforts to institutionalize a new style of politics. As well, we stress what seem to be the innovative aspects of Mao's efforts to promote directed social change in a peasant society, and to prevent the reemergence of traditional social values and political practice.

THE INTERVIEW PROCEDURE

On the basis of our research assumptions that political attitudes grow from childhood socialization, and that Chinese hold distinctive attitudes toward authority and conflict, an interview procedure was developed to explore the evolution of social and political attitudes from early in life, through formal schooling, to their adult elaborations.

Interviews were carried out with the help of five standardized procedures: a set of open-ended questions about social attitudes and life experiences, a biographical schedule, an attitude survey, and two psychological "projective" tests—the standard Rorschach Test and a Thematic Apperception Test (TAT) designed especially for this study.[11]

In order to acquire a broad base of data on social attitudes and on the socialization experiences from which they had grown, a series of sixty-three questions were developed as the core of the interview procedure. These questions begin with early life experiences and attitudes toward family authority, pass on to experiences and attitudes gained through formal education, and then into general social perceptions and experience. There is a concluding section of eighteen questions which is more directly political in quality. "Political" issues had to be handled with some care while interviewing

10. For three particularly instructive statements on the problems of interpreting political communications in Communist countries, see Franz Borkenau, "Getting at the Facts Behind the Soviet Façade," *Commentary,* Vol. XVII, No. 4 (April 1954), pp. 393–400; "The Role of Esoteric Communication in Soviet Politics," in Myron Rush, *The Rise of Khrushchev* (Washington, D.C.: Public Affairs Press, 1958), pp. 88–94; and William E. Griffith, *Communist Esoteric Communications: Explication de Texte* (Cambridge, Mass.: M.I.T. Center for International Studies, 1967).

11. These materials are reproduced in Appendixes I through IV, pp. 527–540 below.

in Taiwan and Hong Kong, however, for merely the use of the word "politics" (*cheng-chih*) was sufficient to raise anxieties in some respondents. This orientation in itself is one of the things we wanted to explore in this study; and it was found in pretests that if we raised general matters of social authority and leadership indirectly, most respondents would discuss political matters at their own initiative. If, however, they were asked highly structured or explicit political questions they would "turn off." Hence, the general interview questions were designed to be as open-ended as possible.

Complementing the general questions were a seventy-three item biographical schedule, and an attitude survey of thirty-two items. The attitude survey items were created with a number of objectives in mind. They provided a standardized set of statements which could be used in group administrations to other Chinese in Taiwan and Hong Kong to test the reliability of our interview data.[12] Also, the survey could be used cross-culturally to test the degree to which attitudes found to be of particular concern to Chinese were truly "Chinese." [13]

A further objective of the attitude survey approach was to measure the degree to which social attitudes might be changing over time as a result of the Communist-promoted cultural changes. Survey responses provided data for comparing the social orientations of the different generations within the interview sample.[14] A basic assumption behind the design of the survey instrument was that as a culture changes certain types of attitudes change more rapidly than others. In particular, we anticipated that attitudes toward authority and interpersonal trust would change less readily than more superficial "value" attitudes which are only a reflection of underlying personality needs.

As an example, we found that a basic need for a strong source of authority might be met through the Confucian tradition, by participation in Christian religious activities, or through acceptance of Communist Party (or Chairman Mao's) leadership. A Chinese who accepted Christianity or Chairman Mao's leadership was a

12. The attitude survey was administered to several hundred Chinese university and high school students in Taiwan and Hong Kong. As no significant variations in attitude related to the interpretations developed here were noted in these groups, the data have not been incorporated into this study.

13. A translation of the attitude survey (modified to be suitable for American respondents) was administered to a sample of 269 American student and adult males. Data from this study have been presented in the author's article, "Mao's Effort to Reintegrate the Chinese Polity," in Barnett, ed., *Chinese Communist Politics in Action.*

14. The generational differences discovered in this study are discussed in detail in *ibid.* As they were not found to be directly relevant to the interpretations developed in this book, they have not been stressed here.

"different" man from his Confucian predecessor; yet it would be our interpretation that the manner in which he responded to authority, or utilized the authoritative writings of these religious or political movements, might be quite similar to that of a "traditional" Chinese.[15]

In order to validate attitude survey responses given by the persons interviewed, we allowed for a period of questioning as to why particular responses to individual survey items had been given. It was found that in explaining their reasons for evaluating a particular question as they had, the respondents provided rich additional information on their social attitudes. Hence, these elaborations were also recorded.

In developing the outline of the general interview, the biographical schedule, and the attitude survey instrument, items and questions were first worked up in English, then translated and pretested with the help of Chinese in both Taiwan and Hong Kong.

To explore in greater depth respondents' attitudes toward authority, their handling of feelings of aggression, and responses to situations of interpersonal conflict, two psychological projective tests were incorporated into the interview procedure: the standard Rorschach Test, and a set of nine Thematic Apperception Test (TAT) cards especially designed to analyze attitudes toward conflict and relations with authority.[16] These research techniques are designed to encourage an individual to reveal or "project" his inner thoughts and feelings. It is assumed that in interpreting the social situations described in the TAT pictures, or the highly ambiguous Rorschach ink-blots, a respondent structures his interpretations and projects his emotional concerns in a way which reveals basic aspects of his personality and world view.[17] As Henry A. Murray, the developer of the TAT technique, has suggested, the interviewee, in

15. This distinction between personality needs and manifest values is drawn from Henry A. Murray, *et al., Explorations in Personality* (New York: Oxford University Press, 1938); David C. McClelland, *The Achieving Society* (Princeton, N.J.: Van Nostrand, 1961); from the study by T. W. Adorno, *et al., The Authoritarian Personality* (New York: Harper, 1950); and from the methodological critique of the Adorno research, Richard Christie and Marie Jahoda, eds., *Studies in the Scope and Method of "The Authoritarian Personality"* (Glencoe: The Free Press, 1954). These studies, and the work by Daniel J. Lerner, *The Passing of Traditional Society* (Glencoe: The Free Press, 1958) provided much of the methodological inspiration for this research.

16. The TAT pictures designed for this study are reproduced in Appendix IV, pp. 538–540.

17. A discussion of the assumptions underlying the Rorschach Test procedure, and interpretive guidelines, will be found in Bruno Klopfer, *et al., Developments in the Rorschach Technique* (2 vols., Yonkers-on-Hudson, New York: World Book Co., 1954–1956).

creating a story in response to the test picture, "expose[s] his own personality, wishes, fears and traces of past experiences." [18] Responses to these psychological tests were analyzed by a trained psychologist who had had a decade of clinical experience.

The TAT cards were also administered to a group of American respondents to test the degree to which this technique was measuring cultural differences. Quantified analysis of these cultural differences has been presented elsewhere.[19]

The Interview Sequence. Each respondent was interviewed on three occasions, each session lasting about three hours. All three sessions, with few exceptions, were held within a period of one or two weeks.

Of the total of 91 interviews, approximately one-third were conducted by the author, without an interpreter. About half the interviews, those with the older and middle-aged respondents, were carried out on Taiwan by two Chinese female social workers, in their 20s, who had been trained to use the interview procedures. The remaining interviews, conducted in Hong Kong with young student emigrés from the mainland, were carried out by a college-educated Chinese female in her 30s, herself an emigré. Female interviewers were found to be particularly effective in gaining the confidence of the respondents.

Before coming to the first interview, each respondent had been asked by a Chinese contact person if he was willing to participate in a study of Chinese social customs and habits sponsored by an American academic. There were two refusals. Each respondent was paid a nominal fee for his time and the transportation costs of coming to the interview sessions.

The first interview began with filling in the biographical schedule and was largely taken up with open-ended questioning about early family life. The last half-hour of the session was devoted to the attitude survey. At the end of the session the interviewee was asked if he would return a second time and was told he would be given an opportunity to elaborate upon the responses he had just given to the survey.

The second session began with the survey response elaborations, and continued with the open-ended questioning on social attitudes. The concluding forty-five minutes to one hour were spent in administration of the TAT test.

By the third session a degree of rapport usually had been established between the interviewer and respondent, and most of this

18. Henry A. Murray, *et al., Explorations in Personality,* p. 531.
19. *See* Richard H. Solomon, "Mao's Effort to Reintegrate the Chinese Polity," in Barnett, ed., *Chinese Communist Politics in Action,* pp. 271–361.

final session was devoted to concluding the open-ended questioning about social and political attitudes. The last hour of the sequence was given to administering the Rorschach Test.[20] In some cases where a respondent had had experiences of particular interest to the objectives of this study, he was invited to return for an additional session.

The five basic interviewing tools developed for this study provided an effective mixture of procedures for exploring each respondent's social orientation. The variety of approaches appeared to give each individual the opportunity to put forward and elaborate upon his own personal concerns and points of view; yet his responses were sufficiently structured to enable us to test our hypotheses through aggregate data analysis.

The interview data were recorded by hand in Chinese during the interviews (except for those conducted by the author, in which responses were recorded in English translation), and later typed into a permanent record on a Chinese typewriter. The biographical and attitude survey data and responses to the open-ended questions were then coded by a team of analysts and punched on data cards for processing by computer. The TAT responses were coded by a trained psychologist according to a variety of standard and special coding systems, with the codes put on data cards for further computer analysis. These data form the base of information for the first two parts of this study.

The Interview Sample. There are obviously basic difficulties in attempting to do interview research on a society inaccessible to direct observation. Interviews with emigrés always carry the danger of biases because, for a variety of personal reasons, these people have left the society.[21] As is discussed in the next section of this

20. The Rorschach Test materials are not directly relevant to the interpretations of this study and will be handled separately in another publication.

21. In practice, our experience with emigré interviews was much like that of Soviet scholars who worked with emigrés in Europe: Despite the various —and usually very personal, not ideological—reasons why the subjects had emigrated, interviews revealed many positive attitudes toward the country the individuals had left. This seems to be a manifestation of strongly ambivalent feelings about leaving one's native society (*See* Alex Inkeles and Raymond A. Bauer, *The Soviet Citizen* [Cambridge, Massachusetts: Harvard University Press, 1959], pp. 41–64).

In the case of the Chinese emigrés interviewed for this study, the older respondents—many of whom had been closely identified with the Nationalists—were more ideological in their criticism of the Communists; yet they frequently expressed grudging admiration for the unity and national power which China had reacquired under Mao's leadership. The young students, mostly of "bourgeois" background, tended to be bitter about life on the

chapter, a number of perspectives have been adopted in interpreting the interview data in order to minimize biases. In constructing the emigré sample to begin with, however, certain procedures were used in selecting respondents to reduce biases in the data gathered.

In order to check for distortions related to place of interview, respondents were located in both Taiwan and in Hong Kong, through a variety of agencies—a Chinese cultural association, an old people's club, educational organizations, and a refugee resettlement agency. By comparing responses given in various locations, and by people referred to us by different organizations, we were able to check for biases which might be associated with the immediate political environment. In one case an interviewee appeared to have been "planted" by a government agency to test the intentions of the author. His interview has not been included in the sample. In general, the questions and procedures were not seen as politically sensitive by the persons interviewed. Indeed, in a completely unanticipated manner, several respondents to whom the author talked in Taiwan were surprisingly critical of the Nationalist government. Apparently the focus of the interviews on family life and social relations, and the physical context in which the interviews were conducted—a mental health center in a public hospital complex—were quite enough to put the respondents at ease.

The fact that a number of interviewers gathered data gave additional opportunity to check for biases which might have been introduced by the use of male and female interviewers, or by the different personalities doing the interviewing. No observable distortions were found in this regard. The respondents seemed anxious to explain their views on Chinese society and culture to an interested foreigner; and the female interviewers were found to be particularly effective in drawing out the more elderly respondents.

Four major criteria—sex, age, place of origin, and level of education—were selected in constructing the sample. Because until recently direct participation in political and social activity has been limited almost exclusively to males in Chinese society, it was decided to exclude females from the interview sample. Given the additional limitations of time and financial resources, the total sample had to be modest in size. The use of respondents of only one sex facilitated intergroup comparisons according to age, place of origin, and educational experience.

---

mainland because they had been singled out for discriminatory treatment because of their "bad" class origins. Their criticism was not so much of the system, but of the fact that they had not been allowed to participate in the process of national development in a manner commensurate with what they felt were their intellectual skills.

A major objective in this study was to acquire "baseline" data on social attitudes from Chinese who had received a traditional up-bringing before the revolutionary turmoil of the twentieth century. By comparing their attitudes with those of middle-aged and younger generational groups, we hoped to test for changes in social orienta-tion which might have developed over more than a half-century of social change. Hence we conceived an interview sample structured into three generational groups: an older and more traditional group aged 55 and above; a middle-aged group between 30 and 54; and then a younger generational group, between the ages of 20 and 29, which had been exposed to some education under the Communists. As Table I indicates, we were largely able to meet this criterion of generational grouping.

To avoid response biases related to regional differences, we at-tempted to select interviewees with a broad range of provincial backgrounds, and avoid overreliance on Chinese from major urban areas who had been strongly exposed to foreign influence. In Table I we summarize the provinces of birth of the interview sample. As the data reveal, in the sample finally gathered there is particular emphasis on respondents from the coastal provinces of central and south China. Apparently people from these areas have greater so-cial mobility, and Nationalist support is stronger in east China. Among the younger generation the preponderance were from Kwangtung Province, bordering on Hong Kong. This is largely a reflection of the difficulties Chinese face in gaining formal permis-sion from the government of the People's Republic to emigrate. Many of the interviewees, particularly those of middle and younger years, left the mainland illegally during the crisis of food produc-tion and political control of 1961–62.

While we were able to select interviewees from a variety of provinces and native places—farming villages, county towns, and major cities—the sample does not have the geographical balance that we would have preferred. Analysis of responses according to the range of provincial origins in the sample, however, does not reveal any strong trend or bias in attitude associated with region. A respondent's generation and sibling position within the family seem to be the major variables which account for the differences in social attitude observable in this sample.

The interview techniques necessitated the adoption of a basic educational criterion of minimal literacy. Respondents had to be able to read the attitude survey and be sufficiently articulate to respond to the open-ended interview procedures. Thus all the in-terviewees were functionally literate. Beyond this basic criterion,

TABLE I:

INTERVIEW SAMPLE BY REGION AND PROVINCE OF BIRTH

PLACE OF BIRTH		AGE GROUP			PROVINCIAL SUBTOTAL	REGIONAL TOTAL
Region	*Province*	*20–29*	*30–54*	*55–85*		
NORTHEAST CHINA	Heilungkiang		1		1	
	Kirin			1	1	
	Liaoning		1	2	3	
						5
NORTH & NORTHWEST CHINA	Hopeh		1	6	7	
	Shansi			1	1	
	Shensi					
	Kansu					
						8
CENTRAL CHINA	Honan		2		2	
	Hopeh			2	2	
	Hunan	2	1	4	7	
						11
EAST CHINA	Shantung		4	3	7	
	Kiangsu	6	3	3	12	
	Anhwei		3	2	5	
	Chekiang	1	2	1	4	
	Kiangsi		1	4	5	
	Fukien	3	1	2	6	
						39
SOUTH CHINA	Kwangtung	12	8	2	22	
	Kwangsi	1	2		3	
						25
SOUTHWEST CHINA	Szechwan	1		1	2	
	Kweichow					
	Yunnan		1		1	
						3
	AGE GROUP SUBTOTALS	26	31	34		91

however, there was a range of education experiences and levels within the sample. One-third of the respondents had not graduated from high school; another third had a high school degree, or the equivalent in trade school education; and the final third had gone to college or had received military education above the high school level. We selected interviewees in the 20–29 age group from those who had had at least one year of formal education under the Communists; and respondents over the age of 54 were selected if they had had traditional education in the Confucian classics in a family or clan school.

In addition to these characteristics of the sample according to sex, age group, geographical origin, and educational background, analysis revealed that the respondents had had a variety of occupational experiences. There were few "pure" peasants; and approximately half the respondents had had some exposure to military life during the war against Japan. There was also a range of what might be termed "urban" occupations ranging from school teachers and merchants to lawyers and government employees.

In terms of economic class background, the respondents were largely from families of the middle to upper income levels of Chinese society.

The upper limit of the sample size was dictated by considerations of time and financial restrictions. The lower limit was set by our objective of selecting a group large enough to permit some statistical analyses of generational and other differences. Obviously gathering by random selection a sample large enough to represent a reliable cross-section of 700,000,000 Chinese was impossible. Yet within the limits of having to build a structured emigré sample over a year of research, it was possible to select 91 individuals who conformed rather closely to the criteria just discussed. And when interpretations developed from this moderate-sized emigré sample are tested against data derived from a variety of other independent sources, there is sufficient convergence to strengthen the major interpretive hypotheses developed in this study.

A number of general remarks should be made about this sample. This group of respondents represents the social base of semiurbanized or urbanized, literate, middle to upper income level Chinese from coastal provinces from which the Nationalist movement drew its support.[22] About one-third of the respondents had been associated with the Nationalist government either directly through participation in governmental or military activities or through family members associated with the former Nanking government. The majority of the remaining respondents' social backgrounds are similar to those with more direct ties to the Nationalists.

Given the particular characteristics of our interview sample, the social and political attitudes explored in the first two parts of this book represent the cultural orientation of that "bourgeois" element of Chinese society which Mao has struggled against most of his life.

22. An analysis of the social background characteristics of the Nationalist elite will be found in Robert C. North, *Kuomintang and Chinese Communist Elites* (Stanford, California: Hoover Institute, 1952).

During the Cultural Revolution Mao asserted that the need for another revolutionary upheaval after two decades of Communist Party rule reflected a continuation of the Party's struggle against the Kuomintang.[23] By this he meant that the style of politics which the Party had fought through long years of civil war was reasserting itself in the social values and behavior of Party and governmental cadres. In this regard, the interview sample—while not necessarily representative of Chinese society as a whole—helps to define the social orientation which Mao is seeking to overcome.

The one major group of Chinese society which this sample does not contain is the "poor and blank," illiterate, and, until recently, socially unmobilized peasantry who form the bulk of China's population. Thus we cannot make direct observations about the relationship between Mao Tse-tung's evolving style of political leadership and the attitudes of the peasants whom Mao and the Party eventually had to make the "main force" of their proletarian revolution. It is worthy of note, however, that there is a high degree of "fit" between Mao's notion of the leadership process needed to mobilize peasants into the ranks of the revolution, and the social attitudes of our "bourgeois" respondents. This finding strengthens our belief that despite differences in the level of consciousness and sophistication with which cultural attitudes are held by people of varying educational levels, and the differences in "interest" associated with economic class and social status, there is a shared core of culture and personality common to those reared within a social tradition like China's, which was stable for many generations.

SOME INTERPRETIVE PERSPECTIVES

Past efforts to interpret the relationships linking individual personality, group processes, and politics have raised as many questions as they appear to have answered. Certain authors have given evidence of a lack of conceptual clarity, or have been imprecise in delimiting the scope of their assertions. Basically, however, the precise nature of personality remains an issue of considerable debate, and the interrelationship between individual behavior and group processes is an even more elusive subject.[24] Our point of view

23. *See* one of Mao's "latest directives," translated in *Peking Review*, No. 19 (May 10, 1968), p. 2.

24. Among the literature which has attempted to develop the level of conceptual clarity in personality and politics studies, I have found particularly useful Nathan Leites, "Psycho-Cultural Hypotheses about Political Acts," *World Politics*, Vol. I (1948), pp. 102–119, and Fred I. Greenstein, *et al.*, "Personality and Politics: Theoretical and Methodological Issues," *Journal of Social Issues*, Vol. XXIV, No. 3 (July 1968).

on some of these issues might be briefly stated for the interested reader.

The Reliability of the Interview Data. The question of data reliability in this study is essentially a matter of the extent to which attitudes found in a structured sample of emigré Chinese reflect those of Chinese now on the mainland, or who lived there in generations past. The basic test of reliability used here has been whether our interview data are supported by a variety of independent sources of information about Chinese social attitudes and behavioral patterns. Thus we have drawn upon the field studies of anthropologists and sociologists, the memoirs of foreign travelers who observed life in imperial China, and a variety of Chinese documentary sources ranging from formal writings of the Confucian tradition to newspapers of the People's Republic. The interpretations advanced here, in our judgment, are supported by these varied materials.

The Validity of Attitude and Behavioral Data Gathered Through Interviews. Data validity in this analysis is a question of the relevance of attitudes expressed in the interviews to behavioral situations in the "real" context of Chinese society. Do respondents' assertions of personal value or behavioral predisposition provide a valid guide to the behavior of those who live on the mainland? Here our measure of validity relies on the same test of convergence used in estimating reliability. We assume our data to be valid when we note observations of the same value orientations and behavioral styles revealed in the interviews in mainland press materials or in the field notes of anthropologists.

One of the more gratifying aspects of this research has been the discovery of a close relationship between attitudes discussed by the interviewees and the political style which Mao Tse-tung evolved to oppose the "reactionary" aspects of China's traditional culture. As one example, interview and social data reveal weak communication linkages between superior and subordinate. Mao has attempted to institutionalize new patterns of communication between the Party and people, and among "lateral" social groupings, in order to overcome traditional weaknesses in social integration.[25]

Reducing Everything to Psychological Causes? In a study such as this which focuses on personal attitudes, there is a tendency to overstress the importance of the psychological dimensions of political action. While such an emphasis could be found equally well in a study of economics or history, some might assume that the

25. This interpretation is developed in the author's article, "Communication Patterns and the Chinese Revolution," *The China Quarterly*, No. 32 (October–December 1967), pp. 88–110.

author sees only psychological factors as relevant to understanding social processes. The environment, however, is a major factor in shaping action, for to varying degrees it "pressures" the individual to respond in certain ways regardless of his personal desires.

The second half of this book is an attempt to place the aspects of Chinese culture and personality explored in the first two parts in the context of larger historical and political events. More specifically, we try to develop a sense of the interplay between one man's personality and the development of the leadership style of a political movement. The chapters which deal with Mao Tse-tung's efforts to institutionalize his conception of a new political process for China against increasing resistance from other Party leaders, reveal with particular clarity the value of personality analysis in political research. To the extent that a man acquires power, he gains the opportunity to promote solutions to social problems which reflect his own personality. Mao's stature as leader of the Chinese Communist Party has given him this opportunity; and we would hold that the great events of Chinese domestic politics of the past two decades —the "Hundred Flowers" movement, the "Great Leap Forward," and the "Great Proletarian Cultural Revolution"—cannot be explained satisfactorily without reference to Mao's personality.

From another perspective, the increasing tensions within the Chinese Communist Party which finally burst forth into the Cultural Revolution reveal the usefulness of a culture and personality approach to political analysis. While policy differences were important factors contributing to the growing split within the Party leadership during the decade 1955–1964, Cultural Revolution documents have revealed that the ultimate breakdown within the leadership was closely related to basic differences in personal leadership style. Mao Tse-tung was unyielding in his belief that only his conception of a new Party "work style" could bring about China's modernization. Yet other leaders and the Party apparatus would not, or could not, use power in the ways that he prescribed. Mao was "fighting the system" in the sense of trying to bring about a radical change in political processes. These changes were not being sustained by the millions of Chinese who participated in the organizational life of Party and state.

One student of the organizational transformations promoted by the Chinese Communists over the past two decades has seen "the resurgence of the forces of Chinese society" in the form of pressures by China's major social groups on the Party's ideology and organization.[26] In other words, despite alterations in institutional

26. Franz Schurmann, *Ideology and Organization in Communist China* (Berkeley: University of California Press, 1968 revised edition), p. 504.

framework, even Party and governmental cadres have gradually modified China's "Communist" political system to conform more closely to their "Chinese" personalities. It was Mao's reaction to this development which led him to see the need for a "Cultural Revolution" against China's "four olds."

Unchanging China? These assertions of the endurance of China's cultural system and social orientation in a sense are "pessimistic," for they imply (and we think rightly) that efforts to bring about social change through organizational transformation will be resisted to the extent that the organizational forms conflict with widely held personal needs. Such a view is perhaps overstressed in this study, only in part because we see Mao so concerned about traditional values and patterns of behavior, and partly because in the first two sections we explore what is termed China's "traditional" social orientation.

To no small degree, however, our use of the term "traditional" is a notational convenience. How might one more easily characterize the attitudes of those elderly Chinese in our interview sample who were educated before the fall of the Ch'ing dynasty? Although these individuals in many respects are "transitional" men, living out their lives in a changing society, we find their social attitudes to be strikingly congruent with those stressed in classical Confucian texts.

Our use of the term "traditional," however, is not intended to slight the evolution of China's historical institutions, or to imply that there has been no change in recent times. "Tradition" is not necessarily an unchanging past. The question is what exactly has changed? On the basis of the limited data which would enable us to gauge the continuity of culture and personality style over the centuries, we would concur with those historians who suggest that change in China—in a society which for thousands of years has been rooted in the stable life style of a peasant social economy— has been a matter of "change within tradition." [27] Institutions have evolved, culture has been modified by the foreign influence of invading nomadic tribes. Yet the "tradition," the basic cultural logic and the personalities shaped by the learning of China's social legacy have shown remarkable continuity over time.

We do not imply that the Chinese are fated to bear the burden of an ancient way of life in a changing world. Our basic assumption of the importance of the socialization experience in shaping personality means that the focus of change will be in the new attitudes and styles of behavior developed in future generations. It should

27. John K. Fairbank, Edwin O. Reischauer, and Albert M. Craig, *East Asia: The Modern Transformation* (Boston: Houghton Mifflin, 1965), p. 5.

be recalled that the men now in positions of political leadership in China were born at the end of the imperial era. Their socialization experiences had only begun to reflect the impact of new values. And those more recent generations for whom the educational experience was significantly altered are only beginning to make their impact felt on China's political and social life.

The foreign observer cannot readily see exactly what changes have come about in the socialization process during the last twenty years of Party rule, and what alterations in social orientation have been produced by a Communist education. As the Cultural Revolution conflict has revealed, there have been strong divisions of opinion within the Party leadership about the educational process. Mao Tse-tung developed doubts that the Party was rearing a younger generation who would be "revolutionary successors," committed to realizing the goals that the Party has not yet attained. And in the Cultural Revolution conflict Mao was to find the Red Guards less than model students of his "thought."

Two points are worth stressing, however. First, when Mao Tse-tung decided to promote his Cultural Revolution, he turned for support to the student generation. Presumably they had been liberated to some degree from the cultural inheritance which Mao saw as still burdening their elders. A second and related point is that a more meaningful time framework for evaluating social change is not the passing of solar years, but rather generational time. It is only as new generations with significantly altered socialization experiences acquire political influence that enduring change will come about.

Unique China? From the stress which this analysis gives to the importance of culture and socialization experience, some may see an implication of Chinese uniqueness. Such an impression is perhaps reinforced by Chinese assertions of the distinctiveness of their own cultural tradition. Our own view is that many areas of social experience, perception, and emotional concern transcend cultural boundaries. However, a culture imparts differences in emphasis to certain emotions, attitudes, and behavioral patterns.

These conflicting perspectives seem best resolved by the view that despite the many areas of common experience and social perception which Chinese share with other people, the total configuration or "mix" of social context, cultural inheritance, and personal orientation gives China's social life a distinctiveness which has been the subject of comment by generations of foreign visitors.

There is much in China's cultural pattern which draws its meaning from the qualities of peasant life which are common to other agrarian societies. As one anthropologist has suggested, food gathering cultures tend to stress attitudes of dependency in their children in order to preserve the integrity of the family group, the organizational guarantor of individual security.[28] Despite this common cultural base which China shares with other peasant societies, however, there is a degree of elaboration to the values of rural life in her traditions which reflects the centuries of vital intellectual life sustained by the material resources of a productive peasant economy.

Any foreigner who has lived and worked in a Chinese social context knows by personal experience the cultural differences in the way conflicts are handled, authority is invoked, and emotions disciplined. For decades Westerners referred to "oriental inscrutability," which was only a way of saying that their own cultural inheritance had not prepared them to "read the signals" of interpersonal relations in Chinese society.[29] The Soviet technicians who worked in China during the 1950s described the Chinese as "vacuum bottles." Unprepared by Russian traditions, which sanction emotional expressiveness, they were unable to sense from external appearances whether "what was on the inside was hot or cold." [30]

Such expressions of cultural difference are usually damned or described as quaint from the observer's perspective. We have tried, however, to approach the distinctive structure of social values and personality configuration in Chinese political life from a Chinese or at least a neutral perspective.

All Chinese Are Alike? In contrast to the view of Chinese uniqueness, some critics of culture and personality analysis see a denial of individual differences in the effort to define that which is shared. The absurdity of such an objection is revealed in large measure by the variations in personal style which are evident in our interview data.

Such an objection is usefully confronted by turning the proposition around. "All Chinese are different." Is there nothing which they have in common? Unless one believes that all generalizations about human social life, or history, are invalid—which we do not—the question is in what respects are Chinese alike, and in what ways is

28. Eric R. Wolf, *Peasants* (Englewood Cliffs, New Jersey: Prentice-Hall, 1966), p. 69.

29. One of the more extreme interpretations of Chinese cultural patterns with a foreign bias is Arthur Smith's *Chinese Characteristics* (New York: Fleming Revell, 1894). For a discerning analysis of changing Western interpretations of the Chinese, see Harold R. Isaacs, *Scratches on Our Minds: American Images of China and India* (New York: John Day, 1958).

30. This Russian characterization of the Chinese was related to the author by Mikhail A. Klochko, a Soviet chemist who worked in China as an adviser during the 1950s. *See* his book, *Soviet Scientist in Red China* (New York: Praeger, 1964).

their individuality expressed? Such a question, it seems to us, is best answered through empirical research. The analysis in this book is an attempt to define the shared cultural dynamic of China's political life, and to examine Mao Tse-tung's efforts to reshape this ancient social tradition.

Part One

THE TRADITIONAL CHINESE SOCIALIZATION PROCESS

"Old Age," one of a collection
of twenty-four ivory carvings illustrating
the twenty-four exemplary acts of Confucian filial piety.
*Courtesy The Wellcome Institute and
Museum of the History of Medicine, London.*

Chapter II

CONFUCIANISM AND THE
CHINESE LIFE CYCLE

The Confucian political order was centered on the notion that the family was the matrix of society's political relations. As is stated in one of the classic texts of this traditionally dominant social philosophy, "The filial piety with which the superior man serves his parents may be transferred as loyalty to the ruler; the fraternal duty with which he serves his elder brother may be transferred as submissive deference to elders; [and] his regulation of his family may be transferred as good government in any official position." [1] Thus, proper political leadership remained rooted in its original social context: "The ruler, without going beyond the family, completes the lessons for the state"[2]; and, "wishing to order well his state, he first regulates his family." [3]

As our analysis will elaborate, there were compelling emotional reasons why the Chinese political tradition was tenaciously linked to its familistic root—why the emperor was seen as "the Son of Heaven" and why local functionaries were termed "father-mother" officials. And for equally cogent reasons the Western political tradition has tended to ignore its roots in family life, to "forget" that an individual's conception of social authority and of the processes which mediate relations between the powerful and the subordinate were first learned within the family.

As cultural contrast can be particularly revealing of a society's habits, we begin by observing how two different social traditions have attempted to solve the difficulties of relations between the weak

1. *Hsiao Ching* [Classic of Filial Piety], trans. James Legge, in Max F. Müller, ed., *Sacred Books of the East* (50 vols., Oxford, England: Clarendon Press, 1879–1910), Vol. III, p. 483.

2. *The Great Learning*, "Commentary of the Philosopher Tsang," in *The Chinese Classics*, trans. James Legge (5 vols., Shanghai: 1935), Vol. I, p. 370.

3. Paraphrased from Section 4 of the "Text of Confucius" in *ibid.*, p. 357.

and strong through an institutional patterning of the human life cycle. Thus, while the political route to Paris may be by way of Peking, an understanding of the politics of China may begin in Greece, by a reconsideration of one of the more revealing social "myths" of Western civilization.

OEDIPUS WAS AN UNFILIAL SON

All cultural traditions express the collective hopes and concerns of their people through artistic or literary communication, thus helping to bind a society together through the sharing of life's frustrations and triumphs. Artistic works provide the social analyst with concentrated statements of a society's particular concerns and the ways in which they have been managed. One example is the Greek drama of King Oedipus, who killed his father and married his mother. In recent times the Oedipal myth has acquired connotations for understanding the emotional life of the Western family that we will consider shortly. But in keeping with our interest in relating a society's political style to roots in the training of its children, it is important to recall that the myth of Oedipus at first reading is more a story of politics than of family life or individual tragedy.

Concerned as Westerners are with the plight of the individual we may forget the problem faced by Oedipus' parents, Laius and Jocasta, who were the political rulers of Thebes: In abandoning their "fated" infant son they were trying to deal with the problem of regicide, as well as patricide and incest. Oedipus appeals to the Horatio Alger in us, for he was a "high achiever," a self-made man who, though rejected by his family, used his intelligence to outwit the Sphinx that had terrorized Thebes and thus, by his own determination, rose to great power and fame. But to the Theban people he was, until his fall, a political hero who had freed them from a community scourge.

In mythical terms, the inexorable working out of Oedipus' fate raises serious community and political problems: How is the ruler (Laius) to deal with a subordinate (Oedipus) who would destroy him and enjoy the pleasures that come with great power? How were the Theban people to deal with the paradox of having a leader whom they loved because he had saved them from the Sphinx but who also brought with him compulsions and an arrogant pride which could plague the community and destroy social order? Oedipus, the man of great courage and wisdom, was also the hot-blood who killed a traveler, his father unrecognized, in a conflict over precedence and prestige at a rural cross-road. He was the popular king who brought a plague down on his people because of a fate-driven violation of social taboo.

Consideration of the various institutional solutions developed by the ancient Greeks to deal with these problems of the relation between leader and led would take us far from our central point, which is to stress that even in the root experience of the Western political tradition family and individual problems have been intertwined with the development of political institutions. Oedipus, the tragic ruler of Thebes, was a man who became conscious of the paradoxes inherent in the human life cycle—for this was the riddle of the Sphinx which he solved. And through the solution of this riddle he was led on to conclude the tragedy of his fate. The story of the Theban king, at this individual level of insight, is a metaphorical expression of the Western life cycle, a symbolic representation of the solution worked out by our root culture to the universal "political" problem stemming from the dependent and unsocialized condition of humans at birth.

In dealing with the oracle's prediction of his son's terrible fate, Laius was facing the paradox that the dependent child must be disciplined if he is to become a participating member of society. But the process of socialization, which is the child's first exposure to "politics"—to the relation of the strong who have and the weak who want—will leave a residue of resentment of authority and a desire to "do in" the one who first forced denial or restriction of the pleasures of life. The solution to this paradox which Oedipus' parents chose, the casting out of the family of the ill-fated child, is in symbolic terms the solution worked out by Western culture: The potentially disruptive dependent is "abandoned," or more correctly, "set forth," after a period of disciplining to seek for himself in new social contexts alternative solutions to his life's most original hates and loves.

The story of Oedipus, of course, represents only one aspect of the Greek social tradition which, as with Western culture generally, had to face the concomitant social problems that arise from individuals aggressively seeking to work out their personal problems and pleasures in a world of other striving individuals. Without being diverted into a consideration of the various Western social institutions which have been developed to handle these problems, we must at least make explicit two assumptions which underlie the development of these institutions: First, the individual is the basic "actor" of society and should be trained in childhood to make do on his own, to be self-disciplining and self-directing. From this conviction have developed Western notions about moral equality and equality of social responsibility and political "rights." Second, there is the assumption that potential social conflict should be handled not by repression of the aggressive impulse so much as by providing the individual with alternative behavioral forms through which hostility can be discharged without endangering the larger society.[4]

The Chinese have since early times been concerned with the same problems of resentment of superior by subordinate and of disruptive social conflict which underlie the Oedipus myth. They have sought their own solution to such problems, as we are informed in the opening lines of the Confucian educational text *The Classic of Filial Piety*: "The ancient kings had a perfect virtue and all-embracing rule of conduct, through which they were in accord with all under heaven. By the practice of it the people were brought to live in peace and harmony, and there was no ill-will between superiors and inferiors." [5] A descriptive statement of this "all-embracing rule of conduct," and of the manner in which it shaped the Chinese life cycle, is significantly not found in a drama to stir human emotions but in an educational text to be memorized and to provide models of behavior for China's children. The "mythical" presentation of the ideal of the Confucian life is not the tragedy of one man but the triumph of twenty-four.

The first of the twenty-four models of filial piety is Yu Shun, who, like Oedipus, was rejected by his family. It is not clear what motivated Yu's father and brother to drop him down a well and

4. In this regard it is worth recalling something about the *form* in which the myth of Oedipus was presented, apart from its content. The Greek drama as an art form, Aristotle tells us in his *Poetics,* had the virtue of producing an emotional excitation or release, a catharsis, in the audience; a stimulation, "correction, and refinement" of emotions mobilized during the course of the play through such behavioral forms as laughter in response to comedy, or pity and horror at tragedy. The popularity of works of art like Sophocles' *Oedipus* was based on their ability to strike responsive emotional chords in a large audience. The performance of such plays served a function of social integration through mobilizing and then discharging in socially harmless ways widely shared emotional tensions. Each member of the audience, in "feeling" his (unconsciously held) fantasies and resentments acted out on the stage, had his own inner state of desire for the tragic act "refined" by enhancing his sense of horror or outrage—guilt—at the fantastic event. The result was that the "occurrence" of the act on the stage made the same act less likely to occur in real life.

In the Western social tradition, then, surrogate forms of emotional discharge, or self-discipline through guilt, tend to replace either the direct release of such emotions against their original objects, a total denial of the emotional impulse, or the application of external controls—group pressures or the authority of a superior individual—to regulate individual behavior. As we shall stress later, however, repression of emotional impulses and group controls over individual behavior are predominant in the Chinese social tradition.

5. *Hsiao Ching*, p. 466.

throw stones upon him, or to set fire to a granary when he was inside; we are only told that his father and brother were "stupid" and "conceited." But, unlike Oedipus, who rewarded his rejecting parents with an inexorable, fate-driven vengeance of death and violation of social taboo, Yu continued a life of toil on his family land and returned his parents' rejection with reverence for them and sincerity in his life-long social obligations as a son. His reward was the moral renovation of his family through his own example: "His parents became pleasant, and his brother more conciliatory and virtuous." [6]

A similar tale of determined filial devotion rewarded with parental abuse was the fate of Min Sun of the Chou dynasty. His mother died and his stepmother and father mistreated him, but Min's stoicism and good nature succeeded in maintaining the integrity of his family:

> In all ages men have exhibited a great love for their wives; but dutiful children have often met with unkindness. Min carefully concealed all his grievances, and refused to indulge in any complaint; even while suffering severely from cold and hunger, he maintained his affection unabated. During the long period in which he endured this oppressive treatment, his good disposition became manifest; and by his own conduct he was able to maintain the harmony of the family unimpaired. His father and mother were influenced by his filial devotion; and his brothers joined in extolling his virtues.[7]

The dutiful son thus will not accept his parents' rejection, but bears his personal pain for the greater good of family "harmony." He endures the *externally* imposed sufferings associated with dependency and subordination—as contrasted with Oedipus' *internal* sense of torment born of the terrible truth of his personal guilt—to fulfill the "fated" and life-long obligations of his social role as a son.

Other models of behavior among the twenty-four instruct us that the filial obligation is conceived as a repayment of the debt of parental nurture a son incurs during his childhood years of dependency. He reciprocates with care for his parents when they enter the dependency of old age. Chung Yu, though exhausted, traveled great distances to bring rice to his parents, and Ts'ai Shun spared his widowed mother the anxieties of years of famine and political unrest by gathering berries in distant forests. "[Ming Tsung's] mother was very ill, and one winter's day she longed to taste a soup made of bamboo shoots, but Ming could not procure any. At last he went into the bamboo grove, and clasping the bamboos with his hands, wept bitterly. His filial love moved Nature, and the ground slowly

6. *The Book of Filial Duty,* trans. Ivan Chen (New York: E. P. Dutton, 1909), p. 34.
7. *Ibid.,* p. 38.

opened, sending forth several shoots, which he gathered and carried home. He made a soup of them, which his mother tasted, and immediately recovered from her malady." [8]

More than a third of these exemplars of the Confucian life pattern are sons who endured hardships to feed their mothers and nurture them in sickness, which suggests in its own way the special relationship between mother and son which is mystically described in the tale of Tseng Ts'an: When his mother was anxious, she had only to gnaw her finger. Tseng immediately felt a pain in his heart even at a great distance and came running home to ease her discomfort.

The twenty-four models provide less frequent or vivid instruction on the relationship between father and son, although we do learn that Huang Hsiang of the Han dynasty, "in summer, when the weather was warm . . . fanned and cooled his father's pillow and bed; and in winter, when it was cold . . . warmed the bed-clothes with his body." [9] And when danger threatened, Yang Hsiang risked his life: "Once a tiger seized his father, and was slowly carrying him off, when Yang, anxious for his father and forgetting himself, although he had no iron weapon in his hand, rushed forward and seized the tiger by the neck. The beast let the prey fall from his teeth, and fled, and Yang's father was thus saved from injury and death." [10]

The nature of the relationship between father and son in the Confucian tradition is more fully revealed in the story of Hsüeh Jen-kuei, a traditional tale which is perhaps the Chinese equivalent of the Oedipus myth. (It has been incorporated in the repertory of Peking opera.) Hsüeh, a soldier of fortune of the T'ang period, had risen from humble status to become a high military officer. His martial skills attracted the attention of the emperor, who assigned him to duties on a distant frontier. The tale focuses on his return and reunion with his wife, whom he had not seen since he left her pregnant eighteen years earlier to join the imperial service.

As Hsüeh approaches his home district, he sees a youth skillfully shooting wild geese at the bank of the River Fen. He challenges the boy to a test of marksmanship, claiming that he can shoot two geese with one arrow. When the challenge is accepted, Hsüeh shoots the youthful rival instead of the geese, exclaiming, "I could have spared the boy, but a soldier like me could not let another live if he was a superior in marksmanship with the weapons in which I excel." [11]

8. *Ibid.*, pp. 54–55.
9. *Ibid.*, p. 45.
10. *Ibid.*, pp. 49–50.
11. Quoted from a synopsis of this tale entitled, "At the Bend of the River Fen," in A. C. Scott, *An Introduction to the Chinese Theater* (Singapore: Donald Moore, 1958), p. 63.

The Confucian exemplar Lao Lai-tzu,
who donned children's clothes and played games
to amuse his aged parents. Adapted from a second-century A.D. (Han
Dynasty) stone engraving.
*Courtesy Houghton-Mifflin Company
and John K. Fairbank.*

Hsüeh finally reaches home and is reunited with his wife, but he brings with him concern and uncertainty about her fidelity during his long absence. These doubts are increased when he discovers a pair of men's shoes under the family sleeping platform. His wife chides him for his doubts and explains that the shoes belong to his son, who was born shortly after he left home eighteen years before. Hsüeh asks his son's whereabouts, and his wife tells him that he is out hunting. The dénouement is the parents' horrified discovery that Hsüeh has killed his son.

This tale provides a revealing counterpoint to the Oedipus myth: It is Hsüeh the father, not the son, who leaves the family to make his fortune; and, of course, it is the father who kills the son unrecognized in an encounter over prestige. In mythical terms Hsüeh Jen-kuei's actions suggest the father's reluctance to let the son grow to his own maturity; his unwillingness to be challenged by him. Hsüeh's doubts about his wife's fidelity reveal a tension in the father-son relationship born of the particularly intense mother-son tie described in the twenty-four models of filial piety. But the father will not let the son challenge him "with the weapons in which he excels."

The son thus is instructed to remain a son all his life, as is explicitly symbolized in the exemplar Lao Lai-tzu, who in the fullness of his maturity donned children's clothing to amuse his seventy-year-old parents. He culminates a life of service and self-sacrifice for his parents with a vigil at their death which reciprocates the parental birth vigil. This dutiful behavior is also emphasized by Huang T'ing-chien: "When his mother was seized with illness he watched her for a whole year without leaving her bedside or even taking off his clothes; and at her death he himself fell ill and nearly lost his life." [12]

But in spite of Huang's extreme grief at the death of his beloved mother he does not die, for to do so would be unfilial; as the Confucian classic instructs, "Our bodies—to every hair and bit of skin—are received from our parents, and we must not presume to injure or wound them: this is the beginning of filial piety." [13]

Oedipus, we must conclude, by Confucian standards was a most unfilial son; not only because he unknowingly murdered his father and loved his mother, but also in that he mutilated himself. In tearing out his eyes, with which he finally saw the horror of his own guilt, he was violating that rule which Confucius tells us is the beginning of filial piety, the inviolability of the body of life which parents give the child. For by mutilating himself, Oedipus was threatening to break the cyclical Confucian life pattern, through

12. *The Book of Filial Duty,* p. 60.
13. *Hsiao Ching,* p. 466.

which life is given to the group and to its future generations rather than to the individual alone.

Here then, in the symbolic forms of cultural ideals, are expressed two polar extremes in the solution of the fundamental political problem of human life, the tie between dependent son and powerful and disciplining father: In the Western solution the parents perceive the potential for conflict born of childhood dependency and its concomitant process of disciplining. They thus set the matured child on his own to seek in adult life alternative social contexts and behavioral forms for the gratification of his hostile and pleasure-seeking impulses. The Confucian solution, however, rejects the "abandonment" of the source of generational conflict in favor of the greater ends of parental security and the integrity of the family group. The son is to realize his social identity in a life-long prolongation of his original state of dependency.[14] The original objects

14. While the son of a Chinese family was reared to remain with his parents, this was not the case with a female child. Indeed, in several respects a Chinese daughter was the "Oedipus" of her family. It will be recalled that as Oedipus was abandoned, his feet were pierced by the shepherd who was to leave him on a mountainside; hence his name, "Oedipus" or "wounded foot." The daughter of a Chinese family was quite literally, like Oedipus, sent forth from her parents with wounded feet, the painfully acquired "golden lilies" or bound feet which, according to traditional conceptions of feminine beauty, made a young girl more attractive to potential husbands and mothers-in-law. As well, female children in Chinese families, particularly in times of scarcity or famine, were sold or occasionally abandoned directly, reflecting at an extreme the generally low valuation which was placed on female children in the traditional culture.

It will also be recalled that despite his abandonment, Oedipus survived to become a great political leader, but a leader who brought tragedy to his family and a plague upon the people of Thebes. Similarly, the traditional Chinese woman was seen as not only a potentially disruptive influence in the family into which she married, but also a source of great political trouble. The Confucian classics and generations of scholar-officials explicitly warned against the influence of women in politics; and the experience of a series of assertive, powerful and often disruptive female rulers including Lady Wu of the T'ang dynasty, the Empress Dowager Tz'u-hsi of the Ch'ing, and Madame Chiang K'ai-shek and Chiang Ch'ing of the present era, indicates that the Chinese woman had the strength of character to assert herself despite (or perhaps because of) her bound feet and all that this physical mutilation symbolized. (For two very different interpretations of the strength and disruptive influence of women in Chinese society, *see* Lien-sheng Yang, "Female Rulers in Imperial China," *Harvard Journal of Asiatic Studies,* Vol. XXIII [1960–61], pp. 47–61, and Warner Muensterberger, "Orality and Dependence: Characteristics of Southern Chinese," in *Psychoanalysis and the Social Sciences,* Vol. III [1951], esp. pp. 54–65.)

Such equivalences between the mythical Oedipus and Chinese conceptions of the influence of women in their social and political life, we must stress, are meaningful because they reflect certain psychological commonalities in

of discipline and love are retained, but hostility toward the stern father is denied and love for the mother is maintained.[15]

The Confucian life pattern thus is "cyclical," for within the *inter*dependence of the family the son reciprocates the nurturance he receives in his childhood dependency by nurturing his parents in the dependency of their old age. In childhood one depends on one's parents, and in old age on one's children; thus for the filial individual, life comes full circle. The filial son in this sense remains a "son" as long as he lives; he never breaks out of his original social matrix to establish an independent life. But he bears the pain and injustice which tradition tells him is an unavoidable part of childhood because he knows that in time he will become a father while remaining a son; and he can thus look forward to a time when his own son will enable him to enjoy fully the pleasures of dependent old age.

The twenty-four models of filial piety are, of course, an ideal of hope, just as the tragedy of Oedipus is a myth of horror. Such stylized expressions of a culture's anxieties and aspirations are meaningful to the extent that they define in an explicit, if highly simplified, manner certain cultural values and conceptions of life role and social relations. By contrasting these two mythical expressions of the life cycle we have tried not only to make the Western reader more conscious of some of the distinctive aspects of Chinese social life but also to make him aware of certain biases he brings

---

the ways in which female and male children have been reared in these two very different cultural settings. Such myths and cultural stereotypes symbolize in a simplified, artistic manner, an underlying psychological reality, certain aspects of which we will explore in subsequent chapters.

15. Put in more direct terms, there was no "Oedipus complex" in traditional Chinese culture in the sense that this tradition explicitly told a son that it was both proper and morally virtuous for him to love his mother. This was not love in its sexual sense, of course, but love in the same form of oral nurturing by which the mother had loved the son as a child.

Consistent with our interpretation of the daughter as the Chinese "Oedipus" detailed in the previous footnote, the "Oedipus complex" in the Chinese family lay in the oft-observed tension between mother and daughter-in-law. The mother feared, at some level of perception, that her son's wife would detract from the affection which filiality said was her due. And the dreaded harshness of the mother-in-law represents the same rivalry for affection which can give father-son relations their tension in a Western family.

From a daughter-in-law's perspective, this competition for the affection of her husband was sufficiently intense to produce, in some instances, anxieties about her husband in fact violating the incest taboo. As is noted in the autobiography of one Chinese woman: "A girl of our village was married to a man of another village whose relationship with his mother was not a clear one. The young wife came home and wept with her mother." (Ida Pruitt, *A Daughter of Han: The Autobiography of a Chinese Working Woman* [Stanford, Calif.: Stanford University Press, 1967], p. 40.)

to the study of China given his own cultural background, which lays such stress on individual autonomy.

A Chinese viewing the Western life pattern, of course, in similar fashion reveals his own cultural biases. He notes that, "The life of a single individual is . . . incomplete. . . . Life exists in social relationships, and the family is the most fundamental of them by nature. . . . How different this is from the Western style, which makes orphans out of children and . . . lonely people out of parents by having the children live apart from their parents; how different this is from the Western style which values not companionship but separation, and condones an unstable relationship of marriage." [16]

Our task in the following chapters will be to try to go beyond interpretations of China which are based on personal judgments weighted with a Western cultural viewpoint. Rather, we shall try to evaluate, through the eyes of individuals raised in the Confucian tradition, the extent to which the myths of filiality reflect an underlying social reality, and the ways in which Chinese themselves see their society and its continuing social and political revolution.

16. C. K. Yang, *Chinese Communist Society: The Family and the Village* (Cambridge, Mass.: M.I.T. Press, 1965), Vol. I, pp. 166–167.

Chapter III

LIFE'S GOLDEN AGE (?)

The cyclical quality of the Chinese pattern of life suggested by the formal literature of the Confucian tradition finds expression in the attitudes of the Chinese we interviewed. They had few doubts that childhood and the years of youth embodied the happiest period of life. As expressed by a school teacher reared in Peking, childhood "is a golden age. You don't have to worry about anything: if you are hungry your parents give you food; if you need a haircut they give you money. You just have to study well and if there is anything you need they give it to you." [1] From the standpoint of adulthood,

1. T-9. Brief biographical sketches of the interview respondents, who are identified in the footnotes by place of interview—"T" for Taiwan, and "H" for Hong Kong—and case number, will be found in Appendix V, pp. 541–558 below.

Approximately 65 percent of our interviewees identified childhood as a happier time of life than adulthood; 15 to 20 percent saw adulthood as the happier time; and the remainder were undecided. This question about the more satisfying period of the life cycle is related to the social dislocations experienced by emigrés, who must have looked back with a degree of longing to the security of their early lives. For example, 75 percent of the thirty-one respondents in the 30–55 age group, all refugees only recently arrived from the mainland, saw childhood as the happier time of life, with few "undecided" responses. Only 56 percent of the thirty-four older refugees in the 56–85 age group, men who had been settled on Taiwan for more than a decade, saw childhood as the happier period.

It would be misleading, however, to attribute this response pattern merely to the immediate problems of being an emigré. In part the emphasis on childhood seems to reflect the bewilderments and tension of social change. Of those eighteen respondents who saw both their own social outlook and the outlook of their father as "traditional" (*shou-chiu*), 78 percent saw childhood as the happier time of life, while 91 percent of the eleven who were unable to define either their own social outlook or that of their father as either "traditional" or "modern" saw childhood as the happier time. Only 59 percent of the seventeen respondents who saw consistency between their own and their father's "modern" (*hsien-tai-hua*) outlook on life identified with childhood. This sample suggests both that these individuals had less emotional need to cling to the security of childhood and that adulthood,

the attraction of the early years of life is partly the condition of having one's desire for food and other material needs effortlessly gratified. It is also a time when one is screened from the complications of life behind the high walls of the family compound and through the intercession of nurturing adults:

> Youth years are happier than adulthood because you don't know or understand anything. All you do is play; you are without worries. When you become an adult then there are problems about studying, marriage, and your working future. These all can get you bothered. I think that life up until you are twenty is a relatively happier time. After you are thirty your superiors make trouble for you; and if you do not manage interpersonal relations well you can provoke people's hatred, so it is very annoying.[2]

This idealization of childhood as a time of "tranquillity" finds expression in China's ancient philosophical traditions.[3] The reasons for this desire to find pleasure and security by being cared for by others becomes evident when seen against a complex background

---

with its greater opportunities for self-realization, is seen by those striving after modernization as life's most significant period.

Our basic interpretation, however, remains that the strong appeal of childhood for the respondents taken as a group reflects a general cultural identification with the security and forms of nurturance and pleasure known most fully in the first years of life. We find no significant variation in this attitude orientation when the sample of respondents is considered in terms of geographical origin within China, socioeconomic status, or educational level.

Cross-cultural comparison is useful here for underlining the distinctive aspect of this orientation toward the life cycle. A group of 225 male American students from two midwestern colleges, and thirty-nine male adults of white-collar occupations from a Detroit suburb, were asked whether childhood or adulthood was the happier time of life. The students were about evenly divided (45 percent "childhood"; 52 percent "adulthood"; the remainder undecided), while the adults had "shifted" in the direction of seeing adulthood as the happier time of life (74 percent). What these data suggest is that a middle-class American, after wrestling with the identity problems associated with a culture that stresses individual autonomy, is able to find a meaningful life and personal fulfillment in a professional career and through the creation of his own family. The Chinese, however, continues to see his identity linked to the life of his original family, and longs for a return to that condition where he was cared for by others. (These comparative data are discussed in more detail in the author's article, "Mao's Effort to Reintegrate the Chinese Polity: Problems of Conflict and Authority in Chinese Social Processes," in A. Doak Barnett, ed., *Chinese Communist Politics in Action* [Seattle: University of Washington Press, 1968], pp. 276–280.)

2. T-49.

3. *See* Donald J. Munro, *The Concept of Man in Early China* (Stanford: Stanford University Press, 1968), Ch. 7.

of the social maturation process experienced by a child as he develops, and the world he knows as an adult. The focus of this chapter
is on a description of the way in which the Chinese reared their
children, and of the basic social attitudes and patterns of interpersonal relations which they inculcated for getting along in the adult
world.

THE INDULGENCE OF INFANCY

Memories of the first several years of life are, for all people, embodied in a diffuse sense of trust and well-being or mistrust and fore-
boding of some unforeseen calamity or evil, rather than in specific
and sharply recalled incidents. Hence we must seek understanding
of the events of these infant years through the field notes of the cultural anthropologist or the attitudes of adult Chinese about the
proper way to rear children. In particular, some insight into how
Chinese children are welcomed into life and educated to appreciate
its pleasures and deal with its dangers can be gained by looking at
the manner in which parents take care of an infant's bodily and
emotional needs and at how adults anticipate children fitting into
the social economy of their lives.

The birth of a child, especially a male, is cause for much satisfaction and celebration in a Chinese household. The mother has
affirmed her generative competence and fulfilled her social role as
a daughter-in-law. The father at last graduates from being a mere
son to one who has added a new generation to the family line and
can now face his eventual old age with a greater sense of security.
Grandparents, as well, delight at the addition to the family of a new
life with whom they can share the dependent leisure of their final
years.

But this time of joy can also be an occasion for anxiety in a
society with a high incidence of infant mortality. In rural Taiwan,
when a child dies his coffin is struck in "anger" before burial. Says
a villager in explanation:

> When you have a child you want him to take care of you when
> you are old and bury you when you die, but it is just the opposite
> when you have to bury him. It is because you are mad at him because
> he failed you [that you strike his coffin]. He wasn't really coming to
> be your child but just to waste your money. Also, people say that if
> you don't hit the child, the King of Hell will hit him as punishment
> for deserting his parents. If you don't hit him someone else will, so
> you might just as well hit him yourself.[4]

4. Reported in Margery Wolf, "Child Training in a Hokkien Village,"
(mimeographed; a paper prepared for a seminar on "Personality and Motiva-

Parental anxieties about survival of their offspring find expression in oral indulgence, for liberal feeding is about the only recourse beyond prayer that exists for a people with premodern notions about medicine and hygiene. In nursing, the breast is given to the child on demand by the mother or, in wealthy families, by a wet nurse. Weaning is abrupt, but takes place quite late, between one and two years according to most observations. The best morsels of food are frequently given to the youngest child, and many of our interviewees' most glowing recollection of parental love was of the mother who showed special favor through her cooking. A "proper" Chinese baby is one so plump with nourishment that there can be no doubt about his good health—or of his parents' concern that he survive infancy and grow up to take care of them when they return, in old age, to a similar state of dependency.

The considerable indulgence accorded a male child in infancy and early childhood, affection expressed above all through the giving of food, seems to be the basis of an "oral" calculus in the way that Chinese approach interpersonal relations throughout life. The reckoning of their family or population size in terms of "mouths" (*jen-k'ou*) rather than "heads," and the emphasis on eating which has produced one of the world's great culinary traditions, are only part of a view of life in which oral forms of pleasure and pain predominate.[5] Some of these forms might be noted here, not only because this oral calculus is obvious in our interview responses, but also because in important ways discussed throughout this study it colors Chinese political thinking.

A growing child finds that his society rewards achievement and success through eating. An engineer raised in a Kiangsu market town recalled as his most memorable youthful experience: "When I was about nine a little child of about four fell into a river near our house. I rescued her and carried her home. The child's parents were very thankful; and I, too, was very happy. I was given a lot of

---

tion in Chinese Society," Castle Harbour Hotel, Bermuda, January 26–28, 1964), p. 2. The Hokkien people of Taiwan are descendants of mainland Chinese, primarily from the coastal province of Fukien, who migrated to the island during the eighteenth century. Their language and customs have remained similar to those of the mainlanders from whom they are descended.

5. The manner in which sexual practice in China manifests an "oral" quality has been analyzed by John H. Weakland in, "Orality in Chinese Conceptions of Male Genital Sexuality," *Psychiatry*, Vol. XIX (1956), pp. 237–247. Weakland's insights seem borne out by interview and documentary data contained in a recent study of footbinding in traditional China: "When I loved a woman, I went all the way and wished that I could swallow her up. But only the tiny [bound] feet could be placed in the mouth." (Howard S. Levy, *Chinese Footbinding: The History of a Curious Erotic Custom* [New York: Walton Rawls, 1966], p. 135.)

food to eat. Even today I have not forgotten the experience." [6] But the table is also a major focus of punishments: "If my grades were not good, or if I got into fights, I would be physically punished, as by spanking, or being hit on the palm—or sometimes I would not get food to eat, and would have to sit by the side of the table and watch everyone else eat." [7]

The table is also the place where more routine social disciplines are developed; where a child acquires basic concerns about having sufficient material resources in a society traditionally faced with scarcity—anxiety about his ability to "take in" with restraint. As was recalled by an elderly lawyer from Fukien Province, "I remember that from the time we were small [my mother] always taught us to be economical about the things we ate. For example, when eating a fish you should always save a little bit; you should not eat it all at once. Hence today when I eat I am always very economical." [8]

For a Chinese the basic sense of social well-being and security remains linked throughout life to the ritual of eating. Meal-taking in a noisy, bustling setting reaffirms an individual's unity with his primary social group and recaptures the sense of being cared for that was most fully known in infancy:

> (What is the thing you remember with most pleasure about your early life?) My family was a big one, and I remember that mealtimes were very bustling. When it was time to eat someone would ring a bell, and then grandmother would divide up the food. Everyone would pick up his bowl to be served his portion. Everybody crowded in and bustled around. When we were busy with the farm harvest it was even more bustling as we would hire more than seventy people. Aside from this there was nothing in particular.[9]

In present-day Taiwan the descendants of mainland Chinese who emigrated to the island in centuries past see their social identity linked to rituals of eating. "Members of a family are defined as those who share a cooking stove. . . . This identification of stove and family is so important that those who cannot afford to add a new room to house the stove of a newly created family unit [in the compound of an extended family] build a second stove in the same kitchen." [10] And the sad act of breaking up a large family because of conflict or economic difficulty is termed "dividing the stove."

6. T-40.
7. T-9.
8. T-47.
9. T-49. Questions in parentheses were addressed by the interviewer to the respondent. Brackets enclose interpolations added for greater clarity.
10. Margery Wolf, *The House of Lim: A Study of a Chinese Farm Family* (New York: Appleton-Century-Crofts, 1968), p. 28.

As a child matures he discovers that the nurturing quality of food-giving is augmented and transformed: Authority becomes associated with who eats before or better than whom, and who can speak and who must listen. As he goes to school he acquires a sense of the ritualistic qualities of language, and of the importance of using the proper words and phrases in the appropriate social contexts. He also discovers in the world beyond his family that people can "eat" people by turning the oral patterns of respect and care learned in childhood into forms of aggression.[11] Yet throughout life his basic sense of security and social self remain associated with the oral forms of nurturing and social intercourse learned while young.[12]

Although after the first year or two of life the child begins to mature physiologically, the manner in which his needs are met prolongs his dependence on adult care. The breast which was given to the infant whenever he cried is replaced by the indulgence of *amahs* in wealthy families, or grandparents and older siblings among the peasantry, who will pacify the child with food or affection whenever he is unhappy. It is quite common for *amahs* to indulge their young charges by carrying them long after they have acquired the physical capacity to walk—an aspect of the rearing of children of wealth which seems to enhance their belief that both power and pleasure are to be found in a condition of passive dependency. And even in present-day Taiwan or urban Hong Kong it is quite common to see parents or youngsters of seven or eight carrying a child or younger sibling on their backs even though these children are quite able to walk on their own.

Underlying the permissive and indulgent treatment which elders accord young children is the notion that *adults should anticipate the child's needs for him.* As one observer of Chinese family life has phrased it, "[The pre-school] child is considered incapable of learning very much, and the parents' main goal is simply to keep the child from injuring himself or others and from causing his parents too much trouble." [13] A focal activity in the growth of a young child which enables us to affirm this interpretation is bowel training. Development of sphincter control is the first bodily function around which adults might—and in some cultures determinedly do—force onto the child their own anxious concerns for cleanliness, order,

11. *See* pp. 70–71, 99–104 below.
12. As expressed by a lonely working class woman who had traveled from her home in Shantung Province to Manchuria, "I was homesick for the land to which I was accustomed. The people in Manchuria did not talk as our people talked, nor did they eat the same food." (Ida Pruitt, *A Daughter of Han,* p. 131.)
13. Wolf, "Child Training in a Hokkien Village," p. 6.

Woman carrying child,
Taipei, Taiwan, December 1970.
Richard H. Solomon.

and punctuality; their concern that an individual learn to control his own behavior. The Chinese cultural pattern, however, does *not* place undue emphasis on such traits, and the growing Chinese child is not pressured by adults to learn to regulate his bowels by himself —and through such self-control acquire a sense of personal autonomy. Chinese parents are rather permissive about toilet training.[14] "Mothers claim they 'know' when the child wants to urinate or move his bowels and hold him out so that the child soils neither himself nor his caretakers." [15] Before he can walk, a parent, grandparent, or older sibling takes care of a child's eliminative activity "for him" by anticipating his needs and encouraging movement through gentle sounds or whistling; and later on, especially in lower class households, the child is told to emulate the toilet habits of his older brothers and sisters who take him outside for relief.

The impact of this form of cleanliness training would seem to be that the child acquires neither a sense of privacy nor an exaggerated concern with self-control of bodily functions by learning to "hold in" through muscular discipline. Rather, because elimination is such a "public" function in which he moves with the help of an adult or older sibling, failures to perform properly create anxieties about his *relation* to the adult or sibling who was "helping" him. A sense of the interdependent quality of even the most personal activities is developed, and with it a basic concern for how one performs before others—a sensitivity to shame.

In sum, until a male child approaches the age of five or six, when he has become strong enough to do simple chores on the farm or has acquired sufficient intellectual skills to begin formal schooling, life is a period of indulgence and light discipline. Bodily needs are anticipated and gratified within the limits of family resources. The appeals of this "golden age" of childhood dependency remain vital to traditional Chinese throughout life; and as was suggested in the *Twenty-Four Models of Filial Piety,* the hope of the parent and obligation of the filial son or daughter was to bring life full circle to those in old age, so that the pleasures of having one's needs effortlessly fulfilled would usher life out just as the parent had in similar fashion ushered life in for the child. The pattern of infant nurture remained the model by which a true son expressed love for his aging parents:

> Father . . . had a very pure character, he was very filial to his mother. (How did he express his filiality to her?) He was very com-

14. *See* Martha Wolfenstein, "Some Variants in the Moral Training of Children," *The Psychoanalytic Study of the Child,* Vol. V (1949), pp. 313, 326.

15. Wolf, "Child Training in a Hokkien Village," p. 3.

pliant with her wishes. Anything that grandmother liked to eat, things that would help to maintain her bodily health, father would go out and buy and give to her to eat, no matter how expensive they were. Grandmother would have to go to the toilet, and even though she could take care of it herself sometimes father would even help her there.[16]

CHILDHOOD RELATIONS WITH AUTHORITY:
BASIC PATTERNS IN THE USE OF POWER

The change in treatment a traditionally educated male child encountered between the ages of five and seven was radical and painful.[17] Whereas indulgent females previously had been the dominant influence in his life, now males began to exert pressures, both directly and by way of female caretakers, for conformity to social custom. The child quickly learned that he had graduated from the years of indulgence and was confronted with stern demands that he acquire the social habits which would enable him to get along in society and in a world of material scarcity.

As we have noted, the dominant theme or mode of early childhood disciplining in a traditional Chinese family was on proper ways of "taking in" (rather than concern with "holding in," as would be the case with strict toilet training) and that mealtimes were a major focus of such disciplinary activity. In a well-to-do family it was at the table that a child acquired his first view of authority as a provider of security and as a teacher of proper forms.

> (What kind of a person was your father?) Father was a very sincere person. He thought if other people had requests to make of you, you should respond to them. For instance, in the wintertime if other people did not have enough food to eat and came to father to ask his help, he would definitely agree to help them. And he did not worry about whether they returned [the food he had given them]. (How did

16. T-33.
17. In a very helpful analysis of the periodization of the Chinese life cycle, Marion Levy notes that the youth or "*yu-nien* period of childhood ranged . . . from four years or earlier to fifteen or sixteen. During this period the real discipline of Chinese life made itself felt upon the children. . . . In the gentry family . . . the male *yu-nien* was sent to live in his father's section of the house. Nurses and servants continued to care for him, but his father took over his immediate supervision." (Marion Levy, *The Family Revolution in Modern China* [New York: Octagon Books, 1963], pp. 75–76.)
This same phenomenon of an "abrupt, bewildering, and drastic" change in the way a father treats his maturing son has been observed among lower class villagers in Taiwan. (Margery Wolf, "Child Training and the Chinese Family," in Maurice Friedman, ed., *Family and Kinship in Chinese Society* [Stanford, Calif.: Stanford University Press, 1970], p. 41.)

he treat you children?) [Father] dealt with the children very strictly: for instance, when we were eating we could not make a sound with our chopsticks, and when we lifted up food from the serving dish with chopsticks we had to do it from the table directly in front of us, otherwise we would be scolded.[18]

For China's peasant millions, however, concern with "taking in" was developed through the most basic discipline of all, an inadequate food supply. As one farmer from North China recalled:

We came to Yenan from Hengshan when I was five. That was during the great famine of 1928. . . . We went about begging. . . . We had nothing to eat. Father went to Chaochuan to gather firewood and beg food, but he didn't get any. He was carrying elm leaves and firewood when he fell by the roadside. . . . That is my earliest memory: of always being hungry, and of father there dead in the road.[19]

The handling and consuming of food thus, for Chinese of all economic levels, becomes an activity associated with considerable anxiety; anxiety about parental disapproval of one's table manners, or just the elemental concern that one is consuming scarce resources.

The frequent and often emotionally tinged recollections of our respondents about parents or a favored younger brother being given somewhat better food or a larger portion at meal-time suggest that a child's first exposure to social status relationships, to the facts that some people are more important or more highly valued than others, is also associated with table ritual. Self-respect and degree of authority become measured by the quality and amount of food one is given by one's providers:

[Parents] ought to help their children develop a sense of self-confidence and pride . . . Certainly they should see that children do not have a sense of inferiority. (How can they make sure that children do not have any sense of inferiority?) Well, for example, if a child carries a lunch box to school, we adults could eat a little less ourselves and let the child carry somewhat better food to school. In that way the child will not see his friends eating good food but he himself eating food that is not so good, and thus develop a sense of inferiority.[20]

As a child grows older and more articulate—especially in upper class families—concern with proper "taking in" becomes generalized to the more abstract give-and-take of verbal exchange:

18. T-26.
19. Jan Myrdal, *Report from a Chinese Village* (London: Heinemann, 1965), p. 135.
20. T-38.

With [father] things had to be just so; there were rules for everything. At the table we had to wait for the older people to start to eat first, we had to sit there at attention, couldn't talk with our other brothers. (What about the adults talking?) Oh, they could talk as they pleased.[21]

When father was speaking the children could not go on talking. Children were only allowed to listen to the adults speaking because they don't understand; they can only listen to people speaking and if they talk a lot then they will get hit.[22]

The giving of opinions, like the giving of food, is an activity where adults, certain adults, have precedence and take initiative. Children are made to feel that they are incompetent to develop their own opinions, that they "don't understand" and lack sufficient experience in society and hence should rely for guidance on the adults who do have the proper understanding and experience. The communication pattern which the growing Chinese child learns is thus nonreciprocal. Parents are the ones with the authority to give, whether the giving concerns food, opinions, or orders; there is no "giving back" on the child's part; he has to learn to "take in" what is given to him in proper fashion:

(When you were young did you have any differences of opinion with your parents?) Children did not have that freedom so I did not express opinions. My younger brother once had a difference of opinion with my parents. (What difference of opinion?) When we were small our parents ate food that was rather good, but we children ate food that was a bit inferior. My younger brother was rather unruly, he was dissatisfied; he argued that he wanted to eat better food. Father was unhappy, thought he was just a little troublemaker wanting to enjoy the oral pleasures of the older generation. (As a result, how was this difference of opinion resolved?) There was no use in my younger brother talking about it. Quite the contrary, father was unhappy and hence scolded him.[23]

A strong sense of social status and authority thus develops around interpersonal communications, of who may speak first, who must listen, or who is left speechless.[24]

Chinese sum up their expectations regarding relations between adult and child—as with other relationships between an authorita-

21. T-9.
22. T-26.
23. T-38.
24. A Chinese household servant recalls, "My master was a very tall man and well grown. . . . We were all afraid of him. . . . We were so much afraid . . . that when he gave orders we stood meekly and stuttered." (Pruitt, *A Daughter of Han,* p. 107.)

tive individual and his subordinates—in the notion of *modeling* or emulation. The superior is supposed to behave in such a way that the subordinate can "study" or imitate the superior's example. A child may occasionally be led to believe that he should receive the same treatment as an adult, as in the example above, but in most of our respondents' recollections, the superior took the initiative in communication, or gave cues as to what was acceptable behavior on the subordinate's part.

Of course emulation as an aspect of the childhood learning process is not unique to China. Children of all cultures learn from behavioral models and copy the actions of adults who are significant in their early lives. What seems distinctive about Chinese notions of model emulation is the parents' conviction that the child should sustain his deferential relationship to the "model" adult as he matures. Furthermore, this form of learning is generalized into the adult world.[25] The traditionally reared child was told to *rely upon* the greater wisdom and experience of family elders or an older sibling rather than being urged to formulate his own *internalized* set of behavioral controls. He was not encouraged to test out, within the limits of his developing physical and mental faculties, his ability as an individual to direct his own actions and to make personal judgments.

This adult expectation permeates many other aspects of the growing child's life. Interview respondents, when asked to recall the most pleasurable moments of childhood, frequently mentioned episodes of tree-climbing and swimming, or running and playing with friends. They also recalled that such activities were very likely to bring them a beating from an anxious parent, who feared that they would injure themselves or make some kind of trouble. The child yearns to test and develop his own physical and mental capabilities, but adults continually tell him that he is incompetent. He will get hurt or do something bad, and hence should either inhibit his capacity for individual activity or develop his talents in areas where adults can guide and protect him. The strength of such a point of view is, in part, a continuing expression of the parents' anxiety that their male offspring might die—as by drowning or in a fall from a tree. An adult's concern with receiving care during his own old age and his doubts about a child's competence to act apart from the guidance of more experienced elders, thus shape with great emotional force the way he trains his children.

Punishments reinforce parental pressures for reliance on adults.

25. The important place that model emulation occupies in Confucian philosophy, and in Chinese theories of learning, is discussed in Munro, *The Concept of Man in Early China*, pp. 90–96, 108–109, 167–171.

Traditionally, and particularly in lower class families, it was considered necessary and proper to beat children so that they would develop a sense of fear if they did not obey adult commands. The majority of the adults in our sample recall having been beaten with boards, whips, or rulers, or having received other forms of physical punishment.[26] Such punishments were not given *indiscriminately,* but resulted from disobeying parental orders or from failure to meet their standards of performance (especially in school). Through it all, the child can perceive a rationale and predictability behind adult power and is presented with alternatives whereby through his own behavior he can avoid punishment.[27] Yet because his parents allow him no opportunity to "talk back" or reason with them in the matter of discipline, the child learns that it is safer and less painful to ac-

26. Of the seventy-nine interviewed persons who provided information on how they had been punished in childhood, sixty-two (79 percent) recalled receiving frequent physical punishments. Twenty-one percent asserted they had received only nonphysical punishments. These data do not show any strong association with information on the respondents' economic class level. (*See* additional information on childhood punishments in Appendix VI, pp. 559–560.)

27. In an analysis of the political culture of Burma, Pye has found that a Burmese child experiences erratic and willful treatment from his parents, which establishes a sense of unpredictability, danger, and impermanence in social relationships and the expectation of a lack of congruence between personal effort and outcome in social action. (Lucian W. Pye, *Politics, Personality, and Nation Building: Burma's Search for Identity* [New Haven: Yale University Press, 1962], pp. 182–183, 195–203.) This cultural pattern contrasts with the stress on unambiguous role relationships, predictability, and a sense of purposefulness in action which Pye finds in the Chinese political culture: "Children [in China] are made to feel that in spite of constant harassment and criticism they can still demonstrate their ultimate worth by showing they are not lacking in the vital ingredient of willpower. . . . To demonstrate correct desires to act purposefully so as to reveal one's willpower is thus the most assured way that the Chinese child has of proving his worth to others. It is also the way to demonstrate dutiful compliance with authority and to receive the emotional rewards of security." (Pye, *The Spirit of Chinese Politics: A Psychocultural Study of the Authority Crisis in Political Development* [Cambridge, Mass.: M.I.T. Press, 1968], p. 141. Also see pp. 94–99, 137–143.)

These expectations of predictability and the efficacy of willpower in Chinese attitudes toward social action have an important relationship to the individual's sense of indebtedness and relationship to the family group. Having called the child's attention to his obligations to parents and family, these adults then provide a clear path by which, through his own efforts, he can repay his social "debts." Educational achievement or business success traditionally were ways in which a Chinese could "honor" his family. The compulsive work habits which give Chinese society or communities of overseas Chinese their industrious air seem the most concrete expression of the concern for fulfilling family obligations which the Chinese carry throughout their lives—even if they are separated by great physical distances.

cept parental injunctions in a passive manner. This pattern of passivity is expressed succinctly in the Chinese phrase for obedience, *t'ing-hua,* to "listen to talk." Attempts by the child to question the guidance of authoritative elders, or to reason and develop independent judgments, can only invoke parental displeasure. He learns to "take in" parental guidance without question, and is firmly discouraged from "giving out" on his own.

Certain cross-cultural research on childrearing practices has indicated that harsh physical punishment may actually increase rather than decrease a child's sense of autonomy.[28] Our interview data provide limited evidence that this may be so. Those respondents who recalled being punished physically were somewhat less likely to exhibit a dependency type of social orientation than were those who recalled nonphysical forms of punishment. In response to the interview question of whether they considered childhood or adulthood a happier time of life, those who described harsh physical punishments in early family life were somewhat less likely to look back with longing on childhood than were those who mentioned being punished primarily through emotional pressures. Because of our small number of respondents, however, this pattern must be considered suggestive only.

Our provisional interpretation, which will be elaborated in the next chapter, is that through a combination of physical and emotional sanctions Chinese parents developed in their children considerable anxiety about disobeying their instructions, and indeed fear of direct contact with a stern father. The legacy of this pattern of childhood punishments and anxiety in the face of family authority which it developed was that the child acquired an attitude of passivity toward those with power over him. He tended to follow their guidance rather than internalize their standards of behavior so that he might act independently of their control. When authority figures were not present he would feel himself "freed" of controls which he had not been encouraged to maintain on his own. From such a childhood pattern of relations with family authority seems to grow the adult Chinese concern for the presence of a strict, personalized, and unambiguous source of (political) authority who will impose order on potentially unruly peers and provide a clear source of guidance for all.[29]

28. *See* John W. M. Whiting and Irvin L. Child, *Child Training and Personality: A Cross-Cultural Study* (New Haven: Yale University Press, 1953), pp. 240–246.

29. These Chinese political attitudes are discussed in more detail in a quantitative and cross-cultural framework in the author's study, "Mao's Effort to Reintegrate the Chinese Polity," in Barnett, ed., *Chinese Communist Politics in Action,* pp. 280–285, 301–306.

The emotional pressures by which Chinese parents seek to control their children reinforce the dependency needs instilled during the first years of life. The threat of *isolation* from family approval and resources is a particularly potent parental sanction.

The recollections of our interviewees suggest that isolation can involve either being made conspicuous before the family group ("For big mistakes we would have to kneel in front of the after-dinner group and be scolded" or, as noted previously, be forced to "sit beside the dinner table and watch everyone else eat" [30]), or being cut off from family resources.

> (What kinds of punishments did you receive at home?) If I did not study well then I would be hit or isolated. (How would you be isolated?) My parents would not buy clothing for me, nor give me presents; or they would say, "All right, if your behavior is going to be that way then you won't be able to study any more. You can go out and work." [31]

The use of such sanctions to control an individual's behavior provides an important point of intersection between the sense of social interrelatedness and the dependency needs developed in a young child, the life of the family group, and paternal authority. The father invokes the solidarity of the group to shame the child, and to raise his anxieties about not fitting into group life properly; or for more serious transgressions confronts him with the ultimate horror of being cut off from family resources and having to face life alone, "like an orphan." [32]

When the child enters school such forms of control over the individual are reinforced by the teacher's invocation of group pressures. In a study of educational practices in contemporary Taiwan it was observed that, "In a first grade class . . . a child who was crying . . . was told by the teacher that he should not cry in school because it was not nice looking or sounding. Then the teacher, pointing out the weeping child, made the other students imitate the sound of crying and laughing." [33] Throughout this study we shall

30. T-9. Other observations of parents' use of family group pressures to discipline an erring son are reported in Martin C. Yang, *A Chinese Village: Taitou, Shantung Province* (New York: Columbia University Press, 1945), pp. 129–130.

31. T-11.

32. Parents' use of the threat of abandonment or adoption to control their children is reported in Wolf, *House of Lim*, p. 42.

33. This, and other examples of group shaming techniques are discussed in a discerning and well-documented study of educational practices in Taiwan by Richard W. Wilson, *Childhood Political Socialization on Taiwan* (unpublished Ph.D. dissertation, Princeton University, 1967), Ch. I.

see that to be isolated (*ku-li ti*)—in the two senses of being made
to stand out in shame before one's group, or being threatened with
alienation from the group and its resources—is an emotionally compelling sanction invoked widely in adult Chinese social and political
life. This is most clearly seen in the use of the cangue or penal col-
lar, a form of public shaming of social offenders which has now
been institutionalized by the Chinese Communists.

While group pressures may be used to control his behavior, a
growing child soon learns that his relations with other members of
the family are clearly structured in hierarchical fashion and that
group authority derives from the authority of the family head,
usually the father. Each family member has a social role to perform, and these roles are interrelated in rank order.[34] The pattern
of authority and deference the son learns in dealing with his father
is primary: yet this "submission-dominance" style influences most
other relations between males. There are no "brothers" in the
family, only *ko-ko* and *ti-ti,* elder and younger brothers, and their
relations are shaped by the pattern of father-son interaction:

> "The ruler should be a Ruler, his minister a Minister, the father a
> Father, and his son a Son" [a famous quote from the *Analects* of
> Confucius]. If a father doesn't understand the proper way to be a
> Father, then naturally his sons and daughters will not understand
> morality or the proper relationship between elder and younger brother.
> If the father is kindly then the son will be filial. The same kind of
> rationale lies behind the relationship of an older and younger brother.
> "The older brother should be kindly and the younger brother patient"
> [another Confucian quotation]. The older brother should be lenient
> and generous, and his younger brother should . . . accept his older
> brother's guidance.[35]

This response adds an important dimension to usual descriptions
of the hierarchical authority of the Chinese family. In one sense the
child was taught that the authority of his father was absolute and
that he owed him unwavering obedience. Yet the son also learned
that authority had responsibilities and that his own behavior was
in some measure conditional upon the actions of those with authority over him. The formal Confucian tradition told him that while he

34. While this "role-relationship" pattern of interpersonal deference and
obligation was first learned implicitly within the family, when a child began
his formal education he was taught that it carried the legitimacy of the
Confucian tradition. The Classics explicitly identified the *wu-lun* or five
dyadic social relationships of father to son, elder to younger brother, husband to wife, friend to friend, and ruler to minister, as a reciprocal pattern
of responsibility and deference which was both "natural" and morally just.
   35. T-32.

Man in a penal cangue,
in a Shantung village, 1890s.
Courtesy New York Public Library.

was to give filial submission, his father or elder brother *should* be generous or kindly. In practice, our respondents recounted that fathers or elder brothers frequently did not live up to their family roles, and great resentment could grow in the gap between performance and obligation. As we will see in the next chapter, grievances toward family authority were seldom translated into openly expressed hostility or opposition; yet at some limit, when father or elder brother failed to perform as Father or Elder Brother should, when the dependent's minimal needs were not met, then "rebellion" had a certain legitimacy. In the sense of injustice which dependents saw in authorities who failed to fulfill the obligations of their social role lies the psychological root of the "right of rebellion" expressed in the philosophy of Mencius.

As a child approaches his teens, and the time when he will begin to have frequent contacts outside the family, his relation to paternal authority, which at the end of infancy had become stern and controlling, becomes more distant. His father increasingly *cuts himself off* from direct interaction with him, and the child experiences only the taking of orders, the unquestioning reliance on a more distant and unapproachable source of control.[36] He is told in deeds as well as words that his position is to *depend* on adults, who will both make decisions for him and take care of him; and he will gain their approval, if not their affection, by conforming to their demands:

> Father was very conservative; everything was old-fashioned. (In what way was he conservative?) For example, his style of life was regulated, he did not want to have contact with people on the outside. He was a bit selfish and rather lacking in concern for us children. . . . (What was his personality like?) Father's personality was very strong, stubborn; this was all a matter of the influence of the environment because he was a farmer and seldom had contact outside [the family]. (How did he treat you children?) He did not worry very much about us children. By temperament he liked to be alone, he did not like to

36. Of the eighty-one respondents to the question, "When you were young and had problems, with whom would you discuss them?" 46 percent replied "Mother," only 10 percent replied "Father," and 11 percent indicated "both Father and Mother." Fourteen percent replied "no one" or said they considered problems by themselves. The remaining respondents identified siblings, friends, or other relatives, with a frequency in each case of less than 8 percent. This communication pattern suggests that the mother played a key role in relating the child to paternal authority. Responses to Thematic Apperception Test (TAT) Card III [See Appendix IV, p. 538 below] indicate that the mother's role was usually that of a mediator who attempted to prevent the father from venting hostility against the son. From this pattern the child learned that intermediaries were helpful in dealing with conflict-laden social relationships. (See pp. 128–129, 134 below.)

be together with the children; he would be annoyed with their bawl-ing.[37]

Because father was very stern when we were small we would not dare to talk with him. . . . If you asked him something he would just say, "Children shouldn't ask so many questions!" . . . He might say, "Just you go and study!" [38]

Several important patterns in relations between superior and subordinate which find clear manifestation in Chinese political behavior seem to have their roots in the harsh and distant treatment a father accords his growing sons. First, the child learns there is a distinction between decision-making and action in his relations with authority. The father passes judgments regardless of the child's will, yet the child must obey when informed of paternal decisions. Authority becomes associated with thought and word; subordination with the need to act or execute the will of others.[39] This pattern seems to be rooted in the concept in Confucian political philosophy that "superior men" (*chün-tzu*) with "cultivated" minds are to rule over those who labor with their hands.[40]

Second, the child's contacts with authority become laden with anxiety. Chinese parents believe that the inculcation of fear is necessary in rearing filial children. The severe (*yen*) father or elder

37. T-38.
38. T-47.
39. Pye writes: "Historically the tempo of Chinese politics was lethargic and cautious. The picture one has of imperial offices and *yamen* is one of slow-moving and heavily clad officials, the only bustle of activity coming from the purposeful but anxious movements of flunkies who, however, could not be part of politics precisely because they were so active. The more important the man, the slower his pace." (*The Spirit of Chinese Politics*, p. 129.)

The Chinese inclination to rely on intermediaries in interpersonal rela-tions, discussed elsewhere in this chapter, seems further to separate thought from action: a plan is conceived, but its execution requires the assistance of a third party. As one analysis has suggested, "Sequences of behavior di-rected toward aims involve a considerable differentiation of preparation and execution. The preparation is largely private or undisclosed. . . . Overt ac-tive preparations toward the protagonist's end are largely made for him by others on whom he has some claim and who react to the immediate need he reveals to them." (John H. Weakland, "The Organization of Action in Chinese Society," *Psychiatry*, Vol. XIII [1950], p. 364.)

40. ". . . there is the saying, 'Some labour with their minds, and some labour with their strength. Those who labour with their minds govern oth-ers; those who labour with their strength are governed by others. Those who are governed by others support them; those who govern others are supported by them.' This is a principle universally recognized." ("The Works of Mencius," Book III, Part I, Ch. IV, sect. 6, in *The Chinese Classics*, trans. James Legge, Vol. II, pp. 249–250.)

brother saw respect as naturally related to the anxiety his presence evoked in son or younger brother:

> (How did you get along with your older brother?) I feared him; respected him. (Why did you fear him?) Well, he had his experience, his knowledge, and could help me. He also had his power, and if my parents were not around he could direct me or punish me if I did something bad—for example, if I was reading a novel when I should have been studying.
>
> (What is the most important aspect of relations between brothers?) The older brother should correct the younger brother's errors and encourage his good points. The younger should respect the elder. . . . I really feared my older brother.[41]

As revealed by our interviews, most respondents sought to reduce the anxiety of dealings with authority either through avoidance or, when contact was unavoidable, by prompt obedience to authority's demands: "You can say that father never was angry with me. If I did not obey him in the least way it would just take one look from his face, a blink of his eyes, or a few words of instruction, and we would not dare [disobey him]. We just feared him and that was it. As a result we obeyed him." [42]

The reliance on intermediaries in social relations, so pronounced in adult Chinese social behavior, seems to have its roots in the child's desire to dilute or "buffer" his contact with anxiety-provoking authority. A Chinese recalls his childhood attempts to gain favorable decisions from his mother:

> We never had the courage simply to ask [her] to take us somewhere, since we felt certain that our request would be categorically refused. . . . So we sent my fourth brother, Ch'un, who was seven or eight, to act as mediator, not with full authority, but merely to report to Mother what we had said, and to bring back her answer. He was not to voice any opinion of his own, or to misreport what we had said, or to forget what Mother said in reply.[43]

A child's ability to manipulate the family social environment, of course, is in no small measure a function of the willingness of various adults to be "used" by, or to use, the child. Evidence suggests that the mother could play a particularly critical role in the constellation of family relationships in giving her son the encouragement to respond to the demands of the father. *The Twenty-four Models of Filial Piety*, discussed earlier, and interview data pre-

41. T-9.

42. T-43.

43. Chow Chang-cheng, *The Lotus Pool* (New York: Appleton-Century-Crofts, 1961), p. 59.

sented in this chapter, indicate that the relationship between mother and son could be particularly close. When a mother found that her needs for affection, respect, or security were not fulfilled by her husband—who was very likely committed to fulfilling his filial obligations to his mother—the wife would seek solace in her relationship to her son. As one analysis has put it: "The early deprivation and submissiveness which as a young girl and a young daughter-in-law, a woman has to observe, can be gradually given up after she has borne a son. . . . She has the need to establish her superiority [in her husband's family, and so she uses her son as] a highly esteemed extension of herself, a narcissistic tool." [44] Thus, the ego strength which a male child develops is in part related to the support and encouragement he acquires from his mother, who may seek to use him for her own ends.

Both the status differences within the Chinese family and the particular affection which could characterize mother-son or grandparent-grandchild relations provided emotional support and leverage which a child learned to manipulate. He found that *indirectly* he could influence the behavior of those with immediate authority over him.[45] The status and affection of a family elder could be invoked to modify the behavior of a father or elder brother: "My brother would sometimes hit me. I would get mad and say, 'You shouldn't hit me; you should help me!' I would tell mother and she would hit him." [46] Similarly, as observed in a Taiwan village, children learned to control the behavior of offensive peers, not by a direct response, but through invoking the authority of someone with superior status. "Village children . . . developed a technique for taking revenge on an attacker that is both safe and rewarding. They report the transgressor to his parent. . . . The mother of the naughty child then either beats her own child in the presence of his victim or promises to do so when she finds him." [47]

Despite the tension surrounding direct dealings with those in

44. Warner Muensterberger, "Orality and Dependence: Characteristics of Southern Chinese," p. 64.

45. It was precisely this type of family constellation which seems to have characterized Mao Tse-tung's early life. Mao told Edgar Snow in 1936 that while he hated his father, his mother was "kind, generous, and sympathetic." She formed a "united front" with Mao and his brother against the father, encouraging her sons in a strategy of "indirect attack" against the family "ruling power." (Edgar Snow, *Red Star Over China* [New York: Grove Press, 1961], p. 125.) From such indirect evidence one can infer the emotional origins of Mao's willingness to challenge established political authority as an adult.

46. T-18.

47. Wolf, "Child Training and the Chinese Family," p. 55.

authority, a child did learn that family elders were nurturant as well as severe. He knew that his physical needs would be taken care of and that he could win their implicit approval through obedience and dependence on their guidance. This experience left the child with a strong sense of ambivalence toward authority; a feeling of wanting to be protected by it, yet anxiety at approaching too near. As expressed by the son of a Ch'ing dynasty scholar-official from Chekiang:

> [Father] loved his children with all his heart, but his love was *in* his heart. He would not express it. He was concerned that we had enough to eat, that we were properly clothed, and whether we were hot or cold. Every time he would go away from home he would definitely bring back something for us to eat. But his attitude was very stern. *When you saw him you would both fear him and want to get near him.*[48]

The manner in which this ambivalence to authority is handled, both in adolescence and in adulthood, tells much about the style of Chinese political behavior, as will be elaborated in subsequent chapters.

48. T-43. Emphasis added.

Chapter IV

EMOTIONAL CONTROL

One would expect that the change in treatment from indulgence to strict control encountered by a young child as he entered the period of training for life in society would initially produce some bewilderment and frustration, if not rage. As Chinese tend to guard the intimate details of family life and personal feelings behind high walls and polite social forms, there have been few direct and systematic observations of relations between parents and children which would make possible a detailed description of the child's reaction to this change in treatment. However, a number of Western observers have noted tantrums of uncontrolled anger in young Chinese children. Rage is possibly the child's initial response to the sudden imposition of adult control.

On the basis of field observations of life in a fishing village near Hong Kong, one anthropologist has suggested that these fits of anger, in which the child will drop to the ground and kick and scream, are a reaction to fear of being abandoned by his parents, to an inability to get his way from adults (who had previously been so indulgent), and a reaction—often delayed—to teasing or bullying by older children or adults.[1] The fact that such tactics of violent loss of control are used affirms in one more dimension what we saw in the last chapter: the child finds he has little room for "talking back" or influencing the behavior of adults who control him. It appears that his *initial* reaction to this unpleasant confrontation with an unyielding source of control is to express frustration and rage in a tantrum.

What is of greater significance for the emotional development of the child than simply having tantrums is the way these and other

1. Barbara E. Ward, "Temper Tantrums in Kau Sai: Some Speculations upon Their Effects" (mimeographed; a paper prepared for a seminar on "Personality and Motivation in Chinese Society," Castle Harbour Hotel, Bermuda, January 26–28, 1964), p. 2.
Lucian Pye also notes frequent parental teasing of their children, and a general adult "fascination in observing the emotional outbursts of children who have been teased." (*The Spirit of Chinese Politics,* p. 100.)

expressions of emotionality are dealt with by adults. In the setting of the Hong Kong fishing village it was observed that, "as a general rule the child is left to cry himself out." [2] Adults neither comfort nor scold the raging youngster, with the result that after a number of ineffectual tries at influencing the offending elder, the child gives up the tactic as useless.

In describing attempts to strike back at the abuse of older siblings, respondents recalled that efforts to vent hostility at those due "respect" could only invoke greater pain: "[My brother] was five years older than I. Sometimes he would pull my hair and we would fight. I would sometimes try to hit back, but then he would only hit me harder. Mostly I had to obey him. I feared him." [3]

These observations and recollections suggest that the growing child soon learns that emotional expressiveness is dangerous because he lays himself open to manipulation by adults or older siblings. If avoidance of contact with these offending family elders is not possible, then at least a holding in of the feelings by which they seek to use him becomes the most effective way to prevent humiliation or the pain of a rage. Also, the child learns from observing the ways in which adults handle their own feelings that reserve and emotional impassiveness are appropriate ways to discipline these inner urges.

THE DANGERS OF "DROWNING A CHILD WITH LOVE" (NI-AI)

The general emotional tone of early family life that is recalled by adult Chinese suggests that there is considerable reserve in the expression of affection between parents and children. The parental models from which children learn tell them that inner feelings are not to be expressed, except in highly guarded ways, and that in public, emotions should be masked behind the forms of propriety (*li-mao*): "(How did your parents get along?) They lived off in a separate house. (Were they very natural to each other, or very courteous?) They were very mannerly; they treated each other like guests. They were very considerate to each other, and never fought or argued in front of us children." [4]

The son of a small merchant in rural Hupeh Province, when recalling his aloof father, observed, "People in the countryside very seldom expressed their love anyway. (To your mother?) Love between a Chinese husband and wife is very reserved; it is deep in one's heart. They just would not express their love in front of the

2. Ward, "Temper Tantrums in Kau Sai," p. 5.
3. T-18.
4. T-9.

children or the older generation. (Why not?) This is an old Chinese tradition." [5]

Even in matters of the "bruises and scratches" of growing up, parents seem to give children little sympathetic treatment or open emotional support. As one Hokkien mother on Taiwan told an anthropologist:

> They don't dare come crying back to me [if they hurt themselves]. I always scold them and say, "I called you to do something so why didn't you do it instead of staying here and getting yourself hurt?" Or sometimes I say, "Why don't you sit at home? Why do you have to go out and play and get hurt?" [Laughing] Really, sometimes they get a big cut, but they never tell me about it. They just go and get some medicine and put it on themselves. Besides, they shouldn't come crying to me. They are already this old [seven and nine] so they shouldn't do that any more.[6]

Adults act as if emotions are dangerous (not an unreasonable assumption in a society which traditionally has lived in dense population settlements). If expressions of affection are not restrained, once such feelings come into the open the individuals involved might lose all control. As expressed by a middle-aged teacher reared in rural Shantung, "Young people's recreation shouldn't necessarily include dancing. When I see people holding hands on the street I find it very repulsive. . . . This can lead to not maintaining order; it means that anything goes." [7]

Parental emotional reserve and "distance" communicates to the child that his expressions of feelings should be limited. If his parents are too permissive with him, his emotions might overwhelm him and disorder would follow:

> (Were you very close to your parents?) In China parents have their dignity. It is an old custom. If they are just "do as you please" (*suipien*) with the children, then probably they won't be obedient. For example, if they told me I had done something well I might get all excited and would think I could just do as I pleased, such as playing ball anywhere in the house. So for this reason they wouldn't allow any rude or disorderly behavior.[8]

Underlying the development of emotional control is the same adult attitude we encountered previously concerning the child's re-

---

5. T-33.
6. Margery Wolf, "Child Training in a Hokkien Village," p. 14. This attitude has also been noted by Richard Wilson in his study of socialization in Taiwan elementary schools. *Childhood Political Socialization on Taiwan,* p. 61.
7. T-26.
8. T-9.

lations with authority: A growing person is considered by family elders to be incapable of learning to discipline his own behavior, his own emotions, *by himself*. Hence parents must provide discipline for the child. In the case of controlling emotions this requires that the parents do not express their own inner feelings. If they should show their feelings to the child, his emotions might be stimulated, leading him to some "disorderly" action.

There is, of course, a circular argument here: Parents do not believe that children can learn to handle their emotions in open, if disciplined, ways; hence they educate them to reserve their feelings (and the behavior which emotions might motivate). The child thus grows up believing he can have no control of himself once these evils[9] within him come into the open—or once external controls are taken away. As a result *in fact* he may not have well-developed control over *released* emotions as an adult, both because he has not been trained for such control and because he thinks control is not possible. Logically, of course, this argument is tautological, yet it becomes a self-fulfilling prophecy when transmitted from one generation to the next through childhood socialization.

Parental concern that letting the child know he is valued will lead to loss of control and "doing as one pleases" carries with it an echo of the golden years of infancy—when the new baby was highly valued, when adults *did* openly express affection to the child, when the child obtained material satisfaction and pleasure without discipline or personal effort. That such an existence should be appealing is not strange, especially when it is followed by the imposition of stern parental controls. But yearning for such an indulgent life can appear very dangerous to people living not far above subsistence, or not far away from fallen gentry neighbors who once had been wealthy.[10] As a result traditional Chinese felt that to love a child

9. An ancient Chinese medical text asserts that, "The inner causes of diseases consist of seven types of emotion." (Cited in Pye, *The Spirit of Chinese Politics,* p. 153.) And in folk wisdom, emotions, particularly those of anger and aggression, could cause death. A Chinese working-class woman recounted to a foreign friend an incident in which a man became so "angry that he died of heat in the intestines." She also noted with sadness the death of a grandchild: "It was my daughter who destroyed the life of her own child. The foreign doctors said that she died of typhoid fever, but I knew that she had died of shame and the anger that her mother put on her." (Pruitt, *A Daughter of Han,* pp. 26, 223–224.)

10. There is much evidence in the records of clans, great families, and even popular sayings, that traditional Chinese were quite conscious of the rise and fall of family fortunes; of humble or impoverished origins and a determined advance to wealth and power, but then a decline into renewed penury within a few generations. Such "elite circulation," which has been documented in several recent studies, was often seen as related to the ma-

openly or "too much" after the years of infancy was very dangerous for both the child and his family group in a world of material scarcity and insecurity.

The Chinese expression for "spoiling" children is *ni-ai*, literally "to drown in love." Drowning is an "oral" kind of death; suffocation by taking too much in through the mouth. As we saw earlier, indulgence through the mouth was precisely the way parents expressed their love and concern for a new infant. But such "taking in" is also the form of behavior about which adults first imposed discipline on the maturing child. It is not surprising that in a world of scarcity parents should fear that if discipline is not imposed, the child (the one who is being trained to depend on his parents, and on whom parents hope to depend in old age) will "eat up" the family resources through undisciplined consumption. Therefore, since love was most fully known and expressed through eating, both eating and love must be restrained or else it could mean impoverishment, for the group if not the individual. As a result, in the rearing of Chinese children there traditionally has been a tension between "loving" the child with food so that he will survive, yet controlling him so that he will not grow up to "eat one out of house and home." This tension is clearly expressed in the following revealing comments by an elderly upper class Chinese from Shantung:

> Father's weak point was that he was excessively strict with the children. Take, for example, the son of my father's concubine: He went away to study. He was already twenty. Father gave him his tuition, but when he would return home Father would make him account for the money he had spent. If things did not tally up then Father would think that he had not used his money correctly and would beat him with a stick. Parents should be warmer than this; then you can have some emotional exchange. Being so strict is not right, the children will just fear their parents.
>
> Mother's weak point was that she "drowned her children in love." After my older sister got married her family situation turned bad; her husband gambled money. Mother would practically risk her life to give them more money, and afterwards even my sister's whole family moved in to live with us. This kind of excessive love is not good. Mother should have helped [my sister] to manage her own household properly; then she would not have been so dependent.[11]

The father expresses his anxiety that one of his offspring—significantly enough the fruit of his own pleasure—will consume family

---

terial indulgence and lack of self-discipline of the children of those who had attained wealth and status. (*See* Ho Ping-ti, *The Ladder of Success in Imperial China* [New York: John Wiley, Science Editions, 1964], Ch. IV.)

11. T-36.

resources without discipline. Yet the mother risks invoking the rage of her husband so that she can "love" her children by feeding them money to satisfy their craving for easy living (and as well her own concern that the children appreciate home life enough to remain with her?).

This type of problem was one which primarily burdened China's wealthy few. For most of the peasantry and impoverished urban dwellers the relationship between family resources and the desire to consume was not a balanced one; life in a subsistence economy imposed its own limits and offered little alternative to disciplined consumption. But the *source* of the problem was common to all those educated to depend on others. Without the responsibility for disciplining their own behavior, children were unlikely to limit their own consumption when family resources were plentiful, particularly when they saw their parental models enjoying such pleasures as concubines and good food. For the poor, dependency posed no such problem. Indeed, it was a solution to the problem of how to maintain life through family solidarity in an economy of scarcity.

The common resolution of these divergent concerns, according to our respondents, was the conviction that "too much" love, or affection too openly expressed, was bad for a child as he would become "selfish" or "lazy" and overconsume family resources. A stern parental exterior was felt to be necessary for imposing discipline on one incapable of self-discipline. Love was expressed by *implication,* indirectly from behind a strict parental "face," through concern for a child's physical well-being. As expressed in a statement noted earlier: "[Father] loved his children with all his heart, but his love was *in* his heart; he would not express it." [12]

We have traveled a circuitous route in tracing the logic behind our respondents' conviction that stern discipline is necessary for a growing child, and that "too much" love is dangerous both for the child and for the family. Inasmuch as the reasoning behind these attitudes is basic to the logic of the "dependency" social orientation, and to filial relations with authority, it is worthwhile retracing our analysis to make this cultural logic explicit: The traditional Chinese orientation to childrearing embodied a strong concern that the child grow up to provide for his parents' future security. Parents loved their young child in the manner appropriate to infancy, through oral indulgence, and they expected the same expression of love in dependent old age. Once the child had outgrown infancy, however, the concern of the parents became a matter of insuring that the maturing youngster did not grow up to leave them. To this end they imposed a strict external discipline on the child and discour-

12. T-43.

aged his explorations of autonomous behavior. The child became emotionally dependent on parental guidance and discipline. His maturation was arrested at a stage where love was expressed through oral forms, and where behavioral controls were still externally imposed by personalized sources of authority.[13]

Having educated the child to be dependent on their guidance, the parents were now caught up in the logic of the "filial" relationship: Strict discipline had to be maintained or the child would have doubts about what was appropriate behavior on his part (and parents might begin to doubt his "filial" commitment to them). Too much parental love in the sense of relaxed affection or emotional exchange would conflict with the child's need to receive external discipline and with the parents' expectation that the child could not control his own behavior once his emotions became mobilized (as indeed he had not been trained to do). Also, love in its form of feeding and material support had to be disciplined, or else—given the understandable desire of the child to recapture pleasures known in infancy—he would overconsume scarce family resources and raise doubts about his commitment to provide for his parents in what they hoped would be a return to that "golden age" of dependent security in their elderly years.

Strict authority (and guarded displays of affection) thus became the binding and guiding force of "filiality." Yet as we shall now see, this very strictness produced further reasons for seeing danger in the outward display of emotions.

THE IMPERMISSIBILITY OF HOSTILITY

In the Confucian family tradition there is no behavior which is more likely to invoke swift punishment than a child's quarreling or fighting with siblings or neighborhood peers:

13. Our interview data indicate that, in contrast to a sample of middle-class American adults, Chinese retain a personalized image of political authority, and continue to believe that their own actions in society must be guided by an external source of control to be effective. (*See* the author's "Mao's Effort to Reintegrate the Chinese Polity," pp. 280–284.)

This interpretation is supported by a recent study of the development of political attitudes in American adolescents. Through interviews it has been found that after the ages of 11, 12, or 13, children's political thinking develops beyond a conception of authority as a personalized "he" preoccupied with preventing people from doing bad things to that of a set of abstract institutions operating according to general principles intended to bring about some positive improvement in community life. (*See* Joseph Adelson and Robert O'Neil, "Growth of Political Ideas in Adolescence: The Sense of Community," *Journal of Personality and Social Psychology*, Vol. IV [1966], pp. 295–306.)

If I fought with other children [Mother] would pull us apart and hit me, and would then apologize to the parents of the other child. (Even if the other child had started the fight?) Even then; after all I had had contact with him and so the fight started. [She would] pull me into the house by the ear, make me kneel down and then hit me with a stick.[14]

There is no right or wrong concerning the point of contention. Merely having exposed oneself to the possibility of conflict is sufficient grounds for a thrashing.[15] Among more highly educated Chinese many can recall being hit by their parents *only* for fighting with a sibling or peer. Yielding and "harmonious" behavior are presented to the child as great virtues:

Our people have always loved peace; Chinese consider harmony valuable. From the time we are small we are taught to be yielding. . . . Harmony has a bit of the idea of yielding. For instance, if a husband and wife are not harmonious then the children will not be, and the outcome would be unthinkable. If you think ahead a little bit you can reduce trouble. Chinese also stress manners. If you are mannerly to a superior then we consider that an expression of peace. If you are mannerly then there is "harmony." [16]

Anxious parental reactions to interpersonal conflict, to expressions of hostility, work to develop in the child fears of aggressive impulses, both his own and those of other people. Such feelings should be masked behind ritualized forms of behavior, "good manners" (*li-mao*).

The reason for this uncompromising effort to inhibit expressions of aggression in children—an attitude which finds formal justification in the Confucian stress on "harmony" in interpersonal relations

14. T-18. This parental response to expressions of aggression in their children has been observed in present-day Taiwan. (*See* Wolf, "Child Training and the Chinese Family," pp. 54–55.)

15. Our interview data indicate that for our respondents as a whole, quarreling or fighting was the most frequently recalled cause of parental punishment (44.5 percent of seventy-four responding). The next most frequent causes were for doing poorly in school (33.4 percent) and disobedience of parental instructions (30.6 percent). The frequencies of other responses given were all lower than 18 percent. In some cases respondents mentioned more than one cause of punishment, which is why the percentages do not add up to 100. This punishment pattern shows some association with economic class level. (*See* Appendix VI, pp. 559–560.)

Further evidence on the importance which Chinese parents attached to inhibiting expressions of aggression in their children, based on interviews with Chinese reared on the mainland, is reported in Robert W. Scofield and Sun Chin-wan, "A Comparative Study of the Differential Effect upon Personality of Chinese and American Child Training Practices," *Journal of Social Psychology,* Vol. LII (1960), pp. 221–224.

16. T-47.

—is basic to the psychological logic of filial piety. In cultures which tolerate or encourage the development of a sense of autonomy in children, aggressive impulses play an important role in the child's efforts at self-assertion, his attempts to establish an identity for himself independent of the adults who bore and reared him.[17] But as we have stressed, self-assertion was the one thing which Chinese parents would not tolerate. Hence every indication of willful, assertive, or aggressive action on the part of the child would be severely discouraged. By inhibiting the expression of aggression in their children, Chinese parents (consciously or unconsciously) were seeking to insure the continued dependence of these guarantors of their future security. Self in the Confucian tradition was not to be considered apart from the relationships of filiality, the *wu lun*.

As is so often the case, however, the anxieties or good intentions which drive parents to attempt to develop certain behavioral patterns in their children can at times produce contradictory results. Parental efforts literally to beat the aggression out of their offspring and insure their obedience, tend to reduce the appeal of the dependent role. And they certainly teach the child that to have authority means, in part, to have the power to express aggression against inferiors. This interpretation is clearly revealed in our interview materials, where respondents indicated that they learned to repress hostility or aggressive feelings before father or elder brother, but would then release such emotions on younger siblings or weaker peers:

> (What would you say your father's weaknesses were?) When we were young we didn't think about that; we didn't know what weakness was. All I knew was that my father made me kneel every day [as a punishment]. He was very strict. As I was always being made to kneel it would get my anger up. (How did you express your anger?) How could you express it?! He is your father! You can't scold him! (Where did your anger go then?) We just wouldn't dare say anything to him. You just don't talk as you please to your father.[18]

17. An English psychoanalyst writes: "If there were no aggressive drive towards independence, children would grow up into and remain helpless adults so long as anyone could be persuaded to care for them, a fate which actually does befall some individuals who either lack the normal quota of assertiveness or else who have been subjected to regimes of childhood training which makes any kind of self-assertion seem a crime." (Anthony Storr, *Human Aggression* [New York: Atheneum, 1968], p. 44.)

The negative tone of these remarks bespeaks the deviant quality attributed to strong dependency needs in a society which values personal independence and self-reliance. In contrast, Chinese characterize strivings for autonomous behavior on the part of their children as nothing more than "selfishness."

18. T-18.

The respondent then indicated that his elder brother, who received similar treatment from the father, would turn around and play the part of a "father" with him, by hitting him or pulling his hair.

This "submission-dominance" pattern is evident in the recollections of childhood of the third son of a Kwangsi merchant. After describing how strictly his father had treated him, the respondent said that of all the people in his family he was closest to his little brother, "because he would obey me when I told him to do something." [19] The treatment received from more powerful elders provides a model of behavior which the individual, living within the Confucian social pattern of hierarchical relationships, applies to those subordinate in status. Aggression or hostile behavior is proscribed for the one dependent, but is resorted to with considerable frequency by adults anxious for the maintenance of "filiality."

"EAT BITTERNESS" (CH'IH-K'U)

The notion that feelings, especially sentiments of aggression, should not be released against authoritative individuals is expressed by Chinese in an interesting manner. As one sensitive young man explained it, "We hold things in our hearts, *in our stomachs.* . . . We hold hatred in, but we shouldn't do this." [20] Similar language was used by the son of an Anhwei peasant in recounting how a point of contention was dealt with among his brothers: "You would just put [the disagreement] in your stomach and not say anything. Everyone would try to work out a compromise. Otherwise quarreling would develop and everyone would be in a bad way." [21] The same concept is used in the peasant's interpretation of the Confucian ideal of "self-cultivation" (*hsiu-yang*):

> (How does one become a cultivated person?) You have to be patient and yielding. (When you get mad what do you do?) I very seldom get mad; *I swallow my anger, put it in my stomach.* (What is the bad point about being angry?) It never can have a good outcome. (What do you do when you try to control your anger?) Nothing in particular, just "eat a loss" (*ch'ih-k'uei*).[22]

19. T-6. Observations of this phenomenon are also reported in Wolf, *The House of Lim*, pp. 42, 130–131.

20. T-4. Emphasis added.

The same concept is used by a woman who recalls the bitterness of her first days living with her new husband's family: "I had never done much heavy work before, but after [moving in with the in-laws] I had to do all kinds of hard work, even in the fields. I cried a lot in my stomach in those days, but I didn't complain." (Wolf, *The House of Lim*, p. 54.)

21. T-27.

22. *Ibid.* Emphasis added.

This phraseology is meaningful in a number of respects. Earlier we pointed out that love and care in the Chinese tradition were above all expressed through feeding, yet from the combination of paternal harshness and nurture grew a strong sense of ambivalence toward authority. This ambivalence shapes perceptions of the act of feeding, which can become a form of aggression as well as of care: the father can make the child "eat bitterness" (*ch'ih-k'u*) as well as good food by being hostile or provoking bad feelings that the child knows must be put "in the stomach" and not expressed.

There may also be a physiological counterpart to the notion of putting hostility "in one's stomach" or "eating bitterness." The well-known phenomenon of intestinal ulceration resulting from tension indicates that feelings which must be strictly disciplined have their effects on bodily health; and unreleased rage may indeed make one's stomach tense, filled with bitterness.[23] Thus, the combined Confucian stress on filial submission, paternal unwillingness to tolerate a child's expression of hostility, and physiological mechanisms seem to work in concert to make the forced feeding of dependency an experience which combines aggression with love. The maturing child carries into his perceptions of social life the awareness that oral forms of nurturance, and the social rituals of filial deference, can be vehicles of hostility as well as of respect.[24]

This conception of dealing with hostility by holding it in one's stomach also brings to mind something pointed out earlier, that the major form of *early* childhood disciplining focuses on the develop-

---

23. Chinese speak of an individual becoming "white with rage" or "fainting with anger," which indicates that constriction of the vascular system is in some manner related to the "holding in" of aggression. (*See* Otto Kleinberg, "Emotional Expression in Chinese Literature," *Journal of Abnormal and Social Psychology,* Vol. XXXIII [1938], pp. 517–520.)

To exercise great caution or self-discipline is spoken of as being *"hsiao-hsin"* (literally, "small heart"), while to be relaxed is to *"fang-hsin,"* to "release the heart." In this culture to become "red with anger," that is, to expand one's vascular system, is viewed with great alarm, apparently because it communicates that hostile feelings are not being "held in." A Chinese servant recalls: "The master was so angry that his face became red even down his neck. If they had been ordinary people there would have been a fight. But because he was an official and because there were so many of us [servants] around he dared not beat nor revile [his offending wife]. But his anger was too great for him to bear. He jumped up, seized his whip, and began to thrash the dogs." (Pruitt, *A Daughter of Han,* p. 80.) Thus, a Chinese "signals" how aggressive impulses will be handled by becoming "white" (holding in) or "red" (mobilizing hostile feelings).

24. Interesting descriptions of how table ritual and the apparent politeness of a formal banquet can be used to offend or humiliate will be found in Wolf, *The House of Lim,* p. 53, and Pruitt, *A Daughter of Han,* pp. 15–17.

ment of proper forms of "taking in"—while little parental anxiety is expressed about the child "holding in" the products of his consumption. At the stage of development that begins at about four or five, however, it appears that "holding in" does become an important mode of discipline; but rather than being focused around a physiological or muscular "holding in," which would be the case with strict sphincter discipline, the child is taught to retain his emotions, particularly anger, hostility, and hatred. Such a pattern of discipline implies that to a Chinese an important aspect of social identity, of self-discipline and self-respect, is the control of emotions rather than of actions.[25] Self-control means restraining improper feelings more than improper behavior, especially where one has been taught to depend on external authority for guidance as to what is correct or incorrect behavior.

How does a child learn to "hold in" his emotions? The parental example of reserve in expressing feelings undoubtedly is an important factor. It also appears that teasing or bullying teaches the child the virtue of defense through emotional impassivity. Furthermore, our TAT responses suggest that an important psychological mechanism of defense in this culture involves learning to prevent the mobilization of bad feelings, to separate the perception of having been mistreated from the emotions of rage or resentment which such treatment would provoke, particularly where the offending individual is a powerful authority.[26] The oft-noted passive or indif-

25. "Holding in" conflict has its counterpart for the family group as well as the individual. Group disciplining of aggression, and its relationship to social identity, is indicated in the following recollection of childhood: "If any quarrel spread beyond our walls it was considered a blot upon the entire household. Everyone tried to curb his irritation and any inclination to quarrel." (Chiang Yee, *A Chinese Childhood* [New York: John Day, 1952], p. 302.)

26. This way of handling emotions is illustrated by one interpretation of TAT Card IV. The respondent, T-12, sees an older man directing a younger subordinate to do something improper. The younger man obeys, fails, and will evidently be punished by the authorities for his misdeed. However, he feels "nothing in particular" towards the superior who gave him the illegitimate orders. For the full story, see below, Ch. VII, p. 113.

In one effort to analyze the psychological defense mechanisms characteristic of different cultures, Francis Hsu suggests that this way of handling emotions be termed "suppression." Because Chinese parents do not force the child to internalize standards of behavior so much as to rely upon their (external) guidance, the child does not develop mechanisms of "repression" in which control can be maintained over forbidden emotions only by putting them well out of consciousness. He learns to "hold in" or to suppress sentiments which he knows will bring censure if expressed in the immediate presence of parental authority. But the forbidden feelings or thoughts remain

ferent reaction of a Chinese youth or peasant to mistreatment or misfortune is in fact such a strategy of defense. Where one has learned through painful experience that nature is beyond one's control, or that powerful individuals are beyond one's influence, emotional mobilization can at best produce personal torment and frustration and at worst the increased pain of retaliation from those who seek to keep child or peasant "in his place."

THREE "CONTRADICTIONS" IN THE FILIAL PATTERN

While Chinese recall much that is painful about the disciplining of childhood, it should be stressed that such treatment had a logic which made it meaningful within the cultural tradition. While the child undoubtedly would have preferred avoiding the pain, he came to accept it as necessary. This is clearly illustrated in the way that our respondents described their childhood dealings with authority.

> Father was very strict. If I was out playing at night and he called me to come in to study, he would hit my hand with a bamboo and make me kneel in front of President Chiang's picture if I didn't come in right away. But now I guess it was needed; I was unruly. There is a Chinese proverb: "A strict father produces a filial son." (From the point of view of personality what was your father like?) To use

within his consciousness. (*See* Francis L. K. Hsu, "Suppression Versus Repression," *Psychiatry*, Vol. XII [1949], pp. 223–242.)

Our data suggest that the defense termed "isolation" perhaps more aptly describes this mechanism, for what is involved is the isolation of the emotional state from the perception. Chinese, in recalling paternal mistreatment, usually do not deny that they were wronged; they just don't relate the feelings of anger which one would assume to be associated with such treatment to the recollection. (*See* Otto Fenichel, *The Psychoanalytic Theory of Neurosis* [New York: Norton, 1945], pp. 155–164.)

Whatever the best technical description of this phenomenon, it is particularly important for the present analysis because of its relation to problems of political motivation. In the traditional society, both father and political ruler sought to establish their authority by developing feelings of "awe" (anxiety, fear) in their dependents and subjects. They seem to have assumed that through the workings of such emotions they would be inviolate to expressions of hostility or aggression. As we shall see in Ch. XII, one of the problems Mao Tse-tung dealt with in developing popular support for the Communist movement was that of bringing large numbers of peasants, by tradition fearful of dealings with authority, into political participation. The techniques of political control that he helped develop to make people politically "conscious" represent, in part, efforts to reestablish the linkage between popular perceptions of authority as harsh and unjust, and the forbidden emotions of hostility and hate which tradition said must not be expressed against those in positions of power.

another common expression, he was "hard on the outside but gentle within." He was always polite to older people, and he would not just turn away the poor but would help them out with food or money. (How was he to you children?) Very strict. . . . [But] when we grew up we knew we had learned moral truth from him. We saw all parents rearing their children in that manner. And then we saw some bad children: thieves, juvenile delinquents, and bullies. It was said that their parents had loved them too much and had harmed them. They had not reared them strictly, but just let them do as they pleased. They got bad friends and learned [improper habits] from them.[27]

The pain of childhood disciplining is thus readily acknowledged, but it had a significance which the child, in time, could understand and accept. The adult, in retrospect, recalls that he was incapable of controlling himself in the face of his emotions, and affirms that strict parental authority was required to impose orderly behavior.

In addition, society was seen as rewarding with responsibility and respect those who successfully endured the pain of becoming a filial son.

When I was young I didn't like to study, to have to kneel in punishment [when my grades were poor]. I wanted to play. But when I would go out with father and see other people really respecting him [for his learning] that was really impressive! Hence if you are not strict, your children won't study. They won't grow up to be asked by others to assume responsibility for some job. They won't be respected by them.[28]

Strong authority is thus accepted as a source of personal security, particularly because the child has been told in the diverse and often indirect ways by which parents communicate with their children that an individual is incapable of managing his behavior or emotions by himself. It is also a source of security in a world where certain people have not been properly disciplined:

There are a small number of children who, no matter how strictly they are raised, will be bad—like juvenile delinquents. (Why is that?) They learn from a bad environment. (Is it easy to learn from a bad environment?) Very! Their wills are weak and they might start to steal; and then if they get excited it can lead to fighting.[29]

Because adults know that people have been trained from childhood to depend on more powerful elders for guidance, rather than to act according to a discipline within, there remains an apprehen-

27. T-19.
28. T-18.
29. T-9.

sion that others (or they themselves?) might be led astray by evil or enticing external forces: "They got bad friends and learned from them"; "They learn from a bad environment." Trusting others becomes problematical when one is uncertain about abilities for self-control and discipline. Suspicions are easily aroused that another individual is being manipulated by some unseen authority, or that his control of dangerous feelings may not be secure. Strong authority is thus a blessing, insofar as it protects against external (or internal) threats and gives clear and proper guidance.

Filiality, the relationship between strong and experienced parent and dependent child, can be conceived as a security pact, a social contract which establishes reciprocity between the generations: Parents "agree" to nurture, protect, and discipline the child when he is a vulnerable infant so that he may mature; and the child in return "agrees" to remain dependent within the family to care for those who raised him. And as the *Classic of Filial Piety* assured, "By the practise of this . . . all embracing rule of conduct . . . the people were brought to live in peace and harmony, and there was no ill-will between superiors and inferiors." [30]

In reality, of course, a child has no choice in the matter of how his parents rear him. Parents, as well, by the nature of the way cultural attitudes and values are incorporated within their personalities, do not choose, or "agree to," such a reciprocal set of life obligations. As we have seen in the recollections of adult Chinese, the filial pattern was maintained and transmitted to each new generation through the workings of such robust sentiments as anxiety and fear, feelings tempered by affection and a sense of responsibility. But it is evident that fear or anxiety within the filial tie notwithstanding, a child could come to accept the relationship in which he sacrificed a large measure of autonomy in social matters if he received a sense of security and social worth in return.

However, there is a major vulnerability in the all-embracing and self-renouncing pattern of filiality. Should the dominant member of the relationship fail in his obligations to the dependent, or should there be discipline without nurture, then feelings of having been cheated of one's proper share, or fears about being abandoned, can easily arise in the child or dependent adult and turn to great resentment or hatred for the dominant one who failed. In the world of material scarcity and insecurity known to traditional Chinese, and given the universal frailties of the human will, such failures must have been all too common.

Of the many examples we might draw upon to illustrate this vul-

30. *Hsiao Ching*, p. 465.

nerability of the filial authority pattern, it seems useful to look at a
childhood recollection of the man who has now taken the lead in
the Chinese social revolution, as we will in time be referring in detail to his efforts to reshape Chinese attitudes toward authority and
conflict. Mao Tse-tung, in a 1936 interview with the American
journalist Edgar Snow, recounted of his early family life:

> My father wanted me to begin keeping the family books as soon as
> I had learned a few characters. He wanted me to learn to use the
> abacus. As my father insisted upon this I began to work at those
> accounts at night. He was a severe taskmaster. He hated to see me
> idle, and if there were no books to be kept he put me to work at farm
> tasks. He was a hot-tempered man and frequently beat both me and
> my brothers. He gave us no money whatever, and the most meagre
> food.
>
> My mother was a kind woman, generous and sympathetic; and
> ever ready to share what she had. She pitied the poor and often gave
> them rice when they came to ask for it during famines. But she could
> not do so when my father was present. He disapproved of charity.
> . . . I learned to hate him.[31]

The failure of the severe taskmaster is all too clear: He hated idle-
ness (or insecurity?) but rewarded the diligent efforts of his dependents with castigation and stinginess. The young Mao sensed no
reciprocity, only exploitation: "I learned to hate him."

As was the cultural norm, Mao was discouraged by his mother
from openly venting hostility toward his father or directly challenging his authority: "My mother advocated a policy of indirect attack. She criticized any overt display of emotion and attempts at
open rebellion against the Ruling Power [the father]. She said it
was not the Chinese way." [32] But as we indicated earlier, her support of Mao and his brother in "a policy of indirect attack" evidently developed in the boys a strength of character which in time
enabled Mao to rebel against this and other harsh and unjust social
authorities.

The cultural norm, however, was that family or political author-

---

31. Snow, *Red Star over China,* pp. 125–126.
   To cite another example, Chu Teh, Mao's military cohort during the years
of struggle for power, recalled of his early life: "I loved my mother, but I
feared and hated my father. . . . I could never understand why [he] was
so cruel." (Agnes Smedley, *The Great Road: The Life and Times of Chu
Teh* [New York: Monthly Review Press, 1956], p. 10.)
   As is probably common to all revolutionary social movements, the Communist Party, in its formative years, seems to have drawn much vital leadership from individuals with very personal "authority problems" which motivated them to challenge established social authority through violence.

32. Snow, *Red Star over China,* p. 125.

ity should be inviolate to criticism or other expressions of hostility which might weaken its "prestige" and threaten the integrity of the filial relationship. In rearing their children, Chinese parents sought to develop attitudes and emotions which would sustain a system of authority in which initiative, guidance, and responsibility to care for dependents were vested in a dominant individual, while submissive loyalty would characterize those subordinate. To allow dependents to vent hostility at authority would threaten the security of the entire family group by placing in jeopardy its source of guidance. Who could say what confusion might reign if the source of authority were removed from individuals who had been trained to depend?

Yet, in the real world of material scarcity and human frailty the reciprocal obligations of the filial bond were not always realized[33]; and the disciplines of learning to be filial were not far removed from emotions of hostility or hate. Any father or official who him-

33. It is, of course, difficult to estimate just how effective Confucian family life was in meeting the needs of individual family members. Young Chinese had been educated to believe that this family pattern was natural and morally just; and the socialization process developed in them the attitudes and emotional needs which helped to bind the individual to his family group. It is only in such phenomena as the suicide of a young girl protesting an arranged marriage, or the running away from home of a son fearful of paternal punishment that we see individual cases of the failure of this family pattern.

Of the sixty-two cases in our particular sample for whom we have sufficient data, ten (16 percent) report that they ran away from home largely because of fear of punishment or the restrictions of family life. Six respondents recall other close family relatives who ran away.

Because this is an emigré sample, we can hardly generalize this ratio to the entire population, if for no other reason than that "running away" from adversity may be a particular characteristic of this kind of a group. One important characteristic of those respondents, however, might be noted. All of the ten who ran away from home grew up in the social dislocation which characterized Chinese society between the collapse of the Ch'ing dynasty and the founding of the Communist state. Our respondents' discussions and additional biographical data suggest that the new forms of social organization which appeared in the early twentieth century—political parties, "modern" armies, new forms of schooling, and new employment opportunities in the cities—provided alternatives for discontented young men which had not existed in the old social order. In traditional times, "eating bitterness" was probably the more frequent way in which a discontented son handled his frustrations with family life.

The fact that none of these runaways were from the younger generation reared under the Communists suggests that the Party has provided outlets for youthful frustration other than running away from home, and indeed may have begun to modify in significant ways the quality of Chinese family life. Later we will suggest that the "Cultural Revolution" was one such outlet for China's youth to vent their frustrations, although the source of discontent may have been the Party itself rather than family life.

self had been reared to filiality intuitively knew all the reasons why a son or subject might not appreciate such a position. In self-protection (and to insure maintenance of the tie which was a guarantee of its own future), authority would impose discipline and restrict expressions of dissatisfaction with firm determination. In circular fashion increased dissatisfaction would only lead to greater discipline.

This was a basic contradiction in the Confucian system of authority: The very harshness which was deemed necessary to keep children and subjects in awe could produce resentment as well as anxiety, particularly when dependence on authority was not balanced by a minimal level of support and justice. And where an authority had doubts about the filial submissiveness of his dependents he was likely to resort to even harsher measures to elicit submission, thus compounding the sense of resentment. As we shall show in later chapters, it was this pattern of authority and the ways of handling the emotions of hostility and aggression which Mao Tse-tung learned to tap and utilize in the Communist Party's struggle for power.

For most individuals living within the Confucian social tradition, however, there were a variety of strategies far short of rebellion by which they might seek to avoid injustice and reduce the pain of filial subordination. As disclosed in our interviews, such strategies primarily affected the ways in which an individual related to those with authority over him, how he tied his personal interests to those of the family or peer group which was his basic social affiliation, and how he handled such emotions as anger or hostility.

By way of summarizing the analysis in Chapters II and III, we might characterize these tensions between individual needs and social values as three "contradictions" inherent in the Confucian tradition:

1. *Dependence on hierarchical authority versus self-assertion.*—This first area of tension reflects the basic authoritarianism of China's social tradition. In the Confucian conception of society, order was maintained through a structuring of social relations into hierarchical dualities, the *wu-lun*. The father-son relationship was a model structural unit which, if properly realized and emulated throughout society, would insure the interdependence of the generations, social harmony, and personal security.

As we detailed in the preceding analysis, however, the paternal harshness which was seen as necessary to the rearing of filial children produced in a maturing son a strong sense of ambivalence to authority, a desire to be nurtured and protected by it, yet anxiety about approaching too near.

While he was young, a child learned a variety of strategies for dealing with anxiety-provoking authority: avoidance of contact, ready obedience, and appeals to stronger third parties for intercession. But when older, a son discovers there are situations in which he has authority over "loyal dependents." He must submit before his father, but he can play the part of a "father" to a younger brother. Thus the ambivalence of dealings with authority can find resolution by seeking out social roles in which one is the authority. The individual in this tradition seeks to affirm the potency of the self through the submission of others.

This striving for the dominant position in social relations, however, conflicts with the concern of those already in positions of leadership to insure social order and to affirm their own authority. It competes with the desires of other would-be leaders to attain positions of dominance. From such contradictions develop the uncompromising struggle for power when authority is dead or in doubt, and the concern in peer relationships that someone is always trying to put others down.

2. *Social harmony and peace versus hostility and aggression.*— Aggressive behavior plays an important part in a child's efforts at self-assertion. This is a phenomenon most obviously seen in the generational conflict present in many cultures when youngsters, approaching their full maturity, seek to break away from the family group to establish an independent social identity. Such conflict, however, runs counter to parental and group purposes in the Chinese tradition, and parents sternly discourage expressions of self-assertion, willfulness, or hostility in their children. According to most observations, Chinese parents quite literally attempt to beat the aggressiveness out of their youngsters through physical punishment. It is the parents' attempt to deny any legitimacy to the limited release of any aggressive emotions in their children—sentiments which are often heightened by the very harshness of parental discipline—that accounts for this second "contradiction."

What children in fact seem to learn from their parents' stern training is that sentiments of hostility must not be expressed against those in positions of authority. A sense of fear of paternal authority is developed. The child learns to "put into his stomach" the pain of parental discipline, to "eat bitterness," or prevent the mobilization of dangerous emotions even when provoked by an older member of the family. Yet he also learns from the very aggression which these family authorities invoke to insure his own filial submission that hostile feelings are appropriately released against those subordinate in status or power.

To be sure, such aggression is usually masked behind the forms of propriety (*li-mao*): the subtle twisting of good manners into an insult; the verbal abuse before a subordinate who must passively *t'ing-hua* and eat the bitterness of bad feelings he knows must be repressed. But this pattern sets up a tension between cultural ideals of peace and harmony within the (family) group, and a reality of bickering and tensions which are only masked by the social rituals of Confucian cultivation. As one Chinese expressed it: "If you look at the face of our family, it looks good, but if you look at its bones, it is not like that. In the 'bones' of the family there is ceaseless friction." [34]

This polarization of harmony and conflict is further reinforced by the contrast between the indulgence with which adults treat young children and the subsequent harshness by which parents attempt to restrict desires for pampering and to instill discipline in maturing youngsters. In the way in which parents handle their own aggressive impulses the child learns a basic social rhythm of *ho-p'ing* and *hun-luan,* the alternation between "harmony" and the "confusion" of vented aggression.

3. Self versus group.—This third area of tension reflects the way in which Chinese tradition sought to have the individual find security through group solidarity. The basic impulse which shaped the manner in which parents reared their children was the hope that, in particular, the elder male would survive the dangers of infancy to mature and remain within the family group, giving continuity to the blood-clan over the generations and providing for the security of family elders in the dependency of old age.

It is the tension between the indulgence of infancy and the subsequent harsh discipline of youth which creates the contradiction between individual and group life. Cross-cultural evidence on child-rearing practice indicates that generous breastfeeding and other forms of oral gratification develop in a child a strong sense of trust and self-esteem, a feeling of his own worth.[35] But such attitudes, if perpetuated, would run counter to parental goals of developing in their children a strong commitment to the purposes of the family group, not to the self. Thus, the subsequent harsh disciplines of youth represent the parents' effort to arrest the development of that self-esteem which is the legacy of an indulged infancy. The child matures with a "selfish" longing to recapture the oral pleasures and the sense of power known early in life. He seeks to enjoy once again

34. Wolf, *The House of Lim,* p. 35.
35. *See* Erik H. Erikson, *Childhood and Society* (New York: Norton, 1950), pp. 67–76, 219–222; and Robert Sears *et al.,* "Some Child-Rearing Antecedents of Aggression and Dependency in Young Children," *Genetic Psychology Monographs,* Vol. XLVII (1953), pp. 135–234.

the "lazy" indulgence of consuming without effort. The parents, in fear of these strivings, find that they must discipline the child's desires to consume. What had been oral nurturance now becomes oral discipline, and the child comes to see that love is mixed with aggression in those who would forcefully feed him filiality.

As we shall see in subsequent chapters, these three areas of tension between individual and society in the Chinese tradition pervade adult social relations and shape the pattern of China's politics.

Chapter V

THE PAIN AND REWARDS

OF EDUCATION

The skills of literacy, and the opportunities available to a literate individual in traditional China, were a distant goal for most of China's peasant millions. Although formal education was "available" to the rural population by virtue of the Confucian openness to class mobility, in practice a peasant's son had little opportunity for study simply because of limited family resources. The life of subsistence farming imposed disciplines which gave individuals and families little choice in career selection or education. Sons were needed on the farm for their labor. Whatever surplus family capital might have financed education was usually allocated first to savings as a hedge against the threat of flood or drought, and then to additional security through the purchase of new land. While clan schools or imperial academies provided some educational opportunity for impoverished families, the political and economic systems of landlordism, the state bureaucracy, and merchant activity concentrated the wealth sufficient for supporting the formal education of children in the hands of only a small fraction of the population.[1]

Before a peasant child entered his teens the grinding and repetitive labor pattern of rice or wheat farming would become for him a severe taskmaster, a "teacher" who would make meaningful the virtues of yielding patience and diligence which parents had stressed. A child of the gentry was fortunate to be spared this compulsion for physical labor, yet in becoming a member of the "great tradition" of Confucian scholarship, he faced disciplines and repetitive-

1. Estimates of the total literate population are necessarily approximate, and fluctuate over time with changing economic conditions and political manipulation of either examination quotas or the actual purchase of academic degrees. A rough estimate of the literate segment of the population between 1600 and 1900 puts it at between one and two percent of the total. (Statistics on population and degree holders will be found in Ho Ping-ti, *The Ladder of Success in Imperial China*, pp. 181–182 and *passim;* and Robert M. Marsh, *The Mandarins: The Circulation of Elites in China, 1600–1900* [Glencoe, Ill.: The Free Press, 1961], esp. pp. 14–15.)

ness often no less demanding.[2] There is an almost contrived equivalence between the monotony and physical discipline of agricultural life and the mental repetitiveness and unquestioning acceptance of the teacher's authority required to become literate in the Classics.

The Chinese political tradition required a rigorous and demanding period of training in language and scholarship before one could enter the political class, that small literate percentage of the population from which a large proportion of imperial administrative officials was selected. Because the Confucian educational tradition was conceived to be training for political administration, its methods and the attitudes it sought to develop give us a rather explicit picture of the behavior considered appropriate to politics and of the values and goals which Confucian government sought to attain.

Formal education in traditional China was not so much a public process which sought to bring individuals into the larger society, as a private or family function that linked the members of each generation to the Confucian great tradition. The authority of the teacher was that of the philosopher sages who extolled the virtues of family life as the pattern of the state, and more immediately of the parents who sought education and a successful career for their children. The primary institutional form of education was private instruction in a family or clan school, termed a *szu-shu*—the first character explicitly emphasizing the private nature of formal learning. The authority of the teacher reinforced parental authority, not only directly through preaching filiality, but also indirectly by maintaining for the adolescent the same image of authority as the stern and unapproachable source of control which he knew at home.

As this relationship was expressed by a respondent from the northern province of Liaoning:

> Teachers ought to take responsibility for their students and they should treat them like their own offspring. To run a school like a business is really not good. (How should students behave toward their teachers?) Students ought to respect the teacher. (How do they express this respect?) They obey the teacher; if they don't trust the teacher how can they learn things?[3]

Another, who had been the principal of a secondary school elaborated:

> The teacher . . . must be correct in his behavior. If he himself is not correct then there is no way he can teach his students. A teacher

2. Interview data concerning punishments received in childhood indicate that performance in school was the area of a child's activities on which parental anxieties focused in upper class families. (*See* Appendix VI, pp. 559–560.)

3. H-7.

A Confucian schoolroom, Hong Kong, ca. 1910.
Radio Times Hulton Picture Library.

educating his student does not mean just broadening his knowledge; at the same time moral cultivation is very important. The student must respect the teacher and the right way of doing things. But the most important thing is that the teacher's personal morality must be very good.[4]

The teacher becomes an additional source of morality for a child to emulate, a model of behavior that he must trust and obey, or else "how can he learn things?" Establishing a proper relationship with a teacher means above all expressing dependence upon him by way of submissive "respect": "You have to respect the teacher, because if you want to learn things from him but don't respect him then he won't reveal the secrets of his craft." [5]

Parents accorded a teacher the same range of authority over their children as they themselves had. After a home education which stressed dependence on adults for discipline and guidance, children were seen as requiring even more of the parental type of control to prevent them from becoming "bad":

> (What attitude did your parents have to your teachers?) While I was in primary school my parents thought the stricter the teacher was with me the better. They thought they should give the school all power and responsibility over me—some children are unruly, and if teachers are too affable they will be bad. The teacher has to be strict.[6]

As in the relation of father to son, the teacher reinforced a one-way pattern of communication. The student learned to "take in" but was strongly discouraged from talking back:

> The ancient relationship between a teacher and students has been the spreading of knowledge. If the teacher says something the students must definitely obey him . . . a teacher himself must explain his students' doubts. I remember once when I was a student and didn't understand a mathematics lesson I asked the teacher [for an explanation]; but the teacher just got mad at me. This is very wrong. Afterwards I wouldn't dare to ask questions of the teacher.[7]

> (Did you or your fellow students ever make jokes or play tricks on the teacher?) I never did! How could I dare? That's just too much! (Why?) "The teacher has to be strict and his students must respect him" [a common aphorism]. When the teacher teaches he stands in front of the blackboard as a representative of Confucius. You just wouldn't dare make jokes. We don't even have to talk about playing tricks on him; you would get your palms slapped. However, when it comes to studying perhaps the modern type of teacher is more en-

4. T-32.
5. T-1.
6. T-14.
7. T-35.

lightened. You can joke with him and it is relatively easy to get close to him.[8]

During the first years of formal schooling, education was a painful process of blind learning through memorization of the sound patterns of classical texts. This form of instruction was primarily a course in self-restraint. For young adolescents it was an onerous business, as is described in one anthropologist's field observations of life in a Shantung village during the 1940s:

> . . . most of the boys did not like the school. They learned their lessons by rote without understanding the meaning of what they were required to read. Except for the *Jih Yung Za Tze,* all the textbooks were completely incomprehensible to them, but they were compelled to read and to remember what they had read. It was painful work. Unfortunately, neither the teacher nor the boys' parents had any interest in remedying the situation, and the boys were forced into endless memorizing and were punished severely if they failed in this dull task. Fear of punishment also made school hateful. Once a six-year-old boy, who was reading his *San Tze Ching,* fell asleep at his table. The teacher woke him with a thunderous call, scolded him harshly, and then asked him to recite his lesson. The boy was too frightened to do it well, and for this failure he was beaten. This sort of thing used to occur very frequently.[9]

Such instruction overwhelmed the child with an adult's curriculum rather than encouraging him to develop intellectual skills commensurate with his growing mental capabilities. The effect was to reinforce the sense of anxiety before authority which had been learned at home. It sustained the child's belief that he was incapable of handling adult demands without their guidance. He learned to discipline his impulses for autonomous or exploratory thinking and behavior, and his sources of authority and guidance remained external. Responsibility for discipline in the classroom remained with the teacher, and at home with the parents, for the overwhelming task of rote learning required too much self-discipline for a lively and growing child. As was observed in the Shantung village:

> The old-fashioned school offered no recreation. As a rule, a schoolboy had to sit in his seat and keep quiet all the time. When he heard the noise, the laughter, and the wild running of the boys on the street, he and all the other pupils felt a great longing to join them but did not dare. The only chance for fun was when the teacher was not in school. On these rare occasions the boys' energy, imagination, and joy broke forth immediately and simultaneously. They overturned tables and piled up benches as a stage for an impromptu "show." *They threw*

8. T-32.
9. Martin Yang, *A Chinese Village: Taitou, Shantung Province,* p. 147.

paper balls and water holders in a game of "war." They stole into the vegetable garden near the schoolhouse to pick fruits, cucumbers, or radishes. The shouting, swearing, and laughing could be heard even by distant neighbors. One or two small boys stood guard at a far corner to watch for the teacher's coming. As soon as he was sighted and the signal was given, all the boys ran wildly back into the schoolhouse and put everything in order. Occasionally they were discovered and punished.[10]

Such a scene of undisciplined adolescence is, we must stress, not unique to Chinese society. Youngsters the world over respond to the presence, or absence, of adults who are significant in their early lives. Two aspects of this traditional educational process, however, do seem of particular importance. First, the child was not presented with opportunities for testing out in *limited* ways methods for mediated control of his urges toward aggression (as in competitive sports), or for limited intellectual achievements consonant with his capabilities. It seems likely that the child developed doubts about his own abilities for self-control and achievement as a result of the demands made upon him for memorization and physical discipline. Second—and related to this point—the child continued to be taught to depend on adults, his parents or teacher, for the discipline of which he was incapable. Rather than developing abstract principles of behavior which were gradually internalized by the growing adolescent, the boy remained bound within his relationships to those specific individuals—parent or teacher—who nurtured and disciplined him to maturity.

More specifically, the child came to identify authority with "the power of the word." At home he had learned that one manifestation of paternal authority was precedence in speaking and the right to formulate opinions. In the classroom he saw that the teacher could compel the memorization of sounds and phrases which were defined as "proper" in terms of tradition and family aspirations. To exert authority came to mean having the right both to speak and to "educate" inferiors; while to be compelled to memorize and repeat the words of a teacher became a mark of subordination, a ritual of social control. As we will detail in Chapter VII, this identification of power and control with words and the process of education was given formal legitimation in the Confucian doctrine of the "rectification of names." And as will become evident in the conclusion of this study, when a Chinese political leader has doubts about his authority, the technique he instinctively selects to reaffirm his status is "education," compelling his subjects to commit to memory his words, his "thought" (*szu-hsiang*).

10. *Ibid.* Emphasis added.

While the process of formal education thus reinforced the pattern of authority first learned at home, it also provided an individual (and his family) with the opportunity to attain the most respected identity of Chinese society, that of a cultivated *literatus* or Confucian scholar-official. Parents of the gentry or would-be gentry put great demands on their children for successful scholarship, for they saw their future well-being and the prosperity of future family generations as contingent upon the achievements of their young. In the world of the traditional Chinese social elite, all prestige and potential power and wealth were concentrated in the role of the scholar-official. Merchant or militarist might come to attain power or fortune, but so potent was the appeal of literatus status that succeeding family generations would be encouraged to seek the ultimate of social achievement through scholarship and public service in the Confucian tradition. Thus parents, and to some degree teachers, transmitted their concerns for status, security, wealth, and power to their children through demands for good scholarship.

For a maturing child these adult pressures for educational achievement brought together the authority pattern of the society and the highest opportunity for self and group realization. Parents and teachers raised his anxieties about fulfilling obligations to the family through their strict demands for performance and harsh punishments for failure; yet they also provided him a clear if painful path, and distant yet appealing goal, by which he could relieve these anxieties, meet his filial obligations, and make a name for himself:

> (When you were young how did you feel about studying?) In those days I felt I would die from studying. For instance, when I was in grammar school I would memorize to death a book no matter what the ideas inside were. The teacher would not explain [what we were memorizing]. Then we were interested in studying because we always thought that it was a way to develop a name for yourself. Father and mother thought that in the future you could become an official.[11]

Earlier we suggested that control of emotions has been central to Chinese conceptions of self-identity. In the classroom the student was taught that emotional restraint was an essential part of the Confucian tradition. The "superior man" (*chün-tzu*) was one who had learned to discipline his feelings through "self-cultivation." Social order was a function of the discipline—"equilibrium" and "harmony"—of popular emotions:

> While there are no stirrings of pleasure, anger, sorrow, or joy, the mind may be said to be in the state of EQUILIBRIUM. When those

11. T-35.

feelings have been stirred, and they act in their due degree, there ensues what may be called the state of HARMONY. This EQUILIBRIUM is the great root *from which grow all the human actings* in the world, and this HARMONY is the universal path *which they all should pursue.* (Emphasis in source cited.) [12]

Where parents had indicated implicitly by their own behavior that guarded reserve was the proper way to deal with feelings (and had punished the child's failures at emotional restraint), the Sage openly condemned expressions of emotion:

> Confucius said, "There are three things which the superior man guards against. In youth, when the physical powers are not yet settled, he guards against lust. When he is strong and the physical powers are full of vigor, he guards against quarrelsomeness. When he is old, and the animal powers are decayed, he guards against covetousness. [13]

The remedies which the Confucian tradition formally developed to cope with troublesome human emotions were "cultivation" and "rectification."

> What is meant by, "The cultivation of the person depends on rectifying the mind," *may be thus illustrated:* If a man be under the influence of passion, he will be incorrect in his conduct. He will be the same, if he is under the influence of terror, or under the influence of fond regard, or under that of sorrow and distress.
>
> When the mind is not present, we look and do not see; we hear and do not understand; we eat and do not know the taste of what we eat.
>
> This is what is meant by saying that the cultivation of the person depends on the rectifying of the mind. [14]

And while attainment of knowledge was the evident purpose of education, the Classics made it clear that knowledge and learning were in the service of personal "cultivation" and "rectification," the virtues by which the wise kings of ancient China had maintained social order.

Popular interpretations of the term "cultivation" indicate more explicitly than formal philosophical works that this basic concept of the Confucian political tradition was closely related to the concern with aggression and social conflict. As a teacher reared in Peking explained the meaning of the term "cultivation":

> Well, for instance, if I am at a bus stop waiting in line, two or three people may get in front of me. If I remonstrate with them it might

12. "Doctrine of the Mean," Ch. I, in James Legge, trans., *The Chinese Classics,* Vol. I, pp. 385–386.
13. "Analects," Book XVI, Ch. VII, *ibid.,* pp. 312–313.
14. "The Great Learning," Ch. VII, *ibid.,* p. 368.

lead to a fight. They might say, "Why are you remonstrating with me? What authority have you?" If I have cultivation, then I would just say "Let's forget it." Or if you are in a group and a person is unmannerly, you just hold in your anger and in this way avoid conflict.[15]

Through the stress that "cultivation" placed on emotional restraint, formal education reinforced a student's already developed distrust of expressions of emotionality and conflict. The examples of China's history which he learned in school, the murders and factious turmoil documented in the annals of the "Spring and Autumn" period or the writings of Mencius, and the histories of the "Warring States," gave him ample proof that conflict was an ever-present possibility. But most fundamentally, a student had learned in his own early life experience that quarreling among his peers or expressions of hostility toward adults could only invoke parental wrath. Latent anxieties about conflict were thus formalized and given the legitimacy of official doctrine in the classroom.

How was a child's immature anxiety about expressing aggression developed into a "cultivated" adult restraint?

> To become cultivated requires that you read many books. This is so that you will be able to control your emotions with your intelligence. The seven emotions of man—happiness, anger, sympathy, joy, sadness, fear, and apprehension—can be controlled by cultivation. This is the so-called "middle way" (*chung-yung*). I have seen that many friends have succeeded in their work because they can control their emotions. The most capable kind of person is one who can control the seven emotions and not be used by them.[16]

> People who are cultivated have an enlightened attitude about getting along in the world; they are fair, reasonable, and not selfish. Cultivated people are not emotionally impulsive. (How does one become cultivated?) Read many books, and study the examples of cultivated ancients. You have to forgive people, and don't get angry easily.[17]

The development of personal "cultivation" is certainly related to the process of education; but is it just a matter of "reading many books"? Perhaps the ability to hold in one's emotions is acquired more as a result of the *form* of traditional teaching methods than of their content. To a certain degree, ideas were irrelevant to the training of young students; after all, the first few years of instruction were devoted to the blind memorization of sound patterns. It seems most likely that the process of subjecting students in the full physical

15. T-9.
16. T-30.
17. T-38.

vigor of adolescence to the rigorous demands of memorization of lengthy texts, or reproducing hundreds of complicated characters by brush within the squares of a copybook, was a powerful disciplinary experience in controlling impulses to take action or vent emotional frustration.[18]

In addition, as within the family, the teacher presented a model of emotional reserve which a student would fail to emulate only on pain of being "misunderstood":

> Eastern people don't like to express friendliness to others; they want the other person to express it first and then they will express it. In college, it is the same thing with the professor and his students. The students won't necessarily say hello to the teacher, they want to wait until the professor expresses himself and then they will. Probably this is because from primary and middle school experience the teacher does not pay much attention to the students. Therefore, the students do not dare to express friendship or say hello to the teacher. It's the same with your neighbors: each side wishes to maintain its dignity. Another thing is that they are afraid the other party will not understand them.[19]

The Classical books and the Confucian classroom thus gave official sanction to the logic of filiality, or the interdependence of the generations. And how striking it is to find in the enduring texts of this millennial civilization the same concerns with laziness, over-indulgence, lack of concern for parents, and conflict which we find so prominent in the attitudes of Chinese interviewed in the 1960s! As Mencius tells us:

> There are five things which are said in the common practice of the age to be unfilial: The first is laziness in the use of one's four limbs, without attending to the nourishment of his parents. The second is gambling and chess playing, and being fond of wine, without attending to the nourishment of his parents. The third is being fond of goods and money, and selfishly attached to his wife and children, without attending to the nourishment of his parents. The fourth is following the desires of one's ears and eyes, so as to bring his parents

18. An interesting example of the manner in which the forms of traditional education became an integral part of an adult's equipment for emotional discipline is found in the use of calligraphy. In the diaries of Lin Tse-hsü, the famous "Commissioner Lin" sent to Canton by the emperor in 1839 to suppress the opium trade, it has been noted that during the time he was awaiting an imperial investigation of his failure to stop the British trading activity—an investigation which carried with it very serious professional consequences—he devoted days on end to calligraphic practice as a way of calming his nerves. (*See* Arthur Waley, *The Opium War through Chinese Eyes* [London: Allen and Unwin, 1958], pp. 124–127.)

19. T-37.

to disgrace. The fifth is being fond of bravery, fighting and quarreling so as to endanger his parents.[20]

The important question which remains is whether the social attitudes and emotional concerns of China's small stratum of literate elite, as expressed in the life style and ideology of the Confucian "great tradition," were shared by illiterate peasants enduring poverty and toil in the "little tradition" of the villages.

Since almost all historical materials on China have come from the "great tradition" of Confucian scholarship and public service, our view of Chinese society has tended to be filtered through the values and world-view of this elite social stratum. Students of China, in recent years, have become concerned about the possibility of biased interpretations resulting from the unrepresentative quality of their data sources.[21] Unfortunately the material on Chinese social and political attitudes gathered for this study do not provide a complete refutation of these concerns. The individuals who participated in this research project were chosen, in part, to reflect the attitudes and life experiences of "ordinary" Chinese who are not fully a part of the formal Confucian tradition. But as we mentioned in the introduction, our tools of analysis required minimal literacy and sufficient social poise to be able to respond to an interview situation. Hence we do not have direct evidence of the social attitudes of illiterate peasants.

What our data do clearly reveal, however, is that the values inculcated as part of the "great tradition," spread beyond those who received formal training in the Confucian classics. The social outlook and values of that portion of our sample who had had only elementary schooling or who were educated decades after the abolition of the Confucian educational system are very similar to those of the elderly respondents who had been educated before the turn of the last century in Confucian schools.

As we have tried to emphasize in the first part of this study, the formal values and ideology of China's traditional political elite found expression in the daily life and verbal culture of peasant villages, and in common socialization practices. Furthermore, studies of social mobility in China indicate that there was a rapid rise and fall of family fortunes associated with uncertain attainment of a scholar's status through the imperial examinations. Access to an

20. "Mencius," Book IV, Part II, Ch. XXX, in James Legge, trans., *The Chinese Classics*, Vol. II, p. 337.

21. A recent historical text by Edwin O. Reischauer and John K. Fairbank, for example, is explicitly titled, *East Asia: The Great Tradition,* perhaps to disclaim any intention of speaking for the social history of China's voiceless peasant millions.

official position within the governmental bureaucracy was equally uncertain. While this "elite circulation" was uneven throughout the society, it did promote the interpenetration of "great" and "little" traditions.

Hence while the data marshaled for this study can only be viewed as suggestive of the distribution of social attitudes across lines of economic class and educational level, the following interpretation seems justified as a working hypothesis: The general set of attitudes toward self and interpersonal relations which we have characterized as the "dependency social orientation"—in particular a hierarchical conception of authority, a strong group sense, and anxiety about aggression and conflict—had an enduring rationale in the context of China's social and economic pattern of family and village-centered agriculture. Since the elite continued to rise from and return to this social base and maintained its source of wealth in the systems of land tenure and agricultural taxation, it sustained strong links to the pattern of rural life. One senses that the formal logic of Confucianism and the life style of the scholar-official represented an *elaboration* and ideological justification of the peasant cultural pattern, rather than being divorced from it.[22] Our data reveal no significant variation in concern with social conflict or differences in conception of authority associated with socioeconomic class or educational level. Direct observations of peasant life by anthropologists support this data. China's elite seems to have used its wealth to gratify culturally developed inclinations for oral indulgence and a "tranquil" life—luxuries which an impoverished peasant could not afford.

The full extent of continuity in basic "cultural linkage" between the elite of Chinese society and the peasantry will become clearer in the next two parts of this study. First we shall explore the elaboration of our themes of childhood socialization into adult social and political attitudes. We shall then relate these adult attitudes to the strategy of revolution developed by Mao Tse-tung and the Chinese Communists in their efforts to develop a mass following in the struggle for power.

22. The notion of "great" and "little" traditions within a cultural area was developed by the anthropologist Robert Redfield, who wrote: "The two traditions are interdependent. Great tradition and little tradition have long affected each other and continue to do so . . . . The teachings of Confucius were not invented by him singlehanded; on the other hand, [such] teachings have been and are continually understood by peasants in ways not intended by the teachers. Great and little tradition can be thought of as two currents of thought and action, distinguishable, yet ever flowing into and out of each other." (*Peasant Society and Culture: An Anthropological Approach to Civilization* [Chicago: University of Chicago Press, 1956], pp. 71–72.)

Part Two

ADULT PERCEPTIONS OF SOCIAL RELATIONS: "CONFUSION" (LUAN) AND THE NEED FOR STRONG AUTHORITY

Rice merchant's wife and starving boy, 1940s.
George Silk, Life *Magazine*, © *Time, Inc.*

Chapter VI

"PEOPLE EAT PEOPLE"

The social concerns which have dominated the development of China's political institutions, and which still suffuse interpersonal relations, center about the polarity of "unity versus conflict." Historians perceive a rhythm in Chinese political life which reflects this polarity, the so-called "dynastic cycle": the alternation of periods of ordered peace and social stability with episodes of disintegration and violent conflict.[1] One of the philosophers of the Confucian tradition in centuries past saw this rhythm as elemental to human society: "A long time has elapsed since this world of men received its being, and there has been along its history now a period of good order, and now a period of confusion."[2]

Ordinary Chinese see this alternation of order and confusion in the context of conflict between the centralized authority of the emperor versus regional, clique, or clan groupings. Confucian philosophers relate this social rhythm to the moral qualities of the man who wields imperial power. Both philosopher and peasant share common ideals of peace, harmony, political unification and "The Great Togetherness" (*ta-t'ung*), and fear of confusion (*hun-luan*), social disintegration, and violence.

The historical records of the Confucian tradition amply document the civil disorder which this tradition of government has long sought to remedy. As a basis for considering the system of authority which characterized the Confucian political order, we shall first look at the attitudes toward social relations which made this pattern of political leadership meaningful to Chinese for more than two millennia.

Consonant with their perception of a tendency for political disintegration and turmoil in social life, Chinese express apprehen-

---

1. A useful collection of materials detailing the "dynastic cycle" concept will be found in John Meskill, ed., *The Pattern of Chinese History: Cycles, Development, or Stagnation?* (Boston: D. C. Heath, 1965).

2. "The Works of Mencius," in James Legge, trans., *The Chinese Classics* (Shanghai: 1935), Vol. II, p. 279.

sion at the ever-present possibility of conflict in interpersonal relations. One of our interviewees, a semiliterate young man of peasant background from Kwangtung Province, expressed this anxiety in a distinctive, and now familiar, manner in responding to one of the TAT pictures. He saw in Card IX [3] three students threatened by a group of ruffians. The students were undecided as to the best way to deal with the threat:

(Interviewer's question) So these fellows in the foreground disagree as to what they should do?

(Respondent's reply) They are not of one opinion. The other two fellows are thinking of a way to deal with those ruffians (*liu-mang*). [One says], "I have my method." The other one is thinking, "I will have no difficulty [in dealing with this situation]. As for the government, although there are police, they, ah!—they want money. They won't deal with our problem. This small matter—they probably won't have anything to do with it."

[This student in the foreground] feels he is not strong enough, however. He has had no experience in dealing with such affairs of the world, and so he can't manage such a situation by himself. "It would not do *not* to have a government," the student is thinking, "because there is always fighting. *If there were no government, people couldn't live in society. People eat people, the big ones eat the small; they will eat them all up. Although people don't really eat people, society could eat you up. If there were no government, naturally people would eat each other; eat each other all up.*" [4]

Now it is most unlikely that this semiliterate peasant had ever read Lu Hsün's *Diary of a Madman* (published in 1918), in which a leading intellectual of China's "May Fourth" era, protesting the Confucian tradition, also characterized Chinese society as one which "ate men." This way of conceptualizing the threatening aspects of social life seems to tap common roots about the way interpersonal tensions are handled.

Lu Hsün related the "man eating" quality of Chinese society to the demands of filiality, which consumed the life of the younger generation in self-sacrifice for their elders: "I remember when I was four or five years old, sitting in the cool of the hall, my brother told me that if a man's parents were ill, he should cut off a piece of his flesh and boil it for them if he wanted to be considered a good son. . . . I have only just realized that I have been living all these years in a place where for four thousand years they have been eat-

3. *See* the Thematic Apperception Test pictures in Appendix IV, pp. 538–540 below.
4. T-15. Emphasis added.

ing human flesh." [5] The Kwangtung peasant more generally relates this conception to problems of social authority and conflict; to the fact that people with power take advantage of those who have none. "The big ones eat the small."

We noted in Chapter III that Chinese are taught to hold in aggressive impulses, and to put frustrations "in the stomach." This terminology implies that interpersonal tensions, which Chinese see handled in such "oral" terms as back-biting and verbal abuse, making an adversary "lose face," and masking hostility behind the "polite" forms of *k'o-ch'i* verbal exchange and table ritual, can make an individual feel "consumed" with restrained anger. And as we shall see in Chapter IX on political perceptions, social power is conceived in the image of a tiger who quite literally devours the most precious and life-sustaining substance of all, food. Taxation, the usurious rents of the landlord, or a foraging army can, almost literally, "eat" one by consuming a limited food supply.

Whatever the psychological mechanism which lies behind the concept that "people eat people," it is clear that this is one verbal manifestation of an anxiety, widely shared in Chinese society, about conflict in interpersonal relations. Children of all social classes are taught that they must not fight with siblings or peers. Parental punishments build up in a growing child considerable anxiety about releasing hostility or being aggressive. This stress on avoiding conflict arouses in Chinese the apprehension that there is a fund of bad feelings within other people which should not be provoked, lest it lead to hostility or violence.

Our interview respondents consistently expressed the belief that it is proper to interfere in the behavior of other people to prevent them from doing bad things which would be harmful to society. This attitude, however, is in tension with the fear that in so doing resentment or hatred "held within" the offending person will be provoked into the open, leading to conflict. As expressed by the son of a shopkeeper from rural Kwangtung:

> At first I thought I should [remonstrate with a bothersome neighbor], but then I got to thinking about the Chinese sayings, "Sweep the snow in front of your own door," and "An enlightened person guards himself." Today in China you have the tradition of minding your own business. (Why is it this way?) If you don't, if you don't consider a man's power, you can bring out his resentment. (In what way?) You might get into a fight, or get beaten up in a dark alley at night. So you have to be very careful not to say anything in front of other people when it isn't your business. [6]

5. "A Madman's Diary," in *Selected Works of Lu Hsün* (Peking: Foreign Languages Press, 1956), Vol. I, p. 20.
6. T-12.

Inasmuch as children are taught to hold in their resentments and frustrations, it is not strange that they grow up *assuming* that other people are bottling up bad feelings too. Whether harmful emotional energy or hatred actually *is* pent up is less important than the belief that it is there, for the belief shapes behavior.

In the discussion of doctrines and processes of formal education in Chapter V we noted that the Confucian tradition viewed personal "cultivation" as an important method for insuring social harmony. "Cultivation" was viewed as the personal discipline which would limit social conflict.

The majority of China's peasant population, of course, had no opportunity to become "cultivated" through the long and intensive disciplinary process of traditional education. Probably part of the aloofness with which the "cultivated" literati held themselves apart from the peasantry, and their stern use of authority in dealing with the common people, was based on the apprehension that these uneducated souls lacked self-discipline. Just as a child required stern paternal authority to keep him from becoming bad, so the common people required the harshness of "father-mother officials" (*fu-mu kuan*) to keep them from being unruly.

Activities which would tend to foster aggressiveness or conflict, such as athletic competition or militarism, were viewed by the literati as threatening to social order—perhaps because such stimulation tended to draw out an individual's capacity for aggression. Thus competition in most of its forms was discouraged in the traditional society. Competitiveness came to be closely identified with the unrestrained aggressiveness of interpersonal violence and war. A law professor from Hunan Province answered the question, "What is the effect of interpersonal competition on society?" thus: "Initially competition between people is not bad. For instance, two people may cooperate in doing something, but in the middle of things they may get to fighting over their personal interests, and then it's 'I'll kill you or you'll kill me.' " [7]

This notion that conflicts of personal interest can easily lead to deadly violence, even in the context of cooperation, seems to reflect an idea we saw earlier regarding childrearing: Human emotions are considered dangerous and uncontrollable once mobilized. Hence, interpersonal relations are laden with anxiety for they always contain the possibility of serious conflict.

Then too, in a subsistence agricultural economy, the insecurities of life undoubtedly contributed to the serious consequences of conflict. Avoidance of conflict became a matter of survival in a situa-

7. T-31.

tion where family energies were fully committed to the basic task of producing enough to eat.

Given this set of perceptions and emotional concerns, China's difficulty in becoming a well integrated national society is understandable. Reluctance to face up to points of dispute and avoidance of contact out of fear of aggression fragment the society into suspicious family groupings. This phenomenon was described by a respondent from a well-to-do rural family of Anhwei Province:

> (What kind of a relationship did your family have with the neighbors?) Most of our neighbors were farmers. Those who got along well had contact rather often, and those who didn't get along too well usually understood [what the situation was] and went out of their way to avoid having contact. (Why didn't some get along?) For instance, because their children fought. *Everyone in general avoided contact so as to avoid quarrelsome situations.*[8]

There is an all-or-nothing quality about this style of social relations: either the full trust and reliance characteristic of "dependency," or apprehension and avoidance of outsiders. Extending the range of social transactions beyond a close circle of known and trusted individuals is unlikely when there is an expectation that one will be cheated, or where the striving for personal interests seems to lead to violent conflict.

With such a view of social relations, it is not surprising that the world of childhood seems a safe and tranquil "golden age":

> Youth is a relatively happy period of life because you have no responsibility. In those times society was relatively simple, not so complicated (*fu-tza*) as today. Now if people seek to make friends they have some [ulterior] motive. Relations between friends usually have some political or economic flavor. There are many people who are not so talented but who have bad motives creating a lot of confusion (*luan*) for their own selfish interests.[9]

The particular vocabulary which this young man from Kwangtung uses to express the difficulties of interpersonal relations, of "complications" and of conflict leading to social "confusion," is encountered again and again in the responses of our interviewees. It suggests that Chinese conceptualize social conflict within a formula of *"complicated"* (*fu-tza*) *interpersonal relationships leading to competition, producing conflict and violence which creates social chaos or "confusion"* (*hun-luan*).

"Complications" imply emotional tension, conflicting desires,

8. T-27. Emphasis added.
9. H-7.

unresolved issues of great importance, and interpersonal hostility. It can be said of an individual, "That man is complicated." A relationship with another person, or a social situation, can be characterized as "complicated," all with the implication that conflict is a likely possibility just behind the face of social custom.

In this second part of the study, which focuses on adult Chinese attitudes toward authority, social relations, and politics, we will explore the roots of the social tension between unity and conflict in basic Chinese cultural patterns, some of which were identified in Part One as growing from childhood educational experiences. More specifically, we will suggest that Chinese hold a paradoxical orientation to social authority which draws its inspiration from this tension between unity and conflict. On the one hand, they look to authority for security against conflict and material deprivation, and willingly accept as "natural" a unitary, dominant, and personalized political leadership. On the other hand, however, they express concern with the manipulative and harsh qualities of that same authority, and seek to avoid contact with what is seen as the "tiger" of governmental power.

Chapter VII

INSTITUTIONAL PATTERNS
OF AUTHORITY

The philosopher Yu said, "They are few who, being filial and fraternal, are fond of offending against their superiors. There have been none, who, not liking to offend against their superiors, have been fond of stirring up confusion (*luan*)." [1]

A pervasive concern with social disorganization and interpersonal conflict gave enduring meaning to the authoritative institutions of Chinese society, and an individual's early-life experiences with family authority prepared him for commitment to these social institutions as an adult. The major patterns of relations with authority which we found in our investigation of childhood recollections—dependence, emulation, and the power of the word—are encountered again in the more elaborate dress of Confucian political concepts. Thus early life experiences and political orthodoxy combined to give coherence to what has been one of the world's most enduring political systems.

THE IMPORTANCE OF NAMES

The structure of interpersonal relations was embodied in society's five moral or natural relationships (*wu-lun*): the pattern of deference and obligation linking ruler and minister, father and son, husband and wife, brothers, and friends. This concept differs significantly from the Western notion of an individual's social "role," because unlike a role, which is defined in terms of the action of the *individual,* the Chinese emphasis is on the *relationship*. In the Confucian tradition an individual's social identity was defined not so

1. From "The Analects," in *The Chinese Classics,* Vol. I, p. 138.

much by what he had achieved, as by those to whom he was related through ties of kinship or personal loyalty.[2]

This social structure is reflected in the Chinese language—in its highly differentiated terminology for identifying social, and specifically family, relationships.[3] More importantly, it is revealed in the way that Chinese *use* language. In any society there are rituals for mediating interpersonal relations, particularly power relationships, the interaction between the superior and subordinate. The Chinese language, with its mystical origins in bone divination, carries great weight in this regard, as is expressed in the Confucian doctrine of the "rectification of names":

> Tsze-lu said, "The ruler of Wei has been waiting for you, in order with you to administer the government. What will you consider the first thing to be done?"
>
> The Master replied, "What is necessary is to rectify names (*cheng-ming*).
>
> "If names be not correct, language is not in accordance with the truth of things. If language be not in accordance with the truth of things, affairs cannot be carried on to success. . . .
>
> "Therefore a superior man considers it necessary that the names he uses may be spoken [appropriately], and also that what he speaks may be carried out [appropriately]. What the superior man requires is just that in his words there may be nothing incorrect." [4]

In the life of an individual, the importance of words was impressed upon him early in his dealings with paternal authority. Words were further invested with considerations of status in the learning of kinship nomenclature. This was no small task:

> [The] *Ta Ch'ing Lü Li* (Laws and Regulations of the Ch'ing Dynasty) distinguished forty-one different groups of kinship members, each group designated by distinct kinship terms. Within a group, each member was designated by an individual term based on sex and age, age being arranged numerically by the order of birth, such as "first

2. The anthropologist Hsu suggests the term "situation-centered" to describe this type of social structure. It would seem that the term "relation-centered" is a more accurate description, primarily because the word "situation" has a strong spatial connotation. The essence of the Confucian system was the set of interpersonal relationships, and more specifically the blood relations, which defined an individual's social identity. *See* Francis L. K. Hsu, *Americans and Chinese, Two Ways of Life* (New York: Henry Schuman, 1953), p. 10.

3. A thorough analysis of Chinese kinship terminology will be found in Han-yi Feng, "The Chinese Kinship System," *Harvard Journal of Asiatic Studies*, Vol. II, No. 2 (July 1937), pp. 141–275.

4. From "The Analects," in *The Chinese Classics*, Vol. I, pp. 263–264.

elder sister" or "third elder brother." These terms were used by kinship members in addressing one another.[5]

The sociologist C. K. Yang observed in a study of life in a south China village,

Learning the complete system of kinship terms constituted an important part of a peasant's training to fit him for social life in a kinship oriented community. . . . The effective operation of this complicated system . . . enabled each individual in the kinship group to identify his own status, to assert his authority or to offer his obedience, to exercise his privilege or to fulfill his obligations.[6]

The concept behind this stress on nomenclature seems to have been that if people acted according to the obligations of the social relationships into which they had been born or matured (a "Son" or a "Father") or of which they had been named a part (a "Prince" or his "Minister"), then society would be properly ordered, each individual would be cared for, and there would be no "confusion." The development of an elaborately differentiated set of status "names" is basic to this conception, for it would make unmistakably clear to everyone who was to show filial deference to whom, and who was to depend on whom.

The practical problem, however, is to insure that a person behaves in accordance with the requirements of his "name." This problem finds expression in the concern shown by both Chinese philosophers and political leaders for "rectification," for insuring that people behave as their status names say they should. Of course, humans have a well-developed ability for maintaining the form of an ideal in the absence of its reality: a minister calls himself a loyal Minister just as he is trying to unseat his prince; or a father does things to his son that no proper Father would do. And the classical literature of Confucianism amply documented the social disruption that resulted when individuals did not act as their status names required.

What then was the reality which developed from Confucius' doctrine that, "There is government when the prince is a Prince, and the minister a Minister, when the father is a Father, and the son a Son"?[7] First, it is clear that political philosopher and official alike, ruling in times when the state was unable to maintain a pervasive presence in society, looked to such basic social organizations as the

5. C. K. Yang, *Chinese Communist Society: The Family and the Village* (Cambridge, Mass.: M.I.T. Press, 1965), Vol. II, pp. 86–87.
6. *Ibid.*
7. From "The Analects," in *The Chinese Classics,* Vol. I, p. 256.

family and clan to assume much of the burden of insuring social order. The sense of respect for authority which Confucian family life sought to instill was seen as basic to the stability of the dynasty; and in times of increasing disorder imperial officials sought to strengthen family and clan life:

> Without the *tsung-tzu* as the clan head, the imperial court has no hereditary official to depend on. If the system of *tsung-tzu* is revived, people will learn to respect their ancestors and value their origins, and then the court will naturally command more respect. In ancient times, young people looked up to their fathers and elder brothers. Now the reverse is true, because people no longer respect their origins. . . . Only recognition of the relationship between superior and subordinate, between high and low, can insure order and obedience without confusion. How can people live properly without some means of control? [8]

If children were reared to respect the system of authority embodied in strict adherence to the nomenclature, imperial officials assumed, then the emperor's subjects would know their places in society. "This is what is meant by the saying, 'The government of his kingdom depends on his regulation of the family.' " [9]

RITUALS OF CONTROL

Deference rituals played an important part in maintaining the hierarchical system of authority ideally defined by the *wu-lun*. An individual used status names in addressing other people, and practiced the rituals of filiality—the *k'ou-t'ou* before parents at New Year's time and the ceremonies of ancestor worship—as a way of indicating his continuing commitment to the social order.[10] Saying the name became a way of reaffirming the authority hierarchy. As one respondent's almost unconscious use of family nomenclature indicates, if the proper verbal symbol has not been invoked the defer-

8. A quote from the Northern Sung philosopher Ch'eng I, cited in Hui-chen Wang Liu, "An Analysis of Chinese Clan Rules: Confucian Theories in Action," in David S. Nivison and Arthur F. Wright, eds., *Confucianism in Action* (Stanford: Stanford University Press, 1959), pp. 64–65.

9. From "The Great Learning," in *The Chinese Classics,* Vol. I, p. 372.

10. The subversive impact on the legitimacy of authority that would result from refusals to perform deference rituals is illustrated with particular clarity in the tensions and drama surrounding early Sino-British diplomatic contact. British unwillingness to perform the kowtow ceremony before the emperor raised anxieties among Ch'ing imperial officials, who feared the effect on the Chinese of this demonstration of lack of respect for the Manchu court. For interesting documentation on Ch'ing official reactions to one of the first English refusals to abide by the tribute system see John L. Cranmer-Byng, *Lord Macartney's Embassy to Peking in 1793 from Official Chinese Documents* (Hong Kong: University of Hong Kong Press, 1961).

ential relationship has been left in doubt: "(How did your father teach you to behave toward family elders?) Naturally we had to respect them. If father's brothers—we called them *shu-shu,* and we were very mannerly (*li-mao*) to them—if they came to visit we couldn't sit down unless they asked us to." [11]

Words thus acquire great "political" weight, for failure to use them properly signals to the individuals involved a person's unwillingness to accept the prescribed power relationships. Conversely, an authority will go to great lengths to make certain that the proper words are spoken before the right people, for it is in the *act* of speaking the name that acceptance of the deference pattern is affirmed.

Family rituals provided the basic model for an individual's efforts to establish relationships with other people. When a parent introduced an acquaintance to his child as "auntie" or "uncle" he indicated the desire to have the individual treated with the same respect and intimacy due those who more accurately bore such titles. And in political life, attempts to establish alliances or stabilize relationships of power frequently took the form of family ritual:

> After his defeat at Kiangsi, Sun Ch'uan-fang went to Tientsin to ask the northern warlords for assistance. He begged Marshal Chang Tso-lin to forgive his previous revolt against the Fengtien Clique. Sun even went through the rites of kowtow and made Chang his adoptive father and Chang Hsueh-liang, son of the Marshal, his sworn brother.[12]

This affirmation of authority relationships through ritualized deference is reinforced by the form of social sanction most characteristic of Chinese society. In Part One we noted how children were educated to acquire great sensitivity to shaming as a form of punishment. They learned to fear "sticking out" from their proper relationships to others. The adult expression of this sensitivity is embodied in the complex calculus of "face," of social approbation for successful management of life's interpersonal responsibilities and ridicule for failures.[13] One could "lose face" by not observing properly the rituals of deference to others and by not fulfilling the obligations which were implied by the social pattern of authority and dependence. If he feared "losing face" before relatives or peers or was anxious to "acquire face," an individual could observe with

11. T-18.
12. From *The Reminiscences of General Li Tsung-jen* (unpublished manuscript of the Columbia University East Asian Institute, Chinese Oral History Project, n.d.), Ch. XXI, p. 1.
13. The most thorough exploration of the meanings of "face" will be found in Hsu Hsien-chin, "The Chinese Concepts of 'Face,'" *American Anthropologist,* Vol. XLVI (January–March 1944), pp. 45–65.

exaggerated correctness those ritualized forms of behavior which would publicly indicate his desire to assume his social obligations.[14]

Students of animal life have observed that ritualized forms of behavior play an important part in the control of conflict among members of a given species, and the affirmation of status relationships within an animal group.[15] Social ritual, the *li,* seems to have played a similar role in Confucian efforts to end social violence and maintain the integrity of authority. As expressed by the philosopher Hsün Tzu: "*Li* is that whereby . . . love and hatred are tempered, whereby joy and anger keep their proper place. It causes the lower orders [of society] to obey, and the upper orders to be illustrious." [16]

The Chinese conception *ch'eng,* usually translated as "sincerity," is closely related to the effort to control troublesome human emotions through social ritual. In the West "sincerity" implies that an individual acts on the "outside" in congruence with his inner feelings. The Chinese, as we saw in Chapter III, have considerable distrust of what is being held inside, of what has been "put in the stomach." The last thing they want is to have inner feelings find public expression. Their conception of "sincerity" is exactly the opposite of the Western meaning. One demonstrates "sincerity" by commitment to one's interpersonal obligations, to society, and not to one's inner feelings. Indeed, one is perhaps most sincere when doing the socially correct thing at precisely the time that inner feelings are urging a different course of action. Sincerity in the Confucian context means bringing social behavior into accord with an external truth of moral or social principles, *not* inner feelings: "[The man] who possesses sincerity is he who, without an effort, hits what is right, and apprehends without the exercise of thought —he is the sage who naturally and easily embodies the right way. He who attains to sincerity is he who chooses what is good, and firmly holds it fast." [17]

14. Western observers of corruption and nepotism in Chinese bureaucratic behavior have tended to overemphasize the element of individual consumption in such practice, without seeing its basic relationship to the interdependent quality of Chinese social life. Such behavior was usually motivated by an individual's desire not to "lose face" before those members of his family and clan who had supported him in his rise to public office. Similarly, conspicuous consumption by Chinese in positions of social leadership represented efforts to "increase face," to obtain the loyalty and respect of dependents by indicating a willingness to care for their needs.

15. *See* Konrad Lorenz, *On Aggression* (New York: Harcourt, Brace, and World, 1966), Ch. V.

16. Cited in Donald J. Munro, *The Concept of Man in Early China* (Stanford, Calif.: Stanford University Press, 1968), p. 33.

17. From "The Doctrine of the Mean," in *The Chinese Classics,* Vol. I, p. 413.

To be sincere is to be socially trustworthy, to demonstrate self-discipline, to conform to the proper pattern of human relationships and thus to contribute to social order.

MODELING

How were individuals raised in this tradition taught to be "sincere," to fit their behavior within the social "box" whose boundaries were formed by familial and social relationships? An important aspect of the development of this form of social discipline seems to have been embodied in the techniques of formal education. Acquiring the self-control for rote memorization of lengthy texts and repetitive copying of characters into the squares of a copybook would seem to develop the discipline for "holding in" emotional impulses and adapting one's behavior to approved social forms. Also, the constant use of models—characters to copy, approved texts to commit to memory—and punishments which made obedience the most painless course of action, must have reinforced the perception gained from family life of the importance of emulating those in authority.

The notion that superiors in status are models of behavior to be emulated is, as was discussed in Part One, quite basic to a child's image of parental authority. The teacher was also presented as one who would make an example of his behavior (*i-shen-tso-tse*) for the child to follow. This conception of authority and leadership applied as well to political life:

> Let the ruler discharge his duties to his elder and younger brothers, and then he may teach the people of the state.
>
> In the Book of Poetry, it is said, "In his deportment there is nothing wrong; he rectifies all the people of the state." Yes; when the ruler, as a father, a son, and a brother, is a model, then the people imitate him.[18]

This image of authority brings to mind subordinates within the cardinal social relationships—ministers, sons, wives, and younger brothers—attentively searching the actions of their superiors for guides to proper behavior. One can see a series of influence hierarchies in which the man at the top carries out a proper action which is then imitated down the line. But in practice how did this idealized conception of leadership function? Our interview materials indicate that people do, in fact, look to superiors for guidance and initiative. Indeed, an important aspect of this system of authority relations is that initiative and precedence in communication are vested in those with power. To describe such a relationship as one

18. From "The Great Learning," in *The Chinese Classics,* Vol. I, p. 372.

of "modeling," however, would be inaccurate, for *within* the tie there is no equivalence or reciprocity; the subordinate does not copy or emulate his superior's action in response. The subordinate, rather, looks to the superior for cues or instruction as to what will be appropriate or permissible behavior on his part. Filiality requires that deference in judgment and decision-making, and communication precedence, be given to the superior within the relationship.

Modeling or imitation of the superior's behavior does seem to occur, however, through the subordinate's adopting his superior's style and judgments of what is proper or permissible behavior *in those other relationships in which he himself is a superior*. In so many of our respondents' descriptions of family life an elder brother is a Son with his father, but a Father with his younger brother. In this sense, the behavior of a prince or a father is transmitted down the hierarchy of social authority. This tendency gave the Confucian tradition its hope that if only a proper leader could be found, his influence would pervade the entire society. But this system of authority also embodied the fear that if the top leader were *not* a "superior man," then the entire society would be vulnerable to the pervasive imitation of a bad model:

> From the loving example of one family a whole state becomes loving, and from its courtesies the whole state becomes courteous, while, from the ambition and perverseness of the One man, the whole state may be led to rebellious disorder—such is the nature of the influence. This verifies the saying, "Affairs may be ruined by a single sentence; a kingdom may be settled by its One man." [19]

ANXIETY IN THE FACE OF AUTHORITY

In terms of the functioning of personality how does this system of leadership seem to have worked? Our findings concerning adult attitudes toward authority follow from the descriptions of how authority was first experienced in childhood. In Part One we emphasized the "dependency" theme in family relations. The traditionally educated male child was taught that he was to depend on his parents, and especially his father, for guidance, initiative, and security. To give emotional force to this conception, parental punishments developed in the child anxieties about either acting independently or contravening parental guidance. Adults reared in this tradition carry with them the legacy of this early-life experience: an anxiety before social authority which produces such behavior as indirection in dealings with superiors, great reluctance to criticize, and an over-willingness to please those in power.

19. *Ibid.,* pp. 370–371.

Perhaps the best way to describe this orientation is a sense of passive impotence before power. The TAT interpretations of our respondents were particularly helpful in exploring this attitude. A typical interpretation of the relation between superior and subordinate was given by a 28-year-old factory worker from Kwangtung Province:

> This [older] person is rather experienced in social matters; an understanding person. This other fellow is relatively young and inexperienced. They have some kind of a relationship. (What kind?) Like commercial people, but yet not like that; like landlords, but yet not. In any case, rather low level in society.
>
> The older man is telling the younger to do something. (What kind of thing?) Not too enlightened a thing. (Why?) You can tell just from their appearances. The younger fellow is fearful; he is unwilling to do it. (What kind of thing might it be?) Just not proper. That could include many things [laughs].
>
> (What does the older man feel about the younger?) He is just telling him to do the job and not to worry about it as the responsibility is all on his shoulders. (How does the younger feel about the older?) He is afraid; he doesn't dare to do the thing.
>
> (What is the result of this situation?) He goes and does it. (Does he succeed?) From his expression he does it and fails, because he is afraid. (Afterwards what is the relationship between the two men?) The older one feels the younger is of no use. (What about the younger?) He thought it could not be avoided, doing that thing, so he did it. (How does he feel toward the elder man?) Nothing in particular; he just had to do the thing. (Then what is their relationship?) The younger man is arrested. (By whom?) The police, another organization, or intelligence group. Then the older man runs away. The younger is very straightforward in telling [his captors] about the thing.[20]

This interpretation is interesting in a number of respects: The initially favorable characterization of the more powerful man—"an understanding person"—changes to one who is manipulating the innocent young man for malevolent purposes. The initial "face" of benevolent authority is quickly dropped, and the respondent reads into the situation his own fears of being manipulated by those with power.[21]

Second, the respondent is unable to face up to the nature of the young man's misdeed. Many of the people we interviewed refused

20. T-12. This interpretation was given in response to TAT Card IV.

21. Other TAT interpretations alter the characterization of authority in the opposite direction: A powerful individual initially is described as being evil or manipulative, but then the respondent "covers over" this disturbing face of authority by making the man benevolent, as if to deny the existence of such exploitation.

to identify improper acts. This "covering over" implies either that whatever the young man in the picture is contemplating is too terrible to articulate or that simply naming the evil deed is tantamount to its execution. Both these factors may be at work, although the second interpretation has particular importance in this tradition. As was observed earlier, Chinese feel that to let people see improper behavior even in the fantasy world of movies or novels brings the act closer to reality, because it may incite others to its performance.

The respondent reveals, as well, an unwillingness to discuss openly the emotional reaction of the young man to such manipulation: "(How does he feel toward the older man?) Nothing in particular. . . ." As we suggested in Chapter III, an individual seems to learn to protect himself against manipulation by divorcing bad feelings from the unavoidable perception that he has been mistreated. By preventing anger from welling up the manipulation may not be avoided, but at least one does not feel so bad about it or become provoked into a rash response against implacable and dangerous power.

Finally, there is described an effortless submission to a new source of authority after the "bad" man has fled. The young man shows no guilt at having done something improper, precisely because in the face of authority he was powerless to do otherwise. The subordinate seeks protection by investing as little of himself in the relationship as possible. There is no sense of personal responsibility; indeed he may have failed deliberately so as to "get back at" the one who promised to bear the responsibility, and who manipulated him into doing something improper.

Now in theory the Confucian tradition did not sanction this passive and uncritical obedience of a subordinate to his superiors. As the *Classic of Filial Piety* instructs:

> . . . when a case of unrighteous conduct is concerned, a son must by no means keep from remonstrating with his father, nor a minister from remonstrating with his ruler. Hence, since remonstrance is required in the case of unrighteous conduct, how can [simple] obedience to the orders of a father be accounted filial piety? [22]

But the formally articulated social ideal runs afoul of the workings of personality. The legacy of learning to be filial carries with it a basic anxiety about dealings with authority, which seems to dominate the behavior of those in subordinate positions.

Interview responses indicate a number of other emotional factors which tend to reinforce a sense of anxiety and impotence be-

---

22. *Hsiao Ching,* in Max F. Müller, ed., *Sacred Books of the East* (Oxford, England: Clarendon Press, 1879–1910), Vol. III, p. 484.

fore power. The fear of conflict, of provoking aggression in the superior, is a theme frequently encountered:

(Why did you agree a little bit with the notion that subordinates should avoid criticizing their superiors?) It's difficult to explain. . . . You don't want to criticize your superiors too directly. The boss might misunderstand, he might think we were opposing him or not obeying his orders. He might get angry and then conflict would develop; and possibly the outcome would be bad for you. Therefore I approve of criticism, but it has to be agreeable. You have to understand the superior's degree of cultivation. If he is insufficiently cultivated, if his personality is too strong, then he will have no way of accepting criticism, and it is just best for you to leave him of your own accord. Don't get near him.[23]

In addition to anxieties about aggression, the complex of emotional concerns we have termed "dependency," of wanting to be cared for and a fear of being "cut off" from a powerful individual who will provide guidance and security, further limit a subordinate's critical ability:

If a subordinate is very polite, very mannerly, and unconditionally obeys his superior [in tasks he is given], the superior will rely upon him and will let him do anything. . . . A subordinate should not express his own opinions in front of a superior; he cannot contradict or contend with him. If you should say that the leader has made some error you will destroy his position. He definitely will be angry with you, will hate you; he will not want to use you again.[24]

There is no dishonor attached to wanting to be used by a more powerful individual, for "being used" (as opposed to "being cheated") implies security—that one has found a relationship within which one gains responsibility and power. And where one's security is intimately related to the status and success of an authoritative individual, criticism comes to be self-destructive, if not directly through rejection by the superior, then indirectly as a result of the superior's loss of position.

Interview data indicate that fear of rejection by authority is predominantly of an economic nature—losing a job or a position of subordinate responsibility—rather than fear of loss of affection or respect. Consonant with the way in which authority was learned in childhood, there is no expectation of such positive emotional sentiments as affection, humor, or warmth in dealings with authority. The subordinate looks only for material security or the status and

23. T-40.
24. T-49.

responsibility that will come to him indirectly through association with a more powerful man.

This tradition of filial or loyal dependence on those with power develops in a subordinate the sense that neither authority nor responsibility can be shared; they are only delegated or acquired indirectly within a superior-subordinate relationship. Hence a passivity, a reluctance to take initiative or to be critical—what the historian Balazs has termed a "panicky fear of assuming responsibility" [25]—becomes the safest course for avoiding the harshness of authority.

DEPENDENCY AND SOCIAL INTEGRATION

The fear that "talking back" to authority, or even airing differences of opinion among family members, will lead to conflict and "confusion" has serious implications for social integration. Respondents' expectations about the manner in which disputes are dealt with both within and beyond the family were revealed in their interpretations of the TAT pictures. The general impression they give is that interpersonal problems are resolved only with considerable difficulty.

The following description of a dispute within the family was given by a 32-year-old government clerk from Kwangtung, responding to TAT Card III:

> This looks like a family. The mother and father are rather conservative from the looks of their clothing. The son is pleading with his father about something. (What kind of circumstance is this?) From their faces *it looks as if they have already split apart. The problem can't be solved.* The father has already decided. The mother is very fearful. (What kind of an affair would this be about?) According to the present situation, it probably is about money. (How does the son feel?) He is very pitiable. You can see it from his face. (What attitude does he have toward his father?) He is beseeching him. (And what attitude does the father have toward the son?) He is trembling with rage. The mother is very much afraid. (What about the father?) He hates the son because he has done some bad thing. (What kind of a thing?) It is about money [laughs].

25. Etienne Balazs, *Chinese Civilization and Bureaucracy*, trans. H. M. Wright, ed. Arthur F. Wright (New Haven: Yale University Press, 1964), p. 18.

Students of Chinese bureaucratic behavior have amply documented the paralysis of initiative and creativity that resulted from the traditional system of authority. *See,* for example, Albert Feuerwerker, *China's Early Industrialization* (Cambridge, Massachusetts: Harvard University Press, 1958), pp. 23–24.

(Afterwards what will be the relation of the father to the son?) The son, for a short period won't have anything to do with the father, as they can't solve the problem. (Ultimately?) *They will get together as before. After all, it is a family.* (How will the father then feel toward the son?) *He will think the son shouldn't bring up money problems.* (What will the son feel toward the father?) The son thinks the father is too conservative, too stubborn. (What about the mother?) She feels very unhappy, out of sorts, but she will try to be good to both of them.[26]

There are two striking aspects of this interpretation: First, there is no meaningful dialogue between the father and son, no attempt to discuss the problem or the son's supposed misdeed. In many TAT characterizations of conflict with authority there is a very ambiguous interpretation of the responsibility for a bad situation. It is seldom *directly* attributed to the authoritative person; yet the implication of responsibility for the problem being with the subordinate is usually ambiguous, almost phrased as, "Yes, the young man did something wrong, but he really isn't to blame." Persons without power or in weaker positions are felt to be blameless; authority is not shared. The subordinate was only following the orders of some powerful individual. In the above story, the father has made a decision, and the relationship has already "split up." The father is about to explode with hostility toward the son, and mother and son fearfully beseech calm and understanding.

Second, there is no meaningful resolution of the problem. For a time the two disputants have nothing to do with one another, as they can't resolve the difficulty; and while they later resume contact, apparently they do so for normative reasons alone. ("After all, it is a family.") The emotional implication of the unresolved dispute is covered over: The father does not want the son to bring up money problems (that is, no attribution of feelings at all, just a desire to cut off communication about the dispute), and the son has only bad *thoughts* about the father.

This set of expectations about the way problems are handled within a family makes more comprehensible the Chinese concern that if differences of opinion are brought into the open it will lead to "confusion" or conflict. Problems really don't get solved; they remain, along with bad feelings, behind the face of filial deference as sources of conflict which might "split up" the family group and hence are better not discussed.

In relations with authority beyond the family the same conception of limited meaningful communication or compromise between superior and subordinate is revealed in TAT responses; and the outcome of differences of opinion frequently is a separation:

26. T-7. Emphasis added.

Here is a superior criticizing this young man's work; he doesn't like the work of his underling. (What is the superior's attitude toward him?) He feels that his technical level isn't high. (What does he *feel* about the young man?) He feels he isn't smart, isn't clever enough. (What does the young man feel toward his superior?) He is expressing his difficulties. (But what does he *feel,* or think, about the superior?) From his facial expression he indicates that the work can't be done. (In the future what will be their relationship, or the situation?) In the future they could split apart. (Why?) He is trying to teach the younger fellow; but he thinks it can't be done. (So what happens in the future?) They split apart.[27]

There is no attempt to come to a meeting of minds, and there is a strong inclination on the part of the respondent to cover over the emotional implications of the conflict. In spite of the interviewer's urgings that he attribute feelings to the characters in the story, the respondent keeps his interpretation at a safe distance from potentially troublesome emotions.

To gauge the extent to which these perceptions of social conflict were shared by the various respondents in our interview sample, interpretations of the three TAT stories dealing with conflict within the family, in superior-subordinate relations, and in dealings among peers, were coded for the entire group. The coding procedure was designed simply to see if the respondent perceived conflict as the immediate outcome of the situation he was describing; and then whether he thought cooperative relations among the major figures in the story would be maintained in the future. For purposes of contrast, responses to these same TAT cards (modified only for dress and facial appearance) given by an American student sample were coded according to the same procedure. The results are summarized in Table II.

The overall pattern one sees in the data from the Chinese respondents is of a level of conflict in family and peer relations approximately twice as high as that in dealings between nonfamily superiors and subordinates. Evidently considerations of career or job security help to dampen down conflict in such situations (although TAT Card IV is somewhat less likely to evoke conflict fantasy than Cards I and III). The most suggestive interpretation, however, is indicated by comparison with the American responses. Not only did the American students see somewhat less conflict in these cards than did the Chinese; they also anticipated that cooperative relations were much more likely to be maintained in the future.

Comparison between the American students and the Chinese emigrés must be handled with care, for reasons of age difference

27. T-10. This interpretation was given in response to TAT Card IV.

TABLE II
PERCEPTION OF CONFLICT AND COOPERATIVE OUTCOMES IN TAT RESPONSES GIVEN AS A PERCENTAGE OF TOTAL RESPONDING*

Group Tested	FAMILY RELATIONS (TAT III)		SUPERIOR-SUBORDINATE RELATIONS (TAT IV)		PEER RELATIONS (TAT I)	
	Present Conflict†	Future Coop-eration‡	Present Conflict	Future Coop-eration	Present Conflict	Future Coop-eration
Chinese emigré males, total sample, N = 88	76.3	25.0	34.5	57.7	79.5	27.4
"Traditional" Chinese adult males,§ N = 29	72.4	30.8	41.3	57.7	75.0	29.4
"Communist" Chinese student males,# N = 30	80.0	18.5	30.8	60.0	75.0	32.0
American student males, ‖ N = 30	64.3	64.3	15.4	76.9	55.2	55.2

* Because of variations in the number of respondents in each sample who did not directly describe either immediate outcomes or future relationships, we have used only those responses which include an interpretation which could be coded in making these calculations. This means there are some minor fluctuations in sample size for the various figures.

† This figure is calculated on the basis of those who attributed conflict, hostile, or "splitting-up" outcomes to the *immediate* social situation they described.

‡ This figure is calculated on the basis of those who attributed cooperative or non-hostile competitive *future* relationships to the people in the social situations they described.

These two columns († and ‡) should not be added together (to obtain 100) as they represent separate calculations. The key to the analysis is the distinction between the respondents' perception of *immediate outcome* and *future relationship*. Americans could see *both* present conflict and future cooperation. Chinese could not.

§ This sample consists of Chinese emigrés who had attended a traditional Confucian-style "home school" (*szu-shu*) when young. Their average age is 60.9 years.

This sample consists of emigré Chinese, mostly from southern and coastal provinces, who had received secondary education in Communist-run schools, or who were in the Communist Party or Youth League. Their average age is 25.3 years.

‖ This sample consists of graduate students from the University of Michigan selected to represent a broad distribution of places of geographical origin and areas of academic interest. They are about evenly divided between urban and small town or rural backgrounds, and come from a range of socioeconomic status families. Their average age is 25.5 years, very close to that of the Communist-trained Chinese student group.

119

if nothing else; yet even when their responses are compared with those of the student element of the Chinese sample, the pattern of less immediate conflict and greater future cooperation is maintained. These data seem to reaffirm our conclusion that Chinese are not taught to see conflict as a legitimate aspect of social life; hence when conflict does develop it becomes most difficult to maintain functioning personal relationships. Indeed, the generally higher level of conflict in the Chinese stories as compared to the American interpretations suggests that the effort to "gloss over" points of dispute makes their disruptive impact on interpersonal relations that much greater.

While the meaning of these data for peer relations and generational change will be discussed in later chapters, we can say at this point that the TAT interpretations, seen in conjunction with material discussed earlier on communication with authority, indicate tensions in the superior-subordinate relationship which tend to weaken "vertical" social integration: The subordinate is reluctant to initiate communication or raise criticism in dealings with his superior.[28] Hence problems are not directly faced, and sources of discontent are not exposed and worked out. The superior may find himself cut off from the reality of problems and popular morale that are his responsibility because of his harshness and the concomitant reserve of subordinates. His effectiveness may be further eroded by passive resistance on the part of subordinates who are unwilling to confront him directly with difficulties or sources of discontent. Finally, he may be "abandoned" by his subordinates, or even subjected to direct retaliation by those who were allowed no moderated redress of grievances.

These disintegrative effects of the dependency orientation toward authority were ameliorated by the Confucian stress on personal "cultivation." To the extent that an individual in an authoritative position could moderate his dealings with subordinates and treat them with "human-heartedness" (*jen*), he could enlist their more active cooperation. As one of our respondents, a governmental official, observed:

> If you are not happy with [the performance of] a subordinate then sometimes you will get angry at him or give him a lecture. But I do not get angry very much any more. I go out of my way to avoid it. (Why?)

28. The weak communication linkages between different levels of Chinese industrial bureaucracies has been noted by Franz Schurmann in *Ideology and Organization in Communist China* (Berkeley: University of California Press, 1968), pp. 230–231. This author's interpretation lays particular stress on the wide "policy-operations" gap created by authority's role conception that he must not involve himself with matters of practical management.

Because no matter at whom you get angry, there always will remain an irritant to keep you apart, and afterwards it will not be easy to cooperate with that person. He will think you are not sufficiently cultivated.[29]

In addition, subordinates could appeal to the "emotions" (*kan-ch'ing*) of those on whom they depended for moderation in treatment. This notion of *kan-ch'ing* reflects the degree to which the relationship between superior and subordinate was personalized and diffuse in content, not mediated by legal norms or considerations of some specified technical function, as tends to be the case in industrial societies. The subordinate would appeal for sympathy or fair treatment on the basis of his past loyalty; and an authority could ignore such requests only at the risk of degrading the cooperation and commitment he might receive in the future. An anthropologist has written of such appeals to emotion:

> *Kan-ch'ing* differs from friendship in that it presumes a much more specific common interest, much less warmth and more formality of contact, and includes a recognized degree of exploitation. It is the common property of all classes. . . . *Kan-ch'ing* operates in the absence of kin ties which can bridge important gaps in status.[30]

Considerate treatment of subordinates not only might make an authority more effective through their active support; it could also enhance his social status through respect and the desire of other individuals to establish relations with him. The willing submission or dependence of people on a powerful individual could increase his power through the skills or resources they might bring to the relationship, and by increasing his prestige, his social "face," in the eyes of others. (This, of course, was the logic behind China's traditional tributary system of international relations.)

The only problem with this approach to wielding authority, from a superior's point of view, was the tendency of subordinates to "eat him up" through claims on his resources, or their tendency to become "unruly" if not under stern control. Weak authority was thus as problematical in its social effects as authority too harshly applied, as is indicated in one respondent's rueful recollection of his mild-mannered father: "He was very honest; and many people in the countryside took advantage of him. When I was small and saw this happen I really felt very upset." [31]

29. T-33.
30. Morton Fried, *Fabric of Chinese Society* (New York: Praeger, 1953), pp. 226–227.
31. T-45.

THE ENDURING AMBIVALENCE TOWARD AUTHORITY

The sum of these institutional aspects of authority embodies the same sense of ambivalence which we noted in Part One. Individuals in the Confucian tradition had come to expect guidance and initiative from superiors early in life, and they looked to the wealthy and powerful to provide for their material well-being and security from social conflict. Uncertain application of power would lead to squabbling among subordinates or "unruly" demands for support. Superior and subordinate alike saw the necessity for strong authority.

The harshness with which authority was applied, however, reflected the concern of those in positions of leadership that their subordinates might show insufficient filial respect and loyalty. Dependents needed to be told what was expected of them, or else they would become demanding, lazy, and hard to control.

Given these contradictions in the orientation toward authority, it is not surprising that we find Chinese seeking an idealized, non-hierarchical brotherhood of friendship as a solution to their problems. As we shall see in the next chapter, however, the idealization of the bond of friendship contrasts with a more somber set of expectations about dealings with peers. In the final chapter in this section, an analysis of Chinese attitudes toward politics, we find that the concern with peer conflict gives renewed meaning to strong political authority, and the sense of ambivalence remains unresolved.

Chapter VIII

FRIENDS AND PEERS

THE HOPE OF FRIENDSHIP . . .

Chinese pride themselves on the degree to which their traditions have developed the bond of friendship to a high art. "We *really* know how to be friends," is a comment frequently addressed to foreigners. Within the society there is a glorification of friendship ties that in quality is not unlike the American idealized conception of romantic love.

Relations among friends constitute one of the five Confucian natural or moral human relationships (*wu-lun*), and is the only one which is nonhierarchical. In expounding on the meaning of friendship, our interview respondents indicated that, in part, the appeals of this relationship represent a breaking away from the harsh controls and emotional restrictions of their society's rigid structure:

> Relations between friends are without restrictions, very free and casual. They are without limits and tend to stress emotions. You can say anything to your friends. For example, if you have some problem with another person you can talk about it with a friend, get his help; he may help you deal with the situation. But superior and subordinate relations are not that way. You do not dare to say many things to a superior. If you talk a lot then your superior will easily be dissatisfied with you.[1]

Unlike dealings with authority which are laden with anxiety, among friends there is relaxation, a "stress on emotions" and an openness in communication. In recalling the learning of authority within the family, respondents repeatedly used the expression, "You can't be just 'do as you please' (*sui-pien*) in relations with Father." The same phrase, to act "as one pleases," occurs repeatedly in descriptions of the appeals of friendship.

Chinese novels reveal a strong element of escapism in the conception of friendship. Note, for example, the bravado of the three sworn brothers in *The Romance of the Three Kingdoms* and the escape from the oppressions of harsh official power into the world

1. H-7.

of banditry recounted in *All Men Are Brothers*. Here, urges for revenge and revelry can find uninhibited expression, and seem to be outlets in fantasy from authority's strict or unjust control. But such novels were read in concealment behind a copy of the Classics, much as the unrestrained behavior they described was intended to be covered over by the social rituals of the Confucian tradition.[2]

Another aspect of the idealization of friendship is its fulfillment of the dependency needs which we have described thus far as central to relations with authority. As one respondent phrased it, "We rely on parents at home, and on friends in society." [3] The belief that a person is not a social individual apart from those to whom he is related, and cannot exist in isolation of the human ties which define his life obligations, is also a part of the conception of friendship:

> (What is the most important thing a person obtains from friends?) [Their] sympathy and support. (Why is that so important?) A person can't take care of things all by himself. If he has friends who come and help him, encourage him, and support him, then things can be dealt with effectively.[4]

This sense of interrelatedness, the belief that the support and encouragement of others is necessary to effectiveness in social life, is expressed most often in the hope of mutual assistance among friends and of cooperation in dealings with one's peers.

. . . AND THE REALITY

Between the idealization of friendship and the manner in which our respondents had experienced dealings with friends in daily life, however, there existed a wide divergence which grew from the excessive hopes they placed in such relations. Almost to a man they agreed that it was most difficult to establish really close friend-

---

2. Mao Tse-tung recalled of his early school days: "I was the family 'scholar.' I knew the Classics, but disliked them. What I enjoyed were the romances of Old China, and especially stories of rebellions. I read the *Yo Fei Chuan (Chin Chung Chuan), Shui Hu Chuan, Fan T'ang, San Kuo,* and *Hsi Yu Chi,* while still very young, and despite the vigilance of my old teacher, who hated these outlawed books and called them wicked. I used to read them in school, covering them up with a Classic when the teacher walked past. So also did most of my schoolmates. We learned many of the stories almost by heart, and discussed and rediscussed them many times. (Edgar Snow, *Red Star Over China* [New York: Grove Press, 1961], p. 127.)

3. T-18.

4. T-36.

ships.[5] Part of the difficulty is in releasing the controls over expression of emotions and thoughts that had been developed from a lifetime of "holding in":

> (Why did you agree [that it is difficult to have friends to whom you can express your innermost thoughts and feelings]?) I think it is very difficult to express [such things]. (Why?) Because they are deep in people's hearts. They can't mutually express them. Isn't that unfortunate? From my experience, of the male or female friends I have had there hasn't been a complete expression of emotions. You have had a common life for several decades but cannot completely have a mutual opening up of what is in your hearts. I think this is very sad.[6]

The most frequent explanation given to the difficulty in having true friends, however, is closely related to the need to rely or depend upon other people, to the hope that one will gain advancement in one's career through the help of a friend or acquire financial assistance when in trouble. As expressed by a university graduate from Hupeh Province:

> It is very difficult to have friends who really understand you, just too difficult. (Why is it so difficult?) It is not easy to explain. For instance, when you both are poor you are good friends. But once your friend makes big money, becomes a big official, he just forgets his old friends. I once had a close friend. Then he became wealthy and the friendship gradually lost its flavor. (Why?) Because he had money. He was afraid that people would go and ask him for money—but I wouldn't do that.[7]

Because in this cultural tradition the obligations of friendship are so intensive, potential friends may shy away from establishing or maintaining a relationship when there is a low expectation of reciprocity. Such a tie strongly implies the acquisition of a dependent who will make demands on one's resources. Thus, as with authority relations, the social implications of dependency work to limit the establishment of interpersonal relationships through fear of being "eaten" by impoverished or demanding friends.

DISTRUST OF PEERS

The conception of friendship is in a sense a special case of contact among peers. Actually, social transactions between people of equal

5. Quantified interview data on this point, and comparative information on American attitudes towards friendship, are presented in the author's article, "Mao's Effort to Reintegrate the Chinese Polity: Problems of Conflict and Authority in Chinese Social Processes," in A. Doak Barnett, ed., *Chinese Communist Politics in Action* (Seattle: University of Washington Press, 1969), pp. 298–301, 360.

6. T-52.

7. T-33.

or near-equal social status were relatively "underdeveloped" in the Chinese tradition. The concern with conflict in social life gave particular emphasis to the hierarchical conception of interpersonal relationships. And much of the effort in dealings among peers was either to place the relationship within a nexus of kin or friendship ties or to "buffer" the transaction, to keep it at a distance through the "politeness" (*k'o-ch'i*) forms of social ceremony or the mediation of a third party.[8]

From the time children begin to have contact with nonfamily peers, they are led to acquire a distrust of other people's motives or of their own ability to deal effectively with interpersonal disputes. We previously noted how anxieties about conflict develop out of parental reactions to quarreling among children. In addition, our respondents frequently observed how important it was that parents choose "proper" friends for their children to play with; for "bad" friends would provoke fighting or lead the child astray into sensual indulgence (a "wine and meat friend" [*chiu-jou p'eng-yu*] or "wine and women friend" [*chiu-se p'eng-yu*]). Again, the basic assumption is that since children cannot discipline their own behavior, parents must limit their social contacts in ways to give them proper guidance:

> (Why do you think it is relatively easy for a child to be influenced by a bad environment?) The attraction of external material things is just too great. This is the same both for children and adults. The Western way of doing things is to try to satisfy your desires, but there is no way completely to satisfy a person's desires. . . . Some people, if they have not had a good upbringing, will just do as they please—even until they are old. They will be muddleheaded and there will be no way for them to correct themselves. You have to give children a good educational environment. This is the idea behind the story of Mencius' mother moving three times: children have a strong sense of modeling [themselves on] the behavior of other people; they imitate the actions of those around them.[9]

The legacy of these early life images of social relations beyond the family is a limited sense of interpersonal trust. One has been led to believe that self-control and guidance of one's own behavior are difficult to achieve, and hence one comes to doubt other people's ability for self-control. As one has been taught to rely upon family elders for guidance, there remains the assumption that peers are not independent social actors, but represent the interests of superiors

8. For an interesting analysis of the Chinese tendency to use intermediaries in social transactions, *see* John H. Weakland, "The Organization of Action in Chinese Society," *Psychiatry*, Vol. XIII (1950), pp. 361–370.

9. T-31.

whose interests may be at variance with those of one's own group. Consequently adults feel that social transactions with peers are safest when they can be placed within the hierarchical framework of mutual obligations and restraints, the "human feelings" (*jen-ch'ing*) characteristic of family life.

Chinese describe the attempt to fit nonfamilial peer relations within the nexus of family or friendship obligations as literally to "speak of human feelings" (*chiang jen-ch'ing*), which might be more formally translated as to "speak on behalf of another":

> (What does it mean to *chiang jen-ch'ing?*) On many occasions Chinese worry about "face." For example, if someone is having a building constructed and the work is going slowly, if the owner of the new building has a friend who knows the contractor, and this friend asks the contractor to help him [the friend] by finishing the building a bit faster for the owner, the contractor will do his best to help. That is *jen-ch'ing* [human feelings]. (What if the owner doesn't have a mutual friend?) Then the contractor may just use talk to rebuff his request.
>
> If you know a person, and he is a friend, then feelings are real. If you don't know him then feelings are false. (How is that?) If you don't know the person, then you don't know the relevance of his requests [for your relationship]. But if you know him then you know the implications of reputation and self-interest.
>
> (What is the importance of *jen-ch'ing* for Chinese society?) Chinese society is based on the inculcation of etiquette (*li-mao*). In interpersonal relations there are certain requirements of etiquette, and these requirements contain *jen-ch'ing*. For instance, we think that the English have no *jen-ch'ing-wei* [sensitivity to other people's feelings]. They are proud, and think China is vulgar and backward. They look down on us. This lacks *jen-ch'ing*.[10]

There are two major points that might be made on the basis of this involved but revealing response. The first is that "human feelings" (*jen-ch'ing*) are the dynamic element in interpersonal transactions; they are the primary test of whether the mutual expectations and obligations of a "face to face" relationship have been met. To accede to that deference which an individual expects to be accorded because of his social "face" or status is to respect him and his social position, and thus give him good feelings. Conversely, to fail to meet these expectations of status deference is to provoke bad feelings. Thus, in the example given by the above respondent, the British are criticized for not according China that respect which she considers appropriate to her proper place in the world. And hence, as the expression goes, the British can no longer properly "face up to" (*tui-pu-ch'i*) China because of British failure (in

10. T-9.

China's eyes) to meet their part of what would be considered appropriate deference. Thus bad feelings are provoked, and the relationship will disintegrate or become hostile unless some "facesaving" solution to the offense can be found.

THE IMPORTANCE OF INTERMEDIARIES

Given the importance which Chinese attach to status deference in social contact, in instances of dealings with unknown individuals they tend to seek out a mutually known third party who understands the "face" expectations of all involved to mediate the relationship. The intermediary who "speaks of human feelings" (*chiang jen-ch'ing*) is thus one who tries to reconcile differences in status by linking the deference hierarchies which are the basic component of the Chinese social structure. If the intermediary is mutually known he understands the expectations of "face" of each party, and hopefully, he can effectively bridge the gap of trust, reconcile differences in status, and prevent bad feelings from being provoked.

In the absence of an intermediary, relations with unknown individuals become problematical, for each party must try to make certain that both the requirements of his own status or "face" and those of his opposite are properly recognized. Failures through mutual ignorance or ill-intention can lead to bad feelings and potential conflict.[11] Such are the difficulties resulting from teaching individuals that their self-respect is based above all on their status relationships to other people, rather than on their personal accomplishments.

Relations with peers thus become caught up in the complex of

11. The ritualized forms of self-deprecation which a Chinese might practice in dealings with peers can thus be viewed as an effort to convince someone of equal status that he has no intention of putting himself "one up"; indeed, he is willing to accept a position of lower status to demonstrate his respect and the desire to maintain a friendly relationship.

An English traveler in China in the early nineteenth century described such ritualized deference at a banquet held in the residence of a literatus: "When all was ready we were led in with great ceremony and placed in the principal seats of honour. We now had the opportunity of seeing the extent to which the Chinese carry their ceremony and politeness amongst themselves when they are about to be seated at table. Our host and his friends were nearly a quarter of an hour before the whole of them were seated. Each one was pressing the most honorable seat upon his neighbor, who, in his turn, could not think of occupying such a distinguished place at the board. However, after a great deal of bowing and flattery, all was apparently arranged satisfactorily and the dinner commenced." (Robert Fortune, *Three Years' Wanderings in the Northern Provinces of China* [London, John Murray, 1847], p. 140.)

feelings and social forms intended to provide security from conflict. One has been taught that there is "order" when everyone knows who is to defer to whom, but the effort to impose this hierarchical calculus on peer relations is beset by the ambiguities of dealing with unknown individuals and the natural tendency to prefer a dominant to a subordinate status. The intercession of a mutually known third party can thus help to fit a transaction within the web of interpersonal status relations and obligations that help to insure "peace."

In addition, the personal obligations and group controls that come with relations of kin or friendship are seen as making people trustworthy, for an individual would make trouble only at the risk of jeopardizing his "face" and place in life's basic social groupings.[12] Thus an intermediary known to friends and kin can insure that an unknown individual becomes subject to these basic sources of social control, and will not create "disorder":

> *"Chiang jen-ch'ing"* means, for example, if you want to find a tenant to live in your house but you don't dare carelessly to let anyone come to live with you, you definitely should find a third party who knows you both, to "speak on both of your behalves," to introduce you. . . . In this way things will be peaceful. You won't have any disorder and no difficulties will develop. If there is someone to introduce you then you won't have any bad people coming in to create confusion (*kao-luan*).[13]

PEER CONFLICT AND CONTROL

The lack of trust and directness in dealings among peers is compounded by fears of conflict; and the social forms of Confucian cultivation—politeness in talk (*k'o-ch'i hua*) and good manners (*li-mao*)—are seen as essential to avoiding conflict. Personal reserve is necessary if one is not to provoke hostility or obstructive behavior in others:

> If a person's cultivation is good it is easy for him to get along with other people, to cooperate with other people. He seldom will develop friction with them, and he will have many friends. If a person's cultivation is not good he will not be easy to cooperate with, he will get into

12. Studies of group life and shaming have indicated that an important aspect of "losing face" is embarrassing one's primary group, and not just oneself, through some personal misbehavior, again indicating the extent to which Chinese social identity is relational, not individual. *See* Richard W. Wilson, *Childhood Political Socialization on Taiwan* (unpublished Ph.D. dissertation, Princeton University, 1967), p. 54; and Hsu Hsien-chin, "The Chinese Concepts of 'Face,' " p. 50.

13. T-38.

conflicts, and because he can't get along with others he will not succeed in his work.

(How does a person become cultivated?) When he runs into some worldly problem he should not be too impulsive, he must be mannerly to people, kindly. He can't just do as he might like to do in some situation, be so aggressive with other people that he turns their faces all red. When speaking to other people he should not be so assertive that he hurts their self-respect.[14]

In evaluating problem-solving situations among peers (through TAT interpretations), our respondents generally indicated that they expected a breakdown in interpersonal communication or cooperative relationships to follow differences of opinion.[15] A typical response to TAT Card I, which deals specifically with peer relations, was given by a former government official from Fukien Province:

These five people are holding a meeting to discuss something. This fellow on the side disagrees with the proposal supported by most of the others, and so he is unhappy. He has stood up and is preparing to leave the group, or is thinking of opposing them. He is not the leader of the group. Probably he just has his own proposal.

(How do these people in the group feel?) Because of the fellow on the side getting up to leave, they have been provoked into feeling tense. Consequently they have put their heads together to discuss the situation and there are many opinions: Some are saying let the fellow go and be done with it; some think that his opinion is not bad and should be reconsidered.

(How does the fellow on the side feel about the others?) He feels that their opinion is nonsense. He wants to support his own proposal but the others won't listen to him. Hence he is unhappy. He is pacing up and down considering whether to participate in the discussion or to leave the group.

(What is the outcome?) This fellow is very unhappy; and so he withdraws from the group—indicates his disapproval and goes.

(In the future what relationship do these people have with the fellow who left?) They have no mutual concern: "You take care of yours, and I'll take care of mine."[16]

Differences of opinion among peers result in a breakdown of cooperative relations, obviously limiting social integration and opening the door to the "bad feelings" which usually accompany

14. T-33.
15. As summarized in Table II, p. 119 above, the full sample of persons interviewed saw conflict outcomes in 79.5 percent of their interpretations of TAT Card I, with future cooperation being maintained in only 27.4 percent of the cases.
16. T-28.

such disputes. As this was phrased in one interview record: "(What happens when, as you have described it, two people 'split apart?') They have resentment (*fan-kan*). (Why do they have resentment?) Because in their basic positions they are not alike." [17] Thus to problems of resolving differences of opinion is added the possibility of conflict based on emotional resentment.

Competition among peers is seen to be as troublesome for social unity as differences of opinion, for the expectation is that rivalry will bring out bad feelings and lead to unrestrained conflict:

> (What is the greatest effect of interpersonal competition on society?) If it is aggressive or emotional then it is not good. It can lead to hatred or jealousy, and the outcome would be too bad! (What would the outcome be?) It can lead to bad emotions on both sides. In lower class society this kind of competitive struggle leads to killing, and so the outcome is not peaceful.[18]

The pattern of peer conflict which our respondents saw resulting from differences of opinion has the same polarized quality of either apparent "peace" or unrestrained violence which we have noted earlier. If a neighbor is troublesome it is best to avoid a confrontation and maintain a "face" of harmony, for the outcome of a critical interchange could only be bad feelings and open conflict:

> If you try to correct the neighbor and are too assertive, you may not succeed. You may create strife. For example, if the neighbor plays mahjong, and you ask him to be quiet, it can develop into conflict. It can lead to a fight [laughs]. Another way of handling this situation would be just to move away—that would be a bit better. If you talk to him about it and he does not accept your point of view, there is nothing you can do.[19]

One can hope that one's neighbors are "cultivated" and can accept criticism; but the concern always remains that even if the "face" reaction is not hostile, underneath there will be hatred to poison the relationship:

> If the neighbor is so objectionable he must have a low educational level. If he was cultivated he wouldn't act that way. If his educational level is low, if you try to correct him it won't have any good effect. He'll just be more objectionable. If he is really bad he might on the surface say, "Good," and then [underneath] he'll hate you. But a cultivated person would thank you for helping him out.[20]

17. T-10.
18. T-47.
19. H-2.
20. T-14.

Observers of daily life in China have consistently reported the unrestrained, "confused" quality of conflict which occasionally breaks through the "face" of cultivated reserve:

> While Chinese in their normal intercourse with each other observe the greatest courtesy, they go to the other extreme once the restraints of polite behavior are thrown aside. Then the foulness of the language, the depths of the insults hurled back and forth can find few parallels. . . . A couple of women who have had a disagreement over some trivial matter will entertain the neighborhood for hours with the picturesque but unprintable phrases that they fling at each other. Each accuses the other of every moral depravity which comes in mind. . . . This often continues until one or both are physically exhausted.[21]

In a society that teaches its children that avoidance of a dispute is preferable to moderated resolution of interpersonal differences, there is little between the poles of "harmony" and "confusion," *hop'ing* and *hun-luan*.

The effort to control conflict among peers often includes the disputants' involvement of neighbors and friends. Foreign observers have frequently noted that "quarrels in China take place by preference before an audience, and the attention of the combatants is directed as much to the effect of their words on the observers as upon each other." [22] The practice of "cursing the street" (*machieh*),[23] of airing one's grievances in a public place or initiating a conflict where friends will be forced to intervene will, it is hoped, bring down on one's opponent the sense of shame and group pressures which will right the wrong.

Fears of conflict and distrust of the unruly behavior of peers, however, lead many to see the only hope of maintaining social order in the external controls of social organization, in which the individual will be "boxed in" by the combined forces of group obligations and ties, and the authority of strong leaders:

> (Please explain what it means to have *chih an hao* [good peace and order]). . . . *Everything has to be well organized.* For example, if a person wants to steal, if you know his motivation you can prevent it. (What kind of organization?) *It is not a special, it cannot be a simple*

21. Carl Crow, *The Chinese Are Like That* (New York: Harper, 1939), pp. 281–282. A more scholarly analysis of the peaceful, docile, yet violent qualities of China's peasants will be found in Hsiao Kung-chuan, *Rural China: Imperial Control in the Nineteenth Century* (Seattle: University of Washington Press, 1960), esp. Chapter 10.

22. Margery Wolf, *The House of Lim: A Study of a Chinese Farm Family* (New York: Appleton-Century-Crofts, 1968), p. 105.

23. *See* Arthur Smith, *Chinese Characteristics* (New York: Fleming Revell, 1894), pp. 219–221.

organization. It has to be united with others. You have to know what a person is doing from the time he is small. . . . *A person cannot be isolated (ku-li ti); he cannot live alone. You have to have 4, 5, 6, 6,000 people around him.* For example, if he gets sick you have to take him to a hospital to get cured—so you have to have things well united. . . . *They ought to have a file on every person from the age of eight,* so if, for example, he comes for a job we will know just what he has done. Also, you have to use good people to implement the plan. For example, Wang Mang in the Han dynasty era, or Wang An-shih: Their methods were good but they failed because they did not have good people to support them.[24]

Interestingly enough, this assertion of the need for organizational control ends with a reaffirmation of the need for highly personalized leadership. The concept of authority remains personified. Social harmony requires the potency of "men of talent" (*jen-t'sai*) who will impose order and control those who in their dependency lack the self-discipline to order their own affairs.

PEER RELATIONS AND PROBLEMS OF LATERAL SOCIAL INTEGRATION

Our argument has come full circle. We began this section of the study by discussing the concern with "confusion" (*luan*)—the ever-present expectation of conflict and disorder—that is the diffuse undertone of Chinese perceptions of social relations. The Confucian concept of social authority attempted to deal with this problem through a hierarchical organization of society in which individuals would submit to the guidance of their elders. Perhaps the most important aspect of the analysis was the implication that this system of authority seemed to trap Chinese society in a vicious circle, where the strength of authority and the dependent submission to it which were designed to prevent confusion actually generated conditions which could produce it: The "holding in" of resentments and hatred of oppressive authority might explode into unrestrained conflict, particularly when individuals were made to feel that they were incapable of acting without guidance. If the necessary superior authority were removed, "confusion" would indeed reign until another powerful individual could institute a new hierarchical ordering of social relationships.

To this analysis we now have added peer relations. The Chinese tradition did not inculcate expectations of trust or rituals of cooperation in dealings among status equals which might have facilitated lateral social transactions. The intense expectations of friend-

24. H-7. Emphasis is added.

ship were such as to limit even that relationship's frequency, in part because it embodied the gratification of dependency needs—for a more powerful "friend" to be a provider in times of difficulty. Thus even friendship took on something of the flavor of hierarchical obligations.

Relations among peers were felt to be most effective if they could be brought within the web of kin or friendship ties and obligations. Intermediaries were seen as necessary for such transactions because they helped to resolve expectations of status or social "face" and overcome distrust by involving primary group ties.

Where intermediaries were lacking, relations among peers tended to be drawn into a competition for dominance: Individuals within this social tradition were made to feel that their self-respect was intimately related to the acquisition of interpersonal authority, and security and stability were felt to reside only within a hierarchical ordering of social relations. This pattern of peer contact reinforced the tendency for unrestrained conflict in the absence of a strong authority, because status equals were not educated to settle disputes effectively on their own.

Dependency needs and anxieties about conflict thus worked to make strong authority a personal necessity; yet strong authority generated its own resentments—in others if not in oneself—which made conflict a continuing possibility. Here is a cultural tautology, a vicious circle rooted in the socialization process which worked to insure the endurance of the Confucian pattern. Nowhere does this circularity of cultural logic find more vivid expression than in perceptions of politics, of the society's highest level of authority, to which we now turn.

Chapter IX

THE TIGER WORLD OF POLITICS:
WILL ONE EAT OR BE EATEN?

> Ever since ancient times China has had too
> much war. When the confusion (*luan*) gets
> extreme people yearn for government. There
> has been just too much war. The people
> really despise war and long for peace.[1]

Chinese attitudes toward political authority and personal involvement in politics betray the same strong ambivalence which we have
traced from roots in childhood to general social perceptions: a paradoxical combination of the desire to depend on those with power
for material support and security from conflict, yet great anxiety
about dealing directly with authoritative individuals because of
their capacity for manipulation and aggressiveness.

Any society's intellectuals tend to articulate through formal, rationalized doctrines attitudes and emotional concerns they share
with less educated compatriots. A good example is the Confucian
concept of "the Mandate of Heaven" (*t'ien-ming*) as the basis of a
ruler's political legitimacy. Simply stated, this doctrine held that
the emperor's claim to be Emperor was *conditional* upon his fulfilling "Heaven's will" in ruling the people. The test of whether Heaven
accorded the emperor its mandate to rule was the reaction of the
people themselves to governmental authority. Social tranquillity
and interpersonal harmony indicated that Heaven was smiling at
the rule of an emperor through his people, while *luan* and rebellion
reflected improper policies and morally degenerate leadership—
and perhaps the need for a new imperial house.

Now it seems true, as historians have argued, that this doctrine
is in part an expression of differences in interest and political objectives among three groups: the scholar officials who directly ad-

1. T-26.

135

"Wu Sung Wrestles the Tiger," an episode
from the classical novel *Shui Hu Chuan* [All Men Are Brothers].
*From a Ming Dynasty (1368–1644 A.D.) collection
of illustrations for the novel.*

ministered the empire for the imperial house; the Confucian gentry who represented the provincial, agrarian life style of China's rural elite; and a central policy-making group (often tied to the "foreign" interests of a militarily powerful border society) who were concerned with maintaining full control of administration and the wealth of the empire.[2]

At another level of perception, however, the doctrine reflects the influence of a culturally normative orientation toward authority: a willingness of the people to be orderly and politically passive under the control of those with power, provided that their material well-being and security were not endangered; but their tendency to withdraw into a potentially explosive hostility when they thought their dependency had been unreciprocated or abused. The actual bursting forth of *luan*, of the unrestrained violence and destruction characteristic of peasant rebellions, was the ultimate expression of popular rejection of existing political authority—and the final judgment of the political lives of numerous officials and dynasties.

The Mandate of Heaven doctrine thus was an expression of the *conditional* nature of the relationship between China's unenfranchised majority and the elite who exercised power, either formally within the state administration or informally through local social leadership roles. The passive deference which China's peasants accorded their leaders provided considerable leeway in policy-making and in the demands which could be made on the population's energies and resources. Yet the Mandate doctrine was a reminder to those with imperial power (from the scholar-officials who administered imperial policy) that there were limits to the demands that could be made on the common people. Those dependent on the powerful expected reciprocity. Even if their methods tended to be passive and indirect, they had ways of influencing the behavior of those in authority.

As we shall now see, political authority was perceived as having two very different faces. There was an ambivalence related to this dual perception which made filial submission conditional upon obligations fulfilled, just as dynastic legitimacy was said to depend upon fulfillment of Heaven's Mandate.

POWER AND THE HOPE OF SECURITY

The hopeful face of political power is viewed through that lens of our respondents' social perception which seeks economic security

2. This point has been developed by Joseph R. Levenson, among others. *See* his *Confucian China and Its Modern Fate: The Problem of Monarchical Decay* (Berkeley: University of California Press, 1964), pp. 97–98.

through reliance on authority in a world of material scarcity and uncertain employment. A respondent from Hopeh Province replied to the question, "What is the most important thing a nation's leaders should do for their people?" as follows:

> They have to be all for the people; like a father, all for the younger generation. The nation is like a family, so the highest leaders have to take responsibility for doing things for the benefit of the people, work things out well for them. (What kinds of problems should they pay attention to?) Problems of the people's livelihood: education, jobs, science. All these things have an effect on the people's livelihood.[3]

This typical attitude is meaningful in two respects. First, the respondent develops his interpretation of political leadership on the basis of an analogy with the family. Social authority has not been generalized to a set of universal principles or laws; the image of state power is still personified and paternal. Just as Confucius instructed, the family is the basic referent of all other social and political relations. Second, the domain of social authority is seen to be as all-inclusive as that of the family. A teacher from Liaoning Province expressed it this way:

> [If] you have enlightened government then you will have good social order. Everyone will have clothing to wear and enough food to eat. Everyone will be able to receive education and you will not have to lock your outer doors. There will be no fear or any more violence. (What methods does the society have to use to maintain this kind of a situation?) You have to use political methods: Raise the level of the people's daily livelihood, extend the period of public education, cultivate public morality. From the time a person is small you have to start educating him, training him. And you might put up slogans in public places stressing public morality.[4]

This willing acceptance of the intrusion of public power into all areas of social activity seems in part a legacy of childhood's teaching that there are few private corners of an individual's life,[5] combined with well-developed needs to be taken care of by a strong external authority.

3. T-19.
4. T-32.
5. A frequent Chinese reaction to American life is discomfort at the strong emphasis on privacy. A recent emigré from the mainland has written, "I am aware that my American hosts, motivated by kindness, ensure that I have privacy and that my social life leaves me regular periods of solitude. Just as they cannot understand *not* needing privacy, I cannot understand the need for it. I suppose one never learns to want what one has never had. In any case I suffer as much from too much privacy as most Americans do from the lack of it." (Tung Chi-ping and Humphrey Evans, *The Thought Revolution* [New York: Coward McCann, 1966], pp. 252–253.)

The positive or constructive image of what public authority can accomplish seems to be overshadowed, however, by the need to control "bad" or destructive tendencies among the people themselves. Concerning the ease with which children are believed to emulate the behavior of their parents, one respondent was asked, "What if a child's parents are bad; what should society do about this kind of a situation?" He replied, "In a well-founded society there ought to be a good leader, an organization which would know what is going on in every house, to help guide children in their weak points." [6]

The notion that the government should intrude even into family life, to "know what is going on in every house," is acceptable when there is a threat to the proper ordering of society. Our respondents frequently used the phrase, "The government must have intimate relations (*mi-ch'ieh kuan-hsi*) with the people"—apparently a popular elaboration of the Confucian idea that social order can be maintained only by "boxing in" people's antisocial potentialities through a hierarchical pattern of deference and obligation:

If the government and people have intimate relations, if the people have vigilance and mutually involve themselves in each other's affairs, then it would not be easy for people to do bad things. If people are uninterested [in social life], if they just "sweep the snow in front of their own doors," if they don't obstruct the bad behavior of others and don't think about its long-term effects, then it will not be good for the nation.[7]

The notion that organization is above all a technique for controlling potentially troublesome individuals is shared by leaders and led alike. Just as Sun Yat-sen felt the Kuomintang party organization would enable him to control the activities of the Communists,[8] so one of our respondents felt that the People's Republic could be controlled through the U.N. organization:

You [Americans] should let China enter the United Nations. (Why?) Because if China is rejected and remains on the outside then she can do bad things. Then there will be no way to control her. If you let her into the United Nations then you can, according to the rules of the organization, give the Communists a kind of education and control.[9]

6. T-9.
7. T-15.
8. *See* Conrad Brandt, Benjamin Schwartz, and John K. Fairbank, *A Documentary History of Chinese Communism* (New York: Atheneum, 1966), p. 68.
9. T-21.

For all the appreciation of the security that can come with strong and intrusive power, however, there is a marked inclination to deny the need for such control in relation to one's own behavior. Apprehensions about dealings with authority combine with fears of conflict to produce an orientation where government is wanted for its ability to impose interpersonal harmony and social tranquillity, yet not for one's self—only for "bad" people:

> (What does *chih-an hao* [good peace and order] mean?) It is a matter of dealing with bad situations: once they break out, immediately doing away with them. (What kinds of things?) Stealing; just excessive incidents—cheating, male-female questions. (How can this kind of a situation be maintained?) There are two aspects: you have to strengthen the moral aspect of life; and then there are a minority of bad social elements—you have to rely on the government to control them.

> (How is it that every now and then a society becomes confused [*hun-luan*]?) What kind of *hun-luan* do you mean? (Whatever you think.) Well let's look at it the opposite way: If there is good governmental power then you can control things—I don't mean like the Communists, they have no morals, no limits. You have to have democracy —but if you don't have [a strong government] then everyone is just out for himself. There will be no limits on people's behavior. (Why do you need a strong government?) *A small group in society is not mannerly (li-mao). They do not abide by social custom, and the government has to use methods to control them—but not for most ordinary people who are mannerly.*[10]

There remains the hope that public morality and merely the distant example of outstanding governmental leaders will make social order and peace a reality. The intrusion of state power is reserved for those individuals who will only submit to the harsh controls of law—a popular attitude that gives continuing meaning in daily life to the philosopher's distinction between Confucianism and Legalism as contrasting approaches to social control in the Chinese tradition.

Government's benign face is thus to a large degree its ability to control society's potential for conflict, to prevent *luan*. And as is indicated in the remark of a peasant's son from Hopeh Province, both the potential for social confusion and the political authority to prevent it are rooted in family life:

> (Why in the early years of the Republic were there warlords?) The central government had no strength. It could not concentrate its power, and the local powers could give orders separately. You see, it is the same thing with a family: If the head of the family cannot manage

10. T-14. Emphasis added.

family affairs, unify family management, then every child will himself think of some way to do things and the family will be split into several cliques. When everyone has his own way of administering affairs then divergencies develop and things become *luan*. Things are the same way with the nation. . . . You have to concentrate power.[11]

THE TIGER OF GOVERNMENTAL POWER

In passing by the side of Mount Thai, Confucius came on a woman who was wailing bitterly by a grave. The Master . . . sent Tze-lu to question her. "Your wailing," said he, "is altogether like that of one who has suffered sorrow upon sorrow." She replied, "It is so. Formerly, my husband's father was killed here by a tiger. My husband was also killed [by another], and now my son has died in the same way." The Master said, "Why do you not leave the place?" The answer was, "There is no oppressive government here." The Master then said [to the disciples], "Remember this, my little children. Oppressive government is more terrible than tigers." [12]

The second face of public authority is perceived in the glaring image of a rapacious tiger, stirring all those concerns about the harshly punitive and manipulative use of power which were acquired early in life. The well-known Confucian anecdote from the *Book of Rites* cited above brings to mind our earlier encounter with the Kwangtung peasant who felt that, "People eat people; the big ones eat the small, will eat them all up."

This perception of authority as "tigerish," as capable of "eating people," we suggested earlier, seems to reflect the way Chinese are taught to control their personal fears and tensions. At a much more obvious level of perception, however, there is good reason why ordinary people saw official power as capable of devouring them and why they characterized entering the local magistrate's *yamen* as walking into "the tiger's mouth." [13] When one's life is spent in neverending toil for subsistence in an insecure world of natural disasters and material scarcity, to have landlords or officials take large parts of a precious and hard-earned food supply can indeed make one feel "eaten." The harsh application of official justice to those unfortunate enough to "disturb the tranquillity of the Empire" (for whatever reason)—examination through torture, punishment by beating and whipping, and execution by the

11. T-38.

12. From "Li Ki" (Book of Rites) in Max F. Müller, ed., *Sacred Books of the East,* Vol. XXVII, pp. 190–191.

13. *See* Jerome Alan Cohen, "Chinese Mediation on the Eve of Modernization," *California Law Review,* Vol. LIV (August 1966), pp. 1213 and *passim.*

thousand cuts or strangulation—can easily consume one with the same fear that might be expected should one encounter a tiger.

For the peasantry, however, direct contacts with governmental officials were rather infrequent. For them the full force of the tiger of power was known through the ravagings of bandit groups or official "pacifying" troops who lived off the land. A Shensi peasant recalls a "bandit suppression" campaign of the 1930s:

> When Hu Tsung-nan [a warlord, and his troops] came, almost every-one left Liu Ling. We went up into the hills. I was in the people's militia then. We had buried all our possessions and all our corn. Hu Tsung-nan destroyed everything, and *his troops ate and ate. They discovered our grain stores, and they stole our cattle.*[14]

Another peasant of the same area describes his enforced service in the warlord's army:

> Our platoon commander was called Liu. He was a bad-tempered man; he hit people when he was angry. I was often beaten. Sometimes he hit me with a stick, and sometimes he took my rifle and hit me with that. I was hit the most of us eleven new ones. Then we began to march. *We marched and marched and everywhere we ate up all the villagers' pigs and poultry. After all, we were hungry too.*[15]

We suggested earlier that within the Chinese tradition there is no expectation of compromise in matters of authority. This perception finds its fullest expression in political conflict, where, as our respondents had known it through the last century of social instability and war, power presents its ugliest visage:

> In the last hundred years China has had so many changes of government, so many changes in political programs, that ordinary people really are disgusted with politics. Each party says that it is the best, it is the only one, and suppresses all others. The people are really fed up with all that confusion (*hun-luan*). It is not surprising that the common people are disgusted with politics.[16]

> [During the 1910s and 1920s, the warlords] held power in their own hands, and so they could do anything they wanted to. . . . These powerful men thought of uniting China—although some, like Tuan Ch'i-jui and Feng Kuo-chang, also thought of competing for the position of emperor. The result was that there were many wars. (Why couldn't the warlords peacefully coexist?) If I want to eat your piece of meat, naturally you won't want to give it to me! [Respondent laughs.] Their fighting was pure avariciousness. Powerful men can

14. Jan Myrdal, *Report from a Chinese Village* (London: Heinemann, 1965), p. 140. Emphasis added.
15. *Ibid.*, pp. 88–89. Emphasis added.
16. H-4.

grab people as they please. They can kill people. This was just competition for power.[17]

When power is unified in the hands of one leader, he can impose a structure of political authority which will control the potential for social "confusion." Personal relations can then be mediated by the customs of civilized society. But the struggle for power, the striving for that dominance which will make a new order possible, causes great disorder. The forms of interpersonal relations appropriate to a peaceful society, such as deference rituals (*li-mao*) and intermediation, must await the creation of the new order.

> (Why is it that some people are interested in politics and others are not?) Those people who are interested have great ambition. People without ambition are not interested in politics. The ambitious ones hope to attain some position through politics, to become an official and get rich. (What do you think should be done about this difference?) This is very difficult; everyone is different; a "third party" [intermediary] can't reconcile this difference.[18]

The competition for power is seen as provoking a hatred which compounds the tendency for violent "confusion," even where there is the appearance of an ordered set of political processes:

> (How is it that a society becomes "confused"?) Everyone is out for status or profit. Take for example competing to be a political representative: If a person is defeated then he will have hate; he will want to destroy the person who defeated him. Now on Taiwan governmental organizations are relatively numerous [and can prevent violence], but before on the mainland this kind of a situation developed just too frequently: If you had been defeated then you would organize some local bandits to go out and kill the person who had won.[19]

But paradoxically, where order and "unity" have finally been imposed, the process of their attainment is seen as having laid the groundwork for further "confusion," as one respondent affirmed in this recollection of China's first political unification:

> Progress [in the Chou dynasty] was very great. Many different kinds of thinking sprang up. (What was the outcome of this situation?) Chin Shih Huang absorbed all of their good thinking. He used talented men and was able to unite China. (But were not all of the books of the famous men burned by Li Ssu?) A part of them. Those that he did not want. (Why didn't he want some of them?) He feared that they would influence people's thinking. (What do you mean by

17. T-26.
18. T-45.
19. T-26.

that?) He feared that people under his control would not obey him, would oppose him and create *luan*. (Why did he fear that?) He had destroyed all those other countries. He feared their people. He thought that by burning all those books he could cause them to forget or not understand what had happened in the past.[20]

What is the way out of this dilemma, the longing for harmony and order, yet realization that the political methods used to impose order themselves produce the "bad feelings" which make *luan* an enduring problem?

I don't think laws have any usefulness, the only thing you can do is to have a highest leader. Having a [good] government includes [the leader] making an example of his own action, and having very strict punishments. If the highest leader can promote good government then the subordinates below him would not dare but do the same thing.[21]

The imposition of a still stronger authority, a "highest leader" who can maintain control over the dangerous world of politics, is the solution most often envisaged by our respondents. Yet for themselves, for their personal relation to the world of politics, avoidance of those in authority is usually seen as the most desirable course to follow.

THE GAP BETWEEN LEADERS AND LED

We have seen avoidance of dealings with the powerful in a variety of contexts, from family life and educational experiences to perceptions of social relations. The growing son fears contacts with a harsh, demanding, and potentially explosive father; a student runs away from school because of the overbearing treatment he receives from a teacher; and in relations with authority an adult uneasily balances the expectation of loyalty with anxious concern that he might be "cheated" or led into trouble by a superior. In the world of politics, maintaining a physical distance has been a time-honored defense for China's rural population. And where avoidance is not possible, creating an "emotional distance" becomes a strategy to guard oneself against the sting of manipulation or of being made to "eat a loss" (*ch'ih-k'uei*) in dealings with the powerful.

The tiger of governmental power was sufficiently distant from the lives of most peasants that even the revolutionary changes of the early twentieth century did not significantly touch their lives.

20. H-7.
21. T-45.

As an elderly peasant from China's northwest province of Shensi recalled:

> When I was nineteen, I got myself sheep and goats of my own and two years after that we heard that there was a revolution. I ran off to the hills. Then we were told that now we were called the Republic of China, and that the Ching dynasty was at an end. That was all. We were old country people, and we seldom went into the town and never talked about such things as the emperor or government. Nobody would have dared do that. And we never saw them either. The officials in the nearest yamen watched over us, and they were the same after the revolution as before it.
>
> Ordinary people did not like going to see the officials. That was a thing one did only if compelled. If one met them, one had to kneel before them. It was exactly the same after the revolution. I could not see that there was any difference at all.[22]

Imperial politics and the "great tradition" of the scholar-officials for the most part were known to the peasantry only indirectly, through contacts with agents of the local gentry who taxed their harvest and the activities of yamen officials who made known the word of the district magistrate. Yet even when a peasant sought to establish more intimate relations with the powerful, so that he might receive some special consideration, authority presented itself in all the harshness first known in childhood and asserted its influence through "the power of the word." As a peasant recalled of dealings with his landlord:

> Any small mistake and he blew up. I had to carry water through the gate. There was a threshold there and a sharp turn. If I spilled some water on the ground, he cursed me for messing up the courtyard. Once I tore the horse's collar. *He cursed me and my ancestors. I didn't dare answer back. I think that was worse than the [bad] food and the filthy quarters—not being able to talk back. In those days the landlord's word was law.* They had their way. When it was

22. Myrdal, *Report from a Chinese Village*, pp. 286–287.
One study has found that there were somewhere between 100,000 and 250,000 people "under the control of" each imperial official during the Ch'ing dynasty. (*See* Hsiao Kung-chuan, *Rural China: Imperial Control in the Nineteenth Century*, p. 5.)
Under such circumstances intimate contact between officials and the population was hardly possible. Indeed, evidence suggests that popular attitudes of fear and avoidance of governmental power were purposefully encouraged by dynastic officials so as to keep the people "in their places," to discourage them from making demands on state resources or causing trouble which would require direct official involvement. (This point is explored in the author's article "On Activism and Activists," *The China Quarterly*, No. 39 [July–September 1969], pp. 77–86.)

really hot and they said it was not, we dared not say it was hot; when it really was cold and they said it wasn't we dared not say it was cold. *Whatever happened we had to listen to them.*[23]

It is not surprising to find the peasantry alienated from those with power, from what was in many respects another world of education, leisure from physical toil, and a degree of material security and comfort. One of the more striking findings revealed by our interview data, however, is that educated and "socially mobilized" Chinese viewed political power with a similar degree of aloofness and anxiety. From early in life they, too, had learned that to show respect and obedience was to *t'ing-hua,* to "listen to talk," and not give out personal opinions.

We find a similar pattern of communication in our interview respondents' contacts with the world of political power. Judging from their newspaper reading habits, political events are of considerable interest to them. Of the sixty-one who were asked how often they read a newspaper, 95 percent indicated daily attention to the news. One respondent said he read a newspaper once a week; and only two said they did not follow the news at all. When asked, "Do you read the national political news?" 86 percent replied they did, and 90 percent indicated that they read news of the international political situation. However, when asked, "With whom do you discuss politics?" only 43 percent of a total of seventy-five admitted that they discussed political matters. The remaining 57 percent denied discussing politics. "Taking in" information is a well-developed habit, but "giving out" opinions about politics is another matter. The respondents showed a strong tendency to deny this minimal level of political involvement.

The reasons given for this apparent lack of interest in political discussion are varied. The feeling that "you can't reach a conclusion" was frequently voiced, recalling the expectation we encountered in nonpolitical social contexts that differences of opinion cannot be resolved. Some respondents emphasized the notion that society is "complicated" (*fu-tza*), that there are important and emotionally explosive issues unresolved behind society's orderly "face," and that talking about them will needlessly provoke hostility and trouble:

I very seldom discuss [political questions]. (Why?) Because society today is very complicated. Each person's thinking, point of view, and opinions are different. If you discuss these differences you won't be able to reach any conclusion. Possibly it would lead to some trouble.

23. William Hinton, *Fanshen: A Documentary of Revolution in a Chinese Village* (New York: Monthly Review Press, 1966), p. 39. Emphasis added.

(What kind of trouble?) People will not understand your thinking. Possibly they will think it is not correct. They might pay special attention to your behavior, or even lock you up.[24]

Of course Chinese society today *does* embody great unresolved political issues related to the civil war and social revolution. But this reluctance to discuss politics cannot be explained merely by the immediate social context in which some of our interviews took place. Respondents interviewed in Hong Kong held attitudes quite similar to those in Taiwan; and the behavior of Chinese who have migrated to more distant cultural areas indicates that they regard open personal involvement in politics as dangerous. The attitudes recalled by our respondents are well *internalized* on the basis of early life experience, in addition to being reinforced by the immediate social context.

Furthermore, it should be stressed that we merely asked respondents whether they *discussed* political issues, and not specific questions about personal political preference. It is also striking that similar attitudes were frequently expressed by elderly mainlanders in Taiwan whose professional careers and political loyalties had at one time placed them in positions of public responsibility. At most we got an admission that political issues were discussed

> with fellow workers or with friends with a similar disposition, or at Party meetings. We discuss these things if our thinking is similar. We don't discuss them with people we don't know, because if you do then you may confuse what is right and wrong. Everyone must be in basic agreement; then you can secretly discuss [politics]. You shouldn't indiscriminately go around [discussing political matters].[25]

Respondents' disclaimers of *any* discussion of politics should not be taken too literally, for when pressed many would admit that current issues were discussed with friends or coworkers in the privacy of home or a trusted group setting. Rather, their responses to the word "politics" (*cheng-chih*) give a further indication of the sense of anxiety about contact with authority. They manifest a fear that if political questions are discussed with people whose thinking is not similar it will lead to conflict or some ill-defined "trouble." Where one's relation to authority is expected to be above all a matter of the personal loyalty characteristic of dependence, rather than social involvement on the basis of specific public issues, the expression of political opinions means submitting one's commitment to a man and group to public scrutiny. Where everyone's "thinking," or political loyalty, is similar, discussion can pro-

24. T-32.
25. T-49.

ceed within a framework of common cause. But where commitment may be uncertain, or where issues threaten to divide, then discussion may "confuse right and wrong" (i.e., loyalties may be called into question), and issues may be evaluated on their own merits rather than in terms of the "truth" of expected deference to the "highest leader." In such circumstances the safest course to follow is outward acceptance of the official view; or better yet, avoidance of trouble through withdrawal and silence.[26]

The sum of these popular attitudes toward politics compounds the problems of vertical and lateral social integration discussed earlier. There was a "gap" in relations between leader and led based on fear of authority. During the dynastic era, the imperial bureaucracy could be paralyzed when local officials feared the consequences of accurate reporting of local conditions to their superiors. In telling the emperor and his ministers what they wanted to hear, local officials literally "cut the emperor off from reality." [27]

In times of political turmoil, when those in official power sought to insure commitment to the public good through deference to established institutions, the harshness of authority would only compound "selfish" popular desires to withdraw into private con-

26. Avenues of political avoidance and withdrawal were well institutionalized in traditional China, not only in "bandit" life and the activities of clan associations and professional guilds which sought to protect their members from official power, but also in the appeals of the Taoist and Buddhist traditions. (*See* Charles O. Hucker, "Confucianism and the Chinese Censorial System," in Nivison and Wright, eds., *Confucianism in Action*, p. 198.) Successful members of the rural gentry often warned their offspring that social success lay in avoiding politics (Ho Ping-ti, *The Ladder of Success in Imperial China* [New York: John Wiley, Science Editions, 1964], pp. 129–130); and within the Confucian tradition itself there was recognition of the legitimacy of withdrawal from society in times of *luan*. (*See* Fredrick W. Mote, "Confucian Eremitism in the Yüan Period," in Arthur F. Wright, ed., *The Confucian Persuasion* [Stanford, Calif.: Stanford University Press, 1960], pp. 202–240.)

27. The famous Ch'ing official, Tseng Kuo-fan, "regarded the lack of communication between official and emperor as the chief cause of the administrative paralysis of his time." He was writing of the period of near collapse of the dynasty in the mid-nineteenth century. (Liu Kwang-ching, "Nineteenth-Century China: The Disintegration of the Old Order and the Impact of the West," in Ho Ping-ti and Tang Tsou, eds., *China in Crisis* [Chicago: University of Chicago Press, 1968], Vol. I, Book 1, pp. 123–124.)

An emperor's concern with being cut off from reality by the distorted reporting of servile or ambitious ministers is revealed in the memoirs of the Ch'ien-lung Emperor. (*See* Harold L. Kahn, "The Education of a Prince: the Emperor Learns His Roles," in Albert Feuerwerker, Rhoads Murphey, and Mary C. Wright, eds., *Approaches to Modern Chinese History* [Berkeley: University of California Press, 1967], pp. 37–40.)

cerns. As Chiang K'ai-shek complained in the difficult year of 1943:

> In the past our adult citizens have been unable to unite on a large scale or for a long period. They have been derisively compared to "a heap of loose sand" or spoken of as having "only five-minutes' enthusiasm." Now incapacity to unite is a result of selfishness, and the best antidote for selfishness is public spirit.[28]

Among peers, the expectation of loyal support for a leader worked to produce a strong "in-group, out-group" orientation, an exclusiveness based on clique affiliation. And as interview data concerning communication habits reveal, there tends to be meager interaction between various factions out of fear of provoking conflict. Differences of opinion can hardly be resolved as they are rooted in exclusive personal loyalties which cause society to fragment along the lines of narrow hierarchies.

The traditional Chinese political culture, as is true of most traditional polities, was nonparticipant for the majority of the people. Involvement in public issues was discouraged by authority's appeals to those elements of personality—anxiety in the face of authority and a willingness to depend on the powerful—which had been developed through childhood socialization. An individual sought security not through his personal efforts, but by adjustment to group norms and interests, and through "obedient respect" for those with authority. The world of political power, for most people, was far away, embodying that sense of "distance" which was acquired in early life relations with authority: "An ordinary person wouldn't see a leader harming the people's welfare";[29] "He would be afraid to do anything [about it]"; "There is nothing he can do to influence politics" (*mei-yu pan-fa*).[30]

This "gap" between leader and led, formally recognized in the Mencian notion that those who use their minds govern those who labor with their muscle, gave reality to the concern of philosopher and political leader about the troublesome distinction between knowledge and action, theory and practice.[31] Those with power

28. Chiang K'ai-shek, *China's Destiny*, trans. in William Theodore de Bary, ed., *Sources of the Chinese Tradition* (New York: Columbia University Press, 1960), pp. 810–811.

29. T-18.

30. T-22.

31. The distinction between "knowledge" and "action" has been an enduring theme in Chinese social thinking. (*See* David S. Nivison, "The Problem of 'Knowledge' and 'Action' in Chinese Thought since Wang Yangming," in Arthur F. Wright, ed., *Studies in Chinese Thought* [Chicago: University of Chicago Press, 1953], pp. 112–141.) This philosophical dis-

asserted their authority through the word, while those who were dependent manifested their loyalty by translating word into action. Where the words of the ruler were "rectified," where there was justice with authority, this relationship could insure social order. But where there was a sense of exploitation or resentment, the conviction of having been cheated or misused could transform anxious dependents into hate-filled rebels. And in the vengeful violence which characterized China's periods of disorder, society's authoritative relationships would be swept away.

THE DREAM OF UNITY

In order to resolve their contradictory feelings about authority, strangely enough the Chinese begin by dreaming about the invocation of a still stronger authority. Even the revolutionary accomplishments of the revered Sun Yat-sen are called into question by the aftermath of *luan* which characterized the warlord period!

> I have a rather strange point of view. It was not too correct for the father of our country [Sun Yat-sen] to have overthrown the Ch'ing Emperor. The people must have a symbol. We have had a dictatorial country for several thousand years, and then in a moment the Em-

---

tinction had its social basis in the relational quality of authority in Chinese society; in the pattern of a superior who in his wisdom was to guide dependents in implementing his will.

As long as those in positions of authority are secure in their values and world-view, "It is not the knowing that is difficult, but the doing," as the Ch'ien-lung Emperor observed. (*See* Harold Kahn, "The Education of a Prince," in Feuerwerker *et al.*, eds., *Approaches to Modern Chinese History*, pp. 34–35.) The literati knew their place in the world; the only problem was to make certain that the people acted as Confucian morality said was proper.

Once the Confucian tradition had lost its aura of efficacy, however, under the combined impact of Western intervention and domestic social change, the "thought" vs. "action" distinction was turned upside down. Sun Yat-sen now phrased it, "Action is easy and knowledge is difficult." (*See* Nivison, "The Problem of 'Knowledge' and 'Action,' " p. 137; and Lyon Sharmon, *Sun Yat-sen: His Life and Its Meaning* [Stanford, Calif.: Stanford University Press, 1966], pp. 232–233.) And a generation of Chinese revolutionaries searched for a new political world-view which would orient their actions— some finding answers in Marxism-Leninism, and others in a resurrected version of Confucianism.

As we will suggest in the second half of this study, one of the aspects of change in China's political culture that has been promoted by Mao Tse-tung has been the effort to resolve the troublesome distinction between thought and action, "theory and practice," by eliminating the gap between a ruling elite that formulates policy, and a dependent population that merely carries out orders.

peror was overthrown and everyone became confused (*luan-le*). If there had been an Emperor in those days then we would not have had the warlords.[32]

While there is a respected leader to impose order, society's divisive forces are kept in check. But once he is gone, competitors for power rise up in a selfish scramble for full control. Such confusion can only be overcome through the action of powerful leaders who establish organizational control over those who would compete for power or make trouble:

> A nation does not develop from tranquillity. You have to govern it, make it peaceful. Therefore the leaders have to have great power and courage. To see if laws and orders agree with the wishes of the people, to manage things well so that there will be peace—these are questions of control. To maintain "peace and order" requires strong political organization.[33]

Our respondents manifest a great distrust of the harshness and impersonality of laws in maintaining an organization, however, for throughout Chinese history imperial Legalism (*fa-chia*) has been associated with oppressiveness. A personalized "highest leader" of talent and moral integrity is seen as society's only way to deal with the possibility of violence and unrestrained competition for power.

How do Chinese see social unity developing from the tension between the hope of a leader whose moral example will be emulated by subordinates, and the belief that only strict controls and punishments will maintain social order? Education as it is related to social control is the usual answer to this problem. Society requires

> a great leader stronger than anyone else to prevent competition for power—like President Chiang. Nowadays there are only a few who will compete for power. They do it in secret. (Why does having President Chiang do away with competition?) It is a matter of education. The leaders pay attention to the thinking of [potential competitors for power]. They make them study "The Three People's Principles," as if President Chiang were their teacher. You don't go against your teacher—after he dies maybe, but not before.[34]

Such an interpretation states clearly the control function of political ideology, the importance of "studying the thoughts of (the

32. T-37.
33. T-49.
34. T-18.

highest leader)." But it also reveals the fragile quality of such ideological unity: "You don't go against your teacher—after he dies maybe, but not before."

Thus, in the popular mind there is no resolution to the problem of how to insure social order without the use of strict authority. A strong leader can prevent *luan* for a time, but the harshness of his rule generates resentment. "Education" can help, but loyal commitment to a teacher must be ended by his death. The argument always comes full circle: When an external authority is removed there will be *luan*.

The longing for social unity remains, however. And the gap between fears of *luan* and the ideal of social harmony ultimately is bridged only by hope. There is hope that somehow all that is painful and threatening in daily life will give way to a condition of "great togetherness" (*ta-t'ung*).

Ta-t'ung is as enduring a concept in the Chinese world-view as the polarity between harmony and conflict from which it draws its inspiration. Taoist recluses read into this idealized condition of the world their search for the ultimate tranquillity, while Confucius saw *ta-t'ung* as China's perfected communal society once known in an early "golden age"—a state of social harmony he sought to reestablish through the political rituals of the Chou dynasty.[35] When the nineteenth-century philosopher K'ang Yu-wei sought to adapt Confucianism to a developmental concept of history, he described Chinese society as evolving from origins of disorder (*shuai-luan*) through "approaching peace" to a utopia of "the great unity" (*ta-t'ung*).[36] Each imperial official hoped to realize *ta-t'ung* in his area of administrative responsibility.[37] The revolutionary Sun Yat-sen impressed foreigners and countrymen alike with his deep desire to make China "an integral part of a world order," and with his devotion to "the Confucian ideal of a world in which men will really get together for the common good."[38]

A variety of translations have been given to the conception of *ta-t'ung* or *shih-chieh ta-t'ung*, "the universal harmony" and "the world commonwealth" among them. From our respondents' elaborations of this term, however, "the great togetherness" seems to

35. *See* Munro, *The Concept of Man in Early China*, Ch. 7.
36. Derk Bodde, "Harmony and Conflict in Chinese Philosophy," in Arthur F. Wright, ed., *Studies in Chinese Thought*, pp. 34–36.
37. *See* C. K. Yang, "Some Characteristics of Chinese Bureaucratic Behavior," in Nivison and Wright, eds., *Confucianism in Action*, p. 138.
38. Sharman, *Sun Yat-sen*, p. 269.

be a rendering which catches its essentially a-political quality:[39] the yearning for social harmony and security, and the desire for an end to interpersonal distinctions. As one respondent put it:

> *"Ta-t'ung"* means mutual assistance; everyone has a spirit of mutual assistance and this means that there will be no conflict among the common people and no war between one nation and another. Everyone has enough food to eat, has clothing to wear, and there can be unity in thinking among everyone. (How can *ta-t'ung* be attained?) Mankind can create this. If everyone has received an education and everyone's point of view is the same, then there will be no disorder, there will be no war. . . . Education must be universal, then everyone's knowledge will be about the same and then you can do away with much nonsensical bother. . . . If everyone's opinions are not the same it can lead to quarreling and confusion (*luan*).[40]

The longing is for an end to all interpersonal conflict, a "togetherness" in which there will be mutual assistance and, as some respondents phrased it, "there will be no difference between you and me." [41] The human condition of conflict based on distinctions of material wealth or differences in status and thinking will, it is hoped, evolve to a tranquil state of interpersonal unity that in quality can only be compared to that "golden age" of early life where, within the unbroken unity of the family, one knew only gratification without conflict.

39. The appeal of group life as "the great togetherness" has also been suggested by Robert J. Lifton in his study, *Thought Reform and the Psychology of Totalism* (New York: Norton, 1963), p. 254.

40. T-28.

41. T-16.

Part Three

THE MAOIST
POLITICAL REVOLUTION

Communist Party Chairman Mao Tse-tung and
Kuomintang General Director Chiang K'ai-shek
toast the beginning of peace negotiations
in Chungking, August 1945.
Jack Wilkes, Life *Magazine,* © *Time, Inc.*

[Political] synthesis is a matter of eating one's enemy. How did we synthesize the Kuomintang? Didn't we take in things captured from the enemy and transform them! We didn't just kill captured enemy soldiers. Some of them we let go, but the large part we absorbed into our ranks. Weapons, provisions, and all kinds of things were taken in. What was of no use we eliminated, to use a philosophical term. . . . Eating is both analysis and synthesis. Take eating crabs for example. You eat the meat and not the shell. One's stomach absorbs the nourishment and expels the waste. . . . Synthesizing the Kuomintang was a matter of eating it up, absorbing most of it and expelling a smaller part.

MAO TSE-TUNG
*(from a speech to
Party leaders at Hangchow,
December 1965)*

Chapter X

POLITICS IS AN
EMOTIONAL STORM

Why does a society have a revolution? This is the kind of broad question which might be approached from an historical perspective, in terms of the sociological or economic dimensions of social change, or at the attitudinal level. One might explore the reasons for the breakdown in acceptability of social traditions for those living in a given society. In this third part of our study we will look at China's twentieth century revolution through the eyes of Communist Party Chairman Mao Tse-tung. This man was to emerge as the most influential political leader of China's search for modern statehood, economic development, and social transformation. How did he mobilize a peasant population to gain political power and bring about a social revolution? As we shall see in the following chapters, there is a complex interplay between the traditional attitudes toward politics and social relations explored in the first two parts of this study, and the institutions of leadership developed by Mao and the Chinese Communists over three decades of struggle for power.

How does Mao Tse-tung account for the success of the Chinese Communist Party after years of bitter conflict with the Nationalists? Some indication of his views on this question is contained in an official Party statement of September 1949, published as the People's Liberation Army was completing its rout of Nationalist military forces and just a few days before the founding of the People's Republic. Mao's statement, entitled "The Bankruptcy of the Idealist Conception of History," began with an attack on Secretary of State Dean Acheson's attempt to explain to the people of the United States the reasons for the impending collapse of the Nationalist government and with it, the failure of America's China policy. Mao cited a passage by Acheson from the State Department's widely publicized "White Paper," distributed earlier in the year. Acheson wrote:

The population of China during the eighteenth and nineteenth centuries doubled, thereby creating an unbearable pressure upon the land. The first problem which every Chinese Government has had to face is that of feeding this population. So far none has succeeded. The Kuomintang attempted to solve it by putting many land-reform laws on the statute books. Some of these laws have failed, others have been ignored. In no small measure, the predicament in which the National Government finds itself today is due to its failure to provide China with enough to eat. A large part of the Chinese Communists' propaganda consists of promises that they will solve the land problem.[1]

Mao's response to this American interpretation of the Chinese revolution was addressed to Chinese, and particularly to those of his countrymen who may have found in Acheson's remarks hope for eventual Communist failure: "To those Chinese who do not reason clearly the above sounds plausible. Too many mouths, too little food, hence revolution. The Kuomintang has failed to solve this problem and it is unlikely that the Communist Party will be able to solve it either. 'So far none has succeeded.' "[2] Mao then added with a characteristic irony:

> Do revolutions arise from overpopulation? There have been many revolutions, ancient and modern, in China and abroad; were they all due to overpopulation? Were China's many revolutions in the past few thousand years also due to overpopulation? Was the American Revolution against Britain 174 years ago also due to overpopulation? Acheson's knowledge of history is nil. He has not even read the American Declaration of Independence. Washington, Jefferson and others made the revolution against Britain because of British oppression and exploitation of the Americans, and not because of any overpopulation in America. Each time the Chinese people overthrew a feudal dynasty it was because of the oppression and exploitation of the people by that feudal dynasty, and not because of any overpopulation.[3]

These remarks carry with them the emotional triumph of a revolutionary at his hour of success; the sense of power and purpose of one who has guided to victory the storm of a people's resentments, frustrated hopes, and threatened security. Yet they also evince the concern of one who knows that destruction is about

1. Mao Tse-tung, "The Bankruptcy of the Idealist Conception of History" (1949), *SW*, English, IV, p. 452.
The notational system used in citing Mao's works is discussed in the bibliography, p. 584 below. "*SW*" stands for *The Selected Works of Mao Tse-tung.*
2. *Ibid.*
3. *Ibid.*

to end and the more demanding trials of rebuilding are soon to begin. And there is a certain pique at the awareness that there are many who do not wish him well, but who look on in hope of his eventual failure:

> The serious task of economic construction lies before us. We shall soon put aside some of the things we know well and be compelled to do things we don't know well. This means difficulties. The imperialists reckon that we will not be able to manage our economy; they are standing by and looking on, awaiting our failure.[4]

At his moment of triumph Mao thus looked forward to the coming period of national reconstruction in terms of a past built on popular resentment of "oppression and exploitation" by established authority. Despite his biting rejection of the interpretation that his success lay in the failure of others to feed the Chinese people, however, he knew well that the legitimacy of authority was in large measure based on fulfilling the needs of its dependents. His own career as a revolutionary had begun in student days nearly half a century earlier when he witnessed the popular outrage that resulted when a governor of the Ch'ing dynasty failed to feed the people in a year of starvation:

> There had been a severe famine . . . , and in Changsha thousands were without food. The starving sent a delegation to the civil governor, to beg for relief, but he replied to them haughtily, "Why haven't you food? There is plenty in the city. I always have enough." When the people were told the governor's reply, they became very angry. They held mass meetings and organized a demonstration. They attacked the Manchu yamen, cut down the flagpole, the symbol of office, and drove out the governor. . . . A new governor arrived, and at once ordered the arrest of the leaders of the uprising. Many of them were beheaded and their heads displayed on poles as a warning to future "rebels." [5]

Such an event becomes a catalyst in the process of revolution, rapidly eroding the aura of legitimacy surrounding established institutions of government. And a revolutionary sees in it the promise of a new era as much as the failure of the old. The people look to constituted authority as a legitimate source of security. It is the responsibility of those with power to provide for those who depend on them. But the starving citizens obtain no redress. As they see it, authority, in well-provided and ignorant isolation, denies

4. Mao, "On the People's Democratic Dictatorship" (1949), *SW*, English, IV, p. 422.
5. Edgar Snow, *Red Star Over China* (New York: Grove Press, 1961), p. 129.

Citizens of Changsha reaching out
for relief grain during the famine of the spring of 1910.
Courtesy of the Bain Collection, Library of Congress.

them their due, and unjustly labels them as "rebels." Indeed the regime in power cuts itself off more irrevocably than ever from the people's problems; reciprocity and communication are fully severed, all too literally in the chopping off of heads.

At such a point the dependent's attitude toward those in power goes through a qualitative change: His sense of acceptability which ultimately is based on the hope that obligations will be fulfilled breaks down into hostility. And for those who have known such use of power in the intimacy of family life, and have the strength of character to rebel, the *public* injustice becomes a *personal* call to action:

> This incident was discussed in my school for many days. It made a deep impression on me. Most of the other students sympathized with the "insurrectionists," but only from an observer's point of view. They did not understand that it had any relation to their own lives. They were merely interested in it as an exciting incident. I never forgot it. *I felt that there with the rebels were ordinary people like my own family and I deeply resented the injustice of the treatment given to them.*[6]

Mao's ability to relate injustice suffered by others to his own experience indeed seems to reflect his early family life, for he recalled similar treatment at the hands of his father.[7]

HOSTILITY: THE EMOTIONAL FUEL OF REVOLUTION

The route traveled by Mao Tse-tung in becoming the leader of the Chinese Communist Party has been told elsewhere by biographers and students of Party history.[8] What is of particular concern to us here is Mao's conception of the political process and the manner in which his style of leadership grew in response to the political attitudes of those the Party has sought to lead. This conception is most clearly revealed in Mao's early political tracts, written before the ideological filters of the Marxist-Leninist dialectic dimmed the clarity of his native style of expression.

In 1926, writing under the pen name of Jun-chih, Mao described a peasant uprising in Chekiang Province:

6. *Ibid.,* p. 130. Emphasis added.
7. *Ibid.,* pp. 125–126.
8. Of particular help in this study have been Jerome Ch'en, *Mao and the Chinese Revolution* (Cambridge, England: Oxford University Press, 1965); Stuart R. Schram, *Mao Tse-tung* (Baltimore: Penguin Books, 1967); and Benjamin I. Schwartz, *Chinese Communism and the Rise of Mao* (Cambridge, Massachusetts: Harvard University Press, 1964).

In recent months there occurred a great insurrection in the Shanpei area of [Tz'u Hsi County]. The peasants of this Shanpei area are violent by nature, and frequently indulge in armed combat. On top of this, in recent years the officials and police have been unreasonably oppressive and the bad landlords have stepped up their exploitation. So *the accumulated exasperation of the peasants was already deep.* By chance the climate this year was unstable, and as a result the rice and cotton crops failed, but the landlords refused to make any reduction whatever in their harsh rents. The peasants' insurrection against famine thereupon *exploded.* . . .

They burned down the police station, and distributed the arms of the police among themselves. They then turned to go to the homes of the village gentry landlords to *"eat up powerful families."* After eating them up, and out of anger at the evils of the village gentry landlords, they destroyed the landlords' screens, paintings, and sculptured ancient doors and windows. They did this every day; they did not listen much to others' exhortation, but *let off their steam* in this manner.[9]

Mao's reaction to such events was elation at injustice meeting its due: "If you are a person of determined revolutionary viewpoint, and if you have been to the villages and looked around, you will undoubtedly feel a joy never before known. Countless masses of slaves—the peasants, are there striking down their man-eating enemies." [10] The accumulated exasperation of years of holding in forbidden feelings and frustration at last explodes; the "man-eaters" are devoured by those consumed with rage.

The energies that are released as a result of these grievances and resentments can be likened only to the elemental violence of nature:

Within a very short time, several hundred million peasants from the provinces of China's central, southern, and northern sections will rise up, and their power will be like a blasting wind and cloudburst so extraordinarily swift and violent that no force however large will be able to suppress it. They will burst through all trammels that restrain them, and rush toward the road of liberation.[11]

9. Mao (under the pen name Jun-chih), "The Bitter Sufferings of the Peasants in Kiangsu and Chekiang, and Their Movements of Resistance" (1926), cited and translated in Stuart R. Schram, *The Political Thought of Mao Tse-tung* (New York: Praeger, 1963), p. 179. Emphasis added. Hereafter this source will be cited as "Schram, *PTMTT.*"

10. Mao, "Report on an Investigation of the Peasant Movement in Hunan" (1927), *SW*, I, Chinese, p. 17. Hereafter this article will be cited as "Hunan Report."

11. *Ibid.*, p. 13.

Mao's basic conception of political motivation is thus that of an emotional storm, in which hatreds, resentment, and a sense of hopeless desperation burst through social restraints in an over-whelming surge. The progress of the revolution has the stormy rhythm of "advancing waves," "upsurges," and "high tides" as the emotions that fuel political involvement rise to crests and then diminish through action.

"MUTUALLY RELATED AND MUTUALLY ANTAGONISTIC"

The calculus of such political action draws its logic from the authority relations of the traditional society, where initiative was fully vested with the powerful, where a subordinate had to disci-pline himself against the expression of frustrations and resentment, and where personal security was felt to be ultimately in other hands. When any hope of just treatment has vanished, dependent "respect" becomes a fused explosive; the greater the sense of re-sentment at injustice or failure of obligation, the greater the ac-cumulated charge. One small added injustice may be the "single spark" that will "liberate" great intrinsic energy.

> At the slightest provocation [the peasants] make arrests, crown the arrested with tall paper hats, and parade them through the villages, saying, "You dirty landlords, now you know who we are!" Doing whatever they like and turning everything upside down, they have created a kind of terror in the countryside. . . . The local tyrants, evil gentry, and lawless landlords have themselves driven the peasants to this. For ages they have used their power to tyrannize over the peasants and trample them underfoot; that is why the peasants have reacted so strongly. The most violent revolts and the most serious dis-orders have invariably occurred in places where the local tyrants, evil gentry and lawless landlords perpetrated the worst outrages.[12]

Mao thus looks for the energy of revolution in the sense of injustice and resentment separating various social groups:

> . . . the industrial proletariat . . . is the most progressive class in modern China and has become the leading force in the revolution-ary movement. . . . They have been deprived of all means of pro-duction, have nothing left but their hands, have no hope of ever becoming rich *and, moreover, are subjected to the most ruthless treat-ment by the imperialists, the warlords and the bourgeoisie. That is why they are particularly good fighters.*

> The third section [of the petty bourgeoisie] consists of those whose standard of living is falling. . . . As such people have seen better days and are now going downhill with every passing year, their debts

12. Mao, "Hunan Report" (1927), *SW*, English, I, p. 28.

mounting and their life becoming more and more miserable, they "shudder at the thought of the future." They are in great mental distress because there is such a contrast between their past and their present. Such people are quite important for the revolutionary movement. . . .

The semi-owner peasants are worse off than the owner-peasants because every year they are short of about half the food they need, and have to make up this deficit by renting land from others, selling part of their labour power, or engaging in petty trading. [They] are therefore more revolutionary than the owner-peasants, but less revolutionary than the poor peasants . . . who are exploited by the landlords. . . .

The shop assistants are employees of shops and stores, supporting their families on meagre pay and getting an increase perhaps only once in several years while prices rise every year. If by chance you get into intimate conversation with them, *they invariably pour out their endless grievances* (*chiao-k'u*).[13]

Mao gave the following revealing perception of class conflict in 1939 as he surveyed the progress of the revolution: "The Chinese bourgeoisie and proletariat, seen as two specific social classes, are newly born; they have been born from the womb of feudal society, and have matured into new social classes. They are two *mutually related and mutually antagonistic* classes; they are twins born of old Chinese [feudal] society." [14]

Such family imagery in the context of an analysis of the relationship between economic classes reveals the linkage in Mao's mind between the relational quality of Confucian social authority, the *wu-lun,* and the hostility which will drive the revolution. His own life had sensitized him to the humiliation and sense of injustice that could come with dependence on those in power, and this sensitivity shaped his perceptions of social action. The notion of "mutually related and mutually antagonistic" was raised to the level of a philosophy of politics and social change in his theory of "contradictions" (*mao-tun*): the belief that "there is internal contradiction in every single thing. . ."; that "contradictoriness within a thing is the fundamental cause of its development. . ."; and that hatred, "antagonism" (*tui-k'ang*) is the motive force behind political action.[15]

13. Mao, "Analysis of the Classes in Chinese Society" (1926), *SW,* English, I, pp. 16–18. Emphasis added.

14. This passage from Mao's 1939 essay, "The Chinese Revolution and the Chinese Communist Party," has been analyzed in a provocative article by John Weakland, "Family Imagery in a Passage by Mao Tse-tung," *World Politics,* Vol. X (1958), pp. 387–407. Emphasis added.

15. Mao, "On Contradiction" (1937), *SW,* English, I, p. 313 and *passim.*

ON BEING "CONSCIOUS"

In 1919, after the impact of World War One had provoked in China the political ferment of "May Fourth," Mao wrote with obvious elation in a popular journal:

> Within the area enclosed by the Great Wall and the China Sea, the May 4th movement has arisen. Its banner has advanced southward . . . the tide is rising. Heaven and earth are aroused, the traitors and the wicked are put to flight. Ha! We know it! We are awakened! The world is ours, the nation is ours, society is ours. If we do not speak, who will speak? If we do not act, who will act? If we do not rise up and fight, who will rise up and fight?[16]

"The tide is rising"; "we are awakened." The notion that the storm of revolution wakes people up, makes them "conscious" was expressed by Mao with greater reservation in 1945 at the conclusion of the anti-Japanese war, when he looked back on the Party's historical development:

> The condition of our Party today is vastly different from what it was in 1927. In those days our Party was still in its infancy and did not have a clear head or experience in armed struggle or the policy of opposing weapons with weapons. Today the level of political consciousness in our Party is very much higher.
>
> Apart from our own political consciousness, the political consciousness of the vanguard of the proletariat, there is the question of the political consciousness of the masses of the people. When the people are not yet politically conscious, it is entirely possible that their revolutionary gains may be handed over to others. This happened in the past. Today the level of political consciousness of the Chinese people is likewise very much higher.[17]

As this passage indicates, political "consciousness" is seen as crucial to the success of the revolution. The objective of the revolution, of course, is "liberation" (*chieh-fang*), as the Chinese Communists characterize life under their leadership. Thus development of the revolution is symbolized as a process of awakening, becoming conscious, and then achieving liberation through struggle. But what does "awakening" really mean? What does "consciousness" bring into mind? And what is "liberated" through revolution?

16. Mao, "Toward a New Golden Age" (1919), cited and translated in Schram, *PTMTT*, p. 105.
17. Mao, "The Situation and Our Policy after the Victory in the War of Resistance against Japan" (1945), *SW*, English, IV, p. 19. Translation revised slightly on the basis of the Chinese text.

In the quotation on p. 168, Mao directly links "consciousness" to the capacity for promoting conflict. As we have seen in preceding chapters, however, the traditional culture taught the individual to deny even mediated expressions of hostility against those in authority and viewed conflict as illegitimate to "proper" social relations. Hostile feelings were supposed to be covered over with the social forms of filial respectfulness; they were to be put "in one's stomach." Thus becoming politically "awake" and "conscious," at one level of analysis, means mobilizing *feelings* which the old society said it was impermissible to express.

"Liberation" (a term which could also be translated as "get rid of" or "release") in the Maoist vocabulary means working up all the bitterness that society has made one swallow and releasing or liberating it through revolutionary struggle with "man-eating" enemies. And as Mao wrote with impatience shortly before the founding of the Chinese Communist Party, if only this emotional fuel of revolution could be tapped, organized, and directed for political ends, the Chinese people could create for themselves a new world:

> We must act energetically to carry out the great union of the popular masses, which will not brook a moment's delay. . . . Our Chinese people have great intrinsic energy; the deeper their oppression the greater will be their resistance, and as their sense of grievance has accumulated for a long time it will burst forth quickly. The great union of the Chinese people must be achieved. Gentlemen! We must all exert ourselves, we must all advance with the greatest effort. Our golden age, our age of brilliance and splendor, lies ahead.[18]

Life's golden age no longer lies in an idealized past, but in a yet-to-be attained future.

In the five chapters of Part Three which follow, we will explore in detail Mao's conception of politics as an emotional storm. In Chapter XI we will see the ways in which traditional attitudes toward leadership and social action influenced the political style of the Party in its formative years, producing what Mao saw to be "deviations" from an effective leadership line. Chapters XII through XIV explore the uses of ideology and organization as tools of leadership: their ability to structure the mobilization of popular support for the Party; their capacity to impose political discipline in the revolutionary struggle, to prevent the "confusion" which Chinese have long associated with conflict over power; and the

18. Mao, "Toward a New Golden Age" (1919), cited in Schram, *PTMTT*, p. 105. Translation revised slightly on the basis of the Chinese text.

importance of organization in giving the peasantry the confidence to oppose those in established authority. In Chapter XV we will look at Mao's tactical strategy for gaining power, a conception which draws on traditional Chinese notions of "divide and rule" as well as popular fears of isolation and the divisiveness which is so much a part of the struggle for power.

Chapter XI

REVOLUTIONARY LEADERSHIP AND
THE DEVIATIONS OF TRADITION

Outbursts of violence by China's peasantry held for an enthusiastic young Mao the promise of mass revolutionary energy. But he knew that for centuries a small but organized rural gentry and imperial bureaucracy had exercised effective control over the fragmented rural population. Mass hostility had to be organized and subject to political direction if revolutionary goals were to be attained. As Mao himself wrote after he had acquired greater experience, "If the masses alone are active without a strong leading group to organize their activity properly, such activity cannot be sustained for long, or carried forward in the right direction, or raised to a high level." [1]

One of the most interesting facets of the history of the Chinese Communist movement has been the development of an effective strategy of leadership: the evolution of organizational forms and a Party "line" appropriate to historical circumstances which could be used to coalesce and direct mass energies for political ends. From Mao's own perspective, in the course of the revolution the Party has had to wage a continuing struggle with tendencies to "deviate" from a proper leadership line in order to remain in the vanguard of the revolution. These deviations have roots in the traditional political culture.

THE PARTY MUST NOT
"CUT ITSELF OFF FROM THE MASSES"

Mao, the son of a Hunan peasant, was an aspiring young intellectual in the years of confusion surrounding the collapse of the Ch'ing dynasty. In his late teens he volunteered for eighteen months of service in a provincial army in order to "help complete the revolution" against the Manchus, but with the establishment of

1. Mao, "Some Questions Concerning Methods of Leadership" (1943), *SW*, English, III, p. 118.

the Republic he returned to an uncertain search for a career. Between 1913 and 1918 he studied to be a teacher at the First Normal School in the provincial capital of Changsha; and for a short time in 1918–19 he worked as a librarian's assistant at Peking University.[2]

In China intellectuals have always been close to the world of power. The Confucian imperial examinations were a major channel for the recruitment of public officials until the system was abolished in 1904. Hence a young man like Mao, seeking to make some personal contribution to the revitalization of China, almost instinctively turned to the world of education and the life of the cities, where "new learning" influenced by Western ideas seemed to hold promise for China's renaissance.

Of the many lessons Mao learned in his student days, one of the most enduring was of the gap between the social status of the intellectuals and the poverty and injustice which were his birthright as a provincial peasant. In part this gap reflected differences in life style between those reared in the cities and their rural compatriots. More fundamentally, however, the intellectuals' arrogant aloofness from those engaged in physical labor reflected a desire to rise above the bitter life of toil and insecurity endured by China's peasant millions. Mao himself recalled for Edgar Snow his own seduction by the Mencian notion of the superiority of mental over manual labor while a student serving in the anti-Ch'ing army: "I . . . had to buy water. The [ordinary] soldiers had to carry [it] from outside the city, but I, being a student, could not condescend to carrying, and bought it from the water peddlars." [3]

Mao's personal response to this time-honored aloofness of the intellectual was shaped by a sense of resentment which came from his own rejection by intellectual leaders who inspired many of his generation. While a library worker at Peking University he sought to question the philosopher Hu Shih after a lecture, only to be ignored because he did not have regular student status.[4] And his efforts to establish contact with other intellectual heroes of the hour met with hardly greater success:

> My office [in the library] was so low that people avoided me. One of my tasks was to register the names of people who came to read

2. Mao's recollections of his early life were recounted to Edgar Snow in a series of interviews held in Paoan, Shensi Province, during 1936. This document remains the basic source of information on Mao's early life and a valuable expression of his personal attitudes rendered in a relatively non-Marxist vocabulary. *See Red Star Over China*, pp. 121–156.

3. *Ibid.*, p. 138.

4. Stuart R. Schram, *Mao Tse-tung*, p. 48.

newspapers, but to most of them I didn't exist as a human being. Among those who came to read I recognized the names of famous leaders of the renaissance movement, men like Fu Ssu-nien, Lo Chia-lung, and others, in whom I was intensely interested. I tried to begin conversations with them on political and cultural subjects, but they were very busy men. They had no time to listen to an assistant librarian speaking southern dialect.[5]

From such incidents grew a bitter distrust of intellectuals as a group which has been a constant theme in Mao's social outlook. This orientation has remained in tension with the needs of a political movement for the leadership skills that traditionally have been the exclusive preserve of China's educated few. Mao has sought to resolve this tension through ridicule of intellectual pretentiousness and the remolding of traditional attitudes toward the use of power.

After the Party's near destruction in 1927, Mao found a number of disgraced intellectuals among the leadership who could be held up for ridicule as "negative examples" to educate Party cadres. Mao told Edgar Snow that Ch'en Tu-hsiu, the Party's General Secretary, suffered from "wavering opportunism [which] deprived the Party of decisive leadership"; and he ridiculed the Comintern representative, M. N. Roy, by noting that "he talked too much without offering any method of realization [of Party goals]." [6] But this tendency of the intellectual to use words, without direct involvement in practical problems, was hardly unique to these early Party notables. In a 1930 essay, "Oppose Book Worship," Mao complained of comrades "who like to make political pronouncements the moment they arrive at a place and who strut about, criticizing this and condemning that when they have only seen the surface of things or minor details. Such purely subjective nonsensical talk is indeed detestable." [7] Others, he noted, "eat their fill and sit dozing in their offices all day long without ever moving a step and going out among the masses to investigate. Whenever they open their mouths, their platitudes make people sick." [8]

In the Kiangsi days Mao sought institutional ways of bringing together power and practice: "No investigation, no right to speak." [9] Yet he seemed mocked in his efforts by the legacy of China's political culture, shared by leader and led alike: "What-

5. Snow, *Red Star Over China*, p. 150.

6. *Ibid.*, p. 165.

7. Mao, "Oppose Book Worship" (1930), *Selected Readings from the Works of Mao Tse-tung* (Peking: Foreign Languages Press, 1967), p. 34.

8. *Ibid.*, p. 39.

9. *Ibid.*, p. 33.

ever is written in a book is right—such is still the mentality of culturally backward Chinese peasants." [10] With the influx of disaffected intellectuals into Communist-controlled Yenan during the war with Japan, Mao attempted to reform through ridicule "those who regard Marxism-Leninism as religious dogma":

> We must tell [such people] openly, "Your dogma is of no use," or to use an impolite formulation, "Your dogma is less useful than shit." Dog shit can fertilize the fields. . . . And dogmas? They can't fertilize the fields. . . . Of what use are they? (Laughter) Comrades! You know that the object of such talk is to ridicule those who regard Marxism-Leninism as dogma, to frighten and awaken them. . . . Marx, Engels, Lenin, and Stalin have repeatedly said, "Our doctrine is not dogma; it is a guide to action." Of all things, these people forget this most important sentence.[11]

Throughout his career this peasant revolutionary has reserved his most bitter, scatological irony for those who threaten to transform the ideology of China's future greatness into a new language of control which would heighten the distinction between an order-issuing elite and a peasant mass that only dumbly obeys—a division of function and status that would lead to the Party's "cutting itself off from the masses" (*t'o-li ch'ün-chung*). Mao expressed his determination to bring together word and action in a philosophy of "Practise," [12] and instructed intellectual cadres that they must not write Marxist analyses of Chinese society in the formalistic style of the Confucian "eight-legged essay." [13]

By Yenan days this concern with insuring communication and contact between Party cadres and the people was institutionalized in the leadership concept of the "mass line" (*ch'ün-chung lu-hsien*):

> All correct leadership is necessarily "from the masses; to the masses." This means: take the ideas of the masses (scattered and unsystematic ideas) and concentrate them (through study turn them into concen-

10. *Ibid.,* p. 34.
11. Mao, "Reform in Learning, the Party, and Literature" (1942), in Schram, *PTMTT,* p. 120.
12. *See* Mao's 1937 essay "On Practise," *SW,* English, I, pp. 295–309.
13. *See* "Oppose Stereotyped Party Writing" (1942), *SW,* English, III, pp. 53–68. This and other essays from the 1942 Party "rectification" campaign deal primarily with problems of maintaining effective communications between the leadership and led. *See also* "Preface and Postscript to *Rural Surveys*" (1941), "Reform Our Study" (1941), "Rectify the Party's Style of Work" (1942), and "Talks at the Yenan Forum on Literature and Art" (1942), all in Volume III of the *Selected Works.*

trated and systematic ideas), then go to the masses and propagate and explain these ideas until the masses embrace them as their own.[14]

But this effort to develop a dialogue between Party and people has been in constant tension with enduring traditional attitudes about the relation of superior to subordinate. Various approaches have been tried. In the post-Liberation development of the periodic *hsia-fang* or "transfer downwards" campaigns, students and government workers have been sent out to labor with peasants in the fields. Another educational innovation is the "half-work—half-study" schools, designed to raise new generations of intellectuals who would know through personal experience a relationship between labor and leadership.[15]

It is perhaps because of his perception of the ability of the intellectual to stifle action with words that Mao has placed such emphasis in his style of leadership on the manipulation of emotions; on the rationale of injustice, not on the rhetoric of scholasticism used so long in China as an instrument of political control.

DARE (KAN)!

While Mao's bugbear among early Party leaders was Ch'en Tu-hsiu, his hero was Ch'en's coequal in founding the Communist movement, the intellectual Li Ta-chao. Li was Mao's mentor in Peking, the man who placed him on the staff of the University library, and who headed the Marxist study group in which Mao received his first exposure to the ideology of the Bolshevik revolution. This personal relationship cemented a common social outlook: a shared commitment to activism; concern about the isolation of China's intellectuals from the practical problems of their society; and acceptance of the direct political action approach that had been rejected by men like Hu Shih and Ch'en.[16] But where Li's career was cut short through strangulation during the nationwide anti-Communist suppression of 1927, Mao had the opportunity, and the commitment, to transform Li's ideals into a technique of leadership.

14. Mao, "Some Questions Concerning Methods of Leadership" (1943), *SW*, English, III, p. 119.

15. *See* Donald J. Munro, "Maxims and Realities in China's Educational Policy: The Half-Work, Half-Study Model," *Asian Survey*, Vol. VII, No. 4 (April 1967), pp. 254–272.

16. These aspects of Li Ta-chao's social outlook are documented and analyzed in Maurice Meisner, *Li Ta-chao and the Origins of Chinese Marxism* (Cambridge, Massachusetts: Harvard University Press, 1967).

The problems Mao faced in creating an activist cadre of leaders were based on more than just the intellectuals' aloofness from the problems of China's peasant masses. Common Chinese attitudes toward authority and conflict continued to bind individuals into the structure of a society which endured beyond the destruction of the Ch'ing state apparatus. For Mao and many of his generation the binding effects of Confucian social relations were symbolized in the matter of marriage choice. The selection of a mate, a problem confronted personally by most young radicals, brought to a focus the clash between the wishes of the individual and family interests. When he was twenty-six, Mao wrote an article about the suicide of a young girl who was unwilling to submit to an arranged marriage. In it he expressed many of the frustrations of his generation, and revealed some of the concepts of social action that later evolved into institutionalized techniques of leadership:

> A person's suicide is entirely determined by circumstances. . . . The circumstances in which Miss Chao found herself were the following: (1) Chinese society; (2) the Chao family of Nanyang Street in Changsha; (3) the Wu family of Kantzuyuan Street in Changsha, the family of the husband she did not want. *These three factors constituted three iron nets, composing a kind of triangular cage.* . . . [But] if in society there had been a powerful group of public opinion to support her, if there were an entirely new world where the fact of running away from one's parents' home and finding refuge elsewhere were considered honorable and not dishonorable, in this case, too, Miss Chao would certainly not have died.
>
> Since there are factors in our society that have brought about the death of Miss Chao, *this society is an extremely dangerous thing.* . . . All of us, the potential victims, must be on our guard before this dangerous thing that could inflict a fatal blow on us. *We should protest loudly,* warn the other human beings who are not yet dead, and condemn the countless evils of our society. . . .[17]

For Mao and others of the "May Fourth" era the "five human relationships" which had bound together Confucian society seemed as cold and restrictive as "iron nets." But as Miss Chao's suicide indicated, old custom still had the potency to force the individual to direct life's frustrations inward as aggression against the self. Unlike Miss Chao, however, who withdrew to a private escape, Mao generalized the problem to a public issue in which he saw everyone threatened. He longed for some organized force to counter the source of danger: ". . . if in society there had been a powerful group of public opinion to support her. . . ."

This passage reveals another dimension of Mao's personal style

17. Cited in Schram, *PTMTT*, pp. 226–227. Emphasis added.

which, in combination with his ability to generalize personal difficulties in terms of social ills, seems to account for his effectiveness as a revolutionary leader: his ability to "protest loudly." Mao's assertiveness is a quality he revealed early in life, in a number of youthful rebellions through which he came to perceive that his father was really dependent on him. At the age of ten Mao ran away from school in fear of the beatings administered by a teacher of the "stern treatment school." Afraid of receiving a beating at home as well, he wandered lost for three days before he was finally located by his family. He recalled with satisfaction, however: "After my return . . . to my surprise conditions somewhat improved. My father was slightly more considerate, and the teacher was more inclined to moderation. The result of my action of protest impressed me very much. It was a successful 'strike.' " [18]

A more serious incident occurred a few years later, revealing to Mao the way that authority could be manipulated through the logic of filial dependence:

> When I was about thirteen my father invited many guests to his home, and while they were present a dispute arose between the two of us. My father denounced me before the whole group, calling me lazy and useless. This infuriated me. I cursed him and left the house. My mother ran after me and tried to persuade me to return. My father also pursued me, cursing at the same time that he demanded me to come back. *I reached the edge of a pond and threatened to jump in if he came any nearer.* In this situation demands and counter-demands were presented for cessation of the civil war. My father insisted that I apologize and *k'ou-t'ou* as a sign of submission. I agreed to give a one-knee *k'ou-t'ou* if he would promise not to beat me. Thus the war ended, and from it *I learned that when I defended my rights by open rebellion my father relented, but when I remained meek and submissive he only cursed and beat me the more.*[19]

The notable aspect of this incident, which Mao characterized as "open rebellion," is that the physical threat still was self-directed; the adolescent was capable of attacking his father only *indirectly* by threatening to drown himself (thus "abandoning" his father by leaving him without a son to depend on) and by making his father "lose face" before the guests. Yet Mao saw that if authority were "dared" its harshness could be mitigated, while "meek and submissive" behavior would only invoke greater pain.

In his personal development, the pond before which Mao had defied his father was transformed into one of this revolutionary's most powerful symbols of opposition to dependence on authority.

18. Snow, *Red Star Over China*, p. 125.
19. *Ibid.*, p. 126. Emphasis added.

In Part One we noted how Chinese parents sought to restrict their children's physical activity, such as swimming, out of fear that they would harm themselves. Aggressive impulses and actions which threatened to break the filial bond were to be held in through physical reserve. But where Mao the child had to "dare" authority through the threat of self-destruction because of his inability to swim, as a young man he expressed his determination to turn aggression outwards by learning how to swim. His self-assertiveness found expression in a keen interest in physical culture:

> In the winter holidays we [student friends] tramped through the fields, up and down mountains, along city walls, and across the streams and rivers. If it rained we took off our shirts and called it a rain bath. . . . We slept in the open when frost was already falling and even in November swam in the cold rivers. All this went on under the title of "body training." [20]

The relationship between such physical disciplining and political assertiveness was first articulated by Mao in an essay written in 1917, "A Study of Physical Education." He saw his nation "wanting in strength. The military spirit has not been encouraged." In seeking to remedy this situation he drew on his personal experience:

> Physical education . . . strengthens the will. The great utility of physical education lies precisely in this. . . . Let me explain with an example. To wash our feet in ice water makes us acquire courage and dauntlessness, as well as audacity. In general, any form of exercise, if pursued continuously, will help train us in perseverance. . . . *Exercise over a long time can produce great results and give rise to a feeling of personal value.* [21]

Within a decade this youthful preoccupation with developing a "feeling of personal value" and the martial spirit through body-building was to be transformed into Mao's first effort to build a peasant military force, an act of personal assertiveness which "dared" the Comintern-backed Party Central Committee and the orthodox, urban-oriented strategy of revolution which was then the official Party line.

In later years the link between Mao's willingness to "dare" authority through swimming and military action became central to the mythology of the revolution:

> To make a revolution and wage a war is often not a matter of learning before doing, but of doing and then learning, for doing is learn-

20. *Ibid.,* p. 146.
21. Mao, "A Study of Physical Education" (1917), in Schram, *PTMTT,* pp. 99, 101.

ing. Only by following Chairman Mao's instructions and putting "daring" and "doing" above everything else, and courageously plunging into the practice of war—tempering ourselves in the teeth of storms and learning to swim by swimming—can we acquaint ourselves with the laws of war and master them." [22]

On the eve of perhaps his last great political battle, Mao was to symbolize his determination to "dare" the Party which had passed beyond his control by swimming in the Yangtze. He called on a new generation to share his own youthful experience of learning to challenge authority by "advancing with Chairman Mao amidst great winds and waves" [23] in the Great Proletarian Cultural Revolution.

While the strength of his own self-assertiveness enabled the young Mao to seek ways of dealing with the harshness of authority, his early writings reveal that he was sensitive to the forms of psychological support which an individual needed to oppose the established social order. He found that an ideology could provide an alternative source of authority to answer the criticisms of those in control: "I discovered a powerful argument of my own for debating with my father on his own ground, by quoting the Classics." [24] He also saw that an organized group could back an individual in protest, overcoming fears of acting in isolation and providing an alternative source of support (". . . if in society there had been a powerful group of public opinion to support [Miss Chao]. . . .")

Perhaps the most important aspect of such incidents is that *even* for a man who in time had the audacity to challenge a social order weighted with "five thousand years of history," attacking authority directly was an extremely difficult thing to do: It invoked those aspects of personality—anxiety in the face of authority, and fears of isolation and conflict—which gave the Confucian social pattern its durability.

THE "RIGHTIST" DEVIATION: AVOIDANCE OF CONFLICT

Mao's personal capacity to accept direct conflict and his distrust of a position of passive dependence find expression in his reading,

22. From a *Liberation Army Daily* editorial, "Study 'Problems of Strategy in China's Revolutionary War,' " trans. in *Peking Review,* No. 3 (December 29, 1966), p. 18.

23. *See* the photographs and news release of Mao's swim in the Yangtze, and the editorial "Advance with Chairman Mao Amidst Great Winds and Waves," in the *People's Daily* issues of July 25 and 26, 1966. *See also* pp. 476–477 below.

24. Snow, *Red Star Over China,* p. 125.

and rewriting of Party history, through which he has used past defeats to criticize deviations from his interpretation of the proper leadership line.

During the first six years of its existence, the Party's Central Committee, under General Secretary Ch'en Tu-hsiu, accepted Comintern pressures to work as a "bloc within" the more powerful Kuomintang. Ch'en's personal attitudes toward this Party dependence on "bourgeois" (and Comintern) leadership are obscured by the complexity of events, but in the most detailed study to date of this period, Benjamin Schwartz has concluded: "In the face of what was considered to be the formidable power of the enemy, [the Ch'en leadership group] wished to conserve its strength for the future"; and, "in the implementation of policy they bowed to the superior wisdom of the Kremlin." [25] In spite of the warning of the vulnerability of the masses implicit in the "February Seventh" 1923 slaughter of organized but unarmed workers by Wu P'ei-fu's army, or the promise of mass energies revealed in the "May Thirtieth" [1925] anti-Japanese outbursts, the Ch'en leadership refrained from developing independent armed power. Even Chiang K'ai-shek's arrest of Party and Comintern leaders in March of 1926 produced no basic change in policy, with the result that the Party organization was nearly annihilated in the 1927 anti-Communist suppression carried out by Nationalist military forces.

The most notable aspect of Ch'en's handling of this situation is that despite his doubts, he was unwilling or unable to translate the perception of a bad Party line into a change in policy. He continued to submit to Comintern pressures rather than organize support for a more effective strategy. The basis for Ch'en's lack of assertiveness, or what Mao once termed his "wavering opportunism," was suggested by Mao in 1936:

> Ch'en was really frightened of the workers and especially of the armed peasants. Confronted at last with the reality of armed insurrection he completely lost his senses. He could no longer see clearly what was happening, and his petty-bourgeois instincts betrayed him into panic and defeat.[26]

Mao characterized Ch'en as an "unconscious traitor," [27] and as we have seen previously, "consciousness" in Mao's political vocabulary is directly linked to the capacity for mobilizing hatreds that will fire revolutionary violence. Like other political leaders, Mao has used history to justify present policy rather than to affirm past

25. Schwartz, *Chinese Communism and the Rise of Mao,* p. 64.
26. Snow, *Red Star Over China,* p. 165.
27. *Ibid.*

fact. His criticism of Ch'en can thus be read as an indication that even within the Party leadership, traditional Chinese fears of conflict and anxieties about challenging established authority require constant criticism lest they undermine the momentum of the revolution.[28] Such attitudes were particularly notable in the early, "urban" days of the Party. For example, the Central Committee, meeting in Shanghai in 1926, expressed its distrust of armed peasants and concern about the "destructive tendencies" of such quasi-military rural secret societies as the Red Spears.[29]

It is noteworthy that these two traditional attitudes, fear of conflict and passivity before the power of established authority, are threads which run through the history of Mao's attempt to develop and maintain a successful revolutionary leadership. One of his criticisms of "bourgeois" parties and leaders is that they fear the conflict of revolution:

> . . . the national bourgeoisie cannot be the leader of the revolution, nor should it have the chief role in state power. The reason it cannot be the leader . . . is that the social and economic position of the national bourgeoisie determines its weakness; *it lacks foresight and sufficient courage and many of its members are afraid of the masses.*[30]

The "bourgeois" tendency to fear conflict and mass upheaval, however, manifests itself even within the Party. The "opportunism" which led Ch'en Tu-hsiu to become passive before Nationalist power becomes evident in "liberalism" (*tzu-yu-chu-yi*):

> Liberalism is one expression of opportunism, [and] is fundamentally in conflict with Marxism. *It is a passive thing, and subjectively serves to aid the enemy.* . . . *We must use the active spirit of Marxism to overcome passive liberalism. A Communist should* . . .

28. The autobiographical writings of Ch'ü Ch'iu-pai, a leader of the Party for a short period in late 1927 and early 1928—and, ironically, a man removed from leadership because of a "left" or adventurist deviation in leadership—reveal a strong sense of discomfort about interpersonal conflict. *See* T. A. Hsia, "Ch'ü Ch'iu-pai's Autobiographical Writings: The Making and Destruction of a 'Tender-hearted' Communist," *The China Quarterly*, No. 25 (January–March 1966), pp. 176–212.

This perceptive article reveals a number of other aspects of one Party leader's emotional life which bear out several of the themes of the traditional political culture explored above: a man's dependence on family assistance even when he detested family life (pp. 184–185); a strong desire to return to childhood (p. 194); and a longing for social unity (p. 193).

29. Cited in Meisner, *Li Ta-chao and the Origins of Chinese Marxism*, p. 244.

30. Mao, "On the People's Democratic Dictatorship" (1949), *SW*, English, IV, p. 421. Emphasis added.

be active . . . and wage a tireless struggle against all incorrect ideas
and actions, so as to consolidate the collective life of the Party and
consolidate the relationship between the Party and the people.[31]

These culture-enhanced impediments to the "revolutionary" use
of power—passivity, and fear of conflict—found particular manifestation in the development of Mao's strategy of guerrilla warfare.
To become "conscious" of one's potential for violent combat was not
sufficient; one had to gain initiative in action and force the enemy
into a passive position:

> Freedom of action is the very life of an army and, once it is lost, the
> army is close to defeat or destruction. *The disarming of a soldier is
> the result of his losing freedom of action through being forced into a
> passive position. . . . For this reason both sides in war do all they
> can to gain the initiative and avoid passivity. . . .* Initiative is in-
> separable from superiority in capacity to wage war, while *passivity is
> inseparable from inferiority.*[32]

Mao sensed that although the invading Japanese possessed superiority in firepower and certain types of communication and
transport, there were a number of objective circumstances—insufficient troops, lack of knowledge of China and contacts with her
people, and a rigid leadership—which would limit their initiative.
Hence if the Party could overcome Chinese tendencies to be passive before power, Japan could be defeated through the "activism"
of superior initiative:

> Japan's general position has become one of only relative superi-
> ority, and her ability to exercise and maintain the initiative, which
> is thereby restricted, has likewise become relative. As for China,
> though placed in a somewhat passive position strategically because
> of her inferior strength, she is nevertheless quantitatively superior in
> territory, population and troops, and also superior in the morale of
> her people and army and their patriotic hatred of the enemy; this
> superiority . . . reduces the degree of China's passivity so that her
> strategic position is one of only relative passivity. *Any passivity, how-
> ever, is a disadvantage, and one must strive to shake it off. . . .*
> Through . . . local superiority and local initiative in many cam-
> paigns, we can gradually create strategic superiority and strategic
> initiative and extricate ourselves from strategic inferiority and passiv-
> ity. Such is the interrelation between initiative and passivity, between
> superiority and inferiority.[33]

31. Mao, "Combat Liberalism" (1937), *SW,* Chinese, II, p. 347. Emphasis added.
32. Mao, "On Protracted War" (1938), *SW,* English, II, pp. 161–162.
Emphasis added.
33. *Ibid.,* p. 163.

While the Party's promotion of guerrilla warfare was hardly a decisive factor in the defeat of Japan, it did serve to build up Communist military strength and create a leadership with skill and experience. After 1945 these weapons of revolution were turned against the Nationalist government in civil war. Yet here again, according to Mao, individuals within the Party manifested the "rightist" deviation of fear of conflict before apparently superior forces, and a reluctance to stimulate to full fury the "political consciousness" of the masses.[34] Yet after more than two decades of military trial and growth, the strength of such a deviation had been eroded:

> The Right deviations consist chiefly in *over-estimating the strength of the enemy, being afraid of large-scale U.S. aid to Chiang Kai-shek,* being somewhat weary of the long war, having certain doubts about the strength of the world democratic forces, *not daring to arouse the masses fully* in order to abolish feudalism, and being indifferent to impurities in the Party's class composition and style of work. Such Right deviations, however, are not the main ones at present; they are not too difficult to correct.[35]

Even in victory, when nationwide power was within grasp, Mao's fear of passivity before power did not vanish: "Just because we have won victory, we must never relax our vigilance against the frenzied plots for revenge by the imperialists and their running dogs. *Whoever relaxes vigilance will disarm himself politically and land himself in a passive position.*"[36]

This enduring, anxious concern with activism in the use of power and fear of passivity in the face of strong enemies seems to reflect Mao's personal reaction to the pain and injustice he had known in the dependent period of his own life. Also, from the vantage point of a leader who wants to revolutionize a tradition-bound society, Mao's preoccupation with passivity reveals a concern that those around him, other leaders and followers, will give in to those anxieties about criticizing established authority and custom that are the legacy of China's traditional political culture. In such circumstances, the revolution would become mired down in enduring social patterns characteristic of a discredited way of life.

34. In 1967 this deviation was attributed to Mao's long-time cohort Liu Shao-ch'i as part of a general attack on Liu for his "passive" approach to leadership. *See* pp. 396, 400–404 below.

35. Mao, "A Circular on the Situation" (1948), *SW*, English, IV, p. 220. Emphasis added.

36. Mao, "Address to the Preparatory Committee of the New Political Consultative Conference" (1949), *SW*, English, IV, p. 407. Emphasis added.

"LEFT OPPORTUNISM" AND LUAN

There is a dialectical partner to the "rightist" deviation of passivity in the face of superior power: a tendency to promote conflict without caution. Such "left opportunism" has manifested itself in Party history in such incidents as the Nanchang uprising of August 1927, the precipitate formation and failure of the Canton Commune in December of that same year, and the abortive attacks on Changsha by military forces from the Soviet areas in September 1927 and again in the summer of 1930. Such tactical failures resulting from the impetuous promotion of conflict have been associated with the early Party leaders Ch'ü Ch'iu-pai, Li Li-san, and Wang Ming.

Mao himself, in student days, had toyed with the anarchist's glorification of violence largely for its own sake.[37] Indeed, in later years he was to affirm the legitimacy of conflict with the slogan, "There cannot be construction without destruction." However, since his 1921 acceptance of the need for a Leninist party organization, and the caution with which he committed to battle the meager military forces under his control in the Kiangsi Soviet areas, one can conclude that early in his career Mao had placed revolutionary violence under the discipline of larger political goals.

An inability to express aggression with control, what Marxist-Leninists term adventuristic "left opportunism" in the use of power, seems closely related to Chinese fears of *luan*. As was elaborated in Part Two, traditionally there has been an expectation that once hostile emotions come into the open a person becomes overwhelmed with his own aggressive impulses, his mind becomes "complicated" (*fu-tza*), and he gets carried away into a "confusion" of interpersonal conflict. In the Confucian tradition "cultivation" was conceived as a way of keeping a "clear head," of holding in the bad feelings which, if mobilized, could destroy social order. In looking back on the Party's political adventures of the 1920s Mao once remarked: "In those days our Party was still in its infancy and did not have a clear head or experience in armed struggle. . . ."[38] Early Party history seems to confirm that learning discipline in the use of violence was almost as much of a leadership problem as overcoming the reluctance to mobilize the hatreds that make revolutionary violence possible.

37. Mao recalled that while in Peking he "often discussed anarchism and its possibilities in China. At that time I favored many of its proposals." (Snow, *Red Star Over China*, p. 151.) On this point *see also* Schram, *Mao Tse-tung*, p. 49.

38. Mao, "The Situation and Our Policy after the Victory in the War of Resistance against Japan" (1945), *SW*, English, IV, p. 19.

The first major manifestation of "adventurism," or the undisciplined promotion of conflict, followed the Party's near annihilation in the urban areas in the spring and summer of 1927. An emergency conference of the Central Committee held on August seventh replaced the "right opportunist" Ch'en Tu-hsiu with Ch'ü Ch'iu-pai as Party leader. Thereafter, under prodding from the Comintern, the new leadership initiated planning for the immediate establishment of urban Soviets through provoking uprisings in provincial cities. A Party investigation team surveying preparations for this precipitate insurrection in Hunan found that "Those who are sufficiently angry to want to overthrow the government are in the minority. Most of them would prefer to be passive and inert." [39] But despite such intimations of incipient defeat, the Central Committee pressed on with its plans. The failure of the uprising was to be repeated in the equally hasty Canton insurrection of December 1927.

As with Ch'en's earlier defeat resulting from submission to Comintern pressure, Ch'ü's misjudgment held for Mao the lesson of the dangers of blind dependence on a "superior" authority divorced from China's immediate social conditions. Yet Mao himself was singled out for criticism by his Party superiors as a "rightist" because of "having done too little killing and burning. . . ." [40]

While the urban-based Central Committee bore most of the blame for the adventures of the latter half of 1927, Mao found that his efforts to build a military force in the mountains of the Hunan-Kiangsi border region were also hindered by "leftist" deviations. In an analysis of 1929 he criticized "the ideology of roving guerilla bands" and those elements of the Red Army who resorted to violence as a form of personal indulgence, who "only want to go to the big cities to eat and drink." And perhaps with the increasingly influential Li Li-san in mind, he attacked those who urged "blind action regardless of subjective and objective conditions." [41]

Where Ch'en Tu-hsiu symbolized for Mao "rightist" revolutionary reticence, Li Li-san came to be the personification of "leftist" impetuosity. Mao's first contacts with the impulsive Li had not gone well,[42] and with Li's rise to major prominence in the Party in

39. Cited in Roy Mark Hofheinz, *The Peasant Movement and Rural Revolution: Chinese Communists in the Countryside, 1923–1927* (unpublished Ph.D. dissertation, Harvard University, 1966), pp. 281–282.

40. Cited from Mao's own recollection of this period in Schram, *Mao Tse-tung*, p. 131.

41. Mao, "On Correcting Mistaken Ideas in the Party" (1929), *SW*, English, I, pp. 114–115.

42. Mao recalled that in student days he once put an advertisement in a Changsha paper, "inviting young men interested in patriotic work to make

1928–29 their differences in personal style found expression in conflict over revolutionary strategy. Li criticized Mao's efforts to create a peasant military force as un-Marxist, and asserted that without urban working class leadership (that is, leadership exercised from the urban areas under Central Committee control) there likely would be "a complete destruction of the revolution and of the Party." [43]

In fact, it was Li's own precipitate commitment of the Chu-Mao military forces to urban insurrection which cost the Party dearly, and seriously threatened Mao's growing power base in the rural Soviet areas. A Comintern directive of October 1929 talked vaguely of an approaching "upsurge" in China's revolutionary situation. Li overinterpreted the language to call for a new round of urban insurrections and ordered attacks on major cities in South-Central China during the summer of 1930. [44] Changsha was held for ten days, but attacks on Nanchang and Wuhan encountered superior Kuomintang forces, and within three weeks the unsuccessful venture was abandoned.

While Mao's reading of the uncertainties of the situation had been accurate, Li's failure only led to a new, Comintern-oriented Party leadership headed by the young Wang Ming (Ch'en Shao-yü), recently returned from studies in Moscow. From Mao's perspective this new leadership once again engaged in "leftist" tactical deviations which nearly led to the total destruction of the Red Army during the fifth Kuomintang "Encirclement and Extermination" campaign of 1934. It was only the "Long March," and Mao's rise to Party leadership after the January 1935 Central Committee conference held in the Kweichow market town of Tsunyi which finally gave Mao the opportunity to assert his own political style.

THE IMPORTANCE OF DISCIPLINED STRUGGLE

Mao's reading of these early deviations in leadership was not that they were solved simply by removing the responsible leaders; rather, these twin dangers of indiscriminate conflict or fear of revolution-

---

contact with me." He received "three and one-half replies. The 'half' reply came from a noncommittal youth named Li Li-san. Li listened to all I had to say, and then went away without making any definite proposals himself, and our friendship never developed." (Snow, *Red Star Over China*, p. 145.)

43. Cited in Schram, *Mao Tse-tung*, p. 139.

44. Evidence that Li Li-san overinterpreted a Comintern directive to suit his personal inclinations is discussed in James P. Harrison, "The Li Li-san Line and the CCP in 1930" (Part I), *The China Quarterly*, No. 14 (April–June 1963), pp. 188–189; and the "Comment" by Richard Thornton, *ibid.*, No. 18 (April–June 1964), pp. 208–211.

ary struggle were widespread and enduring dangers within the Party. Indeed, in a revealing statement of 1928 he indicated that manifestations of "right" and "left" opportunism could be found even in the behavior of one individual:

> . . . in the last twelve months [of 1927–28] manifestations of opportunism continued to be widespread. On the approach of the enemy, some members, lacking the will to fight, hid in remote hills, which they called "lying in ambush." Other members, though very active, resorted to blind insurrection. . . . *On the approach of the enemy, either reckless battle or precipitate flight would be proposed. Often both ideas emanated from the same individual in the course of the discussions on what military action to take. This opportunist ideology has been gradually corrected through prolonged inner-Party struggle* and through lessons learned from actual events.[45]

In his early efforts to build an effective and politicized military force out of uprooted peasants, "bandit" groups, and defectors from Kuomintang military units, Mao had discovered that ideological education could serve to mobilize and discipline otherwise aimless military action. One of his points of conflict with Li Li-san was his conviction that the peasantry, through education, could serve China's "proletarian" revolution.[46] And by 1938 he asserted that, "in the last seventeen years our Party has learned to use the Marxist-Leninist weapon of ideological struggle against incorrect ideas within the Party on two fronts—against Right opportunism and against 'Left' opportunism." [47]

Mao's stress on ideological struggle seems to be a composite of his belief that without efforts to overcome the traditional reluctance to criticize or engage in conflict China will never complete her social revolution, and the concomitant concern that without some form of discipline such conflict will degenerate into *luan*. Criticism of the behavior of Party members in terms of standards of conduct defined by ideology could increase Party discipline and unity.[48]

45. Mao, "Struggle in the Chingkang Mountains" (1928), *SW,* English, I, pp. 92–93. Emphasis added.

46. *See* Schram, *Mao Tse-tung,* pp. 127, 141.

47. Mao, "The Role of the Chinese Communist Party in the National War" (1938), *SW,* English, II, p. 205.

In Chinese Communist ideological notation, "Left" with quotation marks indicates false or extreme revolutionary views, while Left without quotes is a true revolutionary position.

48. Mao's belief that unity can come through ideological struggle is explored in more detail in the author's analysis, "Mao's Effort to Reintegrate the Chinese Polity: Problems of Conflict and Authority in Chinese Social Processes," in A. Doak Barnett, ed., *Chinese Communist Politics in Action* (Seattle: University of Washington Press, 1969), pp. 322–337.

Yet as he noted with concern in 1929, "Inner-Party criticism . . . sometimes turns into personal attack. As a result it damages the Party organization as well as individuals." [49] Above all, Mao saw that ideology could be used to dilute the personalized quality of authority which had contributed to the fragmentation of the traditional polity into hostile cliques. In 1944 he admitted, however, that change was not easily brought about:

> In the history of our Party there were great struggles against the erroneous lines of Ch'en Tu-hsiu and Li Li-san, and they were absolutely necessary. But there were defects in the methods employed. . . . *Too much stress was placed on the responsibility of individuals,* so that we failed to unite as many people as we could have done for our common endeavour. We should take warning from these two defects. This time, *in dealing with questions of Party history we should lay the stress not on the responsibility of certain individual comrades but on the analysis of the circumstances in which errors were committed, on the content of the errors and on their social, historical and ideological roots,* and this should be done in a spirit of "learning from past mistakes to avoid future ones" and "curing the sickness to save the patient." [50]

Mao's belief in the importance of "ideological struggle" was given its most complete institutional expression in the "Party rectification" (*cheng-feng*) movement of 1942–1944, when the leadership attempted to transmit two decades of Party experience in political struggle to a new generation of peasant and intellectual cadres recruited for the continuing struggle against Japan and the Kuomintang. The key to the rectification mechanism is the "criticism–self-criticism" meeting of approximately a dozen Party members, in which each individual's past behavior and attitudes are subject to group and personal attack in terms of Party policy and the ideological inheritance of Marxism-Leninism. Documents from the first great rectification movement reveal, however, that the basic social rhythm of *ho-p'ing* and *hun-luan* manifests itself within the ranks of the Party, threatening either to stifle corrective criticism or to split Party ranks through vicious personal attack. As expressed by Party Vice Chairman Liu Shao-ch'i, who a little more than two decades later was to be purged for the deviations he criticized in 1941:

> A formal kind of peace and unity have been manifest in the Party, for many comrades ordinarily do not dare to speak or criticize. But

49. Mao, "On Correcting Mistaken Ideas in the Party" (1929), *SW*, English, I, p. 110.
50. Mao, "Our Study and the Current Situation" (1944), *SW*, English, III, pp. 163–164. Emphasis added.

once the continued concealment of contradictions becomes impossible, once the situation becomes serious and the mistakes are exposed, they criticize and fight recklessly; opposition, schism, and organizational confusion develop in the Party, and it is difficult to reestablish order.

Some comrades think that the more savage the intra-Party struggle, the better. . . . If the words are louder, the expressions more violent, and the fangs longer . . . they consider this better and the "most revolutionary thing possible." In the intra-Party struggle and self-criticism, they do not endeavor to do what is proper, do not weigh their opinions, or stop when they have gone far enough; they struggle on with no limit.[51]

Such deviations from what Mao saw to be an effective style of leadership only stressed the degree to which patterns of the traditional political culture continued to manifest themselves in the behavior of those the Party sought to recruit into positions of leadership. For Mao, the promotion of "ideological struggle" to keep Party ranks pure became all the more meaningful. And if such deviations continued to exist within the revolution's "vanguard" organization, it is hardly surprising that we find the major techniques of leadership promoted for dealings with the masses also reflecting concern with the endurance of similar cultural patterns.

51. From Liu Shao-ch'i, "On the Intra-Party Struggle," trans. in Boyd Compton, ed., *Mao's China: Party Reform Documents, 1942–1944* (Seattle: University of Washington Press, 1952), p. 208.

Chapter XII

IDEOLOGY AND ORGANIZATION, I:
THE POWER TO MOBILIZE

If political deviations rooted in the traditional cultural orientations toward authority and conflict created tensions within the Party leadership, these same factors have been of even greater significance in the Party's dealings with the masses, those who are to be "liberated." Success in political revolution for the Chinese Communists, from one point of view, has meant the effective implementation of Leninist principles of organization and political struggle. But as is indicated by the failures of several leadership "lines" during the early years of the movement, simple adoption of foreign organizational techniques and policies has been no guarantee of success. Organization and the ideology of the revolution have had to be used in ways peculiar to Chinese society: Social groups other than the working class have been appealed to for support, and techniques of leadership often at great variance with the experience of Soviet Marxism have been developed in the struggle for state power.

THE IMPORTANCE OF IDEOLOGY:
TRANSFORMING ANXIETY INTO ANGER

The period of the "Great Revolution," when in alliance with the Kuomintang the Communists pressed for revolution in China's urban areas, ended in the bloodshed of 1927. The Communist defeat did more than precipitate a change in Party leadership and policy line. Nationalist armies destroyed the organizational linkages—primarily the labor unions—by which the Party had sought to draw support from the working class. This organizational catastrophe was paralleled by changes in mass attitudes which further deprived the Party of proletarian support, as many recoiled from the "tiger" of Nationalist power.

The reluctance of China's workers to involve themselves in the dangerous world of domestic politics was a constant concern to early Party leaders. After the bloody suppression of the Peking-

Hankow railroad workers' strike in 1923 by troops of the warlord Wu P'ei-fu, General Secretary Ch'en Tu-hsiu had complained:

> The Chinese proletariat is immature both quantitatively and qualitatively. Most of the workers are still imbued with patriarchal notions and their family ties and regional patriotism are extremely strong. These former handicraft workers carry over the habits of their previous existence even when they become industrial workers. They do not feel the need for political action and are still full of ancient superstitions.[1]

If this early incident produced political reticence on the part of the workers, the widespread anti-Communist violence of 1927 shocked them into a full withdrawal. As the historian Benjamin Schwartz has written: "Once again that strain of political cynicism which seems such a deep-rooted Chinese tendency asserted itself. The Chinese workers again became immersed in their own private trials and tribulations."[2] This tendency to "privatize," to withdraw from political involvement to a concern with the details of daily existence, seems more than just "political cynicism," for the harshness of politics stimulated all those anxieties about authority and conflict which were the legacy of a Chinese upbringing. The "ancient superstitions" of which Ch'en complained indicate that the "tiger" of political power was still a vital symbol for China's young proletariat. The social class which Marxist ideology assured Party members was the foundation of the revolution was burdened with its own cultural heritage.

Mao Tse-tung's efforts to enlist the peasantry in the ranks of the revolution encountered similar difficulties. Avoidance of landlord and governmental authority was a time-honored technique by which the agricultural population sought to mitigate the harshness of power in the countryside. While Mao, the enthusiastic young provincial Party leader, appealed for support of his organizational activities with promises of the "storm" of power that was to be found in the peasantry, he himself knew well of the peasants' traditional resistance to political involvement.

Mao's political activities during the period of Kuomintang-Communist collaboration initially had been centered in urban organizational work.[3] It was only after he retired to his native village of Shao Shan in 1925, ill and under attack from Li Li-san and other Party members who opposed excessive reliance on the United Front, that Mao grasped the peasants' revolutionary possibilities.

1. Cited in Benjamin I. Schwartz, *Chinese Communism and the Rise of Mao*, p. 48.
2. *Ibid.*, p. 98.
3. *See* Schram, *Mao Tse-tung*, p. 77.

Formerly I had not fully realized the degree of class struggle among the peasantry, but after the May 30 [1925] Incident, and during the great wave of political activity which followed it, the Hunanese peasantry became very militant. I left my home, where I had been resting, and began a rural organizational campaign. In a few months we had formed more than twenty peasant unions.[4]

The very success of these efforts provoked the opposition of local landlords and the provincial military leader Chao Heng-t'i, who forced Mao to flee to Canton. There during 1926–27 he became affiliated with the Peasant Movement Training Institute, which had been established under the reorganized Kuomintang in 1924.

The first Communist efforts to bring the peasantry into the revolution had been carried out at the initiative of P'eng Pai, a landlord's son from Kwangtung Province. P'eng was the first director of the Peasant Movement Training Institute, and his own experiences in organizing peasants reflect problems of which Mao undoubtedly was aware. Anxiety in the face of authority was a major element in the "political enslavement" of the rural population. As P'eng wrote: "The peasants fear the landlords, literati, and government officials just as a rat fears a cat, daily groaning out their lives under the blows of the landlord's grain-measure, the scholar's fan, and the chains of the official." [5] P'eng saw that the peasants' political passivity was not based simply on the grinding material poverty of their lives; the old culture reinforced their sense of hopeless apathy.

P'eng's initial efforts to propagandize the peasants encountered deeply rooted attitudes that rationalized passive acceptance of a miserable life and justified the turning of aggression against a politically ineffectual self:

We talked to the peasants about the political problems of national calamity and popular harm that China had suffered at the hands of imperialism and the warlords. We asked their opinions, but most of them held to their millennial old concepts: "Until a true son of heaven comes, the world cannot be peaceful. When a son of heaven with a true mandate comes, then even guns will not be able to fire. . . ." Concerning economics, if we talked about all the bitterness and oppression of the poor, they would mostly say: "This is fated by heaven," or, "We did not have good *feng-shui* [geomantic influences]." [6]

4. Snow, *Red Star Over China*, p. 160.
5. P'eng Pai, *"Hai-feng nung-min yün-tung"* [The Hai-feng Peasant Movement], in *Ti-yi-t'zu Kuo-nei Ko-ming Chan-cheng Shih-ch'i ti Nung-min Yün-tung* [The Peasant Movement during the First Period of Domestic Revolutionary War] (Peking: *Jen-min ch'u-pan-she,* 1953), p. 40.
6. *Ibid.,* p. 49.

P'eng recalled that merely the differences in attire and physical mien of a young intellectual seeking to propagandize in the countryside were barriers to communication, for such outward characteristics stimulated the peasants' anxiety to avoid contact with those who seemed to represent state power. After days of ineffective efforts to make contact with peasants in his native Kwangtung district of Hai-feng, P'eng analyzed:

I suddenly began thinking about what we had been saying to the peasants: first, it was much too cultured; much of what we had been saying the peasants didn't understand . . . much of the bookish terminology had to be translated into plain talk. Secondly, my face, body, and dress were not the same as the peasants, and as [they] had long been cheated and oppressed by those with different faces and clothing, once they caught sight of me they assumed I was their enemy; and then when they saw the difference in class, the difference in style, they always were reluctant to get close to me. . . .[7]

Eventually, to P'eng's delight, several younger peasants responded to his verbal appeals at a rural crossroad. The peasants explained to this landlord's son the ways of rural life, and suggested methods by which he might reach those who labored in the countryside. P'eng observed of these few men who responded to his revolutionary agitation: "They were all youthful peasants, less than thirty years of age; they spoke with animation, and were all very lively." [8] Here one sees in its most primitive form the archetype of the political activist: the member of the younger generation not fully socialized by career, not fully bound into society by the responsibilities of family life and occupation, who out of his own "liveliness" responds to the Party's propaganda.

P'eng Pai's efforts to enlist the peasants of coastal Kwangtung Province into the ranks of the revolution bore modest fruit during Chiang K'ai-shek's "Eastern Expedition" of 1925 against the regional warlord Ch'en Ch'iung-ming, when peasants assisted Nationalist military movements. And during the turmoil of 1927, Party-organized rural uprisings in Hai-lu-feng during May and September culminated in the formation of China's first, if short-lived, Soviet government in November.[9] But P'eng's efforts were cut short by his death in 1929 at the hands of the Nationalists, who now feared the mass power that was gravitating into Communist hands as a result

7. *Ibid.*, p. 54.
8. *Ibid.*, p. 56.
9. A detailed analysis of this early effort at peasant mobilization will be found in Shinkichi Eto, "Hai-lu-feng—The First Chinese Soviet Government," *The China Quarterly*, Nos. 8, 9 (October–December 1961; January–March 1962), pp. 161–183, 149–181

mien

of their organizing activities among the workers and peasants. Here again, Mao was to carry on the work that others had begun.

The clearest statement of the lessons of leadership which Mao derived from his own efforts at peasant organization is his "Report on an Investigation of the Peasant Movement in Hunan," written in the spring of 1927, on the eve of the Party's flight to the mountains of South China. Combining ridicule of formal education with a recital of the power of slogans to focus peasant anger, Mao revealed that he had grasped what is perhaps his most basic insight into the process of politicizing peasants:

> Even if ten thousand schools of law and political science had been opened, could they have brought as much political education to the people, men and women, young and old, all the way into the remotest corners of the countryside, as the peasant associations have done in so short a time? I don't think they could. "Down with imperialism!" "Down with the warlords!" "Down with the corrupt officials!" "Down with the local tyrants and evil gentry!"—these political slogans have grown wings, they have found their way to the young, the middle-aged and the old, to the women and children in countless villages, they have penetrated into their minds and are on their lips. For instance, *watch a group of children at play. If one gets angry with another, if he glares, stamps his foot and shakes his fist, you will then immediately hear from the other the shrill cry of "Down with imperialism!"*
>
> In the Hsiangtan area, when the children who pasture the cattle get into a fight, one will act as Tang Sheng-chih, and the other Yeh Kai-hsin [two warlords notable for their respective support of, and opposition to, the "Northern Expedition" of 1926–27]; when one is defeated and runs away, with the other chasing him, it is the pursuer who is Tang Sheng-chih and the pursued, Yeh Kai-hsin. As to the song, "Down with Imperialist Powers!" of course almost every child in the towns can sing it, and now many village children can sing it too.[10]

This description of the interplay between Party slogans and children's play indicates that Mao had come to see that *private and apolitical emotions of aggression could be projected into public issues to serve as the driving force of revolution.* What is "political" about the aggressiveness of a child's game? Nothing, until the slogan of "Down with imperialism!" has linked it to a public issue.

Furthermore, Mao perceived that *the anxiety before authority which underlay the millennial political passivity of China's peasants could be overcome if it were transformed into anger and directed*

10. Mao, "Hunan Report" (1927), *SW,* English, I, pp. 47–48. Emphasis added.

outward through the force of ideology expressed in a political slogan:

> Some of the peasants can also recite Dr. Sun Yat-sen's Testament. They pick out the terms "freedom," "equality," "the Three People's Principles" and "unequal treaties" and apply them, if rather crudely, in their daily life. When somebody who looks like one of the gentry encounters a peasant and stands on his dignity, refusing to make way along a pathway, the peasant will say angrily, "Hey, you local tyrant, don't you know the Three People's Principles?" Formerly when the peasants from the vegetable farms on the outskirts of Changsha entered the city to sell their produce, they used to be pushed around by the police. Now they have found a weapon, which is none other than the Three People's Principles. When a policeman strikes or swears at a peasant selling vegetables, the peasant immediately answers back by invoking the Three People's Principles and that shuts the policeman up. Once in Hsiangtan when a district peasant association and a township peasant association could not see eye to eye, the chairman of the township association declared, "Down with the district peasant association's unequal treaties!" [11]

Ideology thus had the power to fuse passion and political purpose. A revolutionary slogan could give a voice to those who by tradition had shown submissive obedience by "listening to talk" (*t'ing-hua*). And as Mao once asserted with all the enthusiasm of the May Fourth era: "As soon as we arise and let out a shout, [our enemies] will get up and tremble and flee for their lives." [12]

"SPEAK BITTERNESS" (SU-K'U)

For a leadership anxious to maintain the momentum of a peasant revolution, the problem is how to transform sporadic outbursts of violence into sustained political involvement. In a 1965 interview with André Malraux, Mao recalled, "You know I've proclaimed for a long time: we must teach the masses *clearly* what we have received from them *confusedly*. What was it that won over most villages to us? The expositions of bitterness [*su-k'u*]. . . . We organized these expositions in every village . . . but we didn't invent them." [13]

The emotions which Mao came to see as the motive force of peasant political involvement were "received from them confus-

11. *Ibid.*, p. 48.
12. Mao, "The Great Union of the Popular Masses" (1919), in Schram, *PTMTT*, p. 171.
13. André Malraux, *Anti-Memoirs* (New York: Holt, Rinehart and Winston, 1968), p. 362. Emphasis added.

edly," with all the *luan* which Chinese have traditionally associated with feelings of aggression. But Mao conceived the Party's job as using its ideological "consciousness" to clarify, discipline, and direct this energy of revolution, and to organize what would otherwise be sporadic and dispersed action. This task became institutionalized in the various forms of political agitation and ideological "study" developed during the struggle for power.

According to Mao the most basic of these techniques, which he asserted "won over most villages to us," was the *su-k'u* or "speak bitterness" meeting, first used during the period of civil war and then adapted to the struggles of land reform. The terminology of this ritual of political mobilization reveals its links to the traditional political culture. In encouraging peasants to "speak of the bitterness" of rural life, and to "vomit the bitter water" (*t'u k'u-shui*) of injustice suffered at the hands of the rural gentry, local bullies, and warlord troops, the Party urged "the masses" to work up all the rage and resentment that by tradition was "put in the stomach." This combination of ideological study and organized class struggle makes people politically "conscious" in the sense of bringing together the *perception* of mistreatment and injustice with the repressed *emotion*. The separation of thought and feeling which Confucian culture had made the basis of "cultivated" behavior was brought to an end.

In developing this form of political mobilization, Mao began with the belief that simply redistributing land to poor peasants was insufficient for destroying the power of the landlords and rural gentry. The status of this elite derived in part from economic wealth, but even more from the prestige of "the word" of the old culture in the ears of the peasants: "It is they [the gentry] who know how to speak, it is they who know how to write." [14] The peasants could sustain their commitment to the revolution only if they participated directly in the humiliation of those who represented the traditional system of authority. The "land verification movement" of the early 1930s was one of the first efforts to apply such political tactics on a large scale.[15] Mao thus institutionalized his belief that only the tension of conflict between those "mutually related and mutually antagonistic" could sustain a peasant revolution.

14. From a 1933 article by Mao on the land verification movement; cited in Schram, *Mao Tse-tung,* p. 167.

15. This movement is discussed in *ibid.*, pp. 166–168; and in Ilpyong J. Kim, "Mass Mobilization Policies and Techniques Developed in the Period of the Chinese Soviet Republic," in A. Doak Barnett, ed., *Chinese Communist Politics in Action* (Seattle: University of Washington Press, 1969), pp. 78–98.

A P.L.A. *su-k'u* [accusation meeting
for "speaking bitterness" against the old society]
during the civil war of the late 1940s.
From China Pictorial, *October 1967*.

The cultural logic behind this form of political mobilization is hardly obscure, yet its full meaning is difficult to communicate through an abstract analysis. It is basically an experience of participation, not perception. William Hinton's description of the humiliation of a Shansi village leader in 1948 by peasants organized by Party cadres gives a clearer sense of the use of hostility to overcome anxiety before power, and the importance of an organized confrontation in destroying the established authority of a rural society:[16]

> T'ien-ming [a Party cadre] called all the active young cadres and the militiamen of Long Bow [village] together and announced to them the policy of the county government, which was to confront all enemy collaborators and their backers at public meetings, expose their crimes, and turn them over to the county authorities for punishment. He proposed that they start with Kuo Te-yu, the puppet village head. *Having moved the group to anger with a description of Te-yu's crimes,* T'ien-ming reviewed the painful life led by the poor peasants during the occupation and recalled how hard they had all worked and how as soon as they harvested all the grain the puppet officials, backed by army bayonets, took what they wanted, turned over huge quantities to the Japanese devils, forced the peasants to haul it away, and flogged those who refused.
>
> As the silent crowd contracted toward the spot where the accused man stood, T'ien-ming stepped forward . . . "This is our chance. Remember how we were oppressed. The traitors seized our property. They beat us and kicked us. . . .
>
> *Let us speak out the bitter memories.* Let us see that the blood debt is repaid. . . ."
>
> He paused for a moment. *The peasants were listening to every word but gave no sign as to how they felt.*
>
> He spoke plainly. His language and his accent were well understood by the people among whom he had been raised, but *no one moved and no one spoke.*
>
> "Come now, who has evidence against this man?"
>
> Again there was silence.
>
> Kuei-ts'ai, the new vice-chairman of the village, found it intolerable. He jumped up, struck Kuo Te-yu on the jaw with the back of his hand, "Tell the meeting how much you stole," he demanded.
>
> *The blow jarred the ragged crowd.* It was as if an electric spark had tensed every muscle. Not in living memory had any peasant ever struck an official. . . .

16. The following quotes are drawn from Hinton, *Fanshen: A Documentary of Revolution in a Chinese Village* (New York: Monthly Review Press, 1966), pp. 112–116. Emphasis added.

The people in the square waited fascinated as if watching a play. They did not realize that in order for the plot to unfold they themselves had to mount the stage and speak out what was on their minds. *No one moved to carry forward what Kuei-ts'ai had begun.*

Despite the agitator's effort to manipulate mass emotions, and the role of the violent act in breaking the prestige of established authority, the peasants still required some further stimulus to step over the awesome line of passivity into direct, violent action. That stimulus was provided by social pressures focused through organization, and the direct incitement of Party activists:

That evening T'ien-ming and Kuei-ts'ai called together the small groups of poor peasants from various parts of the village and sought to learn what it was that was really holding them back. *They soon found the root of the trouble was fear* of the old established political forces, and their military backers. The old reluctance to move against the power of the gentry, the fear of ultimate defeat and terrible reprisal that had been seared into the consciousness of so many generations lay like a cloud over the peasants' minds and hearts.

. . . The mobilization of the population could spread only slowly and in concentric circles like the waves on the surface of a pond when a stone is thrown in. The stone in this case was a small group of *chi-chi-fen-tzu* or "activists," as the cadres of the new administration and the core of its militia were called.

Evidently the activists in the village which Hinton describes did their work of mobilization well, for he observed:

Emboldened by T'ien-ming's words other peasants began to speak out. They recalled what Te-yu had done to them personally. Several vowed to speak up and accuse him the next morning. After the meeting broke up, the passage of time worked its own leaven. In many a hovel and tumbledown house talk continued well past midnight. Some people were so excited they did not sleep at all. . . .

On the following day the meeting was livelier by far. It began with a sharp argument as to who would make the first accusation and *T'ien-ming found it difficult to keep order.* Before Te-yu had a chance to reply to any questions, a crowd of young men, among whom were several militiamen, surged forward ready to beat him.

Thus the peasants' fear-based passivity finally is overcome through the agitator's mobilization of their resentments and hostilities. Political participation in the revolution is no rational consideration of issues, no "dinner party, or writing an essay, painting a picture, or doing embroidery." The cadre finds it difficult to maintain order over the mobilized peasants. But the masses have been "liberated"; the old order is under attack; the Party has its active followers.

THE VIRTUES OF AN ENEMY

In application, this form of political mobilization had to be meshed with the historical rhythm of China's revolution; that is, the Party leadership had to adapt the content of its appeals for popular support to shifting social and political issues. In the period of the Kiangsi Soviet (1927–1934), issues of land distribution and the evil activities of landlords and counterrevolutionary "big tigers" were used to mobilize peasant support; while appeals to warlord troops based on the harshness of discipline within military units were used to gain recruits. In the effort to rebuild the Party and army after the Long March, social grievances deriving from the system of land tenure, usurious taxation and loan interest, the brutality of warlord troops, and the threat of famine were all issues invoked by the Party in its mobilization efforts.[17]

While the Marxist commitment of the Chinese Communists orients them toward the exploitation of economic issues in appeals for support, underlying their stress on "class" interest is the more basic striving to reach an individual's sense of personal grievance and resentment toward established authority. The landlords are not evil simply because they control greater economic wealth, but because they use their power and social position with cruelty and injustice. The "class struggle" of land reform focuses on personal misuses of power—a landlord's raping of a peasant girl, a rich peasant's refusal to reduce or delay the payment of rent in a year of famine, or the violence with which a "local bully" (*t'u-hao*) treats a tenant farmer—rather than on the injustice of the economic relationship *per se*. Activist "tiger beater" cadres in a factory question workers and foremen for instances of personal abuse or injustice suffered at the hands of the manager,[18] for such willful

17. Detailed analyses of Party appeals during the Yenan period will be found in Donald G. Gillin, "Peasant Nationalism in the History of Chinese Communism," *Journal of Asian Studies,* Vol. XXIII, No. 2 (February 1964), pp. 269–289; and Mark Selden, "The Guerilla Movement in Northwest China: The Origins of the Shensi-Kansu-Ninghsia Border Region," *The China Quarterly,* Nos. 28, 29 (October–December 1966; January–March 1967), pp. 63–81, 61–81.

18. One personal account of the way cadres attempted to exploit worker grievances during the *"wu-fan"* movement of 1952 will be found in Robert Loh and Humphrey Evans, *Escape From Red China* (New York: Coward McCann, 1963), pp. 84–94. A scholarly analysis of this process is contained in John Gardner, "The *Wu Fan* Campaign in Shanghai: A Study in the Consolidation of Urban Control," in Barnett, ed., *Chinese Communist Politics in Action,* pp. 495–523.

misuses of authority communicate most effectively to those long dependent on power. Mao believes that the intense sentiment of aggression is the only motive force powerful enough to sustain the involvement of China's peasants and workers in the tasks of social revolution.

It is from this perspective that we may view the Party's most significant period of growth and institutionalization which came during the war of resistance against Japan. The importance of the Japanese invasion of China for the Communist rise to power can scarcely be doubted. After the "Mukden" incident of late September 1931, when Japanese troops moved to establish direct control over Manchuria, Chiang K'ai-shek was forced to call an uncertain conclusion to the third "Encirclement and Suppression" campaign against the Kiangsi Soviet. The diversion and division of Nationalist military resources remained a constant factor in Chiang's efforts to deal a final death-blow to the Communists up to the final defeat of Japan in 1945.

The war against Japan provided a political context which the Communists were able to use effectively to establish the legitimacy of their politico-military insurgency. While they did not take the initiative in kidnapping Chiang K'ai-shek at Sian in December of 1936, their response to this incident enabled them to acquire a measure of formal recognition as a patriotic political movement in the wartime "united front" with the Nationalists.[19]

Perhaps most basically, however, the impact of the Japanese invasion of China proper after the summer of 1937 created the social conditions that the Party had learned to exploit effectively in recruiting and motivating supporters for its cause. In the early days of the peasant movement, Party activities had been most successful in those rural areas where established authority—in the form of clan organizations, secret societies, and gentry-led local militia—was weak or disrupted.[20] Similarly, during the Japanese occupation, the undermining of established political relationships "freed" people for new commitments. And the Party provided one well-organized alternative to submission to the foreigner's political order.

The impact of Japanese military operations in North China was

19. The most recent effort to evaluate the Sian Incident is Lyman P. Van Slyke, *Enemies and Friends: The United Front in Chinese Communist History* (Stanford: Stanford University Press, 1967), pp. 75–91. This analysis stresses the interpretation that the Chinese Communists decided to press for Chiang K'ai-shek's release *before* they received similar instructions from Stalin, because they saw the United Front as essential to their own survival.

20. These findings are presented in Roy Mark Hofheinz, *The Peasant Movement and Rural Revolution: Chinese Communists in the Countryside, 1923–1927* (unpublished Ph.D. dissertation, Harvard University, 1966).

another basic aspect of the period of the War of Resistance which enabled the Party to consolidate its new base in the Shensi-Kansu-Ningsia border region. In the most detailed study of this period of Party history, Chalmers Johnson indicates that it was the cruelty of the Japanese, their inability or unwillingness to apply military force with discrimination and establish that degree of security and order which was the limited expectation of China's peasants toward political authority, which mobilized those who traditionally had been passive before power:

> . . . Japan had earned the hatred of the Chinese people. This hatred derived from Japanese attempts to subjugate the countryside by force. . . . The threat of terror and devastation was a constant ingredient in Chinese rural life for seven years; the party that met this challenge with an effective policy and the organizational ability to make this policy work won the support of the peasant population as no other political group has done in recent times.[21]

It is clear from the extent of direct Chinese collaboration with the invading Japanese, and the passive resistance policy which Chiang K'ai-shek adopted in a situation of indigenous political fragmentation and military weakness, that the traditional attitude of accommodation to a superior power remained a durable political tactic even in the China of the 1940s. One can only speculate as to what would have happened had the Japanese been more discriminating in their use of power, or had they not involved themselves at the same time in a multi-front war in the Pacific and Southeast Asia. Chinese history provides the precedents of Mongolian and Manchurian invaders successfully allying themselves with indigenous Chinese to establish durable "alien" dynasties.

To the Communists at the time, the prospect of such accommodation had all the reality of Wang Ching-wei's collaborationist regime at Nanking; and the strategic threat to themselves inherent in further Chinese concessions to the Japanese was very great. As Mao wrote in 1938:

> The enemy will go all out to wreck China's united front, and the traitor organizations in all the occupied areas will merge into a so-called "unified government." Owing to the loss of big cities and the hardships of war, vacillating elements within our ranks will clamour for compromise, and pessimism will grow to a serious extent.[22]

21. Chalmers A. Johnson, *Peasant Nationalism and Communist Power: The Emergence of Revolutionary China, 1937–1945* (London: Oxford University Press, 1963), p. 49.

22. Mao, "On Protracted War," (1938), *SW,* English, II, p. 139.

By mid-1940 the increasing isolation of the limited forces of active resistance within China compounded these tendencies toward political accommodation with the Japanese. The United States was still sixteen months away from Pearl Harbor, and in Europe resistance to German expansion had nearly collapsed, diminishing prospects for outside assistance and making even further isolation an almost certain prospect. To oppose the tendency to "compromise" and to reduce the threat of increased Japanese and Nationalist military pressure on their own base area, the Communists launched what was called the "Hundred Regiments Offensive," forcing the war to a more active level where political accommodation became more difficult for wavering "patriotic" forces within the United Front.[23] As a result of this initiative, Japanese military operations against Communist areas in the Northwest increased sharply, producing serious difficulties in material existence and even a flagging of determination within the Party itself.

It is some measure of the effectiveness of the Party's organizational forms of indoctrination and control—most obvious in the "rectification" or *cheng-feng* procedure developed during this period —that discipline was maintained and economic self-sufficiency made a near-reality through the stress on self-reliance (*tzu-li keng-sheng*) in which even the military was committed to tasks of production. And as Johnson's analysis concludes, in maintaining its own discipline, the Party was able to gain substantial popular support:

23. During the Cultural Revolution supporters of Mao alleged that P'eng Teh-huai had, "without the knowledge of the Party Central Committee . . . waged on his own authority 'the big battle of a hundred regiments,' thereby causing serious setbacks to the development of the North China base areas and of our army." (*See* "Principal Crimes of P'eng Teh-huai, Big Ambitionist and Schemer," Canton *Chingkangshan* and *Kwang-tung Wen-i Chan-Pao* [September 5, 1967]; translated in *Survey of the China Mainland Press* [Hong Kong], No. 4047 [October 25, 1967], p. 9.)

While the allegation is absurd taken at face value, there is additional—if largely indirect—evidence that Mao may not have approved of the Hundred Regiments Offensive. He evidently feared the risks of seriously degrading the Party's military capability, but he was not in full control of military policy in 1940. Semiofficial histories of this period, such as Hu Chiao-mu's *Thirty Years of the Communist Party of China* do not mention the offensive, a strange omission in view of the Party's claim of its leading role in the anti-Japanese war. Mao's own writings of this time criticize "the ultra-Left military policy" of "decisive battles" and those who would "deny the basic role of guerilla warfare" in the resistance. (*See* "On Policy" [December 1940], *SW*, English, II, pp. 441–442.) Mao may not have approved of the conventional military offensive of the summer of 1940, but was probably "outvoted" by collective Party leadership.

In spite of the shrinkage of the guerilla areas and the severe losses suffered in them, the Communists reaped certain advantages from the fact that there was now hardly a village left in Hopei or Shansi that was not half-burned or worse. The revolution spread and became irreversible in the years 1941–42. Instead of breaking the tie between the Eighth Route Army and the peasantry, the Japanese policy drove the two together into closer alliance. This alliance derived partly from nationalism (hatred of the invader), but to a large extent it was purely a matter of survival.[24]

As this passage only parenthetically concludes, it was at base "hatred of the invader" and fear for survival which mobilized the peasants, rather than a more abstract sentiment of Nationalism. Mao has made the same point himself:

> . . . after occupying northern China . . . the enemy everywhere pursued a barbarous policy and practised naked plunder. Had China capitulated, every Chinese would have become a slave without a country. . . . Under the flag of the "Rising Sun" all Chinese are forced to be docile subjects, beasts of burden forbidden to show the slightest trace of Chinese national spirit. This barbarous enemy policy will be carried deeper into the interior of China. . . . [It] has enraged all strata of the Chinese people. *This rage is engendered by the reactionary and barbarous character of Japan's war—"there is no escape from fate," and hence an absolute hostility has crystallized.*[25]

Some scholars have appropriately questioned Johnson's analysis for its stress on the Japanese invasion as the *antecedent* of Party and Red Army expansion,[26] when important periods of growth in these organizations occurred well before the actual invasion. The fact remains, however, that the Party had learned to use effectively issues like the threat of foreign invasion and the injustices of rural life, and to take advantage of social dislocation, in tapping those personal motives of resentment, fear, and hatred which Mao saw to be the driving force of revolution. Party appeals to a sense of "Nationalism," like the earlier stress on issues of class struggle, were important because they helped to give political orientation to an uprooted and threatened rural population and rationalized their commitment to larger political objectives.

For Mao himself, the war against Japan strengthened his earlier belief in the need to involve peasants personally in "struggle" with

24. Johnson, *Peasant Nationalism and Communist Power*, pp. 58–59.
25. Mao, "On Protracted War" (1938), *SW*, English, II, p. 129. Emphasis added.
26. *See*, in particular, Gillin, "Peasant Nationalism in the History of Chinese Communism," pp. 269–289.

[class] enemies, for it was once again the tension between those who were "mutually related and mutually antagonistic" which enabled the Party and army to expand and discipline their ranks. As he phrased it himself in a public statement in 1939: "To be attacked by the enemy is not a bad thing, but a good thing." [27] Enemies are good because they help the Party to sustain popular involvement in the process of social revolution.

DOWN WITH POLITICAL DEPENDENCE!

The years of resistance against the Japanese occupation were a time of major institutional growth and consolidation for the Party, largely because the political context of war against a foreign invader produced a more complete convergence of interests between the Party and people. Where earlier appeals for support of the revolutionary cause had been based on socially divisive issues of class conflict, the Japanese aggression enabled appeals to be phrased on the basis of national unity. Yet Mao's underlying concern was with the unacceptability of a position of passive accommodation to one more cruel and humiliating power. The Japanese effectively dramatized to the Chinese population Mao's personal striving: the desire to eliminate political dependency.

This way of looking at the wartime intersection of interests between Mao and China's millions, however, abstracts the leader's personal objectives from the broad popular appeals for heroic resistance in the face of a foreign threat. It is important not to obscure the very significant differences in perception and motivation with which various people "read" the Party's wartime slogans. Such differences are the basis for understanding why popular support of the Party was to a certain degree partial and temporary and why "con-

27. Mao, "To Be Attacked by the Enemy is not a Bad Thing but a Good Thing" (1939), in *Selected Readings from the Works of Mao Tse-tung*, pp. 130–132.

In a 1964 interview with visiting Frenchmen, Mao told an anecdote which underscores his perception of the positive role which the Japanese enemy played in the Party's rise to power: "Recently a Japanese merchant came to see me and said, 'I very much regret that Japan invaded China.' I replied to him: 'You are not being fair. Of course, the aggression wasn't fair either, but there is no need to apologize. If the Japanese had not occupied half of China, it would have been impossible for the entire Chinese population to rise and fight the Japanese invader. And that resulted in our army strengthening itself by a million men, and in the liberated bases the population increased to 100 millions.'

"That is why I said to him (pause and smile): 'Should I thank you?' "

tradictions" continue to exist to this day within the Communist Party and between the Party and the people. The danger of political passivity was presented to the people by Communist propaganda in a specific manner: "Being passive before *Japanese* power is dangerous; the invading imperialists are cruel and will kill you and destroy your property. You had better stand up and fight." And when the killing and destruction occurred, the Party helped the people to fight. But Mao and certain of his followers read the problem in more general terms: "The condition of being passive and dependent on any power is dangerous and should be destroyed through a revolution in favor of self-reliance."

For most Chinese, the Japanese occupation represented a specific problem of a harsh and humiliating foreign presence, a context in which the security and status of a dependency relationship could not be established. But the normative cultural pattern was to see dependency as the most natural of conditions in relation to authority. The problem was, as it always had been, that the relationship, far from being worthy of destruction, was just not properly implemented. (As was expressed so often in our interview characterizations of dealings with authoritative individuals: "The elder brother *should* be polite and yielding; the younger brother *should* respect the elder." "Teachers *ought* to take responsibility for their students, they *should* treat them like their own offspring. . . . Students *ought* to respect the teacher." "A good leader *should* be just; he *should* solve all the people's problems.") And if the ideals of life's authoritative relationships were not lived up to in practice, at least the dependent individual could bide his time in *hopes* of justice or of one day himself gaining the authoritative position. In sum, many of those who supported the Party did so in order to save a China in which all that their traditional experience told them could be good and proper might be realized. But Mao and certain of his followers sought popular support in the striving for a "new China," a new social order to be realized by a fundamental revolution against the authority system of the old.

During the War of Resistance this discrepancy in objective was obscured behind the symbols of Nationalism. In recruiting people to its wartime cause, the Party created a politico-military organization which was subsequently turned against the Nationalists in the final contest of the unresolved civil war. But as we shall see in Part Four, with the attainment of full power, Mao and his close colleagues faced another series of struggles between their own revolutionary goals and the personal inclinations of the Chinese people—a test of political style and social objective that culminated in the Cultural Revolution of the mid-1960s.

ORGANIZATION: A FRAMEWORK FOR PARTICIPATION

While social injustice and the cruelty of a foreign invader provided the motivational context of Party growth, Mao also found that the organizational forms which the Party had developed to harness this mass energy could be used to heighten popular involvement in the tasks of revolution. His personal rejection of political dependency found expression in efforts to develop a new "work style" (*tso-feng*) in the way Party cadres asserted their authority over "the masses."

In his 1964 recollections to André Malraux, Mao stressed: "You must realize that before us, among the masses, no one had addressed themselves to women or to the young. Nor, of course, to the peasants. For the first time in their lives, every one of them felt *involved*." [28] The capacity of a political organization to involve, and not just to control, was revealed to Mao in the way that members of the traditional "protective" forms of social association found they could express their resentments against the old society through Party-organized peasant associations:

> . . . members of the secret societies have joined the peasant associations, in which they can openly and legally play the hero and vent their grievances, so that there is no further need for the secret "mountain," "lodge," "shrine," and "river" forms of organization. *In killing the pigs and sheep of the local tyrants and evil gentry and imposing heavy levies and fines, they have adequate outlets for their feelings against those who oppressed them.*[29]

A more revolutionary insight into the mobilizing capacity of organizational life was that by altering the traditional dependency relationship—by delegating some responsibility to the individual and by eliminating the physical brutality of traditional military life—the Party could produce a "spiritual liberation" and gain the active commitment of those who had long been politically passive:

> Apart from the role played by the Party, the reason why the Red Army has been able to carry on in spite of such poor material conditions and such frequent engagements is its practise of democracy. The officers do not beat the men; officers and men receive equal treatment; soldiers are free to hold meetings and to speak out; trivial formalities have been done away with; and the accounts are open for all to inspect. The soldiers handle the mess arrangements. . . . All this gives great satisfaction to the soldiers. The newly captured soldiers in particular feel that our army and the Kuomintang army are

28. André Malraux, *Anti-Memoirs*, p. 361.
29. Mao, "Hunan Report" (1927), *SW*, English, I, pp. 52–53. Emphasis added.

worlds apart. *They feel spiritually liberated,* even though material conditions in the Red Army are not equal to those in the White [Kuomintang] Army. The very soldiers who had no courage in the White Army yesterday are very brave in the Red Army today; such is the effect of democracy. The Red Army is like a furnace in which all captured soldiers are transmuted the moment they come over. In China the army needs democracy as much as the people do. Democracy in our army is an important weapon for undermining the feudal mercenary army.[30]

That Mao labels this system "democracy" when it lacks the checks on the use of power basic to Western interpretations of that term seems irrelevant within the social context of China, and in a period of violent revolution. Simply the contrast with the traditional use of power was quite enough to produce a "spiritual liberation" and gain the active commitment of those who by cultural inheritance assumed there was no alternative to the harshness of dependency.

Mao's *insight* into the heightened popular commitment which would come with a new style of authority, however, was far from sufficient for realizing a new Party "work-style," for his perception conflicted with deeply rooted attitudes held by those who joined the movement. As Mao complained:

> People's political power has been established everywhere at county, district and township levels, but more in name than in reality. . . . Authority is monopolized by the Party committees. . . . Not that there are no councils of workers, peasants and soldiers worthy of the name, but they are very few. The reason is the lack of propaganda and education concerning this new political system. *The evil feudal practise of arbitrary dictation is so deeply rooted in the minds of the people and even of the ordinary Party members that it cannot be swept away at once;* when anything crops up, they choose the easy way and have no liking for the bothersome democratic system. Democratic centralism can be widely and effectively practised in mass organizations only when its efficacy is demonstrated in revolutionary struggle and the masses understand that it is the best means of mobilizing their forces and is of the utmost help in their struggle.[31]

While the pattern of authority exercising a monopoly of power and initiative remained rooted in the personalities of Party members, the Maoist leadership was, and continues to be, conscious of the political energies that could be released by altering the traditional relationship to authority, by giving the individual the opportunity

30. Mao, "Struggle in the Chingkang Mountains" (1928), *SW,* English, I, p. 83. Emphasis added.
31. *Ibid.,* pp. 90–91. Emphasis added.

to liberate the grievances that tradition forced him to "hold in," and by delegating certain personal responsibility. The Party has tried to face directly the abuses of power characteristic of the politics of dependency:

> The ugly evil of bureaucracy, which no comrade likes, must be thrown into the cesspit. The methods which all comrades should prefer are those that appeal to the masses, i.e., those which are welcomed by all workers and peasants. . . . Commandism is another manifestation. To all appearances, persons given to commandism are not slackers; they give the impression of being hard workers. But in fact cooperatives set up by commandist methods will not succeed, and even if they appear to grow for a time, they cannot be consolidated. In the end the masses will lose faith in them, which will hamper their development. . . . We must reject commandism; what we need is energetic propaganda to convince the masses . . . and do all work . . . in accordance with the actual conditions and the real feelings of the masses.[32]

To work with the "real feelings" of a people is not easy when their traditions have stressed the holding in of emotions; and to mobilize their active involvement in politics is problematical when traditional attitudes toward authority endure in the personalities of leaders and led alike. The skills of leadership which were the legacy of nearly three decades of political struggle, however, enabled the Party to use its ideology and organization to mobilize popular "consciousness." On the eve of victory in the civil war Mao wrote with satisfaction of the effectiveness of the *su-k'u* and political indoctrination in motivating the People's Liberation Army:

> The correct unfolding of the movement for pouring out grievances (the wrongs done to the labouring people by the old society and by the reactionaries) and the three check-ups (on class origin, performance of duty, and will to fight) has greatly heightened the political consciousness of commanders and fighters throughout the army in the fight for the emancipation of the exploited working masses for nationwide land reform and for the destruction of the common enemy of the people, the Chiang K'ai-shek bandit gang.[33]

32. Mao, "Pay Attention to Economic Work" (1933), *SW*, English, I, p. 135.
33. Mao, "On the Great Victory in the Northwest and on the New Type of Ideological Education Movement in the Liberation Army" (1948), *SW*, English, IV, p. 214.

Chapter XIII

IDEOLOGY AND ORGANIZATION, II:
THE POWER TO DISCIPLINE

Given the burden of passivity before power which was the legacy of China's traditional political culture, problems of mobilization predominated in Party efforts to gain support. Yet maintaining discipline over those mobilized was also a problem, largely because tradition provided no cultural framework for the purposeful, politicized promotion of conflict or for limited ways of challenging established authority.

In earlier chapters we saw that the Confucian social ethic placed all expressions of aggression beyond the pale of respectability. Unlike the Samurai warriors of Japan or the knights of feudal Europe, whose skills in violence became wedded to a moral ethic or code of the established social order, the military in China was an illegitimate element of society in the eyes of the imperial literati. The universal human capacity for aggression remained unallied to any set of abstract social principles which might have tempered or channeled conflict into relatively harmless, if not constructive, social activity. The Confucianists sought no "war" with nature, only accommodation; and China's scientific insights never became translated into attempts to control a threatening physical environment. Commercial activity remained bound within a state-controlled framework of monopoly enterprise, stunting the growth of entrepreneurship which in other societies (and in Chinese communities overseas) developed through the stimulus of competition. And in the realm of politics, the pattern of dependence on the moral wisdom of an elite class of "cultivated" scholar-administrators preempted the development of forms of controlled competition for power which might have checked abuses of authority.

To be sure, the Confucian polity required the application of military power to "pacify" those who disturbed the tranquillity of the empire; but, beyond the scholar-generals who directed such activity, there developed no respected officer corps and military tradition which merited prestige and social meaning among the institutions of imperial China. For the uneducated lower leadership ranks and the peasant boys dragooned into imperial or warlord armies, the military life had little rationale beyond a brotherhood of violence and the security of power.

The only meaning of armed force for the farming population was the apparently aimless foraging and destruction by the "pacification" troops who lived off the land. The military was a tiger which ate up their source of livelihood, turning the world into *luan*. Even the marginal life of banditry was nothing more than the last recourse of desperate men run afoul of the standards of Confucian justice—a tradition of escape in which violence had only the most elemental meaning of self-protection and survival. In traditional Chinese society conflict thus acquired no significance short of "confusion," the breaking away from all social restraints of impulses for hostility. Aggression had no meaning beyond security or self-assertion, no tie to moral values or constructive social tasks.

VIOLENCE FOR THE REVOLUTION

During the early years of Red Army growth this cultural tradition of self-serving, undisciplined violence was manifest in warlordism and the activities of local protective associations which had long provided some relief from the harshness of imperial power. From the perspective of its long-term objectives, a major Party goal was to eliminate the warlords and their undisciplined armies and to make the defensive secret societies unnecessary within a framework of national political unity. But the immediate need to recruit a military force which could be used to attain these goals required that the Party, now isolated from a "proletarian base" in the mountains of south China, draw on these very groups for manpower.[1] And as Mao wrote in 1926, a major problem was how to instill in the new recruits the discipline required to fight for long-term Party goals:

> . . . there is the fairly large lumpen-proletariat, made up of peasants who have lost their land and handicraftsmen who cannot get work. They lead the most precarious existence of all. In every part of the country they have their mutual-aid organizations for political and economic struggle, for instance, the Triad Society in Fukien and

1. *See* Stuart R. Schram, "Mao Tse-tung and Secret Societies," *The China Quarterly*, No. 27 (July–September 1966), pp. 1–13.

One estimate has given the "class" composition of the Red Army in the early 1930s as 57.5 percent peasant, 28 percent soldier, 8.75 percent "bandit," and 5.75 percent worker. Cited in James P. Harrison, "The Li Li-san Line and the CCP in 1930, Part I," *The China Quarterly*, No. 14 (April–June 1963), p. 184.

Kwangtung, the Society of Brothers in Hunan, Hupeh, Kweichow and Szechuan, . . . and the Green Band in Shanghai and elsewhere. *One of China's difficult problems is how to handle these people. Brave fighters but apt to be destructive, they can become a revolutionary force if given proper guidance.*[2]

Organization and the Party's ideology came to be seen as sources of discipline, even as they were used as instruments of mobilization. In his "Hunan Report," Mao listed as one of the fourteen great accomplishments of the peasant associations the elimination of banditry, for the growth of these rural political organizations provided a framework within which indiscriminate violence found social meaning: ". . . [our] armies are recruiting large numbers of soldiers and many of the 'unruly' have joined up. Thus the evil of banditry has ended with the rise of the peasant movement." [3]

A more revolutionary innovation was to seek to discipline these peasant and "bandit" troops through political indoctrination. Mao's military cohort in building the Red Army, Chu Teh, recalled that even the "modern" armies that had helped to overthrow the Ch'ing dynasty sustained the tradition of brutal treatment of the enlisted ranks, an approach to "discipline" that only encouraged the *in*discipline with which the common soldiers treated the rural population:

> . . . the soldiers of the Reform Army [of Yunnan] had been given modern military training, weapons, and uniforms, but nothing had been done to change their minds. No changes had been made in their treatment as men, and they were still subjected to the same brutalizing humiliating beatings and cursings as in past ages. Not even the revolutionary intellectuals could think of the common soldier as anything but a ruffian who had to be treated like an animal.[4]

In developing an organizational style in which officers were not allowed to beat their men, the Party taught a lesson in the disciplining of aggression; and in allowing enlisted ranks to criticize the errors of their officers, conflict found control within the rationale of military effectiveness and the goals of a revolutionary organization:

> Always after each campaign, we held two conferences: the first of commanders and the second of commanders and men together where the battle or campaign was analyzed. . . . Each fighter and each com-

2. Mao, "Analysis of the Classes in Chinese Society (1926), *SW*, English, I, p. 19. Emphasis added.

3. Mao, "Hunan Report" (1927), *SW*, English, I, p. 53.

4. Quoted in Agnes Smedley, *The Great Road: The Life and Times of Chu Teh* (New York: Monthly Review Press, 1956), p. 87.

mander had complete freedom of speech in these joint conferences. They could criticize one another or any aspect of the general plan or the way it had been carried out. . . . Any commander who cursed or struck a fighter or otherwise violated army rules had to answer before this court of public opinion.[5]

Marxist orthodoxy held that industrial workers constituted the only class which was disciplined and politically conscious enough to lead the struggle for Socialism. But this article of revolutionary faith was largely academic after the 1927 rout from the urban areas. Survival required the recruitment of available manpower regardless of class origin. Under the force of these circumstances, Mao came to believe that an army constituted of declassed peasants and defectors from "White" or warlord military units could be "proletarianized" through political indoctrination. As he asserted in a 1928 defense of his unorthodox army-building efforts:

> . . . the Red Army consists partly of workers and peasants and partly of lumpen-proletariat. Of course, it is inadvisable to have too many of the latter. But they are able to fight, and as fighting is going on every day with mounting casualties, it is already no easy matter to get replacements even from among them. *In these circumstances the only solution is to intensify political training.*
>
> The majority of the Red Army soldiers come from the mercenary armies, but their character changes once they are in the Red Army. . . . After receiving political education, the Red Army soldiers have become class-conscious, learned the essentials of distributing land, setting up political power, arming the workers and peasants, etc., and they know they are fighting for themselves, for the working class and the peasantry. Hence they can endure the hardships of the bitter struggle without complaint.[6]

These efforts at political indoctrination were inherently limited, however, by a combination of the cultural background of such recruits and the high casualty rates in Red Army units, which saw the loss of many of those whose attitudes might have undergone real change. The army of the Kiangsi era continued to reflect the traditions of its social environment. As a Party Central Committee report of 1930 complained: "In many of the partisan bands, lumpen-proletarian ideas exist, often expressing themselves in unorganized burning, plundering and killing."[7] In this situation, a political

5. *Ibid.*, p. 292.
6. Mao, "The Struggle in the Chingkang Mountains" (1928), *SW*, English, I, p. 81.
7. Cited in Harrison, "The Li Li-san Line and the CCP in 1930, Part I," p. 184.

commissar system provided an organizational solution to a cultural problem. A cadre of specialists in indoctrination were diffused through the military organization to sustain the discipline and political orientation lacking in the enlisted ranks:

> Experience has proved that the system of Party representatives must not be abolished. The Party representative is particularly important at company level, since Party branches are organized on a company basis. He has to see that the soldiers' committee carries out political training, to guide the work of the mass movements, and to serve concurrently as the secretary of the Party branch. Facts have shown that the better the company Party representative, the sounder the company, and that the company commander can hardly play this important political role.[8]

It is a measure of both the strength of purpose and the organizational skills of the Party leadership that under such adverse circumstances the successes of the Kiangsi period were attained. A group of several hundred would-be revolutionaries was able to build an effective military organization up to a strength of nearly half a million men between 1928 and 1934. Out of this force less than 20,000 survived the Long March; yet these "refugees" remained a cadre of organizational skills and political commitment capable of reconstituting itself. In the thirteen years of Resistance War and civil conflict between 1936 and 1948 this leadership core expanded itself into a force nearly two-and-a-half million men strong.[9]

DISCIPLINE THROUGH ORGANIZED CRITICISM

As was discussed earlier in Chapter XI on "deviations" in leadership, Mao came to believe that the controlled conflict of "rectification"—in which Party members underwent group and self-criticism on the basis of ideological norms and operational performance—provided a way of institutionalizing the discipline necessary to promote revolutionary social change. This organizational innovation was in tension, however, with the traditional image of authority as immune to criticism and the enduring use of aggression as a form of self-assertion. In his 1937 attack on "liberalism" (*tzu-yu chu-yi*) —a concept more accurately translated as "self-ism" or just plain "selfishness"—Mao indicated that the basic impulse behind this "deviation" was

8. Mao, "The Struggle in the Chingkang Mountains" (1928), *SW*, English, I, pp. 81–82.

9. These figures are from Edgar Snow, *Red Star Over China*, pp. 189–191, 215; and Mao, "A Circular on the Situation" (1948), *SW*, English, IV, p. 223.

to let things slide for the sake of peace and friendship . . . and to refrain from principled argument because [a person] is an old acquaintance, a fellow townsman, a schoolmate, a close friend, a loved one, an old colleague, or old subordinate. Or to touch on the matter lightly instead of going into it thoroughly, so as to keep on good terms.[10]

Once such reluctance to engage in "principled argument" was overcome, however, the problem became one of *luan,* the undisciplined release of personal hostility:

> To indulge in irresponsible criticism in private instead of actively putting forward one's suggestions to the organization. To say nothing to people to their faces but to gossip behind their backs, or to say nothing at a meeting but to gossip afterwards. To show no regard at all for the principles of collective life but to follow one's own inclinations. This is a second type [of liberalism].[11]

At its worst, the indiscriminate use of criticism worked to fragment the organization into hostile cliques, for such conflict had no significance beyond the venting of personal grievance or an effort at self-assertion:

> . . . in order to enforce their will, the exponents of the third "Left" line invariably and indiscriminately branded all Party comrades who found the wrong line impracticable and who therefore expressed doubt, disagreement or dissatisfaction, or did not actively support the wrong line or firmly carry it out; they stigmatized these comrades with such labels as "Right opportunism," "the rich peasant line," "the Lo Ming line," "the line of conciliation" and "double-dealing," *waged "ruthless struggle" against them and dealt them "merciless blows," and even conducted these "inner-Party struggles" as if they were dealing with criminals and enemies.* This wrong kind of inner-Party struggle . . . eliminated the democratic spirit of criticism and self-criticism, turned Party discipline into mechanical discipline and fostered tendencies to blind obedience and docility. . . . Such factionalist errors very greatly weakened the Party, causing dislocation between higher and lower organizations and many other anomalies in the Party.[12]

What information is available on the post-Liberation promotion of "criticism–self-criticism" indicates that reluctance to give and accept criticism endures, as does the "left" inclination to criticize irresponsibly or to retaliate against those who have exposed one's

10. Mao, "Combat Liberalism" (1937), *SW,* English, II, p. 31.
11. *Ibid.*
12. Mao, "Our Study and the Current Situation: Appendix: Resolution on Certain Questions in the History of Our Party" (1945), *SW,* English, III, pp. 209–210. Emphasis added.

shortcomings.[13] Yet for all the difficulties in institutionalizing this form of mediated political combat, its persistence represents Mao's conviction that the traditional personalized and family-centered concept of authority can only acquire a larger social meaning if wedded to an ideology, and that social change will endure only in a critical dialogue between those who wield Party power and the creative, yet conservative, "masses."

THE "LUAN" OF LAND REFORM

During the war years of the second United Front with the National-ists, the problem of maintaining discipline over mass energies was inconsequential in relation to the basic problem of sustaining re-sistance to the foreign invader. The Japanese provided a clear tar-get for the promotion of conflict. With the defeat of Japan, how-ever, the civil conflict again became China's main "contradiction"; and the problem of *luan* acquired a new reality.

In resuming attacks on its domestic enemies the Party faced the problem of disciplining the struggle so that its political objective of destroying the power of the Nationalists did not degenerate into a confusion of personalized aggression. After years of decentralized partisan warfare, Mao called for the establishment of a system of centralized political reporting which would tie scattered political and military units to Central Committee control and "overcome any conditions of indiscipline or anarchy existing in the Party and the army." [14]

A more basic problem of maintaining discipline in conflict was presented by the process of land reform, promoted concurrently with the civil war to gain peasant support for the Party and to eliminate Nationalist influence in the rural areas. The personalized hatreds which Party cadres stimulated in the village "speak bitter-ness" struggles were difficult to control. The peasants, lacking the discipline of political "consciousness," tended to be indiscriminate in using the violence of land reform to settle old personal grudges or to embark on an orgy of "eating up" the material possessions of

13. *See* the study based on Party documents and emigré interviews by Martin K. Whyte, *Small Groups and Political Rituals in Communist China* (unpublished Ph.D. dissertation, Harvard University, 1970), esp. Ch. I. Ad-ditional material on this subject will be found in the author's "Mao's Effort to Reintegrate the Chinese Polity," in Barnett, ed., *Chinese Communist Pol-itics in Action,* pp. 322–337, and "On Activism and Activists," *The China Quarterly,* No. 39 (July–September 1969), pp. 92–114.

14. Introductory footnote to Mao, "On Setting Up a System of Reports" (1948), *SW,* English, IV, p. 178.

their class enemies. The Party faced the danger of "tailism"—of becoming a mere appendage manipulated by the peasant violence it sought to use:

> . . . on the question of identifying class status [the Party organization in the Shansi-Suiyuan Liberated Area] adopted an ultra-Left policy; . . . on the question of how to destroy the feudal system it laid too much stress on unearthing the landlords' hidden property; and . . . on the question of dealing with the demands of the masses it failed to make a sober analysis and raised the sweeping slogan, "Do everything as the masses want it done." With respect to the latter point, which is a question of the Party's relationship with the masses, the Party must lead the masses to carry out all their correct ideas in the light of the circumstances and educate them to correct any wrong ideas they may entertain.[15]

A second source of "leftist" *luan* resided within the Party itself. Cadres tended to get carried away with their own revolutionary enthusiasm in the land reform process, leaving the masses behind and excessively broadening the "scope of attack" on rural enemies. The danger inherent in over-enthusiastic or aggressive cadres "broadening the scope of attack" was that the Party would be led into *luan,* into attacking "the People" and not their enemies, thus provoking popular hatred against itself rather than just helping to vent old hatreds derived from "feudal exploitation":

> . . . in the fierce struggles in the land reform of the past year, the Shansi-Suiyuan Party organization failed to adhere unequivocally to the Party's policy of strictly forbidding beating and killing without discrimination [*luan-sha, luan-ta*]. As a result, in certain places some landlords and rich peasants were needlessly put to death, and the bad elements in the rural areas were able to exploit the situation to take revenge and foully murdered a number of working people.[16]

Throughout his career Mao has tended to take the position that revolutionary excesses are better than no revolution at all and that injustices done to individuals in the promotion of class conflict can be corrected at a later date. Nevertheless, it can be said that Mao reveals no personal fascination with violence for its own sake or a compulsive need to assert political control by doing violence to opposition elements. He has seen the Party's task as one of disciplining physical violence, depersonalizing political conflict, and getting people concerned with questions of social change:

15. Mao, "Speech at a Conference of Cadres in the Shansi-Suiyuan Liberated Area" (1948), *SW,* English, IV, p. 232.
16. *Ibid.,* p. 229.

The aim of the land reform is to abolish the system of feudal exploitation, that is, to *eliminate the feudal landlords as a class, not as individuals*. Therefore a landlord must receive the same allotment of land and property as does a peasant and must be made to learn productive labour and join the ranks of the nation's economic life. *Except for the most heinous counterrevolutionaries and local tyrants, who have incurred the bitter hatred of the broad masses, who have been proved guilty and who therefore may and ought to be punished, a policy of leniency must be applied to all, and any beating or killing without discrimination must be forbidden*. The system of feudal exploitation should be abolished step by step, that is, in a tactical way. In launching the struggle *we must determine our tactics according to the circumstances and the degree to which the peasant masses are awakened and organized*. We must not attempt to wipe out overnight the whole system of feudal exploitation.[17]

The Party, in rousing the mass hatreds which give life to the revolution, thus creates for itself a very delicate task of control: If it fails fully to mobilize the masses it may lack the strength to survive the counterattacks of "armed reaction," or it may not be "thorough" in destroying the economic and social roots of the traditional system of authority. But if it is too vigorous in its use of power, it will attack "enemies" where the people do not see them, thus creating new hatreds. This dilemma presents what is probably an impossible task of discernment because of the indiscriminate qualities of power and mobilized emotions. What the Party has chosen to do in the face of this problem is to attempt to drain off any newly generated hatreds by exposing *its cadres* to attack ("criticism") by "the People" for the errors they have made in implementing what are assumed to be inherently correct Party policies:

We must criticize and struggle with certain cadres and Party members who have committed serious mistakes and certain bad elements among the masses of workers and peasants. In such criticism and struggle we should persuade the masses to adopt correct methods and forms and to refrain from rough actions. This is one side of the matter. The other side is that these cadres, Party members and bad elements should be made to pledge that they will not retaliate against the masses. It should be announced that the masses not only have the right to criticize them freely but also have the right to dismiss them from their posts when necessary or to propose their dismissal, or to propose their expulsion from the Party and even to hand the worst elements over to the people's courts for trial and punishment.[18]

17. *Ibid.*, p. 236. Emphasis added.
18. Mao, "Important Problems of the Party's Present Policy" (1948), *SW*, English, IV, pp. 185–186.

As the Party advanced toward the attainment of state power Mao could only hope that it would maintain its "clear head" concerning the use of power and not let Chinese society degenerate into further *luan* because of failures of political control—a weakness in leadership which would generate a new storm of political hatred against the revolutionary vanguard itself.

Chapter XIV

IDEOLOGY AND ORGANIZATION, III:
THE POWER TO OPPOSE

A third major aspect of the significance of Party skills at organization and ideological exhortation is the power to aggregate those who have been mobilized and committed to the revolutionary cause. In a society where for centuries the fragmentation of rural life enabled a proportionately small gentry and imperial elite to exercise effective political control, the ability to concentrate an aroused peasantry represents the power to oppose the traditional social order.

We have already detailed how Mao and other Party leaders found both workers and peasants reluctant to oppose established political authority, especially where it continued to exhibit great strength. The continuing acceptance by those in positions of official leadership of the political culture of dependency meant that opposition in terms other than humble supplication for redress of grievance was viewed as a basic challenge to authority. With little middle ground allowed for criticism, and with all contenders for leadership of one mind in the expectation that power was not to be shared, opposition tended to polarize rapidly at the extremes of either full submission to the established order or total rejection of it.

From Mao's perspective this polarization was in the Party's interest because it eliminated alternatives to the revolutionary cause. The uncommitted were thus forced to choose between support of the Communists and submission to the Nationalists. And in Mao's mind, given the harshness of Kuomintang power, there was no question as to the justice and appeal of the Party's cause. As he wrote after the apparent destruction of the Party's urban base in 1927:

> The masses will certainly come over to us. The Kuomintang's policy of massacre only serves to "drive the fish into deep waters," as the saying goes, and reformism no longer has any mass appeal. It is certain that the masses will soon shed their illusions about the Kuomintang.

In the emerging situation, no other party will be able to compete with the Communist Party in winning over the masses.[1]

END ISOLATION THROUGH ORGANIZATION

While Mao, the contender for Party leadership, revealed little doubt about his ability to win over the masses, in earlier days he had candidly expressed the difficulties confronting those who were forced to choose between submission and rebellion. Previously we noted how he found the authority of the Classics helpful in opposing his father, and how he longed for "a powerful group of public opinion" to support those like Miss Chao who could reject the norms of tradition only through self-destruction. In 1926 Mao expressed a similar lament about the inability of the peasants to sustain opposition to the landlords because of their lack of organization:

> The day after [a peasant outburst], the landlord in question ran to the city to report, and soldiers and police came down to the village and turned everything upside down, but the leaders of the peasants had already mostly escaped. There was widespread propaganda about "Violation of the law" and "Crimes," the farmers became fearful, and thus the movement was suppressed. The reason for the failure of this movement is that the masses did not fully organize themselves, and did not have leadership, so that the movement barely got started and then failed.[2]

The basic problem in promoting an opposition political movement in a society where established authority permits no "talking back" or accepts no open, even if limited, challenges to its policies is that opposition is pushed to totality. The ability to press for limited adjustments of position has been ruled out, and hence full destruction of the position of either opposer or opposed becomes a likely prospect. In this context, to oppose alone, to stand in isolation, becomes little more than self-destruction. In encouraging impoverished peasants to challenge the established authority of the countryside, Mao thus forced them into a most vulnerable position. As a Shansi peasant recalled of his village's early opposition to landlord power:

1. Mao, "A Single Spark Can Start a Prairie Fire" (1930), *SW*, English, I, p. 122.
2. Mao (under the pen name Jun-chih), "The Bitter Sufferings of the Peasants in Kiangsu and Chekiang, and Their Movements of Resistance" (1926), in Schram, *PTMTT*, p. 179.

There were eight households in Liu Ling then, and we made a distribution of the land. Many people were worried and anxious. *They wondered if the communists would be able to stay in power.* "If we take the land and later the Red Army is beaten, we shall have to bear the blame," they said. *They didn't think the Red Army looked strong enough.* One old man called Ai Shen-you said: "I won't touch anyone's land. I have always been a day labourer and farmhand and I intend to go on being one. That's the safest." An old woman called Hsiu said: "I don't want to take any land. I have only one grandson left. He is the last of my family. If I take any of the land, the landowner will kill him when he comes back. And if they cut my grandson's head off, my family will be dead." Stepfather and Mother discussed the question a great deal. Stepfather thought that we ought not to take part in dividing up the land; that that would be dangerous and that it was unnecessary to run such a risk. *The landowners were strong and they always used to win in the long run.* . . . The communists had people making propaganda here, and they talked with people and in the end persuaded them. They said: "We are strong enough to deal with the landowners. If we hadn't been strong enough we should not have begun the revolution. You are all poor and how are you going to be able to live if you don't have any land?" [3]

In the early years of the agrarian revolution, however, the strength of the Red Army *was* uncertain; it was weak in comparison with Nationalist forces and the power of provincial and local authorities. In this context, peasants and wavering Party supporters in rural market towns, feeling themselves isolated and weak, retreated before the *luan* of counterrevolutionary "White terror":

In this period the poor peasants, having long been trampled down and feeling that the victory of the revolution was uncertain, frequently yielded to the intermediate class and dared not take vigorous action. [Action] is taken against the intermediate class in the villages only when the revolution is on the upsurge, for instance, when political power has been seized in one or more counties, the reactionary army has suffered several defeats and the prowess of the Red Army has been repeatedly demonstrated. . . .

When the revolution is at a low ebb in the country as a whole, the most difficult problem in our areas is to keep a firm hold on the intermediate class. . . . *When there is a revolutionary upsurge in the country as a whole, the poor peasant class has something to rely on and becomes bolder, while the intermediate class has something to fear and dare not get out of hand.* . . . Now that there is a nationwide tide of counterrevolution, the intermediate class in the White areas, having suffered heavy blows, has attached itself almost wholly to the

3. Jan Myrdal, *Report from a Chinese Village* (London: Heinemann, 1965), pp. 136–137. Emphasis added.

big landlord class, and *the poor peasant class has become isolated.*
This is indeed a very serious problem.[4]

In developing a solution to this elemental problem of the reluctance of potentially "revolutionary" individuals and groups to
oppose the established order when faced with a sense of isolation,
Mao found himself in opposition both to other Party leaders and to
elements of the Red Army on basic questions of strategy.[5] His effort
to strengthen peasant involvement in the revolution raised fears
among the Central Committee, which was still operating from an
urban base, that the proletarian revolution would be swamped in a
peasant society; and his concern with the sporadic quality of rural
insurrection conflicted with those within the Red Army who tended
to see the revolution as only a *luan* of unorganized destructiveness,
an attitude which found expression in the apparently random violence of "roving guerilla actions." Mao's contention was that only
if the Party established stable and visible centers of revolutionary
power on which wavering supporters could depend for strength
could people acquire the "self-confidence" for action:

> . . . the policy which merely calls for roving guerilla actions cannot
> accomplish the task of accelerating [the] nationwide revolutionary high
> tide, while the kind of policy adopted by Chu Teh and Mao Tse-tung
> and also by Fang Chih-min is undoubtedly correct—that is, the policy
> of *establishing base areas;* of systematically setting up political power;
> of deepening the agrarian revolution; of expanding the people's armed
> forces by a comprehensive process of building up first the township
> Red Guards, then the district Red Guards, then the county Red
> Guards, then the local Red Army troops, all the way up to the regular
> Red Army troops; of spreading political power by advancing in a series
> of waves, etc., etc. *Only thus is it possible to build the confidence of
> the revolutionary masses throughout the country, as the Soviet Union
> has built it throughout the world* . . . only thus is it possible to hasten
> the revolutionary high tide.[6]

4. Mao, "Struggle in the Chingkang Mountains" (1928), *SW*, English, I,
pp. 88–89. Emphasis added.
This type of failure to sustain popular support of the Party's insurgency
was repeated shortly after the Long March in the Wei Pei area of the Shensi-
Kansu border region. Nationalist forces, having access to areas where the
Party promoted land reform from their base at Sian, attacked peasants who
cooperated with the Communists, and the reform movement failed. *See*
Mark Selden, "The Guerilla Movement in Northwest China: The Origins
of the Shensi-Kansu-Ninghsia Border Region, Part II," *The China Quarterly*,
No. 29 (January–March 1967), p. 64.
5. *See* Schram, *Mao Tse-tung*, pp. 135–143.
6. Mao, "A Single Spark Can Start a Prairie Fire" (1930), *SW*, English,
I, p. 118. Emphasis added.

Mao's reference here to the "confidence-building" importance of the Soviet Union carries into the realm of international politics an attitude toward dealings with power which has its roots in childhood: Fears about challenging established authority are most easily overcome when there exists a strong alternative power, an authority on whom a new dependency tie can be established in replacement of the old and a source of support to allay fears of acting in isolation.

We find this calculus in dealings with power affirmed by one of China's peasants, who described to Jan Myrdal how he faced the potentially fatal choice of commitment to either "revolution" or "reaction." As his recollection makes clear, it was at base the issue of power, of which side held the promise of being more effective in providing security from violence and alleviating economic hardship, which determined the direction of choice:

> [The Communists] had their government at Lochuan [in 1935] and the Red Army was commanded by Liu Chih-tan. To begin with, people were afraid of them and said that communists were murderers, but when they came here they were ordinary people and they always said: "Divide up the land and fight against landowners and despots." They talked a lot and held lots of meetings, and *at the meetings we used to stand up and shout "Yes, yes!" but we did not really believe in them or that they had any real power.*
>
> But in April 1935 the Red Army defeated an armed counterrevolutionary landowners' corps ten *li* from here. They killed the leader of the Southern District, Mu Hsin-tsai, and took lots of booty. After that they came more often. They also killed other counterrevolutionaries. *Then the people saw that the Red Army did have power, and so we stopped driving into the town with our taxes and goods. Instead, we organized ourselves into guerilla bands. . . .*
>
> We no longer went to the town and we no longer sold grain to the town and we paid no taxes, and *those who were K.M.T. no longer dared live out in the country, but began to run away. The town was isolated.*[7]

This peasant's use of the term "isolation" is worth noting, for he means by it that the local Kuomintang backers became "cut off" from support, and hence weakened, by Communist military power. With no organized source of strength to rely upon they ran away, isolating the town from Nationalist power.

This notion that in politics, as in society at large, people do not act as self-reliant individuals but only in relation to a source of power on which they can rely is in the most basic sense what we mean by characterizing the main theme of China's political culture

7. Myrdal, *Report from a Chinese Village*, p. 67. Emphasis added.

as "dependency." The expectation is that once you have "cut off" or isolated an individual or group from its external source of power it will lose the strength which gives it political life. No one acts independently; personal integrity is a matter of one's commitment to a *relationship*—"loyalty". This fundamental orientation toward social action is the basis of Mao's strategy for gaining power, which is explored in detail in the next chapter. Here, however, we want to emphasize one aspect of this orientation: the importance of taking political action only when there is an aggregated source of strength which will sustain the confidence to oppose.

The importance of organized and concentrated peasant support as the basis for opposing the established social order was recognized by Mao in his "Hunan Report" of March 1927:

> Almost half the peasants in Hunan have now been organized. . . . *It is on the strength of their extensive organization that the peasants have gone into action* and within four months they have brought about a great revolution in the countryside, a revolution without parallel in history. . . . *This astonishing and accelerating rate of expansion explains why the local tyrants, evil gentry and corrupt officials have been isolated. . . .*[8]

Effectiveness in political action thus depends on a favorable balance between the organizational unity of those in opposition and the concurrent fragmentation of their enemies, who can be isolated and neutralized. As Mao described the problem in the tactics of land reform:

> The main and immediate task of the land reform is to satisfy the demands of the masses of poor peasants and farm laborers. In the land-reform program it is necessary to unite with the middle peasants; the poor peasants and the farm laborers must form a solid united front with the middle peasants, who account for about 20 percent of the rural population. Otherwise the poor peasants and farm laborers will find themselves isolated and the land reform will fail.[9]

Failure to sustain organizational unity exposes one to manipulation: "It is mainly because of the unorganized state of the Chinese masses that Japan dares to bully us."[10] But where that unity has been attained, the mere power of a word shouted in unison will overcome one's enemies: "When this defect [of national fragmentation] is remedied, then the Japanese aggressor. . . will be surrounded by

8. Mao, "Hunan Report" (1927), *SW*, Chinese, I, pp. 15, 24. Emphasis added.

9. Mao, "The General Line of Land Reform: Unite Ninety Percent of the Population" (1948), cited in Schram, *PTMTT*, p. 246.

10. Mao, "On Protracted War" (1938), *SW*, English, II, p. 186.

hundreds of millions of our people standing upright, [and] the mere sound of their voices will strike terror into him. . . ." [11]

From this conviction of the power that comes with unity derives the Party's endless concern with "consolidation" (*t'uan-chieh*) and the belief that the unitary voice of millions of people shouting common political slogans or reciting the words of one great leader represents real political power. And conversely, this belief sustains the notion that all enemies can be controlled if they are made to "stick out" in isolation, whether they be landlords paraded past jeering villagers, tethered with ropes and crowned with tall paper hats,[12] or opponents of a more recent day decked out with signs around their necks revealing their political errors and subjected to angry denunciations before shouting masses.[13]

11. *Ibid.*
12. *See* Mao, "Hunan Report" (1927), *SW,* English, I, p. 37
13. *See* p. 483 below.

Chapter XV

STRATEGY FOR VICTORY:
FOR THE PARTY AND PEOPLE—UNITY;
FOR THEIR ENEMIES—DISINTEGRATION,
ISOLATION, AND DEFEAT

> When [the enemy] is united, divide him. . . .
> Sometimes drive a wedge between a sover-
> eign and his ministers; on other occasions
> separate his allies from him. Make them mu-
> tually suspicious so that they drift apart. Then
> you can plot against them.
>
> SUN TZU,
> *The Art of War*[1]

The basic strategic concept which Mao brought to the revolutionary struggle merges his personal assertiveness with the dynamic of the Chinese political culture. A social tradition which prepared people for a life of dependence on those with authority provided strategies by which the weak could defend themselves against more powerful superiors—just as fears of isolation and conflict enabled those in authority to control their subordinates. Throughout the struggle for state power the Communists operated from a position of rela-tive weakness: in the early years of alliance with the Kuomintang, during the wartime struggle against the Japanese, and in the final period of conflict with the Nationalists. Reality imposed on the Party a strategic ratio of "one against ten"; yet Mao and other lead-ers rejected abandonment of the struggle and developed a tactical style enabling them to pit "ten against one." This technique in-volved the use of initiative, superior organizational discipline, and

1. Sun Tzu, *The Art of War,* trans. Samuel B. Griffith (Oxford: Oxford University Press, 1963), p. 69.

227

manipulation of the vulnerabilities and internal divisions of Party enemies. The weaknesses in social integration which were the legacy of a tradition of personalized, hierarchical authority provided lines of cleavage which could be struck to divide and disorganize opposition forces.

FOR THE ENEMY: DISINTEGRATION AND ISOLATION

In orienting Party members to the difficulties of the war against superior Japanese forces, Mao encouraged doubters to take heart from "the record of defeats suffered by big and powerful armies and of victories won by small and weak armies." [2] In each of a series of foreign and Chinese cases cited, Mao asserted,

> the weaker force, pitting local superiority and initiative against the enemy's local inferiority and passivity, *first inflicted one sharp defeat on the enemy and then turned on the rest of his forces and smashed them one by one,* thus transforming the over-all situation into one of superiority and initiative. The reverse was the case with the enemy who originally had superiority and held the initiative; owing to subjective errors and internal contradictions, it sometimes happened that he completely lost an excellent or fairly good position in which he enjoyed superiority and initiative, and became a general without an army or a king without a kingdom. . . . The fact that every ruling dynasty was defeated by revolutionary armies shows that mere superiority in certain respects does not guarantee the initiative, much less the final victory.[3]

This conception of the strength which could be derived from a position of relative weakness reflects in part Mao's own political style—his fear of passivity and a sensitivity to the "subjective errors and internal contradictions" dividing those holding and competing for power; but also it is a conception which drew reality from the political fragmentation of the era in which the Party struggled for growth. As Mao wrote in an analysis of 1928:

> . . . since the first year of the Republic [1912], the various cliques of old and new warlords have waged incessant wars against one another, supported by imperialism from abroad and by the comprador and landlord classes at home. . . . These prolonged splits and wars within the White regime provide a condition for the emergence and persistence of one or more small Red areas under the leadership of the Communist Party amidst the encirclement of the White regime. . . . In difficult or critical times some comrades often have doubts about the survival of Red political power and become pessimistic. The reason is that they have not found the correct explanation for its emergence and survival.

2. Mao, "On Protracted War" (1938), *SW*, English, II, p. 164.
3. *Ibid.*, p. 165.

If only we realize that splits and wars will never cease within the White regime in China, we shall have no doubts about the emergence, survival and daily growth of Red political power.[4]

The "contradictions" among China's warlords fragmented the Party's opponents, limiting their ability to take concerted action against Red Army forces operating in the political and geographical interstices of the Hunan-Kiangsi border region. Their mutual contention for regional power restricted their willingness to commit troops against Party forces if it would mean a gain in position for some provincial rival. And their common belief that Chiang K'ai-shek sought to destroy unattached units not fully under his control by pitting them against the Red Army further limited initiative within the loose central government coalition.[5]

Within this political context Mao came to see "correct" (successful) leadership as the ability to make an accurate evaluation of the enemy's "contradictions" and to act in accordance with his state of internal unity or disunity:

> The sole reason for the August [1928] defeat was that, failing to realize that the period was one of temporary stability for the ruling classes, some comrades adopted a policy suited to a period of splits within the ruling classes and divided our forces for an adventurous advance on southern Hunan, thus causing defeat both in the border area and in southern Hunan.[6]

And in dialectical fashion, the early military successes of the Chu-Mao forces taught that unity of command and concentration of superior force were needed in the face of the enemy, "so as to avoid being destroyed one by one."[7]

4. Mao, "Why Is It that Red Political Power Can Exist in China?" (1928), *SW*, English, I, p. 65. Emphasis added.

5. Li Tsung-jen recalled in his memoirs: ". . . The Communist suppression policy of the central government was to use the Communist army to eliminate the "unattached units." The major task of the so-called "central armies" was to supervise the "unattached units." . . . Thus, whenever fighting with the Communists began, all armies avoided concrete action and busied themselves with abstract tasks in order to preserve their strength. Meanwhile the Communist Party exploited the situation and became more powerful." (*The Reminiscences of General Li Tsung-jen* [unpublished manuscript of the Columbia University East Asian Institute, Chinese Oral History Project, n.d.], Ch. 44, p. 14.)

A similar evaluation of Chiang's style of political control will be found in Ch'ien Tuan-sheng, *The Government and Politics of China* (Cambridge, Massachusetts: Harvard University Press, 1961), pp. 128–132.

6. Mao, "Struggle in the Chingkang Mountains" (1928), *SW*, English, I, p. 76.

7. *Ibid.*

As was pointed out earlier, Mao analyzed the revolutionary potential of various social classes on the basis of their degree of exploitation. In the same spirit, his "contradiction analysis" of political combat involves a detailed search for those resentments, competitive conflicts, deprivations, and differences in objective which can be used against Party enemies. Such divisive tactics either provoke dissension and thus neutralize one's opponents in mutual conflict, or identify sources of temporary common interest which can be used to gain allies for the Party's cause:

> *The question whether there will soon be a revolutionary high tide in China can be decided only by making a detailed examination to ascertain whether the contradictions leading to a revolutionary high tide are really developing.* Since contradictions are developing in the world between the imperialist countries, between the imperialist countries and their colonies, and between the imperialists and the proletariat in their own countries, there is an intensified need for the imperialists to contend for the domination of China. While the imperialist contention over China becomes more intense, both the contradiction between imperialism and the whole Chinese nation and the contradictions among the imperialists themselves develop simultaneously on Chinese soil, thereby creating the tangled warfare which is expanding and intensifying daily and giving rise to the continuous development of the contradictions among the different cliques of China's reactionary rulers. In the wake of the contradictions among the reactionary ruling cliques— the tangled warfare among the warlords—comes heavier taxation, which steadily sharpens the contradiction between the broad masses of taxpayers and the reactionary rulers. . . . *Once we understand all these contradictions, we shall see in what a desperate situation, in what a chaotic state, China finds herself. We shall also see that the high tide of revolution against the imperialists, the warlords and the landlords is inevitable and will come very soon.*[8]

For Mao the tactician, China's "chaotic state" (*hun-luan chuang-t'ai*) was a condition of promise, for in the tensions among those who were "mutually related and mutually antagonistic" lay the contradictions which weakened opposition unity. An effective revolutionary strategy would use these "contradictions" to disintegrate the forces of the enemy and to increase the unity of "progressive forces" through the polarization of political conflict. As a Central Committee resolution of 1945 put it:

> An important basis for determining our varying tactics is the different impact of the revolution on the interests of different enemies. Consequently Comrade Mao Tse-tung has always advocated that we *"utilize*

8. Mao, "A Single Spark Can Start a Prairie Fire" (1930), *SW*, English, I, pp. 120–121. Emphasis added.

every conflict within the counterrevolution and take active measures to widen the cleavages within it," and "oppose the policy of isolation, and affirm the policy of winning over all possible allies." The application of the tactical principles, *"make use of contradictions, win over the many, oppose the few and crush our enemies one by one,"* was brilliantly developed in the campaigns Comrade Mao Tse-tung led against "encirclement and suppression" and especially, after the Tsunyi Meeting, in the Long March and in the work of the Anti-Japanese National United Front.[9]

Mao's various writings reveal that he conceives the problem of utilizing "contradictions" in two different dimensions. The first is "horizontal"—creating dissension among competitive leadership groups so as to prevent the formation of coalitions against the Party. As he wrote in an analysis of political tactics during the anti-Japanese war:

> Most of the leaders of the regional power groups belong to the big landlord class and the big bourgeoisie and, therefore, progressive as they may appear at certain times during the war, they soon turn reactionary again; nevertheless, because of their contradictions with the Kuomintang central authorities, the possibility exists of their remaining neutral in our struggle with the die-hards, provided we pursue a correct policy. . . . We must [also] know how to exploit the contradictions among the die-hards and must not take on too many of them at a single time, but must direct our blows at the most reactionary of them first. Herein lies the limited nature of the struggle.[10]

And during the final phase of civil war he warned Party members not to forget that the Kuomintang was a "complicated" *(fu-tza)* political party, embodying potentially hostile factions which could be manipulated so as to disintegrate enemy unity.[11]

The second dimension is the "vertical" one of relations between a leadership group and its base of popular support. Through mass agitation, "contradictions" between leaders and followers can be

9. Mao, "Our Study and the Current Situation: Appendix: Resolution on Certain Questions in the History of Our Party" (1945), *SW*, English, III, p. 202. Emphasis added.
A secret Party directive of 1940 which discloses the difficulty of implementing this tactic is presented in Van Slyke, *Enemies and Friends,* pp. 263–265.
10. Mao, "Current Problems of Tactics in the Anti-Japanese United Front" (1940), *SW*, English, II, pp. 424, 426.
11. *See* Mao, "On Coalition Government" (1945), *SW,* English, III, pp. 271–272. The Chinese version of this passage uses the word "complicated" *(fu-tza)* to describe the Kuomintang. The English translation renders *fu-tza* as "not homogeneous."

stimulated into open hostility, thus isolating the elite from the people who might provide them support:

> . . . the Kuomintang's resumption of conscription and grain levies has aroused popular discontent and created a situation favourable for the development of mass struggles. The whole Party must strengthen its leadership of the mass struggles in the Kuomintang areas and intensify the work of disintegrating the Kuomintang army.[12]

The aim of disintegrating enemy forces, whether "horizontally" through stimulating disruptive conflict among leadership factions or "vertically" by encouraging popular resentments against authority, is to induce paralysis in action through mutual antagonism, or to isolate (*ku-li*) elements of the enemy for destruction in piecemeal fashion. Such a tactic can be applied in either military or political action:

> When you are attacking Chinchow, be prepared also to wipe out the enemy forces that may come to its rescue from Changchun and Shenyang. *Because the enemy forces in and near Chinchow, Shanhaikuan and Tangshan are isolated from each other, success in attacking and wiping them out is pretty certain.*[13]

> In order to reduce the number of hostile elements and to consolidate the Liberated Areas, we should help all those landlords who have difficulty in making a living and induce runaway landlords to return and give them an opportunity to earn a living. In the cities, besides uniting with the working class, the petty bourgeoisie and all progressives, *we should take care to unite with all the middle elements and isolate the reactionaries. Among the Kuomintang troops, we should win over all the possible opponents of civil war and isolate the bellicose elements.*[14]

Mao's offensive political strategy, in its simplest terms, is thus a formula of correctly identifying and stimulating contradictions (*mao-tun*) among opponents so as to produce division and *disintegration* (*wa-chieh, fen-san, fen-sui, p'o-lieh*) in which individual elements of the enemy can be *isolated* (*ku-li ti*) and destroyed one by one.

This tactical conception is hardly unique to Mao. As is indicated in the opening quote of this chapter, drawn from the writings of Sun Tzu, a military strategist of the Warring States period (453–221 B.C.), the effort to establish and maintain power through the disunity of one's opponents has been a long-standing approach in

12. Mao, "A Three Months' Summary" (1946), *SW*, English, IV, p. 117.
13. Mao, "The Concept of Operations for the Liaohsi-Shenyang Campaign" (1948), *SW*, English, IV, p. 262. Emphasis added.
14. Mao, "Smash Chiang K'ai-shek's Offensive by a War of·Self-Defence" (1946), *SW*, English, IV, p. 90. Emphasis added.

the Chinese tradition. "Divide and rule" was a basic tactic used to control the nomadic tribes who threatened China's security from her northern frontier; and the playing off of one local power group against another seems to have been the conception which underlay the *pao-chia* system of local security and political control.[15] The enduring reliance placed upon this approach to political rule seems related to its effectiveness within the traditional political culture. Such tactics as playing off various opponents against each other through manipulating their "contradictions," "splitting them up," and "disintegrating" their unity will only work where there are basic conflicts of purpose among opposition leaders (compounded by the belief that power is not to be shared), and where capacities for cooperation and compromise are severely limited. "Isolating" an enemy, or threatening to "cut him off" from a relationship on which he depends, will be an effective tactic only where the sense of dependency or fear of isolation is shared by that enemy, where he, too, finds such a sanction threatening.

We need only recall here in summary that such images as these, which Mao has incorporated into a strategy of power, are precisely the major themes we discovered in our respondents' expectations of dealings with peers and authority. In the Chinese tradition, authority's domain was seen as all-inclusive; its proper function was to establish a noncompetitive and hierarchical social order. There was little sense of cooperation among peers in the resolution of specific issues of mutual interest. Such conflicts were to be resolved through loyal reliance on the initiative of a superior leader. The personalized quality of authority fostered the creation of narrow cliques of loyal subordinates; and equals in power tended to be drawn into competition for full dominance because unitary, personalized leadership was seen as the only effective way to realize an ordered and peaceful society. We found that our respondents had limited expectation of the ability of peers to resolve differences of opinion. Thus Mao shares with those of his countrymen who comprised our interview sample the expectation that with conflict will come a "splitting up."

Furthermore, the effort to cut off a leadership group from its followers can be an effective strategy where there already exists an exploitable gap in communication and sentiment between leaders and led. In our study we have already discussed the early development of this gap in the life of the Chinese child. This problem is further reinforced by anxieties about dealings with potentially aggressive and manipulating power. The limited reciprocity of supe-

15. *See* Hsiao Kung-chuan, *Rural China, Imperial Control in the Nineteenth Century* (Seattle: University of Washington Press, 1960), pp. 72–83.

rior-subordinate relations works to cut off an individual in a position of leadership from his subordinates; and the Communists have been quick to exploit this gap to undermine the mass base of their enemies and to win converts to their own cause.

Finally, we suggested that traditional attitudes toward authority were strongly ambivalent, embodying a paradoxical hatred of its harshness and tendency to be manipulative, yet a longing to find security and guidance under its control. Mao's perception of the importance of stable centers of power from which to oppose forces of "reaction" seems based on an intuitive awareness of the workings of this ambivalence: the desire to strike out at hated power, yet a fear that in so doing one will be cut off from security and subject to an intensely hostile reaction. In a very practical way the Party, by establishing "revolutionary bases" of military and political strength, helped people to resolve this ambivalence, for such centers of power provided an alternative authority on which to depend. From the "liberated areas" hated authority could be attacked: The Party provided ideological justification for the attack and physical security from its consequences.

Mao's revolutionary strategy, derived from this calculus of the Chinese political culture, was succinctly and forcefully summed up on the eve of the civil war:

> . . . we must at all times firmly adhere to, and never forget, these principles: unity, struggle, unity through struggle; to wage struggles with good reason, with advantage and with restraint; and to make use of contradictions, win over the many, oppose the few and crush our enemies one by one.[16]

FOR THE PARTY AND PEOPLE: UNITY

> If we study history, we find that all the movements that have occurred in the course of history, of whatever type they may be, have all without exception resulted from the union of a certain number of people. A greater movement naturally requires a greater union, and the greatest movement requires the greatest union. All such unions are more likely to appear in a time of reform and resistance. . . .

> That which decides between victory and defeat is the solidity or weakness of the union and whether the ideology that serves as its basis is new or old, true or false.[17]

If the first major goal of Mao's strategy is "divide and rule," the second centers around the maintenance of Party and coalition unity

16. Mao, "On Peace Negotiations with the Kuomintang" (1945), *SW*, English, IV, p. 49.

17. Mao, "The Great Union of the Popular Masses" (1919), in Schram, *PTMTT*, p. 170.

while enemies are being "disintegrated." Much of the concern for unity shown by Mao and other leaders has the quality of a reaction against the strategy of disintegration which they seek to impose on their enemies. Seeing their own political action within a calculus of unity opposed to disintegration and isolation, it is but a short step from there to the assumption that the enemy's objectives are similar to those of the Party: ". . . the [Japanese] enemy will not relax his divisive tricks to break China's united front, hence the task of maintaining internal unity in China will become still more important, and we shall have to ensure that the strategic counteroffensive does not collapse halfway through internal dissension." [18]

This perception was fully reinforced by the political fragmentation which had characterized the first decade of the Republic. Sun Yat-sen—who in 1924 was to turn to the Soviet Union for assistance in organization-building—lamented that the post-1911 Kuomintang "was split to pieces and could not agree upon orders." [19] He saw his movement's failure deriving from this fragmentation, and the concomitant unity of his opposition: "Yuan Shih-kai had a firm organization while we in the Revolutionary Party were a sheet of loose sand, and so Yuan Shih-kai defeated the party." [20] This recent history was a powerful lesson to Mao; and it is hardly surprising that he came to gauge success or failure in tactical operations within a framework of isolation versus being isolated:

> The illegal and divisive "National Assembly," which was convened by Chiang K'ai-shek, in order to isolate our Party and other democratic forces, and the bogus constitution fabricated by the body enjoy no prestige at all among the people. Instead of isolating our Party and other democratic forces, they have isolated the reactionary Chiang K'ai-shek ruling clique itself. Our Party and other democratic forces adopted the policy of refusing to participate in the bogus National Assembly; this was perfectly correct.[21]

In Party writings one frequently encounters reassuring little reminders that the "progressive forces" are not really isolated (are they?):

> The broad masses of people in foreign countries are dissatisfied with the reactionary forces in China and sympathize with the Chinese people's forces. They also disapprove of Chiang K'ai-shek's policies. *We*

18. Mao, "On Protracted War" (1938), *SW*, English, II, p. 143.
19. Sun Yat-sen, *San Min Chu I*; cited in Sharman, *Sun Yat-sen*, p. 169.
20. *Ibid.*
21. Mao, "Greet the New High Tide of the Chinese Revolution" (1947), *SW*, English, IV, p. 122.

have many friends in all parts of the country and of the world; we are not isolated.[22]

This concern with "isolation"—with being cut off from one's group or a source of authority and power—as we have seen in both social and political contexts, strikes at the Chinese sense of social inter-relatedness. Its strength is based on emotional needs, shared by subordinate and superior alike, to depend on the support of group life for assistance and security. The preoccupation that Mao has shown throughout his career about the Party becoming "cut off from the masses" betrays the fear of isolation, of standing alone in rebellion apart from popular support. As he wrote in the bleak days of 1928:

> Wherever the Red Army goes, the masses are cold and aloof, and only after our propaganda do they slowly move into action. Whatever enemy units we face, there are hardly any cases of mutiny or desertion to our side and we have to fight it out. . . . *We have an acute sense of our isolation which we keep hoping will end.*[23]

In a similar vein the editors of Mao's *Selected Works,* in an introductory footnote to the "Hunan Report," attacked the "Right opportunist" Ch'en Tu-hsiu leadership for its policy of alliance with the Kuomintang: "They preferred to desert the peasantry, the chief ally in the revolution, and thus left the working class and the Communist Party isolated and without help." [24] The unwavering commitment to mass mobilization which Mao was to display in the years after Liberation reveals, in part, the continuity of his concern with finding himself and the Party alone, without popular support in the process of promoting social change.

An additional reason for the preoccupation with unity lies in the divisive social loyalties which were such an elemental aspect of China's traditional society. The exclusive commitments to family and clan, school class, region, and work group fostered much of the fragmentation of Chinese political life; and in student days Mao had personally known the sting of social isolation which came from such narrow loyalties. As he told Edgar Snow:

> I was disliked because I was not a native of Hsiang Hsiang. It was very important to be a native of Hsiang Hsiang and also important to be from a certain district of Hsiang Hsiang. There was an upper, lower and middle district, and lower and upper were continually fighting,

22. Mao, "On the Chungking Negotiations" (1945), *SW,* English, IV, p. 55. Emphasis added.

23. Mao, "The Struggle in the Chingkang Mountains" (1928), *SW,* English, I, pp. 98–99. Emphasis added.

24. Mao, "Report on an Investigation of the Peasant Movement in Hunan" (1927), *SW,* English, I, fn. pp. 23–24.

purely on a regional basis. Neither could be reconciled to the existence of the other. I took a neutral position in this war, because I was not a native at all. Consequently all three factions despised me. I felt spiritually very depressed.[25]

The political impact of such regional loyalties was brought home to Mao in the early days of army building. In 1928 he wrote with exasperation of the blood feuds which hindered development of a unified base of popular support: "A very wide rift has long existed between the native inhabitants [of the Kiangsi border regions] and the settlers whose forefathers came from the north several hundred years ago; their traditional feuds are deep-seated and they sometimes erupt in violent clashes." [26]

The sum of these varied factors fostering social divisiveness accounts for the determination of Party efforts to maintain internal discipline. Such factors account for the seeming paradox that just as victory in the civil war was approaching, Mao evinced even greater concern with tendencies within the Party and military which threatened to create "indiscipline, anarchy, and localism":

> Because our Party and our army were long in a position in which we were cut apart by the enemy, were waging guerilla warfare and were in the rural areas, we allowed very considerable autonomy to the leading organs of the Party and army in the different areas. This enabled the Party organizations and armed forces to bring their initiative and enthusiasm into play and to come through long periods of grave difficulties, but at the same time *it gave rise to certain phenomena of indiscipline and anarchy, localism and guerilla-ism which were harmful to the cause of the revolution. The present situation demands that our Party should do its utmost to centralize all the powers that can and must be concentrated in the hands of the Central Committee and its agencies,* so as to bring about the transition in the form of the war from guerilla to regular warfare.[27]

Concentration of power thus acquires the weighty justification of overcoming the divisive tendencies inherent in Chinese society. And it seems likely that for a long time to come rational justifications for decentralization of Party, governmental, and economic bureaucracies will be in "contradiction" with fears of *luan* based on anticipated loyalties to family, region, or clique lying below a social face of commitment to nation and Party.

25. Edgar Snow, *Red Star Over China*, p. 132.
26. Mao, "The Struggle in the Chingkang Mountains" (1928), *SW*, English, I, p. 93.
27. Mao, "On the September Meeting" (1948), *SW*, English, IV, p. 273. Emphasis added.

THE UNITY OF RESENTMENT

The approach to maintaining political unity which became most meaningful to Mao apparently is based on the organizational core of the Party:

> Unity within the Chinese Communist Party is the fundamental prerequisite for uniting the whole nation to win the War of Resistance and build a new China. Seventeen years of tempering have taught the Chinese Communist Party many ways of attaining internal unity, and ours is a much more seasoned Party. Thus we are able to form a powerful nucleus for the whole people in the struggle to win victory. . . . Comrades, so long as we are united, we can certainly reach this goal.[28]

This stress on the Party is in part a legacy of the political fragmentation of the period in which the Communist movement had its early growth, and of the influence of Comintern advisers who brought to China the Leninist experience in building a combat organization. If China's "progressive forces" could only maintain their unity, they could make a revolution on the "confusion" which characterized their opponents.[29] A disciplined party came to be seen as the core of this unity.

Yet (as was to become clear only in the days after Liberation) the elite Party institution was less sacred to Mao than the "many ways of attaining internal unity" which were the product of "seventeen years of tempering" in the struggle of domestic revolution. The forms of mobilization and control which comprise Mao's approach to political integration are closely related to his basic concept of political motivation. Unity grows from a shared sense of outrage at exploitation and injustice. Mao told Edgar Snow that the family "United Front" of his childhood grew from hatred of oppressive paternal authority;[30] and in a later day he asserted that the wartime United Front against the Japanese, in similar fashion, drew its cohesiveness from a shared hatred of the aggressor: "We can rally the overwhelming majority of the people to fight with one heart and one mind because we are the oppressed and the victims of aggression." [31]

28. Mao, "The Role of the Chinese Communist Party in the National War" (1938), *SW*, English, II, p. 210.

29. Sun Tzu, too, had seen "unity versus confusion" as a tactical dimension of combat: ". . . if one wishes to feign disorder to entice an enemy he must himself be well-disciplined. Only then can he feign confusion . . . order or disorder depends on organization." (Sun Tzu, *The Art of War*, p. 93.)

30. Snow, *Red Star Over China*, p. 126.

31. Mao, "Problems of Strategy in China's Revolutionary War" (1936), *SW*, English, I, p. 207.

The organizational forms developed by the Party to mobilize resentment at such treatment (discussed in Chapter XII) and the techniques of political study used to rationalize opposition to the common enemy gave structure and control to this basic concept of the unity of resentment. And as Mao asserted on the eve of victory, these forms and techniques accounted for the sharp contrast between the disciplined forces of "revolution" and the disintegration of the "counterrevolutionary" camp:

> In the last few months almost all the People's Liberation Army has made use of the intervals between battles for large-scale training and consolidation. This has been carried out in a fully guided, orderly and democratic way. ["Speak bitterness" meetings and political study have] aroused the revolutionary fervour of the great masses of commanders and fighters, enabled them clearly to comprehend the aim of the war, eliminated certain incorrect ideological tendencies and undesirable manifestations in the army, educated the cadres and fighters and greatly enhanced the combat effectiveness of the army. . . . You can see clearly that neither the Party consolidation, nor the ideological education in the army, nor the land reform, all of which we have accomplished and all of which have great historic significance, could be undertaken by our enemy, the Kuomintang. On our part, we have been very earnest in correcting our own shortcomings; we have united the Party and army virtually as one man and forged close ties between them and the masses of the people. . . . *With our enemy, everything is just the opposite. They are so corrupt, so torn by ever-increasing and irreconcilable internal quarrels, so spurned by the people and utterly isolated and so frequently defeated in battle that their doom is inevitable.* This is the whole situation of revolution versus counterrevolution in China.[32]

The dynamic aspect of Mao's approach to building a unity of revolutionary forces derives from his belief that people are sustained in their political involvement through the tension of conflict with their oppressors: "Struggle is the means to unity and unity is the aim of struggle. If unity is sought through struggle it will live; if unity is sought through yielding, it will perish."[33] The tactical problem confronting the leadership in implementing this conception is first to identify the proper enemy and then to invoke his "contradictions" with uncommitted social groups in order to mobilize and build a base of popular support. As Mao asserted in 1926:

> Who are our enemies? Who are our friends? This is a question of the first importance for the revolution. The basic reason why all pre-

32. Mao, "Speech at a Conference of Cadres in the Shansi-Suiyuan Liberated Area" (1948), *SW*, English, IV, p. 234. Emphasis added.
33. Mao, "Current Problems of Tactics in the Anti-Japanese United Front" (1940), *SW*, English, II, p. 422.

vious revolutionary struggles in China achieved so little was their failure to unite with real friends in order to attack real enemies.[34]

The creative edge of leadership is the ability to perceive the social
issues which can be used to mobilize different social groups and
separate them from the Party's enemies in creating the broadest
base of popular support. This calculus of coalition-building, however, embodies the "deviational" dangers of either excessive exclusiveness ("sectarianism") in mobilizing support—leading to the
isolation of the Party on a narrow base of support—or appealing
for popular backing with such broad and uncontroversial issues
that the revolution flags in moderate "reformism." In Party history
the sectarian deviation was most fully developed in the Kiangsi era:

> Our experience teaches us that the main blow of the revolution should
> be directed at the chief enemy and to isolate him, whereas with the
> middle forces, a policy of both uniting with them and struggling against
> them should be adopted, so that they are at least neutralized; and, as
> circumstances permit, efforts should be made to shift them from their
> position of neutrality to one of alliance with us in order to facilitate the
> development of the revolution. But there was a time—the ten years of
> civil war from 1927 to 1936—when some of our comrades crudely
> applied [Stalin's formula of isolating middle-of-the-road elements] to
> China's revolution by turning their main attack on the middle forces,
> singling them out as the most dangerous enemy; the result was that,
> instead of isolating the real enemy, we isolated ourselves and suffered
> losses to the advantage of the real enemy.[35]

The dangers of working with too broad a base of support were
experienced in 1927, when Chiang K'ai-shek, taking advantage of
the first United Front, seized leadership of the military forces of the
revolutionary coalition and turned them against the Party: "It was
all alliance and no struggle in the latter period of the First Great
Revolution, and all struggle and no alliance . . . in the latter
period of the Agrarian Revolution—truly striking demonstrations
of the two extremist policies. Both . . . caused great losses to the
Party and the Revolution." [36]

According to Mao, it was only under his "correct" leadership
that the proper balance of coalition and struggle was attained during the conflict with Japan and in the ensuing civil war. While an
impartial evaluation of the many reasons for the Party's spectacular

34. Mao, "Analysis of the Classes in Chinese Society" (1926), *SW*, English, I, p. 13.
35. *People's Daily* editorial, "On the Historical Experience of the Dictatorship of the Proletariat" (April 5, 1956), cited in Schram, *PTMTT*, p.
298.
36. Mao, "On Policy" (1940), *SW*, English, II, p. 442.

rise to power must be found in the works of students of Party history, it is at least clear that Mao has sought to present the image of unity versus disintegration as the tactical reality of the Party's rise to power. As he proclaimed in early 1949, when victory was in sight:

> Total power is in the hands of the Chinese people, the Chinese People's Liberation Army, the Communist Party of China and the other democratic parties, not in the hands of the badly split and disintegrating Kuomintang. *One side wields total power, while the other is hopelessly split and disintegrated,* and this is the result of the prolonged struggle of the Chinese people and the prolonged evil-doing of the Kuomintang. No serious person can ignore this basic fact of the political situation in China today.[37]

The unambiguous military successes of the Red Army in the civil war gave weighty support to Mao's assertion, and more sharply defined the polarity between justice and evil, unity and disintegration. As Nanking fell in late April of 1949 and the Liberation Army prepared to cross into south China, Mao brushed a poem which summed the symbols of his revolution, and revealed his elation in *luan:*

> Around Mount Chung a sudden storm has arisen,
> A million courageous warriors cross the great river . . .
> The universe is in turmoil, we are all exhaulted and resolute.
> Let us gather up our courage and pursue the broken foe. . . .[38]

As the Party's "broken foe" prepared to withdraw to an island retreat, Mao taunted the Kuomintang in a farewell of elated satisfaction that nearly leaps from the page: "You are defeated. You have enraged the people. And the people have all risen against you in a life-and-death struggle. The people do not like you, the people condemn you, *the people have risen, and you are isolated; that is why you have been defeated."* [39]

ENDING AN ERA AND "RECTIFYING NAMES"

By early 1949 it had become clear that "Heaven's Mandate" of political leadership was no longer in the hands of the Kuomintang.

37. Mao, "Why Do the Badly Split Reactionaries Still Idly Clamour for 'Total Peace'?" (1949), *SW,* English, IV, p. 344. Emphasis added.

38. Extracted from Mao's poem, "The People's Liberation Army Gains Nanking," of April 1949; translated in Schram, *Mao Tse-tung,* p. 244.

39. Mao, "On Ordering the Reactionary Kuomintang Government to Re-arrest Yasuji Okamura, Former Commander-in-Chief of the Japanese Forces of Aggression in China, and to Arrest the Kuomintang Civil War Criminals —Statement by the Spokesman for the Communist Party of China" (1949), *SW,* English, IV, p. 328. Emphasis added.

And as is the long established tradition in this political culture, the old set of "names" which had represented the underlying realities of power required "rectification."

For the Communists' part, in reacting to the repatriation to Japan of General Yasuji Okamura, Mao declared:

> Gentlemen of the reactionary traitorous Kuomintang government, this action of yours is too unreasonable and is too gross a violation of the people's will. *We have now deliberately added the word "traitorous" to your title, and you ought to accept it.* Your government has long been traitorous, and it was only for the sake of brevity that we sometimes omitted the word: now we can omit it no longer.[40]

In noting a change in the "name" used by the Kuomintang in describing the Communists, Mao rhetorically inquired: "Why has the term 'Communist bandits' been changed into 'Communist Party' in all Kuomintang public documents issued since January 1, 1949?" [41] And in response to an evaluation of responsibility for China's changing political circumstances by the Kuomintang's new acting president, Mao noted with satisfaction:

> If there is nothing else good about Li Tsung-jen, at least it is good that he has made . . . one honest statement. What is more, instead of speaking about "putting down the rebellion" or "suppressing the bandits" he calls the war a "civil war," and this, for the Kuomintang, may be said to be quite novel.[42]

"Names" were being "rectified"; China was about to enter a new political era. And Mao could only hope that with the Party's rise to power it would be possible to "heal the wounds of war and build a new, powerful and prosperous People's Republic *whose reality will be worthy of its name.*" [43]

40. Mao, "Peace Terms Must Include the Punishment of Japanese War Criminals—Statement by a Spokesman for the Chinese Communist Party" (1949), *SW*, English, IV, p. 335.

41. Mao, "On the Kuomintang's Different Answers to the Question of Responsibility for the War" (1949), *SW*, English, IV, p. 352.

42. *Ibid.*, p. 354.

43. Mao, "Address to the Preparatory Committee of the New Political Consultative Conference" (1949), *SW*, Chinese, IV, p. 1471. Emphasis added.

Part Four

THE MAOIST
POLITICAL RECONSTRUCTION

Peasants in a People's Commune Production Brigade
eat lunch between militia drill and the afternoon's labor
during the Great Leap Forward, 1958.
Black Star Agency.

Comrade Mao Tse-tung has said that our direction must be the step by step and systematic organization of industry, agriculture, commerce, education, and the military (militia, that is an armed population) into big communes, thereby forming the basic units of our society. . . . The flag of Mao Tse-tung is the red flag held high by the Chinese people. Under the leadership of this great red flag, the Chinese people, in the not-distant future, will steadily and victoriously advance to the great Communist society.

Red Flag,
July 1958

Chapter XVI

AN END TO THE
POLITICS OF DEPENDENCY?

Since they learned Marxism-Leninism, the
Chinese people have ceased to be passive in
spirit and gained the initiative. The period of
modern world history in which the Chinese
and Chinese culture were looked down upon
should have ended from that moment. The
great, victorious Chinese People's War of
Liberation and the great people's revolution
have rejuvenated and are rejuvenating the
great culture of the Chinese people.[1]

For Mao the attainment of state power was both fulfillment and
promise. He saw in the Party's military and political triumph over
the Nationalists the "liberation" of the Chinese people from a discredited political order and the conclusion of an era of social turmoil and foreign intervention. Yet he expressed awareness that
"countrywide victory is only the first step in a long march of ten
thousand *li,*"[2] in which the Party would have to learn the skills of
social reconstruction. Unlike the founders of past dynasties, however, he did not see China's "golden age" in an idealized past but
in an unrealized future. As the political spokesman for a generation
which had rejected the Confucian heritage, he sought to replace the

1. Mao Tse-tung, "The Bankruptcy of the Idealist Conception of History" (1949), *Selected Works of Mao Tse-tung* (4 vols., Peking: Foreign
Languages Press, 1961–1965), Vol. IV, p. 458. Hereinafter cited as *SW,*
English.
2. Mao, "Report to the Second Plenary Session of the Seventh Central
Committee of the Communist Party of China" (1949), *SW,* English, IV, p.
374.

cyclical historical pattern of China's "feudal" era with the Marxian notion of unilinear social development.[3]

The exact form of China's Communist future was hardly certain in 1949, however. The unexpectedly swift victory in the civil war seems to have caught Party leaders almost unprepared for the constructive dimension of their revolution.[4] The instruments of political and military combat which had brought them to power and the precedent of "socialist transformation" in the Soviet Union, enabled the Party to destroy rapidly the organizational remnants of Nationalist political and economic control. By late 1955, "the socialist transformation of the ownership of the means of production in agriculture, handicrafts and capitalist industry and commerce was in the main completed!"[5] It was only as this period of consolidation of power drew to a close that the attention of Party leaders turned fully to the question of the form of China's future social institutions.

The leadership shared a commitment to realize "communism" in China, but the vagueness of that distant goal was such that on the eve of victory Mao could even compare it to the traditional Chinese utopia of *ta-t'ung*.[6] Between the fact of political and military conquest and the millennium lay an undefined middle range of policies and institutions which would have to implement the transition to China's future greatness.

From the perspective of hindsight, it is now clear that the decade 1955–1964 was a period of experimentation and debate among

3. Mao's mentor, Li Ta-chao, had explicitly opposed the notion of a "golden age" in China's past, and criticized the cyclical view of history, "for it causes men to lose their faith and hope." (Maurice Meisner, *Li Ta-chao and the Origins of Chinese Marxism* [Cambridge, Mass.: Harvard University Press, 1967], p. 167.) Mao shared Li's concern with subjective views of the world which would hinder social progress. He wrote in 1940, "as far as the masses and young students are concerned, the essential thing is to guide them to look forward and not backward." (Mao, "On New Democracy" [1940], *SW*, English, II, p. 381.)

4. It was only gradually during 1947 that the Communists began to sense victory in the civil war. The decisive battle of the Huai-Hai came in November–December 1948, less than a year before country-wide victory. *See* F. F. Liu, *A Military History of Modern China* (Princeton: Princeton University Press, 1956), pp. 252, 263.

5. Lin Piao, "Report to the Ninth National Congress of the Communist Party of China," in *Survey of the China Mainland Press* (Hong Kong: United States Consulate General), No. 4406 (May 1, 1969), p. 15. Hereinafter cited as *SCMP*.

6. *See* Mao, "On the People's Democratic Dictatorship" (1949), *SW*, English, IV, p. 414.

Party leaders over the most appropriate way to transform Chinese society. Many assumed that the basic question of political control had been solved. They saw China's problems of modernization largely in technical and economic terms. Mao, however, increasingly came to see the cultural and political difficulties of the country's development. As we shall stress in this final part of the study, Mao had a personal sensitivity to the authority pattern of the traditional society and believed that only through controlled conflict could China sustain social change. He sensed in the consolidation of Party, governmental, and army organizations the slow reemergence of old, exploitative political relationships in "bourgeois" or "revisionist" guise.

These personal concerns were heightened by challenges to Mao's policies from the Party and state apparatus which came in part as a result of "de-Stalinization" in the Soviet Union. Mao had been Party Chairman since the 1935 Tsunyi Conference and in 1949 he was elected Chairman of the newly established People's Republic, but his dual role as leader of both Party and state hardly gave him total power. In an altered context of political reconstruction, power diffused to the economic and political organizations of "socialist construction". During the 1950s, Mao became increasingly distrustful of China's new bureaucratic and technical elite. He read into their resistance to his concepts for modernizing a peasant society an attempt to restore the pattern of dependent submission by "the People" to the initiative of a small ruling class. To the degree that Mao's colleagues within the Party leadership did not share his personal concerns, and actively resisted his efforts to institutionalize forms of mass political participation, Mao came to see them as "counterrevolutionaries."

At the end of this decade of experimentation and debate, differences of opinion within the Party leadership—compounded by the economic crisis which followed the Great Leap Forward—had become strong enough to hinder cooperative relations and collective decision-making. Mao, feeling his political influence slipping away, asserted himself by initiating a "cultural revolution" designed to remove from power those long-time comrades whom he now saw as bringing about "a restoration of capitalism." And with the help of China's younger generation, the Party Chairman sought to create new forms of mass political participation which would embody his own strategy of social change.

At another level of perception, the experience of this decade seems to have made it increasingly clear to Mao that simply the destruction of the organizational forms of old China—the governing institutions and the "relations of production" which were their base—and their replacement by new "socialist" institutions, were insufficient to guarantee social change. In time he saw that the "four olds" of China's traditional ideas, culture, customs, and habits were the main obstacles to development. In one sense Mao came to reject the Marxist stress on class conflict as the basis of social development in favor of a stress on cultural conflict. He increasingly emphasized the need to transform people's thinking and not just their social organization. In the Great Proletarian Cultural Revolution of 1966 "the thought of Chairman Mao" was to replace Marxism-Leninism as the major source of ideological guidance in China's political life.

In an indirect way, however, the need for a "cultural revolution" affirmed Marxism in that it emphasized that a society would have to pass through a set of discrete stages of social, economic, and political development to realize "communism." The road to utopia was not to be shortened by organizational short-cuts.

The events of 1966–1969 are in part an admission that in cultural terms China remains largely a traditional peasant society. The organization and ideology have changed; yet the Confucian heritage endures in the personalities of the Chinese people. Mao, however, in his unwavering belief that his own revolutionary experience embodies a way to transform a peasant society—and driven by his intolerance of the traditional political culture—has sought ways of institutionalizing "continuous revolution" (*chi-hsü ko-ming*). Without this effort to sustain the process of social change in a peasant society, Mao came to feel, the revolution would succumb to the burden of the Confucian political heritage. China would see the reemergence of a social polarization between an elite leadership group and an exploited, dependent population; an increasingly antagonistic "contradiction" between modern, urban China, and a majority of the population which remained mired in rural poverty.

In the following sections of this chapter we will emphasize the personal values and political style which Mao brought to the process of defining a strategy for China's national development, and then summarize the main lines of leadership debate during the decade 1955–1964. In the next three chapters, we explore in detail the major events by means of which Mao has attempted to transform his conception of China's modernization process into functioning political institutions.

TOWARD THE AUTONOMY OF THE GROUP

As we saw in Part Three, Mao's personal involvement in the revolution and the resistance against Japan revealed his rejection of the passive and dependent quality of the traditional political order. His own aggressiveness merged with that of an age in which the Chinese people, as a society, were attempting to reassert themselves as a major center of world civilization. In this process, shocked into life by a series of military clashes with commercially ambitious foreigners and a great peasant rebellion, Chinese intellectuals slowly came to question the basic assumptions of Confucian culture.

The literati who led the "self strengthening" movement of the late nineteenth century had initially concluded that China's "spiritual essence" could be defended through the selective use of Western technology. More conservative Confucianists, however, saw with greater clarity the manner in which the adoption of this foreign material culture would begin to undermine established bases of power, and the social values that supported them. And from the treaty ports, missionary participants in the ferment of these times pointed out through Chinese language periodicals some of the basic cultural differences which hindered the adaptation of Western technology to established Chinese purposes. They stressed that "the Western peoples looked to the future for fulfillment while the Chinese wished to return to the past," and asserted that "the Confucian moral culture was defective in that it did not emphasize the autonomy (*tzu-chu,* literally 'being one's own master') of each individual." [7]

It was only in the deepening unrest of the May Fourth era after 1919, however—a period of cultural challenge which followed the failures of "self-strengthening" and efforts to establish parliamentary democracy in China—that there developed a vague awareness among the intellectuals that China's difficulties in adjusting to a new era in some way were related to the social orientation of dependency. The spokesmen for this perception were the angered students who saw in the failures of their elders the corruption and weakness of the Confucian cultural heritage. Writing in the influential radical magazine *New Youth* in 1916, Ch'en Tu-hsiu, who five years later was to be a founder of the Chinese Communist Party, revealed the degree to which rejection of Confucian dependence and self-assertion had become the strivings of a revolutionary generation:

> There are three sacred virtues under this Confucian doctrine: *chung* (loyalty), *hsiao* (filiality), and *chieh* (chastity), which are the morals of a slave and not of an independent person. The conduct of a man

7. Cited in Kwang-ching Liu, "Nineteenth-Century China: The Disintegration of the Old Order and the Impact of the West," in Ping-ti Ho and Tang Tsou, eds., *China in Crisis* (Chicago: University of Chicago Press), Vol. I, p. 140.

should be self-centered. Without this self-centeredness, other acts are meaningless. The morals of a slave are not self-centered, therefore every act of a slave is dependent on someone else. Those who proudly regard themselves as the youth of 1916 should struggle to get rid of this dependency and to restore their independent personalities.[8]

Whatever appeals may have existed for a "Western solution" to these strivings for a new cultural orientation—as in the valuation of individualism—were undermined largely by the Westerners themselves. The first Great European War of 1914–1918, and the sense of grievance which Chinese derived from the Versailles peace settlement—in which German concessions in Shantung Province were turned over to Japanese control—seriously degraded the stature of the West in the eyes of China's intellectuals. And in the Bolshevik Revolution of 1917 some began to see an alternative road to national resurgence.

The 1920s and '30s were decades in which China's social leadership became increasingly divided in the search for a world outlook. The Nationalists, under Chiang K'ai-shek, attempted a Confucian revival;[9] and the first leaders of the Chinese Communist movement adhered closely to the Russian revolutionary precedent. In Mao Tse-tung's political career one begins to see an uncertain but persistent effort to define a Chinese way of national development, combining both rejection and innovation within China's own social traditions.

The assertiveness which Mao has displayed throughout his life underscores the degree to which he personally rejects the tradition of dependence on authority. During the Party rectification movement of the early 1940s Mao urged an end to the tradition of uncritical obedience to those in authority: "In order to get rid of the practise of acting blindly which is so common in our Party, we must encourage our comrades to think, to learn the method of analysis and to cultivate the habit of analysis. There is all too little of this habit in our Party." [10] In his policy planning, Mao has revealed a sensitivity to the dependency needs of the population, and to the possibility of the Party being "eaten up" by those who look to authority for security:

In the big cities, food and fuel are now [1948] the central prob-

8. Ch'en Tu-hsiu, "1916," in *New Youth* (*Hsin Ch'ing Nien*), Vol. I, No. 5 (January 1916), p. 3.

9. *See* Mary C. Wright, *The Last Stand of Chinese Conservatism: The T'ung Chih Restoration, 1862–1874* (New York: Atheneum, 1966), Ch. XII.

10. Mao, "Our Study and the Current Situation" (1944), *SW*, English, III, p. 175.

lems; they must be handled in a planned way. Once a city comes under our administration, the problem of the livelihood of the city poor must be solved step by step and in a planned way. Do not raise the slogan, "Open the granaries to relieve the poor." Do not foster among them the psychology of depending on the government for relief.[11]

In an earlier day, however, Mao evinced the politician's awareness that only by fulfilling the broad popular expectations toward government characteristic of the politics of dependency could the Party gain active support for its cause:

We must lead the peasants' struggle for land and distribute the land to them, heighten their labour enthusiasm and increase agricultural production, safeguard the interests of the workers, establish co-operatives, develop trade with outside areas, and solve the problems facing the masses—food, shelter and clothing, fuel, rice, cooking oil and salt, sickness and hygiene, and marriage. In short, all the practical problems in the masses' everyday life should claim our attention. If we attend to these problems, solve them and satisfy the needs of the masses, we shall really become organizers of the well-being of the masses, and they will truly rally round us and give us their warm support. Comrades, will we then be able to arouse them to take part in the revolutionary war? Yes, indeed we will.[12]

Mao's writings thus reveal a paradoxical orientation toward the dependency theme in Chinese culture which is based on the demands of power: The leader seeking revolutionary change finds a valuable goal in the strength and dignity of critical self-integrity; yet the practical politician perceives that dealing effectively with the needs and habits of the people must be the Party's role if power is to be attained.

Mao's resolution of this "contradiction" between his own valuation of self-reliance and the legacy of a culture which stressed dependence on authority has been to stress the autonomy of the group —to have the individual find self-realization in a mutually supporting community of equals, rather than through submissive reliance on hierarchical authority. Like his cultural forebears Mao rejects as "selfishness" the assertion of the individual apart from collective purposes; yet his personal sensitivity to the oppressiveness of authority has led him to seek ways of shifting power away from one dominant individual to the group.

11. Mao, "Telegram to the Headquarters of the Loyang Front after the Recapture of the City" (1948), *SW*, English, IV, p. 248.
12. Mao, "Be Concerned with the Well-Being of the Masses, Pay Attention to Methods of Work" (1934), *SW*, English, I, pp. 147–148.

This stress on the self-reliant group has been most obvious to foreign observers in Mao's assertion of national independence. As he wrote in 1945, when even the Soviet Union had proven itself to be an uncertain ally through its declaration of continuing recognition and support for Chiang K'ai-shek's Nationalist government:

> On what basis should our policy rest? It should rest on our own strength, and that means regeneration through one's own efforts (*tzu-li keng-sheng*). We are not alone (*pu ku-li,* not isolated), all the countries and people in the world opposed to imperialism are our friends. Nevertheless, we stress regeneration through our own efforts. Relying on the forces we ourselves organize, we can defeat all Chinese and foreign reactionaries. Chiang K'ai-shek, on the contrary, relies entirely on the aid of U.S. imperialism, which he looks upon as his mainstay.[13]

And in an attempt to destroy with his pen whatever hopes educated and Western-oriented Chinese might have had of depending on United States intervention in the final phase of the civil war, Mao contemptuously wrote of the "belly ache" that would come from eating foreign fish:

> The Americans have sprinkled some relief flour in Peiping, Tientsin and Shanghai to see who will stoop to pick it up. Like Chiang Tai Kung fishing, they have cast the line for the fish who want to be caught. But he who swallows food handed out in contempt will get a belly ache.[14]

Mao's stress on the autonomy of the group was to find varied expression in the years after Liberation: in the domestic effort to build self-reliant agricultural communities through mass mobilization; in the full assertion of independence from the Soviet Union; and in the attempt to maintain the People's Liberation Army as a mass fighting and production organization, in which hierarchical authority would be played down through abolition of the symbols of rank and promotion of regular social contact between officers and enlisted ranks.

THE LEGACY OF THE REVOLUTION

Mao provided a combination of personal values and institutional forms in defining a strategy of national development which has characterized his leadership of the revolution. Three aspects of his conception of the political process seem to define the areas where

13. Mao, "The Situation and Our Policy after the Victory in the War of Resistance against Japan" (1945), *SW*, English, IV, p. 20.
14. Mao, "Farewell, Leighton Stuart!" (1949), *SW*, English, IV, p. 437.

he departs from or merges with China's traditional political culture, and where he has put himself in conflict with other Party leaders.

1) *The Importance of Struggle.* The area where Mao most notably departs from Chinese tradition—and where he brushes aside Confucian fears of *luan*—concerns his stress on mobilization and struggle. As was explored in Part Three, Mao saw political conflict as "awakening" people out of that passivity which characterized political dependency. He came to believe that if the Party forced confrontations with sources of social resentment and discontent even peasants could become "conscious" and mobilized to the revolutionary cause. Grievance-telling and study were institutionalized during the Yenan period and were designed to enhance people's awareness of their social enemies. The criticism and struggle meetings which were a product of both Party rectification and land reform formalized conflict with opponents of the revolution.

Military action, of course, most fully expressed Mao's commitment to struggle; yet the martial spirit has been no end in itself. By merging military organization with the tasks of economic production—another Yenan development which was to be reapplied during the Great Leap Forward—Mao has sought to institutionalize the "liberation" of those aggressive emotions which, denied legitimate expression in Confucian society, could promote social change.[15]

In the post-Liberation period, the continuing series of political and economic campaigns (*yün-tung*) express most fully Mao's commitment to struggle. By mobilizing the resentments and energies of an entire population for concerted action in periodic surges of activity, and by requiring individuals to criticize the erroneous thinking and behavior of themselves and their cohorts, Mao has attempted to sustain the momentum of social revolution.

2) *The Authority of the Group.* A second dimension of Mao's political style is his effort to shift authority away from its personalized, hierarchical form to group processes. Where Confucian culture placed authority beyond criticism, Mao merged his commitment to struggle with a belief that authority was generated from group life, and he sought to institutionalize forms which would subject even Party authorities to group pressures.

In student days Mao revealed a belief that those in power should be criticized for their errors, but on the basis of principles, not per-

15. Franz Schurmann has suggested that the merging of "war and production" through organization was one of the great innovations of Chinese Communist leadership. See *Ideology and Organization in Communist China* (Berkeley: University of California Press, 1968), p. 425.

sonal attack.[16] And as a Party member he came to see that an ideology could further depersonalize authority, by providing standards for criticism. The experience of the revolution, however, revealed how difficult it was both to sustain criticism and to keep it depersonalized; and in the post-Liberation era Mao eventually came into conflict with other Party leaders who resisted his efforts to subject the Party to criticism from "outside" groups.

When his own control over China's political institutions began to slip away after the failure of the Great Leap Forward, Mao saw that he had to repersonalize authority in order to maintain his impact on the shaping of China's new social institutions. But as we shall see in Chapter XIX, even in this effort he was seeking ways of subjecting those in authority to group criticism. The image of the Paris Commune has remained for Mao and other radical Chinese leaders a vital symbol of the people creating and criticizing their own leadership, just as the People's Commune became an ideal of group self-reliance in economic productivity. The problem has been, and remains, how to institutionalize these ideals in a society with enduring traditions of hierarchical leadership.

Group processes have provided some of the most potent forms of social control in post-Liberation China; and they further merge Mao's commitment to struggle with collective authority. In Part Three we saw that Mao's basic strategy of political conflict has been to unite as large a group as possible against a handful of isolated enemies. In terms of the workings of personality, the effectiveness of this approach is based on individual fears of being isolated from group support and standing alone before the angered "masses." In this process, Mao draws on the traditional dependence of the individual on group life, and anxieties about aggression, as bases of political integration.

Group processes also provided a way of generating the authority which traditionally had stood above those in subordination. The search for individual models of revolutionary behavior in group activities who can be used as objects of mass emulation, in Mao's view, enables the people to produce leaders from their own midst. And in post-1949 China there has been a constant search for and propagation of model citizens and workers—individuals used by the Party as authoritative examples of how the people in new China are to build a modern society.

Model production experiences have also played a key role in the leadership process by providing lower-level cadres with examples

16. This incident is recounted in Jerome Chen, *Mao and the Chinese Revolution,* p. 43.

to follow in the promotion of their work. And as we shall see, it was in terms of competing models of the development process that China's leaders came to express their increasingly divisive conflict in the 1960s.

The stress on learning through model emulation draws on traditional forms of education, just as the stress on group life adapts enduring themes in China's political culture to contemporary political tasks. As we shall stress in the conclusion, the need for those in authority to be increasingly manipulative in the use of model experiences and "thinking" reveals the distance between Mao's objective of well-institutionalized group processes which will give genuine authority to the people, and the increasing reliance which, in fact, has been placed on traditional forms of political control. The dividing line between innovation and restoration is often very thin, and at the end of his career Mao has had to make increasingly greater adjustments to the fact that for all his revolutionary insights, China's traditional culture persists in the personalities of his people.

3) *The Need for Study*. A third major aspect of Mao's political style which was institutionalized during the period of revolution is his stress on mass political education. Unlike the traditional deference and loyalty to an individual teacher, Mao has sought to make ideology a more impersonal basis for "rectifying" the social outlook of the Chinese people. One senses that his conviction is that if only China's seven hundred millions would learn the insights about society and politics which were central to his own political awakening, they would be able to build a new society based on coordinated group life. Hence, he has sought to propagate his "thought," his own social experience, as a model worthy of emulation.

Ideological unity, moreover, serves as the basis of group solidarity and provides the people with standards of behavior by which they can criticize those leaders who "deviate" in their use of authority. As was true in traditional China, there is no legitimacy given to divergence of opinion; and Mao, like imperial leaders of an earlier time, assumes that social unity is possible only on the basis of unified thinking. Here again, the dividing line between ideological study as a foundation for personal initiative and the traditional assertion of authority through memorization of the word is very thin. In the early 1960s conflict between Mao and Liu Shao-ch'i was to develop over whose "word"—whose book and thought—was to serve as the basis for China's new socialist unity and national development. And in the turmoil which followed the first months of the Cultural Revolution Mao was increasingly to use study of his little red book of quotations as a method of reimposing social order and discipline.

TOWARD A STRATEGY OF NATIONAL
DEVELOPMENT: A DECADE OF DEBATE

The major dimensions of Mao's political style are continually visible throughout the increasingly divisive debate among Party leaders during the decade 1955–1964. The question first at issue was the most appropriate strategy for China's national development; but by the end of this decade, the Party leadership was to be rent by an uncompromising struggle for control of the decision-making process in the People's Republic, and conflict over who was to be Mao's "revolutionary successor" to Party leadership.

The initial differences among Party leaders concerned whether China's problems in national development were primarily political and social in nature, or whether a major emphasis on economic reconstruction would produce a nation-state of power and wealth. Many of the leaders apparently felt that the question of "who will win" in the revolutionary struggle had been solved by the mid-1950s, and that primary emphasis should be given to economic development through technical change. The Party, through its army, the public security forces, and the newly created governmental system and mass organizations, seemed successfully to have replaced the structures of Nationalist control in both the urban and rural areas. Mao, however, increasingly came to define the problems of development in political and cultural terms. As his chosen successor Lin Piao recalled, Mao had asserted in 1956 that "the question of which will win out, socialism or capitalism, is still not really settled." [17]

Mao's personal sensitivities made him ever aware of those traditional misuses of authority which he had spent a lifetime opposing. With the creation of the Party's own political system, he increasingly came to see the danger of the emergence of a new exploitative ruling elite which would resort to the old traditional abuses— material self-indulgence, suppression of criticism, and bureaucratic entrenchment—forms of asserting authority which would "cut the Party off from the masses." To the degree that his life-time colleagues did not share this sensitivity to misuses of power—as he was to discover in the Hundred Flowers episode of 1957—Mao came to question their commitment to revolution. And as they resisted those of his policies which were designed to eliminate such problems, he came to see them as "right opportunists" or "revisionists" and eventually as active "counterrevolutionaries."

17. Lin Piao, "Report to the Ninth Party Congress of the Communist Party of China," *SCMP*, No. 4406 (May 1, 1969), p. 15.

This polarization of good and evil reflects the sharpening of the leadership conflict that emerged from the failure of the Great Leap Forward; but in the mid-1950s differences among Party leaders were still "non-antagonistic." Documents from this period indicate that different individuals and groups within the leadership looked to different social problems as the focal areas of national reconstruction. They tended to define their strategies in terms of which social class was to be the Party's main ally during the period of transition to socialism. And in a striking manner, the evolution of Party policy during this period replays the pattern of class coalition and leadership "deviation" which characterized the decades of struggle for power.

The years from the Liberation to mid-1957 were a period of reliance on China's intellectuals, the "bourgeoisie" (in the sense of an urbanized, technical elite educated before the revolution), in an attempt to build the economy on the Soviet Union's pattern of modernization. "Heavy industry received the bulk of investment funds (including Soviet aid) and made notable advances, while agriculture and consumer goods were relatively neglected."[18] Like the revolutionary period of 1921–1927—when Comintern advisers played a key role in Party construction, in formulating the alliance with the "bourgeois" Kuomintang, and in the urban focus of the revolution—Soviet advisers exercised a heavy influence over China's post-Liberation economic, military, and social policies.

Mao was leader of both Party and state during this period, but evidence indicates that he was only first among equals in his influence over policy-making. Furthermore, his leadership may have come under serious challenge. In 1955 it was revealed that Kao Kang, head of the Party's Northeast Bureau and Chairman of the State Planning Commission, had formed an "anti-Party" clique with Jao Shu-shih of the Shanghai Party apparatus, and had attempted an "unprincipled" takeover of the leadership from their "independent kingdoms."[19] Mao seems to have drawn two lessons from this challenge which later expressed themselves in coherent policies:

18. Audrey Donnithorne, *China's Economic System* (London: George Allen and Unwin, 1967), p. 17.

19. The exact nature of the Kao-Jao affair has remained obscure, and what little evidence is available suggests that Mao was not directly challenged but that Kao and Jao directed their activities at men like Liu Shao-ch'i and Chou En-lai. There has been speculation that Mao was sick at this time, and that the factional struggle in late 1953 and early 1954, culminating in the Fourth Plenum of the Seventh Central Committee, was on the order of a premature succession crisis. *See* Frederick Teiwes, "The Evolution of Leadership Purges in Communist China," *The China Quarterly*, No. 41 (January–March 1970), pp. 122–126.

First, it was clear that the modernized sectors of Chinese society—in this case the relatively small centers of industrial economy in Manchuria and Shanghai—could make powerful claims on limited state resources. The highly organized nature of these sectors (as was also to be the case with the army and Party) enabled them to serve as ,influential bases from which the political leadership could be challenged. Second, one may speculate that Mao saw in Kao's challenge one more indication of Russian interference in China's domestic leadership struggles. At least he had another example of Chinese leaders being "misled" by Soviet policy precedents.[20]

In any event, it is clear that by mid-1955 Mao began to express concern publicly about the stress on industrialization at the expense of the agricultural sector and about the tendency of Party members blindly to emulate the Soviet development experience. In his first major post-Liberation statement on agricultural policy he warned, "on no account should we allow . . . comrades to use the Soviet experience as a cover for their idea of moving at a snail's pace." [21] As with his earlier reaction to Ch'en Tu-hsiu's "rightist" deviation, Mao saw some of his colleagues endangering the progress of the revolution by adhering too closely to the Russian precedent. In this case the stress on industrial development conflicted with his own evaluation of the agricultural sector as the focal area of China's development problems. And in response to those who dragged their feet in finding a radical solution to problems of production in the countryside, Mao invoked his characteristic irony by observing

20. There has been speculation that Stalin, distrustful of the assertive Mao, attempted to encourage Kao Kang as an alternative Party leader. Kao emerged as the dominant figure in the "Northeast People's Government" established in Manchuria in 1948, and went to Moscow several months before the founding of the People's Republic to sign a trade agreement with the Soviet Government on behalf of the Manchurian regime.

After Liberation, almost all of his public appearances were associated with official Russian visitors. There has been no direct evidence, however, that Stalin actively interfered in leadership struggles within the Chinese Party through Kao, as he had done earlier in the case of Wang Ming—and as Khrushchev encouraged P'eng Teh-huai in 1959 (*see* pp. 390–392 below). The most detailed examination of evidence on this subject to date is Frederick C. Teiwes, *Rectification Campaigns and Purges in Communist China* (unpublished Ph.D. dissertation, Columbia University, New York, 1970), Ch. X.

Franz Schurmann has documented the relationship between the rise of the "one man management" system of industrial organization in Manchuria and the career of Kao Kang. See *Ideology and Organization in Communist China*, pp. 266–287.

21. Mao, "On the Question of Agricultural Co-operation" (1955), in *Selected Readings from the Works of Mao Tse-tung* (Peking: Foreign Languages Press, 1967), p. 331.

that, "some of our comrades are tottering along like a woman with bound feet and constantly complaining, 'You're going too fast.' " [22]

Mao's estimation was that this major problem area in development required a "vertical" alliance between the Party ("the working class") and those who constituted a majority of the population, the peasantry. He asserted that without a radical effort to attain "socialist" ownership in China's countryside, a capitalist, rich-peasant economy would soon emerge and bring about a new polarization between rich and poor in the villages. Only by creating "common prosperity"—that is, by eliminating wide disparities in income among the rural population—could the Party hold the loyalty and gain the active support of the poor and lower-middle peasants. ". . . this is the only way to consolidate the worker-peasant alliance. Otherwise, this alliance will be in real danger of breaking up." [23]

Mao's position, formally expressed in a twelve-year program for agricultural development which was presented in draft form in January 1956, apparently was overruled by a majority of those in the Party leadership who saw the key to China's progress in industrialization. These "economic" developers held that the major problem lay in encouraging China's precious few intellectuals to lend their skills to the Party's cause. Stress on the technical aspects of economic progress called for a "horizontal" alliance with the urban intellectuals who held such skills. These "economic" leaders saw the major deviational danger as "leftist" in the sense of sectarianism or exclusive attitudes toward non-Party intellectuals by those within the Party (like Mao) who tended to look with suspicion or contempt on this "bourgeoisie."

When Soviet Party First Secretary Nikita Khrushchev unexpectedly attacked Stalin and the "personality cult" in February 1956, opponents of Mao's "worker-peasant" alliance acquired the issue of an overly-assertive Party leader whose abandonment of collective leadership had brought great harm to a Party. This event in the Soviet Union apparently strengthened the collective decision-making process in China and led to the overruling of Mao's agricultural development plan in April of 1956.[24] The impact of Khrushchev's anti-Stalin attack on leadership conflict within the Chinese Communist Party can hardly be overstressed. In fact, Mao has dated the inception of the Sino-Soviet dispute from this event.

22. *Ibid.*, p. 316.
23. *Ibid.*, p. 334.
24. *See* Schurmann, *Ideology and Organization in Communist China*, pp. 142–143.

The upheavals in Poland and Hungary in the fall of 1956 (events also triggered by de-Stalinization) appear to have shifted the coalition of power within the Party leadership more in Mao's favor in the development debate. While the public Party interpretation of these events was that "counterrevolutionary" elements had taken advantage of domestic problems in Hungary, Mao drew the conclusion that even in a country which was in the process of "building socialism," the Party and governmental systems were vulnerable to "degeneration." [25] And he stressed to Chinese Party members that, "in order to get rid of the root cause of disturbances, we must stamp out bureaucracy." [26]

With his hand thus strengthened by the events in Eastern Europe, Mao sought to apply his conception of controlled struggle between those social groups still "mutually related and mutually antagonistic." His aim was to check "conservatism" and abuses of authority by lower-level Party and government cadres and to criticize "antisocialist" attitudes held by people both within and outside the Party. He apparently felt that if the intellectuals were given a constructive role in China's new socialist political process, their energies would be "liberated" in the service of Party rectification and national development. In the Hundred Flowers period of public "blooming and contending" during the spring of 1957, Mao sought to establish a critical dialogue between the Party and the intellectuals.

The criticism encouraged by Mao and his supporters, however, came to exceed the bounds of attack on lower-level cadres. Many intellectuals and students challenged the Communist Party's basic monopoly of decision-making power and the appropriateness of

25. This perception was eventually expressed formally in public polemics with the Soviet Union. (*See* "On Khrushchev's Phoney Communism and Its Historical Lessons for the World" [1964], *Polemic on the General Line of the International Communist Movement* [Peking: Foreign Languages Press, 1965], p. 468.) And when "revisionism" had revealed itself even within the leadership ranks of the Chinese Party, Mao was to claim that through the Great Proletarian Cultural Revolution "a new era in the history of the international Communist movement" had opened. Through this mass movement he had found a solution to the problem of leadership degeneration—a danger not perceived before in the history of the movement. (*See* the *People's Daily* and *Red Flag* joint editorial, "Carry the Great Proletarian Cultural Revolution through to the End"; trans. in *Peking Review* [Peking], No. 1 [January 1, 1967], p. 8.)

26. Mao, "On the Correct Handling of Contradictions among the People" (1957); trans. in *Communist China, 1955–1959* (Cambridge, Mass.: Harvard University Press, 1962), p. 291. Hereafter, this collection of documents will be cited as *CC 1955–59*.

some of the Party's most fundamental policies. Party leaders characterized the events of the spring of 1957 as the "betrayal" of April 1927 all over again:[27] The "bourgeoisie" were unreliable allies in the development process; and an urban-centered strategy which stressed their skills would only put responsibility and resources in disloyal hands and undermine Party leadership. In the "anti-rightist" reaction to the events of the spring the Party reasserted its leading role, and Mao "retreated" to a rural-centered strategy of development.

While Mao's personal sponsorship of the Hundred Flowers policy may have temporarily diluted his political influence among those leaders who questioned his approach to Party rectification through criticism from the "outside," the events of the spring (and continuing problems of agricultural production) strengthened his assertion that development could not proceed through a strategy which placed primary reliance on the skills of disloyal "bourgeois" intellectuals. His earlier call for a twelve-year program of agricultural development, which placed primary reliance on the mass energies of China's majority rural population, was revived in October 1957; and in the years of 1958–1960, Mao sought to convince those colleagues who were tottering along with "bound feet" that through mobilization of the peasantry the country could make a "great leap forward." This was a new "Kiangsi" era in its stress on rural action: The peasants were organized into military units for production, and on all fronts there was a "leftist" effort to wage an adventuresome war with the forces hindering social and economic change in the countryside.

Through the "three red flag" policies of the Great Leap period, Mao attempted to adapt the methods of political mobilization and control developed during the struggle for power to the tasks of economic development. In effect, he was saying that where the Soviet experience was inappropriate to China's specific conditions and problems, the precedent of China's (Mao's) own revolutionary experience provided the shortest road to national greatness. In suggesting that the People's Communes had placed China on the verge of realizing communism[28]—and by implication ahead of the Soviet Union—Mao was trying to reassert the legitimacy of his revolution

27. This characterization was explicitly drawn by P'eng Chen, First Secretary of the Peking Party Committee. (*See SCMP,* No. 1588 [August 12, 1957], p. 2.)

28. The most detailed analysis of Chinese claims that the communes would enable the country to realize communism in the near future—and the impact of these claims on Sino-Soviet relations—will be found in Donald S. Zagoria, *The Sino-Soviet Conflict, 1956–1961* (Princeton: Princeton University Press, 1962), Ch. III.

in the wake of the attack on Stalin, with whom he had so closely identified himself.

The production crisis which resulted from the overly-ambitious and ill-planned Great Leap effort produced, however, a new "long march," both in the sense of a seven-year period of recovery to the level of production which had been reached in 1958,[29] and in Mao's loss of influence among his top Party colleagues. The failures of the Great Leap revealed that there were new critics like Wang Ming among the Party leadership, men who continued to see the Soviet experience as an appropriate developmental model.

Evidence suggests that as with Stalin's earlier sponsorship of Chinese Party members as a way of gaining influence in a potentially rival Party, the Russians probably encouraged first P'eng Teh-huai, and then other "revisionists" within the Chinese Party, to criticize Mao's leadership. Mao was beginning to present a major challenge to their own national policies and their primacy within the International Communist Movement. The period 1959–1966 was a time of increasing conflict among Chinese Party leaders. The escalation in Sino-Soviet tensions during this period seems intimately related to Mao's effort to undercut the arguments of his domestic critics who may have sought to justify less radical approaches to China's national development in terms of "socialist" precedents in Yugoslavia and the Soviet Union.

At the 1959 Lushan Central Committee Plenum Mao successfully met P'eng Teh-huai's challenge to his development policies; but in the deepening leadership crisis Mao apparently was compelled to repeat the earlier pattern of his rise to Party control. He turned to the army to rebuild a power base as his influence over Party and governmental organizations slipped away. Under the leadership of the ever-loyal Lin Piao, who replaced P'eng as Defense Minister, the People's Liberation Army became a new source of support for the aging leader and a testing ground for new approaches to political indoctrination and control which would institutionalize Mao's conceptions of political action and social organization.

During the "three difficult years" of food shortage and natural disasters which forced a pullback from the Great Leap effort, Party control was relaxed in the villages. Mao apparently watched with growing concern as the peasants asserted their own approaches to restoring production in the countryside. Many sought to withdraw

29. *See* Alexander Eckstein, "Economic Planning, Organization and Control in Communist China: A Review Article," *Current Scene* (Hong Kong: United States Consulate General), Vol. IV, No. 21 (November 25, 1966), p. 1.

from collective farming, and resumed traditional social practices. Local cadres took advantage of their positions to increase their own incomes while others were verging on starvation.

At the Tenth Central Committee Plenum in September 1962, Mao called for renewed promotion of "socialist education" in the countryside to combat the reemergence of "capitalist tendencies" and stated forcefully that the Party must continue to wage "class struggle" with traditional practices still evident among its cadres and the population at large.

The ensuing years of the Socialist Education Campaign were a time of qualitative change in relations among Party leaders. Some who disagreed with Mao's policies on Party rectification and leadership in the rural areas apparently expressed their disagreement by applying the Chairman's line in such an extreme way that support would be lost. Even though Mao remained the symbol of national resurgence, he complained that his opponents' practices were "left in form but right in essence"; they "waved red flags" of deference to him even as they "opposed the red flag" of his policies.

In the summer of 1964 which apparently was *the* critical period of change in relations among Party leaders, Mao publicly raised the issue of "cultivating revolutionary successors." He thus reopened the question of who was to follow him in the leadership of Party and nation. The army was put forward as a model organization in a national campaign that by implication slighted the leading role of the Party. Organizationally, political departments patterned on army practice appeared in the Party and in governmental agencies; and in the next two years army personnel were increasingly to fill these supervisory roles. In retrospect it is clear that Mao, through Lin Piao and the army, was explicitly challenging the power base of those whom he now considered to be his opponents.

The precise reasons for the timing of the breakdown in relations among Party leaders and the opening of public conflict during 1966 —a period when the war in Viet-Nam seemed to involve serious threats to China's security—remain obscure. However, from the vantage point of 1970 it seems clear that Mao's objectives in the Cultural Revolution were to remove from power those leaders whom he saw opposing his development and foreign policies and to reestablish his "thought" as the guide to China's national development. Now in his seventies, and reportedly in uncertain health, Mao saw this effort as requiring both the aid of the loyal and more youthful—if scarcely more healthy—Lin Piao, and the support of China's younger generation.

In the Cultural Revolution of 1966–1969 Mao vicariously relived his own political career in the struggles of the student Red

Guards whom he set against "revisionists" within the Party. In declaring to the young intellectuals that Marxism's essence was the notion that "to rebel is justified," Mao was trying to transmit to a new generation the spirit of his own youthful rebellion against established authority. But now the "establishment" was a Party and governmental system which had proven itself increasingly resistant to his influence.

The Eleventh Central Committee Plenum of August 1966 was for Mao another Tsunyi meeting in that it reaffirmed his control over Chinese political life. And the Ninth Party Congress of April 1969 was a new Seventh Congress, reestablishing the guiding role of "the thought of Mao Tse-tung" in the life of the Chinese Communist Party.

*   *   *

The emphasis in this overview on the parallel political rhythms of the periods of revolution and post-Liberation reconstruction is a way of stressing the continuity that Mao has revealed in his personal political style. Also, many of the social issues which Mao confronted as he sought ways of transforming Chinese society have shown remarkable endurance. The conflict over a development strategy which characterized Party leadership relations from the mid-1950s also emphasizes that Mao has remained determined to prevent what he sees as the "restoration" of China's traditional political culture in either elite abuses of authority, a new class polarization in the villages, or an increasing disparity between urban and rural life. The Hundred Flowers period of 1957, the Great Leap Forward of 1958–1960, and the Cultural Revolution of 1966–1969 are the three post-Liberation periods when Mao's personal style has had its greatest impact on China's political life. In the following chapters, we will explore in greater detail aspects of these periods which reveal Mao's efforts to institutionalize the political legacy of the revolution.

Chapter XVII

ONE PARTY AND
"ONE HUNDRED SCHOOLS":
LEADERSHIP, LETHARGY, OR *LUAN?*

Bourgeois reactionary thinking has invaded
the militant [Chinese] Communist Party!
Certain Communist Party members claim to
have learned Marxism. Where has it gone?

MAO TSE-TUNG.
May 1951.[1]

With consolidation of basic military and political control of the
China mainland the Communist Party leadership faced a problem
that had confronted the founders of past dynasties: how to "dis-
mount from the horse" of military conquest and administer a vast
peasant empire. Traditionally this problem had embodied a great
paradox, especially for those dynasties established by nomadic invaders committed to a martial style of life. If control of this extensive, decentralized society were to be achieved, the dynasty had to
gain the active cooperation of the Confucian-oriented rural gentry
who provided the major source of literate imperial administrators.
Yet in gaining the cooperation of this indigenous elite, concessions
had to be made to their style of life and control of local resources,
thus perpetuating a life style which was an appealing—and "corrupting"—alternative to the martial virtues of a conquest genera-

1. *People's Daily* editorial, "We Must Give Attention to Discussing the
Film 'The Life of Wu Hsün' " (May 20, 1951).
During the Cultural Revolution of 1966–1969 it was revealed that this
editorial was one of several written personally by Mao Tse-tung in the early
1950s criticizing the "bourgeois reactionary thinking" of Party intellectuals.
This fact emphasizes the continuity of Mao's concern with the problem of
intellectuals "corrupting" the Party's revolutionary commitment because of
their "backward" or "antisocialist" attitudes.

tion. If given sufficient time, the Confucian gentry could "absorb" —or more accurately, "convert"—their conquerors.

For the Chinese Communists this old paradox was sharpened with a new and double edge. Basically, the Party leadership was committed to a program of national resurgence through social change and economic modernization, yet the necessary political commitment and technical skills were in exceedingly short supply. Party membership in 1956 represented less than 3 percent of China's total population, more than 80 percent of which still eked out a living by ancient agricultural techniques in the rural districts. The "vanguard of the proletariat" was more than 70 percent a peasant organization, and workers comprised only 15 percent of total Party membership.[2] Hence, in the modernization effort there was a basic danger that the revolution might become submerged in the habits and life style of China's peasant majority.

The other edge of this problem was that only a small fraction of China's intellectuals, her small but highly-trained technical, administrative, educational, and artistic elite, appeared committed to the Party's cause. Hardly more than 10 percent of all Party members in 1956 were classified as intellectuals; and less than half of the country's total of approximately four million "high" and ordinary intellectuals were considered to be politically "progressive."[3] If development efforts were to proceed, considerable reliance would have to be placed on their skills; yet such reliance would give political influence and control of scarce resources to this small, urban, and largely foreign-trained "bourgeoisie."

In short, a small political elite committed to social and economic change saw its revolution threatened from both peasant conservatism and the life style of a small urban skill group. As Mao Tse-tung and his supporters phrased it in the mid-1950s, "Rightist conservative ideology . . . presents a most serious threat to our Party."[4]

There was significant divergence of opinion within the Party leadership, however, as to the actual strength of this threat, and

2. These figures are drawn from Franz Schurmann, *Ideology and Organization in Communist China,* pp. 128–139.

3. This evaluation was presented by Chou En-lai in his report, "On the Question of Intellectuals" (January 14, 1956); trans. in *CC 1955–59,* pp. 130–131.

4. *Ibid.,* p. 128.

Mao had stressed the dangers of "right opportunism" and "rightist conservatism" in his report of late July 1955, "On the Question of Agricultural Co-operation" (*see* the text in *Selected Readings from the Works of Mao Tse-tung,* esp. pp. 322, 330), and in his editorial notes of December of that same year in *Socialist Upsurge in China's Countryside* [Peking: Foreign Languages Press, 1957], esp. pp. 10, 12).

whether the greater danger was the "conservatism" of the peasantry or that of the intellectuals. Furthermore, there was disagreement as to the best method for dealing with these challenges to the primacy of "proletarian" values and goals. During the period of the First Five Year Plan (1953–1957) majority opinion within the Party leadership held that China's social revolution could best be promoted on the basis of a program which placed primary emphasis on rapid industrialization.[5] As a consequence, most Party leaders were willing to subordinate any sense of threat of "corruption" by the intellectuals to the need to gain their precious skills for the development effort. Hence, in contrast to Mao's emphasis on the danger from the "right," a number of important documents published during 1956 stressed the "leftist" danger of sectarianism on the part of Party members which would hinder cooperation with non-Party intellectuals.

An attitude of tolerance toward the intellectuals was most obvious at the Chinese Communist Party's Eighth Congress of September 1956. The Party's Vice Chairman Liu Shao-ch'i, in the main political report to the Congress, asserted: "The question of who will win in the struggle between socialism and capitalism in our country has now been decided," and he criticized "some members of our Party who hold that everything should absolutely be 'of one colour.' "[6] Perhaps the clearest expression of a conciliatory attitude toward "class" differences was contained in the report of the Party's Secretary-General, Teng Hsiao-p'ing, on the revision of the Party Constitution. In justifying less stringent standards for admission to Party membership Teng stressed:

> The difference between workers and office employees is now only a matter of division of labor within the same class. . . . The vast majority of our intellectuals have now come over politically to the side of the working class. . . . What is the point, then, of classifying these social strata into two different categories? And even if we were

5. This point of view was detailed in Li Fu-ch'un's report on the First Five Year Plan, delivered in July 1955, and reiterated in Liu Shao-ch'i's political report to the Party's Eighth Congress held in September of 1956.

6. Liu Shao-ch'i, "The Political Report of the Central Committee of the Communist Party of China to the Eighth National Congress of the Party" (September 15, 1956), in *Eighth National Congress of the Communist Party of China* (Peking: Foreign Languages Press, 1956), Vol. I, pp. 37, 74.

Liu was to be attacked for these words of tolerance toward class differences during the Cultural Revolution. *See* "The Third Confession of Liu Shao-ch'i," in *Chinese Law and Government*, Vol. I, No. 1 (Spring 1968), pp. 77–78.

to try and devise a classification, how could we make it neat and clear-cut? [7]

Teng's rhetorical question was very likely addressed to Mao who continued to hold different views. Within six months, the Party Chairman was to assert, "There can be no development without differentiation and struggle." [8] Such conflicting evaluations of the Party's relationship to the intellectual skill group which it sought to use in national development were the basis of leadership debates over the question of Party rectification during the years 1956–57. With the perspective of more than a decade of hindsight, this conflict can be seen to be part of a larger debate over the issue of the most appropriate "road" to China's national resurgence. Should there be moderately paced development, emphasizing economic construction in the urban areas, or should there be an intensely paced, politicized effort aimed primarily at bringing China's rural majority into the modern world through socialist forms of collective work organization?

In the following pages we will trace the evolution of leadership conflict over the question of Party rectification, and the effect on the mobilization of China's intellectuals in support of the development effort during the years 1956–57.

Mao's personal position in this period of debate seems to have been shaped by his enduring distrust of the intellectuals, although his major concern was a matter of the Party's "alliance" with this technical and administrative "bourgeoisie." He saw the stress on Soviet-style industrialization as giving excessive influence to "bourgeois" values *within* the Party and leading to a slighting of development in the rural areas.

In its simplest terms, the argument explored in this chapter is that in late 1955 Mao was persuaded of the need to win greater support from intellectuals in order to develop the economy, but that he was unwilling to accept passively their "rightist conservatism." Their working conditions should be improved, but they also should be expected to "remold" their bourgeois world outlook. This policy was considerably liberalized in application, however, as a result of "de-Stalinization" in the Soviet Union. Other Party leaders, some of whom were opposed to Mao's policies for developing the rural

7. Teng Hsiao-p'ing, "Report on the Revision of the Constitution of the Communist Party of China" (September 16, 1956), in *Eighth National Congress of the Communist Party of China,* Vol. I, pp. 213–214.

8. Mao Tse-tung, "Speech at the Chinese Communist Party's National Conference on Propaganda Work" (March 12, 1957), in *Selected Readings from the Works of Mao Tse-tung,* p. 399.

economy, used Khrushchev's February 1956 attack on Stalin to restrict Mao's influence over policy in the spring of 1956; and they diluted the struggle against "rightist conservatism" as they pressed their own conservative economic line. It was only after the upheaval in Hungary in late 1956 that Mao was able to reassert a policy of "unity and struggle" in the Party's relationship with the intellectuals. Then, however, as a result of the thwarting of his agricultural policies and the lesson of Hungary, the Party Chairman turned his attention to "right opportunism" within the Party itself.

The essence of Mao's "Hundred Flowers" policy, as he sought to apply it in the spring of 1957, was the effort to set intellectuals and Party cadres against each other in a critical debate which would expose and "rectify" improper behavior and attitudes held by each group. What at the time appeared to be an unprecedented move toward liberalization was really Mao's first major effort since the 1949 Liberation to combat "bourgeois" influences within the Party. This was a strategy—to use a phrase of the Cultural Revolution— which was "right in form but left in essence."

Mao's strategy of "unity and struggle" was resisted, however, by the Party apparatus, by cadres who objected to criticism "from the outside," and by other Party leaders who did not want to jeopardize the active support of non-Party intellectuals in the industrialization effort. Thus during 1956–57 there developed a shifting interplay between events in the Soviet Union and Eastern Europe, the balance of political influence within the Chinese Communist Party leadership, and the Party's relationship to the intellectuals.

"DE-STALINIZATION" AND DEVELOPMENT

In late 1955, as part of the promotion of the revised First Five Year Plan for the economy, the Party began efforts to improve relations with non-Party intellectuals. Apparently the initiative lay with such men as Li Fu-ch'un, Chairman of the State Planning Commission, and State Premier Chou En-lai. After several years of "thought reform" and recently concluded national campaigns to discredit as "counterrevolutionaries" the writer Hu Feng and philosopher Hu Shih, the intellectual community showed signs of serious demoralization and a tendency to withdraw from active social involvement.[9]

9. Mao's close personal involvement in these campaigns has been revealed in Cultural Revolution materials. He is now identified as the author of editorial critiques on the Hu Feng affair which appeared in the *People's Daily* on May 20th, 24th, and June 10th, 1955. (*See* the pamphlet, *Mao Tse-tung Szu-hsiang Wan-sui!* [Long Live the Thought of Mao Tse-tung!] [n.p., April 1967], pp. 11–12, hereinafter cited as *Long Live the Thought of*

The Party's united front organizations, the National People's Congress and the Chinese People's Political Consultative Conference, made a survey of the nation's intellectuals and their working conditions. On January 14th, 1956, Chou En-lai addressed a select group of Party and non-Party intellectuals in an effort to improve the utilization of the country's scant technical, educational, and artistic resources.

Chou's report was a "Maoist" document to the extent that it stressed "opposition to rightist conservative ideology" as the Party's major task. He emphasized that the intellectuals needed to be given "political and professional leadership" by the Party. A policy of "unity and struggle" was evident in his presentation, for while he called for improved working conditions and a rationalization of the job assignments of non-Party intellectuals, he made it clear that their incorporation into the ranks of the revolution, "was a process that cannot possibly be free from certain struggle." [10]

Chou admitted that a major aspect of the problem of Party relations with the intellectuals was a matter of "sectarianism" on the part of Party cadres: "Some comrades easily get themselves estranged from intellectuals outside the Party, and even adopt the attitude of respecting them but keeping them at a distance. In this way, there is a lack of mutual understanding, and estrangement becomes the easier." [11] But he also emphasized "a tendency of passivity and an inclination towards compromise" with the intellectuals' political defects. And in a curious example of ideological juggling which seems to reveal Mao's hand in a compromise policy, the State Premier observed of "sectarianism" (a "left" deviation) and "rightist" tolerance: "The two tendencies are opposite to each other in form, but both of them in practise lead to a kind of rightist conservatism." [12]

Chou went on to note with indignation that some non-Party intellectuals

> refuse to study Marxism-Leninism, and even slander Marxism-Leninism. They belittle labor, belittle the laboring people, belittle the cadres who grew from the ranks of laborers, and are not willing to get together with workers, peasants, and worker and peasant cadres. . . .

Mao Tse-tung!) Analysis of these campaigns will be found in Merle Goldman, *Literary Dissent in Communist China* (Cambridge, Massachusetts: Harvard University Press, 1967), pp. 129–157.

10. Chou En-lai, "On the Question of Intellectuals," in *CC 1955–59*, p. 138.

11. *Ibid.*, p. 134.

12. *Ibid.*, p. 132.

They are vainglorious and look upon themselves as the best in the world, and will not accept the leadership and criticism of any other.[13]

Chou's report concluded with an attack on the "baseless view" that "the Party is not capable of leading intellectuals in scientific and cultural construction." [14]

In short, as of January 1956 the Party sought to combine political pressures and strengthened Party leadership with improvements in working facilities in an effort to "use" more effectively the nation's scanty scientific, intellectual and administrative resources in the process of "socialist construction."

Chou En-lai's encouraging, yet patronizing air was to receive three sharp jolts during the next eighteen months: Khrushchev's criticism of Stalin, the Polish and Hungarian uprisings, and the outspokenness of China's intellectuals against Communist Party rule. The first of these shocks came within six weeks when the Russian Communist Party leader Nikita Khrushchev, at the Twentieth Congress of the Soviet Communist Party, launched his unanticipated and officially secret attack on Stalin and the "cult of personality."

The Chinese Party's reaction to this Russian attack on Stalin's abuses of power was defensive, for in both organizational form and personal commitment it had closely identified itself with the man and his system of authority. In a major editorial on April 5th, 1956, the Party paper *People's Daily* summarized discussions held by the top leaders who admitted that,

After the victory of the revolution . . . the leading personnel of the Party and state, beset by bureaucratism from many sides, face the great danger of using the machinery of state to take arbitrary action, alienating themselves from the masses and collective leadership, resorting to commandism, and violating Party and state democracy.[15]

The editorial went on to reaffirm the Party's commitment to the style of leadership which had brought it to power:

. . . if we want to avoid falling into such a [Stalinist] quagmire, we must pay fullest attention to the use of the mass line method of leadership, not permitting the slightest negligence. To this end, *it is necessary for us to establish certain systems,* so as to ensure the thorough implementation of the mass line and collective leadership, to avoid elevation of oneself and individualist heroism.[16]

13. *Ibid.*, p. 136.
14. *Ibid.*, p. 143.
15. *People's Daily* editorial, "On the Historical Experience of the Dictatorship of the Proletariat" (April 5, 1956); trans. in *CC 1955–59*, p. 149.
16. *Ibid.* Emphasis added.

Mao Tse-tung was "ducking his head"—or having it ducked. His name was not mentioned once in the long editorial; and a quotation from his 1943 article "Some Questions Concerning Methods of Leadership," in which he had first spelled out the "mass line" concept, was cited only as "a Central Committee Resolution." The question in the minds of Party leaders was how serious would be the tendency of people within China to develop doubts about the Party and Mao as a result of Khrushchev's revelation of Stalin's errors.

The response of the Party "center" to this threat to its own legiti-macy was two-fold: First, collective leadership was strengthened so as to avoid as much as possible the tendency to compare the "cult" of Stalin with the glorification of Mao.[17] And second, the

17. The Party's shift to collective leadership was emphasized by Teng Hsiao-p'ing in his report on the revision of the Party constitution delivered to the Eighth Party Congress in September 1956. Teng observed that, "It has become a long-established tradition in our Party to make decisions on important questions by a collective body of the Party, and not by any individual. Although violations of this principle of collective leadership have been frequent in our Party, yet once discovered, they have been criticized and rectified by the Central Committee." Teng then went on to quote from a Central Committee decision of late 1948 [only in 1960 identified as having been drafted by Mao—*see* pp. 398–399 below] which stresses the importance of the Party committee system in strengthening collective leadership. (*See* Teng's report in *Eighth National Congress of the Communist Party of China*, Vol. I, esp. pp. 192–195.)

It is open to interpretation whether Teng's remarks were intended to exonerate Mao of any "personality cult," or whether they were purposefully ironic. That the 1956 stress on collective leadership was "anti-Mao" in quality is suggested by other indications of opposition to the Chairman in that year: in the blocking of his twelve-year program for agricultural development in April; in the elimination of "Mao Tse-tung's thought" from the revised Party Constitution passed at the Eighth Party Congress; and more generally in Liu Shao-ch'i's dominant role at this Congress. Liu placed notable emphasis on collective leadership in his lengthy political report. (*See Eighth National Congress of the Communist Party of China*, Vol. I, pp. 103–104.)

Furthermore, during the Cultural Revolution, several leaders prominent at this time, such as Teng Hsiao-p'ing, were attacked for "parroting Khrushchev and in the name of 'opposing the personality cult,' [directing] the spearhead straight at Chairman Mao." (From a Red Guard pamphlet, "Thirty-three Leading Counterrevolutionary Revisionists," reprinted for circulation in the Canton area in March 1968; trans. in *Current Background* [Hong Kong: United States Consulate General], No. 874 [March 17, 1969], p. 5.) P'eng Teh-huai, the Defense Minister and a man who was to criticize Mao's "Great Leap" policies in 1959, was said to have been the one who suggested that "the thought of Mao Tse-tung" be deleted from the Eighth Party Constitution.

leadership tried to modify its relations with non-Party people so as to reduce tensions resulting from "sectarian" or "dogmatic" behavior on the part of Party cadres.

This latter effort merged with the leadership's earlier desire to enlist the support of the intellectuals in the development process. The key operative passage in the *People's Daily* editorial of April 5th sustained Chou En-lai's earlier call for an attitude of "unity and struggle" with the bourgeois intellectuals, but the emphasis was modified to the need for efforts to "shift them from their position of neutrality to one of alliance with us, for the purpose of facilitating the development of the revolution." [18]

The editorial's most obvious point of disagreement with Mao's position was its stress on the danger of Stalin's "leftist" error of directing the main blow of political struggle against "the middle-of-the-road social and political forces of the time." [19] The political implication in 1956 of this reevaluation of Stalin's policies seems to have been that a majority within the leadership feared that Mao's line of continuing to oppose "rightist conservatism" among the intellectuals would only create added problems for the Party in its relations with non-Party people.[20] These relations were already tense in the wake of the campaigns against Hu Feng and Hu Shih and now were given the added strain of Khrushchev's attack on Stalin with all that it implied for popular questioning of a Communist Party's right to a monopoly of political leadership.

The passage in the editorial which hinted that in order to sustain the "mass line" style of leadership it was "necessary for us to establish certain systems" does not appear to have reflected a clear conception or consensus within the leadership. Indeed, much of the

18. "On the Historical Experience of the Dictatorship of the Proletariat," in *CC 1955–59*, p. 149.

19. *Ibid.*

20. While I do not interpret this editorial as unequivocally "anti-Mao," it appears to be a collectively produced document—written on the basis of an enlarged meeting of the Politbureau—which checks Mao's influence on Party policies. The evidence for this interpretation is based on the opposition to Mao's "leftist" agricultural line, which built up as the "high tide" of co-operativization was pressed in the winter and spring of 1955–56. This opposition is documented in Ch. XVIII, pp. 351–356 below.

Furthermore, the eventual bitterness of Chinese attacks on Khrushchev for having "subverted" the leaderships of other Parties indicates that Mao came to see the Soviet leader's attack on Stalin as having undermined his personal authority within China after the Soviet Twentieth Party Congress. (*See* the *People's Daily* and *Red Flag* joint editorial, "On the Origin and Development of the Differences between the Leadership of the CPSU and Ourselves" [September 6, 1963], in *Polemic on the General Line of the International Communist Movement,* p. 63.)

debate within the Party over the next twelve months as related to the organization of Party power, policy toward the intellectuals, and Party rectification seems to represent an effort to evolve such a conception and consensus.[21]

Mao himself appeared to take the first step in this process, perhaps as a way of trying to regain the initiative. On May 2nd, Mao delivered a speech to a meeting of the Supreme State Conference in which he apparently spelled out his own views on how to deal with the intellectuals. In this speech, which has never been published, Mao first invoked the full slogan, "Let a hundred flowers bloom, let a hundred schools of thought contend." We do not know all the arguments which Mao presented at this time, but the main lines of his speech[22] apparently served as the basis for an address

21. Six months after publication of the editorial, the Eighth Party Congress made certain structural changes in the formal Party organization. A Standing Committee was created within the Politbureau, a separate post of General Secretary of the Central Committee was established, and a General Political Department set up. Very little is known about the thinking, or politicking, which underlay the promotion of these changes, and whether proposals for reorganization were advanced before or after the onset of "de-Stalinization."

The main argument advanced here, however, is that the major pressure for strengthening "collective leadership" came from Party leaders who objected to Mao's economic initiatives of 1955. As Mao sought to regain the political initiative in late 1956, he had to utilize a variety of non-Party organizational forums—the Supreme State Conference, a national conference on propaganda work, and criticism of the Party from the intellectual community—to implement his own notion of "mass line" politics. In these policy differences of 1955–1957 lie conflicting conceptions of the leadership process, and of cadre rectification, which in the 1960s were to grow into the open political conflict of the Cultural Revolution.

22. Given the fact that Mao's May 1956 speech has never been published—while his February 1957 "contradictions" analysis has been given wide publicity—it seems that his views on the intellectuals and on "class struggle" in a socialist society were going through a process of evolution under the impact of events during 1956. My own reading of Lu's speech is that it represents a very liberal interpretation of Mao's views. And if one assumes that Mao was increasingly "boxed in" during 1956 as a result of "de-Stalinization," the fact that Lu spoke for Mao could be read as an indication that Party leaders with primary influence at this time were pulling Mao's line on the intellectuals "to the right," that the Chairman could not "speak for himself" publicly on this issue, but had to accept a collective interpretation of his views.

In any event, Lu's speech is clearly more liberal than Chou's report on the intellectuals of the preceding January. Gone is the stress on opposition to "rightist conservatism." Where Chou had stressed Party leadership over intellectual matters, Lu goes to great pains to separate them from politics. ("We cannot fail to notice that although art, literature and scientific research have a close bearing on the class struggle, they are not, after all, the

by the Director of the Central Committee's Propaganda Department, Lu Ting-yi, delivered three weeks later in Peking to a selected group of intellectuals.

Lu's speech, which emphasizes the Party's commitment to the encouragement of scientific and artistic innovation, began by invoking the image of a new "golden age" in Chinese intellectual life:

> During the epoch of the Spring and Autumn Annals and the Warring States two thousand years ago, there emerged in China the phase of "letting all schools contend in airing their views" in the academic field. It became the golden era of academic development in the history of our country. The history of our country has proved that if there were no encouragement of independent thinking and if there were no free discussion, then academic development would stagnate. The epoch of the Spring and Autumn Annals and the Warring States was very different from the situation we are facing today. At that time, society was in a chaotic state (*tung-luan ti*). The contention of all schools in airing their views in the academic field was spontaneous and had no conscious, unified leadership.[23]

This striking introduction reveals all too clearly the bind in which the Party felt itself to be: There had to be unfettered intellectual creativity if China was to develop, yet Chinese history confirmed that intellectual diversity was associated with war and social chaos, with *luan*. And both Party members and non-Party intellectuals must have wondered whether the encouragement of intellectual freedom would lead to a new golden age or to another fearful era of "confusion." [24]

---

same thing as politics.") And where Chou had observed rather sourly that "intellectuals in many units . . . have been slow in making changes," Lu warmly observed: ". . . in the course of [the struggle against bourgeois idealism] most intellectuals have given a very good account of themselves and made remarkable progress." (*See CC 1955–59*, pp. 131, 153–154.)

From such differences in attitude toward the intellectuals apparently grew the Cultural Revolution charge that Lu Ting-yi, among others, had "prettified the bourgeoisie."

23. Lu Ting-yi, "Let a Hundred Flowers Bloom, a Hundred Schools of Thought Contend," *People's Daily* (June 13, 1956); trans in *Current Background*, No. 406 (August 15, 1956), p. 3.

24. The intimate association between intellectual diversity—differences in "thinking" or opinion—and *luan* in the Chinese social orientation is amply revealed in our interviews. Most notable is the following interpretation of the question, "Why since the time of Confucius has Chinese society placed such emphasis on 'Peace'?" by a 50-year-old shop-keeper and former soldier from the North China province of Liaoning: "In that era you had the Warring States period: there were seven or eight countries; they were all scattered, all split up; society was all confused (*luan*). But that was also a very enlightened period, very vigorous. You had all of those "*tzu*"; Confucius (*Kung-fu-tzu*), Mencius (*Meng-tzu*), Han Fei-tzu, etc." (Why, if

Lu's speech tried to answer this implicit question by stressing that intellectual freedom was limited by the bounds of the revolution and permitted only for those who accepted the leadership of the Communist Party and its objective of "socialist transformation":

> We advocate that the counterrevolutionaries should be denied freedom. We hold that we must practice dictatorship over counterrevolutionaries. But among the people we take the stand that there must be democracy and freedom. This is a political line. In politics, we must distinguish ourselves from the enemy.
>
> The line of "letting all flowers bloom together and all schools contend in airing their views" which we advocate stands for freedom inside the camp of the people. We advocate the broadening of this freedom in accordance with the consolidation of the people's regime.[25]

Lu also made it clear that the Party's objective was the elimination of "bourgeois idealism" and acceptance by all of Marxism-Leninism and dialectical materialism as the bases of a new and "correct" social orientation. These were the conditions under which "intellectual freedom" would be prevented from degenerating into *luan*. For those who accepted these conditions there would be free-

that was an enlightened period, was there also the *luan*, the warring?) "It is like when a person is about to die, he will have a last period of great spirit. The Chou dynasty was dying, and in its last years all those men came out; and then, like a man, the dynasty died." (H-7)

25. Lu Ting-yi, "Let a Hundred Flowers Bloom, a Hundred Schools of Thought Contend"; trans. in *Current Background*, No. 406, p. 6.

Lu's use of the term "the People" indicates how vital remains the old Confucian notion that social order can be maintained by "naming" or defining a "proper" relationship between authority and its subordinates. To accept or be worthy of one's "name" means to accept the relationship of power, to play one's social role as authority has defined it. Mao has updated the "naming" conception of political control by indicating that the term "the People" is a variable conception which should be defined or "rectified" under given historical circumstances. As he wrote in 1949, at the conclusion of the "bourgeois-democratic"- stage of the revolution: "Who are the people? At the present stage in China, they are the working class, the peasantry, the urban petty bourgeoisie and the national bourgeoisie. These classes, led by the working class and the Communist Party, unite to form their own state and elect their own government; they enforce their dictatorship over the running dogs of imperialism—the landlord class and bureaucrat-bourgeoisie, as well as the representatives of those classes, the Kuomintang reactionaries and their accomplices—suppress them, allow them only to behave themselves and not to be unruly in word or deed. . . . The right to vote belongs only to the people, not to the reactionaries. The combination of these two aspects, democracy for the people and dictatorship over the reactionaries, is the people's democratic dictatorship. (Mao, "On the People's Democratic Dictatorship" (1949), *SW*, English, IV, pp. 417–418.)

dom of inquiry, discussion, and criticism—and freedom to be countercriticized as well.

To a foreign observer this paradoxical point of view—in which "intellectual freedom" is permitted only with the prior acceptance of the truth of an exclusive doctrine—is difficult to see as much more than arrogant hypocrisy. The prior condition negates the objective. Seen within the context of Chinese society, however, the willingness of the Party to advance this apparently cynical point of view drew meaning from the experience of the Party's rise to power: The recently concluded century of internal chaos undoubtedly seemed sufficient justification for placing social order at the top of the Party's list of political priorities. Popular fears of *luan,* amply documented in our interviews with Chinese of all present generations, would have strengthened the Party's conviction that by maintaining social order it would win wide approval from "the People."

In addition, there was the still vivid contrast of Party discipline with the corruption and demoralization of the Nationalist regime; the phenomenal attainment of power from the low ebb following near destruction in south China; the grueling Long March; and expansion in the face of powerful Japanese invaders—feats which the Party associated with its ideological commitment. It would have taken extremely powerful counterarguments to convince a Party member that his position was not "correct." Hence there was little trace of self-consciousness in Lu's speech at the paradox which underlay the Party's call for "open debates" in the struggle to overcome "idealist thinking."

Apparently the Party leadership believed that the intellectuals would become willingly committed to the Party's cause, to its inherently "correct" policies, if given a constructive professional role in China's national development and the opportunity to criticize unthinking, doctrinaire attitudes on the part of Party members. Lu's speech thus went on to elaborate Mao's conviction that political unity and social development, not *luan,* would grow from a critical dialogue between Party and non-Party intellectuals within the general framework of commitment to the "socialist" path of national resurgence.

Lu's discussion picked up themes raised by Chou En-lai in his January report on the intellectuals. Like Chou, he noted that some non-Party intellectuals adopted "the lordly attitude of the bourgeoisie to oppress the young Marxist academic workers"; but his stress was clearly on

the habit of certain Party members to look upon themselves as the "authority," their intolerance of criticisms made against them and their abstention from practicing self-criticism; the practice of restraint by certain Party members in criticizing others for fear of wrecking the united front and unity; the habit of certain Party members to refrain from criticizing or even to shelter the mistakes of other people on account of personal friendship.[26]

Where Chou's report had stressed "rightist conservatism" as the Party's main problem, Lu—in line with the *People's Daily* editorial of early April—stressed that "the main defect is a tendency toward doctrinairism" on the part of Party members. In short, in the wake of Khrushchev's attack on Stalin there was a clear shift of responsibility onto the shoulders of Party members to encourage the co-operation of non-Party intellectuals. They were to raise their own ideological standards and level of professionalism so as to be able to win, on intellectual grounds, the "struggle" against "idealism."

Lu's speech also revealed a new degree of Party toleration for intellectual diversity. He asserted that, "As everyone knows, the natural sciences, including medicine, have no class character." [27] Such an official line, repudiated in the "anti-rightist" reaction of the summer of 1957 and then revived briefly in 1961–62, was to be scathingly denounced by the Maoists during the Cultural Revolution.

Lu's speech concluded with a discussion of how to promote criticism, giving added emphasis to the contention of the Party leadership that it intended to subject its own cadres to the test of open debate with non-Party colleagues. The promotion of such a dialogue, however, was seen to be no easy matter. Lu rhetorically raised the question, "The present forms of criticism make people afraid. If they do not make people afraid they are banal. How is this problem to be solved?" [28] His answer was that there were two kinds of criticism, one directed at the enemy and, "meant to kill with one stroke or attacking criticism. The other kind is directed against good people which is constructive criticism based on comradeship." [29] Lu indicated that the problem was that among "the People" there still existed "the wrong belief that criticism means attack." And he made a plea for the proper distinction between hostile criticism to be directed at enemies, and rational criticism to be used for constructive and unifying purposes among "the People":

> It is common for good men to commit mistakes. Nobody in the world can be completely free from mistakes. Such mistakes should

26. Lu Ting-yi, "Let a Hundred Flowers Bloom," in *Current Background,* No. 406, p. 10.
27. *Ibid.,* pp. 7–8.
28. *Ibid.,* p. 11.
29. *Ibid.,* p. 14.

be distinguished rigidly from counterrevolutionary utterances. Criticism of such mistakes should be well-intended, calm and cool-headed reasoning by taking the whole matter into consideration, and should only proceed from unity with a view to reaching unity. . . . The criticized people have basically nothing to fear.

It is easy to commit mistakes, but such mistakes should be corrected as fast as possible. Persistence in such mistakes would lead to heavy loss. Those who are subject to criticism should stick firmly to truth. They should voice their disagreement if they feel that the criticisms directed against them are wrong. But they should rectify their mistakes and should humbly accept the criticisms rightly made by other people. . . . This can have only advantages but no disadvantages to ourselves and the development of our cause of science and literature and the arts.[30]

This speech is notable for its indication of the groping efforts being made within the Party to deal with the most basic problems of innovation, social integration, and interpersonal cooperation, and with control of abuses of authority—issues all tinged with a concern about *luan*. The Party's strategy of calling for active political participation and controlled criticism of abuses of authority bore the stamp of Mao's personal leadership. He had learned in the mountains of south China that people would actively commit themselves to the movement if given some personal responsibility instead of being told to remain passive and obedient before authority. The opportunity to criticize abuses of power could "liberate" great reserves of popular emotional energy which, through Party direction, could propel history forward.[31]

To make this strategy work in the new context of peaceful reconstruction, and in relations between people both within and outside the Party, however, required some radical changes of attitude. As our interviews revealed, and as Lu's speech confirms, authority does not expect to be criticized and those in subordinate status do not tend to criticize—except when resentments can no longer be held in and burst forth in a "confusion" of emotional attack. Thus there would appear to have been some wishful thinking behind Lu's call for rational, "well-intentioned, calm and cool-headed reasoning . . ." in criticism within the ranks of "the People."

Lu's speech of late May set one of the main themes for speeches delivered to the Third Session of the First National People's Congress which met during the month of June. Li Wei-han, Director of the Party's United Front Work Department, spoke of continuing class conflict, but he diluted the form of this "struggle" by stressing

30. *Ibid.,* p. 15.
31. *See* pp. 207–209 above.

that it was now a matter of "reasoning, emulating, of criticism and self-criticism and encouragement coupled with criticism." [32] And he invoked words of Mao on the need to "unite all possible forces" for the tasks of "socialist construction." The relation of "blooming and contending" to scientific advancement was given particular emphasis by Kuo Mo-jo, President of the Chinese Academy of Sciences. Kuo observed that, "the 'let diverse schools of thought contend' policy is really the best way of encouraging scientific workers to unleash a high degree of activeness and creativity." [33]

Despite this concentrated effort on the part of the Party leadership to overcome lethargy in the intellectual community, doubts persisted. Non-Party people were confused about the intentions of the campaign, coming as it did after several years of struggle with "counterrevolutionaries" in their midst. How far could open "contending" proceed if the Marxist point of view, by Party precondition, was destined to triumph in the end?

Shortly after the adjournment of the National People's Congress, Kuo Mo-jo attempted to air these doubts about the limits of intellectual freedom, and fear of *luan* resulting from genuine expression of opinion, by affirming that the "symphony" of contending schools was to play under the Party's unified direction:

> The present "contending of a hundred schools" is different from the wasp-like swarming of all kinds of schools during our country's Warring States era. The "hundred contending schools" of that period concerned the change from slave society to feudal society. . . . The "contending of a hundred schools" today is based on the motive of establishing a socialist society, and, with progress, the establishment of communism. We want to safeguard this motive in organizing our "symphony orchestra," and play historically unprecedented powerful symphonies. Let there be ten thousand different kinds of instruments playing together, but they should always play according to a definite score. We want "contention" (*cheng-ming*); we don't want "confused cackling" (*luan-ming*).
>
> . . . If there is some confused blowing and striking of instruments (*luan-chiao luan-ta*) other people may cover up their ears, or even ask you to leave the stage.[34]

Some within the Party leadership, however, were evidently displeased with the reticence of the intellectuals to voice opinions and

32. Li Wei-han, "The Democratic United Front in China"; trans. in *Current Background,* No. 402 (July 24, 1957), p. 3.

33. Kuo Mo-jo, "Development of Scientific Research in China"; trans. in *ibid.,* No. 400 (July 17, 1956), p. 3.

34. Kuo Mo-jo, "Play Powerful Symphonies," *People's Daily* (July 1, 1956), p. 7.

to strike out on new paths of investigative research, for an authoritative "Commentator," writing in the Party paper only a few weeks later, on July 23rd, indirectly challenged Kuo's cautious interpretation of the "contention" policy:

> All the various schools ought to create their own music, and not just play according to the music indicated by the conductor. As long as the melodies they play are not counterrevolutionary they will have freedom to contend. We have only one expectation of the contenders, and that is that they genuinely do academic research. . . . Many people have suggested that contention is not "confused cackling." But what is "confused cackling?" No one's understanding about this is the same. Of course, if there is to be "contention" it cannot be guaranteed there will be "no confusion." If "confused cackling" is a matter of, "the masses say it is confusing," or "establishing theories of the new and unusual," this kind of "confused cackling" isn't necessarily bad.[35]

"Commentator" then concluded with the hopeful assertion that "the condition of Marxism as the leading thought of the academic and cultural world has already been established." [36]

The manner in which these contrasting interpretations of the "blooming and contending" policy were expressed in the press suggests that strong differences of opinion were unresolved within the Party leadership.[37] During the remainder of the summer of 1956, and into the fall, the effort of the first months of the year to mobilize the intellectuals into the national development effort remained a low key operation devoid of political content. At the Eighth Party Congress held in September, Mao—in a brief opening speech which, in contrast to Liu Shao-ch'i's lengthy political report, only seemed to emphasize the degree to which the Chairman's power remained circumscribed—stressed the need for "determined action to get rid of any unhealthy manifestations in any part of our work that are detrimental to the unity between the Party and the people." [38]

Liu's political report, however, gave scant attention to the call for

35. Commentator, "An Interpretive Discussion of 'Let a Hundred Schools of Thought Contend,' " *ibid.*, (July 21, 1956), p. 7.

36. *Ibid.*

37. Kuo Mo-jo is one of the few intellectuals of national prominence in China who over the years has maintained close personal ties with Mao. During the 1960s his public statements and writings were to be the precursor of Mao's political initiatives (*see* pp. 418, 484 below). Hence, one senses that Kuo's 1956 exchange with "Commentator" may be a veiled debate between Mao and other Party leaders.

38. Mao Tse-tung, "Opening Address at the Eighth National Congress of the Communist Party of China" (September 15, 1956), in *Eighth National Congress of the Communist Party of China*, Vol. I, p. 8.

"blooming and contending," mentioning it only once in the context of the need to foster the development of science and the arts. His discussion of Party rectification stressed the strengthening of Party leadership over state organs, and "supervision over subordinates by superiors." "Criticism and exposures from below" was ranked last in his discussion; and the need for "supervision" by the "democratic parties" was brushed aside.[39] Similarly, the report by Teng Hsiao-p'ing on the revision of the Party Constitution mentioned only the need to "greatly intensify criticism and self-criticism *within the Party*." [40]

In his January report on the intellectuals, Chou En-lai had revealed that "the Central Committee of our Party has decided to make opposition to rightist conservative ideology the central question for the Eighth National Congress of the Party. . . ." [41] Documents from the Congress, in striking contrast, hardly mention this danger on the "right." Liu Shao-ch'i repeatedly called attention to the "leftist" errors of doctrinairism, impetuosity, and rashness; and he recalled with emphasis the great harm that had been done to the Party's revolutionary cause by the various "leftist" lines of the 1930s.[42] Similarly, the final resolution of the Congress stressed the "mistake of adventurism" in China's development effort.[43] And just as "the thought of Mao Tse-tung" was no longer mentioned in the revised Party Constitution, an open, critical debate between Party members and non-Party intellectuals was no longer part of the content of "blooming and contending."

THE MEANING OF "HUNGARY"

The second shock to the Party and its effort to establish better relations with the intellectuals came in October and November of 1956, and again came from within the Communist world. The riots and liberalizing ferment in Poland and the upheaval of the Hungarian

---

39. Liu Shao-ch'i, "Political Report of the Central Committee of the Communist Party of China to the Eighth National Congress of the Party," *ibid.,* pp. 76–77.

40. Teng Hsiao-p'ing, "Report on the Revision of the Constitution of the Communist Party of China," *ibid.,* p. 207. Emphasis added.

41. Chou En-lai, "On the Question of Intellectuals," in *CC 1955–59,* p. 129.

42. Liu Shao-ch'i, "The Political Report of the Central Committee of the Communist Party of China to the Eighth National Congress of the Party," in *Eighth National Congress of the Communist Party of China,* Vol. I, pp. 98–102.

43. "Resolution of the Eighth National Congress of the Communist Party of China on the Political Report of the Central Committee," *ibid.,* p. 124.

"counterrevolution" exposed to Party contemplation outbursts of *luan,* fears of which had dampened reaction to Mao's call for "blooming and contending." Did these events prove that a policy of encouraging "intellectual freedom" and criticism was foolish, or that it had become necessary?

The Party leadership's initial reaction to these events was largely in the realm of international relations. The Chinese were clearly concerned about the erosion of cohesion in the "socialist camp," which continued to provide them both international security and a sense of legitimacy at home. Hence China continued to support the leading role of the Soviet Union in the International Communist Movement, and warned of the need to "overcome nationalist tendencies in smaller countries [i.e., Hungary]." [44] But at the same time, the Chinese, who were well acquainted with Russian interference in their own domestic political life, supported Poland's desire for greater independence within the bloc—to the exasperation of the Russians. [45] This Chinese position of walking between the dangers of bloc disintegration and oppressive Russian control was manifest in Chou En-lai's mediation trip through Eastern Europe in January 1957, an initiative which heightened Soviet sensitivities to China's role in the International Communist Movement and set the stage for subsequent escalation in Sino-Soviet tensions.

The significance of "Hungary" for China's domestic political life took some time to become apparent. The initial impact of the events of the autumn in Eastern Europe was to strengthen Mao's contention that deviations to the "right"—"rightist conservatism" and "revisionism"—were the main dangers to China's revolution. His earlier exasperation with those who blindly followed the Soviet precedent (expressed in his mid-1955 report on agricultural cooperation) seemed justified by events. The first official Party editorial in response to the developments of the fall warned that "indiscriminate and mechanical copying of experience that has been successful in the Soviet Union—let alone that which was unsuccessful there—may lead to failures in another country." [46] Mao's earlier

44. *People's Daily* editorial, "More on the Historical Experience of the Dictatorship of the Proletariat" (December 29, 1956), in *CC 1955–59,* p. 270.

45. Chinese initiatives within the "socialist camp" in reaction to the developments in Poland and Hungary, and Soviet responses to them, are analyzed in Zagoria, *The Sino-Soviet Conflict, 1956–1961,* pp. 54–65.

46. "More on the Historical Experience of the Dictatorship of the Proletariat," in *CC 1955–59,* p. 266.

My basic interpretation of this editorial is that it is a "compromise" document, reflecting uncertainties within the Party leadership as to the full relevance of the events of the fall in Eastern Europe for China's domestic

belief that toleration of non-Marxist views held by the "bourgeois" intellectuals would weaken Party leadership, and should be the object of struggle, seems also to have been strengthened.[47] Whereas earlier in the year his desire to promote ideological struggle had been characterized as "leftist" sectarianism which would isolate the Party from the intellectuals, Mao now could stress that "opposition to doctrinairism has nothing in common with tolerance of revisionism"; and he warned that "in the present antidoctrinaire tide" the Party must not compromise with those who would "attempt to weaken or renounce the . . . leading role of the Party." [48]

The key issue which divided Party leaders in the wake of the events in Poland and Hungary concerned the most appropriate way to strengthen the "leading role of the Party." As events of the winter and spring of 1957 unfolded, one group of Party leaders, apparently centered around Liu Shao-ch'i and P'eng Chen, continued to adhere to the position that "class struggle should not continue to be stressed as though it was being intensified, as was done by Stalin." [49] Mao, on the other hand, increasingly saw the events in Eastern Europe, and their reflection in China, as basically a product of Party misuses of power which required correction. Against increasing resistance from within the Party he continued to stress that

> we need a rectification movement. Will it undermine our Party's prestige if we criticize our own subjectivism, bureaucracy and sectarianism? I think not. . . . Even great storms are not to be feared. It is amid great storms that human society progresses.[50]

---

political life. No clear line on internal policy is expressed, in contrast to the detailed evaluation of international developments. Indeed, most of the subsequent analysis in this chapter concerns the attempt of the leadership to reach consensus on a domestic political line in the wake of "Hungary."

47. In the 1960s Mao was to make repeated references to the Hungarian "Petofi Circles"—groups of Party and non-Party intellectuals who had provided much of the leadership in the 1956 "de-Stalinization" movement in Hungary—as an example of the corruption of a Party organization by "revisionists" (*see* p. 450 below). The major lesson which Mao evidently drew from the Hungarian upheaval was of the danger for a revolutionary party of close ties with non-Marxist intellectuals. Or perhaps more precisely, Mao may have used the Hungarian example to assert to other Party leaders the correctness of his earlier concern about "bourgeois reactionary thinking" within the Chinese Communist Party.

48. "More on the Historical Experience of the Dictatorship of the Proletariat," in *CC 1955–59*, p. 266.

49. *Ibid.*, p. 267.

50. Mao, "Speech at the Chinese Communist Party's National Conference on Propaganda Work," in *Selected Readings from the Works of Mao Tse-tung*, pp. 394, 400.

The playing out of these differing interpretations of the meaning of the Hungarian events for the Chinese revolution provides much of the tension and drama of domestic Chinese politics in the spring of 1957. From a retrospective evaluation of press materials published during this year we can reconstruct the main lines of leadership conflict which were only dimly revealed in official editorials, postponed meetings, and the public appearances and statements of various Party leaders.

AN EARLY COMPROMISE

Early January 1957 apparently was the first point of decision at which Mao attempted to turn the "blooming and contending" policy into a rectification movement which would stress criticism of the Party from *outside* groups—particularly the intellectuals. This effort, however, met with determined resistance within the Party leadership. On January 7 an article was published in the *People's Daily* by Ch'en Ch'i-t'ung, a Vice Director of the Cultural Section of the General Political Department of the People's Liberation Army, and three other senior army political workers. In view of the criticism which this otherwise obscure piece received in subsequent weeks, it evidently reflected the leadership debate of the moment.[51]

51. Following Mao Tse-tung's "contradictions" speech to the Supreme State Conference on February 27th, Ch'en and his colleagues were to be criticized by name no less than five times in the *People's Daily*: on March 1st by one Ch'en Liao (perhaps a pseudonym); on March 18th by Mao Tun, Minister of Culture; on April 4th in an article compiled from readers' letters; on April 10th in an official editorial (*see* p. 302 below); and on April 11th in a published interview with Chou Yang, Deputy Director of the Party Propaganda Department.

In the inner-Party rectification which followed public "blooming and contending," Ch'en Ch'i-t'ung was relieved of his duties and sent to his home village for "self-reform."

In a note of political irony, Mao Tse-tung himself praised Ch'en and the three other PLA critics of "blooming and contending" for "commendable courage" in expressing criticism of his policy. This was in early 1958 when Mao had reasserted his influence in matters of Party leadership, and hence his remarks have the air of a graceful winner. His speech, moreover, continues to stress the virtue of public criticism of the cadres as a way of mobilizing popular support for the Party leadership's cause. Ch'en's error was probably in opposing the Chairman's *method* of leadership. He and Mao may not have had differing views on the intellectuals. (*See* "Chairman Mao's Speech at the Ch'eng-tu Conference" [March 22nd, 1958], in Joint Publications Research Service, *Translations on Communist China*, No. 90 [Washington, D.C.: 1970], pp. 48–52.)

By 1959 Ch'en was back at work in army cultural and political affairs, where he remained active and increasingly influential until the Cultural Rev-

Opening with one of those expressions of humility which usually signals that someone in higher authority is being challenged, Ch'en and his colleagues observed that, "our views are immature because we have no time to delve deep into theories." [52] Nevertheless, they went on to attack in detail Mao's "blooming and contending" policy, arguing that non-Party intellectuals still were not loyal to the socialist cause. They noted that among the intellectuals there were those who "tried to avoid the word 'socialist' and used 'realistic' only, or replaced the term with the obscure concept of 'realism of the socialist era.' " And in an effort to shift the focus of political struggle onto the intellectuals (and away from the Party) they asserted: "We should not keep silent in front of certain sceptics and countermandists, nor should we play the sycophant; instead, we should raise our bright colors high, be steady in our battle array, and proceed with the struggle." [53]

The immediate outcome of the leadership debate reflected in this article, however, seems to have been a compromise decision in favor of a mild rectification. The need for a Party *cheng-feng* was affirmed in a Central Committee directive, but it was to be an *internal* Party matter which would proceed at a slow pace. The year 1957 was to be devoted to the study of materials based on the Party's Eighth Congress documents (not a meeting at which Mao was influential), with rectification to proceed only in 1958.[54]

Mao, however, had the "time to delve deep into theories," and in the face of this resistance to a rectification movement which would confront both Party abuses of power and "revisionism" among the intellectuals, he wrote one of his major theoretical statements on the relationship between political struggle and social change. He affirmed that Marxism-Leninism provided the guiding

olution. He was one of the first army leaders purged in 1966. One can only wonder who had been his protectors within the PLA and/or Party, for by all appearances he had served as a "mouthpiece" for those in positions of greater authority who were opposed to "blooming and contending."

52. Ch'en Ch'i-t'ung, *et al.*, "Some of Our Opinions on Current Literary and Art Work," *People's Daily* (January 7, 1957); trans. in *Union Research Service* (Hong Kong), Vol. VII, No.7 (April 23, 1957), p. 84.

53. *Ibid.*, p. 85.

54. As is the case with much of the limited information available to foreign observers about important policy developments within China, the rectification campaign directive was revealed initially by references to its implementation gleaned from relatively obscure press materials. (*See* Chi Lu, "Some Questions on the Work Style Rectification Movement," *China Youth*, No. 2 [January 16, 1957]; trans. in *Extracts from China Mainland Magazines* [ECMM] [Hong Kong: United States Consulate General], No. 70 [February 18, 1957], p. 1.) This publication is currently titled *Selections from China Mainland Magazines*.

theory and political structure of China's development effort, and tried to convince Party members that encouragement of popular criticism of cadre abuses of authority was the best way to prevent "contradictions" between Party and people from going unresolved. *Suppression* of criticism, Mao held, would lead to "confusion"; while a critical dialogue between Party members and "the People" would resolve points of tension, promote social change, and prevent the Party from "cutting itself off from the masses."

Mao formally presented his position on China's proper political course to another session of the Supreme State Conference held on February 27, 1957, developing those ideas which had found indirect public expression in Lu Ting-yi's speech of the preceding May. He began his discussion "On the Correct Handling of Contradictions among the People" with what must have seemed, in the face of events in Hungary, a note of uncertain reassurance: "Never before has our country been as united as it is today. . . . The days of national disunity and chaos (*hun-luan*) which the people detested have gone, never to return." [55]

The major import of this highly revealing speech—even in its edited form[56]—was Mao's conviction of the error in equating po-

55. Mao Tse-tung, "On the Correct Handling of Contradictions among the People" (February 27, 1957), in *Selected Readings from the Works of Mao Tse-tung*, p. 350.

A basic question affecting efforts to interpret Mao's speech is an evaluation of whether he was "optimistic" or "pessimistic" in calling for criticism of the Party from non-Party people. Did he fear a Chinese "Hungary," or did he call for public criticism with an air of confidence over the solidarity of the People's Republic? My personal interpretation straddles both extremes: Mao most likely did not expect the degree of criticism which was to be expressed by the intellectuals in May and early June; yet he was very concerned about the significance of the Hungarian rebellion for other ruling Communist Parties. Mao probably had few illusions about either the commitment to "socialism" of the *older* intellectuals, or of the effects of bureaucratism and "sectarianism" on Party relations with "the People." Yet he apparently felt that patriotism and the power of the state were both strong enough to bind the Party and intellectuals together in "unity and struggle." Mao evidently underestimated the degree of resentment toward Party authority which was latent in the intellectual community—especially among the younger generation—and the strength of resistance to "blooming and contending" which the Party apparatus was to display throughout the spring.

56. The official version of the "contradictions" speech must be handled with some care, for it was published only on June 18th, 1957, and then with "certain additions" by the author.

What was reported as a summary and extracts from a transcript of the original speech—which apparently Mao delivered as a rambling verbal presentation, several hours in length—was published in the *New York Times* on June 13th, 1957 on the basis of a version "leaked" to American correspondent Sidney Gruson by sources in Poland. And a recollection of the majo

litical unity with the absence of all social conflict. He saw China's political danger as one of falling into the traditional trap of stagnation and disunity out of fear of conflict. Many people still carried with them anxieties about *luan,* which in the past had hindered progress and had actually contributed to social divisiveness and political passivity through fear of resolving outstanding problems:

> Many dare not openly admit that contradictions still exist among the people of our country, although it is these very contradictions that are pushing our society forward. Many do not admit that contradictions continue to exist in a socialist society, with the result that they are handicapped and passive when confronted with social contradictions; they do not understand that socialist society will grow

points of the original speech, which were noted by a Chinese industrialist who heard a tape-recording of the February 27th presentation, was published in 1962. (*See* Robert Loh and Humphrey Evans, *Escape from Red China* [New York: Coward McCann, 1962], pp. 289–293.)

A comparison of these accounts of the "original" version of the speech and the authoritative version published in June—after attacks on the non-Party critics had begun—suggests that two major types of editorial changes had been made: First, it appears that the official version contains six additional criteria which define more explicitly the limits of acceptable criticism of the Party. Secondly, certain specific information about Party mistakes, and the intention to rectify them, apparently was omitted.

It would seem that Mao's original speech was designed to justify to Party members the need for public criticism in the light of their past errors and of the effects which failure to rectify such errors could have on domestic political life—as illustrated by events in Hungary. Furthermore, the speech seems to have given added encouragement to non-Party people to voice criticism; even against the weight of a political tradition which did not sanction criticism of authority. In these respects the original version of the speech seems to have been more "liberal" in its admission of Party errors and in the encouragement of public criticism.

There has been considerable speculation as to the motivation behind publication of the edited version in mid-June. The most plausible explanation, suggested by Michel Oksenberg, is that the Party leadership had by now reached a decision to initiate attacks on "anti-Party rightists" and would use the immanent session of the National People's Congress as a forum for these attacks. Hence publication of Mao's revised speech was a way of reshaping the "blooming and contending" so as to focus on the critics of the Party. (*See* Michel C. Oksenberg, *Policy Formulation in Communist China: The Case of the Mass Irrigation Campaign, 1957–58* [unpublished Ph.D. dissertation, Columbia University, New York, 1969], pp. 423–439.)

A further factor which may have affected the timing of publication of the speech was the "leaking" of an unofficial version through Eastern Europe (perhaps by the Russians, who later were said to have been upset by Mao's "blooming and contending" line). An "official" version of the speech would tend to supplant the one which was circulating in the Bloc and which had been extracted in the *New York Times* only five days before release of the "official" version.

more united and consolidated through the ceaseless process of the correct handling and resolving of contradictions. For this reason, we need to explain things to our people, and to our cadres in the first place, in order to help them understand the contradictions in a socialist society and learn to use correct methods for handling these contradictions.[57]

Mao's personal orientation had long been that conflict could be a force for progress, and not simply the cause of *luan*. But in this new era of "socialist unity," with military conflict at an end, could he convince the many doubters of the importance of *controlled* conflict? His speech went on to outline the way in which conflict could be kept within bounds, and how it could help to unite China and promote her progress.

Essentially, Mao asserted, the "storm" of revolution "has basically concluded." And while "class struggle is by no means entirely over," the Party need not fear that "counterrevolutionaries" will unleash a new storm against it, for class enemies have been effectively destroyed. Even the provocative influence of events in Hungary had caused only minor restlessness among a portion of the intellectuals; they had not been able to raise anything approaching "winds and waves."

In these conditions of basic Party control, Mao seemed to be saying, the Party could only blame itself for any new condition of *luan:* If it continued to see enemies everywhere and used only methods appropriate for dealing with enemies, then trouble would be *created:*

> The fact is, there still are counterrevolutionaries (of course, that is not to say you'll find them everywhere and in every organization), and we must continue to fight them. . . . If we drop our guard, we shall be badly fooled and shall suffer severely. Counterrevolutionaries must be rooted out with a firm hand wherever they are found making trouble. But, *taking the country as a whole, there are certainly not many counterrevolutionaries. It would be wrong to say that there are still large numbers of counterrevolutionaries in China. Acceptance of that view would also end us up in a mess (kao-luan)*.[58]

There also remained the old tendency of those in positions of authority to use their power exploitatively for personal advancement, consumption, and a life of ease:

> A dangerous tendency has shown itself of late among many of our personnel—an unwillingness to share the joys and hardships of the

57. Mao, "On the Correct Handling of Contradictions among the People," in *Selected Readings from the Works of Mao Tse-tung*, pp. 358–359.
58. *Ibid.*, pp. 364–365. Emphasis added.

masses, a concern for personal fame and gain. . . . We must see to it that all our cadres and all our people constantly bear in mind that ours is a big socialist country but an economically backward and poor one, and that this is a very great contradiction. To make China rich and strong needs several decades of intense effort, which will include, among other things, the . . . policy of building up our country through diligence and frugality.[59]

Mao's basic problem was to convince the Party that manifestations of popular discontent, "disturbances," should not be anxiously suppressed as in the past, but should be openly accepted and dealt with in order to solve problems stemming from abuses of power on the part of Party cadres: "In a large country like ours, there is nothing to get alarmed about if small numbers of people create disturbances; on the contrary such disturbances will help us get rid of bureaucracy." [60]

Party members must learn to wield their power with discipline, to accept popular criticism, and to criticize both "the People" and Party comrades with reason and restraint, not with the hostility which in the past had produced resentments and generated *luan*. Mao emphasized that in the rectification campaign of 1942 the Party had developed ways of preventing criticism from leading to *luan*:

> The "Left" dogmatists [of the revolutionary period] had resorted to the method of "ruthless struggle and merciless blows" in inner-Party struggle. This method was incorrect. In criticizing "Left" dogmatism, we discarded this old method and adopted a new one, that is, one of starting from the desire for unity, distinguishing between right and wrong through criticism or struggle and arriving at a new unity on a new basis. . . . *The essential thing is to start from the desire for unity. For without this desire for unity, the struggle is certain to get out of hand (tou-luan)*. Wouldn't this be the same as "ruthless struggle and merciless blows?" And what Party unity would there be left? It was this very experience that led us to the formula: "unity, criticism, unity." [61]

Unity, however, Mao made clear, was reserved for "the People," for those who accepted Party leadership and socialism. Hostile criticism could and should be expressed against enemies, but within the ranks of "the People" criticism should be divorced from antagonism. This approach is perhaps the essence of Mao's strategy for institutionalizing progress by bringing conflict into the open.

59. *Ibid.*, p. 384.
60. *Ibid.*, p. 381.
61. *Ibid.*, p. 356. Emphasis added.

By divorcing bad feelings from criticism in dealings with people who accept the larger order and goals of Chinese society (recognizing contradictions among "the People" as "non-antagonistic"), *but sanctioning the release of bad feelings in dealings with "the enemy"* ("antagonistic contradictions") Mao hopes to make criticism less fearful by preserving society's order. At the same time an outlet is provided for the hostility which, "held in" by tradition, had been one of the sources of *luan*.

One of the problems associated with this approach, of course, is to "distinguish clearly between self and enemy." As Mao admitted:

> Quite a few people fail to make a clear distinction between these two different types of contradictions—those between ourselves and the enemy and those among the people—and are prone to confuse the two. It must be admitted that it is sometimes quite easy to do so. We have had instances of such confusion in our work in the past. In the course of suppressing counterrevolutionaries, good people were sometimes mistaken for bad, and such things still happen today. We are able to keep our mistakes within bounds because it has been our policy to draw a sharp line between ourselves and the enemy and to rectify mistakes whenever discovered.[62]

Despite such past mistakes, Mao seemed genuinely convinced of the correctness of his approach, of the importance of allowing hostility to be vented in a disciplined manner, of airing popular grievances against abuses of power by lower-level cadres, and of doing away with the "holding in" of bad feelings, which in the past had provided the motive force of *luan*.[63] He undoubtedly sensed that

62. *Ibid.*, p. 358.

63. To gain some idea of how people felt about the compulsory and highly institutionalized system of criticism which Mao and the Party have developed, we asked those of our interview respondents who had experienced this system about their reactions to it. One of the more revealing responses, affirming how criticism can help to overcome the disunity of the past, was given by a man who had been a member of the Kuomintang and a Nationalist military officer before Liberation, and subsequently had served as an instructor in the PLA: (I have heard that the Communists use the people to criticize the cadres. What is this about?) "They use the ordinary people to oversee the cadres; and also use the cadres to oversee the ordinary people. This is a political method; [both these groups] are equal, and [their mutual criticism] can prevent problems from developing." (But can the ordinary people criticize high level cadres?) "They have criticism meetings among themselves; they talk about their problems and develop a sense of unity. The Communists are always encouraging people to talk, to express their opinions. Originally there is no enmity among people, and if you talk about problems you can prevent misunderstandings and can maintain unity in work. During the Nationalist era things were not this way; you would hold back your

any such feelings which now were held in would in time burst forth
—as in Hungary—to threaten the Party itself. And above all Mao
seemed convinced of the justice of his cause. He could slide over
the basic paradox that "Marxism is accepted as the guiding ideology
by the majority of the people in our country . . ." while at the
same time noting that "Marxists are still a minority among the
entire population as well as among the intellectuals." [64] His conviction was born of the irrefutable argument that the Party had attained power. Obviously the methods used to attain that power had
been both correct and the cause of its success. Hence he affirmed:

> Marxism is scientific truth and fears no criticism. If it did, and if it
> could be overthrown by criticism, it would be worthless. . . .
> Marxists should not be afraid of criticism from any quarter. Quite
> the contrary, they need to temper and develop themselves and win
> new positions in the teeth of criticism and in the storm and stress of
> struggle. Fighting against wrong ideas is like being vaccinated—a
> man develops greater immunity from disease as a result of vaccina-
> tion. Plants raised in hot-houses are unlikely to be sturdy. Carrying
> out the policy of letting a hundred flowers bloom and a hundred
> schools of thought contend will not weaken but strengthen the leading
> position of Marxism in the ideological field. [65]

Mao's determination to press for a policy of public "blooming
and contending" can be interpreted as a summation of both immediate political objectives and personal political style. In terms of
basic political approach, the struggle to resolve "contradictions"
could be the vehicle for confronting "rightist conservative" ideas
held by people both within and outside the Party. Mao's emphasis
on a policy of "unity and struggle" in the Party's "alliance" with
the intellectuals could serve as a way of incorporating non-Party
people, in particular the intellectuals, into the revolution on the
Party's own terms. It could also expose errors on the part of Party
cadres. Mao's personal commitment to "struggle" thus seemed to
find expression at this time in an attempt to set the Party and the
intellectuals against each other in a controlled conflict which would

---

opinions and they would continuously get greater. The distance between you
would get greater and eventually you would become enemies." (Does criticism lead to hating the other person?) "People would not dare to develop
hatred, or they would not dare to express it. If they did, they would just
receive more criticism or eventually be punished." (Which do you think is
a better method, the Communist or the Nationalist method?) "During the
last hundred years China has been very *luan*, people didn't obey the laws.
This method enables everybody to understand the law and obey it." (H-7)

64. Mao, "On the Correct Handling of Contradictions among the People,"
in *Selected Readings from the Works of Mao Tse-tung*, p. 376.

65. *Ibid.*, p. 375.

expose and "rectify" errors or "incorrect" attitudes held by people within each social group. Mao was to use this technique of provoking a confrontation in order to test or expose a political situation again in the Taiwan Straits crisis of 1958, and most notably in the Cultural Revolution of the mid-1960s.

In the area of immediate policy objectives, it seems likely that Mao was trying to use the events of the fall of 1956 in Poland and Hungary to reassert his leading role within the Party. Whereas opponents of his economic and social policies had earlier used the attack on Stalin to restrict his influence within the context of collective decision-making processes, Mao could now point to the events in Eastern Europe as justification for the view that Party errors were more a function of "bureaucratism, subjectivism and sectarianism" on the part of a Party-governmental apparatus than the result of one leader's mistakes. And by invoking the danger of "revisionist" attacks on a Party leadership (as had occurred in Hungary) Mao could restrict the influence of more conservative Party leaders within the context of an "anti-rightist" struggle, and in this way reassert the legitimacy of his previous plans for a more rapidly-paced, rural-centered development strategy.

Finally, Mao's resolve to press for a public rectification movement seemed to carry the conviction born of earlier successes in the revolutionary struggle that a leadership style of merely trying to suppress criticism of those in authority would only lead to the holding in of resentments and the lack of resolution of the social tensions that were the cause of *luan*. Only now if the mass hostility on which the Party had risen to power were generated anew, the emotional storm of politics would be turned against the Party itself.

TO OVERCOME PARTY RESISTANCE

Given these varied concerns, Mao and his supporters within the Party leadership resorted to a variety of organizational means to make public "blooming and contending" an institutional reality. The intellectuals continued to be reticent, and there was increasingly determined resistance within the Party. During the two months of March and April 1957, support for this policy was pressed through the numerous united front organizations of "the new democracy." Members of the Chinese People's Political Consultative Conference who had heard Mao's February speech to the Supreme State Conference discussed implementation of the policy at a National Committee meeting held between March 5th and 20th. The Central Committees of the various "democratic parties" were convened from March 11th to the 26th to discuss promotion of the policy of "long-term coexistence and mutual supervision." And between March 6th and 13th the Propaganda Department of the Party Central Committee convened a national conference on propaganda work, attended by almost 500 Party and non-Party intellectuals, to discuss promotion of "blooming and contending." On March 12th Mao addressed the conference, elaborating on his "contradictions" speech of the previous month.

Coming as it did at the end of this meeting of propaganda workers, Mao's speech seems to reveal major points of concern which he felt had to be overcome if public rectification was to become a reality. His analysis balances concern about the prospect of "antisocialist" attacks on Party rule by non-Party intellectuals with an effort to overcome resistance to the policy within Party ranks.

Mao observed that a majority of the intellectuals still "wavered" in their attitudes toward Marxism-Leninism. While many had studied the new ideology, they still were "very conceited, and having learned some book-phrases think themselves terrific and are very cocky; but whenever a storm blows up, they take a stand very different from that of the workers and the majority of the peasants." [66] Hence he warned that in the coming period of public criticism "the basic principles of Marxism [i.e., Party leadership] must never be violated, or otherwise [political] mistakes will be made." And he reiterated that, "in present circumstances, revisionism [a "rightist" deviation] is more pernicious than dogmatism." [67]

Mao went on to point out that the Party itself resisted public exposure of its errors. He concluded by emphasizing that, "In many places, the Party committees have not yet tackled the question of [incorrect] ideology, or have done very little in this respect. . . . The first secretaries of the Party committees in all localities should personally tackle this question." And Mao conspicuously noted that, "The Central Committee of the Party is of the opinion that we must 'open wide' (*fang*), not 'restrict' (*shou*)" in promoting criticism of both Party errors and non-Marxist ways of thinking.[68]

This assertion of the unity of the Central Committee in support of public "blooming and contending" seems more a statement of Mao's hopes than of political fact, for there is considerable indirect evidence that the leadership was divided over the wisdom of Party

66. Mao, "Speech at the Chinese Communist Party's National Conference on Propaganda Work" (March 12, 1957), in *Selected Readings from the Works of Mao Tse-tung*, p. 391.
67. *Ibid.*, pp. 400, 401.
68. *Ibid.*, pp. 401, 398.

rectification through criticism from outside groups.[69] These differences of opinion were so strong as to become obvious to cadres beyond the Party "center" and to certain leaders in the intellectual community. And as the movement progressed, appeals were made to Party leaders who favored either "opening wide" or "restricting" the public criticism by opponents and proponents of the rectification.

For many of the intellectuals, the lack of leadership unanimity over the rectification issue was highly unsettling. What would happen to non-Party critics if Mao's protection of their "opening wide" were removed by the opposition of other Party leaders? The vulnerable position in which the intellectuals felt themselves was expressed in late March by the American-trained sociologist Fei Hsiao-t'ung. In an article published by the _People's Daily_, Fei invoked the imagery of the intellectual ferment of the preceding year in Eastern Europe. He asserted that as far as the older intellectuals were concerned, there was only a feeling of "early spring" in the air. In fact, he noted, "The weather of early spring, when there are still sudden changes between warmth and cold, is actually the most difficult season in which to relax." [70]

Fei asserted that following Chou En-lai's report on the intellectuals of the previous year there had been some improvement in the material condition of the intellectuals, "but this only had made them too obvious [because of their relative advantages], made others feel uncomfortable, and even had produced resentments among the masses." [71] There had been a heightening of their professional activism, but they feared that without unified and explicit leadership by the Party, their enthusiasm for work would be without direction and they would become "confused." Finally, Fei asserted that while the activism of the intellectuals had been stimulated,

> depressing factors are numerous. Their anxieties about a hundred schools contending are heavy; they don't dare to contend or struggle,

69. Some measure of Party opposition to Mao's policy is found in the Cultural Revolution assertion that Lu Ting-yi and Hu Ch'iao-mu suppressed publication of Mao's talk at the national conference on propaganda work, which revealed resistance to "blooming and contending." (*See* "Liu Shao-ch'i Is Guilty of Heinous Crimes in Staging Counter-Revolutionary Seizures of Power on Three Occasions in Our Country's Journalistic Circles," in *Jen-ta San-hung* [People's University Three Reds, Peking], May 11, 1967.)

This speech was finally published in 1963 when, after the Tenth Plenum of the Eighth Central Committee, Mao began to press his "thought" as a test of the loyalty of long-time colleagues within the leadership.

70. Fei Hsiao-t'ung, "The Intellectuals' Early Spring Weather," *People's Daily* (March 24, 1957), p. 7.

71. *Ibid.*

even to the point that many of them clam up about questions having a relatively close relationship to politics.[72]

Fei observed that he had encountered no great stirring among higher level intellectuals in response to the events in Poland and Hungary; and while in one respect this was good as an indication of the firmness of their political standpoint, in another sense it only revealed their alienation from matters of politics. They kept silent through fear of being "capped" or labeled as rightists for their "idealism," and attacked as "anti-Party" elements for raising criticisms of Party leadership. In short, Fei and other non-Party intellectuals sensed that they were pawns in a game whose rules they did not fully understand, and in which they were powerless to protect themselves against being used.[73]

Apprehension among the intellectuals was paralleled by growing resistance to the rectification from within Party ranks at all levels. Much had transpired during the early months of 1957 to indicate to a Party member that he was to be a major target of "blooming and contending." At about the same time that the Central Committee announced a rectification campaign for 1958 it also issued a directive temporarily halting the recruitment of new Party members during 1957.[74] Further tension followed another article by Propaganda Director Lu Ting-yi, released just after Mao's February "contradictions" speech. In commemoration of the fifteenth anniversary of the first inner-Party rectification, Lu noted that more than 60 percent of the Party membership had joined Party ranks after Liberation. While these new cadres constituted fresh blood,

they have not been ideologically transformed by the Party's work style rectification movement of 1942. . . . Many of them still preserve the undesirable ideologies of the old society and have not given up the

72. *Ibid.*

73. As with the articles critical of "blooming and contending" written by Ch'en Ch'i-t'ung and the other PLA officers, the intriguing but unanswerable question is who may have "encouraged" Fei Hsiao-t'ung to write his article for the *People's Daily,* and who on the editorial staff of the paper allowed it to be published?!

74. The existence of this Central Committee directive was revealed in scattered reports in the provincial press during the spring. These reports were published as local Party organizations tried to prevent demoralization among non-Party "activists" by explaining to them the reasons for the policy. *See,* for example, Li Shen-sheng, "Clearly Explain to Activists the Reason Why Temporarily No New Party Members Are Being Accepted this Year," *Kung-jen Sheng-huo* (Wuhsi, Kiangsu Province), March 21, 1957; trans. in *SCMP,* No. 1521 (May 2, 1957), p. 20.

stand of the petty bourgeoisie to make way for the stand of the proletariat.[75]

Even veteran Party cadres were warned that they "were liable to be
contaminated by bureaucratism. Among our veteran Party members, some have become vain because of their meritorious feats and
some have forgotten the historical experiences of the Party." [76]
It would not have taken a particularly devious mind to sense that
Mao was trying to use the intellectuals to hit at what he saw to be
"rightist conservatism" and the three evils of "bureaucratism, sectarianism, and subjectivism" within Party ranks.

While we do not know precisely the forms which inner-Party
debates and opposition to public rectification took at this time,
press materials do reveal something of the nature and evolution of
Party resistance to "blooming and contending." In late March an
article appeared in the Peking *Ta Kung Pao* by Chang Chih-yi,
Deputy Director of the United Front Work Department of the Central Committee and the Party's delegate to the meeting of the
Chinese People's Political Consultative Conference, then in session.

Like the army officers who had criticized "blooming and contending" in January, Chang began a discussion of united front work
with an expression of humility—"my understanding of the people's
democratic united front not being deep, I can only set forth some
immature views" [77]—which only seems to emphasize that he was
challenging Mao's policy line. He then invoked words which Mao
had delivered to the Eighth Party Congress almost a year earlier
(as if nothing had happened in the meantime to strengthen the
position of the Party Chairman). Mao had talked then of the primary importance of uniting all possible forces in order to strengthen
the Party's worker-peasant alliance.

Chang's basic contention was that given the country's immediate
development problems, the Party's most pressing need was to win
the active support of the "bourgeois" intellectuals. He stressed the
necessity of maintaining the Party's *two* class "alliances"—with both
the peasantry and the bourgeoisie. He contradicted Mao's assertion
of the primary importance of the worker–peasant alliance by noting that

75. Lu Ting-yi, "In Commemoration of the Fifteenth Anniversary of the
Party's Work Style Rectification Movement," *People's Daily* (March 5,
1957); trans. in *ibid.,* No. 1511 (April 16, 1957), p. 36.
76. *Ibid.*
77. Chang Chih-yi, "Problems Concerning the People's Democratic
United Front," *Ta Kung Pao* [Peking] (March 31, 1957); trans. in *ibid.,*
No. 1522 (May 3, 1957), p. 1.

at a certain period or in a certain locality where the masses have not gained a predominance it is necessary to establish the second alliance [with the bourgeoisie] in order to gain gradually the predominance of the masses under the cover of the second alliance.[78]

In a line that expresses the heart of his challenge, Chang asserted, "It goes without saying that, if the second alliance is established because of strategic demand, such an alliance should not be lightly broken." [79] This was evidently Chang's way of stressing that if the "blooming and contending" policy were pressed, it would bring into the open differences in political "standpoint" which would force the Party to break the worker-bourgeoisie alliance through attacks on the "idealist" or "anti-Party" views of the intellectuals. Instead he called for attention to "the legitimate interests and reasonable aims" of these class allies, and asserted that such concessions "genuinely accord with the interests of the working class [i.e., the Party]." [80] Finally, Chang urged moderation in the political struggle, and in a contradiction of Mao's view that the main danger was on the "right," he noted that in past periods of stress on the united front, "the 'leftist' dangers were the main ones," and that "if we [now] commit gross errors in these respects [Party] leadership will not be stable and may even be lost." [81]

Chang, like his immediate superior in United Front work, Li Wei-han, and many other Party notables of this period, was to fall from power during the Cultural Revolution under charges of having advocated a "dying out of class struggle" and for "glorifying the bourgeoisie";[82] but his article of late March 1957 seems to reflect a widely held sentiment within the Party that the promotion of open criticism would endanger Party interests. We can only speculate as to whether Chang perceived these interests narrowly as the security of incumbent Party members, or more broadly as the need to encourage the cooperation of the intellectuals in the development effort.

In any event, the month following publication of Chang's article was apparently a period of increasing effort by Mao and his supporters to push through the "blooming and contending" policy against a most resistant Party apparatus.

78. *Ibid.,* p. 2.
79. *Ibid.,* p. 3.
80. *Ibid.,* p. 4.
81. *Ibid.,* p. 9.
82. *See* "Towering Crimes of Enrolling Capitulationists and Renegades by Li Wei-han and Hsü Ping," in *Pursue the Desperate Foe* [Peking], No. 4 (May 20, 1967); trans in *SCMP,* No. 3970 (June 29, 1967), pp. 1–2; and "Thirty-three Leading Counterrevolutionary Revisionists" (March 1968); trans. in *Current Background,* No. 874 (March 17, 1969), pp. 32–33.

On April 10th the *People's Daily* once again attacked the anti-"blooming and contending" line of Ch'en Ch'i-t'ung and the other army political workers by noting that "their criticism could only cause ideological confusion, and in fact certain confusion in thinking [has] indeed been brought about." [83] In an unusual self-criticism that apparently reflects the resistance to "blooming and contending" which had come from those engaged in propaganda work, the Party paper observed, "We should admit that the fact that this paper has delayed in commenting on their article after its publication is one of the major reasons for this confusion." [84]

The next day these army critics again were criticized in the Party paper through the device of an interview with Chou Yang, Deputy Director of the Central Committee's Propaganda Department. Since Chou had previously opposed expressions of liberalism among the intellectuals, his conspicuous support of the "blooming and contending" line, and his criticism of the army opponents, appears to represent the "winning over" of one source of opposition to Mao's cause.[85]

On April 13th the *People's Daily* published a major editorial urging the vigorous promotion of measures to resolve "contradictions among the people." Beginning with a detailed review of all the meetings since late February at which "blooming and contending" had been *discussed*, the paper went on to stress the need for active Party support in *implementing* the policy. The editorial observed that, "if it is claimed that no contradictions exist inside a thing, that will be the strangest of tales";[86] and in a clear identification of the form which inner-Party resistance to the rectification was taking, it was stressed that

> Party committees of all levels, especially the first secretaries of Party
> committees, must take up this task earnestly. . . . We must urge the

83. *People's Daily* editorial, "Continue to Implement Thoroughly and with a Free Hand the Policy of 'Letting All Flowers Bloom and All Schools of Thought Contend' " (April 10, 1957); trans. in *Union Research Service*, Vol. VII, No. 7 (April 23, 1957), p. 79.

84. *Ibid.*

85. *See* "Comrade Chou Yang Replies to Questions of a *Wen Hui Pao* Correspondent about 'A Hundred Flowers Blooming and a Hundred Schools Contending,' " *People's Daily* (April 11, 1957), p. 7.

Chou Yang's shifting position with respect to the "blooming and contending" policy during 1956–57 is discussed in the larger context of literary and artistic policy during this period in Merle Goldman, *Literary Dissent in Communist China*, esp. pp. 162–166, 190–193.

86. *People's Daily* editorial, "How to Deal with Contradictions among the People" (April 13, 1957); trans. in *SCMP*, No. 1512 (April 17, 1957), p. 1.

leadership personnel of the various departments of the Party and the government to act in this manner, and not merely entrust this task to the propaganda departments of the Party and the educational departments of the government.[87]

Since Mao's policy during this period had been articulated by Lu Ting-yi, the Central Committee's Director of Propaganda, it seems likely that resistance to the policy was taking the form of an effort to slough off implementation by entrusting it to those within the Party who had been its primary advocates.

Increasing pressure on the Party organization to implement "blooming and contending" was revealed in two further *People's Daily* editorials. On April 17th, the Party was urged to encourage criticism "based on the wish for unity." The paper admitted that as a result of criticism from outside the Party, "the prestige of certain Party organizations and state organs may possibly suffer." [88] But it stressed that failure to air complaints would hold even more serious consequences:

> If no support is given to the masses in carrying out criticism of bureaucracy and the masses are prevented by long suppression from presenting their correct views and just demands, once such a bureaucratic tendency becomes intolerable to them, they may take extreme actions to oppose bureaucracy, and may even demand the solution of certain questions which cannot for the moment be solved. By this time the contradictions will really become acute and complicated.[89]

In the April 23rd editorial, the heat was fully turned on continuing resistance within the Party. The *People's Daily* asserted that present difficulties lie "in the fact that the leadership personnel of many Party organizations have during the past few years buried themselves in the busy duties connected with socialist construction." [90] It was stressed that "The first secretaries and other responsible cadres of Party committees of all levels must *personally* lead in the discussion of this question, must *personally* lead in ideological work." [91] "When you say that there are no contradictions, it means your sense of detection is wanting, and you have not yet discovered them." And in a direct warning, the paper asserted: "People in leading positions

---

87. *Ibid.*, p. 5.
88. *People's Daily* editorial, "Criticism Based on the Wish for Unity" (April 17, 1957); trans. in *ibid.*, No. 1516 (April 25, 1957), p. 2.
89. *Ibid.*
90. *People's Daily* editorial, "The Whole Party Must Seriously Study How to Solve Contradictions within the Ranks of the People Correctly" (April 23, 1957); trans. in *SCMP,* No. 1518 (April 29, 1957), p. 2.
91. *Ibid.* Emphasis added.

who fail to see or are unable to solve correctly the internal contradictions within the ranks of the people undoubtedly are in danger
politically." [92]

A COMPROMISE DECISION
IN FAVOR OF PUBLIC CRITICISM

By all evidence, the two weeks of late April and early May constituted the period both of greatest conflict and of compromise in pushing ahead with "blooming and contending." Differences within the
Party leadership became so apparent, even to leading non-Party
intellectuals, that both those who supported and those who opposed
involvement in the Party rectification invoked the names of top
Party leaders in support of their positions at public meetings.

Ch'ien Wei-chang, a member of the Central Committee of the
China Democratic League, a leading natural scientist, and a Vice
President of Tsinghua University, later was reported to have said at
a criticism meeting that " 'blooming and contending' is not good
because it is not supported by the line of Liu Shao-ch'i through P'eng
Chen." [93] Party member Hsü Liang-ying, a research scholar in the
Philosophy Institute of the Chinese Academy of Sciences, was accused of asserting: " 'The Party center has split,' 'Chairman Mao is
under the sectarian opposition of high-level cadres. These high-level
cadres want to retaliate against him. It's too immoral.' 'Chairman
Mao has had to compromise.' " [94] And in support of greater strengthening of the policy of "long-term coexistence and mutual supervision," Chang Po-chün, Vice Chairman of the Democratic League
and Minister of Communications, was said to have "twisted" words
of Mao delivered to another (and unannounced) meeting of the
Supreme State Conference on April 30th. Chang's aim was apparently to promote a policy of eliminating Party committees in the

92. *Ibid.*, p. 4.
93. "Firmly Support the Leading Power of the Party in Scientific Work,"
People's Daily (July 17, 1957), p. 2.
As discussed later in the chapter, it is our basic assumption that this information on the policy positions of various Party leaders was published in
the Party press at this time (mid-July) for several reasons: in part to justify
attacks on non-Party "rightists" who were said to have tried to play on such
leadership divisions; partly to make clear to both Party and non-Party people
which leaders had been opposed to public "blooming and contending"; and
perhaps also as an indirect way of other Party leaders expressing subtle
criticism of Mao for his having pressed for a policy which exposed the
Party to public criticism and threatened China's political stability.
94. "Hsü Liang-ying and Li Teh-chi Are Traitors to the Party," *People's
Daily* (August 3, 1957), p. 2.

universities and reducing Party controls over the "democratic parties." [95]

Additional, indirect evidence supports the interpretation that Mao was opposed by Liu Shao-ch'i and P'eng Chen in his advocacy of public "blooming and contending," and that the Chairman had to invoke the authority of his leadership of Party and State in order to gain active implementation of the policy. Mao was said to have been so angered at Party resistance to the rectification that he told friends in Shanghai that "he would prefer not to be chairman in order to get involved [personally] in 'a hundred flowers blooming and a hundred schools contending.' " [96]

Material published between April 26th and May 11th suggests that Mao finally reached a compromise with Liu and P'eng (perhaps "ratified" by a vote of the Politbureau) in which the public rectification would be pressed and leading cadres would engage in physical labor to overcome bureaucratic isolation from the masses, but that those Party leaders who were criticized or found to have committed errors would not be subject to harsh punishment.

This shift to unanimity within the leadership is revealed first in a *People's Daily* editorial of April 26th which explicitly sides with the "democratic parties" in support of the policy of "long-term coexistence and mutual supervision." Party members were criticized for "showing no due respect for the independent and equal position of the democratic parties." [97] Criticisms of the Party raised by these parties were "welcomed" and considered to be "basically correct"; and the Party paper asserted, "we are elated with the success of these meetings [of the democratic parties to foster long-term coexistence and mutual supervision]." [98]

The following day, the 27th, Liu Shao-ch'i delivered an unpublicized address to cadres of the Shanghai Party organization in which he gave rather modest support to Mao's policy of public criticism. Liu's emphasis was on restraining "dogmatists" within the Party "who would compare [their authority] to that of the leadership" and promote an ideological struggle in the style of "striking deadly blows" as had been done by "leftists" in control of the Party in the early 1930s. He asserted that the objective of "blooming and contending" was not to "create a tense situation" and that the Party

---

95. Ma Che-min, "I Want to Renew Myself," *People's Daily* (July 18, 1957), p. 10.

96. *Ibid.*

97. *People's Daily* editorial, " 'Long-Term Co-Existence and Mutual Supervision' Discussed at Meetings of Democratic Parties" (April 26, 1957); trans. in *SCMP*, No. 1524 (May 7, 1957), p. 1.

98. *Ibid.*, p. 2.

Communist Party Chairman Mao Tse-tung
and Shanghai Municipal Party Committee First Secretary K'o Ch'ing-shih
inspect *ta-tzu-pao* [big character posters] during
the Hundred Flowers campaign of 1957.
From China Reconstructs, *December 1957.*

leadership "does not love struggle." However, because the Party "represented the entire nation" it should "adopt the method of gentle breezes and light rain" as a way of dealing with contradictions "among the People." [99]

On this same day the Central Committee made public a directive instructing Party organizations above the county level to initiate implementation of the rectification and affirming that "first secretaries of Party committees must assume personal responsibility and grasp leadership" of the movement.[100] After publication of this directive provincial Party organizations began to fall into line. New China News Agency reported on May 1st that upon receiving the directive, the Shensi Provincial Committee "immediately called an emergency meeting of the secretariat the same evening, to study the implementation of the directive." [101] At 8 o'clock the next morning there was another emergency meeting of the Provincial Party Standing Committee to discuss further promotion of the directive.

In the weeks that followed, other provincial Party Committees, and organizations under the direct control of the Central Government, began to implement public rectification. The United Front Work Department of the Party Central Committee convened forums of the democratic parties to solicit criticisms of the work style of Party cadres; and their remarks were published throughout the month in the *People's Daily*.

As this Party-sponsored criticism proceeded, resistance continued to be manifest from within Party ranks. And in an effort to strengthen the assertion of unanimity within the leadership in support of "blooming and contending," information was released in the press which seems to reveal the nature of the compromise which top leaders had reached. On May 7th the *People's Daily* published a notable editorial entitled, "Why Must We Carry Out the Rectification Movement 'As Gently as a Breeze or a Mild Rain'?" Invoking

99. "Liu Shao-ch'i's Speech to a Meeting of Cadres of the Shanghai Municipal Party Organization" (April 27, 1957), in *Ta-tao Tang-nei Tsui-ta ti Tsou Tzu-pen-chu-yi Tao-lu Tang-ch'uan-p'ai—Liu Shao-ch'i* [Strike Down the Biggest Person in Authority within the Party Taking the Capitalist Road—Liu Shao-ch'i] (Peking: Peking Chemical Engineering Institute, Mao Tse-tung's Thought Propaganda Personnel, April 10, 1967), Vol. IV, pp. 63–71.

100. "Directive of the Central Committee of the Chinese Communist Party Concerning the Rectification Movement" (April 27, 1957), in *Chung-hua Jen-min Kung-ho-kuo Fa-lü Hui-pien* [Legal Compendium of the People's Republic of China], (Peking: Legal Publishing House, 1957), p. 38.

101. New China News Agency, hereinafter cited as NCNA, "CCP Shensi Committee Calls Emergency Sessions to Discuss Rectification of Work Style" (May 1, 1957); trans. in *SCMP*, No. 1527 (May 10, 1957), p. 14.

phrases from the Central Committee Directive of April 27th, the editorial threatened Party resisters even as it sought to provide them "a way out." The paper sternly warned that, "In our Party there do not exist, and there will not be permitted, sects and groups with different interests and opposed to one another." [102] It threatened:

> In dealing with counterrevolutionaries who have infiltrated into the ranks of the Party, class dissidents who persist in acts of disintegration within the Party, and other decadent and depraved elements who are beyond salvation, the Party has always adopted a resolute attitude and expelled them from its ranks.[103]

Finally, the editorial invoked the name of Liu Shao-ch'i—the only personal reference to him in official documents of this period related to the rectification campaign—in a quote from his lengthy political report to the Eighth Party Congress. His words sounded the only conciliatory note in an otherwise stern editorial: ". . . severe punishment will not guarantee that . . . mistakes will not recur in the Party, and it may even lead to greater mistakes." [104] And on these words the editorial concluded with a stress that, "as long as [Party members] are willing to correct their mistakes, they will generally be exempted from disciplinary measures, particularly disciplinary measures of a grave nature." [105]

102. *People's Daily* editorial, "Why Must We Carry Out the Rectification Movement 'As Gently as a Breeze or a Mild Rain'?" (May 7, 1957); trans. in *SCMP,* No. 1529 (May 14, 1957), p. 2.

103. *Ibid.*

104. *Ibid.,* pp. 2–3.

It might be added that Liu's stress on a policy of leniency towards erring Party cadres—coming as it did in a context of his own increasing influence at the Eighth Party Congress, and in the wake of the revelations about Stalin's purges in the Soviet Party—conveys the air of an attempt to strengthen his personal position within the Party organization at Mao's expense. Liu seemed to be appealing to the Party for support on the grounds that he would be no Stalin by promoting a purge of the Party. This may be one of a number of reasons why Mao, in time, was to call Liu Shao-ch'i "China's Khrushchev"; for like Russia's Khrushchev, Liu apparently was attempting to consolidate his position by appealing to the Party organization for support.

In any event, it seems that many Party members tended to equate Mao with Stalin during 1957 for his determination to press for a Party rectification (*see* pp. 322–323 below).

105. *Ibid.,* p. 3.

On the day this editorial was published Liu Shao-ch'i addressed the Higher Party School in Peking on questions of the rectification movement. There is nothing particularly notable about his remarks as they pertain to the rectification. What is remarkable is his discussion of economic matters. Liu called for China to adopt measures which were "more varied and flexible" than the Soviet approach to economic management. He suggested that

Three days later the *People's Daily* carried a report of a meeting of the Peking Municipal Party Committee held on May 8th, at which P'eng Chen also identified himself personally with the policy of rectification in the style of "a gentle breeze and light rain." [106] And on May 9th P'eng was photographed carrying stones at a road-building project in Peking. Other top Party leaders also participated in this demonstration of personal involvement in that aspect of the Central Committee-endorsed rectification movement which called for participation in physical labor; but the fact that P'eng's photograph was the only one of a major Party figure circulated nationally in the *People's Daily* seems to have been intended to emphasize to resistant Party members that the conflict at the "center" had been resolved, that those within the inner circle of power who had resisted "blooming and contending" were now personally involved in the rectification.[107]

Furthermore, the information about P'eng and Liu's support for the policy of leniency toward erring cadres—an aspect of the Central Committee directive not explicitly associated with the names of any other Party leaders—seems intended to make it clear to opponents of the rectification that those within the leadership who had resisted the public campaign were responsible for protecting Party interests in the context of a compromise decision.

THE BREAKDOWN OF THE
COMPROMISE DECISION

The compromise among Party leaders, embodied in the April 27th Central Committee directive, was to prove fragile and short-lived. "Blooming and contending" was promoted by lower level Party organizations; but the evidence suggests that many Party cadres implemented the directive in a grudging spirit. Some may even have hoped to elicit such extreme criticisms of the Party that the move-

---

the Party permit "controlled free markets" and "assent to a certain number of capitalist commercial enterprises, industries, and underground factories." Within four months such economic "flexibility" and toleration of vestiges of "capitalism" were to go by the board as Mao and his supporters began to press for a politicization of the economy that led to the Great Leap Forward. (*See* "A Record of Liu Shao-ch'i's Talk to Personnel of the Higher Party School on Questions of the Rectification" (May 7, 1957), in *Strike Down the Biggest Person in Authority within the Party Taking the Capitalist Road—Liu Shao-ch'i*, Vol. IV, pp. 94–98.

106. *See* "Comrade P'eng Chen Speaks in Support of the Gentle Breeze Mild Rain Method," *People's Daily* (May 10, 1957), p. 1.

107. *See* "Leading Personnel and the Masses Participate Together in Physical Labor," *People's Daily* (May 10, 1957), p. 4.

人民日報

5月9日，中共北京市委第一書記、北京市市長彭眞（中）在豬市大
街同筑路工人一起劳动。　　　　　　　新华社记者　顧德华摄

"May 9 [1957], Communist Party Peking Municipal
Committee First Secretary, Peking City Mayor,
P'eng Chen (center) Labors with Construction Workers
at *Chu-shih* Boulevard."
From Jen-min Jih-pao [People's Daily], *May 10, 1957.*

ment would be wrecked by the "antisocialist" intemperance of the non-Party critics. At all "blooming and contending" meetings criticisms of the Party given either verbally or in "big character posters" (*ta-tzu-pao*) were recorded by special work teams, ostensibly so that the Party would be able to learn from the "supervision" of its non-Party critics. This material, however, was soon to be used both in confidential Party reports and in the press to convince those Party leaders who had had doubts about the public rectification campaign that it was not working, and then later as incriminating evidence to justify counterattacks on the non-Party critics.

Some analysts have seen in this encouragement of criticism from non-Party intellectuals a "trap" designed by Mao to expose and discredit "anti-Party" elements in the intellectual community.[108] Aside from the fact that this interpretation ignores all the evidence that "blooming and contending" was directed above all at the "bourgeoisification" of the Party itself, there are also indications that Mao

108. The "trap" interpretation of the "blooming and contending" policy in part derives from a statement in a *People's Daily* editorial of June 22, 1957 which asserted that "the Party decided not to deal immediate counterblows [to its critics], so that the masses might fully recognize the faces of the bourgeois rightists. . . ." (*See* "Unusual Spring," *People's Daily* [June 22, 1957], p. 1.)

This statement is accurate to the extent that Party opponents of "blooming and contending" may have encouraged, or gone along with, the criticism in the expectation that they could use attacks on Party leadership and "socialism" as a basis for terminating the movement. But it would be an error to assume that the only target of the rectification was the intellectual community. If Mao was out to "trap" anyone, it apparently was those Party members who had "allied" themselves with the "bourgeoisie" in the development effort, or who had manifested an interest in "bourgeois rightist" values and ways of asserting Party authority.

A more intriguing question, given the various warnings which had been made by Mao and other official sources that Party leadership should not be challenged in the criticism, is why did many critics nonetheless fall into the "trap" of excessive criticism? Aside from the fact that most non-Party critics *did* seem to sense the limits of acceptable criticism, some may not have had the political sensitivity or experience to "read" properly the context in which criticism was being promoted, and others apparently "got carried away" once criticism began, motivated by personal resentments which they carried as a result of past Party injustices.

At base, however, our interpretation is that except in the highly unlikely circumstance that the non-Party critics would have observed nearly perfect political discipline (that is, no attacks on Marxism or the Party's leading role), the Party apparatus would have used just about any "anti-Party" criticism as an excuse to terminate the movement. In short, lack of Party leadership unanimity in support of "blooming and contending" was a major political factor behind the termination of public rectification and in the "trapping" of non-Party critics.

personally had gambled that the intellectuals were sufficiently disciplined to limit their criticisms to Party abuses of power, and would
not resort to fundamental attacks on Party rule and the socialist path
of development. This severe criticism of the Party from the intellectual community constituted the third major shock to Party efforts
to incorporate intellectuals into the development effort.

Documents published before June 1957 amply reveal that the
intellectuals had been warned to keep their criticisms within the
bounds of acceptance of Party leadership. Mao had stressed this
limitation in his speech to the national conference on propaganda
work in early March. On April 6th an editorial in the *People's Daily*
again warned the intellectuals that they must diligently study China's
new political ideology: "Only by using the standpoint, outlook, and
methods of Marxism-Leninism in viewing affairs and in dealing with
problems can you avoid committing [political] errors; only then can
you overcome the influence of capitalism, individualism and idealism on your thinking." [109] And again in late May, when the intellectuals' criticism had already begun to undermine his position, Mao
gave public warning that "words and actions which deviate from
the cause of socialism are utterly wrong." [110] Where Mao apparently
miscalculated was in overestimating the "socialist discipline" of the
intellectuals, and above all in underestimating the resistance within
the Party.

That resistance had revealed itself only days after publication of
the Central Committee's April 27th directive. In a May 9th interview published in the Peking *Daily Worker,* Lai Jo-yü, Secretary-
General of the All-China Federation of Trade Unions and a Party
member active in the leadership of the National People's Congress
(of which P'eng Chen was Secretary General), disparaged the
"blooming and contending." He repeatedly observed that "the views
of the masses are, of course, not always or completely correct"; and
he stressed that in trade union work it was not possible to "form
one's own school of thought" as was being done in the academic
field.[111]

This challenge to the rectification movement received a quick
and uncompromising reply in the form of a *People's Daily* editorial

109. *People's Daily* editorial, "The Educators Must Receive Education:
A Discussion of the Remoulding of Intellectuals" (April 6, 1957), p. 1.

110. These remarks were made to a meeting of Youth League delegates,
and subsequently given national publicity. See *SCMP,* No. 1549 (June 13,
1957), p. 20.

111. "How Contradictions within the Ranks of the People Are Handled
by the Trade Unions," *Daily Worker* [Peking] (May 9, 1957); trans.
in *SCMP,* No. 1535 (May 22, 1957), pp. 8–11.

entitled "On Labor Trouble." "Why," the paper asked, "are there strikes and petitions?" [112] According to the editorial, the cause lay in the bureaucracy of leading cadres. And in remarks apparently addressed to comrade Lai and those for whom he spoke, it was observed:

> A number of leading comrades have their "difficulties." When things are difficult and undoubtedly impossible, you dare not say so. Without a doubt things are impossible, but you choose to make promises. Without a doubt things are difficult, but you choose to say "everything is satisfactory." When a mess is made of things, the masses accuse you of cheating them; and as a matter of fact, you do cheat them.[113]

The editorial then concluded with a reaffirmation that encouragement of criticism and "contrary opinions" was necessary to help the Party resolve "contradictions" in a timely manner and eliminate mistakes in leadership.

A further *People's Daily* editorial on May 19th entitled "Continue to Contend, Aid the Rectification Movement," stressed that although "some comrades . . . feel uneasy and panic-stricken" in the face of criticism, it was all the more necessary to pursue the uncovering and solution of "contradictions," for "they can no more be covered up than a fire can be wrapped in a sheet of paper." [114]

After barely three weeks of public "blooming and contending," pressures began to build within the Party leadership to quash the open criticism. Hints of this pressure were revealed on May 20th and again on the 23rd in New China News Agency reports from Shanghai and Canton: "Old workers" were said to have complained that the press was filled only with accounts of the "defects" of the Party. The "blooming and contending," they implied, had produced poisonous weeds, not fragrant flowers.[115] Within three weeks of these reports the period of encouragement of criticism from non-Party groups was to be brought to an end with a counterattack on the critics entitled "The Workers Start to Speak Up." [116] The Party was reasserting "proletarian" leadership.

The reversal of the compromise decision to promote public criticism occurred sometime between May 25th and June 8th; and the process of this reversal can be approximated from materials

112. *People's Daily* editorial, "On Labor Trouble" (May 13, 1957); trans. in *ibid.*, No. 1536 (May 23, 1957), p. 1.

113. *Ibid.*, p. 3.

114. *People's Daily* editorial, "Continue to Contend, Aid the Rectification Campaign" (May 19, 1957); trans. in *ibid.*, No. 1537 (May 24, 1957), p. 3.

115. See *ibid.*, No. 1546 (June 7, 1957), pp. 4–7.

116. See the *People's Daily* editorial, "The Workers Start to Speak Up" (June 12, 1957); trans. in *ibid.*, No. 1553 (June 19, 1957), pp. 6–7.

published in the open press. On the 25th Mao had given his public warning at the Youth League Conference that criticism should not weaken the leading role of the Party. On the same day it was announced that a session of the National People's Congress originally scheduled to open on June 3rd was postponed until June 20th. (On June 19th the meeting was again postponed. It finally convened on the 26th.)[117] Given the fact that this meeting was to be a forum for the public humiliation of anti-Party "rightists" in July, and that P'eng Chen as Secretary-General of the National People's Congress and Liu Shao-ch'i as Chairman of the Congress Standing Committee were directly involved in the planning of the Congress session, it seems most likely that those who opposed public "blooming and contending" were delaying the meeting in order to bring about a reversal of policy.

It was also on May 25th—as the *People's Daily* revealed in its editorial of June 8th signaling a halt to public criticism—that a member of one of the "Democratic Parties" closely identified with the government was sent "an anonymous letter intimidating him" for his support of the Party.[118] Whether this confluence of events on May 25th indicates that it was *the* date on which the Party leadership decided to cut off the public criticism is uncertain. If it was, it confirms the subsequent official line that once the "rightists" publicly exposed their basic opposition to Party rule, the Party held its hand for another two weeks to allow the "poisonous weeds" to sprout fully before turning them into "fertilizer." [119]

In any event, it seems clear that the Party allowed increasingly drastic criticism to be published in the public media in late May and early June in order to mobilize opposition to "blooming and contending" by stimulating fears of *luan*. The most obvious example

117. These reports are translated in *SCMP*, No. 1540 (May 29, 1957), p. 1; and No. 1556 (June 24, 1957), p. 1.

118. *People's Daily* editorial, "What Is This For?" (June 8, 1957); trans. in *SCMP*, No. 1553 (June 19, 1957), p. 3.

Another bit of evidence indicating that May 25th was probably *the* day in which the "blooming and contending" line was reversed is the fact that in 1966 the public phase of the Cultural Revolution began on May 25th with publication of a "big character poster" attacking "bourgeois intellectuals" in control of China's educational system (*see* p. 492 below). The Cultural Revolution seems to have represented for Mao a resumption and carrying to conclusion of attacks on "bourgeois rightist" intellectuals within the Party which was begun, and then thwarted, in 1957.

Roderick MacFarquhar and Michel Oksenberg are to be credited with this interpretation of the significance of May 25th. *See* Oksenberg, *Policy Formulation in Communist China*, pp. 423–428.

119. *See* footnote 108 above. Mao made the same assertion himself, in a *People's Daily* editorial of July 1st, 1957. *See* pp. 319–320 below.

of this purposeful manipulation of criticism in the press to build Party and public opposition to the rectification is found in the case of Ko P'ei-ch'i, a young lecturer in the Department of Industrial Economics at Peking University. On May 31st Ko was quoted in the *People's Daily* as having said:

> China belongs to 600,000,000 people including the counterrevolutionaries. It does not belong to the Communist Party alone. . . . If you [Communists] carry on satisfactorily, well and good. If not, the masses may knock you down, kill the Communists, overthrow you. This cannot be described as unpatriotic, for the Communists no longer serve the people. The downfall of the Communist Party does not mean the downfall of China.[120]

Again on June 8th, the very day that the first official *People's Daily* editorial attacking critics of the Party was issued, Ko was quoted once more: "I want to reiterate once again that the masses want to overthrow the Communist Party and kill the Communists." [121] This verbal violence seems to have been given wide and repeated publicity in order to bring about a reversal of the decision on public "blooming and contending," and then to justify counterattacks on "rightist" critics.

The precise reasoning adopted by the Party leadership in reversing the policy can only be approximated: An unexpected restiveness among university students,[122] scattered acts of physical violence, and the basic criticisms of Party rule by older intellectuals helped to justify fears that "a fire was being lighted" which might indeed produce a Chinese "Hungary." It was revealed later that certain leaders feared that if Party critics gained the forum of the imminent session of the National People's Congress, Party rule would be seriously undermined.[123] Finally, it seems evident that opposition to this form of public rectification continued to remain

120. Cited in Roderick MacFarquhar, *The Hundred Flowers Campaign and the Chinese Intellectuals* (New York: Praeger, 1960), pp. 87–88.

121. *Ibid.*, p. 88.

122. This aspect of the events of the spring of 1957 is documented in René Goldman, "Peking University Today," *The China Quarterly*, No. 7 (July–September 1961); the same author's "The Rectification Campaign at Peking University: May–June 1957," *ibid.*, No. 12 (October–December 1962); and in Dennis J. Doolin, *Communist China: The Politics of Student Opposition* (Stanford: The Hoover Institution on War, Revolution, and Peace, 1964).

123. This reasoning, said to have come from "reliable sources," also appears to have been purposely "leaked" in the Party press during the period of "anti-rightist" attacks in July. *See* "Attempting to Transform the Ministry of Timber Industry into an Independent Kingdom of the Rightists," *People's Daily* (July 22, 1957), p. 2.

active within the Party leadership. Hence resistant Party cadres encouraged the "poisonous weeds" to expose themselves in the expectation that a reversal of Mao's policy could be brought about by an inner-Party opposition mobilized through fears of erosion of the Party's leading role.

This opposition can be said to represent in part the desire to maintain the institutional interests which came with Party membership. Such an interpretation, while necessary, seems hardly sufficient, however, for in other political systems such institutional interests endure amidst public criticism of abuses of power. It seems evident that underlying the formal justifications for terminating open rectification were strong emotional responses, rooted in attitudes toward authority and conflict, which made such public criticism intolerable to most Party members. The old notions were still there—that those in authority were beyond criticism by their subordinates, that criticism would quickly erode the legitimacy of the Party, and that out of this combination of criticism and lack of respect for authority would come *luan*.

Such emotional responses were effectively used by opponents of Mao's policy within the leadership; and some time before the 8th of June, opinion within the Party "center"—perhaps expressed through a vote of the Politbureau—reversed the compromise decision of late April, bringing to a halt public "blooming and contending." As one "rightist" Party member was reported to have said: "Chairman Mao was under very great pressure, and in this domestic crisis the telegrams [from Party opponents of this form of rectification] flew like snowflakes, all demanding restriction." [124]

In the *People's Daily* editorial of June 8th signaling the end of the period of "blooming and contending" and raising the curtain on the "anti-rightist" campaign, some familiar images from China's political past found expression in a new context. The Party paper indignantly declared that some people had sought to characterize the Party as a "fearful man-eating 'tiger.' " And then the editorial noted with predictive satisfaction that "while these rightist elements want to use the rectification campaign for isolating the Communist Party and isolating those who support socialism, the result is that only they themselves are isolated." [125] The subsequent weeks of "struggle" with non-Party critics were to give all too much reality to the "tiger" of Party power, and to the "isolation" of its enemies. Criticism was ended, but the Party was trapped in that old dilemma

124. "The Treachery of Yüan Yung-hsi Being a Rightist and Promoting Attacks on the Party," *People's Daily* (July 22, 1957), p. 2.

125. *People's Daily* editorial, "What Is This For?" (June 8,1957); trans. in *SCMP,* No. 1553 (June 19, 1957), pp. 2–3.

of knowing that behind an apparently docile popular face lay resentments which might burst forth into *luan* if an occasion ever presented itself.

WHO WON?

In the weeks following this editorial inquiry into "What is this for?" Party organizations turned on their non-Party critics in an attempt to reaffirm the inviolability of Party authority. Criticisms expressed in May were republished in the public press as demonstrations of the "antisocialist" perfidy of those now under attack and to define clearly the types of criticism which went beyond the limits of political acceptability.

Even in this reversal of policy, however, there apparently was lack of unity within the leadership, and a very mixed outcome as far as Mao's personal position and his political objectives were concerned.

A documentary revelation of the Cultural Revolution suggests that as the Party leadership debated its response to the public criticism of Party rule, Mao sought to emphasize that the main danger exposed by "blooming and contending" was "right opportunism" *within* the Party. He is reported to have said:

> Within the Communist Party there are various kinds of people. Marxists, they are in the majority. They have their faults, but not serious ones. There is another section of people with dogmatic thinking. The majority of these people are loyal and honest; they are for the Party and nation, but their way of dealing with things suffers from the "left" prejudice. If they overcome this prejudice, they will make a great step forward. *There also is a section of people with the erroneous thinking of revisionism, or right opportunism. These people are rather dangerous, because their thinking is a reflection of bourgeois thought within the Party. They lean toward bourgeois liberalism; they are negative about everything. They have a thousand and one connections with the bourgeois intellectuals in society.*[126]

126. Mao, "Things Are Beginning to Change" (May 1957), in *Long Live the Thought of Mao Tse-tung!* p. 15. Emphasis added.

Unfortunately this pamphlet gives no more specific information as to the exact date on which Mao made this statement, or the audience he was addressing. From its content it appears to have been made late in the month, when the criticism of May had exposed both the intellectuals' opposition to the Party, and "bourgeois liberalism" among Party members. One would assume that such a statement would have been made to other Party leaders, which is why we suggest that it represents Mao's attempt to convince the leadership that the main target of the "anti-rightist" struggle should be the "rightists" within the Party.

Mao then went on to reveal his concern with the manner in which the press had been used by the Party in the "blooming and contending" campaign:

> Our Party has a large group of new members who are intellectuals (they are even more numerous in the Youth League). Among them one portion really has quite serious revisionist thinking. They deny the party and class nature of the newspapers. They confuse the differences in principle between proletarian journalism and bourgeois journalism. They confuse the journalism which reflects the collective economy of a socialist country and that which reflects the anarchy and group competition of a capitalist country. *They admire bourgeois liberalism, and oppose the leadership of the Party. They approve of democracy, but oppose centralism. . . . They echo the rightist intellectuals in society, and are united with them as closely as elder and younger brothers.*[127]

While the setting in which Mao made these remarks is uncertain, it appears that he was responding to the direct criticisms of Party rule which had appeared in the national press as "blooming and contending" proceeded during the month of May. What is clear, however, is that Mao's concern was with the influence of "bourgeois liberalism" *within* the Party. And while no doubt he would have approved of efforts to arrest open attacks on the Party from the intellectual community, he sought to focus the emphasis of the ideological struggle on revisionism within the Party. As he phrased it: "Over the past several months people have been criticizing dogmatism. Dogmatism ought to be criticized . . . but at present we must start to pay attention to criticizing revisionism." And he played down the importance of "leftist" errors by asserting that, "Some of what has been attacked as 'dogmatism' actually is a matter of certain errors in work. Some of what has been attacked as 'dogmatism' actually is Marxism." [128]

As the Party organization turned to cut off the attacks of the intellectuals after June 8th, however, there was a period of several months when it appeared uncertain as to whether "right opportunism" within Party ranks in fact would be the major target of struggle.

After an additional delay for planning sessions, the meeting of the National People's Congress originally scheduled for June 2nd opened on the 26th. Three days after Chou En-lai's opening speech —a defensive document that sought to detail the achievements of "socialist transformation" even as it affirmed that "we still have a severe class struggle" [129]—Mao left Peking for Shanghai. It was at

127. *Ibid.* Emphasis added.
128. *Ibid.*
129. Chou En-lai, "Report on the Work of the Government" (June 26, 1957); trans. in *Current Background*, No. 463 (July 2, 1957), p. 6.

this point that public humiliation of leading non-Party intellectuals like Chang Po-chün and Fei Hsiao-t'ung began, as the meeting turned into a forum for attacks on non-Party "rightists."

Why did Mao go to Shanghai? There does not appear to be a certain answer to this question, but a number of interpretations may be advanced on the basis of the limited evidence available.

On July 1st an editorial entitled "The Bourgeois Trend of the *Wen Hui Pao* Should be Subject to Criticism" appeared in the *People's Daily*. During the Cultural Revolution this editorial was identified as having been written personally by Mao;[130] and in a larger sense this criticism of the Shanghai non-Party paper presages Cultural Revolution developments inasmuch as it was the final blast in an attack which had been launched on June 14th in the *People's Daily* by a young literary critic from Shanghai—Yao Wen-yuan.[131] Mao's editorial makes it unmistakably clear that the non-Party press would not be permitted to serve as a platform for "anticommunist and antisocialist" attacks on the Party, or to become the mouthpiece of non-Party politicians like the soon-to-be humiliated Vice Chairman of the China Democratic League, Lo Lung-chi.

Again presaging a theme of the Cultural Revolution, Mao stressed that the "freaks and monsters" who had appeared during "blooming and contending" would be criticized as negative examples in order to educate the Party through struggle. Yet the Chairman asserted that these non-Party critics "may be leniently dealt with without punishment" as long as they recant their errors and mend their ways. At the same time, however, he observed that "blooming and contending" had exposed "bourgeois rightists" within the Communist Party and Youth League; and he concluded by emphasizing

---

130. *See* "Outline of the Struggle between the Two Lines from the Eve of the Founding of the People's Republic of China through the Eleventh Plenum of the Eighth CCP Central Committee"; trans. in *Current Background*, No. 884 (July 18, 1969), p. 14.

131. *See* Yao's article, "Noted for the Record," and an accompanying *People's Daily* editorial of June 14, 1957 which also has been attributed to Mao, in *SCMP*, No. 1567 (July 11, 1957), pp. 14–16.

Yao was to fire the opening shot of the Cultural Revolution with an article published in the Shanghai *Wen Hui Pao* on November 10, 1965 attacking Wu Han, a literary figure closely associated with P'eng Chen and the Peking Party organization (*see* pp. 478–479 below). During 1966 Yao was to rise to the heights of power as a member of the Small Group of the Central Committee in charge of the Cultural Revolution. He has remained as the youngest member of the Mao-Lin "inner circle" following the Ninth Party Congress of April 1969. The unusual mobility of this otherwise undistinguished young man has led to unconfirmed speculation that Yao is Mao's son-in-law. (*See* Ting Wang, "Yao Wen-yuan: Newcomer in China's Politburo," *Current Scene*, Vol. VII, No. 14 [July 15, 1969], p. 6.)

that the Party would proceed with rectification after it had dealt with the intellectuals.

Given this personal attack on the Shanghai paper, Mao may have gone to the city to investigate the situation there for himself, and to consult with his earlier-mentioned "friends" [132]—perhaps his close supporters K'o Ch'ing-shih, Chang Ch'un-ch'iao, Yao Wen-yuan, and others[133]—about the current state of affairs.

Confusing this straightforward interpretation, however, was the publication of two brief news items on the front page of the *People's Daily* early in July. On the 9th the Party paper carried a notice that Mao had met with a group of non-Party intellectuals for a meal, and had had two hours of "intimate exchanges" with them.[134] And two days later on the 11th a photograph of this meeting—showing Mao seated informally with these intellectuals, at the extreme left edge of the picture—was published on page one of the Party paper without further explanation.[135]

Why should the Party Chairman publicly identify himself with non-Party intellectuals in Shanghai at a time when intellectuals were being publicly humiliated at the National People's Congress meeting in Peking? Was Mao trying to show that he *did* have supporters within the intellectual community? Or was he trying to prove that he was not really "anti-intellectual," only "anti-rightist"? Given the evidence discussed earlier that the Party organization had strongly resisted public "blooming and contending," and that Mao all along had seen his major target in the movement as "rightist conservatism" and "revisionism" within the Party itself, another plausible explanation is that Mao left Peking to disassociate himself from a situation in which the Party organization, under the leadership of Liu Shao-ch'i and P'eng Chen, was trying to "direct the spearpoint" of the struggle at the intellectuals alone. Thus Mao appeared in public with these intellectuals as a subtle expression of

132. *See* p. 305 above.

133. K'o Ch'ing-shih rose to influence in the East China Bureau of the Party in 1954, following the purge of Kao Kang and Jao Shu-shih. He was Chairman of the Shanghai Party Municipal Committee during the Hundred Flowers period. During the Great Leap he was one of Mao's most active supporters. In November 1958 he became Mayor of Shanghai, a post he held until his death in 1965.

Chang Ch'un-ch'iao, like Yao Wen-yuan, was active in artistic and propaganda work as a member of the Shanghai Municipal Party Committee until his rise to national political prominence after 1966 as a Maoist spokesman and influential member of the Cultural Revolution leadership.

134. *See* "Chairman Mao Receives Shanghai Representative Personages of All Walks of Life," *People's Daily* (July 9, 1957), p. 1.

135. *See* the *People's Daily* (July 11, 1957), p. 1.

毛主席接見上海各界代表人士

毛主席7月7日在上海中苏友好大厦接見上海科学、教育、文学、艺术和工商界代表
士。圖为毛主席和他們亲切交談。 新华社記者 侯 波攝（無綫电傳真）

"Chairman Mao Holds Meeting with Representative Personages
of Shanghai's Scientific, Educational, Literary, Artistic
and Industrial and Commercial Circles on July 7 [1957] at Shanghai's
Sino-Soviet Friendship Building. The Photograph Shows Chairman Mao
Having Intimate Exchanges with Them."
From Jen-min Jih-pao, *July 11, 1957.*

protest over the course of events in which the Party was trying to
protect itself against an "anti-rightist" rectification.

A former Party cadre viewing the photograph of Mao with the
Shanghai intellectuals observed that whoever had selected this picture with Mao seated at the extreme left—rather than in the center,
where the Chairman of both Party and State normally appears—
may have been engaging in a subtle ridicule of Mao for his "leftism"
of having pressed the struggle with "right opportunism." The image
of Mao seated at the extreme left of a group of intellectuals does
seem to convey the message "right in form but left in essence," and
this perhaps is the most accurate characterization of Mao's "blooming and contending" policy: establishing a temporary relationship
with the intellectuals by encouraging them to criticize "rightist"
errors of Party cadres who apply the policies of the leadership.

Assuming that such a tactic was Mao's original intention in promoting "blooming and contending," the excessive "anti-Party"
criticism of the intellectuals in May undermined the Chairman's
position and justified the opposition of those Party leaders who had
resisted the movement. This interpretation only stresses that Mao
may have left Peking "in defeat," and gone to Shanghai to mobilize
support from like-minded comrades in the provincial Party organizations for initiatives which the Chairman was to press at the
Tsingtao Conference of Party leaders in mid-July.

These additional developments in July, and the above interpretation of the *People's Daily* photograph, are given added support by
critical material that appeared in the Party paper during the ensuing weeks. As attacks on the intellectuals progressed in Peking,
information was published in the *People's Daily* documenting the
"anti-Party" perfidy of the "rightists." Some of this material appears
to represent an effort by the Party organization to criticize Mao
subtly by exposing him to public ridicule (as they felt he had tried
to do to them). An article recounting the "crimes" of Chang Po-
chün quotes this leader of the Chinese Peasants' and Workers'
Democratic Party and Minister of Communications as having said,
"Socialist democracy ought to exceed capitalist democracy. The
president of a capitalist country has a term of three or four years;
and how many years had Stalin? And who knows how many years
Chairman Mao will want?" [136]

A "rightist" Party member and journalist, Tai Huang, was reported to have "madly attacked the Chinese People's respected and
beloved great leader Chairman Mao, saying that he 'early had had

136. "The Viciousness and Intrigues of the Chang-Lo Alliance," *People's
Daily* (July 22, 1957), p. 6.

his doubts' about Chairman Mao, and that after the Twentieth Party Congress of the Soviet Union he had 'begun to suspect that Chairman Mao had committed errors.' " [137] And Ch'en Ming-shu, a member of the dissident Revolutionary Committee of the Kuomintang, was quoted as having said that Chairman Mao was "hot tempered," "impetuous," and "reckless," and that "these characteristics . . . have often affected his decisions in matters of policy, causing unnecessary deviations in the implementation of governmental policy." [138] Ch'en was said to have added that Mao "lets his temper get the best of him, and is apt to hurt the feelings of ranking cadres despite their high positions."

These and other remarks critical of Mao, placed in the mouths of "anti-Party rightists," seem to convey with biting irony the resentment felt by many within the Party toward Mao for his impulsive policy interventions. Some of these men felt that Mao had betrayed the Party organization by fostering public criticism of cadre errors by disloyal intellectuals. Similarly, the "leak" published at this time about the opposition of Liu Shao-ch'i and P'eng Chen toward "blooming and contending," and the other information about inner-Party decision-making processes discussed earlier in this analysis, seems intended to reveal to all with political awareness the division of responsibility for the decisions of the spring. Party rule had been threatened and those who were willing to tolerate "bourgeois" interests in the development effort were now being forced to promote the public humiliation of the intellectuals.

This interpretation of the political uses of the press is reinforced by later developments. Liu, P'eng and other leaders were to use the writings of intellectuals as voices of veiled criticism of Mao in the wake of the Great Leap Forward;[139] and many of the major actors of the period of "blooming and contending"—Hu Ch'iao-mu, a man long associated with the press and propaganda work, Teng T'o, editor of the *People's Daily,* and Propaganda Director Lu Ting-yi—were to fall from power during the Cultural Revolution under such charges as having used their power over the press to "facilitate attacks by bourgeois rightists." [140] Lu Ting-yi, in par-

137. "New China News Agency Besieges Tai Huang on Successive Days," *People's Daily* (August 8, 1957), p. 2.

138. "Kuomintang Revolutionary Committee Holds Symposium Exposing Ch'en Ming-shu and the Rightists on July 14th," *NCNA* (Peking), in *Current Background,* No. 475 (August 28, 1957), p. 45.

139. *See* pp. 415–418 below.

140. Red Guards alleged in 1967 that, "When bourgeois rightists launched rabid attacks against the Party in 1957, Hu Ch'iao-mu, . . . taking advantage of the power of supervising Party newspapers he had usurped, . . . on

ticular, was accused of having "used stealthy means to castrate the revolutionary soul of Chairman Mao's policy of 'letting a·hundred flowers bloom and a hundred schools of thought contend.' " [141]

What is most notable in documentation from the Cultural Revolution, however, is the almost complete absence of specific charges against leaders such as Liu Shao-ch'i and P'eng Chen related to the 1956–57 period of "blooming and contending." The above vague references to Lu Ting-yi and Hu Ch'iao-mu are two of the infrequent Red Guard allegations of attempts by Party leaders to distort Mao's policy line during this period.

There seem to be a number of reasons for this silence which can be advanced on the assumption that our basic interpretation of the late April 1957 compromise decision between Mao and Liu-P'eng is correct. First, the evidence would indicate that while there was disagreement within the top leadership, it was kept within the bounds of open institutional procedures and processes of decision-making. Unlike the earlier charges against Kao Kang, or those to be made against P'eng Teh-huai in 1959 and later against P'eng Chen and Lu Ting-yi during the Cultural Revolution, there has been no indication that Liu and P'eng resorted to "conspiratorial" methods at this time to resist Mao.[142] Indeed, one should add that they probably had no need to, inasmuch as Party resistance to public "blooming and contending" at all levels was evidently strong and persistent. Mao had been on the political defensive ever since Khrushchev's attack on Stalin, and if anyone would have had to resort to conspiratorial methods to oppose majority opinion within the Party, most likely it would have been Mao himself. In this sense, Mao "lost" an open debate within the Party leadership.

Furthermore, Mao's policy of using the intellectuals to help

---

numerous occasions resisted and defied Chairman Mao's directives and criticisms in a futile attempt to stop propagating the Party's general and specific policies in Party newspapers and to facilitate attacks by bourgeois rightists." (The Revolutionary Rebel Detachment of the Union of Chinese Writers, "Liu Shao-ch'i's Black Hand in the Realm of Literature and Art: The Assorted Crimes of Hu Ch'iao-mu," *Literary Combat Journal* [Peking], No. 4 [April 14, 1967]; trans. in *SCMP*, No. 3942 [May 19, 1967], p. 8.)

141. "Thirty-three Leading Counterrevolutionary Revisionists"; trans. in *Current Background*, No. 874 (March 17, 1969), p. 40.

142. Indeed, Red Guard materials cite Mao as having explicitly stated that, "Liu [Shao-ch'i] and Teng [Hsiao-p'ing] have always done their work in the open," in contrast to the "double-dealers" like Kao Kang, Jao Shu-shih, P'eng Teh-huai, and later P'eng Chen and Lu Ting-yi, who conspired in secret. (Cited from the transcript of a talk which Mao gave in October 1966, in the Red Guard pamphlet, *Long Live the Thought of Mao Tse-tung!* p. 45.

rectify Party errors had been proved wrong, for the non-Party critics had not limited their attacks to individual abuses of authority but had criticized the very basis of Party rule. It seems unlikely that Mao and his supporters would want to recall these events in 1957 at a time when Liu and P'eng were under bitter attack for their past errors.

In several very important respects, however, Mao can be said to have "won" even though his public rectification program was cut off—which perhaps most fully explains the lack of rancor during the Cultural Revolution concerning the events of 1957. Seen in terms of both the larger Party debate on a strategy of national development and policy decisions made before and after 1957, Mao gained in two important policy areas: Party rectification, and the basic approach of the development effort.[143]

Even as the public humiliation of non-Party "rightists" proceeded during the July session of the National People's Congress, Mao was pressing for a continuation of the "anti-rightist" struggle within the Party. A *People's Daily* editorial of July 28th emphasized that rectification was only in the process of expanding at all levels and all places in the country. As a result of the events of the spring, "it cannot be denied that the [political] standpoint of a portion of Party members was neither clear or firm." [144] Another editorial of early September entitled "Handle Inner-Party Rightists Sternly" asserted that, "There are also many 'rightists' who are veteran Party members of ten or twelve years," and that, "If the existence of rightists within our Party is tolerated, these rightists will collude with rightists outside the Party to attack and oppose us from within." [145]

Thus Mao apparently had been able to use the public criticism of the spring—and Party resistance to it—to convince his colleagues

143. Mao has made this assertion himself. In remarks to Chinese students in Moscow in November 1957 he observed; "Some people say that the real victory of the socialist revolution in our country was achieved in 1956, but as I see it this actually took place in 1957. The system of ownership was transformed in 1956, and this was relatively easy to carry out. But in 1957 the socialist revolution was victorious in the political and ideological spheres. Now the rightists have been toppled, although there are still shortcomings in our work. The current rectification campaign is an important event and we must truly reform ourselves." ("Talk at a Meeting with Students and Trainees of Our Country in Moscow" [November 17, 1957], in *ibid.*, p. 16.)

144. *People's Daily* editorial, "The Anti-Rightist Struggle Is a Weighty Test for Every Party Member," (July 28, 1957), p. 1.

145. *People's Daily* editorial, "Handle Inner-Party Rightists Sternly" (September 11, 1957); trans. in *SCMP*, No. 1616 (September 24, 1957), p. 2.

that "rightist conservatism" *was* the main danger, and that the Party had to be disciplined. This shift towards consensus within the Party leadership in Mao's favor appears to have developed between mid-July and September of 1957, culminating in the Third Plenary Session of the Eighth Central Committee. This Plenum agreed to promote a vigorous rectification within the Party and also revived Mao's twelve-year program for agricultural development which had been shelved in April 1956.

Hence, with increasing scope after Teng Hsiao-p'ing's report on the rectification movement delivered to the Central Committee Plenum in late September, the rectification was pressed within the Party.[146] In part this process involved attacks on those Party intellectuals who had opposed the strengthening of ideological controls over artistic life,[147] but it also took a toll of more than seventy-five leadership cadres of ranks as high as alternate Central Committee member, provincial Party secretary, and provincial vice-governor.[148]

One analyst has concluded that in almost every one of these provincial purges rural policy was an issue,[149] which stresses the second respect in which Mao was able to turn the events of the spring to his advantage. To the degree that the "blooming and contending" policy had been conceived by Mao as a way of confronting "bourgeois rightist" ideas within the Party, the criticisms of the spring provided further support for his contention that the "alliance" with the intellectuals in a heavy-industry-oriented approach to development created a threat to the Party's revolutionary goals: Mao had stressed in his 1955 writings on agricultural cooperation the fundamental importance for China's development of increasing agricultural productivity; and this position had been reiterated in his April 1956 analysis, "On the Ten Great Relationships" and again in the "contradictions" speech of February 1957.[150] The

146. *See* Teng Hsiao-p'ing, "Report on the Rectification Campaign" (September 23, 1957), in *CC 1955–59*, pp. 343–363. This document affirms Mao's evaluation of the state of the Party and Chinese society which had been the basis of the public rectification campaign policy, and is notable for its striking contrast in tone with Teng's speech to the Eighth Party Congress of the previous year.

147. *See* Goldman, *Literary Dissent in Communist China*, Ch. IX.

148. The organizational positions and policy errors of the major "objects" of the inner-Party "anti-Rightist" purge of the fall and winter of 1957–58 are analyzed in Frederick C. Teiwes, "The Purge of Provincial Leaders, 1957–1958," *The China Quarterly*, No. 27 (July–September 1966), pp. 14–32.

149. *Ibid.*, p. 17.

150. Mao phrased it, "As China is a large agricultural country, with over 80 percent of her population in the rural areas, industry must

"betrayal" of the intellectuals enabled him to stress that a development strategy which placed reliance on their skills held great dangers for the Party.

This argument, combined with continuing problems of agricultural production, appears to have enabled Mao to bring about
a major reorientation in China's development effort beginning with
the Third Central Committee Plenum of September 1957. Within
a year of this meeting China's entire rural population had been reorganized into township or county-wide amalgamations of Agricultural Producers Cooperatives called People's Communes. In this
respect, the two-year debate over "blooming and contending" prepared the way for the policies of the Great Leap Forward by
breaking the Party's "alliance" with the intellectuals and the development strategy which that "alliance" implied.

In this analysis we have stressed the impact of events in the
Soviet Union and Eastern Europe in shaping the leadership debate
and coalition of forces within the Chinese Communist Party. Mao's
"blooming and contending" policy in large measure was a reaction
to "de-Stalinization" and to events in Hungary as they held meaning
for China. In a notable way Chinese responses to these developments within the Bloc produced their own counterresponses in the
U.S.S.R. and Eastern Europe.

Mao's encouragement of public criticism of the Chinese Communist Party set a disturbing precedent for other Bloc Parties (as
initially had been the case with Khrushchev's criticism of Stalin).
At the Fortieth Anniversary celebrations of the October Revolution
in November 1957, both Mao (in Moscow) and Liu Shao-ch'i (in
Peking) gave speeches which *inter alia* attempted to explain and
justify to other "fraternal Parties" the policy of public "blooming
and contending." [151] It was later revealed that Khrushchev had

---

develop together with agriculture. . . . Without agriculture there can be
no light industry. But it is not yet so clearly understood that agriculture provides heavy industry with an important market." And then he noted cryptically that there was a "contradiction between the objective laws of economic development of a socialist society and our subjective understanding
of them—which needs to be resolved in the course of practise. *This contradiction also manifests itself as a contradiction between different people,* that
is, a contradiction between those with a relatively accurate understanding
of these objective laws and those with a relatively inaccurate understanding
of them." However, as of early 1957, Mao was able to add that this "contradiction" was one among "the People." (Mao, "On the Correct Handling
of Contradictions among the People," in *Selected Readings from the Works
of Mao Tse-tung,* pp. 385–386. Emphasis added.)

151. These speeches are reproduced in *CC 1955–1959. See* esp. pp. 392,
397–398.

been upset by the Chinese Party's rectification line,[152] and his displeasure with Mao was to be increased by Chinese claims made during the fall of 1958 that the People's Communes had placed China on the verge of realizing communism (and by implication ahead of the Russians).[153]

Khrushchev's attack on Stalin had undermined the legitimacy of the Soviet experience for other Communist Parties, and the People's Commune experiment can be seen as an effort by Mao and other Chinese leaders to evolve an approach to national development adapted to local circumstances and derived from their own revolutionary traditions. This effort was further to erode Soviet leadership of the Bloc, and heighten Sino-Soviet tensions. In dialectical fashion, political developments within the International Communist Movement in the wake of Stalin's death produced reactions and counterreactions which have continued to disintegrate Stalin's empire.

In the matter of differing approaches to Party rectification, the Chinese "blooming and contending" of 1957 was to have a disturbing influence within the Bloc; yet one that was mild relative to Soviet horror in reaction to Mao's greatest Party "rectification," the Great Proletarian Cultural Revolution of 1966–1969. The full impact of these most recent events in China on other ruling Communist Parties has yet to be felt fully.

In terms of domestic Chinese political developments of the next decade, the Hundred Flowers period of 1956–57 reveals in muted outline some of the key issues which were to grow into the Cultural Revolution. Liu Shao-ch'i's attenuated appeal at the first session of the Eighth Party Congress—and again in the spring of 1957— for support on the basis of his protection of the Party apparatus against a Maoist public rectification was to be repeated in the "four clean-ups" movement after 1962. Thus resistance within the Party to another rectification was to be a major stimulus to the Cultural Revolution.[154] The public "blooming and contending" of 1957 presaged the Cultural Revolution in the sense that in 1966

152. *See* Edward Crankshaw's summary of Khrushchev's attack on Mao at the Bucharest Party Congress of June 1960, in Jerome Ch'en, ed., *Mao* (Englewood Cliffs, N.J.: Prentice-Hall, 1969), p. 148.

153. Soviet displeasure with the Chinese Commune experiment is analyzed in Zagoria, *The Sino-Soviet Conflict, 1956–1961*, Ch. III.

154. *See* Charles Neuhauser, "The Chinese Communist Party in the 1960s: Prelude to the Cultural Revolution," *The China Quarterly*, No. 32 (October–December 1967); Richard Baum and Frederick C. Teiwes, "Liu Shao-ch'i and the Cadre Question," *Asian Survey*, Vol. VIII, No. 4 (April 1968); and the "Comment" and "Reply" by Neuhauser in *The China Quarterly*, No. 34 (April–June 1968), pp. 133–144.

Mao was to turn again to groups outside the Party to force a large-scale attack on those who resisted rectification.

The efforts of P'eng Chen and other leaders to shield the intellectuals from Mao's policies of "unity and struggle" and opposition to "rightist conservatism" was to be another major theme in leadership conflict after the Tenth Central Committee Plenum of September 1962. And the indirect use of the press to snipe at Mao was to grow into encouragement of but lightly-veiled ridicule following the failure of the Great Leap Forward. But in the dialectic of inner-Party politics, the Great Leap would have to run its course before opponents of the Chairman's policies would have an issue of sufficient strength to enable them to attempt, once again, to limit Mao's influence on the course of China's revolution.

Chapter XVIII

TO LEAP FORWARD:
THE RELATIONSHIP OF
POLITICAL CONFLICT
TO SOCIAL CHANGE

The struggle in the socialist countries between the road of socialism and the road of
capitalism—between the forces of capitalism
attempting a comeback and the forces opposing it—is unavoidable. But the restoration of
capitalism in the socialist countries and their
degeneration into capitalist countries are certainly not unavoidable. We can prevent the
restoration of capitalism so long as [we] . . .
wage a prolonged, unremitting struggle. *The
struggle between the socialist and capitalist
roads can become a driving force for social
advance.*[1]

In one of his earliest philosophical writings, "On Contradiction,"
Mao stressed the relationship between conflict and social change:

The fundamental cause of the development of a thing is not external
but internal; it lies in the contradictoriness within the thing. . . .
Changes in society are due chiefly to the development of internal contradictions. . . . [It] is the development of these contradictions

1. Editorial Departments of *People's Daily* and *Red Flag,* "On Khrushchev's Phoney Communism and Its Historical Lessons for the World," in
Polemic on the General Line of the International Communist Movement, p.
470. Emphasis added.

[through struggle] that pushes society forward and gives the impetus for the supersession of the old society by the new.[2]

One of the major aspects of Mao's impact on the course of the Chinese revolution has been the effort to institutionalize forms of conflict—methods for resolving "contradictions"—in a society where traditional attitudes toward authority inhibit criticism of the old and established, retard innovation, and slow the pace of social and economic advance.

In the previous chapter we explored Mao's attempt to establish a critical relationship between "the People" and the Party as a way of subjecting conservative ideas to "rectification." Here we shall examine the period of recent political history which most clearly manifests the Maoist approach to promoting controlled social conflict as a way of changing the organization of work and of forcing people to clarify their political "standpoint." The policies of the Great Leap Forward—formulated in the fall and winter of 1957–58 and applied through 1960—are a particularly concentrated expression of Mao's political values and methods of operation: The People's Commune system of rural social and economic organization which was instituted during these years embodies Mao's belief in the virtues of self-reliance and popular "activism." In the Taiwan Straits crisis of 1958, the Party Chairman resorted to another political confrontation in order to test the international balance of power and to force China's major ally to clarify its stand in relation to the revolution and China's national defense. And in the combined policies of the Great Leap Forward, as they were promoted in the fall of 1958, Mao revealed his continuing commitment to that style of political action which intertwines war, social change, and economic production.

As with the Hundred Flowers period preceding these developments, the Party leadership was not in agreement as to whether the rapid effort to establish the People's Communes was the most appropriate way to promote the country's social and economic advance. The conflict over a proper strategy of national development had found increasingly sharp expression after Liberation over questions of land reform, industrial organization, and agricultural collectivization. By 1958 Mao and other leaders had become conscious of a temporal rhythm in the evolution of Party policy and the process of social change. Mao appears to have used the outcome of the 1957 "blooming and contending" (the discrediting of the intellectuals, and the inner-Party rectification), as well as the uncertain state of the

---

2. Mao, "On Contradiction," *SW*, English, I, pp. 313, 314.

economy in the fall of 1957, to play consciously on what the Party leadership characterized as a "saddle shaped" pattern of social advance. The Chairman sought to mobilize support for policies designed to organize the Chinese people into self-reliant economic and political communities which would see them through the transition to communism.

Also in common with the events of 1956–57, Sino-Soviet relations were an important element in the evolution of Chinese domestic policy during the period of the Great Leap Forward. Now, however, Mao was on the offensive. He was searching for a *Chinese* solution to the problems of social change in an underdeveloped peasant society. He conceptualized organizational solutions for rural reconstruction which the Soviets saw as a deliberate challenge to their preeminent position in the International Communist Movement. During the years 1958–59 Mao does not seem to have challenged Soviet leadership of the Bloc directly; rather, he seems to have gone his own way in domestic policy and to have promoted international policies which would force the Russians to take a more militant stand in dealings with "imperialism."

In the Taiwan Straits crisis of 1958 Mao was apparently deliberately testing what the Soviet Union's new intercontinental ballistic missile capability implied for China's national defense. From the outcome of this confrontation, as well as from Russian reactions to the Sino-Indian border conflict of the following year, Mao was to find Khrushchev sorely lacking in "proletarian internationalism." When the Russian Party leader came to Peking in October 1959— just after a tour of the United States—to attend celebrations marking the Tenth Anniversary of the People's Republic, Mao became fully convinced of the necessity of promoting struggle with "revisionism" within the International Communist Movement. He saw that China's national interests and her social revolution needed to be safeguarded against external political pressures and ideological subversion.

Foreign and domestic developments during the period of the Great Leap were most clearly linked in the actions of the Chinese Defense Minister, P'eng Teh-huai. It may have been with Khrushchev's encouragement that P'eng challenged Mao's economic and defense policies in the wake of the unsuccessful Taiwan Straits venture and the increasingly serious economic difficulties resulting from the Great Leap Forward. Mao weathered P'eng's challenge at the Eighth Central Committee Plenum in the summer of 1959, and brought the Chinese Communist Party to the point of open conflict with Soviet "revisionism." Yet in the context of increasingly serious difficulties for China in both her domestic economy and international relations, Mao's political authority was to become seriously eroded—thus setting the stage for a more serious leadership conflict in the 1960s.

As with other agricultural societies seeking to become industrial states, China's problems in economic modernization are basically related to the transformation of the peasants' productive capabilities. Increased agricultural output is the key to economic development, as products of the rural economy provide almost 80 percent of the raw materials for light industry. Increases in food production are necessary to support urbanization and to feed a growing rural population. And the sale of food grains is a major source of foreign exchange.

Conversely, stagnation in the rural economy will inhibit the importation of certain foreign products necessary to promote industrialization, slow down domestic industry because of the lack of raw materials, restrict the rural market for industrial products, and aggravate all the social problems associated with population growth under conditions of decreasing standards of living. But until the late 1940s, China's peasants still followed ancient social and technical patterns. *How* should the country proceed to increase agricultural productivity? This issue is still one of the most contentious facing the Party leadership.

During the first years after Liberation the Soviet experience in economic development exercised a major influence over the thinking of the Chinese leadership on the question of the relationship between agricultural growth and industrialization. Specifically, while industrial expansion was seen as closely related to agricultural productivity the full development of agriculture's productive potential was assumed to be dependent upon mechanization—itself a function of industrialization. In Maoist terms, here was a "sharp contradiction."

In the Soviet Union socialization of the rural economy into large-scale, collectivized production units had occurred on the basis of the technical reform of agriculture. Increases in labor productivity and per-acre yields were brought about through the introduction onto state farms of the tractors, pumps and irrigation equipment, chemical fertilizers, and so on, which are the products of an established industrial economy. Industrialization had *preceded* the social transformation of rural life.

It was this experience which shaped Chinese thinking during the early stages of social change in the rural areas: land reform between 1947 and 1952; the formation of mutual aid teams during

1952–53; and then the establishment of "primary stage" Agricultural Producers' Cooperatives (APCs) in 1954–55 (in which the peasants pooled their land for management by the cooperative, but retained private ownership and the right to withdraw). A powerful element within the Party leadership assumed that the "socialist transformation of agriculture"—the elimination of private ownership and management by individual peasant families—would occur *after* China's industrial capacity had grown to the point of making possible the mechanization of agricultural production.

This view of the relationship between industrialization and agricultural growth was challenged during 1954–55, in part as a result of two years of poor harvests. The agricultural sector was not meeting its targeted contributions to the First Five Year Plan (1953–1957), with the result that industrial goals could not be attained. In the now apparent contradiction between the rural and urban economies, agriculture increasingly came to be seen as the bottleneck in China's overall economic modernization.

Beginning in 1954 there was an attempt to rethink China's strategy of economic development.[3] In contrast to the Soviet experience, China's industrial base was small relative to the size of her agricultural sector. There was little unused land which could be brought into production (unlike the vast tracts of "virgin land" in the Soviet Union). And China's rural population density and her underemployed agricultural labor force were both high, in contrast to Soviet labor scarcity. The process of reconsidering the relevance of the Soviet precedent for China's economic and social conditions began with a rethinking of the relationship between mechanization of the rural economy and the social transformation of peasant life.

According to Mao's one-time personal secretary Ch'en Po-ta, it was Mao himself who challenged "the old concept originally held by some comrades that without the mechanization of agriculture it would be very difficult to realize the large-scale cooperativization of agriculture."[4] Mao evidently came to believe that the "contradiction" between China's industrialization and her agricultural growth could be resolved by bringing about the social transformation of rural life *before* its mechanical revolution. Agricultural

3. In this discussion I have found particularly helpful Kenneth R. Walker, "Collectivization in Retrospect: The 'Socialist High Tide' of Autumn 1955–Spring 1956," in *The China Quarterly*, No. 26 (April–June 1966), pp. 1–43; and Alexander Eckstein, *Communist China's Economic Growth and Foreign Trade* (New York: McGraw-Hill, 1966), esp. Chs. I–III.

4. Ch'en Po-ta, "Under the Flag of Comrade Mao Tse-tung," *Red Flag*, No. 4 (July 16, 1958), p. 4.

productivity could be increased through the intensive application of peasant labor power, mobilized through socialist (collective) forms of work organization and political control. Mao's program thus implicitly challenged the Soviet development precedent, and the thinking of many colleagues within the Party leadership. In the second half of 1955 the Chairman began to press for rapid completion of "primary stage" collectivization, the immediate socialization of these larger production units into "advanced stage" cooperatives, and the promotion of a basic form of technical change through the widespread introduction of a double-wheel double-shared plow.

Mao's initial efforts to rethink a development strategy suited to Chinese conditions—expressed, in part, in a twelve-year program for agricultural development drafted in late 1955—generated strong resistance within the Party leadership. His efforts in the first months of 1956 to follow on cooperativization with measures to bring about a "leap forward" in production under the slogan of "more, better, faster, and more economically" were blocked by those who saw this continuous pressure for progress as the promotion of "reckless advance." They saw his policies for "continuous revolution" as not allowing sufficient time to consolidate the organizational changes brought about by collectivization, producing economic imbalances, and shifting emphasis away from the high-priority industrialization effort. And as we suggested previously, this opposition to Mao's policies was strengthened by the process of "de-Stalinization" in the Soviet Union.

The outcome of the Hundred Flowers experiment, and disappointing harvests in 1956 and 1957, however, gave Mao and his supporters the added political influence needed to reinvoke these thwarted plans of 1956 for increasing agricultural production. With the convening of the Third Plenum of the Eighth Central Committee in September 1957, the "reds" within the leadership began to reestablish their control over China's pattern of economic development. This reassertion of Mao's influence was promoted through the "anti-rightist" Party rectification which was intensified in the fall of 1957 and continued well into the fall of 1958, when the movement to establish People's Communes throughout China was fully under way.

The details of the process by which Mao came to the full conception of the Great Leap Forward and the People's Communes as the basis for China's national development are not fully known by foreign observers, but the concept and its relationship to an altered strategy of economic development are not difficult to describe.

In its simplest terms, the policy of "developing industry and

毛主席观看新式农具——双轮双铧犁　　侯　波摄（新华社稿）

"Chairman Mao Inspects a New Type
of Agricultural Tool—a Double-Wheel, Double-Shared Plow."
From Jen-min Jih-pao, *October 25, 1955.*

agriculture simultaneously on the basis of priority to heavy industry" which was advanced following the Third Central Committee Plenum in September 1957 represented an effort to promote China's economic growth without paying the price of a slowdown in the rate of industrialization.[5] Heavy industry was to continue to receive priority in the investment of capital, while agricultural productivity was to be increased through more intensive application of the "capital" of peasant labor. The State was not to provide investment funds. Rather, there was to be local financing of capital construction through the accumulation and investment of local production surpluses. What was to become known as the policy of "walking on two legs" in economic development represented an effort to rely on local resources to increase productivity in the rural areas, while using China's scarce "hard" capital and technically advanced manpower in the urban economy to promote rapid industrialization. One senses that this policy may have reflected a compromise within the Party leadership: Mao was given support for his "political" policies in the countryside in return for his continued acceptance of such "economic" considerations as priority in capital investment for the development of heavy industry.

In any event, the "three red flags" of policy during the period of the Great Leap Forward (1956–1960)—the "general line" for socialist construction of "more, better, faster, and more economically";[2] the effort to achieve a "great leap" in production;[3] and the formation of People's Communes—were presented as an integrated set of policies designed to promote the pace of China's development fast enough to overtake Britain's level of economic productivity within fifteen years.

The organizational core of these policies was the People's Commune, which was to be the instrument for mobilizing peasant labor and capital in order to create self-reliant rural communities and to

5. This new economic line was formally promoted after a two-week National Economic Planning Conference held in early December 1957. It replaced the formula of "step by step, to bring about socialist industrialization of the country, and step by step, to accomplish the socialist transformation of agriculture, handicrafts and capitalist industry and commerce" which was stressed by Li Fu-ch'un in his mid-1955 report on the First Five Year Plan, and reiterated by Liu Shao-ch'i in his political report to the first session of the Eighth Party Congress.

The "simultaneous development" line of 1958–1960 was replaced at the Ninth Central Committee Plenum of January 1961 with a formula of "agriculture as the foundation of the national economy, and industry as the leading factor," in which still greater efforts and resources were concentrated on development of the rural economy in the context of the Great Leap production crisis.

strengthen economic and political leadership over the peasants. The Commune concept reflects both Mao's values of self-reliance and activism and his continued commitment to the successful experience of the revolutionary period.[6] As early as 1956 Mao had asserted the continuing relevance of the Party's pre-Liberation experience for the period of economic construction:

> To mobilize all the active factors and all the available strength has always been our principle. Formerly, this principle was applied to winning the people's democratic revolution and terminating the imperialist, feudalist, and bureaucratic-capitalist domination. Now it is [to be] applied to a new revolution—the socialist revolution and the construction of a socialist country.[7]

Self-reliance and local initiative are the two dominant themes that run through the rationale advanced by the Party for the Communes. In line with the "walking on two legs" concept, the cadre journal *Study* (*Hsüeh-hsi*) stressed, "it is impossible for the State to provide all the capital required for agricultural development and we must depend primarily on the cooperatives [later to be renamed Communes] for the accumulation of such capital."[8] The rural economy was thus to "pay its own way" in the purchase of machinery and fertilizer from its own production surpluses (after paying taxes to the State). The farmers were also to pay the costs of any destruction of farm machinery and animals, such as had occurred on a limited scale in 1955–56 as a result of peasant resistance to the "high tide" of collectivization.

This approach to mechanization was also seen as a way of encouraging the development of initiative and of managerial and technical skills at the local level. In 1956 Mao had complained about the increasing bureaucratization of economic planning:

> Now there are dozens of hands interfering with local administration, making things difficult for the region[s]. Although neither the Center nor the State Council knows anything about it, the Departments [of the Central Government] issue orders to the offices of the provincial

6. A detailed analysis of the experiments in political and economic organization of the "Yenan" period which were reapplied during the Great Leap Forward will be found in Mark Selden, "The Yenan Legacy: The Mass Line," in A. Doak Barnett, ed., *Chinese Communist Politics in Action* (Seattle: University of Washington Press, 1969), pp. 99–151.

7. Mao, "On the Ten Great Relationships" (April 1956), in Jerome Ch'en, ed., *Mao*, p. 66.

8. Yüeh Wei, "Capital Accumulation in the Agricultural Producer Cooperatives," *Hsüeh-hsi* [Study], No. 7 (April 3, 1958); trans. in *Extracts from China Mainland Magazines* (hereinafter cited as *ECMM*), No. 132 (June 16, 1958), p. 32.

and municipal governments. . . . Forms and reports are like floods. This situation must change and we must find a way to deal with it.[9]

Mao's "way to deal with it," as policy evolved in the fall and winter of 1957–58, came to embody fundamental changes in the pattern of work and administration in the rural areas. In 1956 the Party Chairman had (unsuccessfully) called for a "cut of two-thirds of our party and government organizations." [10] In 1958 this call was manifest in a large-scale *hsia-fang* or "down to the countryside" campaign which involved millions of Party and government office workers in rural labor.[11] Mao seemed determined to prevent the formation of a huge bureaucratic superstructure with such a vested interest in centralized economic planning that all initiative in the rural areas would be quashed under a weight of departmental directives. And as with his 1955–56 effort to prevent a reemergence of class polarization in the villages by forming fully socialized collectives, his decentralization of economic decision-making to the provinces and communes seemed designed to prevent polarization between town and countryside. He could see the dangers of the entrenchment of a small, urbanized political and economic elite, increasingly "cut off from the masses" by physical distance and bureaucratic routine.

Mao's effort to strengthen local economic leadership also manifested itself in rejection of Soviet agricultural institutions. In Russia the Machine Tractor Stations had been a major vehicle by which the State had taxed the collective farms. Mao sought to dilute the "contradictions" in taxation and technical skill between state and society by giving the rural producers direct control over agricultural machinery, and by allowing them greater choice in the investment of their own production surpluses.[12]

To be successful as an experiment in economic self-reliance, the rural management and production organizations had to be large enough to include sufficient labor, capital (chiefly land, agricultural tools, animals, and machinery), and raw materials to enable them to be self-supporting economic units. Thus, the essential

9. Mao, "On the Ten Great Relationships," in Ch'en, ed., *Mao*, p. 75.
10. *Ibid.*, p. 77.
11. *See* Rensselaer W. Lee III, "The *Hsia Fang* System: Marxism and Modernization," *The China Quarterly*, No. 28 (October–December 1966), esp. p. 47.
12. *See* the excellent analysis of the extended leadership debate over state control versus local initiative in agricultural mechanization in, The Editor, "The Conflict between Mao Tse-tung and Liu Shao-ch'i over Agricultural Mechanization in Communist China," *Current Scene* (Hong Kong: United States Information Service), Vol. VI, No. 7 (October 1, 1968), esp. pp. 8–12.

institutional transformation of the Communization drive was the amalgamation of "primary stage" APCs (approximately 30–40 households; roughly comprising a small "natural agricultural village") and the "advanced stage" APCs (approximately 300 households) into Commune units of somewhere between 5,000 and 8,000 households.[13]

This basic pattern of amalgamation in rural organization was seen as one of the great strengths of Communization. In practice, however, it embodied some of the major weaknesses of the movement. Theoretically, this larger scale of production activity would overcome the fragmentation which traditionally had accounted for the low level of China's agricultural productivity, and break down the strong sense of local interest in opposition to that of the political "center." As Franz Schurmann has phrased it, Communization was seen as a way of penetrating to the "inaccessible core of Chinese social organization," the kinship groups and small villages, and of establishing an institutional "bridge on which state and society would meet and merge."[14]

In application, however, the Communes were to alienate the peasant from his most basic social ties and remove from him both initiative in the making of production decisions and economic reward commensurate with personal effort. Thus the human relationships which integrate a society were seriously weakened, and some of the most basic motives for work and innovation—personal responsibility and remuneration according to effort—were eliminated. Similarly, while the objective in forming Communes was to replace a centralized economic bureaucracy with local decision-making units, in fact the reorganization was brought about by a political command structure which was as insensitive to local conditions as any metropolitan economic ministry. Thus, ironically, what Mao saw from the "center" as an effort to promote greater local initiative in fact took initiative out of the hands of the primary producers, the peasants. Power passed "up" from the villages to the Communes and regional Party organizations.

From a social perspective, the Commune concept was seen by its advocates as a way of eliminating enduring sources of social

13. The best discussions of what the amalgamation of APCs into Communes implied for agricultural planning, management and commodity exchange will be found in Kenneth R. Walker, *Planning in Chinese Agriculture: Socialization and the Private Sector, 1956–1962* (Chicago: Aldine Publishing Co., 1965); and G. William Skinner, "Marketing and Social Structure in Rural China, Part III," *Journal of Asian Studies,* Vol. XXIV, No. 3 (May 1965), pp. 363–399.

14. Schurmann, *Ideology and Organization in Communist China,* pp. 471, 496.

inequality. By decentralizing industrial activity—most notably in the mass campaign for the smelting of iron and steel and in the creation of local light industry—the Communes would moderate the social distinctions separating industrial and agricultural workers, urban and rural residents. And by involving governmental bureaucrats and Party cadres directly in economic production several months each year, the Communes would help to bridge the gap between mental and manual labor which traditionally had reinforced the "contradiction" between state and society.

Furthermore, the Communes were supposed to foster popular socialist consciousness through a restructuring of the pattern of property ownership and daily living. Class distinctions in the countryside, already weakened by land reform, were to be reduced further by eliminating all major forms of private ownership of the means of production (private plots, small farm animals, and agricultural tools). As one writer observed, Communization was intended "thoroughly to overcome the desire for private property and private interest on the part of the upper-middle peasants." [15]

The "liberation" of women from household activities for productive labor, and the concomitant formation of communal mess halls, nurseries, kindergartens and boarding schools, and "homes of respect for the aged," were seen as weakening male-female distinctions and aiding in "obliterating the role of family head and the bourgeois authoritarian ideology in respect to family relations." [16]

Mobilization of labor for production was one of the major economic objectives of Commune formation; and here the links of the movement to the Party's revolutionary past, as well as to its hopes for the future, become most apparent. As we have noted, one of the basic characteristics of Chinese Communist political organization during the Yenan period was the intertwining of war, production, and social change. Peasants in the Liberated areas were both producers and guerrilla fighters, mobilized by Party cadres for both war and production through Party control of the peasant associations and militia, and through the manipulation of land rent and interest rates—and later the system of land ownership.

This close linkage between Party leadership, local defense, and the organization of production had weakened after land reform. On the eve of the 1955–56 "high tide" of collectivization, Mao had

15. Wang Yen-li, *et al.,* "An Investigation and Study of the Problems of Transition from Higher Stage Cooperatives to People's Communes," *New Construction,* No. 9 (September 3, 1958); trans. in *ECMM,* No. 145 (October 13, 1958), p. 8.

16. T'ien Sheng, "The Outlook of Communism as Seen from the People's Communes," *Political Study,* No. 10 (October 13, 1958); trans. in *ECMM,* No. 151 (December 22, 1958), p. 10.

attacked local Party organizations for showing "a spineless attitude toward agricultural cooperation," and for not exercising active leadership in promoting social change in the villages.[17] It was such a situation which Mao sought to correct through the varied policies of the Great Leap Forward.

The institutional forms by which Mao sought to have the Party reassert leadership over rural life embody the two major organizational innovations of the Commune movement. First, Party control over operational economic decisions was effected through the merging of township (*hsiang*) government and Commune economic unit—an amalgamation which placed the organs of local government under the control of Party committees directed by the provincial Party organization. In this way Mao sought to shift power away from the bureaucrats and "experts" discredited in the "blooming and contending" of 1957, and place it in the hands of a politically mobilized Party organization. Thus power moved "down" from the central government ministries to the provincial Party organizations. At the same time power was being pulled "up" from the primary producers, the peasant families and villages, to the levels of township/Commune and province.

Second, the Party sought to exercise control over peasant labor power through the militarization of the labor force. Drawing on the wartime experience of embattled Yenan, when the Party successfully rebuilt its strength in a poor agricultural region under conditions of economic blockade by Nationalist and Japanese troops, the Party now sought to organize the rural population into "regiments," "battalions," "companies," and "squads." The peasants, "who have for several thousand years lived in a scattered state, [were thus to be transformed] into a highly organized and disciplined group of new people with an increasingly high degree of Communist awareness." [18]

While the public press gave partial justification for the militarization of work and the expansion of the People's Militia (*min-ping*) in terms of the strengthening of national defense,[19] the primary

17. See Mao, *Socialist Upsurge in China's Countryside*, pp. 136–139, 206–207.

18. "Countless Advantages of Militarization: An Account of the Militarization of Hsü-Shui People's Commune," in *Double Collection of Works on the National Defense of China*, Vol. IV, trans. in Joint Publications Research Service, *Strengthening of National Defense and Socialist Construction and Advantages of Militarization*, No. 22,800 (January 20, 1964), p. 86.

19. Prior to mid-September of 1958 the formation of militia units had been carried out without fanfare in selected areas of China. It was only after the Taiwan Straits crisis had passed its peak of military danger and entered a diplomatic phase that a nationwide campaign for "everyone a soldier" was launched, and a national conference on militia work convened.

rationale advanced for this change in the organization of production was the more effective mobilization of labor. As the newly published Party journal *Red Flag* stressed:

> To "get organized along military lines" of course does not mean that [peasants] are really organized into military barracks, nor does it mean that they give themselves the titles of generals, colonels, and lieutenants. It simply means that the swift expansion of agriculture demands that they should greatly strengthen their organization, act more quickly and with greater discipline and efficiency, so that like factory workers and army men they can be deployed with greater freedom and on a larger scale.[20]

In China's "war" on her poverty, Mao sought to invoke the heroic spirit and work style of pre-Liberation military actions which had brought the Party to power. A *People's Daily* editorial exhorted "Secretaries of Party committees regularly [to] mobilize the masses to examine their thinking, energy, working style, plans, measures, and coordination. Like fighting a war, we must win one battle after another and must, on the completion of one target, immediately put forward another." [21]

The "blooming and contending" of 1957 had exposed conservative or antisocialist attitudes in the cities, and now Mao sought to invoke the same technique of public debate to reshape the peasants' attitudes toward their involvement in the development process. He revealed his belief in "the power of the word" in a celebrated statement of April 1958 in which he referred to China's people as "poor and blank":

> On a blank sheet of paper free from any mark, the freshest and most beautiful characters can be written, the freshest and most beautiful pictures can be painted. The big character poster is a very useful weapon, which can be used . . . wherever the masses are to be found. It has already been widely used and should always be used. A poem by Kung Tzu-chen of the Ching Dynasty reads:
>
> *Only in wind and thunder can the country show its vitality;*
> *Alas, the ten thousand horses are all muted!*

20. *Red Flag* editorial, "Greet the Upsurge in Forming People's Communes," No. 7 (September 1, 1958); trans. in *Current Background,* No. 517 (September 5, 1958), p. 3.

There is perhaps no clearer symbolic indication of Mao's effort to shift China's development pattern away from one of bureaucratic administration to an emphasis on "mass line" popular mobilization than the change in title of the cadre theoretical journal in the summer of 1958 from *Study* to *Red Flag.*

21. *People's Daily* editorial, "Push Forward Steel Production by Every Means" (August 27, 1958); trans. in *SCMP,* No. 1855 (September 17, 1958), p. 6.

"CHAIRMAN MAO INSPECTS HONAN FARM VILLAGES
Repeatedly Praises the Good Growth of Cotton in a People's Commune:
'If There Is This Kind of a Commune, Then There Can Be Many Communes.'"
From Jen-min Jih-pao, August 12, 1958.

> *O Heaven! Bestir yourself, I beseech you,*
> *And send down men of all the talents.*

Big-character posters have dispelled the dullness in which "ten thousand horses are all muted." [22]

The "word" which was to bestir China's people was Mao's conception of the People's Commune, which was put forward during the summer of 1958 with propaganda rather than planning. The cadres drew their policy guidance from the national press. In August, Mao made a widely publicized tour of the provinces during which he asserted, "It is best to form People's Communes." [23] And he was quoted as having told Wu Chih-p'u, his supporter in the Honan Party organization, "If there is this kind of a Commune [in Honan], then there can be many Communes." [24] From such assertions of oracular simplicity, Party cadres learned of the major objectives of institutional reform which they were expected to adapt to their local conditions, and the production targets which they would be required to meet in the coming year.

In the air of tension which surrounded the convening of the enlarged Politbureau meeting at Peitaiho in August of 1958—as gunfire was breaking over the offshore islands—it was claimed that Mao's conception would be the basic unit of society to take China rapidly through the transition to Communism. A *Red Flag* editorial declared with incautious elation that "people can easily see the budding sprouts of Communism," [25] thus strengthening Ch'en Po-ta's earlier assertion:

> It is very obvious that under the guidance of Mao Tse-tung's thought, under the flag of Comrade Mao Tse-tung, in this time of a universal high tide when the nation's economy and culture are developing as if "one day equals twenty years," people already can see a future in which the step-by-step transition from socialism to communism will not be long.[26]

Mao's spokesman, Wu Chih-p'u, stated in the national press that the People's Communes would be "not very different from" the old Marxist ideal of the Paris Commune; and he asserted that with hard work China's people could create the material conditions

22. Mao, "Introducing a Co-Operative" (April 1958), in *Selected Readings from the Works of Mao Tse-tung*, pp. 403–404.

23. *People's Daily* (August 13, 1958), p. 1.

24. *Ibid.* (August 12, 1958), p. 1.

25. *Red Flag* editorial, "Greet the Upsurge in Forming People's Communes" (September 1, 1958); trans. in *Current Background*, No. 517 (September 5, 1958), p. 2.

26. Ch'en Po-ta, "Under the Flag of Comrade Mao Tse-tung," *Red Flag*, No. 4 (July 16, 1958), p. 9.

which would enable them to be remunerated according to the Communist principle of "to each according to his need," in "six or seven years, or somewhat longer." [27]

IN THE "SADDLE" OF SOCIAL CHANGE:
THE "U-SHAPED" PATTERN OF PARTY LEADERSHIP[28]

The inflated rhetoric and exaggerated claims which accompanied the movement to form People's Communes in the fall of 1958 seem to have been advanced purposefully by the leadership to raise the enthusiasm of Party cadres and "the People" for one more great organizational transformation of Chinese society. Yet the process by which Mao attained the power to implement his conception of the People's Commune was hardly without conflict or opposition. Indeed, as the Great Leap increased in momentum, official Party documents revealed a consciousness among the leaders of a temporal pattern in policy formation. This pattern was commented upon by Liu Shao-ch'i in his political report to the second session of the Party's Eighth National Congress held in May of 1958:

> The development [of the economy] is U-shaped [literally, "horse-saddle shaped," *ma-an-hsing*], i.e., high at the beginning and end, but low in the middle. Didn't we see clearly how things developed on the production front in 1956—1957—1958 in the form of an upsurge, then an ebb, and then an even bigger upsurge or, in other words, a leap forward, then a conservative phase, and then another big leap forward?
>
> The Party and the masses have learned a lesson from this U-shaped development.[29]

27. Wu Chih-p'u, "On People's Communes," *China Youth Daily* (September 16, 1958); trans. in *Current Background,* No. 524 (October 21, 1958), pp. 5, 14–15.
It was such statements as this, and earlier ones by Ch'en Po-ta—issued by highly authoritative Party spokesmen—which stimulated Khrushchev's ire by intimating that the Chinese expected to attain "Communism" before the Soviets. *See* Chinese and Soviet differences on this point documented in Zagoria, *The Sino-Soviet Conflict, 1956–1961,* Ch. III.
28. The analysis in this section draws much inspiration from two earlier studies of cyclical patterns in Communist Chinese political and economic life: G. William Skinner and Edwin A. Winckler, "Compliance Succession in Rural Communist China: A Cyclical Theory," in Amitai Etzioni, ed., *Complex Organizations: A Sociological Reader,* pp. 410–438; and Alexander Eckstein, "Economic Fluctuations in Communist China's Domestic Development," in Ping-ti Ho and Tang Tsou, eds., *China in Crisis,* Vol. I, Book 2, pp. 691–729.
29. Liu Shao-ch'i, "Report on the Work of the Central Committee of the Communist Party of China to the Second Session of the Eighth National Congress," trans. in *CC 1955–59,* p. 427.

The nature of the "lesson" to which Liu referred, however, seems more political than economic in quality.[30] Liu himself had been a major spokesman for the "go slow" approach to agricultural development which had predominated in the spring of 1956, shaped the policies of the first session of the Eighth Party Congress, and persisted as a "conservative phase" through the first half of 1957.[31] The second session of the Eighth Party Congress of May 1958 must be seen as a new start for Mao, a reassertion of the economic line which had been thwarted by more cautious leaders after the "high tide" of collectivization. Liu's report to the Congress represents the *mea culpa* of those leaders who had opposed Mao's mass mobilization approach to breaking the agricultural bottleneck to China's economic development.

The "saddle-shaped" pattern to which Liu referred is more political than economic also because underlying the economic policies of these years (1955–1958) is a sequence of leadership debates and policy shifts which shaped the Party's approach to promoting social change. This repetitive pattern can be described simply as follows: First there is a phase of conflict between radical and conservative

30. *See* Liu Kuo-tung, "How May We Understand the 'U-Shaped' Curve?" in *Study,* No. 12 (August 3, 1958); trans. in *ECMM,* No. 145 (October 13, 1958), pp. 38–39.

31. At the Lushan Central Committee Plenum in the summer of 1959 Mao referred back to "those people who opposed venturesome advance" in 1956. He noted that, "The wavering of 1956 and 1957 was not given a dunce cap but was described as a question of method of thinking." He ridiculed their conservatism as "representing the dreary, tragic disappointment and pessimism of the petty bourgeoisie," but made light of their opposition by noting that, "They merely had no experience, and once there were signs of trouble, they were unable to stand firm and turned to oppose venturesome advance."

These opponents of 1956–57, while on Mao's side during the Great Leap, evidently again became the focus of growing resistance as the Commune movement ran into trouble. Perhaps referring to former Minister of Commerce Ch'en Yün, and to Liu Shao-ch'i, Mao warned at Lushan: "The road taken by the comrades who made mistakes in the second half of 1956 and the first half of 1957 has been repeated [in 1959]. They are not rightists, but they have cast themselves toward the brink of rightism. . . . It will be strange indeed if the tune of these comrades is not welcomed by the rightists. Comrades of this kind adopt the policy of brinkmanship. This is rather dangerous, and for those who have any doubts about this, the future will be my witness. My saying these things in public will hurt some people, but it will be [more] harmful to these comrades if I do not speak out now." (Mao Tse-tung, "Speech at the Lushan Conference" [July 23, 1959], in *Mao Chu-hsi tui P'eng, Huang, Chang, Chou Fan-tang Chi-t'uan ti P'i-p'an* [*Chairman Mao's Criticism and Repudiation of the P'eng, Huang, Chang, and Chou Anti-Party Clique*] [n.p., n.d.], pp. 8–9.) This publication is hereinafter cited by its English title.

groups ("reds" and "experts") within the Party leadership over proper policies for social advance—a debate in which several years of poor economic performance enable the radicals to build support for a basic institutional restructuring of society. The radical claim is that they will "liberate the productive forces" (popular energies) through a rearrangement of the "relations of production" (the pattern of property ownership and work organization).

This change in policy line within the leading councils of the Party is followed by an inner-Party rectification campaign, in which lower level opponents of a more radical line are criticized or purged, and the Party organization is mobilized for the leadership tasks of a new mass campaign. A period of public "study" and discussion ensues, in which the objectives of the campaign are propagated to "the masses" and objections are refuted. On the basis of these preparations, a period of intense institutional change or labor mobilization then takes place.

In the period of "upsurge" in organizational change or work activity, excesses are committed by over-zealous Party cadres. These excesses produce economic or organizational difficulties which more conservative leaders invoke in order to shift opinion within the Party "center" toward a period of consolidation. The radicals thus begin to lose their influence in policy-making. "Expert" considerations reemerge and a more moderate orientation persists until further economic or social problems once again enable the "reds" to reassert their influence over Party policy. Thus another round of the pattern or cycle begins.

To grasp fully this "saddle-shaped" pattern, as it led to the Great Leap Forward of 1958, it is necessary to retrace the major agricultural policy decisions since mid-1955. As noted previously, Mao's July 1955 speech on agricultural collectivization came at a time of increasingly uncertain Party leadership over the rural economy. As Marshal of the Army Ch'en Yi recalled in late 1955, this speech "settled the arguments on the question of cooperativization of agriculture during the past three years, [overcame] the rightist vacillating ideology, and enabled certain comrades to turn from their mistaken paths to the correct road of Marxism-Leninism." [32] More exactly, Mao's speech—in combination with decisions of the Sixth Plenum of the Seventh Central Committee which followed in October—reversed a trend toward dissolution of those coopera-

32. Ch'en Yi, "Comrade Mao Tse-tung's Report on Agricultural Cooperativization Is a Classic Example of Combining Theory and Practise," *People's Daily* (November 13, 1955); trans. in *SCMP*, No. 1177 (November 24–25, 1955), p. 45.

tives which already had been formed. Mao derided the fact that "some comrades" had disbanded cooperatives "in a state of panic," and he observed that continuing problems in the rural areas derived from the fact that certain Party leaders had "become scared of the several hundred thousand small cooperatives." [33]

In this state of uncertainty in Party leadership, and in what Mao saw to be a situation of the increasing reemergence of class polarization in village life, the problem was how to mobilize the Party into an effective instrument of leadership in the rural areas. This process began with the creation of consensus within the leadership over plans for a period of rapid formation of "primary stage" APCs. Mao personally exercised direction over the collection of reports from regional areas where cooperativization had already progressed in the early months of 1955, and "advance copies of these articles were printed and distributed to responsible comrades from provincial, municipal, autonomous regional, and regional Party committees" who attended the October enlarged Central Committee Plenum.[34] This documentary summation of "advanced experience," and a revised version of the collection which was published in December of 1955, was to serve as the "model" for study by those who would be guiding the "upsurge" in cooperativization.

Mao's effort to disseminate the experiences of selected regions in organizing APCs, however, trailed behind the actual formation of cooperatives, for political pressures now far outweighed practical concerns. The level of political tension within the Party was substantially heightened at the October enlarged Central Committee Plenum. A resolution on cooperativization, based on Mao's July report, stressed that in the new stage of the revolution the Party had to deal forcefully with "the struggle of the peasants against the rich peasants and other capitalist elements," and that the essence of cooperativization was "a struggle over the choice between two roads—the development of socialism or of capitalism." The resolution also reaffirmed that "the criticism made by the Political Bureau of the Central Committee against Right opportunism is absolutely correct and necessary." [35]

Such remarks, coming as they did in the last stages of a nationwide campaign for the "liquidation of counterrevolutionaries" (*su-*

---

33. Mao, "On the Question of Agricultural Co-Operation," in *Selected Readings from the Works of Mao Tse-tung*, p. 322.

34. *See* Mao's "Preface" in *Socialist Upsurge in China's Countryside*, p. 7.

35. "Decisions on Agricultural Cooperation," adopted at the Sixth Plenary Session (Enlarged) of the Seventh Central Committee of the Chinese Communist Party; trans. in *CC 1955–59*, pp. 106–107.

Agricultural
Producers'
Cooperatives

fan), made it clear to Party cadres that failure to press for the formation of APCs would hold the very serious consequences of "right opportunism." Or still worse, a laggard might be accused of being one of the "landlord, rich peasant, or counterrevolutionary elements" who were alleged to "have already wormed their way in various guises into cooperatives." [36]

The shift within the Party leadership from economic to political considerations was further emphasized by the temporary eclipse of the cautious Director of the Party's Rural Work Department, Teng Tzu-hui. In pre-1955 statements on agriculture, Teng had revealed a concern about not repeating the errors of collectivization which had occurred in the Soviet Union in the early 1930s. [37] Mao, in his report on cooperativization, conspicuously downplayed the significance of the Soviet difficulties by noting that they had been "quickly corrected." And it seems likely that he had Teng in mind when he noted that "on no account should we allow . . . comrades to use the Soviet experience as a cover for their idea of moving at a snail's pace." [38] Teng's eclipse was made obvious to Party members by the fact that explanations on the draft of the Plenum resolution on cooperativization were presented to the Central Committee not by Teng, but by Mao's close associate Ch'en Po-ta.

Finally, it appears that determination within the Party leadership to press for rapid formation of APCs was enhanced by reports of a bountiful summer harvest (a 9 percent increase over the 1954 level, in contrast to the meager increases of 1.6 percent and 2.1 percent for the two previous years). [39] The harvest provided a resource margin which would help to cushion any temporary dislocations which might result from disruptions in the organization of rural life.

This combination of a mobilized Party organization and a population tense in the wake of efforts to root out "counterrevolutionaries" in the rural areas established the political context for the first big surge in the "high tide" of cooperativization. At the October Plenum it was estimated that about 15 percent of all peasant households in China were already in APCs. By December Mao observed with satisfaction that this figure had swelled to more than 60 percent, making the planning of the summer and fall already out of

36. *Ibid.*, p. 114.
37. *See* the "General Introduction" to *CC 1955–59*, p. 3.
38. Mao, "On the Question of Agricultural Co-Operation," in *Selected Readings from the Works of Mao Tse-tung*, p. 331.
39. Alexander Eckstein, "Economic Fluctuations in Communist China's Domestic Development," *China in Crisis*, Vol. I, Book 2, p. 716.

date. The Party Chairman stressed: "All must be appropriately expanded and accelerated." [40]

A second surge in the formation of cooperatives was initiated with a meeting of the Supreme State Conference in late January 1956. Mao now pressed for a "leap forward" in production which would bring about early completion of the First Five Year Plan. It was also at this meeting that his twelve-year program for agricultural development was first presented—and elaborated upon by Minister of Agriculture Liao Lu-yen. The fact that the press release of this session of the Supreme State Conference identified Liao by his Party position as Deputy Director of the Central Committee's Rural Work Department seems intended to emphasize the continuing eclipse of the Director of that Department, Teng Tzu-hui, who was thus all the more conspicuous by his absence from among those leaders identified as having attended the meeting. Teng was to resume his public role as Party spokesman on agricultural matters only after the meetings of the Politbureau in April of 1956, at which Mao's influence over economic policy was restricted.[41]

Between January and April of 1956, however, a mobilized Party and peasantry raised the socialist organization in the Chinese countryside one further level. In December of 1955 only 4 percent of all rural households had been organized into the "higher stage" cooperatives. By the time the Politbureau met in enlarged session in late April 1956 this figure had risen to 58 percent, where it temporarily stabilized.

While the rapidity of this expansion can be accounted for in part by the harvest cycle—the effort to complete organizational changes before the spring planting season—it would also appear that Mao, sensing opposition within the Party leadership to rapid change in the rural areas, pressed ahead to present his more cautious colleagues with a *fait accompli*. And by all evidence the late April meeting of the Politbureau, which was not publicly disclosed until Liu Shao-ch'i and Wu Chih-p'u made passing references to the session in subsequent publications,[42] represented the culmination of

40. Mao's "Preface" to *Socialist Upsurge in China's Countryside*, p. 8.

41. The role of the cautious Teng Tzu-hui in formulation of agricultural policy, and the waning of his influence in times of political radicalization, is documented in Michel Oksenberg, *Policy Formulation in Communist China*, pp. 145–155, 578–580.

42. Wu Chih-p'u has indicated that April 25th, 1956 was the date on which Mao delivered his economic analysis, "On the Ten Great Relationships." (*See* "Contradictions Are the Force that Moves a Socialist Society Forward," *People's Daily* [June 14, 1960]; trans. in *SCMP*, No. 2285 [June 27, 1960].)

a period of decision during which Mao's influence over the Party's political and economic policies was temporarily restricted.[43]

The particular significance of the April 25th meeting as a point of major conflict and opposition to Mao is further reinforced by the disclosure—as a result of the Cultural Revolution—of the full text of an analysis of the economy which Mao presented to his Party colleagues at this time. Entitled "On the Ten Great Relationships," Mao spelled out the contradictory choices which faced the Party in its efforts rapidly to modernize China's economy. He also gave his judgments as to how those contradictions should be resolved.

Most notable is his analysis of the "contradiction between industry and agriculture." The phrasing of his discussion suggests that the Party Chairman faced strong opposition from those leaders who were determined to prevent a reallocation of capital away from investment in heavy industry. As he called for a rise in the proportion of capital invested in agriculture and light industry Mao stressed: "Does this mean that heavy industries are no longer important? They are still important. Is this to shift our focus of attention from them? Let me put it this way: most of our investment will continue to go to heavy industries." [44]

In the wake of the Hungarian uprising a year later when he was in a stronger political position, Mao more forthrightly stressed the paradox that by giving greater investment priority to agriculture and light industry in the short run, "what may seem to be a slower pace of industrialization will actually not be so slow, and indeed may even be faster." [45]

In the spring and summer of 1956, however, opposition to Mao's economic line seems to have been a composite of economic consid-

43. As noted earlier (*see* pp. 275–276 above) this period of restriction in influence began in the wake of Khrushchev's "de-Stalinization" effort. The Party leadership met at the end of March or early April, and issued the editorial interpretation of Stalin's errors on April 5th. At the same time, a Central Committee and State Council joint directive was published attacking "extravagance and waste" in the new APCs, and criticizing local cadres for "making a show of their work." (*See* "CCP Central Committee and State Council Issue Joint Directive on Running of Cooperatives," NCNA [April 4, 1956]; trans. in *SCMP*, No. 1268 [April 16, 1956], p. 3.) In late April Mao presented his comprehensive analysis of China's economic problems, "On the Ten Great Relationships." One infers from the lack of publicity given to this speech at the time, and the silence on references to the twelve-year agricultural plan which Mao had presented in January, that the Chairman's influence had been restricted.

44. Mao, "On the Ten Great Relationships," in Jerome Ch'en, ed., *Mao*, p. 67.

45. Mao, "On the Correct Handling of Contradictions among the People," in *Selected Readings from the Works of Mao Tse-tung*, p. 385.

erations cemented together by institutional interests and the impact of "de-Stalinization." Mao's critics stressed the dangers of "disequilibrium" and "weak links" in the overall pattern of development, together with the existence of supply shortages in certain construction materials, especially steel. The fiasco of the 1955–56 program for wide application of the double-wheel double-share plow, which had proven to be unusable in the soft mud of south China's paddy fields, had wasted large quantities of steel. And even as stalwart a Maoist spokesman as Chou En-lai subjected this early experiment in the technical reform of agriculture to criticism at the Eighth Party Congress as being an example of "reckless zeal." [46] Peasant opposition to the formation of "advanced stage" APCs, while mild in comparison to the violence and dislocation of rural life which had occurred during the similar period of Soviet collectivization,[47] prompted some Party leaders to characterize the "high tide" of the fall and spring as "reckless advance." They were able to mobilize sufficient support to throw "doubts" and "misgivings" on Mao's plans,[48] and on his general line of "more, better, faster, and more economical" increases in production.[49]

The determination of more conservative leaders to thwart Mao's political pressures, to consolidate the changes brought about by the

46. Noted in "The Conflict between Mao Tse-tung and Liu Shao-ch'i Over Agricultural Mechanization in Communist China," *Current Scene*, Vol. VI, No. 17 (October 1, 1968), p. 8. *See also* Roy Hofheinz, "Rural Administration in Communist China," *The China Quarterly*, No. 11 (July–September 1962), p. 148.

47. Thomas P. Bernstein, "Leadership and Mass Mobilization in the Soviet and Chinese Collectivization Campaigns of 1929–30 and 1955–56: A Comparison," in *The China Quarterly*, No. 31 (July–September 1967), pp. 1–47.

48. Noted by Liu Shao-ch'i in his political report to the Second Session of the Eighth Party Congress. *See CC 1955–59*, pp. 426–427.

In view of the evidence that Liu himself had had "misgivings" about Mao's policies of "reckless advance" in 1956, his remarks of 1958 have the ironical quality of a public self-criticism.

49. Given the particular significance which swimming has had for Mao (*see* p. 178 above, and p. 476 below), it may be some reflection of the frustration which the Chairman apparently felt during the late spring and summer of 1956 at his inability to sustain the drive to form APCs that he swam in the Yangtze several times in May and June. After these occasions he wrote a poem on "Swimming" which seems to express his impatient "pacing" outside the room of political influence:

> Heedless of boisterous winds and buffeting waves,
> Better this seemed than leisurely pacing home courtyards,
> Today I have obtained my release.

(Extracted from Mao's June 1956 poem, "Swimming," in Wong Man, trans., *Poems of Mao Tse-tung* [Hong Kong: Eastern Horizon Press, 1966], p. 50.)

drive to form agricultural cooperatives, and to sustain the primary emphasis on industrialization, gained political momentum with the publication of a *People's Daily* editorial on June 20th, 1956, entitled "Oppose Both Conservatism and Hastiness." Subsequently identified as the work of Teng T'o, Hu Ch'iao-mu, and Lu Ting-yi writing under Liu Shao-ch'i's direction,[50] the editorial gives an ironical twist to words taken from Mao's preface to *Socialist Upsurge in China's Countryside*: ". . . one should not indulge in idle fantasies unrelated to reality, plan one's actions beyond the conditions dictated by the objective situation or force oneself to do the impossible." [51] It observed that, "The forty articles of the National Program for the Development of Agriculture are supposed to be put into effect separately in five, seven and twelve years, but some comrades, being hasty, try to do all things in two or three years." [52] And in a nearly direct identification of those "some comrades," the editorial noted:

> That hastiness is a serious question is due to the fact that it exists not only among the cadres of the lower levels but *primarily among the cadres of the higher levels,* and that in many cases the hastiness manifest at the lower levels is the result of pressure applied by the higher levels.[53]

The phrasing of this editorial and subsequent political and economic developments suggest, however, that there was a significant discrepancy between the efforts of certain leaders at the Party "center" to bring about a period of consolidation in the rural areas and the determination of Mao and his supporters within the regional Party apparatus to complete the work of organizing "advanced stage" APCs.[54] Between May and December of 1956 the percentage

50. *See* "Outline of the Struggle between the Two Lines from the Eve of the Founding of the People's Republic of China through the Eleventh Plenum of the Eighth CCP Central Committee," *Liberation Daily* (Shanghai); trans. in *Current Background*, No. 884 (July 18, 1969), p. 11. Also, "Confession by Counter-Revolutionist Wu Leng-hsi," *Worker's Review*, No. 5 (June 1968); trans. in *SCMM*, No. 662 (July 28, 1969), p. 5.

51. *People's Daily* editorial, "Oppose Both Conservatism and Hastiness" (June 20, 1956); trans. in *SCMP*, No. 1321 (July 3, 1956), p. 11.

52. *Ibid.*

53. *Ibid.*, p. 12. Emphasis added.

54. This division within the leadership influenced many areas of economic activity. For instance, Minister of Water Conservancy Fu Tso-yi, complained in early 1957 of the lack of clear policy guidelines during the spring and summer of 1956: "Some people [within the leadership] spoke of blind advance and others did not speak of blind advance. There was much confusing discussion." (Cited in Oksenberg, *Policy Formulation in Communist China*, p. 270.)

of rural households in the fully socialized cooperatives increased from 62 percent to 88 percent.[55]

In contrast to this completion of cooperativization after the harvest season, documents from the Party's Eighth Congress of September 1956 reveal continuing disagreement with Mao's economic policies, and they deprecate through silence his contributions to Party leadership. Liu Shao-ch'i's political report began by recalling the Party's accomplishments since the Seventh Congress held at the end of the War of Resistance against Japan. In line with the stress on collective leadership, Liu gave hardly a mention to Mao's leading role in formulating the Party's policies which had led to a successful prosecution of the Civil War against the Nationalists, and to the recently concluded "socialist transformation" of the rural economy.[56]

Liu referred to the continuing movement to form APCs, but he phrased his comments in a manner that obscured the impact of Mao's July 1955 intervention on the question of agricultural policy. He noted that the recent formation of the cooperatives had "followed on the correction by the Party's Central Committee and Comrade Mao Tse-tung of the rightist conservative ideas within the Party which had tended to stifle the peasant masses' enthusiasm for agricultural cooperation." [57] And as if there had been no "upsurge" in the formation of APCs in the fall and winter/spring of 1955–56, he noted ironically that the Party's policy of "step-by-step" advance in the socialization of rural life had enabled the peasants "gradually [to] accustom themselves to the ways of collective production." Such a policy, he asserted, meant that "losses

55. These figures, based on Chinese sources, are drawn from Kenneth R. Walker, "Collectivization in Retrospect," *The China Quarterly,* No. 26 (April–June 1966), p. 35; and the same author's *Planning in Chinese Agriculture,* p. 14.

56. This slighting of Mao in 1956 contrasts with Liu's political report to the Party's Seventh Congress in 1945, where he had invoked Mao's name and policies more than one hundred times. In his Eighth Congress report Liu cited Mao by name on only four occasions. (Noted in Roderick Mac-Farquhar, "Communist China's Intra-Party Dispute," *Pacific Affairs,* Vol. XXXI, No. 4 [December 1958], fn. 21, p. 333.)

57. Liu Shao-ch'i, "Political Report of the Central Committee of the Communist Party of China to the Eighth National Congress of the Party," in *Eighth National Congress of the Communist Party of China,* Vol. I, pp. 25–26.

This phrasing contrasts with Liu's use of the formulation "the great Chinese Communist Party and its leader Comrade Mao Tse-tung," as well as his repeated references to the leading role of "the thought of Mao Tse-tung" and Mao's "guiding principles" in his political reports of 1945 and 1958. (*See* p. 359 below.)

which might have resulted from sudden changes could be averted, or greatly reduced." [58] And even as Party cadres in the provinces were continuing to press for completion of the movement to form the "advanced stage" APCs, Liu stressed,

> we have to win over, on the basis of the policy of voluntariness and mutual benefit, a small number of peasant households still outside cooperatives to join the cooperatives, and give guidance to the transformation of elementary cooperatives into cooperatives of the advanced type. But we have to be patient and give them time; coercion or commands in any form will not be allowed. The most urgent problem awaiting solution now is that all possible efforts must be made to ensure an increase in the output of about a million cooperatives now existing and in the income of their members. [59]

Concerning the contentious issue of competing investment priorities between industry and agriculture, Liu bluntly stated,

> Some comrades want to lower the rate of development of heavy industry. This line of thinking is wrong. We put this question to them: If we do not very quickly establish our own indispensable machine-building industry, metallurgical industry and other related branches of heavy industry, how are we going to equip our light industry, transport, building industry and agriculture? [60]

Mao gave a public reply to this rhetorical challenge five months later in his "Contradictions" speech:

> Without agriculture there can be no light industry. But it is not yet so clearly understood that agriculture [also] provides heavy industry with an important market. This fact, however, will be more readily appreciated as gradual progress in the technical improvement and modernization of agriculture calls for more and more machinery, fertilizer, water conservancy and electric power projects and transport facilities for the farms, as well as fuel and building materials for the rural consumers. [61]

Then Mao observed:

> We must realize that there is a contradiction here—the contradiction between the objective laws of economic development of a socialist society and our subjective understanding of them—which needs to be resolved in the course of practise. *This contradiction also manifests itself as a contradiction between different people,* that is, a contradic-

58. *Ibid.*
59. *Ibid.*, p. 37.
60. *Ibid.*, pp. 49–50.
61. Mao, "On the Correct Handling of Contradictions among the People," in *Selected Readings from the Works of Mao Tse-tung,* p. 385.

tion between those with a relatively accurate understanding of these objective laws and those with a relatively inaccurate understanding of them.[62]

Mao added in conclusion, however, that this conflict in understanding "between different people" was still "a contradiction among the people"—that is, "nonantagonistic" in quality.

Mao's opportunity to resolve this leadership conflict over economic policy "in the course of practise" grew from the political and economic developments of the spring and summer of 1957: the "anti-Party, anti-Socialist" attacks of the "bourgeois rightists," and the second year of meager growth in agricultural productivity following the bumper harvest of 1955. All evidence indicates that the Third Plenum of the Eighth Central Committee, held in late September of 1957, was the major turning point in several months of effort on Mao's part to reverse the "conservative phase" which since the spring of 1956 had thwarted his plans for agricultural development.[63] Less than a week before the Third Plenum a Central Committee directive was issued strengthening the trend toward a scaling-down and consolidation of the "advanced stage" APCs. In contrast to Mao's long insistence on the superiority of large-scale cooperatives, this directive observed that "large collectives and large [production] teams are generally not adaptable to the present production conditions"; and it called for a rationalization of their size, which in most cases would mean that they should "be divided into smaller units in accordance with the wishes of the members." [64] In conclusion, the directive stressed: "After the size of the collectives and production teams has been decided upon, it should be publicly announced that this organization will remain unchanged in the next ten years." [65]

This trend toward division of the "advanced stage" APCs and stabilization of the pattern of work and administration in the countryside was sharply reversed by the Plenum. Mao's twelve-year plan for agriculture was revived by Tĕng Hsiao-p'ing in his report

62. *Ibid.*, p. 386. Emphasis added.

63. The influence of harvest estimates on policy debate, and Mao's efforts to radicalize agricultural policy in mid-1957 beginning at a leadership conference held in Tsingtao in July and running through the Third Central Committee Plenum in September, is discussed in Oksenberg, *Policy Formulation in Communist China,* pp. 442–446, 635–636.

64. "Directive of the Central Committee of the Chinese Communist Party Concerning Doing Well the Work of Managing Production in Agricultural Cooperatives" (September 14, 1957); cited in Choh-ming Li, "The First Decade: Economic Development," *The China Quarterly,* No. 1 (January–March 1960), p. 43.

65. *Ibid.*

on the rectification movement;[66] and the Plenum agreed to press the "anti-rightist" purge within the Party, while at the same time promoting a nationwide campaign of popular "socialist education."

The People's Commune, both as an organizational solution to the strengthening of Party leadership in the rural areas and an instrument for mobilizing peasant labor power, hardly came full blown from the meeting of the Third Plenum. Indeed, the Plenum communiqué indicated that Mao's agricultural plan had only been "basically adopted" and would be brought up again before a Party Congress for discussion and adoption, and then sent to the National People's Congress for final approval. Between October 1957 and the enlarged meeting of the Politbureau at Peitaiho in late August of 1958—at which time a Party resolution launching Commune formation on a nationwide scale was passed—there was a constant series of meetings between high Party officials and regional leaders which seems to reveal a "feedback" process in which Mao's evolving ideas on a reorganization of the pattern of rural work and administration were put into operation and tested in selected areas in a winter mass water conservancy campaign and later in the spring planting and summer harvest.[67]

66. As Franz Schurmann has suggested, the fact that the Party's General Secretary should have reinvoked this agricultural plan—seen in conjunction with the fact that the Plenum speeches of such "economic" leaders as Minister of Commerce Ch'en Yün and Premier Chou En-lai, who reported to the Plenum on wages and welfare, were never made public—indicates that a line of "political economy" won out over strictly economic considerations during the course of the Plenum. *See Ideology and Organization in Communist China,* pp. 195–199.

67. The most important of these meetings were: a secret leadership conference at Hangchow in December–January 1957–58 which dealt with the mass water conservancy campaign and other economic policies designed to bring about a "great leap" in production in 1958; a meeting to consider similar issues held at Nanning in late January; and a conference on agricultural mechanization and amalgamation of APCs convened at Chengtu in March.

Two months later came the second session of the Eighth Party Congress which formally presented Mao's economic line to the Party (although without its organizational form specified). From late May through July there was a continuous series of meetings of the Central Committee's Military Affairs Committee which apparently dealt with issues of militia formation and the role of amalgamated APCs in a new strategy of national defense—as well as China's defense relationship to the Soviet Union and ways of developing an independent nuclear weapons capability.

The term "commune" was first used authoritatively in Ch'en Po-ta's *Red Flag* article of mid-July (*see* p. 247 above). The full phrase "People's Commune" was invoked by Mao for the first time in the national press on August 13th.

Here was the "mass line" approach to leadership embodying a combination of centralized direction and local initiative in its most developed form.[68] From this period of experimentation evolved the concept of the People's Commune which Mao presented to the August meeting of the Politbureau, and shortly thereafter published nationally as the "Tentative Regulations (Draft) of the *Weihsing* [Sputnik] People's Commune"—a model for nationwide emulation.[69]

This period of experimentation in rural organization evidently proceeded on the basis of some form of compromise or understanding among top Party leaders. Such a development was stressed by Liu Shao-ch'i in his political report to the second session of the Eighth Party Congress which met in May of 1958. In striking contrast to his silence on Mao's contributions to Party leadership which had marked his report to the first session of this Congress in 1956, Liu made repeated reference to "guiding principles laid down by Comrade Mao Tse-tung," and revealed in detail speeches and policy guidelines advanced by Mao that had not been given previous publication (or implementation).[70]

In view of Liu's opposition to Mao's economic and social policies during 1956–57, in which the question of investment priorities had been prominent, it can be hypothesized that Liu's renewed support for Mao reflects, in part, a compromise among Party leaders in which Mao was backed in his plans for organizational changes in the countryside inasmuch as his "general line for socialist construction" continued to give investment priority to the development of heavy industry. One does not know if Mao would have preferred to see more State-supplied capital invested in agriculture and light industry in the short run (as he had suggested in his February 1957 "Contradictions" speech)—and hence had evolved the "walking on two legs" approach as a way of compromising with his op-

68. Mao's repeated use of the provincial Party organization to promote policies which had limited support from other leaders, or were actively resisted by them, is documented in Parris H. Chang, *Patterns and Processes of Policy Making in Communist China, 1955–1962* (unpublished Ph.D. dissertation, Columbia University, New York, 1969).

69. These regulations had been issued without publicity in early August, and were published in the *People's Daily* on September 4th, after the Politbureau meeting at Peitaiho. *See CC 1955–59*, pp. 463–470.

70. Most notable was his revelation of aspects of Mao's comprehensive analysis of the "contradictions" in China's economic development, the April 1956 speech, "On the Ten Great Relationships." *See* Liu's speech in *CC 1955–59*, esp. p. 426. This emphasizes that the second session of the Eighth Party Congress was for Mao a reassertion of his authority and influence over policy which had been restricted in the spring of 1956.

ponents within the leadership. Or did he genuinely believe that a policy of social mobilization in the rural areas would be sufficient to enable agricultural production to keep pace with the develop- ment of industry?

In any event, the process of translating this new consensus within the Party leadership into operational policies which would bring about an upswing from the "conservative phase" of 1956–57 re- peats the mobilization pattern of the "high tide" of cooperativi- zation of the fall and winter of 1955–56. The "anti-rightist" purge within the Party mounted in intensity during the late fall of 1957, heightening tension among the cadres and removing certain leaders who had opposed the implementation of Mao's agricultural poli- cies.[71] This Party rectification was advanced in conjunction with a mass "socialist education campaign," in which "landlord" and "capitalist" elements in the villages were subjected to public criti- cism. Political tension was thus heightened nationwide.

On the basis of these developments, the first large-scale mobili- zation of peasant labor occurred during the winter of 1957–58 in a mass campaign to build irrigation and water-control facilities with local labor and capital resources. During this campaign the first experiments in the running of public mess-halls were carried out, as women were "liberated" from family kitchens to make up for farm labor shortages. And the virtues of militarizing the rural work force were perceived in the need to direct the activities of large numbers of laborers in the winter-spring campaign.

With spring came the first efforts to amalgamate APCs into township-scale production and administrative units. One of the most widely publicized of the early Commune experiments took place in Honan, where Mao's close supporter in the provincial Party apparatus, Wu Chih-p'u—with power enhanced as a result of the provincial "anti-rightist" purge—was promoting "advanced experience" which would be used as a model in the late summer and fall when the People's Communes were organized throughout rural China.[72]

As the summer progressed political tension within the country was further heightened. There were massive public demonstrations to protest American and British interventions in the Middle East.

71. The workings of this rectification campaign, and its removal of Party leaders who had opposed Mao's agricultural policies, are detailed in Fred- erick Teiwes, *Rectification Campaigns and Purges in Communist China*, Ch. XV.

72. *See* Chang, *Patterns and Processes of Policy Making in Communist China*, pp. 180–185, and Oksenberg, *Policy Formulation in Communist China*, pp. 409–422.

And as air clashes and artillery bombardments escalated in the Taiwan Straits the Politbureau held an enlarged meeting at Peitaiho which—with the assurances of a bumper harvest for 1958—agreed to press ahead with the country-wide formation of People's Communes.

By all evidence, in coming to this decision Mao had presented reluctant colleagues within the Party leadership with another *fait accompli*. In mid-September Wu Chih-p'u disclosed that sometime prior to the late August meeting of the Politbureau Mao had issued a "directive" on Commune formation.[73] It is unclear whether this was anything more than an assertion of the Chairman's personal authority; yet this "directive," combined with Mao's public approbation of People's Communes in the national press in mid-August, served as the political basis for local initiative in Commune formation. By late August virtually the entire province of Honan had been reorganized into township and county-wide amalgamations of APCs.[74] And a year later the State Statistical Bureau revealed that by the end of August 1958, 30 percent of all peasant households throughout China had already been Communized.[75]

The fact that this momentous restructuring of rural life proceeded with no more official direction than a cautiously worded Politbureau resolution—no Central Committee decision, no plan approved by the National People's Congress, legally the highest national political authority—strongly suggests that Mao was pressing against continuing resistance within the upper levels of the Party and government, and forged ahead through the support of the provincial Party organization. Furthermore, it would appear from the context of these times that Mao used the political climate of the Taiwan Straits confrontation to make open opposition to Commune formation and militarization of the peasant labor force—developments closely related to his new national defense line—appear to be virtually an act of treason. The Chairman apparently mobilized all the political weapons at his disposal to push Communization through to completion and to prevent the reemergence of a conservative opposition which would thwart his plans—as *had* occurred in the spring of 1956.

73. Wu Chih-p'u, "On People's Communes," *China Youth Daily* (September 16, 1958); trans. in *Current Background*, No. 524 (October 21, 1958), p. 4.

74. "Questions and Answers on People's Communes," *Daily Worker* [Peking] (September 8, 1958); trans. in *SCMP*, No. 1860 (September 24, 1958), p. 7.

75. From *Ten Great Years*. Cited in Kenneth R. Walker, *Planning in Chinese Agriculture*, p. 14.

Massed peasant laborers at the
Miyun dam and reservoir project north of Peking, 1958.
Henri Cartier-Bresson, from Magnum.

In the late summer and fall of 1958, war, production, and social change thus merged once again. And as the Party journal *Red Flag* observed in an editorial of mid-September, the emotions of hatred and aggression released in the military confrontation with "American imperialism" provided the motive power for China's "war" with her own poverty:

> *The [Dulles] policy of hostility toward the Chinese people . . . has constantly aroused in them a swelling tide of anger* against the United States and an ever greater will to rise energetically and become strong themselves. On this count alone, *it can be said that Dulles has done something useful indirectly for the Chinese revolution* and the revolution of other countries of the world. He ought to be given a medal.

> The U.S. policy of hostility toward the Chinese people has failed to prevent the gigantic advance of new China. On the contrary, *it has proved advantageous to China's economic construction* which is based on its own resources.[76]

An important question concerning these events of 1958 is whether Mao had been purposefully manipulative in creating the Taiwan Straits crisis (in part) as a context for Commune formation, or whether the Chairman had used a situation largely beyond his control to his own domestic political advantage. The evidence now available on the offshore island events most strongly suggests that Mao took the initiative in escalating the existing confrontation between Communist and Nationalist forces in the Straits (*see* pp. 386–388 below). And while Mao appears to have had a number of political goals in mind when pressing the confrontation, one important objective seems to have been the creation of a motivational climate in which resistance to Commune formation from both Party leaders and peasants would be minimized. In April 1956 Mao had told a meeting of the Politbureau, "We must do something to raise the self-confidence of our people. We must do what Mencius said: 'When talking about a big man, belittle him.' We must develop the kind of contempt of American imperialism shown during the anti-American war in aid of Korea." [77]

In the spring of 1956 Mao's plans for developing this national confidence and bringing about a "leap forward" had been cut short by resistant Party leaders. In 1958 the Chairman was determined

76. *Red Flag* editorial, "The U.S. Aggressors Have Put Nooses around Their Own Necks" (September 14, 1958); trans. in *SCMP*, No. 1856 (September 18, 1958), pp. 2–3. Emphasis added.

77. Mao, "On the Ten Great Relationships," in Ch'en, ed., *Mao*, p. 84.

that a "conservative phase" should not reemerge and thwart Communization. The Straits confrontation appears to have been one important phase of his strategy for pressing ahead with his plans.

In these events of 1955 through 1958 one sees the outline of a pattern which seems to embody the essential elements by which Mao has promoted "struggle" in the process of leadership and social change. In both 1955 and 1957 Mao's personal inclination to promote collective forms of social organization and to raise the "activism" of China's population was given political weight by poor harvests in two preceding years.[78]

With more conservative "experts" within the leadership thus on the defensive, the Party organization is prepared for an upsurge in social transformation through a rectification campaign. Tension increases as "objects" (*tui-hsiang*) are singled out for criticism, struggle, or purge. The actual removal of leadership cadres, however, is usually restricted in scope, for the basic objective of the rectification is to mobilize the majority of Party members: to increase their understanding of the goals of the new campaign by criticizing the "objects" and their own errors in attitude and to raise anxieties about committing "rightist" errors, thus motivating them for the tasks of leadership.

This air of tension within the leadership is transmitted to "the masses" through a public criticism campaign, which subjects "objects" or targets of past error to public criticism. With both leadership and population thus oriented and emotionally "primed," the movement proceeds.

In Part Three we suggested that one of the major characteristics of the leadership process which Mao evolved during his years in the countryside was the transformation of peasant anxieties in the face of established authority into hatred, thus motivating the rural population for involvement in the revolution. One senses that the post-Liberation use of Party rectification campaigns and mass movements is an effort to sustain this motivational basis of past Party successes. We do not know, however, just how conscious and purposefully manipulative the leadership has been in relying upon this procedure in mobilizing people for political involvement. It is a

78. Ironically, however, it was good harvests in 1955 and 1958 (the result, in part, of more conservative economic policy), which enabled the radicalized leadership to press ahead with organizational changes designed to cope with the poor agricultural performances of the two preceding years (1953–54, and 1956–57). A good harvest on the eve of a period of change provides a margin of security in resources which can limit opposition and make up for disruptions in production stemming from organizational changes.

process which over the years seems to have become second nature to Mao and other leaders.

Mao observed to comrades at a Central Committee Plenum in 1959, "When one is not anxious, one has not the spirit and enthusiasm, and cannot do a good job." [79] And it seems evident enough that in post-Liberation years Mao has shown a determination to sustain a style of leadership which will make people anxious and "active"; a political climate in which popular anxieties about committing errors (*fan tso-wu*) before authority are transformed into anger or indignation over some social evil or enemy, thus creating the motivational basis for change through political struggle.

The intimate relationship between motives of aggression and social change in the development of China's social revolution is nowhere more clearly revealed than in the association of major periods of social upheaval with the violence of war. With only one major exception—the "high tide" of cooperativization of 1955–56—the periods of major institutional change promoted by the Chinese Communists also have been times of war or threatening foreign intervention: The first periods of land redistribution occurred during the War of Resistance against Japan (also a time of continuing civil conflict with the Nationalists). Land reform was promoted during the final phase of the Civil War and completed during the Korean War. The socialization of industry and commerce proceeded in the context of the patriotic movement to "Resist America and Aid Korea." Communization was carried out during the Taiwan Straits crisis of 1958. And the Great Proletarian Cultural Revolution has run its uncertain course while the Viet-Nam War and border clashes on the Sino-Soviet frontier have held the possibility of involving China in a foreign conflict.

With the exceptions of the Civil War, the Taiwan Straits crisis of 1958, and the Sino-Soviet border incidents, these periods of military violence have been the result of developments almost completely beyond Chinese control; hence, the major pattern one sees is how the Communist Party leadership has learned to *respond to* and cope with a war environment. The one sure conclusion that can be reached is that the leadership has not viewed such situations as occasions for inaction. On the contrary, the tension of a violent confrontation is a context which they have learned to use to further their social and political goals. Consistent with interpretations developed at various points throughout this study, we would observe

79. Mao, "Speech at the Lushan Meeting," in *Chairman Mao's Criticism and Repudiation of the P'eng, Huang, Chang and Chou Anti-Party Clique,* p. 10.

that a political or military confrontation with an enemy provides the Party with the most appropriate context for promoting the natural translation of anxiety about conflict with a powerful authority into aggressive emotions and legitimated "struggle."

For Mao the problem of leadership in post-Liberation China has been how to sustain the momentum of social change in a non-wartime environment. The Party Chairman's policy preferences in the period of "socialist transformation" reveal an enduring commitment to the forms of political action which were evolved during the years of struggle for power. One must ask (as did other Party leaders), however, whether the techniques of "struggle" and mass movement which are the legacy of the revolution remain appropriate after the assumption of state power, after foreign military intervention has been eliminated from the mainland and the most blatant forms of social injustice have been reduced through the Party's social reforms?

From the mid-1950s on, Mao himself was to assert with ever greater vehemence that the Party's organizational transformation of Chinese society was in danger of subversion by "bourgeois reactionary" attitudes and patterns of behavior as they endured in the life style of the population, and even in the behavior of Party cadres. This, of course, was the meaning for Mao of the "blooming and contending" experiment; and from the summer of 1957 on, the Chairman was to assert the continuing relevance of struggle politics as a way of sustaining China's revolution in the political and ideological spheres. It was the eventual resistance of other Party leaders to this effort which was to lead to a breakdown in the unity of the leadership. The increasingly divisive factional conflict within the Party during the 1960s grew from Mao's efforts of the late 1950s to speed the pace of China's social advance by sustaining the interrelationship between war and political conflict, production, and institutional change.

One notable aspect of the post-Liberation periods of institutional change within China, particularly those directly promoted by Mao, is their intensity and brief duration in time. In the 1955–56 cooperativization drive it took just six months to organize 45 percent of all rural households into the "primary stage" APCs; and just over four months in the spring of 1956 to bring almost 50 percent of these households into the "advanced stage" organizations. During the Great Leap Forward of 1958 it took only a month to raise the proportion of rural households in People's Communes from 30 percent to 98 percent.[80]

80. The figures are from Walker, *Planning in Chinese Agriculture*, p. 14.

There seem to be two interrelated reasons for the intense quality of these periods of institutional change: First, Mao's belief that it is necessary to "strike while the iron is hot";[81] to move while the "activism" of the masses and political tensions within the Party are high. A second reason is the determination of more radical leaders to bring about change before opposition within the Party can be mobilized to block the movement. As we have detailed previously, Mao has faced strong resistance from within the Party to his major proposals for Party rectification and social and economic reorganization in the rural areas. It is a measure of both his determination as a revolutionary and his skill as a political tactician that he has pressed his proposals despite the opposition. One can only speculate as to whether China's social revolution would be less characterized by periods of intense upheaval if the Party leadership were fully united behind Mao's policies; yet it does seem clear that as a result of this opposition Mao has had to "move fast" to bring about change.

It is the very rapidity of the periods of institutional transformation, however, which produces the excesses and dislocations which strengthen the conservative opposition within the Party leadership. The period of Communization was no exception. There was a notable discrepancy between public Party directives which called for earnest efforts by the local cadres to adhere to the principle of voluntariness in reorganizing society, to avoid "commandism" and overcome popular doubts and resistance through "patient reasoning," and a reality marred by coercion and the rapid and indiscriminate application of "model experiences" propagated by the "Center" when local conditions required variations in approach. The politicized quality of the periods of revolutionary change makes any cadre determined to be "red," not "right"; "left," not a laggard. And in the excesses and disruptions which follow, more conservative leaders acquire the political leverage to bring about a period of "consolidation of gains."

Thus the political balance within the Party leadership swings back to the "right." "Expert" considerations replace those of the "reds," and there is a shift away from calls to the heroic, or coer-

81. As Mao was reported to have told a meeting of the Supreme State Conference in January 1958: "There are two methods of leadership and two styles of work. On the question of [agricultural] cooperation, some advocate that it should be carried out at a faster rate and some at a slower pace. I think the former one is better. It is better to strike while the iron is hot. It is better to accomplish something at one stroke than to resort to procrastination." (From *Chairman Mao's Criticism and Repudiation of the P'eng, Huang, Chang, and Chou Anti-Party Clique*, p. 2.)

cive threats, to renewed appeals to the material interests of the population—wage incentives, increases in living standards—combined with greater toleration of such "capitalist" and "bourgeois" social remnants as private plots, free markets, family life, and choice in job. These moderations of policy, in time, correct the excesses of the period of upheaval, yet set the stage for the renewed emergence of "rightist conservatism" in its many guises. Thus the political context evolves toward a new round in the cycle of leadership debate over the need for radical social change as "spontaneous tendencies toward capitalism" emerge once more, again strengthening the cause of the radicals.

The two cycles of this "saddle-shaped" pattern of leadership debate and policy change which began in 1955 and were played out with the purge of "leftists" in the period of recovery from the Great Leap Forward during 1961–62,[82] should not be viewed as either a highly stable or easily manipulable political process. The pattern described above is not a consciously fabricated rhythm of policy change controlled by one man or a small group of Party leaders. It is the natural result of political conflict within a party whose ideology enhances the tension between "right" and "left," and the effect of techniques for asserting political influence which have become part of the Chinese Communists' methods of operation. How long this pattern will endure seems largely a function of how long the Party leadership will sustain the ideological and institutional legacy of the revolution. And this question itself was raised by the excesses of the Great Leap Forward.

THE "RIGHTIST" REACTION TO THE GREAT LEAP

Within the ranks of the Party there is a small group of right opportunists antagonistic to the Party and the people. They are opposed to the Party's general line and are waging a frantic attack on it. . . . The attack which the bourgeois rightist elements launched against the Party from without in 1957 and the present attack which the right opportunists are waging from within have this in common: To oust the proletarian class and place the bourgeois class in political command.[83]

82. *See* Frederick C. Teiwes, *Provincial Party Personnel in Mainland China, 1956–1966* (New York: Columbia University, East Asian Institute Occasional Paper, 1967), Ch. IV.

83. Shang Chen, "Who Is Supposed to Take Command?" *People's Daily* (November 30, 1959); trans. in *SCMP*, No. 2155 (December 14, 1959), pp. 1–2.

The author's name, which does not appear in other mainland publications, apparently is a pseudonym. In translation its meaning is "On the Truth" or "Toward the Truth"; and as with more frequently encountered pseudonyms it probably masks the identity of a key political leader, or leaders.

In promoting the policies of the Great Leap Forward, Party spokesmen made it clear from the very beginning that doubters and opposition persisted within the leadership. In his May political report to the second session of the Eighth Party Congress Liu Shao-ch'i made this direct assertion:

> Many of those comrades who expressed misgivings about the principle of building socialism by achieving "greater, faster, better and more economical results," have learned a lesson [from political and economic developments since the Third Plenum of 1957]. But some of them have not yet learned anything. They say: "We'll settle accounts with you after the autumn harvest." Well, let them wait to settle accounts. They will lose out in the end! [84]

It is uncertain whom Liu had in mind when he used such threatening language. It may not have been the opposition which eventually emerged at the Lushan Central Committee Plenum of July and August 1959. To some degree Liu may have been raising the spectre of a strong opposition in order to silence doubters within the Party. Yet the evidence of the "anti-rightist" struggle, as it continued through 1958, indicates that opposition remained active at all levels of the Party apparatus. During his tour of the countryside in September 1958 Mao himself was said to have encountered criticism of the mass movement and the militarization of work by local Party officials, who disparaged the drive with epithets of "rural work style" and "the guerrilla habit." [85]

In order to counter such attitudes, the formal termination of the "anti-rightist" rectification in August of 1958 was followed by publication of a Central Committee directive launching a winter and spring campaign of "socialist and communist education." [86] The directive stressed:

> We must lead the masses to recall the historical lessons of the "U-shaped" development of the situation in the past three years, and thoroughly criticize the "Theory of Conditions" which places reliance on nature for existence, and the "Theory of Custom" which calls on the people to walk in the footsteps of those who have gone before. We must break down rightist conservatism, which leaves us satisfied with remaining at the half way point, and promote the ideology of exerting the utmost effort to press forward consistently. The "tide-watching

84. Cited in *CC 1955–59*, p. 427.
85. Fan Jung-k'ang, " 'Rural Work Style' and 'Guerilla Habit' Are Orthodox Marxism," *Political Study*, No. 10 (October 13, 1958); trans. in *ECMM*, No. 150 (December 8, 1958), pp. 1–3.
86. *People's Daily* editorial, "For a Still Bigger Leap Forward in Agriculture Next Year" (September 13, 1958); trans. in *SCMP*, No. 1857 (September 19, 1958), p. 12.

group" and the "post-autumn-account-settlement group" must not only be made to remain silent before the facts of the big harvest, but also become thoroughly bankrupt ideologically.[87]

This effort to sustain mass enthusiasm for the Commune drive through another "education" movement was accompanied by continued warnings to leadership cadres that "rightist conservative ideology" must not again emerge and thwart the pace of social advance. In the *People's Daily* editorial which initiated the "summing up" phase of the rectification movement, it was stressed that inasmuch as the Party was an advocate of the theory of "continuous revolution," cadres should look forward to further revolutionary struggles and rectifications—and conduct themselves accordingly. And there were somber references to "problems concerning some of the leadership cadres that have not yet been solved." [88]

While the exact composition of leadership groups which opposed Mao's policies remains obscure—as well as their procedures for urging caution in forming Communes, and modifying Great Leap policies—hints of their resistance are evident in public press materials.

Pressures for a period of consolidation increased in the fall of 1958 as the political excesses of the drive to form Communes became apparent. The radicalized Party leadership in late August and September had not only stimulated a furious pace in the formation of Communes (over 90 percent of all rural households were reported to be in Communes by the end of September),[89] it also loaded political rewards in favor of the creation of enormous organizations. The Peitaiho Politbureau resolution on the formation of Communes of late August had suggested that, "at present it is better to establish one commune to a township with the commune comprising about two thousand peasant households"; and while the resolution noted that the creation of larger organizations "need not be opposed," it was urged that "for the present we should not take the initiative to encourage them." [90] This caution was thrown

87. "Directive of the CCP Central Committee on the Universal Development of a Socialist and Communist Education Movement in the Rural Areas in the Coming Winter and Next Spring" (August 29, 1958); trans. in *ibid.*, p. 2.

88. *People's Daily* Commentator, "The Rectification Movement Must Be Properly Wound Up" (August 15, 1958); trans. in *SCMP*, No. 1851 (September 11, 1958), p. 10.

89. *See* the NCNA dispatch, "Nearly All Peasant Households in People's Communes" (September 30, 1958); in *SCMP*, No. 1872 (October 16, 1958), pp. 14–15.

90. "Resolution of the Central Committee of the Chinese Communist Party on the Establishment of People's Communes in the Rural Areas" (August 29, 1958); trans. in *CC 1955–59*, pp. 454–455.

to the winds by Mao's more enthusiastic supporters in the regional Party apparatus; and in a *Red Flag* article of mid-September, Honan's Governor and Party First Secretary, Wu Chih-p'u, repeatedly invoked Mao's name in support of huge cooperatives. He boasted that in his province the People's Communes contained an average of 7,500 households.[91]

After a tour of Honan and other provincial areas in late September, the more cautious Minister of Finance and Central Committee member Li Hsien-nien gingerly criticized the Honan Communes. They had grown well beyond the bounds of the township (*hsiang*) to include entire counties (*hsien*); and radicalized cadres had pressed for the more advanced level of property ownership "by the whole people." Management decisions thus went well beyond the control of the local Party and government organizations—not to mention taking them out of the hands of the peasants. Li observed: ". . . all the communes will follow this road *in the future*. But I think that this category of communes may, at present, involve problems which require careful consideration." [92] Li then attempted to rein in Wu's "advanced" initiatives by citing him personally as having stressed the need "to strengthen management and step up planning." In his conclusion, he appealed for more thoughtfulness and caution in the emulation of Honan's experience: "As the situation differs in various places, the concrete practices may also be different, and not necessarily unified." [93]

In fact, however, political considerations outweighed those of economics. As G. William Skinner has shown, it was the indiscriminate application of a few model experiences to areas of China where they were inappropriate, and the creation of very large Commune organizations, which produced much of the dislocation of rural economic activity during the Great Leap. Communes larger than the township (*hsiang*) disrupted the "natural" pattern of rural administration and commodity exchange.[94]

Political momentum for a period of consolidation of the organizational changes of the early fall increased as examples of excess and mismanagement became more apparent. The pressures on basic level cadres to bring about huge increases in grain production had

91. Cited in G. William Skinner, "Marketing and Social Structure in Rural China, Part III," *Journal of Asian Studies*, Vol. XXIV, No. 3 (May 1965), p. 392.

92. Li Hsien-nien, "A Glance at the People's Communes," *Red Flag*, No. 10 (October 16, 1958); trans. in *ECMM*, No. 149 (December 1, 1958), p. 34. Emphasis added.

93. *Ibid.*, pp. 38, 39.

94. Skinner, "Marketing and Social Structure in Rural China, Part III," pp. 383–392.

led them to ignore vegetable growing and the raising of pigs and chickens (activities now socialized as a result of the abolition of private plots and the free-market system). Thus there developed a serious drop in the production of the peasants' major sources of protein and carbohydrates; and social tensions increased as the quality of food and service in the public mess-halls succumbed to cadre concern with meeting production quotas in those crops for which they would be held politically accountable. In a fall editorial urging that Party secretaries personally take charge of the running of public mess-halls, the *People's Daily* stressed: "If we do not properly run the public mess-halls and nurseries, then we shall not be able to consolidate the collectivization of daily living." [95]

A related set of problems came from the mass campaign to smelt iron and steel. In their determination to meet Mao's production quotas, cadres had commandeered all available sources of "scrap" metal, including cooking pots, iron doors, and in one North China Commune even the heating pipes of a secondary school. The popular resentments generated by such measures were intensified by the fact that with poor quality food and service in the public mess-halls, many who would have preferred to eat at home now were unable to do so for lack of cooking implements. Furthermore, the quality of the "native" steel was so low because of its high sulphur content that it was virtually unusable for fabrication into new products.

A further cause for social discontent was generated by the cadres' determination to establish the most "communistic" forms of food supply and wage payment possible. Being more "progressive," such developments would win greater support from radical Party leaders. "Free food" was provided in some Communes, although with limited grain supply and vegetable shortages this tended to mean a poorer diet for those who worked harder. Privately-owned farm animals and family-grown vegetables were commandeered for community consumption; and in some areas the total abolition of wage payments further reduced labor incentives. This was what Mao himself was to criticize in 1959 as "blowing the wind of communism," a "left-opportunist" deviation that he attributed to the excessive political enthusiasm of Commune and county-level cadres.[96]

It was such excesses which the Sixth Central Committee Plenum

95. *People's Daily* editorial, "Run Public Mess Halls Properly" (October 25, 1958); trans. in *Current Background,* No. 538 (December 12, 1958), p. 1.

96. "Mao Tse-tung's Speech at the Eighth Plenary Session of the CCP Eighth Central Committee" (July 1959); in *The Case of P'eng Teh-huai* (Hong Kong: Union Research Institute, 1968), pp. 17–18.

of November–December 1958 sought to correct. Its resolution calling for a consolidation of the changes of the fall did not yet shift the level of management and accounting back "down" to the natural villages,[97] but it did stress the need for the Communes to "plan their production, exchange, consumption and accumulation," and emphasized the importance of maintaining wage incentives, an eight-hour working day, and a high level of social services.[98] Furthermore, cadres were urged to accept the fact that the process of increasing production to a level at which everyone could be remunerated "according to his needs" and where ownership would be by "the whole people" was one which would "take fifteen, twenty or more years to complete, starting from now." [99] In the interim, however, cadres were "reminded" that the peasants should not be overworked and that "exaggeration" in setting production targets and reporting harvest yields to superiors was not permissible.

An important question which is not yet answered concerns the amount of political pressure on Mao at the end of 1958. While the resolution of the Sixth Plenum calling for consolidation of the People's Communes sought to eliminate the air of politicized euphoria prevalent during the summer and fall, it was not hostile to "good-hearted" but "over-eager" comrades who wanted to push the revolution faster than objective circumstances would permit. With the entire rural population now organized into Communes, there is no reason to believe that Mao would not have been in favor of a period of consolidation in order to "even up" the advances of the fall.

On the other hand, the Plenum approved "the proposal of Chairman Mao that he not stand as candidate for Chairman of the People's Republic for the next term of office." [100] During the Cultural Revolution Mao was reported to have remarked that he "was not satisfied with the [results of the] Wuchang Conference" at which the decision that he step aside as State Chairman had been made.[101] Some have interpreted this statement to mean that he had been forced to relinquish the post.

In conflict with this interpretation, however, is a Central Committee document drafted by Mao in January of 1958 in which he

97. This was to come about only in late 1960. *See* Schurmann, *Ideology and Organization in Communist China*, pp. 490–492.

98. "Resolution on Some Questions Concerning the People's Communes" (December 10, 1959); trans. in *CC 1955–59*, pp. 490–503.

99. *Ibid.*, p. 492.

100. *See* the Sixth Plenum resolution of this title in *CC 1955–59*, pp. 487–488.

101. Mao, "Speech at a Report Meeting" (October 24, 1966), in *Long Live the Thought of Mao Tse-tung!* p. 45.

raised the issue of giving up the chairmanship in terms almost identical to those of the Plenum communiqué of December of that same year.[102] In addition, there is one report that in the original presentation of his 1957 "Contradictions" speech Mao had hinted that he might step aside for other leaders.[103] Mao apparently had raised this issue a number of times, perhaps for tactical political reasons: to deflate the argument that he was another Stalin, or to "remind" the Party of his authority when there was opposition to his policies.

Also in support of the interpretation that Mao was not "forced aside" in 1958 are statements attributed to the Party Chairman in October of 1966, in which he reveals that sometime in the 1950s he had conceived of "two lines" of leadership—one at the operational level, and a second "policy" line—as a way of training other top leaders and avoiding a succession struggle, as well as of diminishing the security problems which would come with overly centralized leadership.[104] Furthermore, with the basic social organization which was to see the Chinese people through the transition to communism now created on a nationwide scale, Mao—in his mid-sixties—might indeed have thought of giving greater day-to-day responsibility to other leaders.

From the context of events prior to the Great Leap Forward and developments thereafter, however, one senses that Mao's decision was not so politically innocent. If nothing else, the experiences of 1956–57 (in which Liu Shao-ch'i, Teng Hsiao-p'ing, and P'eng Chen had differed with Mao on important issues of economics, Party rectification, and the treatment of intellectuals) meant that Mao was well aware of disagreements over policy and personal commitment. The Party Chairman may have been anticipating coming political battles in making a "voluntary" withdrawal. Mao may have sensed the likely scope of opposition to his leadership as

102. *See* "Sixty Work Methods (Draft)," issued by the General Office of the Central Committee of the Communist Party of China (February 19, 1958); trans. in *Current Background,* No. 892 (October 21, 1969), p. 13.

103. *See* Loh and Evans, *Escape from Red China,* p. 292.

104. *See* the remarks attributed to Mao from two political conferences of October 24 and 25, 1966; published in the Cultural Revolution pamphlet *Long Live the Thought of Mao Tse-tung!* pp. 40–42, 44–46.

The phrasing of Mao's remarks suggests that the division of the leadership into "two lines" grew from the separation of the Party "center" into two groups in mid-March 1947 for reasons that seem basically related to the security of the leadership during the final phase of the Civil War. (*See* Mao, *SW,* IV, English, footnote 3 on page 132 for a description of this separation.) Yet the exact timing of the creation of the "two lines" after 1949 remains obscure.

a result of communization and the outcome of the Quemoy confrontation (to be discussed below), and hence stepped aside as State Chairman as a way of deflating his opposition. Perhaps he wanted to strengthen his support from Liu Shao-ch'i, who was to succeed him as State Chairman in April of 1959. The exact meaning of this development remains uncertain.

There is no doubt, however, that the "rightist" reaction to the Great Leap Forward did emerge during the spring and summer of 1959, when it was already apparent that a combination of natural disasters, mismanagement, and the disruption of rural life brought about by the changes of the preceding year had led to a drastic drop in grain production. It also had become evident that the production figures for the bumper harvest of 1958 had been highly inflated as a result of "exaggerations" by the cadres reporting local yields. At the Central Committee Plenum held at Lushan, Kiangsi Province, in July and August of 1959, Mao was to see an attempt to unseat him from the "saddle" of influence over China's social development.

At the time the public press gave only indirect indication of the seriousness which Mao attached to the challenge to his policies which was launched at Lushan by a group led by Defense Minister P'eng Teh-huai. On August 6th the *People's Daily* carried an editorial exhorting cadres to fulfill their production targets for the year, and urgently requiring them to "take a determined stand against the rightist-inclined sentiment which has found its way into some of the cadres." [105] At the end of this month an article entitled "The 'Chronic Disease of Right Deviation' and Its 'Remedy' " appeared in the Party paper and stated more forcefully that

> It is a downright crime to ridicule, attack or slander this great, new thing [the Communes], to raise the charge that the commune movement has been "too early," "too quick" and that it has "ended in a mess," or to say that the commune movement is "a fanatical movement of the petty bourgeoisie." [106]

105. *People's Daily* editorial, "Overcome Rightist-Inclined Sentiment and Endeavor to Increase Production and Practise Economy" (August 6, 1959); trans. in *CC 1955–59*, p. 531.

106. Wu Ch'uan-ch'i, "The 'Chronic Disease of Right Deviation' and Its 'Remedy,' " *People's Daily* (August 30, 1959); trans. in *SCMP,* No. 2108 (October 2, 1959), p. 5.
The curious phrasing "chronic disease" reflects Mao's successful defense at Lushan: He has tended to describe political errors as "diseases," and has stressed the necessity of "curing the disease to save the patient" through the method of "criticism–self-criticism" (*see* Mao, "Rectify the Party's Style of Work," *SW,* English, III, p. 50). Also, and more specifically, Mao, in a bit-

Exactly who had "slandered" the Leap policies in this manner remained unstated, although there were several exceedingly sharp references to "frantic attacks" on the Party and the "general line of socialist construction," and the need to obey Chairman Mao. One astute yet cautious observer suggested shortly afterwards that the "rightist opposition within the Chinese Communist Party had been a considerable force, with growing grievances against the leadership." [107]

It was only a year or two later that sufficient information had "leaked" from China (perhaps by way of the Soviet Union) to enable government analysts to begin to piece together the linkage between the dismissal of Defense Minister P'eng Teh-huai—announced in a government proclamation of September 17th, 1959, over the signature of the new State Chairman Liu Shao-ch'i—and the emergence of a new national "anti-rightist" campaign after the Lushan Plenum of the summer.[108] And only during the Cultural Revolution, when documentation on the affair was published by the Maoists for reasons of contemporary political need, did inner-Party information begin to add detail to this incident.

On the basis of the version of P'eng's "Letter of Opinion" to Mao of mid-July 1959 which was made public in 1967, it appears that the Defense Minister criticized the policies of the Great Leap in a way that would draw maximum political leverage from the now apparent economic consequences of Mao's "general line." P'eng's attack, assuming that the letter is an authentic revelation of his arguments, is a detailed *economic* critique of the results of the first year of the Great Leap. But why should the Defense Minister be the one to promote such an attack, and not one of the more conservative economists within the leadership?

A number of interpretations might be advanced. Assuming that P'eng spoke on his own initiative,[109] that his critique had not been

---

ingly ironic letter to Chang Wen-t'ien, one of P'eng Teh-huai's co-conspirators, in early August 1959, told him: "In my opinion, you have relapsed into your old illness" (*The Case of P'eng Teh-huai*, p. 315). Ostensibly this referred to malaria, which Chang had contracted during the Long March; yet Mao's political meaning was a reference to the old "disease" of Chang's policy deviations which were part of his association with the "Internationalist" or pro-Soviet Party faction during the 1930s.

107. From *CC 1955–59*, p. 36.

108. *See* David A. Charles, "The Dismissal of P'eng Teh-huai," *The China Quarterly*, No. 8 (October–December 1961), pp. 63–76.

109. The one shred of direct evidence that P'eng may have been a spokesman for other Party leaders—P'eng Chen and Liu Shao-ch'i in particular—is the revelation of 1965 that on June 16, 1959 (three days after P'eng's

"ghost-written" by other Party leaders more familiar with economic matters, one can see an attempt by P'eng to appeal for support from the Central Committee in terms which were meaningful to all, and hence would gain wide backing. But even assuming that P'eng's letter was not fully his own creation, why should the Defense Minister be the spokesman for such an attack? Conflicting personal styles or political rivalry may have been an element in the confrontation,[110] yet policy issues were clearly a major factor in P'eng's challenge. In particular, it was changes in Mao's military policy in 1958 and the increasingly strained defense relationship between China and the Soviet Union which seems to account for the Defense Minister's actions.

To explore this dimension of the "rightist reaction" to the Great Leap Forward it is necessary to retrace one aspect of the events of 1958–59 which in its own way reveals how Mao has used "struggle" and confrontation politics to further his own policies and position.

---

return from Eastern Europe and the Soviet Union) the *People's Daily* published an article "Hai Jui Scolds the Emperor." The ostensible author of this piece, Liu Mien-chih, in fact was Wu Han, a close associate of P'eng Chen in the Peking Municipal Government. It could be that this article was intended to "prepare opinion" for the Lushan confrontation; yet one does not know whether at this early date it was known that "Hai Jui" would be P'eng Teh-huai. (*See* the *People's Daily* editor's note to Yao Wen-yuan's article "On the New Historical Play *The Dismissal of Hai Jui*" [November 30, 1965]; trans. in *Current Background,* No. 783 [March 21, 1966], p. 1.)

Shortly after P'eng Teh-huai's removal, Wu Han wrote another article "On Hai Jui," published in the *People's Daily* on September 21, 1959, which indirectly defended P'eng's action. And in 1961 Wu Han wrote a play in the style of Peking Opera, "The Dismissal of Hai Jui," which more directly criticized "the emperor's" action against P'eng.

As is discussed throughout the next chapter, the issue of P'eng's dismissal runs through leadership debates leading right up to the Cultural Revolution (*see* esp. pp. 417–421, 425–429 below). P'eng's criticism of Mao was a major factor in the transformation of leadership conflict from matters of policy to that of Mao's personal authority after 1959. Yet at present there is only slim evidence that at Lushan P'eng spoke with the direct backing of leaders other than those who were purged with him at the time.

110. Personal rivalry between Mao and P'eng during the late 1920s was rumored repeatedly in the context of conflict over military policy. (*See* Benjamin Schwartz, *Chinese Communism and the Rise of Mao* [Cambridge, Mass.: Harvard University Press, 1964], pp. 174, 176, 182); and in his confession before Party leaders in 1959, P'eng admitted that he had long adopted a "quarrelsome attitude" towards Mao and had a "prejudice" against him. ("P'eng Teh-huai's Speech at the Eighth Plenum of the Eighth CCP Central Committee" [Excerpts], in *Current Background,* No. 851 [April 26, 1968], p. 28.)

TESTING THE WIND

Either the east wind overpowers the west wind or the west wind over-powers the east wind; on the question of line there is no room for com-promise.[111]

We hold that to defend world peace it is necessary constantly to expose imperialism and to arouse and organize the people in struggle against the imperialists headed by the United States, and it is necessary to place reliance on the growth of the strength of the socialist camp.[112]

The Soviet Twentieth Party Congress of 1956 was a major water-shed in Sino-Soviet relations. Not only did Khrushchev's attack on Stalin produce reactions in China which tended to undermine Mao's personal authority, but the Russian leader also put forward basic policy guidelines which conflicted with Mao's own policy positions —"peaceful coexistence" and "peaceful competition" with non-So-cialist states, and the possibility of "peaceful transition" to social-ism. The Chinese Party leader and his supporters watched with in-creasing distress as Khrushchev's "peace" line went through a proc-ess of "emergence, formation, growth and systematization" during the years 1956–1959.[113] Here was an authoritative alternative to Mao's view of the importance of sustaining political struggle, put forward by the leading Party of the International Communist Move-ment. And by all evidence, Khrushchev's line found sympathetic response within the Chinese Party leadership, for in time Mao was to charge that there were "Chinese Khrushchevs."

Even from Mao's perspective, however, there were many positive dimensions to the Chinese relationship with the Soviet Union, not the least of which was the degree of national security which came from membership in the "Socialist Camp" defended by Soviet nu-clear weapons. Furthermore, the strength of the "Camp" appeared to have increased substantially over that of its "imperialist" adver-saries in 1957 with the Soviet development of an intercontinental ballistic missile capability for its nuclear weapons. The launching of the Russian Sputniks in October and November, on the eve of

111. *People's Daily* editorial, "The Bourgeois Trend of the *Wen Hui Pao* Should Be Subjected to Criticism" (July 1, 1957). As noted in footnote 130, p. 319 above, this editorial has been identified as written by Mao himself.

112. *People's Daily* and *Red Flag* joint editorial, "Two Different Lines on the Question of War and Peace" (November 19, 1963), in *Polemic on the General Line of the International Communist Movement*, p. 254.

113. *People's Daily* and *Red Flag* joint editorial, "The Origin and De-velopment of the Differences between the Leadership of the CPSU and Ourselves" (September 6, 1963), in *ibid.*, p. 59.

the Fortieth Anniversary of the Bolshevik Revolution, seemed to imply greater security for China, and to prove the correctness of the socialist path of national development with its now demonstrated superiority in scientific achievement. As Mao proclaimed to representatives of Communist and Workers' Parties assembled in Moscow in November 1957:

> I consider that the present world situation has reached a new turning point. There are now two winds in the world: the east wind and the west wind. . . . I think the characteristic of the current situation is that the east wind prevails over the west wind; that is, the strength of socialism exceeds the strength of imperialism.[114]

Behind this public expression of faith in the socialist system, however, was Mao's uncertainty about how Khrushchev might use this Russian scientific and military superiority, for Sputnik had been preceded by the launching of the "peace" line. Did "peaceful coexistence" now mean that the hand of "imperialist aggressors" could be stayed by Soviet defense superiority? Or were the Russians preparing to take a less militant line in resolving outstanding issues of great importance for the "Camp" like Berlin and—at least for the Chinese—Taiwan? Did the increased possibilities of "peaceful transition" to socialism as a result of the Soviet scientific breakthrough mean that Communist Parties around the world would gain greater prestige through association with the Socialist system, or that the Russians would back off from aiding struggling revolutionary movements? It was such questions which Mao sought to test during the years 1957–1959.

Mao headed a delegation to Moscow in early November of 1957 —only his second trip abroad—to attend celebrations marking the Fortieth Anniversary of the October Revolution, and to participate in an historic meeting of representatives of Communist and Workers' Parties from all over the world. Mao made the trip with renewed political strength. His period of defensiveness after the "de-Stalinization" drive had ended only weeks earlier with the Third Central Committee Plenum of September–October. Khrushchev, as well, was in a strengthened position. He had recently defeated an "anti-Party" group which included Stalin's old associate Molotov, and had ousted the popular army leader, Marshal Zhukov. The triumph of Sputnik, moreover, appeared to have diverted attention away from the difficulties in Poland and the Hungarian intervention of the preceding fall.

114. From the collection of Mao's statements, "Imperialism and All Reactionaries Are Paper Tigers," *People's Daily* (October 31, 1958); trans. in *Current Background*, No. 534 (November 12, 1958), p. 8.

By all evidence the meetings between Mao and Khrushchev in November of 1957 embodied discussion of political and military issues of primary importance to both countries. Only two weeks before Mao's arrival in Moscow, the Chinese later revealed, the Russians had signed an agreement with the People's Republic to aid in the development of "new technology for national defense." [115] The Chinese also implied that they had requested (unsuccessfully) that the Soviets supply them with "a sample of an atomic bomb and technical data concerning its manufacture." [116] Whether such a request had been made at the time of the October negotiations on the agreement for aid in developing "national defense technology," when Mao met Khrushchev in early November, or at some point subsequent to the world meeting of Communist Parties, is unclear. Yet only two days after Khrushchev's first meeting with Mao and P'eng Teh-huai, a high-level Chinese military delegation suddenly went to Moscow at the invitation of the Soviet Defense Ministry. Evidently defense matters of the highest importance were under discussion.[117]

Whether these Sino-Soviet military contacts involved joint defense planning, the sharing of military and technical information, or bargaining over aspects of either or both issues, cannot be estimated from the public record. Yet it seems evident that both countries were trying to make adjustments in military strategy and defense liaison in the wake of the Soviet ICBM breakthrough. In addition, Khrushchev appeared anxious to be more generous to the Chinese as a way of gaining political backing from Mao. Khrushchev wanted to consolidate his domestic political position and shore up Russia's leading role within the Bloc in the wake of "de-Stalinization" and Hungary.[118]

At the November meeting of representatives of Communist and Workers' Parties, Mao apparently "did a great deal of work" to cor-

115. *People's Daily* and *Red Flag* joint editorial, "The Origin and Development of the Differences between the Leadership of the CPSU and Ourselves" (September 6, 1963), in *Polemic on the General Line of the International Communist Movement*, p. 77.

116. *Ibid.*

117. This delegation was composed of fourteen of China's top generals, including Chief of the General Staff Su Yü. It was headed by Defense Minister P'eng Teh-huai, who was already in Moscow. The delegation remained in the Soviet Union for nearly a month. The long duration of this visit suggests that detailed planning discussions were held.

118. This point is discussed and documented in Ellis Joffe, *Party and Army: Professionalism and Political Control in the Chinese Officer Corps, 1949–1964* (Cambridge, Massachusetts: Harvard University, East Asian Monographs, 1965), pp. 94–95.

rect what he considered to be the erroneous views of the Soviet leadership on the questions of "peaceful transition" and their attitude toward capitalist countries. He is said to have "waged struggles" against the Khrushchev leadership, successfully pressed the world meeting to adopt the thesis that "U.S. imperialism is the center of world reaction and the sworn enemy of the people," and urged other more militant changes in the Soviet draft of the conference document. The Chinese delegation was said to have desisted from pressing their viewpoint only "out of consideration for the difficult position of the leadership of the CPSU at the time." [119]

This belated Chinese admission of a policy of "unity and struggle" with the Soviets in 1957–58 is borne out by documentation published at the time. The "stalking horse" in Chinese efforts to resist the reconciliation themes in Khrushchev's evolving political line was the issue of Yugoslav "revisionism." In mid-1955 Khrushchev had partially repaired Stalin's 1948 open break with the Tito government; and one of the key issues surrounding the 1957 Moscow meeting was whether the Yugoslavs would return to the Socialist Camp on terms acceptable to the Russians. On the eve of the world conference Tito developed, as one analyst has put it, a "diplomatic illness." [120] He apparently feared that if he attended the conference he would either be pressured into signing a conference declaration which would go against his domestic and foreign policies, or be subject to public attack from more militant Parties.

Tito's decision to send to the meeting a lower-level delegation (which was, in fact, subjected to threats and pressures, even from the Russians) meant that Khrushchev's reconciliation efforts within the Bloc had met a serious setback; and following the November conference a partial break in Soviet-Yugoslav relations reappeared. The evidence indicates, however, that at the beginning of the winter of 1957–58 the Russians limited public attacks on the Yugoslavs in hopes of eventually reaching some accommodation with Tito.[121]

It was in this context of political uncertainty that the Chinese intervened in early May of 1958 by launching a blistering public attack on Yugoslav "revisionism"—ostensibly in response to the April publication of the Yugoslavs' "Draft Program" discussed at their Seventh Party Congress. The Chinese termed this political

119. *People's Daily* and *Red Flag* joint editorial, "The Origin and Development of the Differences between the Leadership of the CPSU and Ourselves," in *Polemic on the General Line of the International Communist Movement,* pp. 72–74.

120. Zagoria, *The Sino-Soviet Conflict, 1956–1961,* p. 178.

121. *Ibid.,* pp. 178–184.

program "out-and-out revisionist," and of such danger to the International Movement that the new "sacred task" before all Parties was to "wage an irreconcilable struggle against modern revisionism." [122]

The second *People's Daily* editorial in this attack, however, noted that "some people" thought such a struggle might be "going too far," and would bring harm to the International Movement.[123] In response to this objection, the Chinese detailed the extent of American efforts to split the Socialist Camp—in part by giving military and economic aid to the Yugoslavs—and stressed that, "Those who do not see the danger of Yugoslav revisionism should give careful consideration to this." [124] In conclusion the editorial asserted: "We hold that modern revisionism must be fought to the end and there can be no room for concession here." [125]

The third article in this series came from the pen of Ch'en Po-ta, over the years Mao's closest political spokesman. Ch'en detailed the degree to which the Yugoslavs had blurred the lines of struggle between "imperialism" and "socialism," and had given in to bureaucratism and capitalist tendencies within their own country. His conclusion was that, "It is impossible to cease this struggle [against revisionism]." [126] Ch'en then rhetorically asked: "Is this struggle good for Marxism-Leninism?" His answer was that a continuing political confrontation would "enable people to distinguish still more clearly between Marxism-Leninism and anti-Marxism-Leninism. Marxism-Leninism has always grown and developed by combating opportunism of every description." [127]

To readers of this polemic in Moscow there would have been little doubt that Chinese references to "some comrades" and to the need to struggle against "opportunism" were directed above all at the Soviet Party leadership. Indeed, at a later date the Chinese were to admit publicly that during this period, "for the sake of the larger interest, we refrained from publicly criticizing the comrades of the CPSU and directed the spearhead of struggle against the imperialists

122. *People's Daily* editorial, "Modern Revisionism Must Be Repudiated" (May 5, 1958); trans. in *Peking Review*, No. 11 (May 13, 1958), p. 6.

123. *People's Daily* editorial, "Modern Revisionism Must Be Fought to the End" (June 4, 1958); trans. in *Peking Review*, No. 15 (June 10, 1958), p. 7.

124. *Ibid.*, p. 9.

125. *Ibid.*

126. Ch'en Po-ta, "Yugoslav Revisionism—Product of Imperialist Policy," *Red Flag*, No. 1 (June 1, 1958); trans. in *Peking Review*, No. 16 (June 17, 1958), p. 12.

127. *Ibid.*

and Yugoslav revisionists." [128] But in 1958, in a period of increasingly uncertain Soviet militancy, the Chinese were trying to force the Russian Party leadership to "distinguish clearly between friend and enemy," and to assume those obligations of active aid to "fraternal Parties" which were implied by their leadership of the International Movement (at least in Chinese eyes).

The declining militancy of the Soviet Party's domestic and foreign policies created great problems for Mao, and as he saw it, for the future of China's revolution and state interests. If the Russians were willing to accept as true socialism such modifications of the "dictatorship of the proletariat" as the Yugoslav experiments in economic and political reform and their acceptance of aid from "the sworn enemy of the people," "U.S. imperialism," what would be the impact within China in leadership debates?

We have noted above that there had been strong opposition to Mao's policy of combating "rightist conservatism" in the intellectual community and within the Party, and to his progam of social mobilization in developing the rural economy. Would Soviet toleration of Yugoslav "revisionism" enhance the legitimacy of less radical approaches to social change and strengthen the political position of Mao's domestic opponents? At a time when American support for the Nationalists on Taiwan and the offshore islands of Quemoy and Matsu continued to hold China's revolutionary struggle in abeyance, and when American diplomatic efforts tended to strengthen the reality of "two Chinas," would Soviet nuclear superiority help to solve this basic political and defense problem, or would it lead to an easing of Soviet-American tensions?

Mao's response was a characteristic promotion of open confrontation with the issues. Politically, he launched an ideological polemic against "modern revisionism"—initially personified in the Yugoslav Party leadership—in order to "draw a line" between acceptable and unacceptable forms of social organization and political policies. At best he could force the Russians to draw a similar line; but at least he could make it very difficult for "revisionist" sentiments within the Chinese leadership to be expressed as policy alternatives to his own political line.

In the matter of national defense policy Mao also chose to promote a confrontation, both with domestic military leaders and with the Soviets. Military developments of 1958 reflect several goals: to

128. *People's Daily* and *Red Flag* joint editorial, "The Origin and Development of the Differences between the Leadership of the CPSU and Ourselves," in *Polemic on the General Line of the International Communist Movement,* p. 78.

encourage greater Russian militancy in the international struggle; to test the limits of both Soviet and American power as it affected China, and to invoke the temporary Soviet missile advantage in resolving the Taiwan issue.

Such objectives, intimately related to China's national defense, provoked an intense debate within the Party leadership in the spring and summer of 1958 and were the subject of an extraordinary meeting of the Military Affairs Committee of the Party Central Committee between May 27th and July 22nd. The final communiqué of this exceptionally lengthy convocation—attended by more than a thousand officers, and addressed by the highest political and military leaders—revealed little more than that the sessions had "decided on the principle for future development" of the People's Liberation Army [PLA].[129]

From later developments, however, it seems evident that after debating the price which the Soviets expected the Chinese to pay for a strengthened defense relationship, Mao was able to establish the "principle" of complete Chinese independence of the Soviet Union in matters of both military organization and national defense strategy. As Mao is reported to have said to high-ranking military officials during the meetings: "We cannot feed on meals cooked for us, otherwise, defeat will be our lot. This point must be clearly explained to the Soviet comrades." [130]

The Russians evidently had pressed the Chinese for a strategy of "united action," [131] which in practical terms meant a proposal for a joint Sino-Soviet naval command in the Far East,[132] more closely

129. NCNA, "CCP Military Committee Holds Enlarged Conference" (July 25, 1958); in *SCMP*, No. 1822 (July 30, 1958), p. 1.

130. Mao, "Speech at the Symposium of Group Leaders of the Enlarged Meeting of the Military Commission (Excerpts)" (June 28, 1958), in *Chairman Mao's Criticism and Repudiation of the P'eng, Huang, Chang, and Chou Anti-Party Clique*, p. 4.

131. "The Criminal History of Big Conspirator, Big Ambitionist, Big Warlord P'eng Teh-huai," in *The Case of P'eng Teh-huai*, p. 202.

132. *See* Alice Langley Hsieh, *Communist China's Strategy in the Nuclear Era* (Englewood Cliffs, New Jersey: Prentice-Hall, 1962), p. 117. According to Cultural Revolution disclosures, the Soviets made the proposal for a joint naval command in "the second half of 1958," which apparently means while the Military Commission was in mid-session. Mao is reported to have denounced this proposal at the Tenth Plenum in 1962 as having been an attempt "to dominate the coastal area, and to blockade us." And in an apparent reference to Khrushchev's hasty and secretive visit to Peking of late July and early August 1958, Mao noted: "Khrushchev came to China because of this problem [of China's rejection of the plan]." (From Mao's "Speech at the Tenth Plenary Session of the Eighth Central Committee" [September 24, 1962], in the pamphlet *Chairman Mao's Criticism and Repudiation of the P'eng, Huang, Chang, Chou Anti-Party Clique*, p. 25.)

integrated air defenses, and perhaps base agreements and control arrangements for stationing Soviet rockets and nuclear weapons on Chinese territory.[133] The Chinese later indignantly recalled that "these unreasonable demands designed to bring China under Soviet military control" had been "rightly and firmly rejected by the Chinese Government." [134]

In the face of Soviet conditions which in Mao's eyes would have made China a military dependency of the Russians, the Party Chairman urged his colleagues to make the most of a difficult situation through self-reliance. It was during this period that Mao stressed the importance of China developing an independent nuclear weapons capability based on her own resources.[135] Conversely, he apparently proposed rejection of an attempt to keep up with China's enemies in the development of conventional weaponry (aircraft, tanks, a naval fleet, etc.)—which would tax her limited industrial capacity to the extreme—in favor of reliance on the guerrilla warfare defense strategy which was the Party's revolutionary legacy. The formation of a decentralized political and economic system— the Communes—and the strengthening of popular military organization through expansion of the People's Militia were central to this new defense strategy of nuclear weapons to deter attack and "people's war" to resist invasion.

As with his efforts of the preceding three years to break China's dependence on the Soviet experience in economic development, the assertive and independent-minded Mao thus resisted Russian proposals which would have increased China's dependence in matters of national defense.

This shift in defense policy had hardly proceeded without struggle, however. As the communiqué of the Military Affairs Committee meetings disclosed, the sessions had been carried out "using the method of the rectification campaign." [136] The meaning of this cryp-

133. *See* Raymond L. Garthoff, "Sino-Soviet Military Relations, 1945–66," in Raymond L. Garthoff, ed., *Sino-Soviet Military Relations* (New York: Praeger, 1966), p. 90.

134. *People's Daily* and *Red Flag* joint editorial, "The Origin and Development of the Differences between the Leadership of the CPSU and Ourselves," in *Polemic on the General Line of the International Communist Movement*, p. 77.

135. On the occasion of China's first successful hydrogen bomb test in June of 1967 an official press communiqué crowed: "Chairman Mao Tsetung pointed out as far back as June 1958: 'I think it is entirely possible for some atom bombs and hydrogen bombs to be made in ten years' time.' " (*People's Daily*, June 18, 1967, p. 1.)

136. NCNA, "CCP Military Committee Holds Enlarged Conference," in *SCMP*, No. 1822 (July 30, 1958), p. 1.

tic remark was first suggested in a speech by Chu Teh on Army Day, August 1st. After stressing that the army "absolutely follows the leadership of the Communist Party," and that the Party "has established a complete set of systems whereby the Party exercises leadership over the army," Chu revealed: "There are people who advocate an exclusively military viewpoint, who have a one-sided high regard for military affairs and who look down upon politics." [137]

The identity of the people to whom Chu Teh alluded would have been suggested to a careful observer by personnel movements and changes at this time. The political significance of the unexplained disappearance from public view of Chief of the General Staff Su Yü and senior generals Liu Po-ch'eng and Yeh Chien-ying—men "who over the years had been identified with professional [military] thinking" [138]—became clear when Su Yü was removed from office in October. Whether these changes in personnel reflected opposition to Mao's military "principle" of independence from the Soviets or conflicting judgments over the feasibility of events which were shortly to take place in the Taiwan Straits is difficult to estimate. The reemergence of all three men as Mao's supporters during the Cultural Revolution suggests that their opposition had been related to tactical considerations.

In any event, it seems certain that the issue of Taiwan and the offshore islands (Quemoy and Matsu), still occupied by Nationalist forces, was discussed in detail by the Military Affairs Committee during its long deliberations. A week after the meeting concluded, on July 29th, Communist and Nationalist aircraft clashed over the Taiwan Straits; and two days later Khrushchev, accompanied by his Defense Minister, Malinovsky, secretly arrived in Peking for three days of talks. It seems unlikely that such a visit would have taken place had not the Soviet leaders had some idea of Chinese plans for an attempt to "solve" the offshore island problem through military action.

The press communiqué which was issued at the end of Khrushchev's hasty and initially undisclosed visit made no mention of the Taiwan Straits situation, but instead focused on the current Middle East crisis. Events there were hardly of such importance to Sino-Soviet relations that they would account for the Khrushchev-Malinovsky visit. It seems most likely that the Soviet leaders came to define the limits of their support for the Chinese, if not to cool Mao's ardor for a test in the Straits.

137. Chu Teh, "People's Army, People's War," NCNA (July 31, 1958); in *Current Background,* No. 514 (August 6, 1958), pp. 1–2.
138. *See* Hsieh, *Communist China's Strategy in the Nuclear Era,* p. 122.

The fact that the Mao-Khrushchev communiqué eventually was issued—publicly revealing the Russian leader's presence in Peking —can be explained in terms which would account for conflicting interests on both sides: The failure to mention Taiwan in the communiqué would have made it clear that the Soviets were unwilling to give Mao direct backing in the coming confrontation over the offshore islands; yet the fact that the Soviet visit was revealed probably helped to sustain in American minds the air of uncertainty as to whether the Russians, in fact, might become involved—which is possibly all that Mao felt he needed in the coming test.[139]

One suspects that Mao tried to convince Khrushchev and Malinovsky that the confrontation could be localized and that artillery fire directed at the offshore islands would run only a limited risk of involving the Americans directly. Yet one cannot rule out the possibility of a major political confrontation between Mao and Khrushchev at this time. It may be that the real "test" of Soviet reliability in aid of China's national defense concluded with this meeting.

Whatever the exact explanation for the visit, it is clear from subsequent developments that Mao was determined to act. He probably estimated that the United States, beset by an economic recession at home,[140] and distracted by its current intervention in the Middle East, would find it difficult to respond to a limited and indirect action in a distant theater. Further, merely the knowledge of Soviet missile superiority and the possibility of Russian intervention would have seemed enough to give the Americans additional cause for inaction. Hence, as Cultural Revolution materials later revealed:

> After bald-headed Khrushchev left [Peking on August 3rd], Chairman Mao ordered the shelling of Quemoy. This was a forceful reply to Soviet revisionism, and traitor P'eng Teh-huai was very dissatisfied over this. Chairman Mao personally directed this important military action, but traitor P'eng Teh-huai stealthily slipped away on the grounds of making an inspection tour.[141]

In the event, of course, the military aspect of Mao's calculated gamble failed, initially because the Americans deployed a military

139. Shortly after Khrushchev's August visit to Peking, rumors began circulating in Warsaw that the Russians had granted the Chinese nuclear weapons and missiles. These reports, which have never been substantiated, are thought to have been planted by Chinese agents. *Ibid.*, p. 123.

140. The first issue of *Red Flag* (June 1, 1958) carried a lengthy analysis of the deteriorating state of the American economy by Chang Wen-t'ien entitled, "On the Economic Crisis of the United States."

141. "The Criminal History of Big Conspirator, Big Ambitionist, Big Warlord P'eng Teh-huai," in *The Case of P'eng Teh-huai,* p. 202.

task force to the area and showed themselves willing to take the risks of convoying Nationalist supply vessels to the offshore islands. A further factor in the playing out of this challenge, however, was the demonstrated Soviet unwillingness to invoke their nuclear weapons in support of the Chinese initiative. The shelling of Quemoy began on August 23rd, and by the last days of the month it was clear that the United States was actively mobilizing naval strength for the confrontation. On September 6th Premier Chou En-lai issued a statement asserting that the Government of the People's Republic was willing to discuss the dispute with the United States through the ambassadorial talks at Warsaw; and the next day the *People's Daily* carried a defensive editorial asserting that the "U.S. imperialists' attempt to impose war on the Chinese people comes at a time when they are making a big leap on the road to socialist construction" (i.e., they are not interested in a military confrontation), and that the Chinese people "have every right to liberate their own territory by all suitable means at a suitable time" (that is, not at present).[142]

It was only after this public expression of Peking's willingness to seek a political solution to the crisis that Khrushchev sent a message to President Eisenhower warning that "an attack against China is tantamount to an attack against the Soviet Union"—a tardy and ambiguous response in its military implications that was nonetheless given wide publicity in the Chinese press.

As the Straits crisis thus entered a diplomatic phase, Mao emphasized the turning of this confrontation with "U.S. imperialism" into a context for motivating still greater "leaps" in the areas of production and social reorganization by promoting a nationwide campaign to make "everyone a soldier." [143] Mao thus speeded the militarization of the rural work force and the implementation of his new national defense line which called for large militia units. His personal support for these developments was emphasized by a publicized tour in late September of production facilities in newly communized areas of central China.

Whether or not one assumes that Mao had consciously exacerbated the confrontation in the Taiwan Straits in part as a test of Soviet and American responses, it seems evident that as a result of the demonstrated Soviet reluctance to back a "fraternal Party" in a confrontation with the "imperialists and their lackeys," Mao could

142. *People's Daily* editorial, "Six Hundred Million People Mobilize to Crush the U.S. Aggressors' Military Threats and War Provocations!" (September 7, 1958); trans. in *SCMP,* No. 1851 (September 11, 1958), pp. 3, 6.

143. National publicity was given to this movement beginning on September 11th. *See* NCNA dispatches in *SCMP,* No. 1856 (September 18, 1958), pp. 17–19.

affirm the correctness of his earlier judgment that China should be independent of the Soviets in matters of defense. Yet as with the "blooming and contending" confrontation with the intellectuals of the preceding year, one cannot be certain that Mao had manipulated a "struggle" situation to make a political point clear to resistant colleagues within the Party leadership.

While in a strategic sense Mao could claim his judgment vindicated by these developments, tactically the Russians had seriously let him down by requiring a retreat before a "paper tiger." Mao's rage at Khrushchev for this further betrayal of "proletarian internationalism" was hinted at after the crisis had passed into its political phase. A *Red Flag* editorial of September 16th, entitled "The U.S. Aggressors Have Put Nooses around Their Own Necks," stressed that the "tense situations" created by the Americans around the world only helped to mobilize "the People" to make revolution. But the editorial went on to observe that

> up to now there are still some people who have failed to understand this reality. They often overestimate the strength of the enemy and underestimate the strength of the people. . . . They often only see the fact that some ice-bound rivers are not yet thawing as a whole, but fail to see the torrential streams underneath which will soon break up the ice completely and rise in mighty waves.[144]

The unusual imagery of the "ice-bound rivers" would seem to have been intended to evoke in Chinese minds the picture of the "allies" to the north across the frozen Amur and Ussuri rivers, and to make it clear to politically sensitized minds that those "some people" who failed to understand the weakness of "imperialism" included Khrushchev. This theme was to be repeated in late October with the republication of Mao's 1945 work, "Imperialists and All Reactionaries Are Paper Tigers." The introductory editorial again observed that, "At present there are quite a few people who still fail to see [that the United States is a paper tiger], and still remain in a state of passivity." [145]

The full extent of Mao's rage at the now lengthy record of Soviet failures to assist their "fraternal allies" in China—a record that Mao, with no little justice, could contrast with evidence of repeated Chinese sacrifices on behalf of Soviet security going back to the 1920s—erupted publicly in the open polemics of 1963. The

144. *Red Flag* editorial, "The U.S. Aggressors Have Put Nooses around Their Own Necks" (September 14, 1958); trans. in *SCMP*, No. 1856 (September 18, 1958), p. 4.

145. "Comrade Mao Tse-tung on 'Imperialists and All Reactionaries Are Paper Tigers,' " *People's Daily* (October 31, 1958); trans. in *Current Background*, No. 534 (November 12, 1958), p. 1.

Chinese gave a blistering reply to Soviet charges that in the Straits crisis they had tried to provoke a "head-on clash" between Russia and the United States:

> Our answer is: No, friends. You had better cut out your sensation-mongering calumny. The Chinese Communist Party is firmly opposed to a "head-on clash" between the Soviet Union and the United States, and not in words only. In deeds too it has worked hard to avert direct armed conflict between them. Examples of this are the Korean War against U.S. aggression in which we fought side by side with the Korean comrades and our struggle against the United States in the Taiwan Straits. We ourselves preferred to shoulder the heavy sacrifices necessary and stood in the first line of defense of the socialist camp so that the Soviet Union might stay in the second line.[146]

The clear implication of this expression of controlled rage was that the Soviets had not "shouldered heavy sacrifices" on behalf of the socialist camp, but had repeatedly hidden themselves behind Chinese skirts. And in a direct refutation of Soviet assertions that they had invoked their nuclear weapons in behalf of Chinese security during the off-shore island confrontation, the Chinese detailed:

> What are the facts? In August and September of 1958, the situation in the Taiwan Straits was indeed very tense as a result of the aggression and provocations by the U.S. imperialists. The Soviet leaders expressed their support for China on September 7 and 19 respectively. Although at that time the situation . . . was tense, there was no possibility that a nuclear war would break out and no need for the Soviet Union to support China with its nuclear weapons. It was only when it was clear that this was the situation that the Soviet leaders expressed their support for China.[147]

Mao had thus "tested the wind" and found the Russians unwilling to translate their temporary superiority in a nuclear weapon delivery system into efforts to resolve an outstanding political-military issue of great importance to the Chinese. Yet the initiative in the events of the fall had been with Mao, and there were both domestic and international prices which would have to be paid for this exposure of Soviet reticence.

The meaning of the fall confrontation for the Sino-Soviet defense relationship almost certainly was one of the issues which Defense Minister P'eng Teh-huai had to deal with in a tour of the

146. *People's Daily* and *Red Flag* joint editorial, "Two Different Lines on the Question of War and Peace," in *Polemic on the General Line of the International Communist Movement*, p. 246.

147. "Statement of the Spokesman of the Chinese Government" (September 1, 1963), in Garthoff, ed., *Sino-Soviet Military Relations*, p. 233.

Soviet Union and Eastern Europe between April 24th and June 13th, 1959. P'eng was in Albania during Khrushchev's visit to what within a few years was to become China's lonely "fraternal ally"; and the Defense Minister's critics were later to charge that, "He informed baldheaded Khrushchev of the shortcomings of the Great Leap Forward, and the latter encouraged the former to go home and oppose Chairman Mao." [148]

The Chinese later revealed that one week after P'eng's return from his trip to Eastern Europe, on June 20th, the Soviets "unilaterally tore up the agreement on new technology for national defense." [149] It seems likely that this development was somehow related to P'eng's trip, although it is not yet known whether the Defense Minister had engaged in secret negotiations with the Soviets concerning the now strained defense relationship between the two countries. Perhaps the Russians presented the Chinese Party leadership with certain demands through P'eng which they refused to accept, and then broke the agreement. It seems likely, however, that the Russians timed the breaking of the agreement to try to strengthen the hands of those within the Chinese leadership who might oppose Mao on economic and military issues at the coming Central Committee Plenum.

Such was the political climate after P'eng returned to China, and within a month he circulated his "Letter of Opinion" to the Party leaders at Lushan. What has been reported as P'eng's letter of self-criticism to Mao contains no reference to his dealings with Khrushchev, and the excerpt from the Central Committee Resolution condemning P'eng's "anti-Party clique" suggests that the "Party should continue to adopt an attitude of great sincerity and warmth" toward P'eng.[150] Furthermore, the Defense Minister—in contrast to Kao Kang—was given lenient personal treatment after his dismissal. Hence, it seems most likely that P'eng's errors had

148. "The Criminal History of Big Conspirator, Big Ambitionist, Big Warlord P'eng Teh-huai," in *The Case of P'eng Teh-huai,* p. 204.

The 1961 study of the P'eng case by David A. Charles indicates that P'eng had been charged with giving a "letter" of criticism of Mao's policies to Khrushchev during their meeting in Tirana. (*See* "The Dismissal of P'eng Teh-huai," *The China Quarterly,* No. 8 [October–December 1961], pp. 67, 74.) This "letter" was not mentioned in Cultural Revolution documents on the P'eng affair.

149. "Statement by the Spokesman of the Chinese Government" (August 15, 1963), in *SCMP,* No. 3043 (August 20, 1963), p. 36.

150. "Resolution of the Eighth Plenary Session of the Eighth Central Committee of the Communist Party of China Concerning the Anti-Party Clique Headed by P'eng Teh-huai (Excerpts)," in *The Case of P'eng Teh-huai,* p. 44.

been to engage in excessively critical or indiscreet discussions with the detested Khrushchev and Russian military leaders concerning China's internal affairs, and to present criticisms to the Eighth Plenum which "objectively" placed him on the same political ground as the increasingly "revisionist" Soviets.[151]

Behind Mao's uncompromising response to P'eng's critique of the Great Leap Forward was the complex set of issues of personal authority, development strategy, and national defense line which Khrushchev had raised beginning with the Soviet Twentieth Party Congress. P'eng was said to have *"depended entirely on the Khrushchev revisionist clique* for the improvement of our army's equipment and the development of up-to-date military science and technology, in a futile attempt to *turn our army into a dependency of that clique."* [152] The Defense Minister's actions had tapped the intense emotionalism of a leader rebelling against a political culture of dependency:

> . . . the attitude Comrade Khrushchev has adopted is patriarchal, arbitrary and tyrannical. He has in fact treated the relationship between the great Communist Party of the Soviet Union and our Party not as one between brothers, but as one between patriarchal father and son.[153]

The assertive Mao, for his part, had now alienated Khrushchev through the exaggerated claims which had been made for the People's Communes, and his initiative in the Taiwan Straits. Following the Lushan Plenum it was little more than a matter of time before the strains between the two leaderships became public. The Chinese claimed that the Russians brought the dispute "right into the open before the whole world" by verbally siding with the Indians in Sino-Indian border clashes which grew from the rebellion in Tibet in the spring of 1959.[154] And when Khrushchev came to China to

151. The lenient treatment accorded P'eng may also reflect the efforts of his supporters within the Party leadership to mitigate Mao's counterattack. As we shall stress in the next chapter, evidence strongly supports the interpretation that during the 1960s there was continuing pressure from within the leadership to "reverse the verdict" on P'eng once the aftermath of the Great Leap Forward had more fully vindicated his criticism of Mao's policy.

152. "Settle Accounts with P'eng Teh-huai for His Crimes of Usurping Army Leadership and Opposing the Party," in *The Case of P'eng Teh-huai,* p. 165. Emphasis added.

153. "Statement of the Delegation of the Communist Party of China at the Bucharest Meeting of Fraternal Parties" (June 26, 1960), in *Polemic on the General Line of the International Communist Movement,* p. 110.

154. *People's Daily* and *Red Flag* editorial, "The Origin and Development of the Differences between the Leadership of the CPSU and Ourselves," in *ibid.,* p. 77.

attend celebrations marking the Tenth Anniversary of the founding of the People's Republic—just after his September meeting with Eisenhower at Camp David—he is said to have "read China a lecture against 'testing by force the stability of the capitalist system.' "[155]

Before long, the "unbreakable" Sino-Soviet alliance was sundered by these fully developed strains over defense and development strategies, leadership, and political line. The Chinese escalated the dispute to the level of ideological polemics with publication of the April 1960 theoretical challenge "Long Live Leninism!" and three months later the Soviets suddenly began to remove from China all their scientific and technical experts working on aid projects.

Thus Mao had pushed his differences with Khrushchev to the point of an open break between the two countries rather than compromise on issues which he felt would sacrifice China's interests and the future of the revolution. And while this confrontation brought with it great costs in the areas of economic assistance and national defense, Mao sought to turn even these losses to advantage by mobilizing hatred for the "revisionist" Soviets in order to build China's "revolutionary vigor." The *People's Daily* observed as the Soviet advisers were being withdrawn:

> Where does revolutionary vigor come from? . . . Only when you are conscious of having been oppressed and cheated, and don't want to be placed in this kind of a position, and because of this suppress a stomach full of anger—get angry enough to want to go and change the situation —only then can you produce a lot of revolutionary vigor. To use a Chinese proverb, this is "drawing strength from anger" (*fa-fen t'u-ch'iang*), this is revolutionary spirit.[156]

THE DEEPENING CRISIS OF LEADERSHIP

Mao was able to mobilize sufficient support at the Lushan Central Committee Plenum in the summer of 1959 to turn P'eng Teh-huai's criticisms of his "general line" for modernizing China into an attack on "right opportunism," and to have the Defense Minister replaced by the loyal Lin Piao.[157] Yet the deepening economic

155. *Ibid.,* p. 78.

156. "If You Want to Make Revolution You Must Have Revolutionary Spirit," *People's Daily* (August 13, 1960), p. 7. This article is an abridgment of the original version which appeared in the Shanghai periodical *Liberation*, No. 15 (1960).

157. The circumstances under which Mao was able to bring about P'eng's replacement as Defense Minister by Lin Piao remain one of the most obscure, yet important, aspects of political developments in the late 1950s leading to the Cultural Revolution. The fact that within three years after

Communist Party Chairman Mao Tse-tung Welcomes
Soviet Premier and Party First Secretary Nikita Khrushchev
at Peking Airport, September 30, 1959.
Brian Brake, from Rapho Guillumette.

crisis which grew from the Great Leap Forward was to serve as a powerful defense of P'eng's critique. By 1962, when the crisis reached its depth, the coalition of power which had enabled Mao to weather the Lushan challenge began to disintegrate.

Mao made a self-criticism before his Central Committee colleagues at Lushan. He observed: "Now I should be attacked because I have not exercised supervision over many things." [158] And he expressed awareness of how, in practice, the power of the word and popular activism had not justified "the abandonment of planning":

> Diseases enter by the mouth and all disasters come through the tongue. I'm in great trouble today. . . . I decided upon and promoted the target of 10,700,000 tons of steel, and as a result 90 million people were thrown into battle. . . . Next, the People's Communes. I did not invent the People's Communes, but I promoted them. When I was in Shantung a correspondent asked me: "Are the People's Communes good?" I said, "Good"; and on the basis of this he published a report in a newspaper. From now on, I must avoid reporters.[159]

The tension of the Plenum had been very great, and not all of Mao's comrades had, in Chinese fashion, put the bitterness "in their stomachs." Using his characteristic scatology, Mao revealed a hope that the "disasters of the tongue" would—like some evil air—pass away. He concluded: "This trouble I have brought on is a great one, and I hold myself responsible for it. Comrades, you also should analyze your own responsibilities, and you will all feel better after you have broken wind and emptied your bowels." [160]

Despite Mao's candor before his colleagues within the leadership, the question remained just how the Party organization and "the People" would assign responsibility for the deepening economic crisis. It was perhaps in response to this nagging question that the fourth volume of Mao's *Selected Works* was published in Septem-

---

Lin's rise an attempt was made to "reverse the verdict" on P'eng suggests that by 1962 other Party leaders were quite concerned about Mao's increasing reliance on the army as his base of power. Yet whether this possibility had been foreseen at Lushan is uncertain. At the same time that Liu was promoted, Lo Jui-ch'ing—who was to be purged in the early stages of the Cultural Revolution—was advanced to the position of Vice Minister of National Defense; but whether he had been elevated as part of a "deal" to balance off Lin's new power remains uncertain.

158. Mao Tse-tung, "Speech at the Lushan Conference" (July 23, 1959), in *Chairman Mao's Criticism and Repudiation of the P'eng, Huang, Chang and Chou Anti-Party Clique*, p. 10.

159. *Ibid.*

160. *Ibid.*, p. 11.

ber of 1960.[161] As a contemporary political document this book appears to be an attempt to reaffirm Mao's preeminent contribution to the Party's attainment of power. It contains the veiled assertion that leaders other than Mao had been responsible for "leftist" errors in the application of Party policy in the rural areas, and reaffirms the collective responsibility of the Party "center" for leadership decisions. Such an interpretation of Volume Four is most clearly seen if the editorial footnotes elaborating each article are taken as the main text, with the historical materials serving as documentation to affirm the continuity of accurate judgment or political error on the part of various Party leaders.[162]

Earlier we noted that Liu Shao-ch'i's political report to the Eighth Party Congress of 1956 had been notably silent on Mao's role in shaping Party policies which led to final victory over the Nationalists. The first twenty-three articles in Volume Four give clear emphasis to the position that only Mao's correct assessment of the balance of forces within China in 1945–46 led to the Party's successful prosecution of the Civil War.

The editorial notes stress that it was Mao, in August of 1945, who "unmask[ed] the counterrevolutionary face of Chiang K'ai-shek [in order to] teach the whole people to be on guard against his civil war plot." [163] "Some comrades [had] overestimated the strength of imperialism . . . [and] showed weakness in the face of the armed attacks of the U.S.-Chiang K'ai-shek gang and dared not resolutely oppose counterrevolutionary war with revolutionary war." [164] But

161. Publication of this volume may also have been timed to coincide with the November meeting of eighty-one Communist Party delegations in Moscow, as a way of emphasizing Mao's stature as a leader and theoretician.

162. I am indebted to Mr. John Gittings for having called my attention to the contemporary political relevance of the editorial footnotes in the fourth volume of Mao's *Selected Works*.

163. Introductory note to "Two Telegrams from the Commander-in-Chief of the Eighteenth Group Army to Chiang K'ai-shek" (August 1945), in *SW*, English, IV, p. 34.

164. Introductory note to "Some Points in Appraisal of the Present International Situation" (April 1946), in *ibid.*, p. 88.

The "some comrades" apparently include Stalin, for as Mao recalled to Party leaders in 1962, "Stalin tried to prevent the Chinese revolution by saying that there should not be any civil war." (Mao, "Speech at the Tenth Plenum of the Eighth CCP Central Committee" [September 24, 1962], in *Chairman Mao's Criticism and Repudiation of the P'eng, Huang, Chang, and Chou Anti-Party Clique*, p. 25.) Liu Shao-ch'i may have supported Stalin's position by claiming in 1945–46 that China was about to enter "a new era of peace and democracy" in which the Communist Party would challenge the Nationalists for power through political rather than military means. (*See* the *Red Flag* and *People's Daily* editorial, "Along the Socialist or Capitalist Road?" [August 17, 1967]; trans. in *Peking Review*, No. 34 [August 18, 1967], p. 13.)

"in accordance with the strategic plan laid down by Comrade Mao Tse-tung, the People's Liberation Army went over to the offensive" in the fall of 1947. And finally, as if to emphasize that it was Mao's sole responsibility to have mobilized the PLA for the Civil War, the notes reveal that it was after the Central Committee had divided into two groups—with Mao heading the Party Secretariat which went to northern Shensi Province, while a "working party" of the Central Committee headed by Liu Shao-ch'i went south to Hopei[165] —that Mao drafted the "Manifesto" of the PLA's victory offensive.[166]

The contemporary political purpose of this historical analysis seems to have been to recall to Party members in the strained situation of 1960 that the Party owed its power to Mao's correct judgments of the late 1940s. It also seems intended to recall the heroic contributions of various comrades at the Party and army's hour of triumph, and thus to reevoke a spirit of collective unity.

A second group of articles and editorial notes in Volume Four appears to express the view that a share of the blame for the "left opportunist" deviations of the Great Leap Forward was the responsibility of those Party members on the "first line" of leadership who held the authority for implementing policy. This is done through historical analogy, by revealing that in the past Liu Shao-ch'i had committed adventurist mistakes when promoting the Party's land reform policies. According to the editorial notes, Mao's December 1947 article, "The Present Situation and Our Tasks," had been described by the Central Committee at the time of its adoption as "a programmatic document . . . for the entire period of the overthrow of the reactionary Chiang K'ai-shek ruling clique and of the founding of a new-democratic China." [167] Party members were exhorted to apply this Party resolution strictly in practice.

Then with a series of personal references which make it clear that Liu Shao-ch'i was responsible for implementing Party policy in the Shansi-Suiyuan Liberated Area,[168] the articles reveal that serious "leftist" errors had occurred in areas under Liu's jurisdic-

165. "On the Temporary Abandonment of Yenan and the Defense of the Shensi-Kansu-Ningsia Border Region—Two Documents Issued by the Central Committee of the Communist Party of China" (November 1946, and April 1947), in *SW*, English, IV, p. 132, fn. 3.

166. Introductory note, "Manifesto of the Chinese People's Liberation Army" (October 1947), in *ibid.*, p. 148.

167. Introductory note to "The Present Situation and Our Tasks" (December 1947), *ibid.*, p. 158.

168. *See* especially the introductory note to "Different Tactics for Carrying Out the Land Law in Different Areas" (February 1948), p. 194; and the passage from "Speech at a Conference of Cadres in the Shansi-Suiyuan Liberated Area" (April 1948), *ibid.*, pp. 231–232.

tion. A telegram which Mao sent to Liu in February 1948 warns that, "Haste will certainly do no good" in promoting the Party's Land Law.[169] And an inner-Party directive instructs unnamed cadres: "Do not be impetuous" in carrying out land reform; "Do not start the work in all places at the same time, but choose strong cadres to carry it out first in certain places to gain experience, then spread the experience step by step and expand the work in waves." [170] The inference which Party members might draw, reading these documents in the wake of the communization drive, would have been that Liu, Mao's enthusiastic supporter on the "first line" of leadership, had been responsible once again for "leftist" errors —for the breakneck speed in Commune formation, and the indiscriminate application of a few model experiences throughout the country.

Finally, an article of April 1948 stresses:

> . . . while many comrades remember our Party's specific line for work and specific policies, they often forget its general line and general policy. If we actually forget the Party's general line and general policy, then we shall be blind, half-baked, muddle-headed revolutionaries, and when we carry out a specific line for work and a specific policy, we shall lose our bearings and vacillate now to the left and now to the right, and the work will suffer.[171]

It is clear that at the Lushan Plenum in the year before republication of these words of 1948, Mao's "general line" of 1958 had been challenged. Hence, this document seems to be significant as a warning to comrades that they must not abandon Mao's policy or else serious problems will arise on the economic front. And unless the Party learns to manage the nation's productive enterprises effectively, Mao asserted through this old article, "you cannot be called good Marxists." [172]

Whatever the justice of these historical insinuations that Liu Shao-ch'i bore much of the responsibility for the "leftist" errors of the Great Leap, it seems evident that Mao was concerned about being held responsible in isolation for the difficulties which resulted from implementation of the policies of 1958. Accordingly, a third group of articles in Volume Four deals with problems of consolidating Party unity on the eve of nationwide victory. Beginning

169. "Different Tactics for Carrying Out the Land Law in Different Areas," *ibid.*, p. 194.

170. "Essential Points in Land Reform in the New Liberated Areas" (February 1948), *ibid.*, p. 202.

171. "Speech at a Conference of Cadres in the Shansi-Suiyuan Liberated Area," *ibid.*, p. 238.

172. *Ibid.*, p. 33.

with a gratuitous editorial identification of Teng Hsiao-p'ing's responsibilities in this area of work,[173] Mao republished an article of May 1948 which noted with concern:

> There are people who, without authorization, modify the policies and tactics adopted by the Central Committee. . . . There are also people who, on the pretext of pressure of work, adopt the wrong attitude of neither asking for instructions before an action is taken nor submitting a report afterwards and who regard the area they administer as an independent realm.[174]

The republication of these words would have had doubtful political significance in 1960 were it not for the fact that during the Cultural Revolution Teng Hsiao-p'ing was to be attacked for precisely this error: After 1959 "he took arbitrary action in all things, and never made reports to or asked for instructions from Chairman Mao, who once criticized him for acting 'like the emperor.' " [175] Mao himself is reported to have complained at a meeting of the Party leadership in the fall of 1966, "Teng Hsiao-p'ing never consulted with me. He has never consulted with me about anything since 1959. In 1962 four vice premiers . . . came to Nanking to consult me. Later they went to Tientsin [to consult with me again]. I forthwith gave them my approval. . . . But Teng Hsiao-p'ing never came." [176]

Finally, the editorial notes reveal that in 1956 Teng Hsiao-p'ing had invoked a Party decision of 1948 which had been drafted by Mao as justification for the stress on collective leadership which Party leaders had used to restrict Mao's influence at the Eighth Party Congress.[177] In 1960, when Mao apparently feared that he alone would be blamed for the deepening economic crisis, the Party Chairman turned this argument of 1956 back on his critics. In an introductory note to the republished Central Committee resolution of 1948, the editors of Volume Four cite Teng Hsiao-p'ing by name and quote his words of 1956 on the need for "conscientious practice of collective leadership." [178] "The meaning of this citation for 1960

173. See the introductory note to "Tactical Problems of Rural Work in the New Liberated Areas" (May 1948), *ibid.*, p. 252.

174. "The Work of Land Reform and of Party Consolidation in 1948" (May 1948), *ibid.*, p. 258.

175. "Thirty-three Leading Counterrevolutionary Revisionists," trans. in *Current Background,* No. 874 (March 17, 1969), p. 5.

176. Mao, "Speech at a Report Meeting" (October 24, 1966), in *Long Live the Thought of Mao Tse-tung!* p. 45.

177. *See* p. 275 above.

178. Introductory note, "On Strengthening the Party Committee System" (September 1948), *SW,* English, IV, p. 268.

was that the Party leadership had to take collective responsibility for the Great Leap Forward, and that no one leader should be singled out as a scapegoat.

Mao's effort to sustain the unity of the leadership through collective responsibility, however, was to fail for two major reasons. First, Mao had been too obvious as the primary formulator and promoter of the "three red flags" of the Great Leap Forward, the People's Communes, and the "general line" of socialist construction. Second, the food and production crisis of the winter of 1961–62 was a powerful spokesman in support of P'eng Teh-huai's defeated Lushan critique. And according to later Maoist revelations, it was Liu Shao-ch'i himself who in early 1962 at a Central Committee work conference defended P'eng by observing of his 1959 "Letter of Opinion": "much is in conformity with the facts." [179] Liu was also accused of having encouraged P'eng to write "a document running into a full 80,000 words aimed at reversing the verdict passed on him." [180]

Such charges suggest that the P'eng issue contributed substantially to the eventual breakdown in the Mao-Liu coalition. The Party Chairman was able, once again, to defend his position at the Tenth Central Committee Plenum of September 1962—as is indicated by the Plenum communiqué's assertion that the "great historic significance" of the Lushan Plenum of 1959 had been that it "victoriously smashed attacks by right opportunism." [181] Nevertheless the increasing strains within the Party leadership were revealed by new assertions of the inevitability of class struggle, which was said to be "very sharp" at times, finding expression even "within the Party." [182] Thus the "saddle-shaped" rhythm of policy swing from "right" to "left" and back which Mao had tried to "ride" in pushing China's social advance began to fall apart as the Party leadership became increasingly polarized over basic questions of personal authority and social vision.

THE SEARCH FOR A CONFLICT MANAGER

One of the major themes in Parts Three and Four of this study has been Mao's effort to institutionalize forms of disciplined political

179. *Red Flag* editorial, "From the Defeat of P'eng Teh-huai to the Bankruptcy of China's Khrushchev," No. 13 (1967); trans. in *Peking Review,* No. 34 (August 18, 1967), p. 20.

180. *Ibid.*

181. "Communiqué of the Tenth Plenary Session of the Eighth Central Committee of the Chinese Communist Party," NCNA (September 28, 1962) in *Current Background,* No. 691 (October 5, 1962), p. 4.

182. *Ibid.,* pp. 3–4.

conflict in order to attain power and promote social change. This effort was to become a central issue in the deepening leadership crisis which grew out of the Great Leap Forward.

In 1960 Mao had republished an article of 1948 which seems to express his view of the pattern of Party leadership over the preceding five years:

> The history of our Party shows that Right deviations are likely to occur in periods when our Party has formed a united front with the Kuomintang and that "Left" deviations are likely to occur in periods when our Party has broken with the Kuomintang.[183]

Mao was apparently drawing a parallel between this earlier era and his perception of the two periods we have been describing in these last two chapters: In 1956–57 the Party had "allied" itself with the bourgeois intellectuals in a manner which he felt was producing "right opportunism" within the Party; and in 1958, after the "break" with the intellectuals in June of 1957, the Party had committed "leftist" deviations in promoting the "three red flag" policies for economic development.

Who was responsible for these deviations? In the largest sense perhaps the Party as a whole, for as we have tried to show, it was resistance to Mao's political initiatives by other Party leaders or by lower level cadres which produced the abrupt swings in policy between "right" and "left." Mao apparently found that the political tensions of rectification campaigns and mass movements were needed to goad cadres and the population as a whole into institutionalizing the "transition to socialism." Yet as he revealed in his editorial observations in *Socialist Upsurge in China's Countryside,* Mao saw the deviations of lower-level cadres as resulting from "opportunism" within the Party leadership.[184] In Volume Four he sought to stress that deviations in leadership were the responsibility of those on the "first line" who were charged with implementing Party decisions.

In regard to these policy swings between "right" and "left" there remains one important matter of interpretation which we have not yet confronted: How was it that Liu Shao-ch'i, who had had "misgivings" about Mao's economic policies and the "blooming and contending" line in 1956–57, also could have been one of the Chairman's most vocal supporters during the Great Leap Forward? This question evidently bothered Mao, too. Possibly a major issue in the breakdown of relations between these two leaders—which

183. "A Circular on the Situation" (March 1948), *SW*, English, IV, p. 219.
184. Mao, ed., *Socialist Upsurge in China's Countryside,* p. 138.

was to become apparent only during the Cultural Revolution—was Mao's feeling that Liu was not an effective "conflict manager," and that over the years he had not promoted the social conflict necessary to sustain the revolution.

Previously we noted that Mao reserved his most biting criticism for those Party leaders who had not dealt successfully with conflict situations: He disparaged Ch'en Tu-hsiu for his fear of armed struggle, and criticized Li Li-san for impulsively pressing conflict where it led only to defeat.[185] In one of his writings from the late 1920s Mao had observed that "right" and "left" opportunism sometimes were evident in the behavior of one individual.[186] This pattern was personified first in the policy lines of Wang Ming, and later in the behavior of P'eng Teh-huai[187] and Khrushchev.[188] Liu Shao-ch'i drew Mao's ire for a similar pattern of policy misjudgment: a "wavering" between avoidance of conflict when it was opportune, and the inability to promote struggle with discipline when it was necessary.

The Maoist critique of Liu's errors in leadership, as it came to be expressed publicly in 1967, stresses his misjudgment of the situation in 1945 as "a new phase of peace and democracy" in which the Party would limit itself to a "parliamentary" struggle against the Kuomintang.[189] Subsequently Liu is said to have been responsible for "leftist" errors during the period of civil war land reform: for permitting "excessive burning and killing" in the struggles against the landlords, and for allowing undue strictness to be used in assigning class status in the rural areas, thus disrupting agri-

185. *See* pp. 180, 185 above.

186. *See* p. 187 above.

187. In a denunciation of P'eng in 1959, Lin Piao is reported to have told unspecified Party members: ". . . Comrade Mao Tse-tung cannot tolerate his [P'eng's] Right opportunism, nor his 'Left' opportunism." ("Vice Chairman Lin's Talk about P'eng Teh-huai [Excerpts]" [October 12, 1959], in *Ko-ming Tsao-fan Pao* [Revolutionary Rebellion Journal] [November 25, 1967].) Examples of rightist tendencies were said to be his support of Kao Kang in 1953 and his activities at Lushan; while his leftism was illustrated by his initiative in promoting the "Battle of a Hundred Regiments" in the winter of 1940. (*See* additional documentation on these charges in *The Case of P'eng Teh-huai*, pp. 136, 160.)

188. After Khrushchev fell from power the Chinese jeered: "Pursuing an adventurist policy at one moment, he transported missiles to Cuba, and pursuing a capitulationist policy at another, he docilely withdrew the missiles and bombers from Cuba on the order of the U.S. pirates. . . . In so doing, Khrushchev brought a humiliating disgrace upon the great Soviet people unheard of in the forty years and more since the October Revolution." (*Red Flag* editorial, "Why Khrushchev Fell" [November 21, 1964], in *Polemic on the General Line of the International Communist Movement*, pp. 485–486.)

189. *See* note 164 above.

cultural production through excessive restriction of the rich and middle peasant economy.[190]

During the land reform after Liberation, Liu apparently swung well to the "right" in handling class struggle—perhaps overreacting to Mao's criticism of his errors of the late 1940s. In his 1950 report on land reform Liu stressed that

> chaotic conditions (*hun-luan hsien-hsiang*) must not be allowed to occur, and no deviation or confusion may be allowed to remain uncorrected for long in our agrarian reform work in the future. Agrarian reform must be carried out under guidance, in a planned and orderly way.[191]

Liu's "rightist" stress on guidance and order—and the playing down of class struggle—was to endure through mid-1957. He was lenient toward the "national capitalists," [192] failed to support socialization of the rural economy when Mao thought the moment ripe, and resisted the struggle with "rightist conservatism" among the intellectuals and within the Party in 1956–57.

Liu's public support for the Great Leap Forward in the fall of 1957 suggests his renewed conversion to the Left; yet as our interpretation of Volume Four indicates, Mao apparently held Liu responsible for failure to guide the mass movement properly. He was "Left," not Left,[193] and incurred Mao's disfavor for his lack of skill in promoting the "mass line" style of leadership.

Liu's willingness to "reverse verdicts" on Great Leap critics in 1962 reveals his swing back to the "right." During the Cultural Revolution he was to be attacked for promoting policies in the rural areas between 1963 and 1965 which were characterized as "left in form but right in essence." [194]

This latter charge suggests the difficulty of relying on categories of "right" and "left" in analyzing Liu's policy positions. Rather, Mao seems to be responding to something much more basic in Liu's style of leadership—his inability to promote conflict with judgment

190. These charges, which Mao revealed in the fourth volume of his *Selected Works* as discussed earlier, were admitted by Liu in his second self-criticism. (*See* "The Confession of Liu Shao-ch'i," *Atlas* [April 1967], p. 15.)

191. Liu Shao-ch'i, "Report on the Question of Agrarian Reform" (June 1950), in *The Agrarian Reform Law of the People's Republic of China* (Peking: Foreign Languages Press, 1959), p. 62.

192. *See* the *Red Flag* and *People's Daily* editorial, "Along the Socialist or the Capitalist Road?"; trans. in *Peking Review*, No. 34 (August 18, 1967), p. 13.

193. *See* above, Chapter X, fn. 47, for "left" vs. left.

194. *See* Richard Baum and Frederick C. Teiwes, "Liu Shao-ch'i and the Cadre Question," *Asian Survey*, Vol. VIII, No. 4 (April 1968), pp. 323–345.

and skill. The attacks on Liu during the Cultural Revolution thus reveal Mao's fear that the style of leadership which he has evolved over a lifetime of struggle, and which he feels is still essential to sustaining China's social advance, will go with his passing. The polemical charges hurled at Liu as "China's Khrushchev" likewise reveal Mao's concern about the continuing appeal for certain Party leaders of "revisionist" policies advocated by Russia's Khrushchev—policies which Mao bitterly rejected as unsuited to China's development needs and likely to sustain the political culture of dependency.

Attacks on Liu in 1967 accuse him of propagating a theory of "cultivation" of Party members which would have turned cadres into "docile tools," "blindly obedient" to their organizational superiors,[195] of advocating a "dying out of class struggle,"[196] and of advising other Communist Parties to lay down their arms and give up the struggle against imperialism and its lackies.[197] These charges reflect Mao's personal assertiveness and his determination to find a "revolutionary successor" committed to sustaining his life-long effort to institutionalize a revolutionary political culture after his death. It is this determination which was to lead Mao in the early 1960s to the Great Proletarian Cultural Revolution, a mass political upheaval directed against "revisionism" in the Chinese Communist Party out of which was to emerge a leader with demonstrated skills as a political "conflict manager"—Chou En-lai.[198] The development and course of the Cultural Revolution is the subject of the next chapter in this study.

195. *See* Red Guards' Regiment of the Philosophy and Social Sciences Department of Mao Tse-tung's Thought under the Chinese Academy of Sciences, "Bury the Slave Mentality Advocated by China's Khrushchev," *People's Daily* (April 6, 1967); trans. in *SCMP*, No. 3920 (April 17, 1967), pp. 1–7; and *People's Daily* editorial, "Refuting the Reactionary Theory of 'Docile Tools' " (April 10, 1967); trans. in *SCMP*, No. 3922 (April 19, 1967), pp. 8–11.

196. *See Liberation Army Daily* editorial, "Fight for the Thorough Criticism and Repudiation of the Number One Person in Authority Taking the Capitalist Road" (April 11, 1967); trans. in *SCMP*, No. 3918 (April 13, 1967), pp. 1–4.

197. *See* Cheng Li-chia, "Down with the Capitulationism of China's Khrushchev!" *People's Daily* (July 6, 1967); trans. in *Peking Review*, No. 31 (July 28, 1967), pp. 19–22.

198. *See* the analysis by Thomas W. Robinson, "Chou En-lai and the Cultural Revolution in China," in Thomas W. Robinson, ed., *The Cultural Revolution in China* (Berkeley and Los Angeles: University of California Press, 1971), pp. 165–293.

Chapter XIX

A CULTURAL REVOLUTION?
THE RECAPITULATION OF A
POLITICAL CAREER

A revolution probably ends only when opportunists join the ranks and undermine it
from within.

LU HSÜN, 1928[1]

Thought, culture, customs must be born of
struggle, and the struggle must continue for
as long as there is still a danger of a return
to the past. Fifty years is not a long time;
barely a lifetime—our customs must become
as different from the traditional customs as
yours [in France] are from feudal customs.

MAO TSE-TUNG,
TO ANDRÉ MALRAUX, 1965[2]

A great revolutionary rebellion must be
launched against the old ideas, old culture,
old customs and old habits and all things opposed to the thought of Mao Tse-tung!

RED GUARDS OF PEKING,
July 1966[3]

1. Lu Hsün, "Wiping Out the Reds—A Great Spectacle," in *Selected Works of Lu Hsün* (Peking: Foreign Languages Press, 1959), Vol. III, p. 42.
2. André Malraux, *Anti-Memoirs* (New York: Holt, Rinehart and Winston, 1968), p. 374.
3. The Red Guards of Tsinghua University Middle School, "Third Comment on Long Live the Rebellious Revolutionary Spirit of the Proletariat," *Red Flag*, No. 11 (August 21, 1966), p. 2.

The years of crisis brought on by the Great Leap Forward heightened the social and political tensions which we have explored in the two preceding chapters. Most basic were the problems in the rural areas. The collective organization of agriculture weakened as peasants sought to "go it alone" either by engaging in "sideline" production on their private plots or by seeking nonagricultural employment—thus swelling the numbers of uprooted rural workers in China's major cities.

This diffusion of economic discipline was heightened by a general relaxation of political controls as the social discontent surrounding the production crisis increased in intensity. As a result of unpopular Party policies, peasants were reluctant to assume the responsibilities of basic Party and governmental leadership in the rural areas. Former cadres complained that to bear the burdens of local leadership was to "eat a loss" (*ch'ih-k'uei*); and in Lien-chiang County, Fukien, almost 10 percent of the basic level cadres expressed the desire to resign from their posts.[4]

This erosion of leadership was compounded by abuses of authority on the part of many of the cadres who remained. They used the power of their offices to weather the hardships of the "three bitter years." Gambling, economic speculation, religious frauds, and a return to the practice of money marriages, were varied manifestations of the deep anxiety generated by the production crisis.[5] As one production team Party branch secretary reported to the county Party committee:

> At present [early 1963], production and standards of living are not good and difficulties remain, even though some persons are demanding and extravagant with everything. The problem of excessive eating and drinking is also very severe and is also prominent among cadre members. As a result, a number of those among the masses have said that if we do not oppose these evil tendencies, it will be difficult to strengthen and expand the collective economy of the people's communes. . . . This is especially so in regard to the problems of excessive eating and drinking, taking of special privileges and conveniences, and excessive spending and borrowing by the cadres.[6]

4. Richard Baum and Frederick C. Teiwes, *Ssu-ch'ing: The Socialist Education Movement of 1962–1966* (Berkeley: Center for Chinese Studies, University of California Research Monograph No. 2, 1968), p. 12, note 4. *See also* Appendix A.

5. Such phenomena stemming from the Great Leap crisis are revealed throughout the "Lien-chiang" documentary collection. *See* C. S. Chen, ed., *Rural People's Communes in Lien-Chiang* (Stanford, Calif.: Hoover Institution Press, 1969).

6. "Report of the Expanded Cadre Meeting of the Ch'ang-sha Brigade" (February 20, 1963), in *ibid.*, pp. 213–214.

The Party was finding itself "cut off from the masses." And that natural political authority which is sustained by success became seriously eroded—for the Party at large and for Mao personally within the Party. It was Mao's own conception of the manner in which Chinese society should be organized during the period of socialist construction which seemed to carry much of the responsibility for the hardships.

This crisis of authority within the Chinese Communist Party was manifest during the years 1961–62 by veiled yet sharp criticism of Mao's policies and his style of leadership. There developed strong pressure to reverse the condemnation of the Lushan critics of 1959, for the reality of events seemed to have proven them right. Mao, however, remained unyielding in his commitment to the conception of the Communes and to the importance of waging struggles against the "right opportunism" of his domestic critics, and the now open political attacks and economic difficulties created by the Soviet "revisionists." During the Party debates in the wake of the Great Leap crisis, Mao increasingly defended the correctness of his "three red flag" policies as a matter of his personal authority. His uncompromising stress at the Tenth Central Committee Plenum in September of 1962 on the need to press "class struggle" at home and to wage an unyielding polemic with the Soviet Party was in part a manifestation of the deepening challenge from within the Chinese Party to his own position of leadership.

In earlier chapters we noted that during the 1950s, Mao had repeatedly challenged the Party to remain true to its revolutionary goals—to prevent a new polarization of class relationships in the villages, to promote the development of a collectivized economy, and to discipline Party ranks against the insidious influence of "bourgeois conservatism" among the intellectuals. In the early 1960s, as his own position within the Party weakened, Mao phrased his concern about the Party's commitment to promote social revolution in more somber terms: He warned that unless a determined effort were made to resist the reemergence of old social habits and patterns of leadership new China would "change color" from revolutionary red to the white of a bourgeois revisionist party. There was the increasing danger, he asserted, of "a restoration of capitalism." [7]

The endurance of the basic social problems the Party had con-

7. This evaluation was given its most developed expression in the programmatic *People's Daily* and *Red Flag* joint editorial, "On Khrushchev's Phoney Communism and Its Historical Lessons for the World" (July 14, 1964), in *Polemic on the General Line of the International Communist Movement.*

fronted during the 1950s seems to have brought home to Mao the
fact that although more than a decade of effort had been devoted to
smashing the state machinery of China's prerevolutionary political
order, the old political culture continued to endure. It was rooted
in the personalities and "work style" (*tso-feng*) of the millions of
Chinese who participated in the organizational life of the Party,
state, and economic system. Hence, he concluded, "class struggle"
had to be sustained. As this idea was expressed in the communiqué
of the Party's Tenth Plenum which met in September 1962:

> Throughout the historical period of transition from capitalism to
> communism (which will last scores of years or even longer), there is
> class struggle between the proletariat and the bourgeoisie and struggle
> between the socialist road and the capitalist road. The reactionary
> ruling classes which have been overthrown are not reconciled to their
> doom. They always attempt to stage a come-back. Meanwhile, there
> still exists in society bourgeois influence, the force of habit of the old
> society and the spontaneous tendency towards capitalism among a
> part of the small producers [peasants]. . . . Class struggle is inevi-
> table under these circumstances. This class struggle inevitably finds
> expression within the Party. . . . [We] must remain vigilant and
> resolutely oppose in good time various opportunistic ideological tend-
> encies within the Party.[8]

This gnawing perception that, despite the great organizational
changes of the 1950s, the forces of habit of the old society were
constantly trying to "stage a come-back," pervades Maoist pronouncements of the 1960s with increasing pessimism. In the rural
areas Party cadres warned of "the power of old customs":

> The peasants have gone through several thousand years of feudal
> control and more than a hundred years of semifeudal semicolonial
> control. . . . Although they have received ten years of education in
> socialist ideology since the liberation, the peasants fall back on the
> old customs when the opportunity occurs.[9]

By 1964 this concern with the reemergence of old cultural patterns was more formally stressed to the entire Party and the International Movement:

> The socialist revolution on the economic front (in the ownership of
> the means of production) is insufficient by itself and cannot be con-

---

8. Cited from the NCNA English translation of the Plenum communiqué;
in *Current Background,* No. 691 (October 5, 1962), pp. 3–4.

9. Wang Hung-chih, "Implementation of the Resolution of the Tenth
Plenum of the Eighth Central Committee on Strengthening the Collective
Economy and Expanding Agricultural Production," in Chen, ed., *Rural
People's Communes in Lien-Chiang,* p. 97.

solidated. There must also be a thorough socialist revolution on the political and ideological fronts. Here *a very long period of time is needed to decide "who will win" in the struggle between socialism and capitalism. Several decades won't do it; success requires anywhere from one to several centuries.* On the question of duration, it is better to prepare for a longer rather than a shorter period of time. On the question of effort, it is better to regard the task as difficult rather than easy. It will be more advantageous and less harmful to think and act in this way. Anyone who fails to see this or appreciate it fully will make tremendous mistakes.[10]

It was the combined perception of the erosion of his authority within the Party and a preoccupation with the fact that despite more than a decade of Party rule traditional customs and habits, culture and thinking continued to endure in the social practice of the Chinese people that shaped Mao's determination in the 1960s to press for a "class struggle" against these backward influences. This struggle was first to be promoted through a new "Socialist Education Movement"; but in time it led to the upheaval of the "Great Proletarian Cultural Revolution."

That Mao came to feel the need for a "Cultural Revolution" is perhaps the most basic reassurance that the underlying assumption of this study—that culture and personality are enduring influences shaping political behavior—is well founded. Although Party leaders continued to use Marxist rhetoric to articulate policy, many had come to question Marxism's basic assumption, that man's economic life determines his social behavior. Mao's stress on the need to "re-mold" people's thinking reveals his awareness that the basic factor shaping social action is the human personality. To be sure, the economic base in some measure shapes cultural superstructure, and culture, in turn, shapes personality. Yet a revolutionary alteration in economic relationships and the pattern of property ownership—in the short run—is likely to have but limited effect on the way people relate to each other, or on the assertion and response to authority.

While it would be too much to say that Mao and his close supporters have come to reject their commitment to Marxism, it is nonetheless noteworthy that as the 1960s progressed the Chairman's closest comrades talked more of the "thought of Mao Tse-tung" and less of the relevance of Marxism-Leninism as a theoretical guide for coping with the problems of China's social development.

10. *People's Daily* and *Red Flag* joint editorial, "On Khrushchev's Phoney Communism and Its Historical Lessons for the World," in *Polemic on the General Line of the International Communist Movement,* pp. 471–472. Emphasis added.

As we will detail, however, an important element within the Party leadership continued to see Marxism-Leninism rather than Mao's "thought" as their guide in charting China's path to Communism. Their policy disagreements with Mao were now considerably intensified as a result of the experiences of the Hundred Flowers episode and the crisis aftermath of the Great Leap Forward. Much of the drama of Chinese domestic politics after 1960 thus reflects the increasingly sharp divergence between those Party leaders who continued to see the social development of their country as but one part of a world revolutionary movement which drew its inspiration from the Soviet Marxist experience and those who "waved the red flag of the thought of Mao Tse-tung" as the guiding standard of China's revolution.

This divergence within the leadership, rooted in earlier disputes over policy, increasingly passed into questions of personal authority: Had justice been done to those who had been branded as "rightists" in the 1959 purge of P'eng Teh-huai? Who would succeed Mao in his position of leadership of both Party and nation? The question of succession ties together many of the political issues explored in earlier chapters of this study. By the Tenth Plenum, Mao came to question the revolutionary commitment of long-time comrades who had become increasingly resistant to maintaining the struggle with "bourgeois rightism" among the intellectuals, "revisionism" within the International Communist Movement, the peasants' "spontaneous tendencies toward capitalism," and deviations in both political orientation and practice by lower-level Party cadres.

The first half of the decade of the 1960s thus replays the major themes of the period 1955–1959 in the sense of reconfronting Mao and other Party leaders with the issues which had been dealt with in the great movements of the preceding decade. Yet there were significant new dimensions to these problems, and to the leadership's response to them. Mao was now in his seventies, and at one time during this period he was reported to be in poor health. In addition, the generation of leaders who had brought the revolution to the attainment of state power was increasingly divided over basic issues of policy for promoting the long period of "socialist construction." Further, for Mao there were disturbing signs that the younger generation was not firm in its commitment to the goals which its elders had struggled for through force of arms.

For Mao the 1960s was the reliving of his career: He had to face again many of the social and political problems of earlier years—a fact that was to be emphasized by the republication of many of his earlier writings, which he felt to be of continuing relevance. In a more direct way, however, as the Chairman lost influence over the

Party in the wake of the Great Leap Forward, he turned once again to the Army as the base of his power. In the period from Lin Piao's appointment as Defense Minister to the Eleventh Plenum of August 1966 he repeated the pattern of his rise to Party leadership from the Chingkang Mountains to the Tsunyi Conference by relying upon the People's Liberation Army as the instrument for insuring his influence over Chinese political life.

Mao's advancing age constituted an important limit on the reassertion of his authority, however. And his determination to institutionalize his own conception of a new political life for China led him to seek a way of passing on the lessons of the revolution to a new generation. He was seeking a way to combine theory with practice without relying on bookish recitations alone. At some point before the summer of 1966 Mao conceptualized a way of confronting in "unity and struggle" both the opposition of long-time Party leaders and the political immaturity of the younger generation. In the Cultural Revolution of 1966 Mao was to relive his political career vicariously by stimulating a new student generation to rebel against a Party organization which the Chairman had come to see as hopelessly compromised by "revisionist" thinking and habits in the use of power. In the "rebellion" of the student Red Guards, the aging Mao was to seek to father a new generation of student revolutionaries and bring them into a place of influence within China's political life.

In terms of this study, the events of the 1960s are also a recapitulation of the major issues we have explored, bringing together in sharp focus the major analytical themes developed in earlier chapters. In Mao's concern with the problems of cadres "overeating," in their vulnerability to "sugar-coated bullets," we see enduring problems with the discipline of power in a society with dominant oral traditions. Mao was to see the Party as increasingly "cut off" from the masses, again exposing that gap between superior and subordinate, state and society, which has been an enduring theme in Chinese political life. In the Party Chairman's isolation atop the Party bureaucracy we see one of the key psychological vulnerabilities of a culture which has laid such stress on interdependence. Mao was to turn his own isolation back upon those Party leaders who opposed his solutions to China's national resurgence by having them dragged out for isolated exposure and humiliation before the angered masses.

The manner in which Mao came to reassert his authority during the 1960s reflects the enduring Confucian concept of the "power of the word." It was through his writings, the "little red book" of *Quotations from Chairman Mao,* and emulation of model students of his "thought," that the Party Chairman sought to sustain his influence over the course of the Chinese revolution. And then, when such measures had proven ineffective, the man who throughout his career had attempted to convince his colleagues that controlled conflict should endure as a vital aspect of Chinese political life, purposefully provoked the "confusion" of a rebellion of youth to disorganize a Party and governmental apparatus that had become impervious to his will.

WILL GHOSTS AND DEMONS STAY BURIED?

Speaking of the internal conditions of . . . a socialist society . . . it has just grown from the old society, and in many areas the scars of the old society are still preserved. Lenin stated well, the corpse of the bourgeois society "cannot be put into a coffin and buried underground." In a socialist society, "the beaten capitalist society will corrupt and decompose in our midst, contaminate the air, and poison our life. From all sides, the corrupt and dead things will encircle the fresh, young and vital things." . . . . In addition to remaining in the minds of the people, bourgeois ideology also through various forms (such as certain cultural heritages) is ingeniously and somewhat attractively preserved, and over a very long historical period, will continue to spread its influence.[11]

The initial reaction of the Party organization to the Great Leap crisis was much the same as its response to the shock of Khrushchev's attack on Stalin: Collective ranks were closed, and the Party sought to affirm the correctness of its policies. Study of Volume Four of Mao's works was promoted nationwide by provincial Party organizations. Liu Shao-ch'i was quoted as deferring to Mao as "the greatest revolutionary and statesman in the history of China, and also the greatest theorist and scientist in the history of China." [12] The Chairman was said to be the Party's "best model" in "educating us not only in applying successful experiences but also in seizing the mistakes in our work and summing up the lessons of mistakes." [13]

11. Commentator, "Put Ideological Work in the Primary Position," *Red Flag*, No. 5 (March 17, 1964); trans. in *SCMM*, No. 412 (April 13, 1964), p. 3.

12. *Ch'ün-chung* [The Masses] editorial, "Build a Powerful Army of Marxist-Leninist Theoreticians," No. 3 (February 1, 1960); trans. in *SCMM*, No. 212 (May 23, 1960), p. 10. This publication is the theoretical magazine of the Kiangsu Provincial Party Committee, equivalent in function to the national publication *Red Flag*.

13. Hsiao Shu and Yang Fu, "The Party's Policy Is a Guarantee for Victory in Revolution," *Red Flag*, No. 22 (November 16, 1960); trans. in *SCMM*, No. 238 (December 5, 1960), p. 20.

Despite these assertions of solidarity and deference to Mao, the Party "center" was faced with very real problems of political discipline in its regional and local organizations. In a situation where the Chairman's policies seemed to be responsible for the difficulties of the Great Leap, regional leaders were proving to be increasingly unresponsive to guidance from the center, prompting the national Party to reaffirm the principle of "democratic centralism":

> In the case of questions which should and must be decided upon and made public by the Central Committee, the local Party organizations must not override their commissions and state their views in advance of the Central Committee. In regard to problems of a national nature, all spokesmen of the Party, including members of the Central Committee, may not state their views without the consent of the Central Committee.[14]

These words of Liu Shao-ch'i were strengthened in organizational terms by the creation, in the late fall of 1960, of six regional Party bureaus under the direct control of the Secretariat of the Party's Central Committee.[15] In one respect this development reflected the desire of the national Party leadership to maintain organizational discipline in the Great Leap crisis. Yet in another sense, it seemed to reflect the desire of certain Party leaders to build channels of political control which would render the provincial Party organizations less susceptible to the pressures of the Chairman.

One affirmation of this interpretation was to be the pattern of political purge during the Cultural Revolution: Mao found himself increasingly isolated by the Secretariat after 1960; and seeing his policies blocked or distorted in their implementation by the Party organization, he was to turn to the Army for political backing in an effort to remove from power those national Party leaders who continued to thwart his political initiatives.

In the immediate context of the Great Leap crisis, however, it appears that many within the Party attempted through subtle criticism to induce Mao to moderate his struggle against the many forms of "right opportunism" within the Party, among the intel-

14. Li Chien-chen, "Strengthen the Organization and Discipline and Consolidate the Solidarity and Unity of the Party," *Nan-fang Jih-pao* [Southern Daily, Canton] (November 26, 1960); trans. in *SCMP,* No 2416 (January 13, 1961), p. 2.

15. The creation of six regional Party bureaus was formally approved by the Ninth Central Committee Plenum in January 1961, along with the promotion of a new Party rectification campaign. (*See* "Communiqué of the Ninth Plenary Session of the Eighth Central Committee of the Chinese Communist Party" [January 20, 1961]; in *Current Background,* No. 644 [January 27, 1961], p. 4.)

lectuals, in rural life, and in the International Communist Movement, while continuing to express deference to the man and to his contributions to the revolution. The Chairman was still a powerful symbol of national unity and political authority, and the Party organization could repudiate him only at the cost of calling into question its assertion of being China's only source of "correct" political leadership. The Party was in large measure a prisoner of the Chairman's prestige and the unity which he gave the organization.

In early 1961 a slim book of ancient fables entitled *Stories about Not Fearing Ghosts* was published under the sponsorship of the Literary Research Institute of the Chinese Academy of Sciences and the All-China Federation of Literary and Artistic Circles. As the noted writer Ho Ch'i-fang indicated in the preface to this volume, the objective of republishing these ancient ghost stories was to publicize Mao's assertion that "all reactionaries are paper tigers" and awaken people to the fact that like ghosts, "imperialism, reactionaries, revisionism and all kinds of calamities" are not to be feared. "As far as Marxist-Leninists are concerned, all these can be beaten and overcome." [16] Ho noted that even China's ancient sage Confucius, in the *Analects,* had shown a progressive social attitude by disparaging the existence of ghosts; and he added that Mao himself, as a revolutionary student, had expressed the same view. Ho applauded this "scientific attitude," and he cited Mao's words on the importance of winning over all possible allies and avoiding "leftist" errors in the continuing struggle against contemporary political "ghosts."

Was Ho's preface actually in praise of Mao, or was it a sly way of turning the Party Chairman's own arguments back on him? Did the words imply, "True, revisionists and reactionaries continue to give us trouble, but let us not overestimate their strength and push the struggle to the point at which it causes us great loss?" As a wealth of Cultural Revolution materials were to affirm, this publication was part of a widespread yet subtle expression of protest from the intellectual community against Mao's policies—sentiments expressed within the context of a limited revival of the "Hundred Flowers" spirit of 1956.[17]

16. Ho Ch'i-fang, "Preface to *Stories about Not Fearing Ghosts,*" *Red Flag,* No. 3–4 (February 1, 1961); trans. in *SCMM,* No. 252 (March 13, 1961), p. 1.

17. The theory that "ghosts are harmless" was said to have been proposed in 1961 by the writer Liao Mo-sha, Director of the United Front Work Department of the Peking Municipal Party Committee, in order to "oppose the thought of Mao Tse-tung and vilify revolutionaries." (*See* "*Notes on San-chia Village* and *Night Causerie at Yenshan* Criticized by *Ch'ien Hsien* and

The 1956–57 slogan of "Let a hundred flowers bloom" was raised again in January 1961 by a *Red Flag* article which stressed the importance of a pragmatic and scientific approach to dealing with China's current problems: "Being Marxist-Leninists, we hold that questions of right and wrong in science are not decided by subjective 'convincing arguments,' but by their conformity or nonconformity to reality." [18] This was but one manifestation of a widespread distrust of revolutionary "spontaneity" brought on by the Great Leap Forward; one indication that certain Party leaders wanted to enforce "democratic centralism" and to have cadres be "docile tools" of the organization. [19]

By all evidence, the Hundred Flowers theme was reasserted at the initiative of Liu Shao-ch'i and other leaders who bore the "first line" burdens of seeing the country through the Great Leap crisis. [20] As had been true before the Great Leap Forward, many high-ranking officials continued to see the intellectuals and their skills as a major national resource in the development effort: The intellectuals should be protected from undue political pressure as long as they gave their services in support of the Party's economic and social policies.

This attitude was restated in early September 1961 by Foreign

Peking Jih-pao," Yang-ch'eng Wan-pao [Canton] [April 16, 1966]; trans. in *SCMP,* No. 3686 [April 28, 1966], p. 2.)

Chiang Ch'ing is said to have organized the publication of articles criticizing this viewpoint after the Tenth Plenum. (*See* Chung Hua-min and Arthur C. Miller, *Madame Mao: A Profile of Chiang Ch'ing* [Hong Kong: Union Research Institute, 1968], p. 95); and it became the subject of public attack during the "Cultural Revolution." (*See* the Red Guard publication, "Chiang Ch'ing's Outstanding Contributions to the Cultural Revolution," in *Hsin Pei-ta* [New Peking University], May 30, 1967.)

18. *Red Flag* editorial, "Stand Firm on the Policy of Letting a Hundred Flowers Bloom and a Hundred Schools of Thought Contend in Academic Research," No. 5 (February 28, 1961); trans. in *SCMP,* No. 2451 (March 8, 1961), p. 2.

19. *See,* for example, T'ao Teh-lin, "Be a Docile Tool of the Party," *People's Daily* (January 14, 1960); trans. in *SCMP,* No. 2184 (January 26, 1960), pp. 3–6.

This particular article observes that "some Party members imbued with serious bourgeois individualism are opposed to being docile tools of the Party," while wanting the Party to be their "docile tool" (p. 4). During the Cultural Revolution Mao was to attack Liu Shao-ch'i for having propagated the "docile tool" concept. (*See* p. 404 above.)

20. Liu publicly identified himself with the revival of the "Hundred Flowers" policy (which Mao did not) in a speech marking the Fortieth Anniversary of the founding of the Chinese Communist Party delivered at a rally in Peking on June 30th, 1961. *See* the NCNA translation of this speech in *Current Background,* No. 655 (July 12, 1961), p. 6.

Minister Ch'en Yi, in a commencement address to university graduates in Peking. Ch'en told the students that "The Party and State need you," and he stressed the importance of specialized knowledge and professional expertise for "the work of building up our country as a great socialist power with modern industry, modern agriculture, and modern science and culture." He also asserted that "there is, in my opinion, nothing wrong about [advanced students] taking part in political activities less frequently." [21] As we shall see, such an attitude was a direct challenge to Mao's concurrent effort to politicize the People's Liberation Army through the study of his writings.[22]

The Party's encouragement of pragmatism and professionalism in 1961 was accompanied by a general political relaxation in artistic and cultural life. During this year there appeared in the public media historical commentaries, anecdotal columns, poems, and plays on historical themes which were veiled yet biting criticisms of Mao for having led the Party and people into the Great Leap crisis. In the first months of the Cultural Revolution in 1966 attacks were to be focused on the authors of this material, with the "spear point" of the conflict eventually turning against those Party leaders who had given them encouragement and political protection.

One of the most notable of these critics of 1961–62 was the former editor of the *People's Daily,* and Cultural Director of the Peking Municipal Party Committee, Teng T'o. In newspapers and magazines under the direct control of the Peking Party Committee —of which P'eng Chen was First Secretary—Teng subjected the Party Chairman to veiled ridicule and political threats in the context of commentaries on historical topics. In a discussion of social difficulties during the Sung dynasty, he quoted an imperial magistrate who exhorted the powerful official Ssu-ma Kuang to heed the suggestions of lower-level officials. And in an oblique reference to Mao, Teng invoked the magistrate's complaint that there are

> some persons . . . who always want to assert their own ideas, attempt to win by surprise and refuse to accept the good ideas of the masses under them. If persons with such shortcomings do not wake up and rectify their shortcomings themselves, they will pay dearly one day.[23]

21. *See* this speech as published in *China Youth Journal* [*Chung-kuo Ch'ing-nien Pao*] (September 2, 1961); trans. in *SCMP*, No. 2581 (September 19, 1961), pp. 1–7.

22. *See* esp. pp. 437–442 below.

23. Cited in Merle Goldman, "The Unique 'Blooming and Contending' of 1961–62," *The China Quarterly,* No. 37 (January–March 1969), p. 77.

In an essay entitled "Talking Nonsense," Teng criticized those who rejected the work of China's scholars and scientific research workers, or who manifested a continuing distrust of the intellectual community. He complained of the Sung reformer Wang An-shih: "[Wang] considered everyone else inferior to himself and used to criticize them vehemently on no grounds at all. His major shortcoming was his lack of humility" [24]—apparently a veiled reference to Mao's attack on P'eng Teh-huai. In a column entitled, "How to Make Friends," Teng criticized Mao's obduracy in pressing the Sino-Soviet conflict to the point of an open break. In the article, "Who Were the Earliest Discoverers of America," he lauded the "long tradition of Chinese-American friendship." And in an essay, "Great Empty Talk," published in *Front Line* (*Ch'ien-hsien*), the theoretical magazine of the Peking Party Committee, he disparaged Mao's dictum that the "East wind" was now prevailing over the "West wind" as being clever words lacking in reality.[25]

In a society where words have been the touchstone of political power, such ridicule of the Chairman for "Talking Nonsense" and "Great Empty Talk" could not be a clearer expression of the erosion of his authority—and a challenge to which Mao was to respond in kind, by reasserting his influence through the "word" of his writings.

Political focus was given to these expressions of discontent through criticism of the programs which had generated the present social crisis, and also through pressures to rehabilitate those who had criticized Mao's policies at the Lushan Plenum. Teng T'o ridiculed the Great Leap Forward as having "substituted an illusion for reality";[26] and he criticized Mao in a published poem for his ignorance of the plight of the peasantry.[27]

These issues were more sharply drawn in the play *The Dismissal of Hai Jui*, written in 1961 by Wu Han, Deputy Mayor of Peking (P'eng Chen was Mayor), former professor of history, and a leading non-Party intellectual.[28] Wu described the suffering of Soochow peasants exploited by rapacious Ming dynasty officials who had confiscated their land. Hai Jui was an upright imperial governor who dared to intervene against the officials on the peasants' behalf

24. *Ibid.*, p. 79.
25. *Ibid.*, pp. 78–82.
26. *Ibid.*, p. 80.
27. *See* Chung and Miller, *Madame Mao*, pp. 50–52.
28. "Cultural Revolution" attacks on Wu Han and his play and various articles related to Hai Jui are contained in the documentary collection, "The Press Campaign against Wu Han," *Current Background,* No. 783 (March 21, 1966).

by appealing to the emperor for the return of their land. For his directness the emperor removed him from office. The analogy of this historical episode to the plight of the peasants under the Commune system and to the intervention and dismissal of P'eng Teh-huai is apparent. Such artistic works, Mao was to contend during the Cultural Revolution, were intended to "prepare public opinion" for a reversal of the judgment against P'eng Teh-huai and abandonment of the Great Leap policies.

In the years 1961–62, however, Mao confined his open response to these expressions of discontent among the intellectuals to poetic assertions of his own determination to press the struggle against political "revisionism." He also resisted, within the framework of Party decision-making procedures, any efforts to bring about a reconsideration of the treatment accorded P'eng Teh-huai and other "anti-Party rightists." In late 1961 Mao's friend among the intellectuals Kuo Mo-jo commiserated with the Chairman over the increasingly bitter and public dispute with "the monk" Khrushchev:

> Confounding humans and demons, right and wrong,
> The monk was kind to foes and mean to friends.
> Endlessly he intoned the "Incantation of the Golden Hoop,"
> And thrice he let the demon escape.[29]

Mao replied that despite the now public "storm" of the Sino-Soviet dispute, the "demon" (*kuei,* ghost) of "revisionism" was so dangerous that the Party's only course was to wage a continuing struggle against its "malignant" influence:

> A thunderstorm burst over the earth,
> And the demon rose from a heap of white bones.
> The deluded monk was not beyond the light,
> But the malignant demon must wreak havoc.

He added:

> The Golden Monkey wrathfully swung his massive cudgel,
> And the jade-like firmament was cleared of dust.[30]

Mao's determination to wield the "cudgel" of class struggle against the influence of revisionism among the intellectuals and within the Party was expressed more directly in a *Red Flag* editorial of mid-May 1962 in commemoration of the twentieth anniversary of his "Talks at the Yenan Forum on Literature and Art." The

29. From Kuo's poem to Mao, "On Seeing *The Monkey Subdues the Demon*"; trans. in *Ten More Poems of Mao Tse-tung* (Hong Kong: Eastern Horizon Press, 1967), p. 29.

30. From Mao's poem, "Reply to Comrade Kuo Mo-jo" (November 17, 1961), *ibid.*, p. 14.

editorial asserted, "It is impossible to fulfill the tasks of socialist construction if we do not persist in carrying out the socialist revolution in the fields of ideology and culture and if we neglect ideological work among the intellectuals." [31] It emphasized that the "Talks" showed "how completely friendly was Comrade Mao Tsetung's attitude in conducting intimate talks, consultations and discussions" with intellectuals. Yet it affirmed that this did not mean toleration of their anti-socialist attitudes. The editorial bluntly stated: "On the question of whether the world should be transformed according to the proletarian or bourgeois outlook, a question of principle, Marxist-Leninists are unequivocal and will never make any compromise." [32]

No doubt responding to the veiled ridicule of his person and the increasingly serious criticism of his policies, Mao thus expressed his determination to press the conflict. And apparently in response to this pressure, Teng T'o's critical columns terminated in the late summer of 1962, on the eve of the Party's Tenth Plenum.

Revelations of the Cultural Revolution suggest that in 1962, as the leadership debated how to modify its policies in the lingering economic crisis, certain Party leaders attempted to resurrect P'eng Teh-huai—with obvious implications for the "burial" of Mao's policies and political stature within the Party.

In January of 1962 the Party Central Committee convened an enlarged work conference, apparently to review the policies which had been adjusted at the Ninth Central Committee Plenum held a year earlier. In this period permissive policy alternatives to Mao's "three red flag" guidelines were said to have been formulated and discussed within the Party. Domestically, a line of "three privates and one guarantee" (*san-tzu yi-pao*) was suggested, extending the peasants' private plots, encouraging rural free markets, and tolerating small scale private business and manufacturing enterprises, while fixing agricultural production quotas on the basis of the labor of individual households. Internationally, a line of "three reconciliations and one reduction" (*san-ho yi-shao*) was proposed in order to moderate China's conflicts with "imperialists, reactionaries, and revisionists," and to reduce the amount of support given to "national liberation" insurgency movements.[33]

31. *Red Flag* editorial, "The Intellectuals' Way Forward," No. 10 (May 16, 1962); trans. in *SCMM*, No. 317 (June 12, 1962), p. 2.

32. *Ibid.*, p. 3.

33. The exact manner in which these policy alternatives to Mao's "three red flags" were formulated and discussed within the Party remains obscure. In a work report to the First Session of the Third National People's Congress in late 1964, Chou En-lai asserted that these policy lines had been put forward between 1959 and 1962, and had been actively advocated by "quite

During the Cultural Revolution Mao's supporters were to charge that at this work conference Liu Shao-ch'i had "openly tried to reverse the verdict on P'eng Teh-huai." [34] Other Red Guard pamphlets of early 1967 more plausibly quote Liu as having said at the meeting: "In respect to persons who share P'eng Teh-huai's views, cases may be reopened provided they are not cases of collusion with a foreign country";[35] and, "Provided the persons concerned lodge an appeal, cases may be reopened if the leading body and other comrades consider it necessary to do so." [36]

It would appear that where P'eng's critique of the Great Leap seemed to have been vindicated by subsequent events, there was strong sentiment within the Party for a rehabilitation of those who had previously been denounced as "rightists." Whether Liu actually made an open appeal directly on P'eng's behalf is much more problematical. Mao's sensitivity on this issue had been clearly revealed at Lushan in 1959; and his poetic exchange with Kuo Mo-jo shortly before the January 1962 meeting reiterated his determination to face up to the storm of criticism whether from the Soviets or from domestic "demons." [37] Liu may have raised the issue of "reversal

---

a number of people." (*See* Chou's speech in *SCMP*, No. 3370 [January 5, 1965], p. 9.) In his third Cultural Revolution confession, Liu Shao-ch'i implied that the *san-tzu yi-pao* line on agriculture had been formulated by Teng Tzu-hui, and that he personally had only "not refuted him." The "three reconciliations and one reduction" in international relations, Liu revealed, "was put forward by [an unnamed] comrade in a rough draft and was not brought up at any Central Committee meeting. At the time I did not know about this proposal. Afterwards, it was removed from the comrade's safe." (*See* "The Third Confession of Liu Shao-ch'i, in *Chinese Law and Government*, Vol. I, No. 1 [Spring 1968], pp. 78–79.)

The fact that Chou En-lai made mention of these policies of 1959–1961 as late as 1964 suggests that certain Party leaders were being warned not to continue to press for alternatives to Mao's "three red flags."

34. *Red Flag* and *People's Daily* joint editorial, "Along the Socialist or the Capitalist Road?" (August 17, 1967); trans. in *Peking Review,* No. 34 (August 18, 1967), p. 20.

35. From an article in the Peking Red Guard publication, *Chingkangshan* [Chingkang Mountains], (January 1, 1967) entitled "Look at Liu Shao-ch'i's Sinister Features!"

36. From the Red Guard pamphlet, *Selected Edition of Liu Shao-ch'i's Counter-Revolutionary Revisionist Crimes* (April 1967); trans. in *SCMM,* No. 652 (April 28, 1969), p. 30.

37. Mao revealed his use of poetry to express political sentiments in a letter to the editors of the poetry publication *Shih-k'an* in January 1959. Commenting on the two poems "Shaoshan Revisited" and "Ascent of Lushan," which he had written at the time of the P'eng Teh-huai challenge, he asserted with a peasant's asperity: "These two poems of mine are replies to those bastards [*wang-pa-tan*]." Translated from *Ko-ming Tsao-fan Pao* [Revolutionary Rebellion Journal] (November 25, 1967). The poems may be found in *Ten More Poems of Mao Tse-tung,* pp. 4, 6.

of verdicts" on "rightists" in general terms, perhaps hoping to prepare the political climate for a further appeal by P'eng himself. It was later claimed that P'eng did issue a long document in June of 1962 aimed at vindicating his actions of 1959.[38]

A more speculative interpretation of these Cultural Revolution charges is that the Party organization—well aware by this time of Mao's increasing reliance upon the People's Liberation Army and Lin Piao for political support (to be commented upon below)—was anxious to dilute Mao's influence within the Army. Party leaders may have hoped for a vindication of P'eng and subsequent personnel changes within the Army which would check Mao's increasing influence.

Whatever the actions and motives related to "reversing verdicts" in January of 1962, later developments reveal increasing conflict over whose influence was to prevail at the Tenth Plenum to be held in September. There was a sharpening of debate in a press campaign on the question of how to strengthen the Party's "democratic centralism."

Mao's own position in this debate had been expressed to Party leaders at the January work conference. Consistent with his views on how to resolve "contradictions" between the Party and "People" as expressed in his writings of 1957, the Chairman held that genuinely centralized leadership could be attained only by allowing "the masses" to air their criticisms of the Party for the difficulties of the preceding years:

> Without democracy, there can be no correct centralism because when people have differing opinions and no unified thinking, it is impossible to establish centralism. . . . If there is no democracy, the conditions of the lower levels are not understood, things are not clear, the views of different quarters are not gathered together to the fullest extent, the higher and the lower levels cannot air their views to each other, and the leading organs at the higher level depend only on one-sided or untrue materials to make decisions on questions. Then it is difficult to avoid subjectivism, it is not possible to achieve unified thinking and action, and genuine centralism cannot be attained.[39]

There must have been strong resistance to this view of how to handle popular discontent, for Mao observed that some "veteran revolutionaries" within the Party leadership

38. *See* the *Red Flag* and *People's Daily* joint editorial, "Along the Socialist or the Capitalist Roads?" trans. in *Peking Review,* No. 34 (August 18, 1967), p. 20.

39. Mao, "Talk on Problems of Democratic Centralism" (January 30, 1962), in *Long Live the Thought of Mao Tse-tung!* pp. 23–24.

still do not understand this question [of how to promote democratic centralism]. . . . Some comrades fear mass discussion very much; they fear that the masses may put forward views different from those of the leading organs and leaders. When problems are discussed, they suppress the enthusiasm of the masses and forbid them to speak out. This attitude is extremely bad. Democratic centralism is incorporated into our Party Rules and our Constitution, but they do not carry it out.[40]

As with the "blooming and contending" policy of 1957, many within the Party evidently feared that to allow public grievances to be expressed in the context of the Great Leap crisis would only bring to the surface great popular resentment and seriously erode the authority of the Party. Yet Mao adhered to his conviction that only by allowing problems to be "talked out" and bad feelings vented through open discussion of how "correct" policies had been misapplied, could a genuine political consensus be achieved.

Was Mao blind to his own responsibility in formulating policies which might not be practicable in application through the Party system? Was he so convinced of the correctness of his conception of how Chinese society should be organized that he assumed "the People"—those who accepted the Commune system and "extensive democracy" under Party guidance—were in the majority? Did he really feel that a new period of "opinion airing" in a time of great social tension could be kept within the bounds of acceptance of Party rule? Such questions remain imponderables. Yet Mao's stature as Party leader and symbol of national unity continued to accord him protection from political attack outside the inner circle of Party leadership. This fact provided much of the tension between the Party and its leader in Mao's call for "extensive democracy."

Mao may have felt that his policies had been correct, while China's current problems were in fact the result of errors on the part of those who had implemented them—compounded by three years of natural disasters and the economic sabotage of the Soviet "revisionists."

The Party organization, however, did not want to be subject to mass criticism for operational errors in implementing policy; the "democracy" wanted by the cadre was the right to criticize plans they had been pressured to implement.

The "centralism" demanded by other Party leaders was the discipline of organizational channels which would protect those on the "first line" of operational responsibility against Mao's lobbying for support within the Party's provincial organizations.

Throughout the spring and summer of 1962 a flood of articles

40. *Ibid.*, p. 23.

appeared in the daily press and in magazines under the control of the Party apparatus giving the organization's interpretation of how "democratic centralism" should be implemented and the unity and authority of the Party sustained. *China Youth* (*Chung-kuo Ch'ing-nien*), the monthly magazine of the Youth League, published an article in early March which called on unnamed comrades to "treat others as equals." [41] It asserted,

If one, having assumed the tasks of leadership, feels that he is better than others and is always right while the masses and lower levels are not good, and consequently takes arbitrary actions and monopolizes things without consulting the masses or convincing others in democratic ways, and uses certain "authority" to humiliate others, then democracy cannot but be damaged.[42]

The article then invoked words of Liu Shao-ch'i delivered to the Eighth Party Congress in 1956:

Each leader must know how to hear patiently and consider dispassionately opposing views and resolutely accept those opposing views which are rational. . . . [He] must not assume an exclusive attitude toward any comrade who, out of a correct motive, puts forward any opposing views according to normal procedures.

The author then asserted that "these words are applicable to our leading body at all times." [43]

An article of April 1 was pointedly entitled "On Modesty." The author, one Yü Chin (apparently a pseudonym) observed that Stalin had praised Lenin because he "always placed himself in the midst of the masses and never behaved as if he were special." [44] Yü Chin urged that those who had made distinctive contributions to the revolution take a broad historical perspective of their accomplishments:

A man may have done many things, and in his own view, in the opinion of his friends, or even in the opinion of his contemporaries, his contributions may be enormous. But if such contributions are observed in the light of the long river of history, their importance will be relatively limited. The modest [leader], by anticipating objective judgments and by making allowance for them in advance, is able instead to win the admiration of others.[45]

41. *See* Wu Ch'iang, "Centralism Based on Democracy," *China Youth*, No. 5 (March 1, 1962); trans. in *SCMM*, No. 307 (April 2, 1962), p. 2.

42. *Ibid.*

43. *Ibid.*, p. 3.

44. Yü Chin, "On Modesty," *China Youth*, No. 7 (April 1, 1962); trans. in *SCMM*, No. 312 (May 7, 1962), p. 15.

45. *Ibid.*, p. 14.

An article by one Pai Yeh pleaded that "Listening to Divergent Opinions Is Essential to Fostering the Democratic Work Style." The author tried to explain just how complicated social problems could be; and how different people, in all honesty, could analyze them quite differently from their varying social perspectives. His illustrative example was the politically loaded image of the Sung dynasty poet Su Tung-po describing Mount Lushan as resembling either a sharp peak or a whole range of mountains, depending on the vantage point from which it was viewed. And he exhorted "some people" with the observation: "If you listen to the opinions of the masses, your own knowledge will become more comprehensive and will get nearer to the truth, and this will give you more prestige"; while, "If you cling to your own one-sided or even erroneous ideas and the truth is not on your side, how can you have prestige?" [46]

Finally, a June article in *Red Flag* entitled "On Whipping and Spurring," observed that such treatment was "meant for horses"; intended to encourage them to go at a fast pace. But "even good horses sometimes slow down." [47] The author then went on to imply that Mao's criticisms of "the horse" of the Party had their usefulness if not taken too far, while Mao himself might benefit from a bit of the "whipping and spurring." "We must make a mirror out of people's criticisms of us and encouragements to us, other people's strong points and foibles, their successes and mistakes, and spur ourselves onward." [48]

Such articles, in retrospect, seem all too obviously to represent the Party organization pleading with Mao to accept well-intentioned criticism of his policies, to show greater personal modesty, and to limit his "whipping and spurring" of critical comrades. Were these articles published at the instigation of high Party leaders in order to prepare the climate of opinion within the Party for P'eng Teh-huai's appeal of the summer and for a sharp reconsideration of Mao's policies at the Tenth Plenum? We don't know.

A Maoist response to these appeals seemed to be expressed in a *Red Flag* article of mid-May entitled "Combine Exacting Demand with Painstaking Persuasion." Author T'ang P'ing-chu called attention to the high ideological standards of the People's Liberation Army in handling "contradictions" within its organizational life.

46. Pai Yeh, "Listening to Divergent Opinions Is Essential to Fostering the Democratic Work Style," *China Youth*, No. 7 (April 16, 1962); trans. in *ibid.*, p. 4.
47. Wu Chieh-min, "On Whipping and Spurring," *Red Flag*, No. 12 (June 16, 1962); trans. in *ibid.*, No. 321 (July 9, 1962), p. 38.
48. *Ibid.*, p. 39.

Such standards, it was asserted, "cannot be lowered, and no make-shift or indulgence can be allowed." [49] Then after stressing that this attitude was good for the work of "other departments and units," the author observed:

> Sometimes the subjection of some persons to disciplinary repression and necessary disciplinary punishment of a coercive nature is also an essential and correct means by which to make the demand [for high ideological standards] exacting, but this is still based upon persuasion and education.[50]

This veiled debate on the justice of the Lushan Plenum decision against P'eng Teh-huai also proceeded throughout the spring of 1962 in the press of provincial Party organizations. On April 4th the *Southern Daily* (*Nan-fang Jih-pao*), organ of the Party's Central-South Bureau, initiated a series of eight articles intended to implement Vice Chairman Liu Shao-ch'i's call to strengthen Party members' knowledge of democratic centralism. The series asserted the right of Party members to raise criticisms of their superiors, even as it criticized "dispersionism"—"a lack of organization and discipline, characterized by free action in the field of politics and disrespect for the leadership *of the Party Central Committee*." [51] In what again appears to be a lightly veiled reference to the P'eng Teh-huai case, the third of these articles observed:

> Some leadership personnel at the higher levels like to put on airs and look dignified. They only criticize others and teach others lessons and cannot persuade themselves to consult those below them, to listen to their criticisms, or to criticize themselves before them. . . . [The] responsible persons of some Party organizations do not protect such just actions by Party members as the airing of opinions at meetings, criticisms of the leadership, and the making of representations to organizations at higher levels in accordance with proper procedures, but criticize such actions as erroneous or even consider them as anti-Party acts or acts of insubordination; and when they take disciplinary actions

49. T'ang P'ing-chu, "Combine Exacting Demand with Painstaking Persuasion," *Red Flag*, No. 10 (May 16, 1962); trans. in *ibid.*, No. 317 (June 12, 1962), p. 17.

50. *Ibid.*, p. 22.

51. "Strengthen the System of Democratic Centralism: Lectures on Basic Knowledge about the Party," *Southern Daily*; trans. in *ibid.*, No. 2750 (June 1, 1962), p. 2. Emphasis added.

The consistent identification of Teng and Liu in these various articles of the period 1960–1962 as advocates of strengthened Party organizational discipline seems one more affirmation that the Party Secretariat was the organizational focus of efforts within the leadership to restrict Mao's influence over policy implementation.

or pass sentences on a Party member, they will not allow him to appear in a tribunal to make representations in person.[52]

A response to this plea for toleration of criticism from subordinates within the Party organization appeared in the same provincial paper in early July—shortly after P'eng Teh-huai is said to have presented a lengthy document to the Party leadership in his own defense. The article was entitled "Distinguish Well-Meant Criticisms from Reactionary Opinions"; and the author Ch'en Yi-yen began, rather curiously, by invoking a quote from a *People's Daily* editorial of 1955 on the Hu Feng affair which asserted that in the case of "reactionaries" it was both right and necessary to "restrain them from carrying out their restoration activities and stop all counterrevolutionaries from utilizing freedom of speech to attain their objective of counterrevolution." [53] During the Cultural Revolution these words of 1955 were attributed directly to Mao. Hence, one senses that in 1962 the Chairman's authority was close to the assertion that

> those who raise questions as to restraint on reactionary opinions have forgotten the viewpoint on the class struggle and the viewpoint on dictatorship over the enemy. They have blurred their vision on what are questions of right and wrong among the people and what are questions concerning relations between the enemy and ourselves.[54]

Finally, this article reveals something of the nature of the appeals which some Party leaders may have been making on P'eng Teh-huai's behalf. Observers of international affairs reported during the spring of 1962 (when the Great Leap crisis was at its peak) that the Nationalists on Taiwan initiated active planning for a possible invasion of the South China coast.[55] Furthermore, the question of possible American support for a Nationalist attack became the subject of a diplomatic exchange between American and Chinese Communist officials at the Warsaw ambassadorial talks.[56] Within China, concern over a possible Nationalist military action seems to account for a reduction in Maoist political pressures on the Party apparatus

52. "Strengthen Democratic Centralism: Lectures on Basic Knowledge about the Party: III. Fully Develop Democracy," *Southern Daily* (April 18, 1962); trans. in *SCMP*, No. 2738 (May 15, 1962), p. 2.

53. Ch'en Yi-yen, "Distinguish Well-Meant Criticisms from Reactionary Opinions," *Southern Daily* (July 6, 1962); trans. in *SCMP*, No. 2789 (July 13, 1962), p. 5.

54. *Ibid.*

55. *See* "Chiang Wants Ban Lifted: Said to Ask for Right to Invade China if Revolt Erupts," *New York Times* (March 16, 1962), p. 14.

56. *See* "U.S. Tells Peiping It Will Not Support Nationalist Attempt to Attack the Mainland," *New York Times* (June 27, 1962), p. 1.

in the spring and summer of 1962 (*see* pp. 443–444 below). One also may speculate that P'eng Teh-huai's supporters within the Party were attempting to gain the rehabilitation of the former Defense Minister in the interests of political unity, if not in order to strengthen Army leadership.

The *Southern Daily* article, however, reaffirmed the necessity of distinguishing "well-meant criticism" from "reactionary opinions" (". . . words uttered against the Party and government and against socialism and the fundamental systems of the state [the Communes]" [57]). In more direct terms it stated:

> It is true that due to Chiang K'ai-shek's reckless planning for an invasion of the mainland, counterrevolutionary sabotage activities have been intensified, and the contradictions between the enemy and ourselves have become more prominent. Despite the confrontation of such contradictions, we will not relax our efforts to resolve the contradictions among the people.[58]

Whether behind such phrases lay the specific issue of reconsideration of P'eng Teh-huai's dismissal is uncertain; yet it was in the context of this active debate in both the national and provincial presses over the question of how to sustain organizational discipline while strengthening Party "democracy" that preparatory meetings for the Central Committee's Tenth Plenum began in late July with a meeting of the leadership at Peitaiho.

The lines of debate at these meetings must have been sharply drawn. The plea of the Party organization for moderation in the policies which had produced the "three bitter years," and for open Party debate on the issues, culminated on August 1st with the republication in the *People's Daily* and in *Red Flag* of a newly edited version of Liu Shao-ch'i's 1939 work, "How to Be a Good Communist" [literally, "On the Cultivation of a Communist Party Member" (*Lun Kung-ch'an-tang Yüan ti Hsiu-yang*)]. During the Cultural Revolution, Mao's supporters were to charge that Liu's work had been edited to delete references to "class struggle," and to negate the importance of the "dictatorship of the proletariat"— which in Mao's eyes meant eliminating the importance of mobilizing "the masses" for active participation in the political life of the state.[59] After the "blooming and contending" of 1957, and the mas-

57. Ch'en Yi-yen, "Distinguish Well-Meant Criticisms from Reactionary Opinions," *Southern Daily*; trans. in *SCMP*, No. 2789 (July 31, 1962), p. 6.
58. *Ibid.*
59. *See* the *People's Daily* and *Red Flag* joint editorial "Betrayal of Proletarian Dictatorship Is the Essential Element in the Book on 'Self-Cultivation' " (May 8, 1967); trans. in *Peking Review*, No. 22 (May 12, 1967), pp. 7–11.

sive mobilization of the Great Leap, Liu was likely to find readers within the Party who would be responsive to a leadership approach which down-played mass campaigns and public criticism of Party errors.

Cultural Revolution charges also indicate that the preparatory sessions for the Tenth Plenum were only the culmination of earlier meetings convened by regional Party leaders during 1961–62 at which—the Maoists alleged—"black material" was gathered to negate the achievements of the Great Leap Forward.[60] Other attacks on Party leaders after 1966 also indicate that there was strong sentiment at the Plenum's preparatory meetings further to ease economic pressures on the peasantry.[61]

The full dimensions of this two-month-long period of reconsideration of the Party's basic economic, social, and political policies which culminated in the brief four-day Plenum have yet to be analyzed in detail in the light of Cultural Revolution disclosures. Yet it is notable that the final Plenum communiqué appears to be an across-the-board approval of Mao's analysis of China's domestic and international situation.

Given all the resistance to Mao's policies and assertive leadership style revealed in the Party press during the years 1961–62, one can only wonder by what process he had been able to mobilize such political support in a time of great economic difficulty. Given the Party's call of the spring for an end to "dispersionism" and the strengthening of "democratic centralism," one can only speculate that, as had been the case in past periods of the Chairman's policy initiatives, Mao and his supporters in "the center" had successfully

60. Such meetings were said to have been convened in the fall of 1961 by P'eng Chen in Peking Municipality, and by T'ao Chu in the Central-South region. (*See* "Events Surrounding the 'Changkuanlou' Counter-Revolutionary Incident," *Tung-Fang Hung* [The East is Red, Peking], April 20, 1967; "Tao Chu Is a Loyal Knave of the Bourgeoisie: The Real Facts Exposed at a Black Meeting," *Hung-wei-ping Ko-ming Tsao-fan Ping-t'uan Ch'uan-tan* [Handbill of the Red Guard Revolutionary Rebel Corps, Canton], No. 1, January 16, 1967.)

In early 1962, Liu Shao-ch'i, Teng Hsiao-p'ing, and Ch'en Yün convened what was said to have been a "black conference" at the "Hsi-lou" (West building) in Peking to discuss financial work in the light of the Great Leap crisis. (*See* "Down with Counter-Revolutionary Revisionist Ch'en Yün," *Tung-fang-hung* [January 27, 1967].)

61. These charges are associated with the names of Liu Shao-ch'i, Ch'en Yün, Teng Tzu-hui, Po Yi-po, and Chu Teh, in a number of Red Guard publications. (*See* the pamphlet, *Selected Edition of Liu Shao-ch'i's Counter-Revolutionary Revisionist Crimes* [April 1967]; trans. in *SCMM*, No. 652 [April 28, 1969], esp. p. 23; and "Down with Old Swine Chu Teh, *Tung-fang-hung* [February 11, 1967].)

mobilized backing from provincial members of the Central Committee by going around the newly formed regional bureaus under the control of the Party Secretariat.[62] The force of Mao's personality and his ability successfully to invoke the authority of his Chairmanship—factors which may have been strengthened by such political issues as the threat of a Nationalist attack, and the need for Party unity in the face of an imminent military confrontation with India—must have helped Mao to carry the day on issues where he indicated a determination not to compromise.

The Plenum communiqué forcefully asserted the necessity of struggling against "revisionism" both domestically and in China's international relations, thus confirming Mao's assertion of the first day of the Plenum that it was necessary to "rename right opportunism as revisionism in China." [63] Mao was ever more directly linking his conflict with the Soviets with domestic leadership debates. The communiqué reaffirms the "great historic significance" of the Lushan decision against P'eng Teh-huai. In his speech to the opening session of the Plenum, Mao reveals his continuing resistance to the political rehabilitation of his critics of 1959: "My advice to you comrades [apparently P'eng Teh-huai and his co-'conspirators'] is that although you have worked hand-in-glove with a foreign country and formed a secret faction against the Party, provided you make a clean breast of yourselves in a down-to-earth manner, we will welcome you and give you work." [64] Yet he continued to stress:

> Recently there has been a tendency to vindicate and rehabilitate people. This is wrong. Only those who have been wrongfully charged can be vindicated and rehabilitated, but those who have been correctly dealt with cannot be so vindicated.[65]

While continuing to be inflexible on the P'eng issue, Mao apparently took a soft line toward those leaders who had continued to

62. The Plenum communiqué notes that in addition to the eighty-two regular and eighty-eight alternate members of the Central Committee who attended the Plenum, "thirty-three other comrades from the departments concerned of the Central Committee and from the provincial, municipal and autonomous region Party committees were also present." (*See Current Background*, No. 691 [October 5, 1962], p. 1.) One does not know, however, if these additional "members present" represented Mao's having "packed the court"—as he appears to have done at the Eleventh Plenum in the summer of 1966.

63. Mao, "Speech Delivered to the Tenth Plenum of the Eighth Central Committee" (September 24, 1962), in *Chairman Mao's Criticism and Repudiation of the P'eng, Huang, Chang, and Chou Anti-Party Clique*, p. 26.

64. *Ibid.*

65. *Ibid.*

raise the matter of "reversing verdicts." Inasmuch as during the Cultural Revolution Mao was to allude cryptically to Liu Shao-ch'i's "right deviation" of 1962,[66] Liu may have been among those whom Mao addressed at the Tenth Plenum with the observation:

> Comrades who have made mistakes must think hard. Provided you admit your mistakes and return to the Marxist side, we will unite with you. I welcome a number of comrades now present. Don't feel shy just because you have made mistakes. We tolerate mistakes. Since you have made mistakes, you also are allowed to rectify them. . . . Many comrades have successfully transformed themselves. This is good! XXX's speech is a confession. Since XXX has rectified his mistakes, we trust him! [67]

The Chairman went on to stress that in leadership conflict it was still necessary to "reason people into compliance"; to adhere to the policy of avoiding forced confessions while emphasizing the method of "curing the disease to save the patient." And he stressed that even in the case of "anti-Party" factions, the "taboo against killing must not be violated." [68]

For all this leniency within the leading council of the Party, the Chairman came down hard on the intellectuals who had sniped at him during the two preceding years:

> Isn't the writing of novels the fashion of the day now? The use of novels to carry out anti-Party activities is quite an invention. To overthrow a political power, it is always necessary first of all to create public opinion, to do work in the ideological sphere.[69]

This intolerance of criticism of his policies or person in the open press, and his determination to propagate the "universal truth" of Marxism in opposition to the "malignant" influence of "revisionism," was to be the focus of Mao's political pressures on the Party in the months following the Tenth Plenum—and the source of increasing leadership conflict.

The Plenum, in retrospect, appears to have been largely a paper victory for Mao; an assertion in words rather than in functioning Party policies of the necessity of sustaining "class struggle." Following the Plenum there was to be an increasing divergence between expressions of deference to the Chairman and his policies,

66. Mao, "Bombard the Headquarters! My Big-Character Poster" (August 5, 1966); trans. in *Peking Review,* No. 33 (August 11, 1967), p. 5.

67. Mao, "Speech Delivered to the Tenth Plenum of the Eighth Central Committee," p. 26.

68. *Ibid.*

69. *Ibid.,* pp. 26–27.

and attempts by the Party organization to restrict his personal influence and dilute the impact of his policies in practice.

WHOSE "WORD" WILL SPEAK FOR NEW CHINA?
WHOSE MODEL WILL THE PEOPLE EMULATE?

Ever since he assumed charge of the work of the Military Commission [in 1959], Comrade Lin Piao has called for holding high the great red banner of Mao Tse-tung's thought. . . . On the other hand, Liu Shao-ch'i came out [in 1962] with his talks about *How to Be a Good Communist,* in which he shunned any mention of Mao Tse-tung's thought. Instead, for ulterior motives, he spoke lavishly of the need to become good pupils of the "creators" of Marxism-Leninism. . . .

Comrade Lin Piao pointed out as early as 1959: "Comrade Mao Tse-tung has comprehensively and creatively developed Marxism-Leninism. . . ." He further pointed out in 1960: "Mao Tse-tung's thought is the apex of Marxism-Leninism." Liu Shao-ch'i has openly opposed Comrade Lin Piao's view. In order to oppose Mao Tse-tung's thought, he even went so far as to invoke help from feudalism and capitalism to "replenish" his revisionist thinking. In *How to Be a Good Communist,* he quoted no fewer than ten times the "maxims" of such dead ancients as Confucius and Mencius down to Fang Chung-yen. On the other hand, it is very difficult to find in his book truisms uttered by Chairman Mao, which are so succinct that one sentence packs in it the import of ten thousand sentences! [70]

Analysis of the evolution of Chinese Communist leadership relations and policy disputes following the Tenth Central Committee Plenum on the basis of published press materials is an increasingly difficult task. There is a growing divergence between words and actions, between assertions of policy and their implementation, and between apparent expressions of deference to Mao and his programs and covert opposition to them. Mao himself during the Cultural Revolution was to express exasperation at this widening gap between appearance and reality by observing that long-time comrades had begun to "wave red flags" of apparent support for his leadership, while in fact "opposing the red flag" by distorting his policies in application.

The years 1962–1964 following the Plenum were a period of rapid polarization within the leadership between those who remained loyal to Mao and his Great Leap concept, and those whose

70. "Thoroughly Smash Liu Shao-ch'i's Counter-Revolutionary Conspiracy: A Brief Commentary on the 1962 Revised and Expanded Edition of *How to Be a Good Communist,*" in *Chingkangshan* (Peking), February 8, 1967; trans. in *Chinese Law and Government,* Vol. I, No. 1 (Spring 1968), pp. 63–64.

commitment was to the Party organization and to the Marxist-Leninist tradition as they understood it. This polarization found expression in the press in the split between those leaders committed to "the thought of Mao Tse-tung," and those who upheld the importance of "Marxism-Leninism" as the Party's guiding ideology. Terminological differences, however, were but the outward expression of an increasingly divisive conflict within the leadership over whose conception of the Party, mass political life, and economic construction would shape the revolution. In Chinese fashion this was a political conflict fought with "words" and "models": Did one promote "ideological remolding" (*szu-hsiang kai-tsao*) through the study of Mao's writings; or the "cultivation" (*hsiu-yang*) of Party members by reading Vice-Chairman Liu's work, *How to Be a Good Communist?* Did one strive to build post-Liberation China's political and economic institutions on the model of wartime Yenan or in terms of the Soviet experience in Party-building and "socialist construction"?

The polarization between Mao's conception of the revolutionary process and Party interests was no more clearly revealed than in the uncertain progress of efforts to rebuild the collective rural economy and peasant political discipline in the wake of the Great Leap crisis. Not long after the Tenth Plenum Mao called a conference which was designed to launch a large-scale Socialist Education Movement in the rural areas. It was a more elaborate development of the effort of 1957–58 to prepare the peasantry for the formation of Communes and to "clean up" cadre abuses of authority. In what was to become known as the "First Ten Points" of policy for Party work in the countryside, Mao stressed that it was necessary to wage an unremitting class struggle in the villages against "landlords and rich peasants who . . . are employing all kinds of schemes in an attempt to corrupt our cadres in order to usurp the leadership and power." [71]

71. "Draft Resolution of the Central Committee of the Chinese Communist Party on Some Problems in Current Rural Work" (The "First Ten Points," May 20, 1963); trans. in Baum and Teiwes, *Ssu-Ch'ing*, p. 61.

During the Cultural Revolution, the "First Ten Points" and the "Twenty-three Article Charter" on rural work of January 1965 were said to have been drawn up under Mao's "personal leadership." They were affirmed by the Eleventh Central Committee Plenum of August 1966 as the Party's authoritative guides to rural work, in contrast to the distortions in policy introduced by Liu Shao-ch'i and others in the "Later Ten Points" (September 1963) and its revision of September 1964. (*See* "Communiqué of the Eleventh Plenary Session of the Eighth Central Committee of the Communist Party of China" [August 12, 1966], in *CCP Documents of the Great Proletarian Cultural Revolution, 1966–1967* [Hong Kong: Union Research Institute, 1968], p. 64.)

Mao's strategy for coping with what he described as a fundamental threat to the socialist economy in the rural areas was to resharpen class lines and set poor and lower-middle peasants against the rich, and the erring cadres, in renewed class struggle.

> To assure this movement [of socialist education and Party rectification] of strong leadership, *we must rely on the organizations of the poor and lower-middle peasants;* we must do the job well in conducting investigation and research on the masses; and *we must set the masses in motion.* Decisions for and disposition of all important problems must be made through *full discussions among the masses.* During the course of the movement, *the masses must be given the opportunity fully to express their views,* to make criticism of errors and shortcomings, to expose bad people and evil deeds.[72]

As in the case of Party resistance to criticism from the intellectuals in 1957, however, cadres were to show themselves highly resistant to this effort at rectification "from below." Some complained, "if the masses criticize the cadres, the cadres will not be able to lead them at all. It's all right for the higher levels to criticize cadres, but if the masses do it, things will become chaotic (*luan*)." [73]

The next major document concerning this combined movement to instill popular "socialist consciousness" and rectify cadre errors has been termed the "Later Ten Points" of September 1963. It reveals the Party's effort to control the development of the movement "from above," and to direct the brunt of mass criticism against non-Party class enemies. This document stressed that the "key to the question of whether [or not] the Socialist Education Movement can be carried out smoothly . . . lies in the leadership. Leading organizations at provincial, district and county levels must pay close attention [to the movement]." [74] These "Later Ten Points" emphasized that while poor and lower-middle peasants should be mobilized, it would be wrong "to brush aside the basic organizations [of the Party] and existing cadres, instead of carrying out work by relying upon them." Furthermore, it was asserted that "we should see that the great majority of basic-level rural cadres are good." [75]

The Party's "class allies," however, were deprecated for their political immaturity. Some of the masses were said to have been

72. *Ibid.,* pp. 66–67. Emphasis added.
73. Cited from a Radio Tientsin broadcast of December 19, 1964 in *ibid.,* p. 33.
74. "Some Concrete Policy Formulations of the Central Committee of the Chinese Communist Party in the Rural Socialist Education Movement" (The "Later Ten Points," September 1963), in *ibid.,* p. 75.
75. *Ibid.,* pp. 76, 85.

utilized by the enemy out of temporary foolishness. Among the peasant masses, there is a small part, including a very few poor and lower-middle peasants, who are backward ideologically and are unable to draw a clear line between classes. Under the enticement of the [class] enemy, they have either committed some crimes which are detrimental to the state or collective interests, or have taken part in some feudalistic or superstitious activities.[76]

This effort of the Party to control the rectification and the reestablishment of discipline in rural life persisted in the movement of mid-1964 to form Poor and Lower-Middle Peasant Associations, which Mao intended to be an organizational counterweight to the Party in the countryside and a concentration of "proletarian" strength in the continuing struggle against rural class polarization. Yet the draft charter of the Associations stresses that these organizations were to be "led by the Party" and were intended to become "a powerful arm of the Party" in raising the class consciousness of the rural population.[77]

The Party's relentless attempt to co-opt the rectification of the "four uncleans" in rural administration (ideological deviations, lack of political discipline, deviations in organizational life, mismanagement of economic affairs) and to lead rather than mobilize the peasants apparently stimulated behind-the-scenes pressures from Mao to open up the movement. A September 1964 revision of the "Later Ten Points," published just three months after the draft rules on Poor and Lower-Middle Peasant Associations had been issued, stressed that "Only by freely mobilizing the masses can this movement achieve complete victory." [78] "The key and prerequisite for correctly launching and leading the Socialist Education Movement is to study the thought of Comrade Mao Tse-tung concerning such questions as classes, class contradictions, and class struggle in a socialist society." [79]

Despite these introductory expressions of deference to Mao and the "mass line," the revision of the "Later Ten Points" continued to stress leadership "from above": "To launch the Socialist Education Movement at any point requires the sending of a work team from the higher level. The whole Movement should be led by work

76. *Ibid.,* p. 78.

77. "Organizational Rules of Poor and Lower-Middle Peasant Associations" (Draft, June 1964), in *ibid.,* p. 95.

78. "Some Concrete Policy Formulations of the Central Committee of the Chinese Communist Party in the Rural Socialist Education Movement" (The "Revised Later Ten Points," September 10, 1964), in *ibid.,* p. 102.

79. *Ibid.,* p. 103.

teams." [80] And while there was a call for "stern" treatment of erring cadres, this was still a matter of "education by persuasion":

> We may also adopt such measures as "recollection" and "comparison" [of how life was in the past] to enlighten them, improve their understanding, and make them repent of their own accord. [But] in dealing with them, no struggle rallies, false accusations, and especially no beatings are allowed.[81]

During the Cultural Revolution, Liu Shao-ch'i was to be attacked for these distortions of Mao's effort to sustain "class struggle" in the countryside. He was said to have promoted policies which were "left in form but right in essence" for their failure to arouse the masses. He was charged with having taken measures to protect "revisionists" within the Party leadership by directing the peasants to struggle against the basic-level cadres, rather than their erring superiors at higher levels of the Party administration. This was said to be a line of "hitting at the many [local cadres] to protect the few [higher leaders]." [82] In a "confession" of October 1966, Liu sidestepped responsibility for these policies. He said he "did not know" how the "Later Ten Points" had been formulated; but he vaguely associated them with the work of P'eng Chen. He asserted that it was only in September 1964 that he "came to discover that the Later Ten Points contained elements which hampered efforts to arouse the masses." [83]

Whatever the justice of these charges and efforts at a defense, within four months after publication of the "Revised Later Ten Points," in January of 1965, a new document on rural rectification termed the "Twenty-Three Articles" was issued. It superseded all previous directives and sharply redefined the objectives of the Socialist Education Movement as an effort to confront the fundamental "contradiction between socialism and capitalism" in China's countryside. The "spear-point" of the rectification was now directed at "those people in authority within the Party who take the capitalist road." [84] Above all, this reformulation of the "Four

80. *Ibid.,* p. 105.
81. *Ibid.,* p. 109.
82. Policy conflict between Mao and Liu on the matter of cadre rectification is discussed in detail in Richard Baum and Frederick C. Teiwes, "Liu Shao-ch'i and the Cadre Question," *Asian Survey,* Vol. VIII, No. 4 (April 1968), pp. 323–345.
83. "The Confession of Liu Shao-ch'i," *Atlas* (April 1967), p. 16.
84. "Some Problems Currently Arising in the Course of the Rural Socialist Education Movement" (The "Twenty-Three Articles" [January 1965], in Baum and Teiwes, *Ssu-Ch'ing,* p. 120.)

Clean-Ups" and "Socialist Education" campaigns stressed the need for a genuine release of mass criticism "from below": "We must let people fully express themselves"; "The most important supervision [of Party cadres] is that which comes from the masses"; ". . . we must boldly unleash the masses, we must not be like women with bound feet—we must not bind our hands and feet." [85] Yet even in this reorientation of the effort to "clean up" the rural Party organization, Mao was to find that there were long-time comrades who continued to block a real "mobilization" of mass resentments against the Party organization.[86]

In contrast to this resistance by the Party, the People's Liberation Army after 1963 became increasingly conspicuous in the public media as an organization embodying Mao's political principles. The center of gravity of Chinese domestic politics after the Tenth Plenum shifted to the steady polarization between Mao and the Army on the one side, and Liu and the Party organization on the other. This conflict was to bloom during the Cultural Revolution of 1966, but its seeds were planted in the years 1959–1962.

Mao's increasing reliance on the PLA grew in the context of efforts to confront the major issues in Chinese political life in the years following the Lushan Plenum: First was the increasing resistance of the Party organization to the Chairman's policy prescriptions; second, Mao's concern—obviously raised by P'eng Teh-huai's challenge—with what would happen should "the Party" (Mao) lose the support of "the gun"; third, the necessity of sustaining Army

85. *Ibid.*, p. 121.

86. Cultural Revolution charges have linked resistance to implementation of the "Twenty-Three Articles" in particular to P'eng Chen's administration of the Socialist Education Movement in Peking Municipality. (*See* the Red Guard pamphlet, *Counter-Revolutionary Revisionist P'eng Chen's Towering Crimes of Opposing the Party, Socialism, and the Thought of Mao Tsetung* [June 10, 1967]; trans. in *SCMM*, No. 639 [January 6, 1969], pp. 18–22.)

In a cryptic remark to Party leaders at a work conference of October 1966, Mao observed of resistance to his policies by the Peking Party Committee: "The time our vigilance was aroused was when the Twenty-Three Articles were drafted." (Mao, "Speech at a Work Conference of the Central Committee" [October 25, 1966], in *Long Live the Thought of Mao Tsetung!* p. 40.)

The exact meaning of this remark, and its relationship to the timing of Mao's personal decision to "get (*kao*) the Party Secretariat" (*ibid.*) is obscure. As is detailed below, there is strong evidence that Mao had decided to challenge the power of other top Party leaders by mid-1964, more than six months before the drafting of the "Twenty-Three Articles." (A recent revelation by Edgar Snow of resistance to Mao at a Party leadership meeting of January 25, 1965 [*see* p. 460, and fn. 185, p. 469 below] adds a bit of light to this question.)

discipline through the social crisis generated by the Great Leap Forward;[87] and fourth, the particular problems of morale which were raised for the military by the dispute with the Soviets—the breaking off of Russian nuclear protection and military and economic assistance, and the increasingly hostile confrontation with a formidable power sharing a long common frontier.[88] Lin Piao was to oversee the handling of these problems; and in Mao's eyes he must have done a successful job, for after the Tenth Plenum the Chairman drew upon the Army's experience in coping with more extensive political difficulties, and on Lin's support in his deepening conflict with the Party organization.

The task of rebuilding the loyalty of the PLA to Mao personally commenced only months after Lin Piao succeeded P'eng Teh-huai as Defense Minister. In the spring of 1960 the Army initiated a "ten year plan" for the cultural development of its troops which stressed inculcation of the old Red Army's "three-eight" work style[89] —one of the legacies of the revolutionary years—and the study of Mao's writings. On National Day, October 1st, 1960, Lin Piao stressed that the victory of the Chinese revolution had been a victory for "the thought of Mao Tse-tung"; and he asserted that the forms of political life which had enabled the Party to attain its power were needed to sustain political discipline in the face of China's present difficulties.[90]

To give organizational life to these assertions, an enlarged meeting of the Party's Military Affairs Committee was convened between September 14 and October 20, 1960 (at the time of publica-

87. Problems of military discipline during the Great Leap crisis are revealed in the secret military "Work Bulletins." *See* J. Chester Cheng, ed., *The Politics of the Chinese Red Army: A Translation of the Bulletin of Activities of the People's Liberation Army* (Stanford, Calif.: The Hoover Institution, 1966).

88. Sino-Soviet border clashes, according to the Chinese, are said to have begun in 1960, initially leading to a serious popular uprising in the Ili region of Sinkiang Province in 1962. The Chinese attributed this uprising to the efforts of Russian agents to undermine the political loyalty of minority groups living in China's Northwest frontier region.

89. "Chairman Mao condensed this working style to three phrases and eight words [characters]. The three phrases are: A steadfast and correct political direction; an industrious and thrifty working style; and a flexible and mobile strategy and tactics. The eight words are: unity; earnestness; seriousness; and liveliness [eight Chinese characters]." (Cited in Hsiao Hua, "Cultivation of the 'Three-Eight' Working Style Is an Important Task in the Building of Our Army [Excerpts]," NCNA [May 22, 1960]; in *SCMP*, No. 2270 [June 2, 1960], p. 1.)

90. Lin Piao, "The Victory of the Chinese People's Revolutionary War Is the Victory of the Thought of Mao Tse-tung," *Red Flag*, No. 19 (October 1, 1960); trans. in *SCMM*, No. 231 (October 18, 1960), pp. 7–20.

tion of Volume Four of Mao's works) to discuss ways of "strengthening political and ideological work in the Army." This conference reaffirmed the line on army-building which Mao had formulated at the Kut'ien conference of 1929 and stressed the need to study and apply "the thought of Mao Tse-tung." With the greatest import for later political developments, the "Central Authorities" of the Party stressed that this directive was

> not only . . . for the work of building up the Army and conducting political activities in the Army. . . . [It] is [also] useful to the Party organizations, government organs, schools, and enterprises at various levels, and accordingly should be distributed to organizations of the local [Party] committee level and above for reference.[91]

While this resolution on military work of late 1960 was only "for reference" by the Party and other organizations, the question which was to be posed with increasing sharpness after the Tenth Plenum was whether the Army was to be a model organization for emulation by the Party, or whether the Party still exercised political predominance over "the gun."

The lines between Party and Army, in retrospect, appear to have been drawn with surprising clarity even in the fall of 1960, as each organization apparently sought to define and defend its areas of operation. While the Party's national media the *People's Daily* and *Red Flag,* as well as the press of the regional Party apparatus, waged a campaign which stressed the need to obey and follow the "Party's policy" [92] (not the "thought of Mao Tse-tung"), the Army launched campaigns to study Mao's works and to strengthen its influence among China's youth. A *Liberation Army Daily* editorial of mid-November 1960, republished in the paper of the Youth League, initiated a movement to develop the "five goods." [93] No-

91. "Endorsement by the Central Authorities of the Chinese Communist Party of the 'Resolution on Strengthening Political and Ideological Work in the Army Made by the Enlarged Meeting of the Military Affairs Commission" (December 21, 1960); trans. in Cheng, *et al., The Politics of the Chinese Red Army,* p. 65.

92. *See* the collection of national and regional press materials, "Emphasis on Party Policy," *Current Background,* No. 646 (February 17, 1961).

93. "Five good" fighters of the PLA, models for Youth League members to emulate, were characterized as good at political ideology, good at military technique, good at the "three-eight" work style, good at fulfilling tasks assigned to them, and good at physical training. (*See* "Conditions for 'Five Good' Fighters," *China Youth Daily* [November 18, 1960]; trans. in *SCMP,* No. 2433 [February 7, 1961], p. 5. *See also* the *Liberation Army Daily* editorial, "Let the Entire Armed Forces Do Youth Work and Further Develop the 'Five Good' Campaign," *China Youth Daily* [November 17, 1960]; trans. in *ibid.,* pp. 1–3.)

tably emphasized as the first "good" was the need to "read assiduously Chairman Mao's works"—a prerequisite to accepting the Party's political guidance. The republication of *Liberation Army Daily* editorials in the press organs of the Party and Youth League was to become one of the more visible signs of the increasing political pressure which Mao was placing on the Party organization through the Army.

In 1961, as the production crisis of the Great Leap deepened, the differing responses of the two organizations to the social and economic difficulties revealed basic differences in leadership technique. The Party called for a new period of "blooming and contending" to encourage the intellectuals to lend their skills to the Party in coping with China's production problems. In direct opposition to this line, the Army stressed that "we must have positive education and not 'blooming and contending' and debating" in stimulating people to greater production efforts.[94] This "positive education," as implemented by the Army, sought to reinstate the form of political motivation which had characterized Mao's leadership from the early days of the revolution—the effort to draw upon people's resentments, indignation, and feelings of hatred.

Beginning after the October 1960 meeting of the Military Affairs Commission, a new "education" movement termed "the two remembrances and the three investigations" was initiated within the PLA.[95] Essentially this was the old technique of "speaking bitterness" adapted to the problems of the 1960s. In order to hold the discipline of the Army, to help officers and men rationalize (emotionalize) their present economic and political difficulties, meetings were organized to enable them to "recall the bitterness of the past and compare it with the sweetness of the present." They were urged to think of "taking revenge" for [Soviet] economic exploitation and imperialist aggression, to express their hatred for the personal hardships and exploitation suffered in "feudal" China, and to compare the old life with the new socialist political order.

In 1963 this same technique was applied throughout China in the context of the Socialist Education Movement. Meetings were held in factories and schools, communes and workshops, to have old peasants and workers recall for the younger generation the bitterness of pre-Liberation life, in order to develop that sense of in-

94. "Several Notable Problems in the Current Educational Movement of the 'Two Remembrances and the Three Investigations'—Summary of a Talk Given by Deputy Director Liu Chih-chien in a Telephone Conference on January 7, 1961," *Kung-tso T'ung-hsün* (January 11, 1961); trans. in Cheng, *et al., The Politics of the Chinese Red Army*, p. 104.

95. Ibid., pp. 97–115.

dignation and hatred which would motivate people to struggle to overcome their present hardships, and to define by contrast the virtues of China under Party rule. "The more one hates the old society, the more will one love the Party and the new society." [96]

Combined with this effort to motivate the Army and people to weather present problems was the commitment of military units to tasks of economic production. Under the Yenan slogan of "regeneration through one's own efforts" (*tzu-li keng-sheng*), the production activities of Red Army military units in the Nanniwan district of the Shen-Kan-Ning border region were held up as a model of economic self-reliance.[97] The PLA was turned out to the fields to cope with the new "blockade" of the Soviet "revisionists" and China's continuing production difficulties.

Mao's increasing personal identification with the PLA was indicated during the summer of 1961 by the publication of an article in the *China Youth Daily* entitled "The Good Traditions of a Certain Company of the Red Army." The author was Chiang Ch'ing—Mao's wife. In terms that from the perspective of Cultural Revolution developments seem laden with political weight, Chiang Ch'ing praised a PLA company because

> on three occasions it had shouldered the most honorable task of safeguarding our great leader Chairman Mao, and was also on guard duty during the Kut'ien Conference [of 1929] which had great historical significance [because of Mao's assertion at the Conference that political indoctrination could establish discipline over insurgent military units].[98]

She added that in the past "this company [also] guarded Marshal Lin Piao and his headquarters, and directly received Marshal Lin Piao's personal instructions and concern."

That Mao's wife should "recall" the glories of the Army in protecting her husband—at a time when Mao was under veiled personal attack in the public media by intellectuals backed by other Party leaders—would almost certainly indicate to politically astute readers in the Party and Army that Mao and Lin were invoking the "protection" of the PLA as their base of political power. The degree of political polarization implied by Chiang Ch'ing's article

96. *Daily Worker* (Peking) editorial, "Never Forget the Past" (September 8, 1963); trans. in *SCMP*, No. 3072 (October 3, 1963), pp. 3–6.

97. *See* Wang Chen, "Self-Sufficiency in Production in Nanniwan Today and in the Past," *China Youth Daily* (September 23, 1960); trans. in *ibid.*, No. 2366 (October 27, 1960), pp. 6–9.

98. Chiang Ch'ing, "The Good Traditions of a Certain Company of the Red Army," *China Youth Daily* (August 26, 1961); trans. in *SCMP*, No. 2581 (September 19, 1961), p. 8.

A peasant describes the sufferings of life
in pre-Liberation China to members of the younger generation
during a "recall bitterness" meeting of the
Socialist Education Campaign, 1963–1966.
From China Pictorial, *November 1967.*

is further manifest in the publication by the same *China Youth Daily* one week later of Marshal Ch'en Yi's permissive graduation address to Peking's young intellectuals.[99] The lines were drawn between a Party adhering to "Marxism-Leninism" and an Army waving the flag of "Mao's thought."

The sudden emergence into political activity of Chiang Ch'ing, who ever since her marriage to Mao in 1940 had been as politically withdrawn as the wives of other Party leaders, was—in Chinese terms—an ominous sign.[100] It indicates the degree of the breakdown in trust and communication between top Party leaders which was to lead to the open conflict of the late 1960s. During the Cultural Revolution Chiang Ch'ing was to reveal that for some time she had acted as a "roving sentinel" for Mao, observing developments in culture and education, and in international affairs.[101] The Chairman evidently did not trust the information which reached him through Party channels.

Chiang Ch'ing's emergence was matched after 1962 by the increasingly frequent public appearances of the wife of Liu Shao-ch'i. Wang Kuang-mei was an attractive and sophisticated younger woman educated at a famous Peking missionary college. As the wife of China's State Chairman she was to assume the role of "first lady" when she hosted the wife of Indonesian President Sukarno during a visit to Peking in the fall of 1962, when she accompanied her husband on a diplomatic excursion through Southeast Asia in 1963, and through frequent contacts with foreigners in the Chinese capital between 1964 and 1966. Also, she was to be Liu Shao-ch'i's "eyes" in observing, and then commenting upon, the progress of the Socialist Education Movement during 1964.

Wang Kuang-mei's public activity contrasts with Chiang Ch'ing's behind-the-scenes efforts on Mao's behalf to bring an end to the public sniping of the intellectuals, and to inject a "proletarian" spirit into Army and civilian artistic life. Madame Mao's activities seemed to culminate in the summer of 1964 with a festival of Peking Opera on revolutionary themes. Yet as Cultural Revolution developments were to confirm, the public appearances of these once politically inactive women marked the beginning of a period of breakdown in cohesion within the Party leadership. During the open political conflict after 1966 the previously muted rivalry be-

99. *See* pp. 415–416 above.

100. *See* the comment on the traditionally disruptive influence of women in Chinese politics on p. 36, fn. 14 above.

101. Chiang Ch'ing, "Do New Services for the People" (a speech of April 13, 1967 delivered to an enlarged meeting of the Military Affairs Committee), in *Tung-fang-hung* (June 3, 1967).

tween these two women was to inject a very bitter and personal note into the Cultural Revolution struggle.[102]

The subtle public indications of political tension between the Army and Party in 1961 were followed by a year in which Lin Piao was inconspicuous in the public "waving of the red flag" of support for Mao. In contrast to his National Day speeches of 1959 and 1960, in which he lavishly praised Mao's contributions to the revolution, and his political activity in the fall of 1961, Lin was notably silent during 1962.

On Army Day, August 1st, Lin was conspicuous by his absence from a reception presided over by Chief of Staff Lo Jui-ch'ing and Foreign Minister and Army Marshal Ch'en Yi. In his reception speech Lo made no mention of "the thought of Mao Tse-tung," while recalling with emphasis the military successes of the PLA in the Korean War.[103] A *Liberation Army Daily* editorial of the day bore the curious title, "Be Ruthless to the Enemy, and Be Kind to Ourselves." In an apparent reference to the P'eng affair, it stressed that "we must unite ourselves properly." [104] And while deference was given to the importance of political indoctrination, the editorial added with the loaded "however" (*tan-shih*): "to strike hard and accurately [at the enemy], and to win a big victory at a small price, we must also learn to use the weapons in our hands skillfully and master flexible tactics." [105] A *China Youth Daily* Army Day editorial, in recalling military heroes of the Long March, stressed that their heroism was due to the fact that "they had in their hearts fervent love for the Party" [106]—not for Chairman Mao.

These signs of an easing of Party-Army political tensions in 1962 seem to be a composite of the domestic political pressures generated by the Great Leap crisis: the issue of "reversing verdicts" which appears to have been actively pressed in the spring and summer, the threat of a Nationalist invasion, and tensions on the Sino-Indian

102. *See,* for example, the transcript of the struggle meeting of April 1967 at which Wang Kuang-mei was humiliated for her "bourgeois" behavior during the diplomatic trip to Indonesia in 1963, "How to Wage 'Revolutionary Struggle': 'Teaching Material' Provided by Red Guards of Tsinghua University, Peking," *Current Scene,* Vol. VI, No. 6 (April 15, 1968).

103. *See,* "Text of General Lo Jui-ch'ing's Speech at [Army Day] Reception," *People's Daily* (August 2, 1962); trans. in *SCMP,* No. 2801 (August 17, 1962), pp. 2–4.

104. *Liberation Army Daily* editorial, "Be Ruthless to the Enemy, and Be Kind to Ourselves" (August 1, 1962; as excerpted in the *People's Daily*); trans. in *ibid.,* p. 5.

105. *Ibid.,* p. 6.

106. *China Youth Daily* editorial, "Show Fervent Love for the PLA and Learn from It" (July 31, 1962); trans. in *ibid.,* p. 8.

frontier which were to explode in the Chinese military initiative of
October. Political conflict thus submerged below the level of press
visibility in a context where the economic, political, and military
issues of the hour were loaded in favor of Party unity and military
professionalism. It was the successful Maoist defense at the Tenth
Plenum, and the devastating attack on the Indians, which put
political initiative back in the hands of Mao and Lin.

That initiative was revealed during 1963 and 1964 over an increasingly wide range of activities with ever greater intensity, as
Mao attempted to translate his Plenum victory into major modifications of Party policy. He used the Army as a prod to push the Party
in a more revolutionary direction by publicizing "models" of Army
practice which the Party was to emulate. Another Army political
work conference was held in February 1963; and it issued a set of
regulations which stressed that even "a slight deviation from the
thought of Mao Tse-tung and we shall lose our direction and experience defeat." [107]

To make fully explicit just how people were to apply "the
thought of Mao Tse-tung" in practice, national campaigns were
initiated in 1963 to hold up for public approbation exemplary individuals who embodied Mao's political principles in their daily
lives. The most widely publicized of these models in the application
of Mao's "thought" was the "great ordinary soldier," the young
martyr Lei Feng, who in his selfless devotion to the people wanted
to be "a rust-proof screw" in the machinery of the revolution.[108]
Lei's selflessness and service to the people were attributed to the
fact that he never forgot his past sufferings. Through the study of
Chairman Mao's words he "knew how to love the people ardently
and hate the enemy. He never forgot the class hatred of the old
society where people perished and families fell apart." [109] He constantly remained on political alert, "never forgetting the pain [of
the old society] when the scars [of exploitation] were healed." [110]

107. *Liberation Army Daily* editorial, "Raise Aloft the Great Red Ban-
ner of the Thought of Mao Tse-tung, Resolutely Implement Regulations
Governing PLA Political Work!" (May 8, 1963); trans. in *SCMP*, No. 2984
(May 22, 1963), p. 2.

108. Liu Chih-chien, "A Great Soldier with a Noble Character," *China
Youth Daily* (February 5, 1963); trans. in *ibid.*, No. 2927 (February 27,
1963), p. 5.

109. *China Youth Daily* editorial, "Fight and Live as Lei Feng Has
Done" (February 5, 1963); trans. in *ibid.*, p. 6.

110. *People's Daily* commentator, "A Great Ordinary Soldier" (February
7, 1963); trans. in *ibid.*, p. 3.

A more extended discussion of the manner in which the model hero Lei
Feng embodied Mao's notion of political motivation through cultivation of
sentiments of hatred is in the author's article, "On Activism and Activists:

A major organizational model propagated at this time was "the Good Eighth Company of Nanking Road." "Armed with the thought of Mao Tse-tung," it had maintained its revolutionary discipline despite the corrupting surroundings of urban life: "Billeted in a big, bustling city for the past fourteen years, warriors of this company have steered clear of all sorts of temptations and have more than once repelled the sugar coated cannon ball attacks unleashed by the bourgeois class, and have stood firm on Nanking Road." [111]

These emulation campaigns reveal Mao's concern that the years of peace following the attainment of victory in 1949 were steadily eroding the legacy of the revolutionary period—a commitment to group life, a willingness to endure material hardships, and a determination to promote social change. In the spring of 1963 authoritative spokesmen began to stress a theme which finally was to express itself in the Cultural Revolution upheaval: "What is really to be feared is political degeneration, separation from the masses of the people, ideological disarmament, and the weakening or the loss of the determination to fight." [112]

How to prevent such political "degeneration," however, was a matter of dispute among Party leaders. Where Mao and Lin Piao, through the Army, gave increasing stress to political indoctrination through the study of Mao's works and emulation of those who incorporated his ideas in their daily activities, Party spokesmen cited Liu Shao-ch'i's writings on the need to stress "cultivation" of Communist morality and submission to the Party's organizational discipline.[113] Even within the Army itself, alternative models to Lei

Maoist Conceptions of Motivation and Political Role Linking State to Society," *The China Quarterly,* No. 39 (July–September 1969), pp. 98–99.

111. A *Liberation Army Daily* correspondent, "An Austere and Hardship-Defying Work Style Passed on from Generation to Generation: An Account of 'The Good Eighth Company of Nanking Road,'" *China Youth Daily* (March 30, 1963); trans. in *SCMP,* No. 2965 (April 24, 1963), p. 1.

112. Hsiao Hua, "Basic Experiences of the Past Two Years Concerning the Creation of 'Four-Good' Companies in the Army" (excerpted in the *People's Daily,* April 1, 1963); trans. in *SCMP,* No. 2971 (May 3, 1963), pp. 2–3.

Hsiao Hua at this time was Deputy Director of the PLA's General Political Department. It was through this department that Mao and Lin Piao asserted their influence over military affairs after 1959. A detailed analysis of the political rivalries and associations within the PLA which contributed to the Cultural Revolution struggle will be found in William W. Whitson, with Huang Chen-hsia, *The Chinese Communist High Command: A History of Military Politics, 1927–1969* (New York: Praeger, 1971).

113. *See,* for example, Ching Ch'ien, "What Is Communist Morality?" *Southern Daily* (April 20, 1963); trans. in *SCMP,* No. 2982 (May 20, 1963), pp. 5–6.

Feng began to appear: An Yeh-min, glorified as a combat soldier on the Taiwan front (rather than as a student of Mao's writings, skilled at production tasks); and Kuo Hsing-fu, a model in the teaching of military technique.[114]

In early 1964 the "advanced experience" of the PLA was propagated even more broadly. Following another lengthy PLA conference on political work which ended in mid-January, a national campaign to "learn from the People's Liberation Army" was initiated, "in the hope that the entire country will study the valuable experience of the PLA in political-ideological work in a more penetrating and extensive manner and obtain a high proletarian and combat character just like the PLA." [115]

In contrast to the stress on study and emulation of the previous year's campaigns, however, the 1964 activity was transformed into direct organizational pressures in areas that had long been the exclusive preserve of the Party and government ministries. In late February a *People's Daily* editorial declared that the government's commercial departments should "humbly and sincerely try to learn from other departments, other localities and other units, in particular from the PLA, which has armed itself with Mao Tse-tung's thinking and is highly vigilant, well organized and disciplined." [116] This "vigilance" and organizational discipline were now not just a matter of something to "study," for the editorial revealed that "since last year" [1963] "a considerable number of military cadres" had been transferred to work in basic-level commercial departments.[117]

This development was reinforced by the creation of political departments, patterned on Army practice, in Central Committee organizations concerned with work in finance, trade, industry, and transportation. By June of 1964 more than twenty ministries of the government were reported to have established such political departments, which subsequently expanded their influence down to pro-

114. "Officers and Men of Naval Units Unfold Activities of Learning the Excellent Character of An Yeh-min, a Great Communist Soldier," NCNA (September 11, 1963); trans. in *SCMP*, No. 3069 (September 27, 1963), p. 10. *People's Daily* editorial, "Inspiration from Kuo Hsing-fu's Teaching Method" (February 10, 1964); trans. in *SCMP*, No. 3175 (March 10, 1964), pp. 1–4.

For comments on the "anti-Maoist" character of these models, *see* pp. 447–449 below.

115. *People's Daily* editorial, "The Whole Country Must Learn from the PLA" (February 1, 1964); trans. in *SCMP*, No. 3164 (February 24, 1964), p. 1.

116. *People's Daily* editorial, "Commercial Departments Should also Learn from the PLA" (February 20, 1964); trans. in *SCMP*, No. 3177 (March 12, 1964), pp. 1–2.

117. *Ibid.*, p. 4.

vincial and local levels. These political departments were staffed, in part, by demobilized Army men, and by Party cadres who received political indoctrination at PLA training centers.[118] Through such developments Mao expressed his determination to inject political discipline into a Party-governmental system which he saw as increasingly unwilling to confront its own bureaucratic "revisionism."

Further propagating the Chairman's political pressures into areas of economic activity was the publicizing of model industrial and agricultural units which had successfully applied "the thought of Mao Tse-tung." Early in February of 1964 the press began to laud the achievements of a production brigade of the Tachai People's Commune, a model of hard work and self-reliance in a barren county of the Northwest province of Shansi. The Secretary of the Party branch of this production brigade, Ch'en Yung-kuei, was to become a major spokesman for Mao's conception of politicized rural administration and production leadership.[119] Similarly, the Taching Oil Field received national press attention beginning in the spring of 1964 as a model of the Maoist virtues of self-reliance and struggle in industrial development.[120]

This pressure, while overwhelming in its press impact, apparently met with continuing, though veiled, efforts by the Party apparatus and Party supporters within the Army to divert or dilute the Maoist initiatives. Only on the basis of Cultural Revolution attacks on leaders of this time do we know that certain "model" experiences publicized in the national press—and others which never received attention in the public media—were advanced by Party and Army leaders as alternatives to those which embodied "the thought of Mao Tse-tung." Other Maoist models were "co-opted" by leaders who sought to dilute the impact of the Chairman's policies by distorting the content of his advanced experiences.

In opposition to the stress of Mao and Lin on the primary im-

118. See John Gittings, *The Role of the Chinese Army* (London: Oxford University Press, 1967), pp. 254–258. I am also indebted to Professor Ellis Joffe for his guidance in interpreting the expanding political influence of the PLA during this period. He has gathered additional documentaton on these organizational changes in an unpublished paper, "The Chinese Army on the Eve of the Cultural Revolution: Prelude to Intervention" (prepared for a conference on Government in China: The Management of a Revolutionary Society, August 1969), pp. 26–28.

119. *See* Ch'en Yung-kuei, "Self Reliance Is a Magic Wand," *Red Flag,* No. 1 (January 6, 1965); trans. in *SCMM,* No. 454 (February 1, 1965), pp. 25–29.

120. Commentator, "On Man as the Primary Factor," *Red Flag,* No. 10 (May 23, 1964); trans. in *SCMM,* No. 422 (June 22, 1964), pp. 5–6.

portance of political study, Chief of Staff Lo Jui-ch'ing was said to have organized weapons competitions within the PLA in January of 1964 in order to emphasize military technique.[121] As noted earlier, Lo's public statements of the 1960s seem to give primary emphasis to combat heroes, rather than to model soldiers in politics and production like Mao's good student Lei Feng. Lo was said to have "borrowed" the Maoist model Kuo Hsing-fu and turned him into a technician in the context of the All-PLA Great Tournament of military skills in the beginning of 1964.[122]

P'eng Chen and Organization Department Director An Tzu-wen were to be attacked for advancing the Tatuho and Nanliu Party branch organizations as model alternatives to "The Good Eighth Company" and the Tachai production brigade.[123] P'eng Chen and Liu Shao-ch'i were criticized for formulating a "hundred key counties" scheme in opposition to Mao's plans for local initiative in advancing agricultural mechanization; while Liu is said to have obstructed publication of the story of the Chinhsing production brigade as a model of self-financed mechanization.[124]

Other provincial Party leaders were accused of having channeled scarce financial resources into local industrial models in order to compete with Taching.[125] Liu and Wang Kuang-mei were to be attacked for publicizing throughout the Party the "Peach Garden Experience" of the "Four Clean-Ups" campaign in a Hopei production brigade as an alternative to Mao's effort to promote "class struggle" in rural rectification.[126] And in the arts, P'eng Chen was said to have promoted certain theatrical productions in oppo-

121. *See* the Cultural Revolution pamphlet, *Chairman Mao's Successor— Deputy Supreme Commander Lin Piao;* trans. in *Current Background,* No. 894 (October 27, 1969), p. 22. Also, "Counter-Revolutionary Revisionist Lo Jui-ch'ing Is Loaded with Crimes," *Chan-pao* [Combat News], January 30, 1967.

122. "Counter-Revolutionary Revisionist Lo Jui-ch'ing Is Loaded with Crimes," *Chan-pao,* January 30, 1967.

A detailed analysis of Lo's opposition to the Mao-Lin military policies, leading to his purge in 1965, will be found in Harry Harding and Melvin Gurtov, *The Purge of Lo Jui-ch'ing: The Politics of Chinese Strategic Planning* (Santa Monica, Calif.: The Rand Corporation, 1970).

123. *See* "Events Surrounding the 'Ch'angkuanlou' Counter-Revolutionary Incident," in *Tung-fang-hung* (April 20, 1967).

124. *See* "The Conflict between Mao Tse-tung and Liu Chao-ch'i over Agricultural Mechanization in Communist China," *Current Scene,* Vol. VI, No. 17 (October 1, 1968), pp. 12–16.

125. *See* "China's Taching Oilfield: Eclipse of an Industrial Model," *Current Scene,* Vol. VI, No. 16 (September 17, 1968), p. 8.

126. "Sham Four Clean-Ups, Real Restoration," *People's Daily* (September 6, 1967); trans. in *SCMP,* No. 4024 (September 20, 1967), pp. 1–20.

sition to Chiang Ch'ing's models of revolutionary Peking Opera.[127] "Model" experiences thus became weapons in the war of words over whose conception of the development process was to shape national social and economic policies.

In addition to the developments of early 1964 in the areas of Party and military life, political indoctrination, and economic activity, there also was a sharpening of issues within the intellectual community, most notably in theatrical work and press debates on apparently obscure issues of philosophy and historical interpretation. As seems to be the case in Communist countries, where the combination of ideologically-oriented politics and the need for the skills of a small, highly educated group charges academic life with political tension, intellectual developments in China during 1963–64 were to be a bellwether for far-reaching changes in Party and Army political alignments. As in 1957 and 1961–62, the intellectuals were pawns in a political conflict; a surrogate for those leaders who did not want to confront Mao directly on issues which would have split the Party "center."

Party use of the intellectuals to resist Mao's Tenth Plenum call for renewed "class struggle" was said to lie behind a "Forum on Confucius" convened by the Shantung Historical Society in November 1962 to commemorate the 2,440th anniversary of the death of China's ancient philosopher-sage. According to Cultural Revolution documents, this forum was encouraged by Chou Yang, Deputy Director of the Party's Propaganda Department and Vice-Chairman of the All-China Federation of Literary and Artistic Circles. His purpose was to reaffirm the ancient Confucian virtues of "human-heartedness" (*jen*) and benevolent government in order to dilute Mao's effort to sharpen political confrontation.[128]

In May of 1963 a national conference of writers and artists was convened to enable China's intellectuals to "play their full militant role" in the intensifying struggle against "modern revisionism" and to help them "identify themselves with the broad masses of the laboring people, with the workers, peasants and soldiers." They were exhorted "not to dodge or cover up the struggle between [political]

127. *See* "Comrade Chiang Ch'ing Leads Us to Struggle," *Hsin Pei-ta,* (May 30, 1967).

Other indications of opposition to Chiang Ch'ing's efforts to create "model" Peking operas by P'eng Chen and other leaders, based on Red Guard materials, will be found in Chung and Miller, *Madame Mao,* pp. 111, 127.

128. "'The Forum on Confucius'—A Black Session of Monsters and Demons for Attacking the Party," *People's Daily* (January 10, 1967); trans. in *SCMP,* No. 3863 (January 19, 1967), pp. 4–13.

contradictions" in their work. "Works devoid of conflict are liked by nobody." [129] This conference was but one of a continuing series of measures initiated by Mao and his supporters to confront the political "revisionism" which they saw propagated by intellectuals backed by Party leaders.

Chiang Ch'ing became increasingly active in artistic matters at this time. She is said to have carried out investigations into the background and intent of the Wu Han play, "The Dismissal of Hai Jui." She found it to have "serious political problems," and initiated a behind-the-scenes campaign to have it banned from the stage.[130]

And with the help of Mao's supporters in Shanghai—K'o Ch'ing-shih, Chang Ch'un-ch'iao, and Yao Wen-yuan—Chiang Ch'ing promoted the publication of an article in the local press attacking the notion that "ghosts are harmless." [131] Her pre-Cultural Revolution influence was to culminate in the summer of 1964 with sponsorship of a national festival of Peking Opera on revolutionary themes.

Such activities reflected Mao's total disaffection with the political orientation of China's intellectuals. As he commented in late 1963 upon reading a report by K'o Ch'ing-shih on artistic matters:

> Problems abound in all forms of art . . . and the people involved are numerous; in many departments very little has been achieved so far in socialist transformation. The "dead" still predominate in many departments. . . .
>
> Isn't it absurd that many communists are enthusiastic about promoting feudal and capitalist art, but not socialist art?[132]

It was such a concern which lay behind the promotion of a rectification campaign in the All-China Federation of Literary and Artistic Circles beginning in June of 1964. In a statement on the campaign, Mao warned: "Unless [these intellectuals] remold themselves in real earnest, at some future date they are bound to become groups like the Hungarian Petöfi Club." [133]

Mao's disgust with what fifteen years of Party rule had wrought in China's intellectual life was also evident in his evaluation of the

129. See "National Conference of China's Writers and Artists," NCNA (May 21, 1963); trans. in *SCMP*, No. 2986 (May 24, 1963), pp. 2–5.

130. "Comrade Chiang Ch'ing's Outstanding Contributions to the Cultural Revolution," *Hsin Pei-ta* (May 30, 1967).

131. Chiang Ch'ing, "Do New Services for the People," in *Tung-fang-hung* (June 3, 1967).

132. Mao, "Comment on Comrade K'o Ch'ing-shih's Report" (December 12, 1963), in *Long Live the Thought of Mao Tse-tung!* p. 25.

133. Mao, "Instructions Concerning Literature and Art" (June 1964), *ibid.*, p. 26.

educational system. In an almost exact repetition of words he had used in an essay on educational methods written in 1917, Mao attacked contemporary teaching practices: "The current method tramples men of talent and young people underfoot. I do not approve of it. So many books have to be read and the examination method is one for tackling enemies. This is harmful and must be put to an end." [134] And in a phrase which reveals how contemporary Chinese life had begun to strike the old anti-dependency themes in his character, the Chairman observed to foreign visitors, "The [teaching] method now used is the forced feeding type, and is not spontaneous." [135]

Mao was to be increasingly negative in his evaluation of the educational system and its influence on China's youth in remarks to foreign visitors after 1964. In January 1965 he told his old acquaintance Edgar Snow that for all anyone knew the younger generation in time might "make peace with imperialism, bring the remnants of the Chiang K'ai-shek clique back to the mainland, and take a stand beside the small percentage of counterrevolutionaries still in the country." [136] In August of the same year he denounced Peking University before a visiting French delegation, adding that "this youth is showing dangerous tendencies"; "youth must be put to the test." [137]

That Mao should express such negative remarks to foreign visitors is only one of a number of indications that the Chairman felt his words were no longer being heeded within the Party. Realizing that his voice was being muffled by an unresponsive bureaucracy, he began to think of ways of giving a political voice to others (and to himself) who would be concerned with the social problems he saw but could not confront. In a comment on educational reform written in the summer of 1965, Mao stressed:

134. Mao, "Instructions Given at the Spring Festival Concerning Educational Work (Excerpts)" (February 13, 1964), in *ibid.,* p. 27.

In his essay "A Study of Physical Education" (*New Youth,* 1917) Mao had written: "In the educational system of our country, required courses are as thick as the hairs on a cow. Even an adult with a tough, strong body could not stand it, let alone those who have not reached adulthood, or those who are weak. Speculating on the intentions of the educators, one is led to wonder whether they did not design such an unwieldy curriculum in order to exhaust the students, to trample on their bodies and ruin their lives." (Cited in Stuart R. Schram, *The Political Thought of Mao Tse-tung* [New York: Praeger, 1963], p. 96.)

135. Mao, "Talk with the Nepalese Educational Delegation on Educational Problems" (1964), *ibid.,* p. 28.

136. Edgar Snow, "Interview with Mao," *The New Republic* (February 27, 1965), p. 23.

137. André Malraux, *Anti-Memoirs,* pp. 375, 366.

Political work must take the mass line. It won't do to rely merely on the leaders alone. . . . [It] is necessary to mobilize everybody to assume responsibility, to speak out, to give encouragement and make criticism. Everybody has a pair of eyes and a mouth. They should be allowed to use their eyes and mouths. It is democracy to let the masses handle their own affairs. . . . Since everybody has a mouth, they must bear two kinds of responsibilities—to feed and to speak. They should speak out and take up the responsibility of fighting against bad deeds and bad styles of work.[138]

It was in the summer of 1965 that Mao remarked to André Malraux: "I am alone with the masses, waiting." [139] The Chairman thus contrasted his own isolation atop the Party bureaucracy with the need to find a political voice through the actions of others. It was such a sentiment that led Lin Piao to exclaim, in a later day when the muffling Party organization had been destroyed:

. . . as Liu Shao-ch'i and his gang of counterrevolutionary revisionists blocked Chairman Mao's instructions, the broad revolutionary masses could hardly hear Chairman Mao's voice directly. The storm [of the Cultural Revolution] made it possible for Mao Tse-tung's thought to reach the broad revolutionary masses directly. This is a great victory.[140]

But before a new Party leadership purged of (some of) Mao's opponents could pass a resolution on the mass distribution of the Chairman's writings,[141] there were decisive political battles to be fought.

THE MATTER OF SUCCESSION

Is our society today thoroughly clean? No, it is not. Classes and class struggle remain, the activities of the overthrown reactionary classes plotting a comeback still continue, and we still have speculative activities by old and new bourgeois elements and desperate forays by embezzlers, grafters and degenerates. *There are also cases of degeneration in a few primary organizations; what is more, these degenerates do their utmost to find protectors and agents in the higher leading*

138. Mao, "Comment on Peking Normal College's Investigation Material Report" (July 3, 1965), in *Long Live the Thought of Mao Tse-tung!* p. 30.
139. André Malraux, *Anti-Memoirs*, p. 375.
140. Lin Piao, "Report to the Ninth National Congress of the Communist Party of China" (April 1, 1969); trans. in *Current Background*, No. 880 (May 9, 1969), p. 31.
141. *See* "Chinese Communist Party Central Committee Decides to Speed Up the Mass Publication of Mao Tse-tung's Works" (August 7, 1966); trans. in *SCMP*, No. 3759 (August 12, 1969), p. 11.

bodies. We should not in the least slacken our vigilance against such phenomena but must keep fully alert.

PEOPLE'S DAILY and RED FLAG, 1964[142]

. . . the question of cultivating successors [to lead the revolution] has become increasingly urgent and important. Internationally, imperialism headed by the United States has placed its hope of realizing "peaceful evolution" in China on the corruption of our third and fourth generations. *Who can say that this way of thinking of theirs is not without a certain foundation?*

RED FLAG, 1964[143]

So many deeds cry out to be done,   Times presses.
And always urgently;   Ten thousand years are too long,
The world rolls on,   Seize the day, seize the hour!

MAO TSE-TUNG, 1963[144]

Following the Tenth Plenum in the fall of 1962 more than three years were to elapse before Mao's voice was heard in national political matters with anything like the assertiveness of the years 1955 through 1958. And even when his influence was reasserted, "the thought of Mao Tse-tung" was to be invoked by other voices, Lin Piao and Yao Wen-yuan. A key question in the interpretation of Chinese domestic politics during the 1960s is the point at which Mao came to realize that if his influence on the Chinese revolution was to endure, basic issues related to the control of the policy-implementing process would have to be raised.

According to Lin Piao, it was as early as 1962 that Mao was "first to perceive the danger of the counterrevolutionary plots of Liu Shao-ch'i and his gang." [145] As we suggested earlier, it may have been Liu's unwillingness to sustain his support of Mao on the P'eng Teh-huai issue which undermined the political relationship between the two men.

A second poetic exchange between Mao and Kuo Mo-jo in early 1963 suggests that shortly after the Tenth Plenum the Chairman

142. *People's Daily* and *Red Flag* joint editorial, "On Khrushchev's Phoney Communism and Its Historical Lessons for the World" (July 14, 1964); in *Polemic on the General Line of the International Communist Movement*, p. 470. Emphasis added.

143. *Red Flag* editorial, "The Cultivation of Successors Is an Unending Great Task of Revolution," No. 14 (July 31, 1964), p. 34. Emphasis added.

144. Mao, "Reply to Comrade Kuo Mo-jo" (January 9, 1963), in *Ten More Poems of Mao Tse-tung*, p. 20.

145. Lin Piao, "Report to the Ninth National Congress of the Communist Party of China" (April 1, 1969); trans. in *Current Background*, No. 880 (May 9, 1969), p. 24.

was quite conscious of a coming political "storm." Kuo wrote to Mao in what seems almost a spirit of optimism, given the nation's economic problems and the Sino-Soviet conflict:

> When the seas are in turmoil,
> Heroes are on their mettle.
> Six hundred million people,
> Strong in unity,
> Firm in principle,
> Can keep the falling heavens suspended,
> And create order out of the reign of chaos.
>
> . . .
>
> Four great volumes
> Show us the way.[146]

Mao, however, was not so certain of the "firmness in principle" of the people or Party. He certainly had doubts about the willingness of certain Party leaders to follow the "four great volumes" of his political thought. Mao replied to Kuo that "shrilling, moaning" insects were plotting "to topple the giant tree"; that it was necessary to "seize the day, seize the hour!" of confrontation.[147] And he concluded impatiently:

> The Four Seas are rising, clouds and waters raging,
> The Five Continents are rocking, wind and thunder roaring.
> Away with all pests!
> Our force is irresistible.[148]

Just how much of this poetic imagery of early 1963 reflects Mao's sentiments about domestic leadership conflicts, as opposed to the Sino-Soviet dispute, is uncertain. As we have tried to document, however, Mao's domestic political influence in the wake of the Great Leap Forward hardly justified the assertion that "Our force is irresistible." On the basis of evidence in the public record, it appears that it was not until the summer of 1964 that Mao felt he had sufficient organizational power—based on his strengthened influence within the Army—to raise political issues related to the erosion of his control over Party policy. The present section is an effort to document the timing and manner of Mao's confrontation with those who resisted his leadership within the Party.

In late May of 1964 an obscure article on philosophical concepts appeared in the Peking paper of the intellectuals, the *Kuang-ming*

146. Kuo's poem, untitled and undated, is translated in *Ten More Poems of Mao Tse-tung*, p. 31.

147. Mao, "Reply to Comrade Kuo Mo-jo" (January 9, 1963), in *ibid.*, p. 20.

148. *Ibid.*, p. 22.

Daily. The apparently esoteric assertion of the two authors, Ai
Heng-wu and Lin Ch'ing-shan, was that "two combining into one"
—or "the unity of opposites"—was the universal law of materialist
dialectics, whereas "one dividing into two" was a matter of the
analytical approach used by Marxists in comprehending the natural
world and man's social life.

Among the examples they gave to illustrate their interpretation
was the matter of evaluating the contributions and errors of Party
members: The best comrades were bound to have their flaws; and
those with defects still had their good points. "Some comrades,"
however, made the "metaphysical" mistake of seeing only the bad
points in other people's work.

> They see only the contradictory aspect of the problem, but fail to
> see the other aspect. When things are observed, they often tend to be
> absolute, holding that good things are absolutely good, and bad things
> absolutely bad. . . . When this method is used to size up other
> comrades, units, sectors, or localities, only the shortcomings, mis-
> takes, and bad points will be noticed. The driving force for develop-
> ment and progress is thus missing in one's work, and harmful feelings
> of self-importance, arrogance, self-satisfaction and conservatism are
> bound to be engendered.[149]

This article drew indignant replies from other writers who reminded Comrades Ai and Lin that according to Chairman Mao the
struggle between opposites, "dividing one into two," was the fundamental law of human progress.

By the end of the summer more than ninety published articles in
the national press had carried this debate to a furious pitch; and the
editorial department of the Party's theoretical journal *Red Flag* had
convened a special two-day forum on the issue, so that students and
cadres of the Higher Party School could debate the relative merits
of "two combining into one" or "one dividing into two."

After three months of exchanges in the press, *Red Flag* gave
some inkling of what the debate was all about in an article which
attacked by name the Director of the Higher Party School, Yang
Hsien-chen. Yang was said to have deliberately provoked the contro-
versy by disseminating the idea among his students that the reconciliation of "contradictions"—"two combining into one"—was the
fundamental law of Marxist dialectics. After invoking threatening
phrases and historical images from the era of Stalin's purges, *Red
Flag* asserted:

149. Ai Heng-wu and Lin Ch'ing-shan, " 'Dividing One into Two' and
'Combining Two into One,' " *Kuang-ming Daily* (May 29, 1964); trans. in
Current Background, No. 745 (December 2, 1964), p. 3.

It is no accident that Comrade Yang Hsien-chen should at this time have made public the concept of "two combining into one." He has done this with the aim and plan of pitting the reactionary bourgeois world outlook against the proletarian world outlook of materialist dialectics.[150]

Yang and his cohorts were said to have been "actuated by ulterior motives" in asserting that "an academic question should not be turned into a political question." The manner in which this debate on philosophical concepts was related to political matters was left unstated; but *Red Flag* asserted that "whenever a sharp class struggle develops in the political and economic fields, there is bound to be acute class struggle in the ideological field as well." [151] It was recalled that during the 1920s in the Soviet Union, during the political struggle against the "anti-Party" faction of Trotsky and Bukharin, "antidialectical philosophical views became the ideological weapon of the anti-Party group." *Red Flag* observed that this debate was "still far from being concluded. Step by step it is deepening. Truth always develops in struggle." [152]

Only from the perspective of Cultural Revolution developments can one infer that behind these veiled assertions of the emergence of an "anti-Party" group, and a debate over the question of whether "contradictions" would lead to division or reconciliation, was the question of whether the leadership of the Chinese Communist Party would be split. Would the unitary Party "divide into two," or could underlying conflicts over policy and leadership approach be resolved?

It remains obscure why the lines of conflict within the Party leadership became so tightly drawn in the early summer of 1964. In part it must have been a reflection of the organizational pressures which Mao and Lin Piao were putting on the Party through the "learn from the PLA" campaign. The key question seems to be why Mao had come to feel the press of time, the need to "seize the day, seize the hour." Why did he now choose to press issues related to personnel and political organization to the point of "dividing one into two"?

150. *Red Flag* correspondent, "New Polemic on the Philosophical Front," *Red Flag*, No. 16 (August 31, 1964); trans. in *ibid.*, p. 29.

151. *Ibid.*, p. 31.

During the Cultural Revolution one Red Guard publication hinted that a *coup* attempt against Mao and Lin Piao had its origins in the Peking Higher Party School in June of 1964. (*See* "The February [1966] Coup," *Chan Pao* [Combat Bulletin], April 17, 1967.) This document, however, has not been supported by additional evidence.

152. *Ibid.*

In 1964 the Chairman was in his seventy-first year; and beginning in the fall, rumors began to circulate that he had had a stroke, was suffering from Parkinson's disease, or had some other serious health problem.[153] Edgar Snow was struck by Mao's repeated observation that "he was soon going to see God," and his musing on how, in a career filled with the violence of revolution, he had so long escaped death.[154] In August 1965 André Malraux observed a nurse at the Chairman's side.[155]

While Mao's subsequent political vigor tends to belie these rumors of ill health and indications of a personal awareness of imminent death, it nonetheless may be that medical problems heightened for Mao the sense that he had only limited time in which to insure that his style of leadership would endure in the institutions of new China. For almost a decade, Khrushchev's denunciation of Stalin and the "personality cult," had been one source of the erosion of his authority. It was now compounded by the direct experience of P'eng Teh-huai's challenge and continuing pressures from within the Party leadership for "reversing verdicts" and reconsideration of the policies of the Great Leap Forward.

In short, Mao's faith in his "claim to immortality" [156] through the permanence of policies and political institutions which were the sum of a life of struggle was being undermined. Perhaps burdened with what Robert Lifton has termed "death anxiety," the Chairman was seeking to sustain the meaning of his life in the support of those who would survive his passing.[157]

It is not known whether the debate over "two into one" or "one into two" reflects a confrontation within the leadership in the spring of 1964 which raised basic questions of policy or personal status. Perhaps Mao invoked his authority in an uncompromising way in order to reassert influence over developments now beyond his con-

153. A French delegation which visited Mao at his Hangchow retreat in September 1964 observed him shaking in a manner which reminded one of the observers of his own father's Parkinson's disease. (*See* Edward Behr, "Red China Face to Face," *Saturday Evening Post* [November 14, 1964], pp. 21–28.) Other reports from China reaching Hong Kong during late 1964 and 1965 rumored that Mao was recuperating from a mild stroke, or had high blood pressure and a heart condition. (*See* Stanley Karnow, "Status of Vanished Mao—Dead, Ill, or Lively—Stumps Experts," *Washington Post* [May 8, 1966], p. 1.)

154. Edgar Snow, "Interview with Mao," *The New Republic* (February 27, 1965), p. 23.

155. André Malraux, *Anti-Memoirs,* p. 372.

156. *See* the suggestive essay by Robert Jay Lifton, *Revolutionary Immortality: Mao Tse-tung and the Chinese Cultural Revolution* (New York: Random House, 1968), p. 93.

157. *Ibid.,* pp. 19–20.

trol. The polemic over Yang Hsien-chen's philosophical concepts, however, does convey the sense of a Party organization appealing for reconciliation, with Maoist spokesmen responding with an uncompromising determination to "divide one into two." Other developments which followed in late May also strongly suggest that the Chairman had invoked the one issue on which his own attenuated authority within the Party still carried considerable influence: the matter of his public approbation of a successor to his leadership of the Party. Mao apparently decided that the test of who was to receive that approbation was to be a matter of unquestioned loyalty to his person and unwavering commitment to his conception of the revolution, his "thought."

Ten days after the *Kuang-ming Daily* published the first article supporting Yang Hsien-chen's thesis of the fundamental importance of "two combining into one," the same paper republished a *Liberation Army Daily* editorial of June 6th. This editorial was apparently a veiled warning to Liu Shao-ch'i and his supporters that the basic issue of loyalty to the "thought of Mao Tse-tung," was now at stake. The editorial quoted from Liu's *How to Be a Good Communist* on the need to hold firm to political principles "at a time when the [political] situation is complex, the environment is beset with sharp changes, and there is need to follow a zigzagging road." [158] Yet which political principles were to guide one through such a complicated environment, Marxism-Leninism or "the thought of Mao Tse-tung"?

> *To study Chairman Mao's works is a shortcut to the study of Marxism-Leninism.* Chairman Mao is a great standard bearer of Marxism-Leninism in the contemporary era, and Mao Tse-tung's thought is an important development of Marxism-Leninism. Now, many revolutionary people are studying Chairman Mao's works.[159]

The editorial then pointedly observed:

158. *Liberation Army Daily* editorial, "Study Chairman Mao's Works with a Profound Class Feeling," *Kuang-ming Daily* (June 8, 1964); trans. in *Current Background,* No. 739 (August 24, 1964), p. 60.
This passage cited from Liu's book appears to be a politically "loaded" addition to the 1962 revision. During the Cultural Revolution this particular passage was to be singled out for criticism as an example of Liu's political deviousness. (*See "How to Be a Good Communist* Is a Revisionist Program Opposed to the Thought of Mao Tse-tung," *Ching-kang-shan,* reprinted in *Kuang-ming Daily* [April 8, 1967]; trans. in *Current Background,* No. 827 [June 1, 1967], pp. 1–16.) Hence, one senses that in 1964 Liu was indirectly being called to account for his opposition to Mao.
159. *Liberation Army Daily* editorial, "Study Chairman Mao's Works with a Profound Class Feeling." Emphasis added.

. . . not every comrade understands clearly what must be done before a success can be made of the study [of Chairman Mao's works]. Some comrades hold that the mentality of a person and his ideological cultivation (*hsiu-yang*) have something to do with whether or not he is able to study Chairman Mao's works well. This view is incorrect.[160]

The implication of these assertions of the PLA paper was that Mao's writings and his emphasis on "thought reform" (*szu-hsiang kai-tsao*) took precedence over Liu's efforts to establish the "cultivation" (*hsiu-yang*) of Party members as the basis for their "rectification." The test of political commitment in the coming period of trial was to be whether one deferred to Mao's "thought" or to Marxism-Leninism as the basis of one's political life.

Later in June, the Party's Youth League held its Ninth National Congress. Mao used the Congress to raise publicly the issue of "cultivating" (*p'ei-yang*, not *hsiu-yang*) a new generation of "revolutionary successors" (*chieh-pan jen*).

The "important directive" in which the Party Chairman discussed the succession problem has never been made public; yet its major arguments appear to be included in the ninth of a year-long series of polemical exchanges with the Soviet Party leadership which was published in mid-July. In an evaluation of the lessons for China of "Khrushchev's Phoney Communism," Mao revealed his concern with "careerists and conspirators like Khrushchev" "usurping the leadership of the Party and government at any level." The article hinted that political degenerates with influence at high levels within the Chinese Party were violating the "mass line" style of leadership, were "despotic like Khrushchev," and were likely to "make surprise attacks" on their comrades—"like Khrushchev." [161]

By raising the issue of succession within the Chinese Party in the context of a public polemic with the Soviets, Mao thus revealed just how interwoven in his own mind had become the erosion of his authority which followed Khrushchev's "surprise attack" on Stalin, P'eng Teh-huai's "surprise attack" on his Great Leap policies at Lushan, and continuing conflicts within the Chinese Party leadership over policy and personal status. One also infers from the Cultural Revolution characterization of Liu Shao-ch'i as "China's Khrushchev" that by mid-1964 Mao had developed strong doubts about Liu's status as his successor. The Chairman saw his

160. *Ibid.*, p. 61.
161. *People's Daily* and *Red Flag* joint editorial, "On Khrushchev's Phoney Communism and Its Historical Lessons for the World" (July 14, 1964), in *Polemic on the General Line of the International Communist Movement*, pp. 478–479.

life's work as vulnerable to repudiation by disloyal comrades; and he was trying to preempt their attacks, to avoid Stalin's posthumous degradation, by selecting new and loyal successors.

How directly did the Chairman challenge Liu Shao-ch'i's authority within the councils of the Party at this time? As reported by Edgar Snow, it was not until a meeting of the Party leadership on January 25th, 1965, that Mao finally "decided Liu had to go" (see fn. 185, p. 469 below). Given all the indications of policy differences between the two leaders explored in these last three chapters, however, it seems most unlikely that this meeting was anything more than a final, explicit confrontation between the two men; an exchange on the question of how to rectify a "revisionist" Party in which Mao found Liu fully beyond his influence. It seems more likely that by raising in mid-1964 the general problem of succession, Mao was giving Liu a last chance to "stand on his side," and using the succession issue to drive a wedge between opponents within the Party leadership.

At the Youth League Congress in June 1964, although Mao had intimated that there were political degenerates "at all levels" of the Party, he had raised the issue of cultivating "revolutionary successors" in very general terms. From the point of view of political tactics, for Mao to have drawn the succession issue too explicitly would have provoked a showdown at a time and in a manner in which he was hardly certain to win. Since his earliest days in politics, Mao has shown great discipline in biding his time when out of influence, and an ability to "disintegrate" enemies and "crush opponents one by one." [162] The Chairman apparently was now playing his one remaining source of strength—his ability to confer legitimacy on a successor—for all it was worth. By keeping silent on his choice of a successor, even as he publicly raised the issue, he acquired the political leverage to divide those within the Party leadership who opposed his "thought," and to build a new coalition of supporters for a confrontation with diehard "revisionists."

Such an interpretation is one way of accounting for the pattern of conflict during 1965 and 1966, in which second rank leaders like P'eng Chen, Teng Hsiao-p'ing, and T'ao Chu appeared to rise in political influence. Then with other leaders Lo Jui-ch'ing and Liu Shao-ch'i, they were sequentially purged over the period of a year.

Whatever the accuracy of this interpretation, one sees in editorial reactions to Mao's June initiative on the question of cultivating "revolutionary successors" an effort by the Party and Youth League

162. *See* pp. 228–234 above.

to incorporate the Chairman's pressure into their regular pattern of organizational activity. They either ignored or did not dare to grasp the full implication of the range of issues which Mao and the Army had raised on all fronts since the winter of 1964. An editorial in *China Youth Daily* at the conclusion of the aforementioned Youth League Congress in June asserted that "our socialist new China has all the favorable conditions for turning the youth into proletarian successors of the revolution." [163] Yet a *Red Flag* article of this time spoke with concern of the influence of modern revisionism on youth, "causing them to become pampered little gentry who will only know how to seek after personal pleasure, who will only know how to eat, drink, and play." [164] And within a year Mao was repeatedly to call into question before foreign visitors the political maturity of the younger generation.[165]

A *People's Daily* editorial of early August stressed that the purpose of cultivating "revolutionary successors" was "to strengthen constantly the nucleus of Party leadership at all levels so that the correct line and correct policies of the Party are adhered to at all times." [166] By the end of the year, however, Mao had intervened twice in an attempt to correct what he considered to be the erroneous policy orientation of the Socialist Education Movement, which, under Liu Shao-ch'i's "first line" guidance, was giving stress to Party leadership "from above."

As had happened with so many of Mao's policies since the inception of the Great Leap crisis, the Party took the Chairman's initiative and tried to turn it back on him. The *People's Daily* editorialized on Mao's assertion that "revolutionary successors" must be good at uniting with their colleagues, even those with whom they disagreed:

> Members of the nucleus of leadership must make the best use of collective wisdom and be good at listening to all useful opinions and working with people of differing views, be good at creating an atmosphere of earnestly discussing and studying problems so that comrades with differing views can freely express their opinions, undertake debates and make right and wrong clear, and through such dis-

163. *China Youth Daily* editorial, "Forever Be Firm Revolutionaries" (July 8, 1964); trans. in *SCMP*, No. 3278 (August 13, 1964), p. 2.

164. *Red Flag* editorial, "The Cultivation of Successors Is an Unending Great Task of Revolution," No. 14 (July 1964), p. 35.

165. *See* Mao's comments to Edgar Snow and André Malraux, on p. 451 above.

166. *People's Daily* editorial, "Cultivate and Train Millions of Successors Who Will Carry on the Cause of Proletarian Revolution" (August 3, 1964); trans. in *SCMP*, No. 3274 (August 7, 1964), p. 1.

cussions to raise comrades' ideological level of Marxism-Leninism, raise their ability to discover errors and strengthen unity among them on Marxist-Leninist principles.[167]

The Party paper then pointedly added:

It is necessary resolutely to oppose the arbitrary style of "do as I say," resolutely oppose the rude style of not treating others as equals, and resolutely oppose the style of those who welcome flattery and turn like a wounded tiger on those who raise criticism.[168]

A further response to Mao's initiative on the succession issue which more completely reveals a fear of the growing political polarization between Party and Army was expressed in an article of late September by An Tzu-wen, Director of the Party's Organization Department. In contrast to Mao's insistence on pressing "class struggle," An Tzu-wen declared that

during the socialist period, building socialism is the highest criterion of our unity. All the comrades building socialism should be seriously united with thorough criticism–self-criticism even if they hold different views which conflict with ours over certain concrete problems or when they show certain shortcomings or even make mistakes.[169]

In contrast to Mao's assertion of mid-July that it was "essential to test and know cadres and choose and train succeessors in the long course of mass struggle," [170] An Tzu-wen talked about cultivating successors "on a business-like basis":

. . . with workers and peasants gradually acquiring knowledge and with intellectuals performing labor, fine and cultured workers and peasants and revolutionary intellectuals having close connections [with each other] will be brought up in large numbers. This is a safe and dependable road to bringing up newborn forces of revolution and training revolutionary successors.[171]

Mao evidently had made clear to Party leaders his determination to press for "mass struggle" as the way to rear a successor genera-

167. *People's Daily* editorial, "Educate the Younger Generation to Be Revolutionaries Forever" (July 8, 1964); trans. in *Current Background*, No. 738 (July 30, 1964), pp. 41–43.

168. *Ibid.*

169. An Tzu-wen, "Cultivating and Training Revolutionary Successors Is a Strategic Task of the Party," *Red Flag*, Nos. 17–18 (September 23, 1964); trans. in *SCMM*, No. 438 (October 12, 1964), p. 7.

170. *People's Daily* and *Red Flag* joint editorial, "On Khrushchev's Phoney Communism and Its Historical Lessons for the World," in *Polemic on the General Line of the International Communist Movement*, p. 479.

171. An Tzu-wen, "Cultivating and Training Revolutionary Successors Is a Strategic Task of the Party," p. 11.

tion, and it was increasingly apparent that the Army was to be the guarantor of this intention. An Tzu-wen, however, tried to reinterpret Mao's assertion of the need to confront modern revisionism by reformulating the current conflict as a contest between the "true Marxist-Leninists" (of the Party) and "phoney Marxist-Leninists" (in the Army). In what perhaps is an indirect reference to Lin Piao, Mao's chosen successor to PLA leadership, An Tzu-wen stressed the importance of being able to distinguish those

> who are true Marxist-Leninists and [those] who are phoney Marxist-Leninists. [We] must very carefully select and train revolutionary successors, place the responsibility for leading the revolution in the hands of true Marxist-Leninists, and prevent phoney Marxist-Leninists from usurping the political leadership. It is not easy to distinguish true Marxist-Leninists from phoney Marxist-Leninists. Frequently, a wrong view is taken of a person.[172]

An Tzu-wen then recalled with concern the Kronstadt mutiny of 1921 in Russia, in which a rebellious naval unit had attempted to overthrow Communist Party leadership: "It will be remembered that when the White Guards of Russia staged a counterrevolutionary mutiny in Kronstadt, they raised this pernicious cry: 'Soviets without Communists!' "[173]

Who were the real, and who the phoney "Marxist-Leninists?" The Party organization clearly saw Mao's political reliance upon the Army as creating the danger of "Soviets without Communists." Yet one can only wonder whether as early as the summer of 1964 Mao knew how far his determination to press the conflict with Party opponents was to take him; and whether the Party had any inkling that Mao's "White Guards" of the Army were to be but the protectors of his "Red Guard" rebels among China's younger generation.

VIET-NAM!

On Army Day, August 1st of 1964, a *Liberation Army Daily* editorial seemed to express the degree to which Mao's disenchantment with the course of the revolution had led him back to the earliest

---

172. *Ibid.,* p. 3.

According to Cultural Revolution charges, Lo Jui-ch'ing (and presumably others) attempted at this time to get Lin Piao to step aside as Defense Minister, in the context of new decisions on State personnel which would be taken at the approaching first session of the Third National People's Congress. (*See* "Counter-Revolutionary Revisionist Lo Jui-ch'ing Is Loaded with Crimes," *Chan Pao* [January 30, 1967].)

173. *Ibid.,* p. 4.

battles of his political career. Entitled "Long Live the Firm and Complete Revolutionary Spirit of Chingkang Mountain," the editorial revealed that despite China's isolation within the International Communist Movement, military tensions on the country's southern border, and domestic political opposition, the Chairman remained determined to press the revolution through to the end.[174] Lines were invoked from a 1928 poem by Mao:

> Flags and banners flared at the mountain's foot
> While drums and bugles sounded from the peaks.
> The enemy army encircled us in countless cordons,
> But like the peaks I remained unmoved.[175]

The Chairman thus drew inspiration from early successes against great odds in the revolutionary struggle—and confidence from his renewed political support from the PLA.

In this context where Mao had pushed his differences with life-long Party cohorts to the point of "dividing one into two," the escalation of the war in Viet-Nam—sharply emphasized by the Tonkin Gulf clash between North Vietnamese and American naval vessels on August 5th—must have produced a political explosion within the Chinese Party leadership.

As the Viet-Nam conflict continued to expand over the next year, Mao and his supporters faced two related dangers: If the war enlarged in scope as a result of American participation to the point of directly threatening China's national security, the PLA—the Chairman's base of power in the recently escalated domestic political confrontation—might very well be dragged from his hands as a political instrument into military action against the United States. Concurrently, if pressures from within the "socialist camp" for "united action" in support of the North Vietnamese in their conflict with the Americans intensified, China might be forced to abandon the political confrontation with Soviet "revisionism." Renewed Sino-Soviet military and political cooperation in aid of the Vietnamese was likely to bring with it further Russian efforts to strengthen the hands of Mao's domestic rivals and new Soviet influence in Chinese military affairs.

The impact of the American escalation on China's internal politics was revealed in the months following the Tonkin Gulf incident in a predictable shift to military preparedness by the PLA, and

174. *Liberation Army Daily* editorial, "Long Live the Firm and Complete Revolutionary Spirit of Chingkang Mountain," *People's Daily* (August 1, 1964), p. 1.
175. *Ibid.*

a blurring of the lines of conflict between Party and Army. On September 8th a *People's Daily* "short comment" noted apprehensively: "We must brighten our eyes and keep a close watch against all conspiracies of the U.S. imperialists and class enemies at home and abroad. We must prepare for the worst and make all kinds of preparations." [176] The New Year's Day editorial of the *Liberation Army Daily* more explicitly revealed the shift to war preparations and collective Party (versus Maoist) influence in Army policy by its dominant emphasis on "training for combat." [177] It was stressed that the PLA was "able to fulfill any tasks assigned to it by the Party and the state" (not Chairman Mao). In a clear indication of the degree to which the war threat had forced "two to combine into one," the editorial exhorted Party cadres to "study energetically Marxism-Leninism *and* the thought of Mao Tse-tung, particularly Chairman Mao's philosophical works *and* Chairman Liu's book, *How to Be a Good Communist*." [178] Further emphasizing a shift to collective leadership, the editorial stressed that in the work of Party branches within the Army, "decisions [must not] be made by a single person, and no individuals should be permitted to change at will the decisions of the Party branch."

The degree to which the war context had forced a (temporary) reconciliation of domestic political differences was revealed in a *People's Daily* editorial and article of late 1964. Entitled "The Interests of the Party above Everything Else," the editorial commented on an article which described how a Party branch leader of a certain PLA platoon—"vexed by family problems"—had carried out his work assignments poorly. The editorial then revealed that by studying Liu Shao-ch'i's *How to Be a Good Communist* he had learned that "the Party's interests are above all else," and was able to subordinate his personal difficulties to the collective interests of the Party.[179]

The accompanying article also described a quarrel between the

176. *People's Daily* short comment, "Persevere in Struggle to the End" (September 8, 1964); trans. in *SCMP*, No. 3307 (September 29, 1964), p. 5.

177. From a *People's Daily* summary of a *Liberation Army Daily* editorial, "Hold Even Higher the Great Red Banner of the Thought of Mao Tse-tung and Carry through in an Even More Thorough-going Manner the Movement of Creating More 'Four Good' Companies" (January 1, 1965); trans. in *SCMP*, No. 3376 (January 13, 1965), p. 3.

178. *Ibid.*, p. 4. Emphasis added.

179. *People's Daily* editorial, "The Interests of the Party above Everything Else" (December 20, 1964); trans. in *SCMP*, No. 3369 (January 4, 1965), pp. 4–5.

leader of a certain PLA company and a member of the company's Party branch committee—apparently an indirect reference to the tensions between Army and Party leaderships—and how the two had resolved their differences through the study of Mao's writings on criticism–self-criticism and the relevant chapters of Liu's *How to Be a Good Communist.* After the argumentative Party member had read a passage from Liu's book on the harmfulness of excessive criticism of other people's errors, "his face turned red with shame and he felt that Comrade Liu Shao-ch'i's criticism had hit his vulnerable spot." [180] Through their combined political study, the two quarreling comrades "united with each other more closely than before."

This indirect revelation of efforts by the Party leadership to bring about a solution of political differences on the basis of the larger interests of Party unity and national security were contrasted in the press by continuing attacks on Yang Hsien-chen for his advocacy of reconciliation in dealing with political "contradictions." Conflicting "signals" in the press through 1965 suggest that despite Party efforts to depoliticize the confrontation within the leadership, Mao persisted in his determination to resolve the issues raised in 1964.

This unwillingness to compromise was reflected in the evolution of China's policy toward the Viet-Nam war. A remarkable public debate in the national press during 1965 on national defense policy revealed that the Viet-Nam situation, far from healing differences, actually increased the political differentiation within the leadership which had begun in the summer of 1964 over the issue of succession.

The question of China's relations with the Soviet Union was a major and highly divisive factor in this debate. The Sino-Soviet conflict had worsened steadily following the 1959 events centered about P'eng Teh-huai and the Chinese ideological challenge to the Russians in the spring of 1960. In June of that year, first at the General Council meeting of the World Federation of Trade Unions in Peking and then at the Rumanian Party Congress in Bucharest, there was public political conflict between Soviet and Chinese Party delegates. And in July and August Soviet technicians and economic aid were suddenly withdrawn from China. A world meeting of eighty-one Communist Parties in Moscow in November of 1960 only papered over the fundamental differences in political strategy

180. "The Party Branch of a Nanking Armed Forces Unit Studies *How to Be a Good Communist* in the Light of Reality," *People's Daily* (December 20, 1964); trans. in *ibid.,* p. 3.

and personal authority which had developed following Khrushchev's initiatives of 1956.[181]

In November of 1961, at the Soviet Party's Twenty-second Congress, Khrushchev had read the Albanians out of the International
Movement, an action which the Chinese interpreted as "killing the
chicken to warn the monkey." In protest, Chou En-lai, the Chinese
delegate to the Congress, staged a walk-out and demonstratively
laid a wreath at Stalin's inconspicuous new grave before returning
to Peking. The Chinese and Albanians were now staunch, if lonely,
fraternal allies in the International Movement.

The collapse of the Soviet-Cuban missile adventure in the fall of
1962, a striking contrast to the Chinese success in their border war
with India (toward which the Russians adopted a stand of "positive neutrality" in favor of the Indians), only increased Chinese
hostility and Russian vulnerability to Chinese attacks. The years
1963 and 1964 saw further unsuccessful efforts to limit the conflict,
and a subsequent expansion into direct public polemics.

There was an abortive bilateral meeting between Soviet and
Chinese Party representatives in Moscow in July of 1963, followed
by a series of press attacks in which both Parties exposed many
previously unknown developments that had led to a deepening of
the confrontation.[182] Beginning in 1963 the Chinese initiated a year-
long series of scathing articles which challenged Soviet leadership
of the International Movement. Khrushchev responded with (unsuccessful) efforts to convene another international conference of
Communist Parties in a "collective mobilization" of opinion against
Chinese factional agitation within the Movement and in other Party
organizations.

Khrushchev's fall from power in October of 1964—on the very
day that the Chinese exploded their first atomic device—must have
occasioned considerable debate within the Chinese Party leadership. A Chinese delegation—with what appears to be a careful
political balance between Chou En-lai and K'ang Sheng as representatives of Mao, and Ho Lung and Wu Hsiu-ch'uan as representatives of Army-Party interests—was dispatched to Moscow within
three weeks of Khrushchev's ouster. But the resumption of public

181. In addition to the study by Zagoria, *The Sino-Soviet Conflict, 1956–
1961*, this brief survey of the major developments in Sino-Soviet relations
after Lushan draws major guidance from the two analytical works on this
period by William E. Griffith, *The Sino-Soviet Rift* (Cambridge, Massachusetts: M.I.T. Press, 1964), and *Sino-Soviet Relations, 1964–1965* (Cambridge, Massachusetts: M.I.T. Press, 1967).

182. *See,* for example, the information on Sino-Soviet military relations
discussed on pp. 378–393 above.

Chinese attacks on the new Soviet leadership shortly after the return of this delegation indicates that the differences between the two Parties had passed well beyond Mao's personalized opposition to Khrushchev.

A *Red Flag* editorial of late November 1964 smugly declared that the Chinese Party, with its true Marxist-Leninist orientation, had "long foreseen" Khrushchev's political demise. It listed twelve policies promoted by the fallen Soviet leader which assertedly had led to the ouster of "this buffoon on the contemporary political stage." [183] The scope of these twelve points embodied a complete defense of Mao's domestic and international policies. For the new Soviet leadership to have accepted the correctness of these alternatives would have meant subordinating their Party and country to Chinese leadership in both domestic and international affairs. Obviously no Soviet leaders would or could accept such a position.

A further intensification of the threat to China's—and Mao's—interests came with the initiation of American air attacks on North Viet-Nam in early February of 1965 and the introduction of large numbers of American ground forces into the south. The bombings began as the new Soviet Premier Alexei Kosygin arrived in Hanoi to negotiate defense arrangements with the North Vietnamese leaders. The combined effect of these developments was to heighten the danger of a Sino-American confrontation as the air war neared China's southern border, to increase Soviet influence within North Viet-Nam through the military and economic aid which they could provide Hanoi, and to strengthen pressures from within the "socialist camp" for "united action" with the Soviets in aid of the Vietnamese.

The following months of debate among Chinese leaders over how to respond to this situation revealed both the diffusion of authority within the Party and the heightening conflict within the leadership. Between February and September of 1965, on a variety of occasions, Party and Army spokesmen revealed through subtle yet significant variations in their evaluation of the Viet-Nam situation, their conflicting views on policy toward the Soviet Union, the United States, and to China's national defense. [184] Chief of the

183. *Red Flag* editorial, "Why Khrushchev Fell" (November 21, 1964), in *Polemic on the General Line of the International Communist Movement*, pp. 483–492.

184. This discussion of the position of various Chinese leaders in evaluating the meaning of the Viet-Nam conflict for China's national security draws much inspiration from the detailed analysis by Uri Ra'anan, "Peking's Foreign Policy 'Debate,' 1965–1966," in Tang Tsou, ed., *China in Crisis* (Chicago: University of Chicago Press, 1968), Vol. II, pp. 23–71; and Donald S. Zagoria, *Viet-Nam Triangle* (New York: Pegasus, 1967).

General Staff Lo Jui-ch'ing appeared to stress the need for an "active defense" against what he characterized as an almost certain American extension of the war to China—a threat that required China to reach some accommodation with the Soviets.[185]

Liu Shao-ch'i, Teng Hsiao-p'ing, and their spokesmen in the Party seemed to call for a relaxation of tension with the Russians for economic as well as military reasons. And P'eng Chen—in a manner which apparently reflected his current domestic political defense of vigorously "waving the red flag"—assumed a virulent anti-Soviet line which foreclosed any possibility of "united action." P'eng may have been seeking to eradicate any doubts in Mao's mind about his own "revisionism" through demonstrative opposition to the Russians. His call for great caution before American strength, however, was to lead to criticism by Mao that he was cowering before "imperialism" just like the Soviet "revisionists."

The position of Mao and Lin Piao in this debate was not formally expressed until early September. In the article "Long Live the Victory of People's War," Lin Piao finally attempted to reassert the correctness of Mao's strategy of national defense which had been evolved in 1958, and the validity of the form of military struggle against superior forces which had brought the Party to power.

Basically, Lin asserted that if the Vietnamese adopted a strategy of "people's war" they would be able to cope with the American intervention without direct Chinese or Soviet assistance (other than the supply of light arms and economic assistance). He revealed an unremitting hostility toward the United States, but stressed that "revolution or people's war in any country is the business of the masses in that country." [186] Similarly he expressed an uncompromising attitude against "united action" with the Soviets by emphasizing that Khrushchev's successors continued to collude with the United States in attempting to "extinguish the flames of revolution."

Thus Mao and Lin tried to establish a policy line which would avoid both confrontation with the Americans and collusion with the Soviets, while encouraging a prosecution of the war in Viet-Nam in such a way that the Vietnamese could slowly drive out American influence through their own efforts. Such a strategy also enabled

185. While this book was in press, Edgar Snow reported that Liu Shao-ch'i himself, during 1965, sought "to reactivate the Sino-Soviet alliance" because of the Viet-Nam situation (if not for domestic political reasons). *See* Edgar Snow, "Mao Tse-tung and the Cost of Living: Aftermath of the Cultural Revolution," *The New Republic* (April 10, 1971), p. 19.

186. Lin Piao, "Long Live the Victory of People's War" (September 3, 1965), as cited in Uri Ra'anan, "Peking's Foreign Policy 'Debate,'" in Tang Tsou, ed., *China in Crisis*, Vol. II, pp. 57–58.

Mao and Lin to sustain the Army's domestic political role and to continue to exclude Soviet influence from China.

Why did it take so many months for Mao and Lin to formulate this alternative to the conflicting evaluations expressed by other leaders during the spring and summer? And why was a debate on matters directly related to China's national security so publicly revealed? In part the policy debate must have reflected uncertainty about the course of events which were largely beyond Chinese control. In this sense the September statement by Lin Piao reflects an evaluation of the impact of the Viet-Nam conflict on China's security after more than six months of watching to see what, in fact, would be the extent of the American escalation and the concomitant ability of the Vietnamese to cope with it.

Given the context of Party leadership conflict in which these differing policies were expressed, however, we would suggest that there were important domestic reasons for both the timing of the debate and the conflicting positions expressed by various leaders. First, Mao and Lin were probably not in a position to impose their view on other Party leaders—as was emphasized by continuing opposition to Lin's policy statement after its publication. The full implications of the war were hardly certain in the spring and summer of 1965, and Mao and Lin would probably have wanted to avoid a showdown on the defense issue when they could not make a strong case for their position through regular Party decision-making procedures. And for obvious reasons, they would not have wanted to force the issue to a point at which Army power would have to be invoked in a domestic confrontation while it was still uncertain whether the PLA might have to assume a direct military role in the war situation.

The fact that the policy debate proceeded in such public fashion is one further indication that power had diffused considerably within the Party. No one leadership group could control the public media, much less set a common defense line. And given all the signs of a heightening of leadership conflict in the early summer of 1964, it is reasonable to assume that the policy alternatives expressed by various leaders reflected their awareness that the defense position eventually adopted would have a major influence on the course of Mao's effort to press the domestic conflict. Thus, the persistent call for a policy of "active defense" by Lo Jui-ch'ing can be seen as a defense against Mao and Lin as well as a position directed against the United States.[187]

187. One Cultural Revolution publication implied that Lo and other leaders who fell from power in 1966 had created a "war scare" over the Viet-Nam situation "from May 1965 to the beginning of 1966" in order

By the late summer of 1965 Mao evidently felt that the Viet-Nam situation had stabilized sufficiently so that he could return to the issues he had raised a year earlier. How did he come to believe that he could divert his own attention, and that of the PLA, to a major domestic political battle with a potential war situation on China's southern frontier? He probably concluded that the Vietnamese could cope with the American ground forces, and that Hanoi would not be pressured into a negotiated settlement of the conflict by the air bombardment. In addition, one suspects that Mao came to see the limits of American escalation. Whether such limits had been communicated to the Chinese through the 126th meeting of the Warsaw ambassadorial talks on June 30th, through some other channel, or simply as a result of a tacit understanding of the situation is not known.

It is telling, however, that after the publication of Lin Piao's September 3rd analysis of the war, official Chinese spokesmen seemed to be at pains to stress the mutual concern shared by both the United States and China about a direct military confrontation. In an exchange with Japanese parliamentarians on September 6th, Foreign Minister Ch'en Yi remarked, "To tell the truth, America is afraid of China and China is somewhat afraid of America. I do not believe that the United States would invade present-day China." [188] And as if appealing to the United States to go no further than her present level of involvement in the war, official Chinese spokesmen continued to reiterate through the end of 1965 and into 1966 that China would not attack unless her territory were directly invaded or the existence of the Hanoi regime were threatened.

On the very day that Lin Piao articulated Mao's position on the war, however, Chief of Staff Lo Jui-ch'ing gave a public statement on the Viet-Nam situation—in the presence of Liu Shao-ch'i and Teng Hsiao-p'ing—which contradicted the Mao-Lin analysis by continuing to stress the danger of a war with the United States and the necessity of relying upon the strength of the "socialist camp" and Soviet nuclear weapons as a deterrent to an American attack.[189]

Punctuating Lo's assertion of the dangers of a Sino-American

to divert attention from their efforts to stage an anti-Mao and Lin *coup* and to involve the PLA in matters of national defense rather than Maoist politics. (*See* "The February Coup," *Chan Pao* [April 17, 1967], and as noted in Franz Schurmann, *Ideology and Organization in Communist China,* p. 555.)

188. These remarks were given wide circulation by Communist publications in Eastern Europe. Cited here from Donald S. Zagoria, "The Strategic Debate in Peking," in Tang Tsou, ed., *China in Crisis,* Vol. II, p. 267.

189. *See* Uri Ra'anan, "Peking's Foreign Policy 'Debate,' 1965–1966," in *ibid.,* Vol. II, pp. 54–56.

war were two clashes between Communist and Nationalist shore patrol craft, first on August 6th and again on November 14th. During the Cultural Revolution, criticism of Lo Jui-ch'ing in a Red Guard publication implied that the Deputy Defense Minister was responsible for provoking these clashes, perhaps as a way of mobilizing support for his assertion of the need for war preparedness against the United States:

> On a certain date in 196x, without consulting Chairman Mao, the Party Central Committee and the Military Commission, Lo Jui-ch'ing acted on his own by giving instructions to the Foochow Military District to the effect that in future sea battles the military region might "actively attack the enemy on its own initiative" according to the situation, and "in order not to lose the initiative in battle, it may go into battle and file a report at the same time." In many other important affairs, Lo Jui-ch'ing often took reckless action without asking the Military Commission for instructions.[190]

Given his public contention with Lin Piao on September 3rd, and this veiled charge of having instituted "active defense" in contravention of Mao's authority, it seems likely that Lo's fall from power after his last public appearance on November 26th was related in some manner to insubordination in matters of defense policy.[191]

That the Viet-Nam issue continued to divide the leadership into 1966—and may have given Mao grounds for taking action against his opponents—is suggested by the final political hours of P'eng Chen and Liu Shao-ch'i. P'eng's last month of public activity, March 1966, was spent in constant contact with a Japanese Communist Party delegation which arrived in Peking on March 3rd for a first round of talks. It went to Korea, and then returned to Peking for further discussions, expanded to include a top-ranking North Vietnamese political delegation which was also in the Chinese capital, between the 22nd and the 30th. P'eng was last seen in public on the 30th, sending off the Japanese group. Subsequent dip-

---

190. "Counter-Revolutionary Revisionist Lo Jui-ch'ing Is Loaded with Crimes," *Chan Pao* (January 30, 1967).

191. It may be significant that Lo's last appearance was at a reception for the naval men responsible for sinking a Nationalist patrol vessel in the November 14th clash. (*See* "Premier Chou En-lai Receives Naval Men," NCNA [Shanghai], [November 26, 1965]; in *SCMP*, No. 3588 [December 1, 1965], p. 22.)

A Cultural Revolution pamphlet asserts that "Comrade Lin Piao decisively exposed Lo Jui-ch'ing's plot to oppose the Party and usurp power in the army at the Shanghai Conference held in December 1965." (*Chairman Mao's Successor—Deputy Supreme Commander Lin Piao,* trans. in *Current Background,* No. 894 [October 27, 1969], p. 22.)

lomatic reports that these discussions may have attempted to work out a compromise formula for "united action" on the war which Mao angrily rejected suggest that the precipitating event in P'eng's fall may have been his "switching sides" on the issues of opposition to the Soviets and Chinese aloofness from the Viet-Nam situation.[192]

Liu Shao-ch'i's last political initiative was a government statement issued during a massive Peking rally in support of Viet-Nam on July 22nd. In language which had not been used in official Chinese statements on the war for over a year, Liu reasserted "proletarian internationalism" as the supreme principle of China's foreign policy, and the importance of condemning "national chauvinism and national egoism which betray the interests of the revolutionary people of the world." [193] He asserted that "the Chinese people are

192. The exact position which P'eng Chen took in these talks, however, remains uncertain. An account of the talks released by the Japanese Communist Party through its journal *Akahata* on January 24, 1967, only adds to the uncertainty about the positions of various Chinese leaders on foreign policy issues.

A further political element in P'eng Chen's fall, as well as that of Lo Jui-ch'ing, may have been responsibility for Chinese policy related to the "September 30" *coup* attempt, and subsequent anti-Communist suppression, in Indonesia in the autumn of 1965. Both men had been actively involved in China's relations with the Sukarno government. There is indirect evidence that Mao may have opposed the policy promoted by Liu and others of working through the "bourgeois-nationalist" Sukarno government. He appears to have favored the Indonesian Communist Party taking power by building its own armed mass base of popular support.

For obvious reasons of national security, the exact manner in which Viet-Nam policy, Sino-Soviet relations, and the Indonesian affair may relate to the fall of Lo, P'eng, and Liu, and other Party leaders, has not been disclosed through Cultural Revolution documents. The interpretation advanced here remains inferential and tentative. It should be emphasized, however, that while these foreign affairs issues may have been important, or precipitating, elements in the leadership conflict, the domestic policy disputes of the preceding decade had established the basic context for the Cultural Revolution.

193. "Chairman Liu Shao-ch'i Issues Statement in Support of President Ho Chi Minh's Appeal," NCNA [Peking, July 22, 1966]; in *SCMP*, No. 3747 (July 27, 1966), p. 27.

A revealing and contrasting Chinese policy statement on the Viet-Nam situation is a *People's Daily* editorial of February 15, 1966 which asserts that "The South Vietnamese people are sure to win and the U.S. aggressor forces and their lackeys will certainly lose. This is now a foregone conclusion." With such an evaluation of the war, China obviously had no need to "undertake the greatest national sacrifices" or to make preparations for direct action, as Liu implied needed to be done in July. (*See* "*People's Daily* Celebrates South Vietnamese Liberation Forces' Anniversary," NCNA [Peking, February 15, 1966]; in *SCMP*, No. 3641 [February 18, 1966], p. 32.)

ready to undertake the greatest national sacrifices" in aid of the Vietnamese, that China was "the reliable rear area of the Vietnamese people," and that "the Chinese people have made up their minds and have made every preparation to take . . . actions at any time and in any place that the Chinese and Vietnamese people deem necessary." [194]

Four days after this statement was issued, Mao publicly reasserted his authority over Chinese political life. The "golden monkey" was not to have his "massive cudgel," the People's Liberation Army, pulled from his hands. It was to be his weapon in the imminent battle with "freaks and monsters."

THE POLITICS OF LUAN

In the last analysis, all the truths of Marxism can be summed up in one sentence: "To rebel is justified."

MAO TSE-TUNG, 1939, 1966[195]

Trust the masses, rely on them and respect their initiative. Cast out fear. Don't be afraid of disorder (*luan-tzu*).

CENTRAL COMMITTEE DECISION ON THE GREAT
PROLETARIAN CULTURAL REVOLUTION, August 8, 1966[196]

I feared confusion (*luan*) and extensive democracy. I feared the rising up of the masses and their rebelling against us.

LIU SHAO-CH'I, 1967[197]

Revolution means rebellion, and rebellion is the soul of the thought of Mao Tse-tung. . . . We want to wield the massive cudgel [of the thought of Mao Tse-tung], express our spirit, invoke our magic influence and turn the old world upside-down, smash things into chaos, into smithereens, smash things *luan-luan-ti,* the more *luan* the better!

STUDENT RED GUARDS OF PEKING, June 1966[198]

194. The communiqué of the Eleventh Plenum, issued on August 12th, reaffirmed the correctness of Lin Piao's analysis, "Long Live the Victory of People's War," obviously a repudiation of the Liu statement.

195. Cited in the *People's Daily* editorial, "It Is Fine!" (August 23, 1966). Mao had first invoked this phrase in 1939, at a celebration in Yenan marking Stalin's sixtieth birthday.

196. "Decision of the Central Committee of the Chinese Communist Party Concerning the Great Proletarian Cultural Revolution" (August 8, 1966); in *CCP Documents of the Great Proletarian Cultural Revolution, 1966–1967*, p. 45.

197. "The Confession of Liu Shao-ch'i" (October 23, 1966), *Atlas* (April 1967), p. 17.

198. Red Guards of Tsinghua Middle School, Peking, "Long Live the Revolutionary Rebel Spirit of the Proletariat" (June 24, 1966), in *Red Flag,* No. 11 (August 21, 1966), p. 27.

The year 1966 began in China as one would expect for a country "building socialism." The *People's Daily* January 1st editorial bore the businesslike title "Usher in 1966, the First Year of China's Third Five-Year Plan." It stated that the continuing campaign for Socialist Education would help to establish the conditions for increasing agricultural output and strengthen the foundation for China's continued industrial development.[199]

A few days later the paper of P'eng Chen's Peking Municipal Party Committee published an editorial on Party building. The editorial stressed the need to expand membership in order to strengthen Party leadership in "first-line basic-level" organizations for the tasks of economic construction set by the new Five-Year Plan.[200] Perhaps the one note of testiness in this otherwise "business-as-usual" expression of policy was the assertion that in recruiting Party members

> we should not impose additional conditions that depart from the established standards specified in the Party Constitution. Rather, we should accept new members strictly according to the provisions laid down in the Party Constitution.[201]

The Party Constitution of 1956 contained no reference to the "thought of Mao Tse-tung"; neither did the editorial.

By the summer of 1966 this air of routine had been shattered by "The Great Proletarian Cultural Revolution." P'eng Chen had disappeared from political view, and his Peking Party Committee and its paper the *Peking Daily* and magazine *Front Line* had been reorganized. High-school and university students of Peking, wearing the red armbands of "Red Guard" units, surged through the capital streets searching for manifestations of "the four olds" and dragging out "freaks and monsters" for public denunciation. In early August a Party Central Committee Plenum, packed with representatives of the new Red Guard organizations, approved a restructuring of the Party leadership that demoted Vice-Chairman Liu Shao-ch'i and affirmed Lin Piao as Chairman Mao's "closest comrade in arms." Even greater reorganization and disorganization followed.

How much of the momentous political conflict that exploded in 1966 had Mao anticipated, or planned? How spontaneous were the

199. *People's Daily* editorial, "Usher in 1966, the First Year of China's Third Five-Year Plan" (January 1, 1966); trans. in *SCMP,* No. 3610 (January 5, 1966), p. 10.

200. *Peking Daily* editorial, "Seriously and Successfully Expanding Party Membership Is an Important Task of Party Organizations" (January 8, 1966); trans. in *SCMP,* No. 3661 (March 21, 1966), p. 1.

201. *Ibid.,* p. 3.

student uprisings? At a leadership work conference in late October, Mao discussed the great changes of the spring and summer months:

> It was I who started the fire. . . . As I see it, shocking people (*ch'ung-yi-hsia*) has its good points. For many years I thought about how to administer [the Party] a shock, and finally conceived [this shock of the Cultural Revolution].[202]

Mao's imagery was telling. His phrase "to shock" (which used the character *ch'ung* with the two-stroke ice radical) implied shock in the way that an individual would react to having a bucket of ice water thrown on him. The man who from youth had seen discipline developed through swimming in icy rivers, who had spent more than a decade trying to find a way to discipline the Party organization, finally decided to rebel against it.[203] In July of 1966, as he moved to reassert his control over China's political life, Mao swam in the Yangtze, and appealed to China's younger generation to re-live with him his own rebellion by "following Chairman Mao and advancing in the teeth of great storms and waves." [204] Thus Mao's career came full circle, as his earliest symbol of rebellion against paternal authority was reenacted in an attack on Party authorities.

The events of 1966 replay, in short compass and great intensity, the major themes of policy conflict and personal political style which have been explored throughout this study. Mao was reliving his lifelong conflict with the "bourgeois intellectuals" and his opposition to a system of authority which expected people to be "docile tools." Yet he was also trying to find a way to pass on his own political experience to a new generation through a ritualized "class struggle," so that his unfinished life struggle against the "four olds" of China's cultural heritage would not die with his passing.

The Cultural Revolution, in its initial conception, was a massive ritual of initiation. It was an attempt to institutionalize "class conflict" so as to temper a younger generation untested in political combat. And through the struggle of the young people, those long-time leaders who Mao felt had substituted "revisionism" for revolution, routine for "remolding," were to be removed from positions of Party authority.

The drama of the Cultural Revolution raises as many questions as it answers. Did Mao see how far the conflict would go? Did he consciously plan to oust long-time comrades in revolution from their leading posts in the Party and state? As a general interpretive

202. Mao, "Talk at a Central Work Conference" (October 25, 1966), in *Long Live the Thought of Mao Tse-tung!* pp. 41–42.

203. *See* p. 178 above.

204. *See* the *People's Daily* editorial, "Follow Chairman Mao and Advance in the Teeth of Great Storms and Waves" (July 26, 1966).

"CHAIRMAN MAO JOYOUSLY SWIMS IN THE YANGTZE."
From Jen-min Jih-pao, *July 25, 1966.*

guideline we would suggest that Mao knew very well the policy changes he wanted to bring about, and that from years of daily contact and conflict, he knew the leadership styles and points of opposition of other leaders. His approach seems to have been to press once more for long-advocated changes in China's educational system, in Party propaganda work, and in rectification, but now to press to the end. If high Party leaders continued to resist his plans—as they had in the past—this time they would be removed from positions of influence.

Backed by the PLA, the Chairman was trying to make certain that his conception of a new China, his "thought" and life-experience, would prevail in the continuing struggle with the old way of life.

The escalation of this conflict into the full-blown Red Guard rebellion of the summer carries certain remarkable echoes of the events of the "blooming and contending" of 1957 and the Lushan Plenum. The beginning of this process was a working conference of the Party leadership held in September and October of 1965— just after Mao and Lin had published their position on China's relation to the Viet-Nam War. At this meeting Mao raised the issue of continuing criticism of his dismissal of P'eng Teh-huai by "giving instructions" that Wu Han, author of *The Dismissal of Hai Jui,* be attacked for his political errors in opposing the Lushan judgment and the Great Leap Forward.[205]

Mao was now forcing those Party leaders, particularly P'eng Chen, who had supported the veiled criticism of the intellectuals either to admit their own political error and repudiate the critics, or themselves become the objects of attack. By all evidence, P'eng Chen and others continued to resist this pressure.

On November 10, 1965 an article "On the New Historical Play *The Dismissal of Hai Jui*" appeared in the Shanghai paper *Wen Hui Pao.* The author of this public criticism of Wu Han for his political error of "making veiled criticism of contemporary people with ancient people" was Yao Wen-yuan. In 1957 Yao had been Mao's public spokesman for a *People's Daily* attack on the *Wen Hui Pao* for its publication of "bourgeois rightist" criticism of Party rule.[206] In 1965, however, Mao had few political supporters in the Party and capital city. The *People's Daily* and the papers of the Peking Party Committee initially refused to publish this attack. As Mao later told Party leaders:

205. *See* "Circular of the Central Committee of the Chinese Communist Party" (May 16, 1966), in *CCP Documents of the Great Proletarian Cultural Revolution,* p. 20.

206. *See* p. 319 above.

Nothing could be done about either Peking or the Center. In September and October of last year [1965] it was asked: If revisionism emerged at the Center, what would the local [Party organizations] do about it? At that time I thought that my suggestions could not be implemented in Peking. Why was the criticism of Wu Han started not in Peking but in Shanghai? Because Peking had no people who would do it.[207]

The Chairman was isolated by the Party leadership at "the Center."

Yao's article was published by the *People's Daily,* apparently after arm-twisting, on November 30th; but the editor's note prefacing the attack on Wu Han stressed that the matter at issue was an academic question of "how to deal with historical characters and plays." [208] Pointed quotes from Mao were invoked: "Our regime is a people's democratic regime which provides advantageous circumstances for writing for the people"; "Our guideline is that both the freedom of criticism and the freedom of countercriticism should be allowed. In regard to erroneous views, we also adopt the methods of reasoning and seeking truth from facts to convince people with reason."

Ten days after this effort to negate the political relevance of the Wu Han play the *Peking Daily* published a defense of the author and his work entitled, *"The Dismissal of Hai Jui* Is a Good Play." [209]

Mao, however, continued to press for politicization of the criticism, to raise this issue to one of political "principle" and personal loyalty. At a meeting of the leadership in Shanghai on December 21, the Chairman stressed: "The crux [of the play is] the question of dismissal from office. . . . In 1959 we dismissed P'eng Teh-huai from office. And P'eng Teh-huai is 'Hai Jui' too." [210]

On December 30th Wu Han published a self-criticism for his political errors in the play; but he avoided the issue of "dismissal from office," and asserted that he was not "beyond remedy" for his mistakes.[211]

Thus by the end of 1965 the issues had been raised and the lines

207. Mao, "Talk at a Central Work Conference" (October 25, 1966), in *Long Live the Thought of Mao Tse-tung!* pp. 40–41.

208. *People's Daily* editor's note to the article by Yao Wen-yuan, "On the New Historical Play *The Dismissal of Hai Jui"* (November 30, 1965); trans. in *Current Background,* No. 783 (March 21, 1966), p. 1.

209. *See* the *Peking Daily* article by Li Chen-yü translated in *SCMP,* No. 3669 (March 31, 1966), pp. 1–5.

210. *Red Flag* editorial, "Two Diametrically Opposed Documents," No. 9 (May 27, 1967); trans. in *SCMM,* No. 581 (June 26, 1967), pp. 11–12.

211. Wu Han, "Self-Criticism on *The Dismissal of Hai Jui,"* *People's Daily* (December 30, 1965); trans. in *Current Background,* No. 783 (March 21, 1966), pp. 28–51.

of conflict which had been established in 1964 were redrawn. The struggle intensified throughout 1966, with Mao ever more directly intruding the authority of the PLA into remaining areas of Party defense.

During the last days of 1965 the Army convened another conference on political work which continued until January 18th. It may have been at this conference that the case of Lo Jui-ch'ing was formally dealt with. His name was not among the conference participants; and the fact that the Deputy Chief of the General Staff, Yang Ch'eng-wu, delivered a speech was the first public hint that Lo was no longer politically active. Furthermore, excerpts of a speech by Hsiao Hua, Director of the Army's General Political Department, published on January 24th, included telling criticisms that whereas "some people say 'Military affairs are politics,' . . . such views are absolutely wrong"; and "One must fight for the military authority of the Party, for the military authority of the people, and not for individual military authority." [212]

This conference apparently represented the consolidation of control over the PLA by the Mao-Lin forces; the final politicization of the Army for the domestic confrontation. Hsiao Hua's speech stressed that a five-point principle put forward by Lin Piao in late November of 1965 on the matter of "bringing politics to the fore" had been adopted by the conference as the guideline for its work in 1966.

With the Army thus oriented, and with a major opponent of Mao's policies removed from influence within the PLA, political pressures were not long in coming. As in 1957, a low-key Party rectification campaign was launched in early February with the propagation of a new model in the study of "the thought of Mao Tse-tung"—the county Party secretary Chiao Yü-lu.[213] And on February 2nd, PLA influence in intellectual matters was heightened

212. Hsiao Hua, "Hold High the Great Red Banner of the Thought of Mao Tse-tung and Resolutely Implement the 5-Point Principle of Bringing Politics to the Fore" (Extracts), NCNA (January 24, 1966); trans. in *SCMP*, No. 3627 (January 31, 1966), pp. 6–20.

Following his detention, Lo Jui-ch'ing evidently was investigated and interrogated for more than two months. On March 12 he completed a self-examination; and on the 18th he attempted to commit suicide by jumping from the upper floors of the building in which he was detained. (*See* "Comment of the CCP Central Committee on the Transmission of the Report of the Work Group of the Central Committee Concerning the Problem of Lo Jui-ch'ing's Mistakes" [May 16, 1966], in *CCP Documents of the Great Proletarian Cultural Revolution*, pp. 31–32.)

213. *See* the *People's Daily* editorial, "Carry on the Study in the Spirit of Rectification" (February 14, 1966); trans. in *SCMP*, No. 3645 (February 25, 1966), pp. 10–13.

with a "Forum on the Work in Literature and Art in the Armed Forces" convened in Shanghai. Chiang Ch'ing directed the work of the conference.[214]

This meeting appears to have been part of the increasingly direct challenge to P'eng Chen. Its work on artistic matters proceeded at the same time that P'eng, head of a "group of five" which since late 1964 had been deputized by the Party leadership to direct the work of a "Cultural Revolution," [215] was preparing a report on guidelines for implementing Mao's Tenth Plenum call for "class struggle" against revisionism within the intellectual community.[216]

Public expression of the increasing political pressure being exerted by the Army was contained in a remarkable series of *Liberation Army Daily* editorials which received nationwide publicity through their republication in the *People's Daily* beginning on February 4th. The very title of the first editorial, "Forever Bring Politics to the Fore," was a clear indication of the way in which Mao was trying to "push" the Party organization through PLA activities. The second editorial stressed that everyone was going to be forced to take a stand in the intensifying "class struggle," that "sectarian" interests were a dangerous expression of "individualism," and that people would have to choose between their own immediate interests and some undefined "common good." (". . . this turbulent conflict [between "the common good" and "self-interest"] will suck everyone into its vortex. There is no escape.")[217]

The third editorial appeared to be a refutation of continuing pressures to divert the Army into a more active defense role in relation to the Viet-Nam War. It stressed that ideological preparation was the most fundamental basis of war-preparedness. Apparently responding to those who continued to press for "united action" with the Soviets, or acceptance of a negotiated understanding with the United States on the limits of the war, it asked incredulously: "Can it be that we should bend our knees and surrender to the imperialists as the modern revisionists have done? . . . Oh no! We say no

214. *See* "Summary of the Forum on the Work in Literature and Art in the Armed Forces with Which Comrade Lin Piao Entrusted Comrade Chiang Ch'ing," in *Peking Review,* No. 23 (June 2, 1967), p. 10.

215. Cultural Revolution material which indicates that P'eng Chen had been placed in charge of the "group of five" probably as early as the latter half of 1964 is discussed in Chung and Miller, *Madame Mao,* p. 127.

216. Mao's use of the Army conference to pressure P'eng is asserted in the *Red Flag* editorial, "Two Diametrically Opposed Documents," No. 9 (May 27, 1967); trans. in *SCMM,* No. 581 (June 26, 1967), p. 10.

217. *Liberation Army Daily* editorial, "Promoting Civic-Mindedness: Again on Bringing Politics to the Fore" (as republished in the Peking *Ta Kung Pao,* February 10, 1966); trans. in *SCMP,* No. 3645 (February 25, 1966), p. 2.

a thousand times, ten thousand times." "We shall not succumb to panic." [218]

The fifth editorial in the series was an uncompromising assertion of Mao's personal authority in China's political life. It directly stated that "the thought of Mao Tse-tung is the peak of contemporary Marxism-Leninism," that Mao's writings were "the highest directive for all our work," and that "the thought of Mao Tse-tung alone is our invincible banner." [219]

Finally, the eighth and last editorial of April 5th threw down the gauntlet to P'eng Chen. It cited Mao's words that "leadership by a Party committee is collective leadership, not personal dictatorship by the first secretary." [220] A further quote from Mao all but directly called on P'eng, the first secretary of the Peking Municipal Party Committee, to accept his responsibilities for having shielded the critics of the early 1960s, Wu Han and Teng T'o:

> When a man assumes the post of first secretary, he must also assume responsibility for any shortcomings or errors in the work of his committee. All those who refuse to assume, or who are afraid of assuming responsibility, who will not allow others to speak, and who, like the tiger's backside, cannot be touched, will fail.[221]

Mao was about to grab the "tiger" P'eng Chen by his "tail," and to do it in true Maoist style. One of the series of *Liberation Army Daily* editorials had asserted:

> If we are mentally lazy, do not seek progress, rely on our "rich store of experience," have blind faith in foreign rules, and are so afraid of being hurt and embarrassed that we will not take off our pants and have our tails removed, our mind will not be properly reformed and the thought of Mao Tse-tung will not take root in our heads.[222]

By year's end P'eng and other Party leaders who proved to be too "embarrassed" to have their "tails" exposed through voluntary confession were to be dragged out in isolation before the masses to have their disloyalty to the "thought of Mao Tse-tung" publicly exposed.

218. *Liberation Army Daily* editorial, "The Most Important and Fundamental War Preparation" (from extracts published by NCNA on February 14, 1966); trans. in *SCMP*, No. 3641 (February 18, 1966), pp. 14, 15.

219. *Liberation Army Daily* editorial, "Regard Chairman Mao's Books as the Highest Directive for All Work Throughout the PLA," NCNA (March 2, 1966); trans. in *SCMP*, No. 3652 (March 8, 1966), p. 2.

220. *Liberation Army Daily* editorial, "The Key Lies in Leadership by the Party Committee," NCNA (April 5, 1966); trans. in *SCMP*, No. 3676 (April 13, 1966), p. 8.

221. *Ibid.*

222. *Liberation Army Daily* editorial, "Regard Chairman Mao's Works as the Highest Directive for all Work Throughout the PLA," p. 5.

PLA cadres jeering at dunce-capped
Party "revisionists" as they are paraded through the streets of Peking
during the Great Proletarian Cultural Revolution, 1966.
United Press International.

P'eng Chen made his last public appearance on March 30th; and the month of April saw a rapid escalation in the political confrontation. P'eng's absence from the meeting of the Standing Committee of the National People's Congress on April 14th was contrasted with a report by the Vice Minister of Culture Shih Hsi-min entitled, "Raise High the Great Red Banner of Mao Tse-tung's Thought, Carry the Socialist Cultural Revolution through to the End." At the same meeting Mao's friend among the intellectuals, Kuo Mo-jo, made a self-abasing speech in which he asserted that all he had written in the past should "be burned to ashes, for it has not the slightest value." [223] If a friend of the Chairman would make such a public self-criticism, what would others be expected to do?

The answer was not long in coming. On April 16th New China News Agency released an article carried by the major national and provincial papers in which the publications of the Peking Party Committee attacked by name "anti-Party" elements Wu Han and Teng T'o for their critical writings of the early 1960s.[224]

These developments took place in the absence of Liu Shao-ch'i and Foreign Minister Ch'en Yi. The two had left the country on March 26 on a curious diplomatic expedition of more than three weeks that took them to countries on China's western and southern borders—Pakistan, Afghanistan, and Burma. During the month of April they returned twice to China's western provinces for stops lasting several days before continuing on to new destinations in Afghanistan and then Burma. Whether this extended diplomatic absence was a convenient way for Liu to disassociate himself from the purge of P'eng Chen—which apparently occurred at the end of the first week of April [225]—or whether the Mao-Lin forces took advantage of the trip for their own purposes, is not known.

223. Kuo Mo-jo, "Learn from the Masses of Workers, Peasants and Soldiers and Serve Them," *Kuang-ming Daily* (April 28, 1966); trans. in *SCMP*, No. 3691 (May 5, 1966), p. 7.

224. *Notes on Sanchia Village* and *Night Causerie at Yenshan* Criticized by *Ch'ien Hsien* and *Peking Daily*: Works by Wu Han, Liao Mo-sha and Teng T'o Are Representative of an Undercurrent against the Party and Socialism" (April 16, 1966); trans. in *SCMP*, No. 3686 (April 28, 1966), pp. 1–3.

225. According to one Cultural Revolution report of the circumstances surrounding P'eng's fall, Chou En-lai convened a meeting of the Secretariat of the Party Central Committee between April 9 to 12 so that K'ang Sheng could "convey Chairman Mao's instructions to the meeting and make a systematic critical review of the many crimes committed by P'eng Chen in the Cultural Revolution." Mao himself is said to have convened an expanded meeting of the Politbureau's Standing Committee on April 16 "to deliberate on the question of P'eng Chen's anti-Party activities." This indicates that

Conflicting political signals continued to be evident in the national press during this time. In late March *Red Flag* published an article commemorating the ninety-fifth anniversary of the Paris Commune, describing it as a "great lesson" in how to seize the machinery of state by way of a mass uprising and establish "proletarian dictatorship" through revolutionary violence.[226] In retrospect, this commemorative article is a remarkable blueprint—by historical analogy—of political events which were to unfold in China beginning in late May.

Early in April, however, the *People's Daily* initiated an interpretive series of articles on "bringing politics to the fore" which appears to represent a last-ditch effort by the Party organization to reply to the nearly concluded *Liberation Army Daily* series on this same subject. The first article by the Party paper tried to emphasize the fundamental importance for China of economic development ("Economy is the foundation and politics is the concentrated expression of economy." "Politics is in the service of the economic base." [227]) It stated that elimination of the social distinctions between town and countryside, workers and peasants, and mental and manual labor was a process that necessarily was gradual, but was being carried out on the basis of existing Party policies.

The second article in the series was a defensive assertion that the Party *was* putting politics to the fore, even while it stressed the concomitant necessity of developing technical skills for "socialist construction." ("Redness must lead expertness, but Redness and expertness must be achieved at the same time." [228]) The third article made a valiant attempt to express deference to Mao even as it contradicted Lin Piao's assertion that the "thought of Mao Tse-tung" was the "peak" of contemporary Marxism: "Comrade Mao Tse-tung has made great contributions to enriching and developing the philosophy and economics of Marxism-Leninism . . ."; "Under the leadership of the Central Committee of the Chinese Communist Party headed by Comrade Mao Tse-tung, the Chinese people are

P'eng was "detained" some time between the 1st of April and the 9th. The pamphlet notes that April 5 was "the eve" of P'eng's collapse. (*See* "Preparation, Release, and Collapse of the Counter-Revolutionary 'February Outline Report,'" *Chingkangshan* [Peking], May 27, 1967.)

226. *See* Cheng Chih-szu, "The Great Lessons of the Paris Commune," *Red Flag*, No. 4 (March 24, 1966), pp. 4–18.

227. *People's Daily* editorial, "Placing Politics in a Prominent Position Is the Root of All Work: On Bringing Politics to the Fore, I" (April 6, 1966) · trans. in *SCMP*, No. 3680 (April 19, 1966), p. 2.

228. *People's Daily* editorial, "Politics Commands Functional Work: On Bringing Politics to the Fore, II" (April 14, 1966); trans. in *SCMP*, No. 3682 (April 22, 1966), p. 5.

holding aloft the banner of Marxism-Leninism . . ." [229]—not the "banner of the thought of Mao Tse-tung."

This continuing Party effort to counterpose Marxism-Leninism against Mao's "thought" was cut short by a *Liberation Army Daily* editorial signaling direct Army intervention into domestic politics. It asserted that the Army "has consistently played a vital role in the proletarian revolutionary cause and will also play an important part in the great socialist cultural revolution." [230] It reiterated that Mao's "thought" was the "highest peak" of contemporary Marxism, and that Mao's writings "will be useful for a long time." It stressed that the Army must rid itself of the influence of the "black line" on the cultural front (a reference to the recently commenced public attacks on P'eng Chen's subordinates Teng T'o and Wu Han) and that "after this black line has been eliminated, there will still be another black line in the future and further struggle will be inevitable."

Finally, anticipating developments of the early summer, the editorial asserted:

> There has been an upsurge in the great socialist cultural revolution and a mass movement is rising in this revolution. The great revolutionary waves will wash away all the filth of the bourgeois trends in art and literature and open up a new epoch of socialist proletarian art and literature. . . . Something must be destroyed and something must be set up in the course of the socialist cultural revolution. Without destruction there can be no construction.

Liu Shao-ch'i returned to Peking sometime after April 19th to a radically altered political scene. Lo Jui-ch'ing, P'eng Chen, and Director of Propaganda Lu Ting-yi had been politically neutralized.[231] Liu's own isolation seemed emphasized by the fact that there was no official reception committee to welcome him at Peking Airport on his return from the diplomatic mission. It appears that Mao was now implementing his assertion of mid-1964 that, "It is essential to test and know cadres and choose and train successors in the long course of mass struggle."

229. *People's Daily* editorial, "To Put Politics in the Forefront It Is Necessary to Put the Thought of Mao Tse-tung Firmly in Command: On Bringing Politics to the Fore, III" (April 22, 1966); trans. in *SCMP*, No. 3688 (May 2, 1966), pp. 2–3.

230. *Liberation Army Daily* editorial, "Hold High the Great Red Banner of the Thought of Mao Tse-tung and Take an Active Part in the Great Socialist Cultural Revolution" (as reprinted in the *People's Daily* on April 19, 1966); trans. in *SCMP*, No. 3687 (April 29, 1966), pp. 5–13.

231. It appears from a Cultural Revolution pamphlet that Lu Ting-yi was not actually detained until the end of April. (*See* "Preparation, Release, and Collapse of the Counter-Revolutionary 'February Outline Report,'" *Chingkangshan*, May 27, 1967.)

The "test" for Liu and Party Secretary-General Teng Hsiao-p'ing was their handling of the Cultural Revolution in the schools of Peking during the late spring and summer months. In mid-May a Central Committee document was circulated throughout the Party organization officially removing P'eng Chen from his position as head of the "group of five" in charge of the Cultural Revolution. The remarkable thing about this circular is the warning it contained to Liu Shao-ch'i that the manner in which he implemented the work of the Cultural Revolution would be the test of his political future:

> Above all, we must not entrust [representatives of the bourgeoisie who have sneaked into the Party] with the work of leading the Cultural Revolution. In fact many of them have done and *are still doing such work,* and this is extremely dangerous. . . . *Some are still trusted by us and are being trained as our successors, Khrushchev-type persons, for example, who are still nestling beside us.* Party committees at all levels must pay full attention to this matter.[232]

A *Red Flag* and *People's Daily* editorial commemorating the first anniversary of this document observed, "The Circular unmasked the P'eng Chen counterrevolutionary revisionist clique. . . . This forced a break in the counterrevolutionary revisionist front headed by the Khrushchev of China, and threw it into confusion (*luan-le hsien-chiao*)." [233]

In essence what Mao was doing was forcing an isolated Liu Shao-ch'i to make a Hobson's Choice: Either he must genuinely "mobilize the masses"—who would criticize him for his past errors against "the thought of Mao Tse-tung," even though he might sustain his political life through an expression of submission to Mao—or continue to play the "revisionist" game and thus suffer the fate of P'eng Chen and Lu Ting-yi. It was a choice which Mao was to force on the entire Party organization. As he told a meeting of Central Committee leaders in mid-July of 1966, when Liu and Teng had failed their "test":

> When you are told to set a fire to burn yourselves, will you do it? After all, you yourselves will be burned. . . . It won't do just to sit in an office and listen to reports. We should rely on and have faith in the masses, and make trouble to the end. Be prepared for the revolution to come down on your own heads. Leaders of the Party and the

232. "Circular of the Central Committee of the Communist Party of China" (May 16, 1966); trans. in *SCMP*, No. 3942 (May 19, 1967), p. 5. Emphasis added.

233. *Red Flag* and *People's Daily* joint editorial, "A Great Historic Document" (May 16, 1967); trans. in *SCMM*, No. 578 (June 5, 1967), p. 6.

government and responsible comrades of the Party must all be prepared.[234]

With the orientation of the confrontation sharpened by the May 16th Circular, and with the national press in Maoist hands,[235] the Chairman retired to his customary retreat near Hangchow to watch the course of events.[236]

As viewed through the national press, the unfolding of the mass struggle phase of the Cultural Revolution, marked by the formation of the first Red Guard units in Peking schools in late May,[237] carried with it all the tension and drama of the early revolutionary years. In a remarkable series of editorials beginning on June 1, the *People's Daily* invoked all the symbols of the revolution for a new student generation. The editorial "Sweep Away All Freaks and Monsters" was a powerful echo of Mao's "Hunan Report":

> With the tremendous and impetuous force of a raging storm, [the revolutionary masses] have smashed the shackles imposed on their minds by the exploiting classes for so long in the past, routing the bourgeois "specialists," "scholars," "authorities," and "venerable masters" and sweeping every bit of their prestige into the dust.[238]

234. Mao, "Talk to Central Committee Leaders" (July 21, 1966), in *Long Live the Thought of Mao Tse-tung!* p. 37.

235. In a speech of early 1967 Mao revealed that the series of *People's Daily* editorials which began on June 1, 1966 to "prepare public opinion" for the Cultural Revolution had been published only after a Maoist faction had "seized power" from the Party-dominated editorial board of the paper. *See* Mao, "Speech at a Meeting of the Cultural Revolution Group of the Central Committee" (January 9, 1967), in an untitled collection of statements by Mao Tse-tung, trans. in *Current Background*, No. 892 (October 21, 1969), p. 47.

236. Mao had been conspicuous by his political absence since the fall of 1965, stimulating rumors that he was seriously ill. After attending a series of receptions for foreign visitors which concluded on November 26, 1965, Mao's presence was not reported in the national press until May 11, 1966, when he received an Albanian delegation at his Hangchow retreat. After more than two further months of public silence, Mao returned to Peking (on July 18th) to launch the Cultural Revolution, as was publicized on July 25th through the reporting of his swim in the Yangtze nine days before.

237. In a description of the evolution of the Red Guard movement designed for foreign audiences, Mao's American friend Anna Louise Strong revealed that the first Red Guard unit had been formed "under cover" at the middle school attached to Peking's Tsinghua University in "late May" of 1966. This student organization came into the open on June 6th, after the Peking Municipal Party Committee had been reorganized and the Maoists had reasserted control over the *People's Daily*. (*See* Anna Louise Strong, *Letters from China*, No. 41 [September 20, 1966].)

238. *People's Daily* editorial, "Sweep Away All Freaks and Monsters" (June 1, 1966); trans. in *SCMP*, No. 3712 (June 6, 1966), p. 2.

The "storm" of this new political struggle was to be an assault on the "four olds" (*szu-chiu*) of China's traditional culture, thinking, customs, and habits as they endured in the minds of a quarter of mankind. The meaning of Marxism, in Mao's words, was reduced to the battle-cry: "To rebel is justified." [239] As the *People's Daily* asserted, "This great task of transforming customs and habits is without any precedent in human history." [240] Mao was calling on seven hundred million Chinese to be "critics of the old world." [241]

All of Mao's hatred of the intellectuals spewed forth in the editorial "Tear Aside the Bourgeois Mask of 'Liberty, Equality, and Fraternity.'" The "scholar-tyrants" who had slighted the Hunanese peasant in the Peking University library, who had ridiculed his conception of China's "leap forward," were pushed to the wall: "We have torn aside your filthy curtain of counterrevolution and caught you red-handed. We shall strip you of your disguises and expose you in all your ugliness." [242]

The lingering spectre of the Hungarian uprising, in Mao's eyes the result of bourgeois intellectuals' corruption of a once-revolutionary Party, found renewed expression:

We must never regard our struggle against [the bourgeois intellectuals] as mere polemics on paper. . . . It was a number of revisionist literary men of the Petöfi Club who acted as the shock brigade in the Hungarian events. The turbulent wind precedes the mountain storm. [China's bourgeois intellectuals] have worked hard to let emperors and kings, generals and prime ministers, scholars and beauties, foreign idols and dead men dominate the stage. This is the prelude to the vain attempt of the revisionists at a counterrevolutionary restoration.[243]

In the initial phase of the Cultural Revolution—the period of public criticism of Wu Han beginning in November 1965—Mao evidently had found the political dialogue still too muted, as Party

239. *See* fn. 195, p. 474 above.
As the Cultural Revolution struggle became increasingly undisciplined, this slogan was modified to read, "Rebellion *against All Counterrevolutionaries* Is Justified."

240. *People's Daily* editorial, "Sweep Away All Freaks and Monsters" (June 1, 1966); trans. in *SCMP*, No. 3712 (June 6, 1966), p. 3.

241. *See* the *People's Daily* editorial, "We Are Critics of the Old World" (June 8, 1966); trans. in *SCMP*, No. 3717 (June 13, 1966), pp. 1–3.

242. *People's Daily* editorial, "Tear Aside the Bourgeois Mask of 'Liberty, Equality, and Fraternity'" (June 4, 1966); trans. in *SCMP*, No. 3714 (June 8, 1966), p. 3.

243. *People's Daily* editorial, "A Great Revolution that Touches People to Their Very Souls" (June 2, 1966); trans. in *SCMP*, No. 3713 (June 7, 1966), p. 2. These quotations have been transposed at the elipsis for the sake of continuity.

leaders sought to ignore the full implications of the Chairman's political initiative. He told Party leaders in the fall of 1966:

> . . . in January, February, March, April, and May [of 1966] many articles were written and circulars were issued by the Central Committee, but they did not draw widespread attention. Attention was aroused only by the big character posters and the Red Guard movement; you would have been in trouble if you had not paid attention to them.[244]

As in 1957, those Party members and their protectors who resisted public criticism sought to fend off Mao's attack: "When the movement was barely initiated and before the masses were mobilized, [the resisters] raised a blast of evil wind, spread rumors, created chaos, shifted the targets, laid one obstacle after another, thus binding the hands and feet of the masses." [245]

But Mao had permitted his voice to be muffled by a bureaucratic political structure long enough. Through the *ta-tzu-pao,* the large-character wall posters which were to be produced in millions by the newly mobilized Red Guards, Mao's "thought" was amplified. The big-character posters were Mao's weapon for rousing the younger generation to political involvement, and for exposing his opposition within the Party.

> Revolutionary big-character posters are a mirror reflecting all freaks and monsters. They constitute the most effective means of mobilizing the masses freely to launch the most powerful attack on the enemy. All anti-Party and antisocialist counterrevolutionary elements are most afraid of big-character posters.[246]

How were the masses to decide who were "freaks and monsters," and who were the remaining revolutionaries within the Party? The standard was a man's past loyalty and present commitment to Mao's "thought":

> Mao Tse-tung's thought is our political orientation, the highest instruction for our actions; it is our ideological and political telescope and microscope for observing all things. . . . The attitude toward Mao Tse-tung's thinking, whether to accept it or resist it, to support it or oppose it, to love it warmly or be hostile to it, this is the watershed between true revolution and sham revolution, between

244. Mao, "Speech at a Central Committee Work Conference" (October 25, 1966), in *Long Live the Thought of Mao Tse-tung!* p. 41.

245. *People's Daily* editorial, "Mobilize the Masses Freely, Knock Down the Counter-Revolutionary Black Gang Completely" (June 16, 1966); trans. in *SCMP*, No. 3726 (June 27, 1966), p. 6.

246. *Ibid.*

Student Red Guards posting *ta-tzu-pao*
[big character posters] at Peking University
attacking University President Lu P'ing and
other "scholar tyrants" and "revisionists,"
June 1966.
From China Pictorial, *November 1967.*

revolution and counterrevolution, between Marxism-Leninism and revisionism, and the touchstone to test them.[247]

Such was the political orientation established in early June as the Party organization, prodded by Mao and the Army, moved to rouse the students of Peking to rise up in criticism of the "scholar-tyrants" who controlled the educational system.

While the student "rebellion" itself must be the subject of other studies, Cultural Revolution documents make it clear that the point of difference between Mao and Liu since the "blooming and con-tending" of 1957—whether or not to release (*fang*) the masses in unrestrained criticism of the errors of those with Party authority—endured, and became the issue on which the Chairman finally sought to settle accounts with "China's Khrushchev."

The initial weeks of the student uprising in Peking were directly supervised by Liu Shao-Ch'i and Teng Hsiao-p'ing. Mao was elated by the spirit of a big-character poster, published on the significant date of May 25th, denouncing Party rule at Peking University. The Chairman later described this poster as "a declaration of the Chi-nese Paris Commune of the sixties of the Twentieth Century [whose] significance surpasses that of the Paris Commune [of 1871]." [248] Yet Mao was to see this expression of revolutionary spontaneity thwarted by continuing Party efforts to impose control on the stu-dent movement "from above."

As had been the case with Liu's direction of the Socialist Educa-tion Movement and the Four Clean-Ups Campaign after 1963, the Party Vice Chairman sought to control the release of mass criti-cism of those in authority through the dispatch of Party work teams. But Mao wanted uprising "from below"; and by mid-July he had confirmed that Liu was unwilling or unable to implement the spirit of "the thought of Mao Tse-tung." As Liu himself was reported to have stated in a confession of October 1966: "If we had been able to understand the Chairman's thoughts, we naturally would have suspended these activities [of the work teams], and we would not have committed a mistake in policy line and direc-tion." [249]

Probably during the first two weeks of July Mao decided to es-tablish direct control over the course of the Cultural Revolution, and to remove from positions of leadership that "small handful of

247. *Liberation Army Daily* editorial, "Mao Tse-tung's Thought Is the Telescope and Microscope of Our Revolutionary Cause" (June 7, 1966); trans. in *SCMP*, No. 3716 (June 10, 1966), pp. 2–3.
248. Mao, "Talk to Central Committee Leaders" (July 21, 1966), in *Long Live the Thought of Mao Tse-tung!* p. 36.
249. "The Confession of Liu Shao-ch'i," *Atlas* (April 1967), p. 3.

people in authority within the Party taking the capitalist road." On July 16th the Chairman swam in the Yangtze as a sign of his good health and a symbol of his determination to press his rebellion against Party authority to the end. On the 18th he returned to Peking, and a leadership conference was convened to reestablish a more permissive policy line on the student rebellion and prepare for a Central Committee Plenum. At the July meeting Mao forcefully declared his determination to let the students "lay seige" to the old educational system and manifestations of Party "revisionism" by siding with the masses against the Party organization (as he had only threatened to do in 1957). He challenged other Party leaders:

> Since you do not show your face [to the masses], I'll show mine. It all comes down to your putting fear above everything else, your fear of counterrevolutionaries, your fear of knives and guns. How can there be so many counterrevolutionaries? [250]

The Eleventh Central Committee Plenum opened on August 1st, Army Day. It was a fitting occasion for the formal inception of this assault on the Party and the civilian "superstructure" of government by Mao and his supporters within the PLA. Press photographs of the Chairman attending the first Red Guard rallies at this time show Mao in simple army fatigues with an armband bearing the single character "soldier." There could not be a clearer statement of the manner in which Mao was seeking to recapture the heroic era of his revolution. A *People's Daily* editorial of the day entitled "The Whole Country Should Become a Great School in Mao Tse-tung's Thought," stressed the bankruptcy of the old educational system in Mao's eyes, and the fact that the Army, not the Party, was the only organization which sustained the legacy of the revolution.[251]

Whereas in 1964 Mao had called on the Party to "learn from the PLA," he now was relying on the Army and the "whole country" to attack through criticism those within the Party who were not loyal to his "thought." As the Plenum decision on the Cultural Revolution stressed: "The main target of the present movement is those within the Party who are in authority and are taking the capitalist road." [252]

250. Mao, "Speech to Regional Secretaries and Members of the Cultural Revolution Group under the Central Committee" (July 22, 1966), in *Long Live the Thought of Mao Tse-tung!* p. 43.

251. *See* the *People's Daily* editorial, "The Whole Country Should Become a Great School in Mao Tse-tung's Thought" (August 1, 1966); trans. in *SCMP,* No. 3754 (August 5, 1966), pp. 6–8.

252. "Decision of the Central Committee of the CCP Concerning the Great Proletarian Cultural Revolution" (August 8, 1966), in *CCP Documents of the Great Proletarian Cultural Revolution,* p. 46.

Communist Party Chairman Mao Tse-tung,
in PLA fatigues and wearing a red armband
with the character *"ping"* [soldier], salutes Red Guards
attending a massive rally at *Tien-an Men*
[The Gate of Heavenly Peace] in Peking,
August 18, 1966.
From **Hung Chi** [Red Flag], *October 1966.*

The Plenum moved to resolve for Mao the remaining political issues of the 1950s concerning the Party's relations with the intellectuals. If the Great Leap Forward was Mao's effort to complete the work of social transformation in rural life that had been blocked by the Party in 1956, the Cultural Revolution can be seen as the Chairman's effort to destroy the Party–urban intellectual relationship which had been unsuccessfully confronted in 1957:

> At present, our objective is to struggle against and crush those persons in authority who are taking the capitalist road, to criticize and repudiate the reactionary bourgeois academic "authorities" and the ideology of the bourgeoisie and all other exploiting classes and to transform education, literature and art and all other parts of the superstructure that do not correspond to the socialist economic base, so as to facilitate the consolidation and development of the socialist system.[253]

In promoting what seems likely to be the last great confrontation of his political career, the Chairman was determined to disorganize the resistant Party organization "beneath him." The Plenum itself was an affirmation of the split with the Party leadership. The demotion of Liu Shao-ch'i from second to eighth place in the order of Party precedence[254] and Lin Piao's rise to second position as Mao's "closest comrade in arms" were probably but the formalization of decisions reached at the leadership meetings which were held after Mao's July 18th return to Peking.

The Eleventh Plenum passed a sixteen-point decision to guide the mass struggle phase of the Cultural Revolution. This document provided the political orientation for the more than twelve million young people who were to make their own "long marches" to Peking between August 18th and late November to participate in a series of eight gigantic rallies. At these meetings, Mao and his supporters within the Party leadership received and encouraged the "revolutionary masses." Mao was isolated no more.[255]

The mobilized millions were to be the embodiment of Mao's effort to generate a new revolutionary generation committed to his "thought" in an incredible "revolution from above and below." Mao was unshakable in his belief that only by "learning swimming

253. *Ibid.,* pp. 42–43.

254. Liu's demotion in the order of Party precedence was made public at the first mass Red Guard rally held in Peking on August 18th. *See* "Peking Mass Rally Celebrates the Great Proletarian Cultural Revolution," NCNA (August 18, 1966), in *SCMP,* No. 3766 (August 23, 1966), p. 1. Compare this listing of Party precedence with the one published on National Day in 1962, just after the Tenth Plenum, in *Current Background,* No. 692 (October 12, 1962), p. 1.

255. *See* the *People's Daily* editorial, "Chairman Mao Is with the Masses" (August 20, 1966); trans. in *SCMP,* No. 3767 (August 24, 1966), pp. 6–7.

Communist Party Chairman Mao Tse-tung
and other Party leaders mingle with the masses
during a massive rally at *Tien-an Men*
[The Gate of Heavenly Peace],
August 18, 1966.
From China Pictorial, *September 1966.*

through swimming," by setting the younger generation against Party "revisionists," would his life-experience survive his passing in the political mobilization of China's youth who were to "grow up in the great storm." [256] Mao was convinced that from such a struggle would emerge consensus, not "confusion":

> I firmly believe that a few months of *luan* will be mostly for the good, and that little harm will result from this confusion. It doesn't matter if there are no provincial Party committees, we still have the district and county committees.[257]

Initiative was being passed to the people. How would they use it?

LUAN FOR THE REVOLUTION?

> In his recent instruction Chairman Mao has said: There is no fundamental clash of interests within the working class. Under the dictatorship of the proletariat, there is no reason whatsoever for the working class to split into two big irreconcilable organizations.
>
> RED FLAG, September 17, 1967 [258]

> *Luan* has a class nature. Before the establishment of the revolutionary committees, *luan* meant causing confusion among the enemy and steeling the masses. For [the class enemy] to propose *luan* after the establishment of revolutionary committees means creating confusion among ourselves and the newborn revolutionary committees.
>
> KWEIYANG RADIO, August 2, 1968 [259]

The Eleventh Plenum of August 1966 reestablished Mao's control over the Party center, but the larger problem of "revisionism" within the regional apparatus remained as a source of resistance to the full reassertion of the authority of "the thought of Mao Tse-tung." Shortly after National Day a Central Committee work conference was convened to promote Party rectification on a nation-wide scale. Against an uncertain degree of resistance from remaining Party leaders, and limited signs that in the growing political upheaval local Party and governmental officials were attempting to protect themselves by encouraging factional conflicts among the Red Guards or by setting workers and peasants against

256. *See* the speech by Ch'en Po-ta, "Grow Up in the Great Storm" (August 16, 1966), *Red Flag*, No. 11 (August 21, 1966); trans. in *SCMM*, No. 540 (September 6, 1966), pp. 12–13.

257. Mao, "Speech at a Central Committee Work Conference" (August 23, 1966), in *Long Live the Thought of Mao Tse-tung!* p. 40.

258. *Red Flag* editorial, "In the High Tide of Revolutionary Criticism, Attain a Revolutionary Great Alliance," No. 14 (September 17, 1967), p. 18.

259. From a transmission by Kweiyang Radio (Kweichow Province), August 2, 1968.

the students,[260] Mao and Lin Piao sought to press the confrontation to its conclusion.

With doubtful candor the Chairman told the leaders attending the October work conference:

> I did something disastrously wrong in the Cultural Revolution. I approved the big-character poster by Nieh Yuan-tzu of Peking University, wrote a letter to the middle school of Tsinghua University, and myself wrote a big-character poster. . . . The time was very brief, but the impact [of these things] was quite violent. It was beyond my expectation that the publication of the big-character poster of Peking University would stir up the whole country. Before the letter to the Red Guards was sent out [on August 1st] Red Guards of the whole country were mobilized and went on charging—charging with such force as to amaze you. I myself caused this big trouble, and I cannot blame you if you have complaints against me.[261]

In a manner reminiscent of his self-criticism at the Lushan Plenum, Mao commiserated with still-loyal comrades over their difficulties and distraction, even as he held firm to the determination to press the policy of disorganizing the regional Party apparatus. In a statement on the last day of the conference, Lin Piao revealed Mao's unwavering belief·that controlled political conflict was the answer to China's continuing struggle with "revisionism" and the "four olds." He characterized the Chairman's "concept of chaos" (*luan-tzu kuan*) as follows:

> Chaos (*luan-tzu*) has a dual character. This was said early on by Chairman Mao. It has a good aspect, and a bad aspect. Don't only look at the bad aspect without seeing the good. The bad aspect [also] can be turned to the good.
>
> The general [political] situation cannot become one of great chaos. Our military forces are very consolidated, and our production is steadily increasing. What kind of chaos was produced by a few students and young people promoting the Cultural Revolution struggle? They can't produce any great chaos. This is our attitude toward the question of *luan-tzu,* this is our "concept of chaos." [262]

260. Mao's awareness that the "class enemy" was likely to "incite the masses to struggle against each other" and to "shift the targets" of the Cultural Revolution struggle was clearly revealed in the Central Committee decision on the Cultural Revolution of August 1966. *See CCP Documents of the Great Proletarian Cultural Revolution,* pp. 45, 48.

261. Mao, "Speech at a Central Committee Work Conference" (October 25, 1966), in *Long Live the Thought of Mao Tse-tung!* p. 41.

262. Lin Piao, "Speech at a Central Committee Work Conference" (October 25, 1966), in *Tzu-kuo* [China Monthly, Hong Kong], No. 65 (August 1, 1969), p. 45.

Such was the attitude of Mao and his chosen successor in late 1966 as they prepared to press the Cultural Revolution throughout the provinces. And with the coming of the new year they called on China's "proletarian revolutionaries" to rise up and seize power from "revisionists" in the regional Party apparatus for Chairman Mao and his "thought." A *People's Daily* editorial of the hour explicitly stated what must have been all too obvious to those within the existing structure of political power, that Mao was intent on seizing direct control of the organization which had become increasingly resistant to his initiatives and had distorted his policies in application:

> Right from the beginning, the Great Proletarian Cultural Revolution has been a struggle for the seizure of power. . . . The revolutionary masses, with a deep hatred for the class enemy, grind their teeth and, with steel-like determination, make up their minds to unite, form a great alliance, and seize power! Power!! And more power!!! [263]

Less certain to all concerned, however, was the extent of conflict and the degree of destruction of two decades of Party-built political order which was to be generated by Mao's country-wide assault. A *Red Flag* article of early February gave some indication of how far Mao felt he might have to go when it stressed the continuing relevance of the Paris Commune experience of smashing the existing state machinery for the Cultural Revolution struggle:

> Since a number of units, in which a handful of Party people in authority taking the capitalist road have entrenched themselves, have been turned into organs of bourgeois dictatorship, we cannot of course take them over ready-made, we cannot accept reformism, cannot combine two into one and cannot effect peaceful transition. We must smash them thoroughly.[264]

A full analysis of the incredible turmoil of 1967 and 1968 which appears to have nearly undermined the ability of Mao and Lin Piao to ride out the *luan* of their effort to wrest political control from the Party organization is beyond the scope of this study. Perhaps the passage of time will give a better perspective to the factional conflict and violence which appears to have brought China to the verge of civil war.

In terms of the interpretations developed throughout this study,

263. *People's Daily* editorial, "Proletarian Revolutionaries, Form a Great Alliance to Seize Power from Those in Authority Who Are Taking the Capitalist Road!" (January 22, 1967); trans. in *SCMP*, No. 3868 (January 26, 1967), pp. 1–2.

264. *Red Flag* editorial, "On the Struggle to Seize Power by the Proletarian Revolutionaries," No. 3 (February 1, 1967); trans. in *SCMM*, No. 563 (February 13, 1967), p. 5.

however, three characteristics of this period of turmoil deserve special comment: the unwillingness of those in authority to tolerate "mass criticism"; the inability of China's younger generation to promote political struggle with discipline; and the eventual disillusionment of Mao and his supporters with the young intellectual Red Guards. These characteristics of the Cultural Revolution struggle became manifest in the great difficulty the Maoists encountered in keeping the political conflict within the bounds of nonviolent struggle and in rebuilding a new political order consonant with their stated goal of a Paris Commune-type of mass organization of "proletarian dictatorship."

It is hardly surprising that as the political purge was pressed throughout the country those in positions of authority resisted. Notably little of this resistance took the form of open opposition to Mao Tse-tung, however. As with so much of the resistance to the Chairman's policies in preceding years, the regional Party apparatus sought to divert or dilute Mao's attack, to turn official policy back on its maker, to discredit it by pushing it to its ultimate extreme, or to co-opt it into their own sphere of authority. Those who suspected that they would be the targets of Mao's *luan* attempted to create a counter-*luan* to disorganize the Chairman's controlled chaos.[265]

Regional Party leaders who were the targets of Red Guard attacks organized their own "Red Guard" units to counterattack Mao's student supporters, or mobilized workers and peasants to attack the young "rebels." In urban areas Party and government authorities granted workers wage increases and other material benefits —what the Maoists came to term "counterrevolutionary economism"—in order to win the support of the local "proletariat" and to force Mao and Lin into the difficult position of having to rescind the workers' economic gains. Union leaders urged laborers to travel to Peking to present demands for further improvements in their working conditions, thus "turning the spearpoint of struggle" away from the regional apparatus of government and clogging a transportation network already burdened with millions of "long-marching" student Red Guards.

Party personnel attempted to control local communication channels so as to prevent the mobilization of opinion against local lead-

265. The numerous ways in which leaders of the regional Party apparatus attempted to resist the purge are revealed in the series of leadership directives. Most of these directives were issued under the name of the Central Committee, the State Council, and the Party's Military Affairs Commission, and were republished in *CCP Documents of the Great Proletarian Cultural Revolution, 1966–67.*

ers. Radio stations and newspapers had to be "seized" from Mao's opponents, and secret personnel files and other political information had to be placed under direct PLA control. The "targets" of attack further resisted by spreading false information about who were the local "revisionists," by fabricating false dossier information, and even by painting city walls with Mao's quotations so that the Red Guards would have to desist from "defacing" the walls with big-character posters attacking local leaders.[266]

In time "fake power-seizures" were attempted, as local leaders sought to limit the struggle by claiming that "revolutionaries" (they themselves) were now in power—having "seized" authority from themselves. They attempted to turn student and worker opinion against the PLA in order to force the basic instrument of Mao's power to struggle against "the masses." In certain areas of China, arms (some stolen from military shipments bound for Viet-Nam) were "made available" to Red Guard units in order to stimulate armed violence against other Red Guard factions, and to force the Army to intervene and fire on the "revolutionary left." [267] In their determination to resist public "struggle" and removal from power, there were few distortions of Mao's policies not invoked by regional "revisionists."

From Mao's point of view a much more serious problem than the resistance of entrenched Party cadres was the degree of political indiscipline shown by the younger generation. The students displayed an inability—for which they can hardly be blamed—to distinguish between Mao's supporters in the now-decimated Party organization, and "the small handful taking the capitalist road." The Red Guards proved to be vulnerable to the political deceptions and provocations of local "revisionists," and uncertain of the objectives of the struggle.

As the Cultural Revolution progressed, the young students came to manifest that age-old Chinese ambivalence toward authority in their combined "fervent love" for Chairman Mao and a growing mistrust of any concrete authority and organizational discipline. As the struggle deepened during 1967, a *People's Daily* editorial complained of a trend toward "counterrevolutionary anarchy":

266. *See* "Circular of the CCP Central Committee and the State Council Concerning Prohibition of the Extensive Promotion of the So-Called 'Red Ocean,'" in *CCP Documents of the Great Proletarian Cultural Revolution,* p. 146.

267. On this point, *see* in particular, "Important Talk Given by Comrade Chiang Ch'ing on September 5 [1967] at a Conference of Representatives of Anhwei Who Have Come to Peking," in *CCP Documents of the Great Proletarian Cultural Revolution,* pp. 529–533.

It is completely wrong to regard all persons in authority as untrustworthy and overthrow all of them indiscriminately. This idea of opposing, excluding, and overthrowing all indiscriminately and its implementation run completely counter to Marxism-Leninism, Mao Tse-tung's thought.[268]

An article attacking anarchism in the same paper during this period observed of some of the "revolutionary rebels":

What [they] want is democracy and freedom, not democratic centralism and discipline. They put the masses in opposition to the leadership. They take advantage of supreme directives and the Party's general and specific policies, applying only those which suit their purposes and not enforcing them to the letter. This tendency is absolutely dangerous.[269]

Such disregard for Mao's authority was compounded by the factional conflict among Red Guard units that intensified throughout 1967. With the old Youth League and Party organizations "smashed" or in poor repute, the student groups and "rebel" organizations in factories, Communes, and government organizations struggled with each other for the position of *the* leading "center" of Maoist authority.[270] These factions often fragmented within a given organizational unit on the basis of leadership "centers" formed at different times and around conflicting individuals. They fought what were termed "civil wars" (*nei-chan*) with varying degrees of violence, destruction of property, and loss of life throughout 1967 and 1968.

Mao's "thought" seemed to provide a fragile basis for political discipline, perhaps because from the perspective of the provinces the conflict which had erupted at the Party center was highly personal, and because Mao's "thought" was so generalized that it provided little concrete guidance in the context of an intense and complicated conflict for power. As Mao's Shanghai supporter, Chang Ch'un-ch'iao, told a meeting of factious university students in early 1968: "The reading of quotations [from Mao's "little red book"] has become nothing but a war of words. I will only read passages

268. *People's Daily* editorial, "A Good Example in the Struggle by Proletarian Revolutionaries to Seize Power" (February 10, 1967); trans. in *Peking Review,* No. 8 (February 17, 1967), p. 19.

269. Hung Yung-ping and Wei Tung-piao, "Down With Anarchism!" *People's Daily* (March 1, 1967); trans. in *SCMP,* No. 3889 (March 15, 1967), p. 14.

270. For analyses of the origins and conflict among student and various "adult" factions, *see:* "Mass Factionalism in Communist China, *Current Scene,* Vol. VI, No. 8 (May 15, 1968), pp. 1–13; Michel Oksenberg, "Occupational Groups in Chinese Society and the Cultural Revolution," in *The Cultural Revolution: 1967 in Review* (Ann Arbor: Michigan Papers in Chinese Studies No. 2, 1968), pp. 1–44.

from the quotations which are favorable to me, but will not read anything which is unfavorable to me." [271]

The factional rivalry and erosion of political authority reached a peak of violence during the spring and summer months of 1967,[272] culminating in a July military insurrection at Wuhan in which Maoist mediators from Peking were kidnapped for a time by rebellious Army authorities. Despite such signs of growing divisiveness within the PLA in reaction to the expanded scope of the purge and the breakdown in public order, Mao and Lin had sufficient control over the Army to ride out the chaos they had provoked. By September enough calm had returned to enable Mao to make a mediating trip through provinces in north, central-south, and east China.[273] And in the wake of this test of Mao's "concept of chaos," Lin Piao reasserted the correctness of the Chairman's political strategy:

> The victory of this Cultural Revolution is very great. The costs are the smallest, smallest, smallest, the victories the greatest, greatest, greatest. Superficially things are *luan,* but this chaos is created by the reactionary line, by reactionary classes, it has burst forth from their actions, [it has been] created by the small handful in authority within the Party taking the capitalist road. This *luan* is necessary, correct. If things were not thrown into chaos reactionary elements would not be exposed. The reason we dare to do things in this way is precisely because we have Chairman Mao's supreme prestige and the power of the Liberation Army. Given these conditions, if we did not let [the opposition] expose itself, when might it then reveal itself [and attack us]? *Luan,* under Chairman Mao's leadership, is nothing to be feared.[274]

Despite such expressions of self-confidence, the available evidence indicates that Mao and Lin have been less than successful in their efforts to balance off the destruction of the Cultural Revolution with the construction of new forms of political organization consonant with Maoist goals and under Mao-Lin control. In early

271. "Comrade Chang Ch'un-ch'iao's Speech at Chiaot'ung University of Shanghai" (January 18, 1968), *Tzu-liào Chuan-chi* [Special Collection of Information Material] (Canton, February 10, 1968); trans. in *SCMP,* No. 4146 (March 26, 1968), p. 3.

272. *See* the *People's Daily* editorial, "Immediately Restrain Armed Struggle" (May 22, 1967).

273. *See* the NCNA press release of September 25, 1967, "Chairman Mao Inspects North, Central-South, and East China, in the Unprecedentedly Fine Situation in China's Great Proletarian Cultural Revolution."

274. "Deputy Supreme Commander Lin's Important Directive" (August 9, 1967), as republished in the Red Guard publication *Chu-ying Tung-fang-hung* (Canton, September 13, 1967); reproduced in *Tzu-kuo* [China Monthly], No. 44 (November 1, 1967), p. 29.

1967 Chiang Ch'ing and Ch'en Po-ta called for the formation of a "Paris Commune" type of political organization in Peking to implement Mao's objective of realizing true "proletarian dictatorship" in China. The sixteen-point decision on the Cultural Revolution of August 1966 had declared that it "is necessary to institute a system of general elections, like that of the Paris Commune, for electing members to the cultural revolutionary groups and committees and delegates to the cultural revolutionary congress." [275] Soon afterwards "Commune" governments were proclaimed in Taiyuan, Peking, and Shanghai.[276] These organizational expressions of faith in the "revolutionary masses," however, appear to have succumbed quickly to factional turmoil and mass violence. In their place appeared "three-way alliances" of PLA representatives, "revolutionary" mass organizations, and trusted Party cadres. Later, "revolutionary committees" of trusted Maoist supporters became the core of organizational efforts to rebuild a new political order in China which would be impervious to "revisionist degeneration." [277]

The first revolutionary committee was established in Heilungkiang Province in late January of 1967. The twenty-one months it took to create loyal leadership cores in all of China's twenty-nine other provinces, municipalities, and autonomous regions is some measure of the difficulty the Maoists faced—and continue to face —in reasserting their authority.[278] In September 1967 Chiang Ch'ing told the feuding "Good Faction" and "Fart Faction" of Anhwei Province,

> At present, a gust of foul wind is blowing. Apart from being directed at the Party Central Committee headed by Chairman Mao and at the People's Liberation Army, it is [also] directed at the revolutionary committee—a newborn thing. . . . A wind is being stirred up with the object of dissolving all revolutionary committees set up with the approval of the Central Committee.[279]

275. "Decision of the Central Committee of the CCP Concerning the Great Proletarian Cultural Revolution" (August 8, 1966), in *CCP Documents of the Great Proletarian Cultural Revolution,* p. 50.

276. *See* "China's Revolutionary Committees," *Current Scene,* Vol. VI, No. 21 (December 6, 1968), pp. 2–3.

277. The authoritative editorial of support for the revolutionary committees is the joint *People's Daily, Red Flag,* and *Liberation Army Daily* editorial, "Revolutionary Committees Are Fine" (March 30, 1968); trans. in *Peking Review,* No. 14 (April 5, 1968), pp. 6–7.

278. For preliminary analyses of efforts to establish revolutionary committees, *see* Parris H. Chang, "The Revolutionary Committee in China: Two Case Studies, Heilungkiang and Honan," *Current Scene,* Vol. VI, No. 9 (June 1, 1968); "Mao Fails to Build His Utopia: A Political Assessment of Communist China," *ibid.,* Vol. VI, No. 15 (September 3, 1968).

279. "Important Talk Given by Comrade Chiang Ch'ing on September

In their efforts to block the reassertion of the authority of Mao and Lin, purged or threatened members of the now-decimated Party organization evidently played on resentments against those who had risen to prominence within Mao's "small group" in the Cultural Revolution. They also stirred up the bitter rivalry for power among student groups, in order to stimulate a diffusion of power away from Mao-Lin's "center." What the Maoists came to attack in the national press as the "theory of many centers" and renewed manifestations of the divisive forces of "departmentalism," "small group mentality," "ultra-democracy," "mountain-top-ism," and "selfishness," were pressures for local political autonomy grown from resentments against more than a decade of Mao's manipulative interventions in domestic political life.[280] Those who had tasted a period of genuine political initiative in Cultural Revolution struggles appeared determined to attain or consolidate a position of local dominance in the new "anti-revisionist" order; while those purged still struggled to make a comeback.

As the trend toward "selfishness" in matters of authority reasserted itself,[281] Mao directed his frustration over this diffusion of authority at the intellectuals. In late 1967 he attacked what he termed an "outpouring of petty-bourgeois and bourgeois ideology from the intellectuals and young students," describing them as "vacillating and amorphous, . . . [and] opportunistic to a certain extent." [282] And in the summer of 1968 he bitterly criticized still-feuding Red Guard leaders. "You have let me down," the Chairman was reported to have told them, "and what is more, you have disappointed the workers, peasants, and Army men of China." [283] Within a month the official political line had shifted away from sup-

---

5 at a Conference of Representatives of Anhwei Who Have Come to Peking," in *CCP Documents of the Great Proletarian Cultural Revolution*, p. 531.

280. *See*, for example, the *People's Daily* editorial, "Unite under the Leadership of the Proletarian Headquarters Headed by Chairman Mao" (August 4, 1968); trans. in *SCMP*, No. 4236 (August 12, 1968), pp. 13–16; and the *Wen Hui Pao* editorial, "Comment on the 'Theory of Many Centers'" (August 6, 1968), in *ibid.*, No. 4253 (September 9, 1968), pp. 11–12.

281. *See* the Red Guard article, "Get Rid of 'Self-Interest,' Forge a Great Alliance of Revolutionary Rebels," and the accompanying *Red Flag* editorial note; trans. in *Peking Review*, No. 7 (February 10, 1967), pp. 20–21, 31.

282. Mao, "Our Strategy" (September 1967); trans. in *Chinese Law and Government*, Vol. II, No. 1 (Spring 1969), p. 6.

283. Cited in Parris H. Chang, "Mao's Great Purge: A Political Balance Sheet," *Problems of Communism*, Vol. XVIII, No. 2 (March–April 1969), p. 3.

port for China's student "rebels." The "working class" was to exercise dominant political leadership, with the Red Guards relegated to the background and subject to PLA and "proletarian" political discipline.[284]

Such indications of the difficulty Mao encountered in propagating his "thought" as the basis for more spontaneous political initiative from "the masses" have also been revealed in an increasing tendency by the Maoists to resort to traditional forms of asserting authority in their attempt to consolidate a new political order. Whereas in the post-Civil War years of Party rule the Army had been relegated to the background as an instrument of social control, in the anarchy of the Cultural Revolution this most basic form of political discipline was reinvoked to support the rebellion of "the left" and then to dampen the conflict among contending Maoist factions.

As we have stressed in previous chapters, in earlier years Mao attempted to depersonalize political authority and make ideology the basis for a more decentralized, self-initiating political order. Yet with the diffusion of authority in the Cultural Revolution, the Chairman has resorted to an ever more direct repersonalization of his power to sustain his influence over Chinese political life. Within the PLA, oath-taking rallies are held in which soldiers swear their personal loyalty to Mao and his "thought." And the renewed use of the traditional character *chung* for loyalty in civilian propaganda themes bespeaks Mao's inability to sustain political discipline solely on the basis of his "thought."

Over the centuries in China, education has been a basic means of asserting authority, and as noted earlier, Mao has attempted to make the study of Marxism and his own writings the basis for mass political initiative. Yet one sees in the Cultural Revolution the subtle transformation of the study of Mao's quotations from an act of creative learning to a new ritual of political control. The establishment of "Mao's thought propaganda teams" under the direction of the PLA has become one of the basic instruments for the reestablishment of political discipline.[285] Although earlier Mao had hoped that ideological education would produce new generations of Chinese able to take initiative in self-conscious political action, now the controlled recitation of Mao's quotations has become a new ritual

284. *See* the authoritative article by Yao Wen-yuan, "The Working Class Must Exercise Leadership in Everything," trans. in *Peking Review,* No. 35 (August 30, 1968), pp. 3–6.

285. *See People's Daily* editorial, "Organize Classes for the Study of Mao Tse-tung's Thought Throughout the Country" (October 12, 1967); trans. in *SCMP,* No. 4045 (October 23, 1967), pp. 1–3.

A PLA cadre leads a study group
in discussing Party Chairman Mao Tse-tung's political writings.
From China Pictorial, *February 1968.*

A "Mao's Thought Propaganda Team"
leads peasants of a People's Commune Production Brigade
in chanting slogans from the "little red book" of
Quotations from Chairman Mao.
From China Pictorial, *February 1968.*

of deference. As the Shanghai paper *Wen Hui Pao* baldly stated after the violent summer of 1967, "We must carry out Chairman Mao's instructions whether we understand them or not." [286]

These indications that the purposeful *luan* of the Cultural Revolution passed beyond Mao's control raise basic questions about his ability to reshape China's political order. In dynasties past a ruler of Mao's stature would have been content to see the establishment of civil order after a period of domestic political strife. In the historical pattern, the *luan* of a time of troubles would give way to *ho-p'ing;* and in the tranquillity of a new dynastic cycle China's rural population would build the material basis of another period of prosperity. Mao's objective, however, has been to transform a peasant society; and he has remained convinced that *ho-p'ing,* in its traditional sense of a period of political amelioration and bureaucratic rule, will hinder China's social transformation through the uncritical acceptance of traditional social values and rule by a small, educated, and paternalistic elite group.

China's problem has certainly not been one of trying to reestablish a period of political tranquillity. As we have shown, it has been Mao himself—in the 1956–57 period of "blooming and contending," in the Great Leap Forward, and in the Cultural Revolution—who has resisted the trend toward reconsolidation of domestic political order out of his fears that the momentum of social change would die. The Cultural Revolution is not a manifestation of the failure of Party rule; quite the contrary, it is a result of Mao's objection to the Party's success.

In Mao's terms the problem has been to institute a new style of politics somewhere between the poles of Cultural Revolution *luan* and Party *ho-p'ing,* in which criticism of the old way of life and those who wield Party authority becomes part of the political life of the Chinese people in their struggle to become a modern nation. The violence and social fragmentation of the Cultural Revolution indicates how difficult it is to institutionalize limited and disciplined political conflict in a society where for centuries interpersonal "harmony" has been stressed as a basic social value. Conversely, the rapid consolidation of bureaucratic Party rule, and the resistance of the Party apparatus to public criticism, bespeaks the ease with which traditional forms of political paternalism reemerge. Only time will tell whether out of the destruction of the Cultural Revolution Mao and his supporters will be able to build a new political order in which controlled "struggle" will become an accepted part of China's political life, and the basis for her social advance.

286. *Wen Hui Pao* editorial (September 30, 1967), p. 1.

Chapter XX

CONCLUSION:
THE ROLE OF AGGRESSION
IN SOCIAL CHANGE

The Ninth National Congress of the Chinese Communist Party, which convened in April of 1969, represented for Mao Tse-tung both the conclusion of more than a decade of struggle with "revisionist" Party leaders and the beginning of a period of efforts to rebuild a national political structure shattered by the Cultural Revolution. The new Party Constitution adopted by the Congress reaffirmed "the thought of Mao Tse-tung" as the theoretical guide to China's national development, *the* expression of Marxism-Leninism in "the era in which imperialism is heading for total collapse and socialism is advancing to world-wide victory."[1] Thus, on the eve of the twentieth anniversary of the People's Republic of China, Mao was able formally to break the influence of the Soviet precedent of national development within the Chinese Communist Party and initiate a new beginning in the long march to free the country of foreign influence and the burden of her past.

This formal development, however, does not warrant the conclusion that Mao has finally established his conception of a new political order for China. Indeed, during the three years following the conclusion of the Cultural Revolution there have been developments which only increase the uncertainty surrounding Mao's influence on China's future. While the Chinese people, by all accounts, have restored daily patterns of disciplined collective labor, rote learning, and directed political participation characteristic of the traditional culture, the Party leadership around Mao has displayed an instability which reflects personal rivalries and resentments exacerbated by the Cultural Revolution struggle.

1. "The [Ninth] Constitution of the Communist Party of China" (April 14, 1969), in *Current Background,* No. 880 (May 9, 1969), p. 51.

510

In the early fall of 1970 the Chairman's long-time comrade and exponent of "the thought of Mao Tse-tung" Ch'en Po-ta was purged at a Party Plenum that shifted China's political line away from the "left" orientation that had characterized policy during the preceding decade[2]; and in September of 1971 Mao's own chosen successor Lin Piao disappeared from view, apparently the loser in a struggle for power between the Army's political leadership and those who would reestablish the preeminent role of the Communist Party. Mao, speaking through the symbol of his old hero Lu Hsün, denounced the "betrayal" of Lin Piao in terms that implied that the Defense Minister—like his predecessor P'eng Teh-huai—had had "illicit relations" with the Soviet Union[3]—perhaps in an effort to moderate the Sino-Soviet dispute, which in 1969 had escalated to near warfare. By late 1971 it was evident that day-to-day leadership in China had passed to the man who had emerged from the Cultural Revolution as Mao's "conflict manager"—Chou En-lai.

Exactly what these developments imply for the succession to Mao Tse-tung's leadership remains uncertain. In terms of domestic policies, the political pendulum has taken at least a temporary swing to the "right," as is evident in the rebuilding of a Party apparatus and renewed stress on relatively non-politicized approaches to economic development. While Mao's opposition to Soviet "revisionism" endures, this "leftist" line became "right in essence" in 1972 as Mao and Chou En-lai promoted a major reorientation of China's foreign policy that included receiving an American President in the People's Republic. Thus the legacy of the *luan* of the Cultural Revolution is an uncertain set of leadership relations, an unresolved succession to the aging but still influential Mao, and shifts in China's domestic policies and foreign relations which give no clear indication of implementing the development concepts which Mao evolved in the mass campaigns of the 1950s and '60s.

Thus, this study concludes on a major note of uncertainty. As an exercise in the still imperfect science of political analysis, our conclusions must focus on Mao Tse-tung's life-long effort to reshape China's traditional political life, on his approach to promoting social change in a peasant society, and on the areas of tension that are likely

2. *See* "Communiqué of the Second Plenary Session of the Ninth Central Committee of the Communist Party of China," in *SCMP,* No. 4741 (September 21, 1970), pp. 18–21.

3. *See* Lo Szu-ting, "Learn the Thoroughgoing Revolutionary Spirit With Which Lu Hsün Criticized the Confucius Shop—In Memory of the 90th Anniversary of the Birth of the Great Revolutionary, Thinker, and Litterateur Lu Hsün," *People's Daily* (September 25, 1971); trans. in *SCMP,* No. 4989 (October 6, 1971), pp. 44–53.

to endure in a country still trying to find its road to renewed greatness.

THE INTERPLAY BETWEEN
REVOLUTIONARY LEADER AND CULTURAL LEGACY

In overview, one has a sense of the complex interplay among China's social and political traditions, popular social attitudes, and Mao Tse-tung's personal political style. In part this complexity reflects the endurance of cultural norms in the personalities of millions of Chinese reared before Liberation, and in part, Mao's adaptation of old behavioral patterns and social values to the demands of leading a quarter of mankind to cope with the challenges of a new era. For all that endures, however, there is also the revolutionary leader's personal determination to overcome what he sees as backward in the national tradition.

The one theme in Mao's personality which stands in sharpest contrast to China's traditional cultural pattern is his strong element of self-assertiveness, in a society which for millennia has stressed social interdependence and personal dependence. Mao's youthful opposition to the role of a filial son, his rebellion against the pain and manipulation suffered while dependent on paternal authority, however, acquired meaning beyond personal assertiveness. Mao's individual struggle merged with that of an age in which millions of Chinese witnessed the increasing ineffectiveness of the Confucian social tradition and suffered humiliation at the hands of exploitative foreign powers. Thus, one unique individual's efforts to break the bonds of personal subordination found larger meaning in a nation's struggle to overcome political subordination. Mao's call for a confrontation with Japanese invaders and rejection of a position of dependence on Comintern and Soviet political guidance were powerful appeals for China to "stand up" against manipulative authority.

Mao's personal style seems to have been a major factor shaping the evolution of the Chinese Communist Party's policies and leadership methods. While other leaders advocated withdrawal from confrontation with the Japanese, acceptance of Soviet political authority, and reliance on non-Chinese models in national development, Mao's policies, with few exceptions, have stressed confrontation and self-assertiveness.

From a psychological perspective, there is no little irony in the fact that in contrast to the unfilial Mao, the ancient philosophers of China's political tradition, Confucius and Mencius, were men who lost their fathers early in life. One is tempted to see in their system of filial deference to authority an effort by these ancient sages to construct a source of authority which was lacking in their personal lives. Mao, however, was a man who knew a harsh reality of filial subordination; and in his political life he has tried to pass on to the Chinese people a system of political participation in which subordinate opinion becomes a powerful element in checking abuses of authority. Whether it be criticism of Party cadres from the intellectuals or from members of the Associations of Poor and Lower-Middle Peasants, or the uprising of the student Red Guards against erring Party leaders, Mao has sought to institutionalize his own rebellion against manipulative authority in the political life of new China—even as he has sought to control the "struggle" and use it as a technique for asserting political discipline.

Rejection of the dependency social orientation finds varied expression in the Maoist political style. Where Confucianism lauded the virtues of tranquillity and interpersonal harmony, Mao has made activism the key to the behavior of the ideal Party cadre. Where fear and avoidance of conflict characterized the "cultivated" response to social tension in the traditional society, Mao has stressed the importance of criticism and controlled struggle in resolving those issues which block China's social advance.

Perhaps Mao's most innovative reaction against tradition has been his effort to liberate in disciplined, politicized fashion the aggressive emotions which were denied legitimate expression in the political culture of dependency.[4] Where the Confucian order stressed emotional restraint as the basis of personal discipline, and "eating bitterness" as the only appropriate response of the subordinate, Mao,

4. While this study has not been cast in comparative terms, we would suggest that the emphasis which Mao has placed on drawing forth emotions of resentment, anger, and hatred as the motivational basis of the revolution is one of the distinguishing characteristics of China's struggle for national development in contrast to other great revolutions of the twentieth century. In the case of Japan, the Samurai tradition apparently provided a basis of value congruence for incorporating the military challenge of the West. And as is readily attested by Japan's aggressiveness during the first half of the century, that country readily emulated the combative expansionism of the European nations. In India, a strong tradition of pacifism has found expression not only in Gandhi's politics, but also in Indian foreign policy in the years after independence. And as Nathan Leites has concluded in his study of Soviet Bolshevism, Lenin's stress on the need for a highly disciplined revolutionary party in part represents a reaction against the emotional "spontaneity" of the Russian character. (*A Study of Bolshevism* [Glencoe: The Free Press, 1953], Ch. V.)

early in his career, saw resentment and hatred as the motivational basis of mass political participation.[5]

Hence among the institutional forms which were evolved in the years of struggle for power, Mao developed the "speak bitterness" meetings, in which the peasants were encouraged to "vomit the bitter water" of repressed hatreds which tradition said should be "put in the stomach." Mobilization of such sentiments of aggression thus constitute a powerful tool of social change, both motivating people to seek change and overpowering that anxiety which is the emotional support of authority and precedent.

A concomitant of the traditional orientation toward authority was Confucian rejection of open social conflict. Conflict, when it did occur, tended to pass beyond the bounds of dispute over specific issues into a "confusion" (*luan*) of personal animosity. Aggression, once released, knew few limits.[6] Mao sought to "liberate" aggressive emotions in the service of political ends by subjecting them to disciplined release. In contrast to the unrestrained violence of a traditional peasant rebellion, Mao has stressed the need for political education as a way of both making men "conscious" of their rage at exploitation *and* disciplining the aggression into purposeful political action. Emotional manipulation and political "education" thus constitute complimentary dimensions of the Maoist approach to mass mobilization.

One of the most profound contradictions facing a political leadership seeking to institutionalize change in a peasant society, however, is centered around this basic motivational mechanism of the Maoist political style. As was revealed in the resistance of certain Communist Party leaders to the "mass movement" approach to political mobilization in post-Liberation China, and in Party opposition to criticism from non-Party groups, there are those who

5. Inhibitions against expressing aggression in limited ways against established authority may very well be a universal aspect of peasant life. (*See,* for example, Frantz Fanon, *The Wretched of the Earth* [New York: Evergreen, 1968], p. 54.) One of the appeals of Maoism to revolutionary groups in other parts of the "underdeveloped" world thus may be Mao's solution to the motivational problem of mobilizing people long accustomed to turning aggression inward into conscious political participants willing to attack established authority.

6. Apparently identifying another universal quality of peasant life, Fanon speaks of "waves of uncontrollable rage" among Algeria's peasants, which a revolutionary leader finds to be "objectively reactionary." (*Ibid.,* p. 111.) Here again, the concomitant aspect of Mao's mobilization technique, the disciplining of aggression through heightening political "consciousness" of the need for limit and purpose in "struggle," may constitute another important dimension of the appeal of Mao's "thought" to revolutionaries in peasant societies.

have questioned the appropriateness of emotional mobilization in the years of "socialist construction." Should a highly emotionalized style of politics be sustained in a period where the Party's goals seem to require a rationalized approach to leadership and the promotion of technical innovation? How relevant is emotional manipulation in an era when the Party has eliminated many of the worst abuses of authority and the sources of social injustice which genuinely fueled the mass mobilizations of the revolutionary years?

In addition, one senses that there endures in the political orientation of many Party cadres attitudes that reject even the limited conflict and tension of political "struggle," and criticism of authority by subordinates. As was indicated in earlier chapters, the question of whether or not to sustain "class struggle" after the consolidation of Party rule was one of the central issues which came to divide the leadership. During the Cultural Revolution Mao managed to remove from power those Party leaders who resisted "struggle" politics. But will the leaders and institutions which emerge from the current efforts to rebuild a national political order sustain Mao's approach to mass mobilization and "class struggle?"

From another perspective, Mao's conception of an emotional mechanism for ensuring political participation in a peasant society is self-defeating, for as the Party moves toward the attainment of its social goals, it eliminates many of the sources of discontent which previously generated popular support for Party programs. One sees a reflection of this contradiction in the Hundred Flowers Campaign, the Socialist Education Movement, and the Cultural Revolution, as strained efforts to make the most of existing social discontent in order to eliminate cadre abuses of authority—even as this criticism is intended to sustain popular support for "correct" leadership.

In the eyes of Party cadres, however, there was little justice in holding them responsible for difficulties in implementing overambitious policies formulated at the Party "center." In addition, one senses that there is likely to be limited effectiveness in encouraging peasants to "recall the bitterness of the past" as the basis for their allegiance to the Party. The landlords were eliminated as a political and economic force two decades ago and the hardships created by the Great Leap Forward are much more immediate—and Party-created—sources of discontent. Such emotional manipulation, in time, can only produce dissimulative responses and political cynicism.

It is in this light that Mao's repeated warnings about the dangers of a "restoration of capitalism" and his calls for "class struggle" reveal a fear that there is insufficient popular commitment to the Party's radical social goals for the revolution to be sustained through a rationalized approach to leadership and stress on economic growth. In post-Cultural Revolution developments, the most significant point to watch is the *manner* in which Mao and his supporters seek to restructure China's political life so as to sustain popular participation and prevent a return to bureaucratic rule by an elite administrative class.

Whatever the contradictions in this approach to political mobilization, however, a major point of departure from traditional Chinese political values has been Mao's effort to institutionalize "the unity of opposites." He has sought to substitute controlled political conflict between the Party's operative cadres and those they lead, as well as between different social and economic groups, for the traditional ideal of "the great unity" (*ta-t'ung*) in which social conflict was denied legitimate expression.

Although Maoist politics are a "dialectical" departure from China's traditional political culture, many of the institutions of the People's Republic continue to bear the stamp of the social traditions from which the revolution has grown. "The power of the word" was a major expression of authority in Confucian China, and Mao has sought to give the long-unenfranchised masses a sense of political efficacy both by popularizing literacy and by institutionalizing the (controlled) mass expression of political opinion. The "big character poster" (*ta-tzu-pao*) is both a sign of efforts to diffuse political authority to the people and a symbol of greater popular political participation. Mao departs from imperial forms in trying to use the critical voice of the people to discipline his officials, even as he merges with Chinese tradition in attempting to assert his authority through the study of his own writings. This contradictory combination of tradition and innovation is no more clearly symbolized than in "the little red book" of Mao's quotations. His words are used to attack established Party authority even as their recitation has now become a ritual of discipline for unruly Red Guards and factious cadres.

The one Maoist political value which fully merges with tradition is an uncompromising stress on the collective good above the interests of the individual; the damning of individualism as "selfishness." The Cultural Revolution call to "destroy self and establish the collective" (*p'o-szu, li-kung*) in part reflects the leadership's response to the indiscipline manifested by Mao's youthful supporters during a period of political combat. Yet it also reveals a paradox which brings our analysis full circle. While Mao calls for China's people to "stand up" and reject the dependency social orientation, he must cope with the need for social order and political discipline in a society where traditions have not prepared people for a critical and participatory role in the affairs of state. The Party Chairman wants to encourage popular innovation in economic matters and mass criticism of cadre abuses of authority, even as he seeks to sustain policy control and initiative from a revolutionary center of national political leadership. The resolution of this contradiction, as with other points of divergence between Maoist ideals and enduring Chinese realities, is in large measure a matter of the extent to which "the masses" come to absorb Mao's "thought" as the basis for social action.

Throughout this study we have been impressed by the close correspondence between the requirements for survival in a social economy of subsistence agriculture, the "eating" themes which predominate in Chinese social imagery, and the dependency style most characteristic of the "oral" stage of personality formation.[7] Apparently all the anxieties associated with having enough to eat in an economy of extreme scarcity had an enduring influence on the manner in which Chinese organized their social relations and reared their children to cope with life's hardships. The great stress on family interdependence is a clear response to the needs of production and security in this type of society. Adults had to rely on the life-long commitment of their children to the family group for both labor power and, eventually, for their material needs in old age. Love was thus suffused with the "oral" qualities of feeding and being fed, while discipline was associated with the "taking in" of scarce resources and the "eating" of emotions which would disrupt the interdependent group. Aggression was conceptualized in terms of "being eaten" by others, or "putting in one's stomach" frustrations and rage which would threaten group solidarity if given free expression.

The dominant forms of authority and social sanction which characterized traditional Chinese society reflect this basic logic of social interdependence. Authority mirrored the harshness of the natural environment; it was hierarchical and had all the sternness of submission-dominance. Social authority remained external to the individual—in the superior experience of family elders and what Max Weber has termed the tradition-based authority of the "eternal yesterday."[8] One might characterize such an authority pattern as one of the "external superego." The major form of social sanction, furthermore, reinforced external controls over an individual's be-

7. Erik H. Erikson, *Childhood and Society* (New York: Norton, 1950), pp. 67–72, 222–224.

8. Max Weber, "Politics as a Vocation," in Hans H. Gerth and C. Wright Mills, *From Max Weber: Essays in Sociology* (New York: Oxford University Press, 1958), p. 78.

havior. The punishments of shame, of "loss of face" and social isolation, reflected the predominance of the interdependent group as well as manipulation of the individual's dependency needs.

While the natural environment sustained for generations of Chinese rural dwellers the relevance of this pattern of social relations, it is clear from our interviews with Chinese of middle and upper-income levels—many of whom had lived in urban areas—that this cultural pattern was not restricted to the countryside. The social logic of an agrarian society became elaborated into a "great tradition" of culture which celebrated the virtues of peasant life and rationalized the status of those who lived off the peasant's produce.

Given the manner in which culture is incorporated within the developing personality through socialization experiences, however, the dependency orientation acquired something of a life of its own apart from the environment which gave it meaning. Chinese sustained this pattern of social relations even when they migrated to distant societies with very different social systems and economic patterns.

It is the endurance of this cultural pattern in the personalities of millions of Chinese that Mao Tse-tung has sought to confront, in part through changes in organizational pattern and "work style," and in part through efforts to promote the "thought reform" of adults socialized before Liberation. The difficulty of changing mature personalities, and the endurance of traditional Chinese social values and behavioral patterns, however, ultimately led Mao to resort to the upheaval of the Cultural Revolution. Between 1966 and 1968, he sought to remove from positions of political authority "revisionist" adult Chinese and replace them either with adults whose behavioral style was consonant with Maoist ideals or with members of the younger generation schooled in Mao's "thought."

There are, of course, a variety of levels at which one might analyze Mao's political style: the organizational forms developed during his leadership of the Party; the economic or political policies he has promoted; or his social and political philosophy. In addition, if one assumes, as we have throughout this study, that a single personality is critical both as a carrier of culture and as an organizer of individual social action, then personal style becomes another major factor in the analysis of societies and social change.

How might one characterize Mao's style of political leadership? In summarizing themes that are only implicitly developed in the preceding analysis, let us begin in proper Chinese fashion by invoking a series of quotations from the Chairman concerning matters of leadership:

It seems that right up to the present quite a few have regarded Marxism-Leninism as a ready-made panacea: Once you have it, you can cure your ills with little effort. This is a type of childish blindness and we must start a movement to enlighten these people. . . . We must tell them openly, "Your dogma is of no use," or to use an impolite formulation, "Your dogma is less useful than shit." We see that dog shit can fertilize the fields and man's can feed the dog. And dogmas? They can't fertilize the fields, nor can they feed the dog. Of what use are they? (Laughter) Comrades! You know the object of such talk is to ridicule those who regard Marxism-Leninism as dogma, to frighten and awaken them, to foster a correct attitude toward Marxism-Leninism. Marx, Engels, Lenin, and Stalin have repeatedly said, "Our doctrine is not dogma; it is a guide to action." [9]

Subjectivism, sectarianism and stereotyped Party writing are . . . gusts of contrary wind, ill winds from the air-raid tunnels. (Laughter) It is bad . . . that such winds should still be blowing in the Party. We must seal off the passages which produce them. Our whole Party should undertake the job of sealing off these passages, and so should the Party School.[10]

With victory, certain moods may grow within the Party—arrogance, the airs of a self-styled hero, inertia and unwillingness to make progress, love of pleasure and distaste for continued hard living. With victory the people will be grateful to us and the bourgeoisie will come forward to flatter us. It has been proved that the enemy cannot conquer us by force of arms. However, the flattery of the bourgeoisie may conquer the weak-willed in our ranks. There may be some Communists, who were not conquered by enemies with guns and were worthy of the name of heroes for standing up to these enemies, but who cannot withstand sugar-coated bullets; they will be defeated by sugar-coated bullets. We must guard against such a situation.[11]

Conscientious practise of self-criticism is a hallmark distinguishing our Party from all other political parties. As we say, dust will accumulate if a room is not cleaned regularly, our faces will get dirty if they are not washed regularly. Our comrades' minds and our Party's work may also collect dust, and also need sweeping and washing. The proverb "Running water is never stale and a doorhinge is never worm-eaten" means that constant motion prevents the inroads of germs and other organisms. . . . Fear neither criticism or self-criticism . . .

9. Mao Tse-tung, "Reform in Learning, the Party, and Literature" (February 1942), in Stuart R. Schram, *The Political Thought of Mao Tse-tung* (New York: Praeger, 1963), p. 120.

10. Mao Tse-tung, "Rectify the Party's Style of Work" (February 1942), *SW*, English, III, p. 36.

11. Mao, "Report to the Second Plenary Session of the Seventh Central Committee of the Communist Party of China" (March 1949), *SW*, English, IV, p. 374.

—this is the only effective way to prevent all kinds of political dust and germs from contaminating the minds of our comrades and the body of our Party.[12]

. . . [Our] aim in exposing errors and criticizing shortcomings, like that of a doctor curing a sickness, is solely to save the patient and not to doctor him to death. . . . So long as a person who has made mistakes does not hide his sickness for fear of treatment or persist in his mistakes until he is beyond cure . . . we should welcome him and cure his sickness so that he can become a good comrade. . . . In treating an ideological or a political malady, one must never be rough and rash but must adopt the approach of "curing the sickness to save the patient," which is the only correct and effective method.[13]

Diseases enter by the mouth and all disasters come through the tongue. I'm in great trouble today. . . . I decided upon and promoted the target of 10,700,000 tons of steel, and as a result 90 million people were thrown into battle. . . . Next, the People's Communes. I did not invent the People's Communes, but I promoted them. When I was in Shantung a correspondent asked me: "Are the People's Communes good?" I said, "Good"; and on the basis of this he published a report in a newspaper. From now on I must avoid reporters. . . . This trouble [of the Great Leap Forward] I have brought on is a great one, and I hold myself responsible for it. Comrades, you should also analyze your own responsibilities, and you will all feel better after you have broken wind and emptied your bowels.[14]

It is evident from the predominantly scatological tone of Mao's humor—ridicule of those who would assert their authority in the time-honored Confucian manner through "the power of the word" as but issuing faeces and "ill winds,"—that "anal" themes have a particular emotional weight in his perception of the world.[15] In his efforts to evolve a new style of political leadership he seems to be reacting against the "oral" characteristics of the traditional political culture, which he symbolizes most vividly in the dangers for the Party of "sugar-coated bullets."

These clues to the organizing emotional theme of Mao's personal style are strengthened when we consider the common dimensions

12. Mao, "On Coalition Government" (April 1945), SW, English, III pp. 316–317.

13. Mao, "Rectify the Party's Style of Work" (February 1942), CW, English, III, p. 50.

14. Mao Tse-tung, "Speech at the Lushan Conference" (July 23, 1959), in *Chairman Mao's Criticism and Repudiation of the P'eng, Huang, Chang, and Chou Anti-Party Clique*, in *Chinese Law and Government*, Vol. I, No. 4 (Winter 1968/69), p. 11.

15. A description of the character traits that psychoanalysts identify as "anal" and "oral" will be found in Otto Fenichel, *The Psychoanalytic Theory of Neurosis* (New York: Norton, 1945), pp. 278–284, 488–492.

of political policies he has promoted, and the manner in which they contrast with themes of the traditional culture and with policies promoted by other Party leaders.

Perhaps the strongest theme in Mao's politics is the stress on "self-reliance," the need for the Chinese people to "stand on their own feet"—a self-assertiveness which contrasts so strongly with the traditional dependency. Mao's glorification of "activism" similarly seems to be a reaction against the passivity inherent in relying on others. His stress on struggle, on "liberating" with political discipline bad feelings which have been "swallowed" and "put in the stomach," indicates that his major mode of self-discipline is associated with "letting go" or "releasing" (*fang,* as in *chieh-fang* "to liberate," or *fang-p'i* "to break wind") rather than the traditional concern with proper "taking in."

In contrast to the oral omnipotence inherent in the traditional style of asserting authority, in which skill in the use of words was the measure of a man's right to assert power over others, Mao has stressed the need to bring together thought and action, theory and practice. Party cadres are no longer to derive their status from skill in manipulating an official ideology, but through effective involvement in the tasks of economic production. Only thus, says Mao, can the Party avoid the traditional "gap" between leaders and led.

Finally, Mao's opposition to the use of material incentives in motivating people for national development, his general concern with the loss of revolutionary vitality that will come with increased consumption on the part of both Party cadres and population, and his stress on the need to develop self-discipline through such physical "struggle" as swimming in the teeth of winds and waves, indicate a determination to overcome the "oral" characteristics of the traditional political culture. Mao might be said to be an "anal" leader seeking to transform an "oral" society.

THE ROLE OF AGGRESSION IN SOCIAL CHANGE

In the Western experience of social change, leadership in the development of new economic and social patterns has been taken by distinctive social subgroups whose culture and personality characteristics provided the motivational basis for innovative activity.[16] In China, efforts to promote economic and social innovation during the late nineteenth century were thwarted by a political elite which

16. This is the central thesis explored in David McClelland's *The Achieving Society* (Princeton, N.J.: Van Nostrand, 1961), and Everett E. Hagen's *On the Theory of Social Change: How Economic Growth Begins* (Homewood, Illinois: Dorsey Press, 1962).

sought to sustain a life style antithetical to commercial and techno-
logical activity and the agrarian social basis of its power.[17] Leadership in social change eventually fell to a revolutionary party committed to the Marxist conception of political and economic development.

In conclusion, what does this study suggest about the motivational basis upon which the Chinese Communists have attempted
rapidly to transform a relatively homogeneous peasant culture
through centralized political leadership? In the first two parts, we
found that individuals reared in the Chinese tradition responded to
authority with a strong sense of anxiety. Such a sentiment helped
to sustain filial dependence, and suppressed challenges to those in
positions of leadership and to the traditions from which they drew
authority. In positive terms, moreover, China's people had been
taught for centuries to draw a sense of security from traditional productive processes and the interpersonal patterns which were the
time-tested cultural distillation of this ancient and enduring society.
The motivational problem of China's revolution at base has been a
matter of how to overcome these emotional roots of tradition and
established authority.

In the West the profit motive, a need to achieve or to attain personal salvation, or the determination to reattain a status denied by
a dominant culture have provided the personal motivation behind
innovative activity. China's traditions, however, gave scant legitimacy to commercial pursuits. The strong emphasis on the group
above the individual and the primacy of ancient traditions dampened that self-assertiveness which might have spurred innovation
and social change.

In the case of Mao's revolution we found sentiments of aggression
to be the distinguishing motivational quality of political activity.
This characteristic reflects, in part, the fact that because of foreign
aggression the development of Chinese society has been a defensive and highly politicized process. The difficulty with which the
Chinese responded to the pressures of assertive Western nation-
states (in contrast to the rapidity with which the Japanese, for example, absorbed foreign military and commercial technology and
social practice), however, is in itself a reflection of the incompati-
bilities of cultural pattern. And finally, the *persistence* of Mao's

17. This interpretation is developed at a philosophical level in Joseph R.
Levenson's *Confucian China and Its Modern Fate: The Problem of Monar-
chical Decay* (Berkeley: University of California Press, 1964), and in terms
of difficulties in promoting new economic patterns in Albert Feuerwerker's
China's Early Industrialization (Cambridge, Mass.: Harvard University
Press, 1958).

stress on political techniques which emphasize emotions of resentment and hatred, his determination to sustain "class struggle" more than two decades after the attainment of state power, leads to the conclusion that Mao sees great motivational problems associated with sustaining social change in a peasant society.

Students of the functions of violence and conflict in social processes have stressed the role of such aggressive behavior in modifying the actions of those in established authority, in signaling the depth of commitment of those who seek change, and—in the extreme—in destroying by force the organizational power of "the establishment." [18] China's revolution suggests, however, that the expression of aggression may be just as important in modifying the behavior *of those who are struggling for change* as it is in influencing, or destroying, the existing order of things.

In the land reform process, Party writings indicate, it was not enough simply to redistribute land to the peasantry to gain their support for the revolutionary cause. If the authority of social traditions and interpersonal relationships which sustained the "feudal" pattern of landholding and agricultural production was to be destroyed, the peasants had to become active participants in attacking the landlords who personified the rural social order. Through the "speak bitterness" meetings, Party cadres worked up the rage of the peasantry over past injustices and economic inequities. It was only through the mobilization of such aggression that the peasants dared to attack those who carried the authority of tradition, and acquired new perceptions of their altered political status and of possibilities for social change.

Mao's particular contribution to the process of promoting social change would seem to be his conception of an institutionalized motivational mechanism for mobilizing a basically conservative and politically reticent peasantry. Sentiments of aggression, when disciplined in their expression through organizational controls and given purposeful direction through a social ideology, become a powerful tool for promoting change where established authority and custom are rooted in personal anxieties. Such emotions apparently are the only motive force powerful enough to overcome rapidly the inhibitions which sustained tradition in the personalities of China's peasants.

In the fourth part of this study we found, however, that Mao's stress on emotionally charged mass campaigns and controlled "class conflict" came to be resisted by other Party leaders. This suggested

18. *See* H. L. Nieburg, "The Threat of Violence and Social Change," *The American Political Science Review,* Vol. XVI, No. 4 (December 1962), pp. 865–873.

that tradition-based fears of social conflict and the expression of aggression—anxieties about *luan*—were at work in many Party members, inhibiting their acceptance of the Maoist approach to promoting social change. Given his "dialectical" view of social processes, Mao has attempted to sustain his influence over Party policies by playing upon the same aggressive emotions which have been used to break the rural population out of their traditional social patterns. By mobilizing popular resentments against Party cadres, as was first done in the 1957 "Hundred Flowers" period of mass criticism, later in the post-1962 "Four Clean-ups" Campaign, and most fully in the Cultural Revolution, Mao has sought to subject to public criticism those Party members who manifest in their leadership style the "four olds" of the traditional political culture. Such criticism was intended to reshape the attitudes of the critics as much as those criticized, by giving them a participant role in the political process, and by propagating new social norms and standards of behavior.

SPEEDING UP THE PACE OF SOCIAL CHANGE

Perhaps there are still children who have
not eaten men? Save the children . . .

LU HSÜN[19]

In the first draft of this analysis, completed on the eve of the Cultural Revolution, we concluded with some speculative observations about the likely psychological impact of a totalitarian political order on Chinese society. We suggested that a political party which sought to exercise total social control by penetrating into all areas of a society, down into the basic social unit of the family, sowed in its striving for total influence the seeds of its own psychological self-destruction. We based this conclusion on the assumption that the roots of a population's submissive acceptance of an authoritarian political order were the anxieties before the powerful which were the product of the traditional family socialization process. By diluting the authority of the stern family head, the totalitarian state would foster the rearing of new generations which would not have in their personalities the emotional inhibitions which were the basis of political submissiveness. And in time, as these new generations entered the political process, they would show greater willingness to challenge established authority than would their elders. In such a

19. Lu Hsün, "A Madman's Diary," in *Selected Works of Lu Hsün* (Peking: Foreign Languages Press, 1959), p. 21.

pattern of generational change, we suggested, lay the long-term possibilities for the erosion of a totalistic state.[20]

The Cultural Revolution, in an unexpected way, would lead us to conclude that not only does this interpretation have certain validity, but that Mao Tse-tung himself has attempted to play upon such a mechanism of social change in order to speed up the pace of China's revolution.

After 1962 Mao repeatedly expressed to other Party leaders his concern about the "restoration" of old social practices in the Communist Party and in Chinese society at large. In essence he was affirming Max Weber's observation that revolutionary leadership eventually becomes routinized into bureaucratic administration, or reverts to traditional forms of authoritarian control.[21] In his struggle against domestic "revisionism" Mao was asserting that the Chinese Communist Party was not sustaining its commitment to social change, but was giving in to the influence of old cultural patterns and a leadership style which in time would stifle the revolution.

In the Cultural Revolution Mao resisted this trend by speeding up the process by which new generations—with new personal styles —are socialized and brought into positions of social influence. The Red Guard movement was in one sense a contrived *rite de passage,* a political ritual of initiation for cultivating "revolutionary successors" by which Mao sought to recreate his own socialization experience for millions of Chinese youngsters. In its initial conception the Red Guard movement, as common to the mass campaign pattern, was to generate new "activists" committed to the Maoist political style; and these bearers of a revolutionary leadership style would be incorporated into a reconstituted Party organization.

At present it appears uncertain whether Mao's effort to speed up the socialization and recruitment processes of Chinese society have worked. What scanty evidence exists indicates that the Red Guards were not simply "little Maos"; that under the influence of their families and the social context they had acquired many traditional or nonrevolutionary behavioral inclinations, and were not the disciplined and selfless fighters for the revolution that Mao had hoped they would be. Moreover, it appears that Mao and his close comrades are hardly in full control of the process of reconstituting the Party and state.

The social composition and leadership style of those who emerge

20. *See* "On the Psychological Self-Destruction of a Totalitarian Society," in Richard H. Solomon, *The Chinese Revolution and the Politics of Dependency* (unpublished Ph.D. dissertation, M.I.T., 1966), pp. 388–397.

21. Max Weber, "The Meaning of Discipline," in Gerth and Mills, *From Max Weber,* p. 253.

from the Cultural Revolution struggle, and the policy commitments of Mao's successors, are uncertain quantities which the foreign observer can only wait to see evolve. Mao sought to use the Cultural Revolution to accelerate the institutionalization of his version of a new Chinese political culture. In practice, however, the endurance of the thought and word of the revolutionary innovator will depend on a myriad future small decisions by millions of Chinese as to whether they will sustain Mao's political legacy in the actions of their daily lives.

Appendix I

INTERVIEW SCHEDULE
(Translation)

I. EARLY FAMILY LIFE

A. RELATIONS BETWEEN PARENTS AND CHILDREN

1. What kind of person was your father/mother?
   How did he/she treat you children?
2. What did you admire most about your father/mother?
3. Naturally, no one is without faults. What would you say were your father's/mother's weak points?
4. What should parents pay closest attention to in rearing a child?
5. What was the most important thing you obtained from your parents?
6. Did your father often take you to play? (In what way?)
7. Naturally there are times when parents and children will have differences of opinion. What kinds of things did you and your parents have differences of opinion about? How did you resolve the problem?
8. a. When you were young, when you made some mistake what would your parents do? For what kinds of mistakes would they punish you in that way?
   b. Who ordinarily punished you at home? What kinds of punishment did you ordinarily receive? For what kinds of mistakes were you punished? Which kind of punishment did you think was the worst?
9. Whom is your personality most like? In what ways?
10. At home to whom were you closest? Why?
11. When you were small, what caused you the most bother?
12. When you had problems, with whom would you discuss them? Why (with that person)?
13. Many people, when they are small, have bad dreams. Do you remember any bad dreams you had when you were small?
14. What kinds of dreams have you had recently?

B. RELATIONS BETWEEN PARENTS

15. How did your parents get along?
16. Who ordinarily made decisions about family affairs?
    How were differences of opinion resolved?
17. Naturally at times in every family there will be differences of
    opinion. What differences of opinion were there in your family?
    How were they resolved?

C. SIBLING RELATIONS

18. How did you and your brothers and sisters get along together?
19. With whom were you closest? Why?
20. When you would get mad at each other, what would you do?
21. What is the most important thing in the relationship between
    an elder and a younger brother?

D. RELATIVES AND NEIGHBORS

22. How many relatives lived near your house? Did they often
    come to your house?
23. What kind of relationship did your family have with the neigh-
    bors? What kind of people were they?

E. GENERAL QUESTIONS ABOUT FAMILY LIFE

24. a. How many rooms were there in your family house?
        How many people lived together?
     b. Did you all sleep together in one room? Where did your
        parents sleep?
     c. What was the approximate population of the village/town/
        city where you grew up?
     d. When members of your family would go out, what kind of
        transportation would they use?
     e. When your parents would go out during the cold time of
        the year, what kind of clothing would they wear?
     f. When you were small, who in the house cooked food for
        you?
     g. Ordinarily at meal time how many dishes and soups were
        there?
     h. Was there a high wall around your family house? Why?
     i. In your home, when you wanted to go into another person's
        room, would you first knock on the door? Why (not)?
25. From the point of view of personality, what is the difference
    between a child and an adult? From the point of view of emo-
    tions?

26. a. Why do you think it is relatively easy for a child to be influenced by a bad environment?
    b. At what age can a child distinguish between right and wrong?
27. What is the thing you remember with most pleasure about your early life at home?
28. Which is a relatively happier period of life, childhood or adulthood? Why?
29. What changes have occurred in family life today? Are these changes for better or for worse? Why?

II. ADOLESCENCE

A. RELATIONS BETWEEN TEACHER AND STUDENT

30. What is the most important aspect of relations between a teacher and his student?
31. What attitude did your parents have toward your teacher?
32. In elementary and middle school, what teaching methods did your teachers use?
33. At that time how did you feel about studying?
34. Did you or your fellow students ever play tricks on the teacher? Did you ever play such tricks on your father? (If "no":) Why? (If "yes":) What was the outcome?
35. a. What is the effect of "cultivation" (*hsiu-yang*) on the way a person gets along in the world?
    b. How does a person become "cultivated"?
    c. What do you do when you get angry?
    d. When you try hard to overcome your anger, what do you do?
    e. What was your father like when he would get angry? What would you children do?

B. IMPORTANT LIFE CHOICES

Career:
36. When you were young, what did you hope to become in the future?
37. What did your parents hope you would do? (If there was a difference of opinion:) How did you resolve this difference?

Marriage:
38. a. How did you and your wife become engaged?
    b. Did your parents object to your choice? (If "yes":) How did you resolve this difference?
39. If a housewife goes out and works, what influence will it have on family life?

III. ADULTHOOD

40. How is it that some people succeed in their careers and others do not? Other people's help?

Friendship:
41. What is the most important thing a person obtains from friends?
42. What is the best kind of friend?
43. What is the difference between the relation of a superior to his subordinate and relations among friends?
44. What is the source of conflict between people?
45. Why is *chiang jen-ch'ing* ("speaking on behalf of another") so important in Chinese society? Could you give me a specific example of what it means to *"chiang jen-ch'ing"*?

IV. GENERAL SOCIAL ATTITUDES

Order:
46. Please explain what *ta-t'ung* ("the great harmony," or social unity) means. How can *ta-t'ung* be realized?
47. Why, in the early years of the Republic, were there warlords? Why couldn't they peacefully coexist? What method can prevent such a situation from developing?
48. Please explain what *chih-an hao* ("law and order") means. What method can a society use to maintain *chih-an*?
49. Why has Chinese society especially emphasized *ho-p'ing* ("peace")?
50. What is the greatest effect of interpersonal competition on society? Are there others?
51. How is it that society becomes *hun-luan* ("confused")? What are conditions like in a *hun-luan* society? In what way can *hun-luan* be avoided?
52. a. Why is everyone at present so concerned about the *t'ai-pao* and *liu-mang* (juvenile delinquents and ruffians)?
    b. Why is their influence on society so great?
    c. How should they be dealt with?

International Order:
53. Please name, in decreasing order of importance, the four most important countries in Asia. How can they maintain peace in Asia?
54. What is your point of view on China having the atomic bomb?
55. What could enable the United Nations to become a more effective organization for world peace?

Leadership:

56. Why is it that some people have an interest in politics and others do not? How do you feel about this difference?
57. Of the things a country's leaders can do for their country, which is the most important?
58. a. If you were mayor of this city, what would be the first policy you would like to promote?
    b. If you were president (a leader of China)?
59. If a newspaper asked you to write an article, one concerning some especially important contemporary social problem, what problem would you select to write about?
60. Under what conditions should the people support their leaders?
61. a. What is the best way of preventing a political leader from engaging in activities that endanger the people's welfare?
    b. If a political leader engages in some activities that endanger the people, what should an ordinary person do?
62. a. With whom do you ordinarily discuss political problems? (If the respondent says he does not discuss them with anyone:) Why not?
    b. With family members? (If not:) Why not?
    c. With co-workers? (If not:) Why not?
    d. With friends? (If not:) Why not?
63. a. When you hear the word "politics" what feeling do you have?
    b. Which problems belong to the sphere of politics?

Appendix II

BIOGRAPHICAL SCHEDULE

Interview Case Number ―――――
(T—interviewed in Taiwan
H—interviewed in Hong Kong)

Date―――――――   Interviewer―――――――――――
Language used―――――――   Interpreter―――――――――――

==

1. Sex: male/female
2. Marital status: single/married/divorced/widow/widower
3. Number of children:―――――――
4. Birth date:―――――――; Age:―――――――
5. Province of birth:―――――――(county, city, or village also may be given)
6. Place where parents lived after marriage:――――――― (Province, county, city, or village)
7. Place where paternal grandparents lived after marriage:―――――― (Province, county, city, or village)
8. Place where maternal grandparents lived after marriage:―――――― (Province, county, city, or village)
9. Province where you grew up:―――――――
10. Reared by: parents/relatives (which)―――――――/other――――――
11. Province where spent adult life:―――――――
12. Date arrived in Hong Kong―――――――and/or Taiwan―――――――
13. Father: alive/deceased, at what age of R.?―――――――
13a. Father's educational level:―――――――
14. Mother: alive/deceased, at what age of R.?―――――――
14a. Mother's educational level:―――――――
15. Siblings: Number of older brothers―――――――
16. Number of younger brothers―――――――
17. Number of older sisters―――――――
18. Number of younger sisters―――――――
19. Primary education: Private family school/home tutor/parents/church/public/other―――――――
20. Secondary education: Public/church/private/tutor/other――――――

532

21. Highest grade attained ————————
22. Activity after leaving school————————
23. College: which————————; where———————— type: public/private/church————————
24. Major subject studied————————
25. Chinese dialects spoken:————————
26. Foreign languages studied in school:————————
    Middle School: which:————————; amount of time devoted to each:———————— College: which:————————; amount of time devoted to each————————; Could you read an article in this language? no/with difficulty/could
27. Radio listening: none/entertainment programs/news programs/other————————
28. Movie attendance; frequency: every week/every month/several times per year/never
29. Percentage of all movies seen which are foreign (estimate):————
30. Newspaper reading: never/daily/several times each week/occasionally
31. First part of a newspaper read: entertainment/sports/business/local social situation/national situation/international situation/editorial
32. Part of a newspaper most likes to read: entertainment/sports/business/local social situation/national situation/international situation/editorial
33. Do you read national political news? Yes/no
34. Do you read news of the international situation? Yes/no
35. Do you read news about the international political situation? Yes/no
36. Travel abroad: Where:————————
37. Travel for: pleasure/work/other reason————————
38. How much time have you spent abroad?————————
39. Occupation————————
40. Father's occupation————————
41. Religion————————
42. Do you actively participate in religious activities? Yes/no
43. Number of times per month goes to church:————————
44. Would you consider your childhood and adolescence to have been: traditional/relatively modern?
45. Would you consider childhood and adolescence to be basically a happy/unhappy time of life?
46. Would you consider your personal attitude to be: traditional/modern?
47. Would you consider your father's attitude to have been: traditional/modern?

Appendix III

ATTITUDE SURVEY

(Translation)

A SURVEY OF PEOPLE'S OUTLOOK
ON CONTEMPORARY LIFE
INTRODUCTION

During the past several decades all our lives have changed very much. Some changes are for the better; some are not so good. Some people approve of recent developments; some object to various aspects of life today.

We are interested in your point of view concerning various aspects of contemporary life. This will give us a better understanding of those recent developments which people in general think are good, as well as those which perhaps are not so popular.

We will appreciate your help and cooperation in this survey of popular opinion. It should be emphasized that in asking for your point of view there are no "right" or "wrong" answers. The best answer is your personal opinion. You can be sure that, whatever your own opinion, some people may disagree, and others are sure to agree with you.

In this survey we have tried to include many aspects of contemporary life as well as various different points of view. You will probably find yourself agreeing strongly with some statements, disagreeing with others, and perhaps agreeing only slightly with still others.

If you are willing to help us in this survey, please answer the questions as follows:

(1) Read each statement carefully, and mark it according to your first reaction. It isn't necessary to consider any one statement too long; each one should take you about a minute. Or in other words, to complete the entire survey should take you not much more than 30 minutes.

(2) Answer every question.

(3) Try your best to give your true and accurate point of view.

(4) Respond to the statements as follows. If you:

534

Strongly agree, mark +3   *Strongly* disagree, mark −3
Agree somewhat, mark +2   Disagree somewhat, mark −2
Agree a *little,* mark +1   Disagree a *little,* mark −1

For example, if you strongly disagree with the statement, "The style of the most recently constructed buildings in the city is ugly," mark −3 in the answer box ☐. If you *slightly agree* with the statement, mark +1; if you agree, but not strongly, mark +2; etc.

This survey, like any study of popular opinion, works just like an election: your answers are private, and you need not write down your name.

1. It is basically a good thing that young people can have more fun these days, such as by going out dancing or walking hand in hand in the park. ☐

2. The nation naturally has its importance; but family life is more important. ☐

3. Schools today put too much emphasis on mathematics, physics, and chemistry, and not enough on such worthwhile subjects as classical literature and calligraphy. ☐

4. In the long run it is a good thing that a young man select his own career for himself. ☐

5. A large part of the crime and immorality around here these days is due to so many strangers and travelers from abroad. ☐

6. Although laws and political programs have their place, what our country needs even more is a few courageous, firm and dedicated leaders in whom the people can put their trust. ☐

7. Although many people think that fortune-telling is nonsense, in the future it just may be proved that it really can explain many things. ☐

8. It is an unfortunate thing that today there are many young women who prefer having a career to remaining at home and having a simple, happy family life. ☐

9. Although the theories of Confucius and Mencius in the past had their value, their works cannot explain the many problems of interpersonal relations in society today. ☐

10. Just as foreigners have come to appreciate many Chinese things, we also ought to adopt various good customs and habits of foreign countries. ☐

11. Obedience and respect for their elders are the most important virtues children should develop. ☐

12. Nowadays a young man can make a valuable and interesting career for himself in commerce. ☐

13. It is more important to prove you are right in a discussion than to take an attitude of "why bother" or "forget it" just for the sake of friendliness or out of a desire not to hurt the other person's feelings. ☐

14. There are few things more enjoyable for entertainment than China's traditional songs and regional operas. ☐

15. It is better, in these modern times, if parents are not so strict in expecting their children to do things just the way they do them. ☐

16. If a neighbor is making a public nuisance of himself, it is best just to try and ignore him or avoid the trouble of involvement than to attempt to correct the situation. ☐

17. If China would place greater emphasis on putting into practice her time-tested customs, habits, and social virtues, then many problems of contemporary society could be solved. ☐

18. Although criticizing the thoughts and suggestions of our superiors is useful for improving our work, it can lead to much trouble, and hence is best avoided. ☐

19. Although Chinese history possibly can provide some good experience, there are many important things we need to learn from modern economics, science, and social research. ☐

20. While it might not be bad for a son to live with his parents after marriage, it is basically better for a young couple to set up their own household. ☐

21. If there were not so many foreigners attempting to help other people deal with their own problems, then the world would be a much more peaceful place. ☐

22. In contemporary society, the professions of a scientist or engineer are particularly interesting and valuable. ☐

23. It is essential for effectiveness in study or work that our teachers or superiors give us detailed explanations and directives. ☐

24. For understanding different social customs and ways of interpersonal relations, as well as various foreign things, foreign movies are worthwhile to see. ☐

25. Human nature being what it is, unfortunately there will probably always be interpersonal disputes, conflicts, or war. ☐

26. History will probably prove that the contribution of the scholar or artist has been more important for society than that of the scientist or manufacturer. ☐

27. It is annoying to hear people always stressing the virtues of patience, compromise, and restraint. We should be bold enough to work for great change and seek to improve things now, even though some people may be opposed. ☐

28. If someone is lying hurt in the street, it is best not to rush right up and help, and thus avoid bringing on a lot of trouble, as someone whose proper job it is will always come along quickly to take charge. ☐

29. It is an unfortunate thing that during one's life it is so difficult to find true friends with whom one can share the thoughts and feelings deep in one's heart. ☐

30. Although sciences like chemistry, physics and medicine have helped in the advancement of mankind, there are many important things which can never be understood by human intelligence. ☐

31. When the national situation gets a bit difficult, it is only natural and proper that people be expected to make a greater contribution, such as by extending the time of military service, controlling consumption, or directing people in their work and study, etc. ☐

32. If two people really love each other but both their parents object, it is better for their long run happiness that they not marry. ☐

Appendix IV

THEMATIC APPERCEPTION TEST
(TAT) PICTURES

I

II

III

IV

V

VI

VII

VIII

IX

540

Appendix V

RESPONDENTS' BIOGRAPHICAL
SKETCHES

These biographical sketches are designed to provide the reader with a general description of each respondent's social background and life history. They have been written on the basis of detailed biographical information contained in the respondent's interview record. A standard biographical data schedule, reproduced in Appendix II above, served as the basis for collecting this information, although supplemental material, gathered during the course of the interview, was also utilized in preparing the sketches.

The interviews were carried out during the year 1965. The fifty-six respondents in the "T" series were interviewed in Taipei City, Taiwan. The thirty-six "H" series interviews were done in Hong Kong. In general, the respondents in the 55–84 age group emigrated to Taiwan during the late 1940s. Those in the 20–29 age group emigrated from the mainland during or subsequent to the large exodus into Hong Kong of 1962, the period of crisis following the Great Leap Forward. The respondents in the 30–54 year old group have mixed times of emigration. Some left the mainland in the late 1940s, and others have come out since 1962.

* * *

T-1: 32 years old at the time of interview; reared in a well-to-do rural family of Heng-hsien, Kwangsi Province. As a young adult the respondent moved to Canton. He taught in an elementary school on the mainland for three years. He now holds a clerical position with the Nationalist government on Taiwan.

His father was trained at the Paoting Military Academy, eventually rising to the rank of major-general in the Nationalist army. He commanded the military district which included the family's old home at Heng-hsien, Kwangsi. The Communists classified this family as "landlord." The father was executed as a class enemy in 1951.

T-2: A 36-year-old former soldier; born at Hoyuan, Kwangtung Province and reared in the market town of Chacheng, Kwangtung. He received a high school education and worked on the mainland as a mechanic. He now works as a mechanic in Taiwan.

His father was a small merchant who owned about 20 *mou* of land in Kwangtung.

T-3: 33 years old; grew up in Shantung Province, but returned to his home province of Kiangsu at the age of 15 where he was tutored in the Confucian classics. He taught at a private elementary school on the mainland for five years, and now works as a clerk for the Nationalist government on Taiwan.

His father, who was singled out for criticism by the Communists, was a wealthy salt merchant whose business was in Shantung.

T-4: 26 years old; born and raised in Shanghai City. The son of a landlord family, he studied public health in high school and worked for one year in a public health clinic on the mainland. He is now a library worker in Taiwan.

His father was a college graduate who later became captain of a ship engaged in international trade.

T-5: 26 years old; reared in Liuchou, Kwangsi Province. From a well-to-do family. He attended a college in South China for two years under the Communists, but the experience consisted primarily of manual labor. He taught himself to read and write music, and now writes music for a broadcasting station in Taiwan.

His father, whose home was in Heng-hsien, Kwangsi, was trained at the Paoting Military Academy and became a lieutenant-general in the Nationalist army. His father was stationed at Liuchou, and was killed by the Communists in the early 1950s.

T-6: 53 years old; from Kueip'ing, Kwangsi Province. He served 19 years in the Nationalist army as a communications specialist. After the Communists attained power he was unable to find a regular job and so supported himself in Canton City by working as a street secretary for three years, and then by running a noodle stand. He now works as a research aide for a cultural organization in Taiwan.

His grandfather had been a classical scholar of some reputation. His father had operated a successful wholesale food business in Kueip'ing.

T-7: 32 years old; born and raised in Canton City, Kwangtung. He had been a cadre in the Communist Party during the land reform period (1950–1953) and up through the failure of the Great Leap Forward (1962). He now works in Taiwan as a statistical clerk.

His father had been the leader of a religious sect in Canton, and died in prison in 1959 after six years of internment by the Communists.

T-8: 53 years old; born in Loting-hsien, Kwangtung, but moved to Canton City as a young man. He spent many years in the Nationalist military. After World War II he began police work, first in Kwangtung and now in Taiwan.

His family was classified as "landlord" by the Communists. His father had been principal of an elementary school for many years in Loting-hsien. He was killed during a "struggle" meeting in 1951.

T-9: A 49-year-old college graduate from a large and wealthy family; born and raised in Peking. He directed the family's private school in Peking for many years. After the Communists attained power he worked as a laborer and spent one year in jail. He now teaches high school in Taiwan.

His father, who was an official at the close of the Ch'ing dynasty, owned many pawn shops in Peking.

T-10: A 63-year-old intellectual and teacher; born and raised in Tientsin City, Hopeh Province. He graduated from Yenching University and spent three years in Japan studying law at Meiji University.

His father, who was a colonel in the Manchu army during the last days of the Ch'ing dynasty, died when the respondent was very young. He was reared by an uncle, also a military man.

T-11: A 38-year-old high school teacher from Mei-hsien, Kwangtung Province. He graduated from Chuhai University in Canton and taught high school biology on the mainland before coming to Taiwan.

His father owned shops in Mei-hsien and Canton which sold rice, tea, and other staples. The father died of a disease shortly after being classified as a landlord and subjected to criticism by the Communists.

T-12: 29 years old at the time of interview, the respondent came from a poor family living in Huiyang-hsien, Kwangtung. After graduating from high school he had five years of training at a trade school on the mainland, and now works as an electrical technician in Taiwan.

His father was a small merchant in Huiyang-hsien.

T-13: Born into a well-to-do family from Sui-hsien, a town of some 200 families in Hupeh Province. The respondent was 63 years old when interviewed. He had worked for many years in a county-level governmental office under the Nationalists on the mainland. After reaching Hong Kong he supported himself for a time by begging. Since arriving in Taiwan he has sold beancake and is now a fortune teller in a public park.

T-14: 26 years old; born in Ningpo-hsien, Chekiang Province and grew up in Shanghai City. He received five years of architectural training in Shanghai and now works as an architect in Taiwan.

His father was a small merchant in Shanghai who now works as an accountant in Taiwan. From the ages of nine to twenty-three the interviewee was separated from his parents as they had been in Taiwan when the Communists gained control of Shanghai and had not returned. During these years the interviewee and his brother were reared by an aunt in Shanghai.

T-15: 35 years old; from Wuhua-hsien, Kwangtung. Although he had had a high school education, the interviewee worked as a farmer and general laborer on the mainland. He now works as a clerk in Taiwan.

His father had been a local official (*hsiang-chang*) in Wuhua-hsien under the Nationalists. The father died of a disease while in jail during the Communist period.

T-16: 26 years old; reared in a farming village of about 2,000 people in Kwangtung Province. After graduating from high school he worked as an accountant in a factory in Canton. In 1957 he was sentenced to two years of labor reform for criticizing the Communist government during the Hundred Flowers Movement. He now works as a clerk in a government bureau in Taiwan.

His father, who was classified as a landlord by the Communists, died when the interviewee was very young. He was reared by his mother who managed to support the family by opening a small provisions store.

T-17: 33 years old; from Ilan-hsien, Heilungkiang Province. He moved to Peking at the age of 18 and spent seven years (during the 1950s) in the People's Liberation Army. He now drives a truck in Taiwan.

His father ran a small inn, and also had served as a superintendent over several thousand forestry workers.

T-18: 36 years old, from a scholarly and respected family in Hokou-chen, a market town of about 300 families, in Loshan-hsien, Honan Province. He served in the Nationalist army during the last days of World War II. After 1949 he ran a wine shop and worked as a manual laborer for several years. He was sentenced to a period of political reform in a labor camp by the Communists in 1955 for having urged his fellow workers to demand higher wages. He escaped from the labor camp which was in

Szechwan Province, and spent three years wandering about China, often working as a truck driver. He managed to reach India via Tibet, and eventually was brought to Taiwan.

His grandfather and father had been teachers of the Confucian classics and occasionally were called upon to settle local disputes.

T-19: 26 years old; born in the small village of Chofang, Wuchiao-hsien, Hopeh Province, and later raised in the town of Kiangtien-lan, Changlo-hsien, Fukien. He graduated from high school in 1957 and worked in administrative jobs until he was selected to receive two years of training at a technical school in Inner Mongolia. Accused of being uncooperative with Party personnel, the Communists sentenced him to two years of labor reform on a farm. After serving his sentence, he escaped to Taiwan.

His father had been an officer in a local unit of the Nationalist security forces near their village in Fukien. The father was killed during a "struggle" meeting in 1950. His mother was a nurse who operated a small clinic.

T-20: 39 years old at the time of interview; born in the village of Koko-chuangtsun (population about 2,000 persons), in Tsaiyang-hsien, Shantung. He was reared in Dairen, Liaoning Province. He received one year of trade school education under the Japanese during their occupation of North China, and later worked as a repairman of electrical machinery for the Communist government. He joined a guerrilla band in Tibet during the middle 1950s to fight the Communists. He escaped to India and then came to Taiwan.

His father was a housing contractor with about 50 employees, whose business was in Dairen.

T-21: A 26-year-old medical student born in Shanghai. His family moved to Kansu Province when he was 12. His parents had separated when he was two years old, and he was reared by his mother's relatives—a grandmother and an uncle. He studied medicine for eighteen months under the Communists at the Changyi Medical School in Kansu, and at the time of interview had continued his medical studies in Taiwan for three years.

His father worked as a hired sailor on a commercial ship. His mother's relatives were also of moderate means.

T-22: A 35-year-old overseas Chinese, born in Singapore and raised both in Yungch'un-hsien, Fukien Province, and Ampenan, Indonesia. In 1948 he decided to join the Communist movement on the mainland after being influenced by an overseas Chinese high school teacher who was a Party member. He traveled from Djakarta to Hong Kong and joined a guerrilla band in Kwangtung Province. He spent three years during the 1950s studying physics at Chungshan University in Canton, but was assigned to labor reform in 1957 for having criticized the secret police system. He succeeded in escaping from the mainland in 1962 after one earlier failure, for which he served a one-year prison sentence. He is now studying physics at a Taiwan university.

His father had worked in a small import-export store in Yungch'un-hsien, Fukien, and later opened a grocery store in Indonesia. The father returned to the mainland in the early 1950s to search for his son, but died there without finding him.

T-23: 46 years old; born and raised in Chinchiang-hsien, Kiangsu Province. As the only male child in his generation, he was eligible to inherit much land that belonged to his family's clan. He was disgusted by the family quarrels over this matter and ran away from home at the age of 20 to join the Nationalist navy. He later returned to his home village and served as village chief for eight years, until the Communists came. He now works as a clerk in the town office of a market center in Taiwan, where he has lived since 1951.

The interviewee's father was a wealthy land owner who concerned himself mainly with his land's agricultural production.

T-24: 54 years old; from a wealthy family in Nanchang-hsien, Hupeh Province. He served in the Nationalist army during World War II and the civil war, after graduation from a military school. He retired in the early 1950s on Taiwan as a lieutenant-colonel.

His father was a college professor on the mainland.

T-25: 46 years old; born in Leishang-hsien, Anhwei. He graduated from the Anhwei Provincial Agricultural College just before World War II. Although his parents hoped he would become a school teacher in the local district, the interviewee left home to join the Nationalist army. Since the early 1950s he has been a special member of the Nationalists' Committee on Tibetan-Mongolian Affairs.

His father was an elementary school teacher in Leishang-hsien and also served for six years as a local official (*hsiang-chang*).

T-26: 44 years old; born in T'anch'eng-hsien, Shantung Province. He taught school for several years, then joined the Nationalist army during World War II. He retired from the army in 1959 and now runs a small grocery store in Taiwan.

His father was a well-to-do farmer.

T-27: 47 years old; born and raised in Hsühsüan-hsien, Anhwei. He grew up in an extended family of 31 persons who lived together in a large house. At the age of 14 he was appointed a minor official (*li-chang*) by his uncle and later was a township functionary (*hsiang-chang*) for three years. He joined the Nationalist army at the age of 24, at the beginning of World War II. He is now a policeman in Taiwan.

His father was a poor farmer, although his grandparents and uncle had some wealth.

T-28: 68 years old; born and raised at Hohsing-cheng, a town of some 10,000 people, in Ch'anglo-hsien, Fukien. He majored in political science at the Foochow Political Science College. After graduation in the early 1920s he served the central government as a secretary in the National Assembly in Peking and in the Judicial Yuan at Hankow. From 1928 to 1935 he was an administrator for the Nationalist government, serving at Shanghai and Foochow. Before retiring on Taiwan in 1952, he was a propagandist for the Central News Bureau.

His father, although poor, became a Ch'ing dynasty scholar (*hsiu-ts'ai*) and taught the classics in a private school. The father died when the respondent was three years old.

T-29: 76 years old; from a gentry family in Hsuanhsing-hsien, Kiangsu Province. After receiving a traditional education from his father, and some additional study in Nanking, the respondent received an M.A. in Western history from the University of Wisconsin and later a Ph.D. from the University of Heidelberg in Germany. He is now a professor of history in a Taiwan university.

His father was a Ch'ing dynasty scholar (*chü-jen*). His mother died when he was eight years old and his father remarried.

T-30: 72 years old; born into a poor family in Chiangtu-hsien, Kiangsu Province. He received a traditional education from his father, and later graduated from the Kiangsu Law College. He then worked as a newspaper editor, a high school teacher, and was general secretary of the Nationalist Party's Central Political Council. He is today a popular writer in Taiwan.

His father ran a dry goods store.

T-31: 56 years old; born to a well-to-do family in Hengshan-hsien, Hunan. He spent eight years in Japan and graduated from Kyoto University where he majored in law. He later worked as a newspaper manager and is now a college professor.

The respondent's father was a "revolutionary" and a member of the *Tung Meng Hui*. Because he spent so much time in political work, the respondent claimed, the father devoted too little attention to his children and was not adequately concerned about their welfare.

T-32: 64 years old; reared by a wealthy family in Kaier-hsien, Liaoning Province. After an early career as a teacher and secondary school principal, the interviewee taught in government police academies. During World War II he joined the Nationalist army and became an officer.

The interviewee had been given by his natural parents to a wealthy family to be brought up. His foster father, who owned much land, also served as a district chief (*ch'ü-chang*) for several years. The interviewee said his foster parents treated him very well.

T-33: 57 years old; born and raised in Hanchou-hsien, Hupeh. He graduated from Chunghua University in Wuchang, majoring in political science. He is now a staff adviser in the Ministry of National Defense in Taiwan.

His father ran a small dry goods shop and was often away from home on business.

T-34: 54 years old; born and raised in Ihuang-hsien, Kiangsi Province. Encouraged by his older brother who was studying in the United States, the respondent worked part time to earn money for his own schooling. He graduated from Facheng University in Nanking, majoring in law. He worked for the Nationalist government as a principal of secondary schools, and now teaches at a political cadre training school in Taiwan.

His father was a small merchant who was often away from home buying cloth in Shanghai. His mother died when the respondent was very young, and he was reared by his maternal grandmother. His father later remarried, but the respondent continued to live with his grandmother.

T-35: 66 years old; raised in Nanch'ang, Kiangsi Province. He majored in law at Facheng College in Nanchang. He has spent many years as the head of various departments of the Nationalist government, and is a member of the National Assembly in Taiwan.

His father was a Ch'ing dynasty scholar (*hsiu-ts'ai*). The respondent described his family's financial situation as difficult. His mother managed family affairs.

T-36: 72 years old at the time of interview; from a wealthy family in the small village of Kaoai-chen in Anch'iu-hsien, Shantung Province. He graduated from Shanghai T'ungchi University. He has worked for most of his life as a civil engineer.

His father was the largest land owner in the area and also ran a small business buying and selling brass.

T-37: 58 years old; from a wealthy family in Nanch'ang, Kiangsi. He majored in education at National Tungnan University in Nanking. He taught high school after graduation and later became supervisor of a Nationalist government educational bureau. He is now a professor in Taiwan.

His father was a financial administrator for the Nationalist government. The respondent said his father was usually working at the office and spent little time at home.

T-38: 56 years old; born in the small village of Shih-chuang in Yung-p'ing-fu, Hopeh Province. The respondent left home to study in Peking at the age of 12. He spent three years in a military training academy and is now an administrative officer for the Nationalist army.

His father was a peasant who owned some land.

T-39: 56 years old; born and raised in a village in Chungchiang-hsien, Szechuan. After finishing high school he graduated from a military school in Nanking, spent one year at the Whampoa Military Academy, and then served as a career officer in the Nationalist army. He retired with the rank of captain.

His parents were peasants who owned some land. The respondent and his parents lived in an extended family which included three paternal uncles and their families.

T-40: 71 years old when interviewed; reared in the city of Wuhsi, Kiangsu Province. He graduated from a high school in Tokyo and then attended Tokyo Industrial University. He was a mechanical engineer.

His father was a Ch'ing dynasty scholar (*chü-jen*) who later became a judge and a lawyer.

T-41: 52 years old; raised in a family of wealth in a village in Shenyang-hsien, Liaoning Province. He graduated from Tungpei University, where he majored in political science. During World War II he followed the Nationalist government to Szechuan. He now teaches mathematics at a government school in Taiwan, and also runs a night school.

His father, who was a grand nephew to the Hsuan-t'ung emperor, was also a Ch'ing dynasty scholar (*chü-jen*).

T-42: 55 years old when interviewed; raised in Kut'ang-chen, Chiuchiang-hsien, Kiangsi Province. He graduated from an accounting school in Kiangsi Province. Most of his adult life was spent as an officer in the quartermaster corps of the Nationalist army. He was retired in 1962 and now runs a small business in Taiwan.

For thirty years his father operated a soap factory in Kiangsi.

T-43: 69 years old; born in a village in Ch'anghsing-hsien, Chekiang. He graduated from the Facheng Academy in Hengchou, majoring in political science and economics. He worked for the Chinese Customs Bureau for several years, then spent fifteen years in the Nationalist army. He retired in 1949 with the rank of lieutenant.

His father was a Ch'ing dynasty scholar (*hsiu-ts'ai*).

T-44: 63 years old; reared in the small village of Hsich'i-lits'un Hsia-hsien, Shansi Province. He graduated from Shansi University in T'ai-yuan, where he majored in law. He spent many years study-ing in Germany and became a translator after his return to China. Five years later he began working for the Nationalist government and is now a specialist in legal and administrative work.

His father was a peasant who owned and farmed his own land.

T-45: 69 years old; raised in Chungshan-hsien, Kwangtung Province. He completed high school in Japan and then graduated from the Imperial University, majoring in law. He spent 40 years working as a specialist in the Railroad Bureau of the Ministry of Trans-portation for the Nationalist government. Although now retired from government service he works as a secretary in a high school in Taiwan.

His father ran a small tea store in Chungshan-hsien.

T-46: 74 years old; from a gentry family in Pailien-ts'un (population about 100), in Huoshan-hsien, Anhwei Province. He taught for ten years in a traditional private school (*szu-shu*) then entered the Provincial Fak'o University in Hupeh Province where he ma-jored in law. Since graduating he has operated Chinese medicine shops.

His father was a Ch'ing dynasty scholar (*hsiu-ts'ai*), who served as a county official (*hsien-chang*) for four years and owned much land.

T-47: 65 years old; born and raised in Foochow City, Fukien Province. He graduated from the private Facheng Academy in Foochow where he majored in law. After spending many years as a judge he became a lawyer. He is now a lawyer in Taiwan.

His father was also a lawyer in Foochow.

T-48: 54 years old at the time of interview; reared in Chiahsing-fu, Chekiang Province. During the course of twenty-two years he served for a time in the Nationalist army, ran a stationery store, and opened an elementary school. Later he rejoined the army and came to Taiwan. He retired in 1963.

His father was an official in the Shanghai municipal govern-ment.

T-49: 57 years old; raised in a village in Linglu-hsien, Hopeh Province. He ran away from home at the age of 14. An uncle in Hankow helped him attend high school. He graduated from a private mili-tary academy in Nanking and for several years worked in a provincial office of the Nationalist Party. He then spent twelve years as a military instructor. In 1949 he retired and now runs a small food store in Taiwan.

His father was a peasant who owned his own land.

T-50: 56 years old; raised in a poor family from the small village of Wuchia-han Mop'ing-hsien, Shantung Province. For over 20 years he worked in records and administration for the Nationalist Party, first at Party headquarters and later in the Fukien provincial government. He is now a political officer in the Nationalist army in Taiwan.

His father was a peasant who owned and farmed his own land.

T-51: 66 years old; reared in the village of Hsiang-ts'un, Tach'eng-hsien, Hopeh Province. He helped his father farm the land until the age of 20, when he left home to join the Nationalist army. After twenty-five years in the army he retired as a lieutenant colonel.

His father was a peasant who farmed his own land.

T-52: 72 years old when interviewed; raised in Fengyang-hsien, Anhwei Province. After graduating from a naval academy, he spent over twenty years in the Chinese navy. He participated in the 1911 revolution, and eventually became a staff officer in the Nationalist armed forces. He also served as a police official. He retired in 1965.

His father was a Ch'ing dynasty scholar (*chü-jen*), who operated a traditional style school for ten years and then opened a "western style" elementary school.

T-53: 57 years old; raised in Ch'angli-hsien, Hopeh Province. He served in the Nationalist army for seventeen years, then worked for five years as a secretary in a police department. He is now a missionary for the Protestant Church in Taiwan.

His father was a carpenter.

T-54: 55 years old at the time of interview; raised in the village of Tali-chuang, Kirin Province. He spent many years working on various railroads in North China as a dispatcher and in railroad administration. He then worked as an accountant in a friend's business for four years. He retired in 1959.

His father was a poor peasant who farmed his own land.

T-55: 83 years old; of a gentry family from a village in Ts'ailing-hsien, Hunan Province. He passed the imperial examinations to become a Ch'ing dynasty scholar (*hsiu-ts'ai*), and also graduated from the Facheng Academy in Ch'angsha, where he majored in law. After serving in the army, he spent the next eleven years at home at the request of his father. He later worked for three years as a secretary in the provincial government of Honan. He has been living in retirement since coming to Taiwan.

His father was a Ch'ing dynasty *chin-shih* scholar.

T-56: 63 years old; reared in Shant'ou (Swatow) City, Kwangtung Province. He spent some years in government service, as chief of the Financial Bureau of the Fukien provincial government and as a police official in Hsiamen (Amoy) City. He entered the import-export business in 1934. Since coming to Taiwan in 1947 he has been a teacher.

His father ran an import-export business.

H-1: 24 years old; from a wealthy family living in Shanghai. After high school he entered Hsiamen (Amoy) University to major in chemistry. After two years of study, upon the death of both parents, he went to Hong Kong. He is now working as a tailor's assistant.

His father was a chemical and electrical engineer who was trained at universities in the United States.

H-2: 30 years old when interviewed; from a former gentry family of the city of Foshan (Fatshan), Kwangtung Province. He received five years of architectural training at Chungshan University in Canton under the Communists, and worked in Canton for a time. He is now a draftsman with a Hong Kong architectural firm.

Both of the interviewee's grandfathers had been officials in the Ch'ing dynasty. His father was an officer in the Nationalist army who attained the rank of major.

H-3: 25 years old; reared in Hsiamen (Amoy) City, Fukien Province. After graduating from middle school he received two years of training in chemical engineering at the Chekiang Chemical Engineering School in Hangchow. After a serious illness he was unable to find work. He arrived in Hong Kong shortly before the interview.

His father was an accountant in a Hong Kong soy sauce factory.

H-4: 38 years old; raised in Shant'ou (Swatow) City, Kwangtung. During World War II he aided his parents in supplying information about Japanese forces to Chinese Communist guerrilla units. He served in the People's Liberation Army, fought in the Korean War, and later became a bodyguard for some of China's highest officials.

His father, who originally ran a boxing school in Shant'ou joined the Chinese Communist Party in the 1930s. Because of the father's activities against the Japanese, he was executed by them in 1942.

H-5: 23 years old; raised in Shanghai. He spent one year studying medicine under the Communists at the Second Medical School in Shanghai. He then came to Hong Kong.

His father, who had studied law in Japan, was at one time president of the Judicial Yuan in the Nationalists' Nanking government.

H-6: 23 years old at the time of interview; reared in Meilung-chen (population about 300), Haifeng-hsien, Kwangtung Province. After graduating from high school under the Communists he worked for one year as a farmer, then came to Hong Kong. At present he is an assistant in a library of classical Chinese materials.

His father was a school teacher and also a county level secretary for the Nationalist Party. He was executed by the Communists in 1951.

H-7: 49 years old; reared in the city of Yingk'ou, Liaoning Province. During World War II he joined the Nationalist army and rose to the rank of colonel. After the Communists gained control of the mainland he joined the People's Liberation Army and served as an instructor, teaching former guerrilla units the tactics of regular warfare. He came to live in Hong Kong in 1957 and now runs a small store.

His father ran a small shipping business along the North China coast, and later opened a jewelry store.

H-8: 25 years old; raised in the cities of Shant'ou (Swatow) and Nanking. He spent one year studying at the Nanking Theological Seminary. In 1958, as a result of having criticized the Communist government during the Hundred Flowers movement of the previous year he was sentenced to four years of labor reform. In 1961 he spent one year studying Chinese art at Nanking Normal University. He is now a student in Hong Kong.

His father was a Baptist missionary who spent sixteen years preaching in Singapore.

H-9: 31 years old; born and raised in Shanghai. He worked as a laborer in a nationalized Shanghai factory producing industrial stoves. He now is employed in a Hong Kong cotton mill as a machinery maintenance worker.

His father was a cook on an American-owned ship.

H-10: 25 years old; from a gentry family of Yangchiang-hsien, Kwangtung. He entered Shant'ou (Swatow) Normal University to study Chinese, but because of his athletic abilities became a prominent track star in China. He later became a track instructor in the Foshan (Fatshan) special district, Kwangtung Province. He also served eight years as a branch secretary in the Communist Youth League. He is now a student in Hong Kong.

His grandfather was a Ch'ing dynasty scholar (*hsiu-ts'ai*) and a man of some wealth. His father was an officer in the Nationalist army.

H-11: 23 years old at the time of interview; born in a market town in Shih-hsing-hsien, Kwangtung Province and moved to Canton City at the age of seven. After graduating from high school he spent one year studying Chinese medicine at the Canton Medical College. He then left China and is at present a student in Hong Kong.

His father was a medical doctor. The interviewee was reared by his mother, a nurse, after his father's death.

H-12: 39 years old; born and raised in the market town of Ch'eng-chen, Yu-hsien, Honan Province. During World War II he fought the Japanese in the Nationalist army. After returning home he eventually obtained a responsible position under the Communists in a local government office handling documents. In 1958 he took an administrative position with a local coal mine. Since coming to Hong Kong in 1961 he has worked as a laborer on construction crews.

His father had been in the Ch'ing dynasty military forces, and later worked at a relative's restaurant.

H-13: 25 years old; from a well-to-do business family of Amoy City, Fukien Province. He received two years of technical training at the Anhwei Mining College in Huainan City. After graduation he worked at the college for two years. He is now studying civil engineering in Hong Kong.

For many years his father operated private food companies. Under the Communists he became an adviser at a food products company.

H-14: 21 years old; reared in Hong Kong and in Suchow City, Kiangsu Province. After graduating from high school on the mainland he returned to Hong Kong. He is now studying civil engineering.

His father works in a thermos bottle factory in Hong Kong.

H-15: 20 years old when interviewed; born and raised in a well-to-do business family in Shanghai. In 1963 he began studying chemistry in Hong Kong.

His father, a graduate of St. John's University in Shanghai, was director of a Shanghai insurance company and later opened an import-export business.

H-16: 64 years old; from a poor peasant family in Liaoning Province. He left his home village at the age of 18 and later studied sociology for two years at Chungshan University in Hankow. He has since worked as a foreman in various factories.

His father farmed his own land. The respondent said he himself was the only member of his family who left home to work away from the family.

H-17: 21 years old; from a wealthy family of Tayung-hsien, Hunan Province. After the death of their father, the interviewee and his older brother moved to Canton where they were reared by an aunt. After graduating from high school he came to Hong Kong, where he works in a wine house.

His father was an officer in the Nationalist army and was executed by the Communists in 1951.

H-18: 22 years old; the older brother of H-17. After graduating from high school he failed to gain admittance to a university. He then worked as a farmer in Anhwei Province. At present he is working at a gas station in Hong Kong.

H-19: 22 years old; reared in Huan-hsien, Kwangtung. He graduated from high school and then worked as a farm laborer for a year. He is now studying civil engineering in Hong Kong.

His father was an officer in the Nationalist army who escaped to Hong Kong just before the Communists gained control of the mainland. He is currently a foreman with a heavy construction firm in Hong Kong.

H-20: 21 years old; from a rich and well-known family in Hsinhsing-hsien, Kwangtung Province. Because of his family's wealth and former association with the Nationalist government, the respondent and his family were under observation by the Communists after 1949. He was brought up in a family from another district of Kwangtung. After graduating from middle school he taught elementary school for a short time, then came to Hong Kong.

His grandfather participated in the 1911 revolution under Sun Yat-sen and was a military officer during China's warlord period. Because of the family's wealth, the respondent's father never had to work.

H-21: 23 years old at the time of interview; born and raised in Yang-chiang-hsien, Kwangtung. In 1960, after graduating from high school, he entered the Kwangtung Chiaot'ung Academy in Canton where he studied water conservancy and dam construction for two years. Since arriving in Hong Kong he has been studying social science topics at a private academy.

His father formerly was a printer for a Nationalist newspaper. He moved to Hong Kong in 1949 and has worked since as an electrical repairman for the British military.

H-22: 28 years old; of a poor family from Lingshan-hsien, Kwangtung. Two years after graduating from high school, in 1959, he entered the Kansu Province Railway Academy in Lanchou where he studied transportation. In 1960 he was unable to obtain food and was reduced to eating weeds and tree bark. He became sick and went to Canton, but was unable to support himself. He then worked as a farm laborer in Paoan-hsien, Kwangtung. In 1962 he came to Hong Kong and now works in a toy factory.

His father was an officer in the Nationalist army during World War II. After 1949 he was accused by the Communists of being a reactionary and spent two years in prison. Since his release he has worked as a factory laborer in China.

H-23: 21 years old; from a wealthy Shanghai family. After graduating from high school he tried unsuccessfully for three years to enter a university. Since coming to Hong Kong he has worked part time while studying chemistry at a local college.

His father had studied in the United States and became an airline pilot in China. After the Communists gained power he opened his own factory but later decided to come to Hong Kong, where he is manager of a factory.

H-24: 31 years old; from a wealthy Canton family. In 1950 he entered Peking Industrial University where he studied civil engineering for six years. He then began working for the Central Chemical Engineering Planning Bureau in a job that required travel to many parts of China. Accused in 1963 of being a rightist, he left his job and returned to Canton. He later came to Hong Kong.

His father was an overseas Chinese from Panama who came to study civil engineering in Canton. Shortly after marrying, the father returned to Panama. The respondent has never seen his father.

H-25: 21 years old at the time of interview; reared in a village in Haifeng-hsien, Kwangtung. He graduated from high school in 1961 but failed to pass the college entrance examinations. He came to Hong Kong in 1962 and is now studying the humanities at a local academy.

His father was a peasant who later worked as a school janitor.

H-26: 60 years old; raised in a peasant family from P'u-hsien, Shantung Province. After finishing primary school his father put him to work on the family farm. He left home at age 15 to become a soldier, and spent his adult life in the Nationalist military.

His father was a poor peasant.

H-27: 57 years old; from a wealthy landowning family of Hangchow City, Chekiang. He entered Chihchiang University in Hangchow to study literature, but because World War II was in progress left school to do political work for the Nationalist government. After the war he continued to work for the Nationalist Party. Before the Communists gained control of the mainland he escaped to Hong Kong, leaving his wife and children in China.

His father, a Ch'ing dynasty scholar (*chü-jen*), died when the respondent was six years old.

H-28: 20 years old; reared in Canton City. After graduating from high school he tried unsuccessfully for three years to enter a university. He then came to Hong Kong and is at present a student.

His father was a businessman in Hong Kong who occasionally visited the interviewee and his mother in Canton.

H-29: 75 years old; brought up in a wealthy land-owning family from Hengshan-hsien, Hunan Province. He graduated from Hunan University in Ch'angsha, where he studied law and government. He began working for the Nationalist government at the county level and eventually became a judge. He came to Hong Kong in 1949 and is now living alone.

His father was a high level county official during the last days of the Ch'ing dynasty.

H-30: 22 years old; from a wealthy family of Haifeng-hsien, Kwangtung. Because he had been classified by the Communists as coming from a landlord family, he was unable to gain admission to a university after graduating from high school. He came to Hong Kong in 1962 along with his mother and younger brother. He is now studying literature and history.

His father, who was a landlord, died when the interviewee was four.

H-31: 49 years old; born and raised in Ch'ingtao (Tsingtao) City, Shantung Province. After receiving an elementary education he became an apprentice in a metal fabricating shop. He later operated his own small plumbing and electrical repair shop and still runs such a business in Hong Kong.

His father ran a small business in Ch'ingtao, but after becoming addicted to opium he left home and moved to Dairen City, Liaoning Province, where he worked in a mine. He returned home after overcoming his addiction.

H-32: 76 years old when interviewed; from a land-owning family in P'ingchiang-hsien, Hunan Province. He was educated at home until the age of 17, when he entered the Hunan First Normal School in Ch'angsha (where he was a few classes ahead of Mao Tse-tung). After six years of study he returned home to become principal of a local school. He left home when the Communists came to power and went to Hong Kong.

His father was a landlord.

H-33: 69 years old; raised in Kanchou City, Kiangsi Province. He graduated from Wuhan Normal University, where he studied history. He participated in the Northern Expedition of 1927–28, and later did administrative work in the Nationalist government. He also taught school for a time.

His family had formerly been wealthy, but his father had both to farm and run a small business to provide for his dependents.

H-34: 51 years old; reared in Wuhu City, Anhwei Province. He studied economics at Futan University in Shanghai and graduated from Nanking's Chengchih University. During World War II he worked for the Nationalist government in Chungking. After the war he sold motor vehicles in Nanking. Since coming to Hong Kong in 1949 he has taught school.

His father had been in charge of a Nationalist government bureau concerned with strategic resources. He later opened a coal mine.

H-35: 54 years old; raised in Chinan City, Shantung Province. He never received a formal education. He left home in his teens and joined the warlord army of Wu P'ei-fu. He now operates a shoe repair stand in Hong Kong.

His father was a poor peasant.

Appendix VI

CHILDHOOD PUNISHMENTS AND
CHINESE SOCIAL VALUES

The pattern of punishments characteristic of a culture is an important indicator of social values, for the pain which parents purposefully inflict on their children reflects both their own social values and personal anxieties, and the areas of concern they develop in their children. As Talcott Parsons has observed, punishments and rewards in the childrearing process play a particularly important role in organizing a maturing personality.[1] Pleasure and pain as administered by parents establish an important link between the generations, providing continuity of value systems. Such sanctions and rewards also help to establish a (partial) congruence between the individual's personality system and the values of the culture and society he will enter when mature.

As is discussed in the first part of this study, our interview data indicate that expressions of aggression were the primary cause of parental punishment in Chinese society, revealing a pervasive concern with social conflict.[2] By way of contrast, the punishment pattern of American culture accepts (disciplined) aggressive behavior, while failures to be self-disciplining or to assume personal responsibility violate the American concern with developing self-reliance in children.[3]

The interview data suggest several variations in the way that parents of different socioeconomic status (S.E.S.) levels in Chinese society punish their children.[4] As the following table suggests, a child's failure to

1. Talcott Parsons, "Social Structure and the Development of Personality," *Psychiatry,* Vol. XXI (1958), pp. 321–340.
2. *See* pp. 67–73 above.
3. Comparative data is presented in the author's, "Mao's Effort to Reintegrate the Chinese Polity," in A. Doak Barnett, ed., *Chinese Communist Politics in Action,* p. 286.
4. Socioeconomic status differences were estimated for the interview sample on the basis of responses to questions 24a–i of the interview schedule. (*See* Appendix I, p. 528.) Because of missing data we were not able to develop a measure of S.E.S. for all respondents, which is why there is only a total sample of 62 in the table.

perform well in school was evidently the focus of parental anxieties in upper class families.

MAJOR CAUSE OF PARENTAL PUNISHMENT,
AS RECALLED IN ADULTHOOD

		Fighting	Doing poorly in school	Disobeying parental instructions	Being lazy	N
	Low	33% (5)	7% (1)	40% (6)	20% (3)	15
FAMILY	Medium	52% (12)	9% (2)	30% (7)	9% (2)	23
S.E.S.	High	29% (7)	38% (9)	25% (6)	8% (2)	24
	Total %	39% (24)	19% (12)	31% (19)	11% (7)	62

This distribution of responses indicates relatively constant parental concern with displays of aggression across lines of socioeconomic status, and slightly higher concern at lower S.E.S. levels with maintaining obedience and overcoming laziness. The low number of cases in several of these categories, however, makes the percentage differences of uncertain stability. It is in the area of performance in school that the major difference seems to lie.

Inasmuch as all these respondents had received at least some secondary-level education, the following interpretation seems justified: At lower S.E.S. levels students probably were highly conscious of the sacrifices parents were making for their education, and the family hopes which resided in their performance. They were probably highly motivated students, striving for the previously unattainable goals of economic security and social status that would come with educational achievement. Their parents, coming from lower social and literacy levels, probably had a certain sense of awe concerning the educational experience.

In well-to-do families, however, students grew up in surroundings where wealth and education were familiar attainments. They lacked that sense of urgency, both for their family and their personal security and status, which motivated students of lower S.E.S. levels. Their parents, however, well aware of the ease with which family fortune and status could be lost, pressured their children for performance in the one area where status and security could be *maintained*—successful scholarship. And as is corroborated by interview recollections of childhood, the educational process was a painful experience, apparently particularly so for the children of well-to-do families where parents and children did not share a common sense of urgency about successful scholarship.

A Glossary
of Chinese Terms and Phrases

amah 阿媽 — A female servant.

ch'eng 誠 — Sincerity; to act according to the obligations of one's social role and society's moral norms.

cheng-chih 政治 — Politics.

cheng-feng 整風 [整风]* — "Party rectification"; an abbreviated form of *cheng-tun tang ti tso-feng* (整頓黨的作風) [整顿党的作风], to rectify the Party's work style.

cheng-ming 正名 — To rectify names. The Confucian concept that if people acted according to the moral obligations of their social status or "name" then society would be well ordered and secure. A ruler was to "rectify names" by clearly defining ·what was proper or improper behavior for each social status, and by making a model of his own actions for others in authority to emulate.

ch'i 氣 [气] — Anger; hostile or aggressive feelings. (See *p'i-ch'i.*)

chi-chi fen-tzu 積極份子 [积极分子] — An activist; one who is motivated to promote Party policy.

chi-hsü ko-ming 繼續革命 [继续革命] — Continuous revolution. A Maoist alternative to Trotsky's heretical theory of "Permanent revolution" (trans. as *pu-tuan ko-ming* 不斷革命 [不断革命]).

* The character forms in brackets are the simplified characters now in common use in the People's Republic of China.

chiang jen-ch'ing 講人情 [讲人情]	To speak on behalf of another; to intercede for a friend in difficulty, invoking one's status or personal associations to help solve his problem.
chiao-k'u 叫苦	To pour or shout out one's grievances.
chieh 潔 [洁]	Chastity.
chieh-fang 解放 [解放]	Liberation, as from an oppressive political order. To liberate, to let go or to release, as to release hostile feelings that have been denied expression by being "put in the stomach."
chieh-pan jen 接班人	Revolutionary successors.
Ch'ien-hsien 前綫 [前线]	*Front Line.* Theoretical magazine of the CCP's Peking Municipal Party Committee.
chih-an hao 治安好	Good peace and order.
ch'ih-k'u 吃苦	To "eat bitterness," to put frustration or hostility "in one's stomach" rather than express such socially improper feelings.
ch'ih-k'uei 吃虧 [吃亏]	To "eat a loss," to suffer some failure or to be mistreated by a more powerful individual.
chin-shih 進士 [进士]	An advanced degree conferred by the imperial examination system (lit. "advanced scholar"). Roughly equivalent to the doctor's degree in the West.
chiu-jou p'eng-yu 酒肉朋友	A "wine and meat friend," a friend who leads one astray into sensual indulgence.
chiu-se p'eng-yu 酒色朋友	A "wine and women friend," a friend who leads one astray into sensual indulgence.
ch'ü-chang 區長 [区长]	A district chief.
chü-jen 舉人 [举人]	An advanced degree conferred by the imperial examination system

(lit. "an elevated man"). Roughly equivalent to a master's degree in the West.

ch'ün-chung lu-hsien 群衆路綫 [群众路线]
The Mass Line, the Maoist leadership concept that the Party should stimulate active popular participation in discussing and applying policies.

chün-tzu 君子
The Confucian concept of a morally cultivated "superior man."

chung 忠
Loyalty, the Confucian concept of personal commitment to one's superior as required by the virtue of filial piety.

Chung-kuo Ch'ing-nien 中國青年 [中国青年]
China Youth, the magazine of the CCP's Youth Corps.

ch'ung-tung 衝動[冲动]
To be impulsive or assertive, implying lack of proper reserve or control of aggressive feelings.

ch'ung-yi-hsia 衝一下 [冲一下]
To shock or startle; to dash against, as to throw cold water against someone or something.

chung-yung 中庸
The Confucian concept of the "Middle Way," implying lack of extremism or aggressiveness in personal behavior.

fa-fen t'u-ch'iang 發奮圖強 [发奋图强]
To draw strength from anger.

fan-kan 反感
Bad feelings, resentment.

fan tso-wu 犯错誤 [犯错误]
To commit an error; in CCP parlance, to make a political mistake.

fang 放
To release, to let go, implying an easing of control. (See *chieh-fang.*)

fen-san 分散
To scatter or disperse, in political terms implying the breakdown of an organization's unity, as in Sun Yat-sen's lament during the early years of the Republic that the Chinese nation was just "a sheet of

scattered sand" (*yi-p'an sha-tzu* 一盤沙子 [一盘沙子]).

fen-sui 粉碎

To disintegrate, to fragment; in political parlance implying the disintegration of the cohesiveness of an organization or coalition.

feng-shui 風水 [风水]

The geomantic forces of the natural environment. If one adjusts one's behavior to these forces they can provide assistance, while to violate them is to bring on trouble.

fu-mu kuan 父母官

"Father-mother officials." An informal designation for local magistrates during the imperial era.

fu-tza 複雜 [复杂]

To be complicated, as of a social relationship. The term implies tension or clashing interests which might lead to open conflict.

han-hsü 含蓄

To be reserved. The opposite of impulsiveness. (See *ch'ung-tung*).

ho-ch'i 和氣 [和气]

To be affable, considerate.

ho-p'ing 和平

Harmony, peace, the absence of social conflict. The opposite of *hun-luan*.

ho-tso 合作

To cooperate.

hsia-fang 下放

To "transfer downward," as to transfer administrative cadres "down" to the countryside to engage in physical labor.

hsiang 鄉 [乡]

The township level of political organization in China.

hsiang-chang 鄉長 [乡长]

A township's chief administrative official.

hsiang-yüeh 鄉約 [乡约]

Lectures on Confucianism delivered to the common people by imperial scholar officials. The title of the local official in charge of such lectures.

hsiao 孝

The Confucian virtue of filial piety.

hsiao-chi ti-k'ang 消極抵抗 [消极抵抗] — Passive resistance.

Hsiao Ching 孝經 [孝经] — *The Classic of Filial Piety.*

hsien 縣 [县] — The county level of administrative organization in China.

hsien-chang 縣長 [县长] — The chief administrative official of a county.

hsiu-t'sai 秀才 — A popular term for holders of the lowest scholarly degree conferred by the imperial examination system (lit., "cultivated talent"). Roughly equivalent to a bachelor's degree in the West. (See *sheng-yüan*.)

hsiu-yang 修養 [修养] — The Confucian concept of moral self-cultivation through study.

hsüeh 學 [学] — To study, with the implication of emulating the object of one's attention, as to "study" a person in order to learn his good points and imitate them.

Hsüeh-hsi 學習 [学习] — *Study,* the theoretical journal of the CCP from 1949 to 1958. At the time of the Great Leap Forward it was superseded by *Hung Ch'i* (紅旗), *Red Flag.*

hua-ch'iao 華僑 [华侨] — An "overseas Chinese," one who has migrated to a country beyond China.

hun-luan 混亂 [混乱] — Confusion, chaos, a breakdown in social order implying conflict and the unrestrained release of aggression.

hun-luan chuang-t'ai, 混亂狀態 [混乱状态] *or hun-luan hsien-hsiang* 混亂現象 [混乱现象] — Chaotic (social) conditions, implying a breakdown of authority and unrestrained conflict.

je-nao 熱鬧 [热闹] — To be bustling, busy, as of an environment; a positive term implying a warm and active group atmosphere, giving the individual a sense of security.

jen 仁

The Confucian virtue of human-heartedness, compassion, a lack of selfishness. A subordinate hopes that *jen* will mitigate the harshness of authority and give him security in job and material amenities.

jen-ch'ing 人情

Human feelings, the emotional sensitivities involved in one's social relations and obligations to others. (See *chiang jen-ch'ing*.)

jen-k'ou 人口

Population (lit. "human mouths").

jen-min kung-she 人民公社

People's Commune.

jen-t'sai 人才

Men of talent and ability, a concept that reflects the personalized image of political authority in the Confucian tradition.

ju-chia 儒家

The Chinese term for the Confucian school of political philosophy.

kan 敢

To dare, to challenge the existing order of things.

kan-ch'ing 感情

Emotions, feelings, particularly as they enter into one's relationship with another person. It can be said, "I have good *kan-ch'ing* with that man," implying that he will be sympathetic and provide both emotional and material support.

k'ang 坑

A clay sleeping platform used in North China. A fire can be built under it to provide warmth during the winter months.

kao-luan 攪亂 [搅乱]

To make trouble, to stir up confusion. (See *hun-luan*.)

k'o-ch'i 客氣 [客气]

To be polite, mannerly, implying lack of aggressiveness or quarrelsome behavior.

k'o-ch'i-hua 客氣話 [客气话]

Polite or mannerly talk.

ko-ko 哥哥	An elder brother.
k'ou-t'ou 叩頭 [叩头]	To kneel and knock one's head on the floor before a person in authority as an expression of filial submission and loyalty.
ku-li 孤立	To isolate.
ku-li ti 孤立的	To be isolated, implying either to be surrounded and exposed to group hostility, or to be rejected and cut off from group support.
kuei 鬼	Ghost, spirit, implying something grotesque, as in the Cultural Revolution phrase used to ridicule Party "revisionists," *niu-kuei she-shen* (牛鬼蛇神) "freaks and monsters" (lit. "ox ghosts and snake spirits").
kung-she 公社	Commune, as in the Paris Commune of 1871. (See also *jen-min kung-she*.)
li 禮 [礼]	The Confucian concept of social ritual used to express deference to those in authority and acceptance of one's social obligations.
li-chang 里長 [里长]	The chief official of a *li*, an administrative subdivision of approximately 100 households used to collect revenue for the central political authorities.
li-mao 禮貌 [礼貌]	Good manners, etiquette, propriety in one's social relations.
luan 亂 [乱]	Confusion, chaos, implying conflict and unrestrained release of aggression. (See *hun-luan*.)
luan-sha, luan-ta 亂殺 亂打 [乱杀 乱打]	To beat and kill indiscriminately.
luan-tzu 亂子 [乱子]	A disturbance; disorder.
luan-tzu kuan 亂子觀 [乱子观]	The Maoist "Concept of Chaos," expressed during the Cultural Revolution, which held that the

	disturbances and confusion caused by the Red Guards would be a positive test of the revolutionary commitment of Party cadres.
Lun Kung-ch'an-tang Yüan ti Hsiu-yang 論共產黨員的修養 [论共产党员的 修养]	*On the Cultivation of a Communist Party Member;* also translated as *How to Be a Good Communist.* Written in 1939 by Liu Shao-ch'i, Vice Chairman of the CCP, in the form of three lectures delivered to Party cadres. First published as a book in 1949. Revised versions, published in 1962 and 1964, were attacked by Maoists during the Cultural Revolution as being Confucian in spirit and for playing down the importance of class struggle.
ma 罵 [骂]	To scold, criticize, or curse.
ma-an-hsing 馬鞍形 [马鞍形]	Horse-saddle shaped, "U-shaped."
ma-chieh 罵街 [骂街]	To "curse the street," to air one's grievances in public so as to expose to public ridicule the individual who caused one difficulties.
mao-tun 矛盾	Contradiction, in Maoist usage implying conflicting economic interests and/or personal grievances and resentment toward an individual or group.
mei-yu pan-fa 没有辦法 [没有办法]	"There is nothing that can be done" (about a situation). A popular expression implying lack of personal ability to deal with a problem or to influence a (more powerful) individual.
mi-ch'ieh kuan-hsi 密切關係 [密切关系]	To have intimate relations (with someone or a group), implying involvement in their affairs as a way of either assisting or controlling them.

ming-che pao-shen 明哲保身   "An enlightened man protects himself."

mou 畝 [亩]   A measure of land area. One acre equals 6.6 *mou*.

Nan-fang Jih-pao 南方日報 [南方日报]   *The Southern Daily.* The press organ of the Kwangtung Province Party Committee, published in Canton since 1949.

nei-chan 內戰 [内战]   Civil war.

ni-ai 溺愛 [溺爱]   To spoil a child with too much love; lit. "to drown with love."

pao-chia 保甲   A form of village political organization used in the imperial era to establish dynastic control at the lowest levels of society through group responsibility for individual misdeeds. One hundred households were organized into *chia* units, with ten *chia* comprising a *pao*.

p'ei-yang 培養 [培养]   To rear or nurture, as a child.

p'i-ch'i 脾氣 [脾气]   Temperament. An irascible individual would be said to be *p'i-ch'i pu-hao* (脾氣不好).

pi-tzu pang-mang 彼此幫忙 [彼此帮忙]   To render mutual assistance; reciprocal support.

p'o-szu li-kung 破私立公   "Destroy selfishness, establish the collective spirit." A Maoist slogan propagated during the Cultural Revolution when factional conflict among Red Guards threatened to undermine all political discipline.

san-ho yi-shao 三和一少   "Three reconciliations and one reduction." A foreign policy line which Maoists attacked during the Cultural Revolution as having been formulated by "revisionist" Party leaders in the early 1960s. It called for reconciliation rather than struggle with Soviet "revisionism," U.S. "imperialism," and all foreign "reactionaries," and reduction of aid to "revolutionary" insurgency movements.

san-tzu yi-pao 三自一包

"The three privates and the one guarantee." An economic policy line attacked by the Maoists during the Cultural Revolution. It was said to have been formulated by "revisionist" Party leaders in the early 1960s, during the period of recovery from the Great Leap Forward. It advocated extension of the peasants' private plots, private enterprise, and the free market system, while guaranteeing the peasants that grain production targets would be fixed at the household level of planning.

sheng-yüan 生員 [生员]

The first level imperial examination degree, which qualified the recipient as a candidate for the higher degrees of *chü-jen* and *chin-shih*. Roughly equivalent to a bachelor's degree in the West. (See also *hsiu-ts'ai*.)

shih-chieh ta-t'ung 世界大同

The Confucian concept of a human utopia, a world commonwealth or universal society without political divisions, conflict, or material insecurity. (See *ta-t'ung*.)

Shih-k'an 詩刊 [诗刊]

Poetry. A magazine published in Peking since 1957.

shou 收

To restrict or restrain, as to restrict criticism.

shu-shu 叔叔

Paternal uncle, i.e., father's younger brother.

su-fan 肅反 [肃反]

"Liquidation of Counterrevolutionaries." The short form of *Su-ch'ing fan-ko-ming fen-tzu* 肅清反革命份子 [肃清反革命分子]. A political campaign of 1955 by which the Party sought to eliminate "counterrevolutionaries" in governmental organizations. (Not to be confused with the *chen-fan* 鎮反 [镇反] or *chen-ya fan-ko-ming fen-tzu* 鎮壓反革命份子 [镇压反革命分子] ["Suppression of Counterrevolutionaries"] movement of 1951.

su-k'u 訴苦 [诉苦] — To speak bitterness, to express one's resentment at personal mistreatment or social injustice.

sui-pien 隨便 [随便] — To do as one pleases.

szu-chiu 四舊 [四旧] — "The four olds," a Cultural Revolution slogan by which the Maoists called for criticism of China's "old customs, habits, culture, and social thought" as they continued to be manifest in the behavior of Party cadres and the population.

szu-hsiang 思想 — Thought, in the sense of relatively formal or systematic ideas about something based on personal experience. A term used in common parlance in the sense of "ideology," *yi-shih hsing-t'ai* 意識形態 [意识形态].

szu-hsiang hun-luan 思想混亂 [思想混乱] — Ideological confusion.

szu-hsiang kai-tsao 思想改造 — Ideological remolding, or thought reform.

szu-shu 私塾 — A traditional Confucian home-school which educated children in the classical literature.

Ta Kung Pao 大公報 [大公报] — A newspaper published in Shanghai before Liberation which since 1949 has been published in Peking. It specializes in economic news.

ta-t'ung 大同 — "The great togetherness," a concept that in popular usage implies social unity, security, lack of divisive conflict, and no distinctions of hierarchy, wealth, or loyalty that would divide people. In Confucian thinking, an idealized state of society in which there is universal brotherhood, mutual assistance, and tranquillity.

ta-tzu-pao 大字報 [大字报]] Big character posters.

tan-shih 但是

However. An adverb used in political discourse to link two clauses of a sentence expressing conflicting policy positions. The clause modified by the "however" usually contains the speaker's criticism of "some comrades," his preferred policy alternative, or a refutation of the argument contained in the first clause.

ti-ti 弟弟

A younger brother.

ti-tui ti 敵對的 [敌对的]

Hostile, antagonistic, as of a relationship or a political contradiction.

t'ien-ming 天命

The Mandate of Heaven. The Confucian political doctrine that a ruler's right to legitimate power is based upon heaven's will, as expressed through popular confidence in the justice of his rule.

t'ing-hua 聽話 [听话]

To obey; lit. "to listen to talk."

t'o-li ch'ün-chung 脫離群衆 [脫离群众]

To be cut off from the masses. A ruling group's alienation from popular support because of bureaucratic procedures and/or unpopular policies.

tou-luan 鬥亂 [斗乱]

To "struggle to confusion." To promote political criticism without limit, producing organizational fragmentation.

tso-feng 作風 [作风]

Work style, as of a Party cadre's manner of applying policy and dealing with the masses.

tsung-tzu 宗族 — A clan.

t'u k'u-shui 吐苦水 — To "vomit bitter water." A phrase used to describe the release of hostility in "speak bitterness" meetings. (See *su-k'u*.)

t'uan-chieh 團結 [团结] — To unite, to consolidate, as an organization.

tui-k'ang 對抗 [对抗] — An antagonism.

tui-pu-ch'i 對不起 [对不起] — To be embarrassed or ashamed; lit., to be unable to face someone (because of a sense of shame).

tung-luan ti 動亂的 [动乱的] — To be confused, chaotic. (See *luan*.)

tzu-chu 自主 — Autonomy, self-direction in behavior.

tzu-li keng-sheng 自力更生 — Self-reliance; regeneration through one's own efforts.

tzu-szu 自私 — To be selfish; selfishness.

tzu-yu-chu-yi 自由主義 [自由主义] — Liberalism; lit., self-ism. (See *tzu-szu*, selfishness.)

wa-chieh 瓦解 [瓦解] — To fragment, to disintegrate, as a political organization or coalition.

wang-pa-tan 王八蛋 — A bastard.

Wen Hui Pao 文匯報 [文汇报] — A paper published since before Liberation in Shanghai. It specializes in intellectual affairs.

wen-nuan 溫暖 — To be warm, nurturing.

wu-fan 五反 — "The Five Antis." A political campaign of 1952 used to gain control of commerce and industry by attacking the "five poisons" of bribery, tax evasion, theft of state property, cheating on government contracts, and stealing of state economic information by members of the business community.

wu-lun 五倫 [五伦] — The five cardinal social relationships—prince and minister, father and son, elder and younger brother, husband and wife, friend and friend—which according to the Confucian conception of society would sustain order and security if each member of the relationship would act according to the obligations of his status.

yamen 衙門 [衙门]

A government office.

yen 嚴 [严]

To be strict, stern.

yi-hsiao-ts'o 一小撮

"A small handful," as of a political faction, implying lack of strength and isolation from popular support.

yi-shen-tso-tse 以身作則

To make a model or example of one's own behavior for others to emulate. Said especially of those in authority, as a ruler, teacher, or father.

yün-tung 運動 [运动]

A political campaign or mass movement.

Selected Bibliography

I. PERSONALITY FORMATION, SOCIALIZATION, AND SOCIAL CHANGE: GENERAL WORKS

Adelson, Joseph, and Robert O'Neil. "Growth of Political Ideas in Adolescence: The Sense of Community," *Journal of Personality and Social Psychology,* Vol. IV (1966), pp. 295–306.

Adorno, T. W., *et al. The Authoritarian Personality* (New York: Harper, 1950).

Almond, Gabriel. "Comparative Political Systems," *Journal of Politics,* Vol. XVIII, No. 3 (August 1956), pp. 391–409.

———, and Sidney Verba. *The Civic Culture: Political Attitudes and Democracy in Five Nations* (Princeton, N.J.: Princeton University Press, 1963).

Atkinson, John W., ed. *Motives in Fantasy, Action and Society* (Princeton: Van Nostrand, 1958).

Atlas (New York: 1961–   ).

Bandura, Albert, and Richard H. Walters. *Social Learning and Personality Development* (New York: Holt, Rinehart and Winston, 1963).

Berkowitz, Leonard. *Aggression: A Social Psychological Analysis* (New York: McGraw-Hill, 1962).

Christie, Richard, and Marie Jahoda, eds. *Studies in the Scope and Method of "The Authoritarian Personality"* (Glencoe, Ill.: The Free Press, 1954).

Coser, Lewis A. *The Functions of Social Conflict* (Glencoe, Ill.: The Free Press, 1956).

Dawson, Richard E., and Kenneth Prewitt. *Political Socialization* (Boston: Little, Brown, 1969).

Erikson, Erik H. *Childhood and Society* (New York: Norton, 1950).

———. "Ego Development and Historical Change," *Psychoanalytic Study of the Child,* Vol. II (1946), pp. 359–396.

———. *Young Man Luther* (New York: Norton, 1958).

Fenichel, Otto. *The Psychoanalytic Theory of Neurosis* (New York: Norton, 1945).

Gerth, Hans H., and C. Wright Mills. *From Max Weber: Essays in Sociology* (New York: Oxford University Press, Galaxy, 1958).

Goode, William J. *World Revolutions and Family Patterns* (New York: Free Press, 1963).

575

Greenstein, Fred I. *Children and Politics* (New Haven: Yale University Press, 1965).

————, et al. "Personality and Politics: Theoretical and Methodological Issues," *Journal of Social Issues*, Vol. XXIV, No. 3 (July 1968).

Hagen, Everett E. *On the Theory of Social Change: How Economic Growth Begins* (Homewood, Ill.: Dorsey Press, 1962).

Hsu, Francis L. K. *Psychological Anthropology* (Homewood, Ill.: Dorsey Press, 1961).

Klopfer, Bruno, et al. *Developments in the Rorschach Technique* (2 vols., Yonkers-on-Hudson, New York: World Book Company, 1954–1956).

Kluckhohn, Clyde, and Henry A. Murray, eds. *Personality in Nature, Society, and Culture* (New York: Knopf, 1956).

Leites, Nathan. "Psycho-Cultural Hypotheses about Political Acts," *World Politics*, Vol. I (1948), pp. 102–119.

Lerner, Daniel J. *The Passing of Traditional Society* (Glencoe, Ill.: The Free Press, 1958).

Levenson, Daniel J., and Alex Inkeles. "National Character: The Study of Modal Personality and Socio-Cultural Systems," in Gardner Lindzey, ed., *Handbook of Social Psychology* (Cambridge, Mass.: Addison-Wesley, 1954), pp. 997–1020.

Lorenz, Konrad. *On Aggression* (New York: Harcourt, Brace, and World, 1966).

McClelland, David C. *The Achieving Society* (Princeton, N.J.: Van Nostrand, 1961).

Mead, Margaret, and Martha Wolfenstein, eds. *Childhood in Contemporary Cultures* (Chicago: University of Chicago Press, 1955).

————. *Soviet Attitudes toward Authority* (New York: McGraw-Hill, 1951).

————, and Rhoda Metraux. *The Study of Culture at a Distance* (Chicago: University of Chicago Press, 1953).

Montagu, M. F. Ashley, ed. *Man and Aggression* (New York: Oxford University Press, 1968).

Moore, Barrington. *Social Origins of Dictatorship and Democracy* (Boston: Beacon, 1967).

Murray, Henry A., et al. *Explorations in Personality* (New York: Oxford University Press, 1938).

Nieburg, H. L. "The Threat of Violence and Social Change," *American Political Science Review*, Vol. XVI, No. 4 (December 1962), pp. 865–873.

Parsons, Talcott. "Social Structure and the Development of Personality: Freud's Contribution to the Integration of Psychology and Sociology," *Psychiatry*, Vol. XXI, No. 4 (September 1958), pp. 321–340.

————, and Winston White. "The Link Between Character and Society," in S. M. Lipset and Leo Lowenthal, eds., *Culture and Social Character* (Glencoe, Ill.: The Free Press, 1961).

Pye, Lucian W. *Aspects of Political Development* (Boston: Little, Brown, 1966).

————. *Politics, Personality, and Nation Building: Burma's Search for Identity* (New Haven, Conn.: Yale University Press, 1962).

————, and Sidney Verba. *Political Culture and Political Development* (Princeton, N.J.: Princeton University Press, 1965).

Redfield, Robert. *Peasant Society and Culture: An Anthropological Approach to Civilization* (Chicago: University of Chicago Press, 1956).

Sears, Robert, *et al.* "Some Child-Rearing Antecedents of Aggression and Dependency in Young Children," *Genetic Psychology Monographs,* Vol. XLVII (1953), pp. 135–234.

Storr, Anthony. *Human Aggression* (New York: Atheneum, 1968).

Whiting, John W. M., and Irvin L. Child. *Child Training and Personality: A Cross-Cultural Study* (New Haven, Conn.: Yale University Press, 1953).

Wolf, Eric R. *Peasants* (Englewood Cliffs, N.J.: Prentice-Hall, 1966).

Wolfenstein, Martha. "Some Variants in the Moral Training of Children," in *Psychoanalytic Study of the Child,* Vol. V (1949), pp. 310–328.

II. CHINESE CULTURE AND SOCIAL RELATIONS

Balazs, Etienne. *Chinese Civilization and Bureaucracy,* trans. H. M. Wright, ed. Arthur F. Wright (New Haven, Conn.: Yale University Press, 1964).

The Book of Filial Duty, trans. Ivan Chen (New York: Dutton, 1909).

Bunzel, Ruth. *Explorations in Chinese Culture* (mimeographed; Columbia University, Research in Contemporary Cultures, 1950).

————, and John H. Weakland. *An Anthropological Approach to Chinese Communism* (mimeographed; Columbia University, Research in Contemporary Cultures, 1952).

Chai Ch'u. "Chinese Humanism: A Study of Chinese Mentality and Temperament," *Social Research,* Vol. XXVI (1959), pp. 31–46.

Chiang Yee. *A Chinese Childhood* (New York: John Day, 1952).

The Chinese Classics, trans. James Legge (5 vols., Shanghai: 1935).

Chow Chang-cheng. *The Lotus Pool* (New York: Appleton-Century-Crofts, 1961).

Crow, Carl. *The Chinese Are Like That* (New York: Harper, 1939).

Dai, Bingham. "Personality Problems in Chinese Culture," *American Sociological Review,* Vol. VI (1941), pp. 688–696.

de Bary, William Theodore, ed. *Sources of Chinese Tradition* (New York: Columbia University Press, 1960).

Fairbank, John K. *Chinese Thought and Institutions* (Chicago: University of Chicago Press, 1957).

————, Edwin O. Reischauer, and Albert M. Craig. *A History of East Asian Civilization:* Vol. II, *East Asia–The Modern Transformation* (Boston: Houghton Mifflin, 1965).

Feng, Han-yi. "The Chinese Kinship System," *Harvard Journal of Asiatic Studies,* Vol. II, No. 2 (July 1937), pp. 141–275.

Feuerwerker, Albert, Rhoads Murphey, and Mary C. Wright, eds. *Ap-

proaches to Modern Chinese History (Berkeley: University of California Press, 1967).

—————. *China's Early Industrialization* (Cambridge, Mass.: Harvard University Press, 1958).

Fortune, Robert. *Three Years' Wanderings in the Northern Provinces of China* (London: John Murray, 1847).

Fried, Morton H. *Fabric of Chinese Society* (New York: Praeger, 1953).

Friedman, Maurice, ed. *Family and Kinship in Chinese Society* (Stanford, Calif.: Stanford University Press, 1970).

Headland, Isaac Taylor. *Home Life in China* (London: Methuen, 1914).

Ho Ping-ti. *The Ladder of Success in Imperial China* (New York: John Wiley, Science Editions, 1964).

Hsiao Ching [Classic of Filial Piety], trans. James Legge, in Max F. Müller, ed., *Sacred Books of the East* (50 vols., Oxford, England: Clarendon Press, 1879–1910), Vol. III.

Hsu, Francis L. K. *Americans and Chinese: Two Ways of Life* (New York: Henry Schuman, 1953).

—————. "Suppression Versus Repression," *Psychiatry,* Vol. XII (1949), pp. 223–242.

Hsu Hsien-chin. "The Chinese Concepts of 'Face'," *American Anthropologist,* Vol. XLVI (January–March 1944), pp. 45–65.

Isaacs, Harold R. *Scratches on Our Minds: American Images of China and India* (New York: John Day, 1958).

Kleinberg, Otto. "Emotional Expression in Chinese Literature," *Journal of Abnormal and Social Psychology,* Vol. XXXIII (1938), pp. 517–520.

LaBarre, Weston. "Some Observations on Character Structure in the Orient: II, The Chinese," *Psychiatry,* Vol. IX (1946), pp. 215–237, 375–395.

Lang, Olga. *Pa Chin and His Writings: Chinese Youth between the Two Revolutions* (Cambridge, Mass.: Harvard University Press, 1967).

Levenson, Joseph R. *Confucian China and Its Modern Fate: The Problem of Monarchical Decay* (Berkeley: University of California Press, 1964).

Levy, Howard S. *Chinese Footbinding: The History of a Curious Erotic Custom* (New York: Walton Rawls, 1966).

Levy, Marion J., Jr. *The Family Revolution in Modern China* (New York: Octagon Books, 1963).

Lin Mousheng Hsi-tien. "Confucius on Inter-personal Relations," *Psychiatry,* Vol. II (1939), pp. 475–481.

Lin Tsung-yi. "Tai-pau and Liu-mang: Two Types of Delinquent Youths in Chinese Society," *British Journal of Delinquency,* Vol. VIII, No. 4 (April 1958), pp. 244–256.

Muensterberger, Warner. "Orality and Dependence: Characteristics of

Southern Chinese," *Psychoanalysis and the Social Sciences,* Vol. III (1951), pp. 37–69.

Müller, Max F., ed. *Sacred Books of the East* (50 vols., Oxford, England: Clarendon Press, 1879–1910).

Nivison, David S., and Arthur F. Wright, eds. *Confucianism in Action* (Stanford, Calif.: Stanford University Press, 1959).

Pruitt, Ida. *A Daughter of Han: The Autobiography of a Chinese Working Woman* (Stanford, Calif.: Stanford University Press, 1967).

Reischauer, Edwin O., and John K. Fairbank. *A History of East Asian Civilization:* Vol. I, *East Asia—The Great Tradition* (Boston: Houghton Mifflin, 1960).

Scofield, Robert W., and Sun Chin-wan. "A Comparative Study of the Differential Effect upon Personality of Chinese and American Child Training Practices," *Journal of Social Psychology,* Vol. LII (1960), pp. 221–224.

Scott, A. C. *An Introduction to the Chinese Theater* (Singapore: Donald Moore, 1958).

Smith, Arthur H. *Chinese Characteristics* (New York: Fleming Revell, 1894).

————. *Village Life in China* (New York: Fleming Revell, 1899).

Ward, Barbara E. "Temper Tantrums in Kau Sai: Some Speculations upon Their Effects" (mimeographed; prepared for a seminar on "Personality and Motivation in Chinese Society," Castle Harbour Hotel, Bermuda, January 26–28, 1964).

Weakland, John H. "Orality in Chinese Conceptions of Male Genital Sexuality," *Psychiatry,* Vol. XIX (1956), pp. 237–247.

————. "The Organization of Action in Chinese Society," *Psychiatry,* Vol. XIII (1950), pp. 361–370.

Wilson, Richard W. *Childhood Political Socialization on Taiwan* (unpublished Ph.D. dissertation, Princeton University, 1967).

————. *Learning to Be Chinese: The Political Socialization of Children in Taiwan* (Cambridge, Mass.: M.I.T. Press, 1970).

Wolf, Margery. "Child Training in a Hokkien Village" (mimeographed; a paper prepared for a seminar on "Personality and Motivation in Chinese Society," Castle Harbour Hotel, Bermuda, January 26–28, 1964).

————. *The House of Lim: A Study of a Chinese Farm Family* (New York: Appleton-Century-Crofts, 1968).

Wright, Arthur F., ed. *The Confucian Persuasion* (Stanford, Calif.: Stanford University Press, 1960).

————. "Struggle *vs.* Harmony: Symbols of Competing Values in Modern China," *World Politics,* Vol. VI, No. 1 (October 1953), pp. 31–44.

————, ed. *Studies in Chinese Thought* (Chicago: University of Chicago Press, 1953).

Wright, Mary C. *The Last Stand of Chinese Conservatism: The T'ung Chih Restoration, 1862–1874* (New York: Atheneum, 1966).

Yang, C. K. *Chinese Communist Society: The Family and the Village* (Cambridge, Mass.: M.I.T. Press, 1965).

Yang, Lien-sheng. "Female Rulers in Imperial China," *Harvard Journal of Asiatic Studies,* Vol. XXIII (1960–1961), pp. 47–61.

Yang, Martin C. *A Chinese Village: Taitou, Shantung Province* (New York: Columbia University Press, 1945).

III. CHINESE POLITICS

The Agrarian Reform Law of the People's Republic of China (Peking: Foreign Languages Press, 1959).

Asian Survey (Berkeley, California: 1961–   ).

Barnett, A. Doak, with a contribution by Ezra Vogel. *Cadres, Bureaucracy and Political Power in Communist China* (New York: Columbia University Press, 1967).

————, ed. *Chinese Communist Politics in Action* (Seattle: University of Washington Press, 1969).

Baum, Richard, and Frederick C. Teiwes. "Liu Shao-ch'i and the Cadre Question," *Asian Survey,* Vol. VIII, No. 4(April 1968), pp. 323–345.

————. *Ssu-Ch'ing: The Socialist Education Movement of 1962–1966* (Berkeley: Center for Chinese Studies, University of California Research Monograph No. 2, 1968).

Belden, Jack. *China Shakes the World* (New York: Harper and Brothers, 1949).

Borkenau, Franz. "Getting at the Facts behind the Soviet Façade," *Commentary,* Vol. XVII, No. 4 (April 1954), pp. 393–400.

Brandt, Conrad. *Stalin's Failure in China, 1924–1927* (New York: Norton, 1966).

————, Benjamin Schwartz, and John K. Fairbank. *A Documentary History of Chinese Communism* (New York: Atheneum, 1966).

Bridgham, Philip. "Mao's Cultural Revolution: Origins and Development," *The China Quarterly,* No. 29 (January–March 1967), pp. 1–35.

The Case of P'eng Teh-huai: 1959–1968 (Hong Kong: Union Research Institute, 1968).

CCP Documents of the Great Proletarian Cultural Revolution, 1966–1967 (Hong Kong: Union Research Institute, 1968).

Chang, Parris H. *Patterns and Processes of Policy Making in Communist China, 1955–1962* (unpublished Ph.D. dissertation, Columbia University, 1969).

Charles, David A. "The Dismissal of P'eng Teh-huai," *The China Quarterly,* No. 8 (October–December 1961), pp. 63–76.

Ch'en, Jerome. *Mao and the Chinese Revolution* (London: Oxford University Press, 1965).

————, ed. *Mao* (Englewood Cliffs, N.J.: Prentice-Hall, 1969).

Ch'en Po-ta. *Notes on Ten Years of Civil War, 1927–1936* (Peking: Foreign Languages Press, 1954).

Chen, S. C., ed. *Rural People's Communes in Lien-Chiang* (Stanford, Calif.: Hoover Institution Press, 1969).

Cheng, J. Chester, ed. *The Politics of the Chinese Red Army: A Translation of the Bulletin of Activities of the People's Liberation Army* (Stanford, Calif.: The Hoover Institution, 1966).

Ch'ien Tuan-sheng. *The Government and Politics of China* (Cambridge, Mass.: Harvard University Press, 1961).

China Monthly [Tzu-kuo Yueh-K'an] (Hong Kong: 1965–   ).

China Pictorial (Peking: 1951–   ).

The China Quarterly (London, 1960–   ).

China Reconstructs (Peking, 1952–   ).

Chinese Law and Government (White Plains, N.Y., 1968–   ).

Chung-hua Jen-min Kung-ho-kuo Fa-lü Hui-pien [Legal Compendium of the People's Republic of China] (Peking: Legal Publishing House, 1957).

Chung Hua-min, and Arthur C. Miller. *Madame Mao: A Profile of Chiang Ch'ing* (Hong Kong: Union Research Institute, 1968).

Cohen, Jerome Alan. "Chinese Mediation on the Eve of Modernization," *California Law Review,* Vol. LIV, No. 2 (August 1966), pp. 1201–1226.

Communist China, 1955–1959: Policy Documents with Analysis (Cambridge, Mass.: Harvard University Press, 1962).

Compton, Boyd, ed. *Mao's China: Party Reform Documents, 1942–1944* (Seattle: University of Washington Press, 1952).

Cranmer-Byng, John L. *Lord Macartney's Embassy to Peking in 1793 from Official Chinese Documents* (Hong Kong: University of Hong Kong Press, 1961).

Current Background (Hong Kong: United States Consulate General, 1950–   ).

Current Scene (Hong Kong: United States Information Service, 1961–   ).

Donnithorne, Audrey. *China's Economic System* (London: George Allen and Unwin, 1967).

Doolin, Dennis J. *Communist China: The Politics of Student Opposition* (Stanford, Calif.: The Hoover Institution, 1964).

Eckstein, Alexander. *Communist China's Economic Growth and Foreign Trade* (New York: McGraw-Hill, 1966).

————. "Economic Fluctuations in Communist China's Domestic Development," in Ping-ti Ho and Tang Tsou, eds., *China in Crisis,* Vol. I, Book 2, pp. 691–729.

————. "Economic Planning, Organization and Control in Communist China: A Review Article," *Current Scene,* Vol. IV, No. 21 (November 25, 1966).

Eighth National Congress of the Communist Party of China (3 vols., Peking: Foreign Languages Press, 1956).

Eto, Shinkichi. "Hai-lu-feng—The First Chinese Soviet Government," *The China Quarterly,* Nos. 8, 9 (October–December 1961; January–March 1962), pp. 161–183, 149–181.

Extracts from China Mainland Magazines (Hong Kong: United States Consulate General, 1955–1960).

Fanon, Frantz. *The Wretched of the Earth* (New York: Evergreen, 1968).

Garthoff, Raymond L., ed. *Sino-Soviet Military Relations* (New York: Praeger, 1966).

George, Alexander. *The Chinese Communist Army in Action* (New York: Columbia University Press, 1967).

Gillin, Donald G. "Peasant Nationalism in the History of Chinese Communism," *Journal of Asian Studies,* Vol. XXIII, No. 2 (February 1964), pp. 269–289.

Gittings, John. *The Role of the Chinese Army* (London: Oxford University Press, 1967).

Goldman, Merle. *Literary Dissent in Communist China* (Cambridge, Mass.: Harvard University Press, 1967).

————. "The Unique 'Blooming and Contending' of 1961–62," *The China Quarterly,* No. 37 (January–March 1969), pp. 54–83.

Griffith, William E. *Communist Esoteric Communications: Explication de Texte* (Cambridge, Mass.: M.I.T. Center for International Studies, 1967).

————. *Sino-Soviet Relations, 1964–1965* (Cambridge, Mass.: M.I.T. Press, 1967).

————. *The Sino-Soviet Rift* (Cambridge, Mass.: M.I.T. Press, 1964).

Harding, Harry, and Melvin Gurtov. *The Purge of Lo Jui-ch'ing: The Politics of Chinese Strategic Planning* (Santa Monica, Calif.: The Rand Corporation, 1970).

Harrison, James P. "The Li Li-san Line and the CCP in 1930, Part I," *The China Quarterly,* No. 14 (April–June 1963), pp. 178–194.

Hinton, William. *Fanshen: A Documentary of Revolution in a Chinese Village* (New York: Monthly Review Press, 1966).

Ho, Ping-ti and Tang Tsou, eds. *China in Crisis:* Vol. I, *China's Heritage and the Communist Political System* (2 vols., Chicago: University of Chicago Press, 1968).

Hofheinz, Roy Mark. *The Peasant Movement and Rural Revolution: Chinese Communists in the Countryside, 1923–1927* (unpublished Ph.D. dissertation, Harvard University, 1966).

Hsia, T. A. "Ch'ü Ch'iu-pai's Autobiographical Writings: The Making and Destruction of a 'Tender-hearted' Communist," *The China Quarterly,* No. 25 (January–March 1966), pp. 176–212.

Hsiao Kung-chuan. *Rural China: Imperial Control in the Nineteenth Century* (Seattle: University of Washington Press, 1960).

Hsieh, Alice Langley. *Communist China's Strategy in the Nuclear Era* (Englewood Cliffs, N.J.: Prentice-Hall, 1962).

Hsin Ch'ing-nien [New Youth] (Peking: 1915–1926).

Hsin-hua Pan-yüeh-k'an [New China Semi-Monthly] (Peking: 1956–   ).

Hsu, Kai-yu. *Chou En-lai: China's Gray Eminence* (Garden City, New York: Doubleday, 1968).

Hsüeh-hsi [Study] (Peking: 1949–1958).

Hu Chiao-mu. *Thirty Years of the Communist Party of China* (Peking: Foreign Languages Press, 1951).

Hung-ch'i [Red Flag] (Peking: 1958–   ).

Inkeles, Alex, and Raymond A. Bauer. *The Soviet Citizen* (Cambridge, Mass.: Harvard University Press, 1959).

Isaacs, Harold R. *The Tragedy of the Chinese Revolution* (New York: Atheneum, 1966).

Jen-min Jih-pao [The People's Daily] (Peking: 1948–   ).

Joffe, Ellis. "The Chinese Army on the Eve of the Cultural Revolution: Prelude to Intervention" (a paper prepared for a conference on "Government in China: The Management of a Revolutionary Society" held in Cuernavaca, Mexico, August 1969).

————. *Party and Army: Professionalism and Political Control in the Chinese Officer Corps, 1949–1964* (Cambridge, Mass.: Harvard University, East Asian Monographs, 1965).

Johnson, Chalmers A. "Lin Piao's Army and Its Role in Chinese Society," *Current Scene*, Vol. IV, No. 14 (July 14, 1966).

————. *Peasant Nationalism and Communist Power: The Emergence of Revolutionary China, 1937–1945* (London: Oxford University Press, 1963).

Joint Publications Research Service, Translations on Communist China (Washington, D.C.: 1960–   ).

Journal of Asian Studies (Ann Arbor: 1956–   ).

Klochko, Mikhail A. *Soviet Scientist in Red China* (New York: Praeger, 1964).

Lee, Rensselaer W. "The *Hsia Fang* System: Marxism and Modernization," *The China Quarterly*, No. 28 (October–December 1966), pp. 40–62.

Leites, Nathan. "Panic and Defenses against Panic in the Bolshevik View of Politics," *Psychoanalysis and the Social Sciences*, Vol. IV (1955), pp. 135–144.

————. *A Study of Bolshevism* (Glencoe, Ill.: The Free Press, 1953).

Lewis, John Wilson. *Leadership in Communist China* (Ithaca, New York: Cornell University Press, 1963).

Li Choh-ming, "The First Decade: Economic Development," *The China Quarterly*, No. 1 (January–March 1960), pp. 35–50.

Li Tsung-jen. *The Reminiscences of General Li Tsung-jen* (unpublished manuscript of the Columbia University East Asian Institute, Chinese Oral History Project, n.d.).

Lifton, Robert Jay. *Revolutionary Immortality: Mao Tse-tung and the Chinese Cultural Revolution* (New York: Random House, 1968).

————. "Thought Reform of Chinese Intellectuals: A Psychiatric Evaluation," *Journal of Social Issues*, Vol. XIII (1957), pp. 5–20.

————. *Thought Reform and the Psychology of Totalism* (New York: Norton, 1963).

Liu, F. F. *A Military History of Modern China* (Princeton, N.J.: Princeton University Press, 1956).

Liu Shao-chi. *Collected Works of Liu Shao-chi* (3 vols., Hong Kong: Union Research Institute, 1969).

Loh, Robert, and Humphrey Evans. *Escape from Red China* (New York: Coward McCann, 1962).

London, Kurt, ed. *Unity and Contradiction* (New York: Praeger, 1962).

Lu Hsün. *Selected Works of Lu Hsün* (3 vols., Peking: Foreign Languages Press, 1956).

MacFarquhar, Roderick. "Communist China's Intra-Party Dispute," *Pacific Affairs,* Vol. XXXI, No. 4 (December 1958), pp. 323–335.

————. *The Hundred Flowers Campaign and the Chinese Intellectuals* (New York: Praeger, 1960).

Malraux, André. *Anti-Memoirs* (New York: Holt, Rinehart and Winston, 1968).

Mao Chu-hsi tui P'eng, Huang, Chang, Chou Fan-tang Chi-t'uan ti P'i-p'an [Chairman Mao's Criticism and Repudiation of the P'eng (Teh-huai), Huang (K'o-ch'eng), Chang (Wen-t'ien), and Chou (Hsiao-chou) Anti-Party Clique] (n.p., n.d.). This pamphlet has been translated in *Chinese Law and Government,* Vol. I, No. 4 (Winter 1968/69).

Mao Tse-tung Hsüan-chi [The Selected Works of Mao Tse-tung] (4 vols., Peking: People's Publishing House, 1960–1964).*

Mao Tse-tung. "Chairman Mao's Selected Writings," *Joint Publications Research Service, Translations on Communist China,* No. 90 (February 12, 1970).

————. *Poems of Mao Tse-tung,* trans. Wong Man (Hong Kong: Eastern Horizon Press, 1966).

————. *Selected Readings from the Works of Mao Tse-tung* (Peking: Foreign Languages Press, 1967).

————. *Selected Works of Mao Tse-tung* (4 vols., Peking: Foreign Languages Press, 1961–1965).*

————, ed. *Socialist Upsurge in China's Countryside* (Peking: Foreign Languages Press, 1957).

* In Parts Three and Four of this study we make numerous citations from official political statements by Mao Tse-tung. Most of these citations have been drawn from Mao's *Selected Works.* We have relied upon two versions of this collection of political statements. The first one, in Chinese, was published between 1960 and 1964 by the *Jen-min Ch'u-pan She* (The People's Publishing House) in Peking in an edition of four volumes. The English language version of the *Selected Works,* published in four matching volumes, was released by the Foreign Languages Press in Peking between 1961 and 1965.

Our general procedure in using these materials has been to compare the English translation of a passage with the Chinese "original" (an edited "original" of the first versions of these statements in some cases), and to cite the English translation where no significant alterations in meaning or tone were found. Where the official translation seems to obscure an important point, we have made a direct translation from the Chinese edition. The language of the version used in any particular citation is indicated in the footnote.

————. *Ten More Poems of Mao Tse-tung* (Hong Kong: Eastern Horizon Press, 1967).

Mao Tse-tung Szu-hsiang Wan-sui! [Long Live the Thought of Mao Tse-tung!] (n.p.: April 1967). This pamphlet has been translated, along with an untitled collection of Mao Tse-tung's speeches and statements from the years 1956–1967, in *Current Background* (Hong Kong: United States Consulate General), Nos. 891, 892 (October 1969).

Marsh, Robert M. *The Mandarins: The Circulation of Elites in China, 1600–1900* (Glencoe, Ill.: The Free Press, 1961).

Meisner, Maurice. *Li Ta-chao and the Origins of Chinese Marxism* (Cambridge, Mass.: Harvard University Press, 1967).

Meskill, Jonathan, ed. *The Pattern of Chinese History: Cycles, Development, or Stagnation?* (Boston: Heath, 1965).

Munro, Donald J. *The Concept of Man in Early China* (Stanford, Calif.: Stanford University Press, 1968).

————. "Maxims and Realities in China's Educational Policy: The Half-Work, Half-Study Model," *Asian Survey*, Vol. VII, No. 4 (April 1967), pp. 254–272.

Myrdal, Jan. *Report from a Chinese Village* (London: Heinemann, 1965).

Nan-fang Jih-pao [Southern Daily] (Canton: 1949–   ).

Neuhauser, Charles. "The Chinese Communist Party in the 1960s: Prelude to the Cultural Revolution," *The China Quarterly*, No. 32 (October–December 1967), pp. 3–36.

New Youth [*Hsin Ch'ing-nien*] (Peking: 1915–1926).

North, Robert C. *Kuomintang and Chinese Communist Elites* (Stanford, Calif.: Hoover Institution, 1952).

Oksenberg, Michel Charles. "Occupational Groups in Chinese Society and the Cultural Revolution," in *The Cultural Revolution: 1967 in Review* (Ann Arbor: University of Michigan Center for Chinese Studies, Papers in Chinese Studies No. 2, 1968).

————. *Policy Formulation in Communist China: The Case of the Mass Irrigation Campaign, 1957–58* (unpublished Ph.D. dissertation, Columbia University, 1969).

Payne, Robert. *Mao Tse-tung, Ruler of Red China* (New York: Henry Schuman, 1950).

Peking Review (Peking: 1958–   ).

Polemic on the General Line of the International Communist Movement (Peking: Foreign Languages Press, 1965).

The People's Daily [*Jen-min Jih-pao*] (Peking: 1948–   ).

Problems of Communism (Washington, D.C.: United States Information Agency, 1951–   ).

Pye, Lucian W. *The Dynamics of Hostility and Hate in the Chinese Political Culture* (mimeographed; Cambridge, Mass.: Center for International Studies, M.I.T., 1964).

————. *The Spirit of Chinese Politics: A Psychocultural Study of the Authority Crisis in Political Development* (Cambridge, Mass.: M.I.T. Press, 1968).

Red Flag [*Hung-ch'i*] (Peking: 1958–   ).

Rush, Myron. *The Rise of Khrushchev* (Washington, D.C.: Public Affairs Press, 1958).

Schein, Edgar H., *et al. Coercive Persuasion* (New York: W. W. Norton, 1961).

Schram, Stuart. *Mao Tse-tung* (Baltimore, Md.: Penguin Books, 1967).

———. "Mao Tse-tung and Secret Societies," *The China Quarterly*, No. 27 (July–September 1966), pp. 1–13.

———. *The Political Thought of Mao Tse-tung* (New York: Praeger, 1963).

Schurmann, Franz. *Ideology and Organization in Communist China* (Berkeley: University of California Press, 1968).

Schwartz, Benjamin I. *Chinese Communism and the Rise of Mao* (Cambridge, Mass.: Harvard University Press, 1964).

Selden, Mark. "The Guerilla Movement in Northwest China: The Origins of the Shensi-Kansu-Ningsia Border Region," *The China Quarterly*, Nos. 28, 29 (October–December 1966; January–March 1967), pp. 63–81, 61–81.

Selections from China Mainland Magazines (Hong Kong: United States Consulate General, 1960–   ).

Sharman, Lyon. *Sun Yat-sen: His Life and Its Meaning* (Stanford, Calif.: Stanford University Press, 1968).

Sheridan, James E. *Chinese Warlord: The Career of Feng Yü-hsiang* (Stanford, Calif.: Stanford University Press, 1966).

Siao, Emi. *Mao Tse-tung, His Childhood and Youth* (Bombay: People's Publishing House, 1955).

Siao Yü. *Mao Tse-tung and I Were Beggars* (London: Hutchinson, 1961).

Simmonds, J. D. "P'eng Teh-huai: A Chronological Re-examination," *The China Quarterly*, No. 37 (January–March 1969), pp. 120–138.

Skinner, G. William, and Edwin A. Winckler. "Compliance and Succession in Rural China: A Cyclical Theory," in Amitai Etzioni, ed., *Complex Organizations: A Sociological Reader* (New York: Holt, Rinehart and Winston, 1969).

———. "Marketing and Social Structure in Rural China, Part III," *Journal of Asian Studies*, Vol. XXIV, No. 3 (May 1965), pp. 363–399).

Smedley, Agnes. *The Great Road: The Life and Times of Chu Teh* (New York: Monthly Review Press, 1956).

Snow, Edgar. "Interview with Mao," *The New Republic* (February 27, 1965), pp. 23–27.

———. *Red Star Over China* (New York: Grove Press, Black Cat Edition, 1961).

Solomon, Richard. "America's Revolutionary Alliance with Communist China: Parochialism and Paradox in Sino-American Relations," *Asian Survey*, Vol. VII, No. 12 (December 1967), pp. 831–850.

———. *The Chinese Political Culture and Problems of Modernization* (mimeographed; Cambridge, Mass.: Center for International Studies, M.I.T., 1964).

———. *The Chinese Revolution and the Politics of Dependency* (unpublished Ph.D. dissertation, M.I.T., 1966).

———. "Communication Patterns and the Chinese Revolution," *The China Quarterly,* No. 32 (October–December 1967), pp. 88–110.

———. "Mao's Effort to Reintegrate the Chinese Polity: Problems of Conflict and Authority in Chinese Social Processes," in A. Doak Barnett, ed., *Chinese Communist Politics in Action* (Seattle: University of Washington Press, 1968), pp. 271–361.

———. "On Activism and Activists: Maoist Conceptions of Motivation and Political Role Linking State to Society," *The China Quarterly,* No. 39 (July–September 1969), pp. 76–114.

Southern Daily [Nan-fang Jih-pao] (Canton: 1949–   ).

Strong, Anna Louise. *Letters from China* (Peking: New World Press, 1963–1970).

Study [Hsüeh-hsi] (Peking: 1949–1958).

Sun Tzu. *The Art of War,* trans. Samuel B. Griffith (Oxford, England: Oxford University Press, 1963).

Survey of the China Mainland Press (Hong Kong: United States Consulate General, 1950–   ).

Ta-tao Tang-nei Tsui-ta ti Tsou Tzu-pen-chu-yi Tao-lu Tang-ch'uan-p'ai –Liu Shao-ch'i [Strike Down the Biggest Person in Authority Taking the Capitalist Road–Liu Shao-ch'i] (Peking: Peking Chemical Engineering Institute, Mao Tse-tung's Thought Propaganda Personnel, April 10, 1967), Vol. IV.

Teiwes, Frederick C. *Provincial Party Personnel in Mainland China, 1956–1966* (New York: Columbia University, East Asian Institute, 1967).

———. "The Purge of Provincial Leaders, 1957–1958," *The China Quarterly,* No. 27 (July–September 1966), pp. 14–32.

———. *Rectification Campaigns and Purges in Communist China* (unpublished Ph.D. dissertation, Columbia University, 1970).

Ten Great Years: Statistics of the Economic and Cultural Achievements of the People's Republic of China (Peking: Foreign Languages Press, 1960).

Ti-yi-t'zu Kuo-nei Ko-ming Chan-cheng Shih-ch'i ti Nung-min Yün-tung [The Peasant Movement During the First Period of Domestic Revolutionary War] (Peking: People's Publishing House, 1953).

Townsend, James R. *Political Participation in Communist China* (Berkeley: University of California Press, 1967).

Tsou, Tang, ed. *China in Crisis:* Vol. II, *China, The United States, and Asia* (Chicago: University of Chicago Press, 1968).

Tung Chi-ping, and Humphrey Evans. *The Thought Revolution* (New York: Coward McCann, 1966).

Tzu-kuo Yueh-k'an [China Monthly] (Hong Kong: 1965–   ).

Union Research Service (Hong Kong: 1955–   ).

Van Slyke, Lyman P. *Enemies and Friends: The United Front in Chinese Communist History* (Stanford, Calif.: Stanford University Press, 1967).

Vogel, Ezra F. *Canton under Communism: Programs and Politics in a Provincial Capital, 1949–1968* (Cambridge, Mass.: Harvard University Press, 1969).

Waley, Arthur. *The Opium War through Chinese Eyes* (London: George Allen and Unwin, 1958).

Walker, Kenneth R. "Collectivization in Retrospect: The 'Socialist High Tide' of Autumn 1955–Spring 1956," *The China Quarterly*, No. 26 (April–June 1966), pp. 1–43.

―――. *Planning in Chinese Agriculture: Socialization and the Private Sector, 1956–1962* (Chicago: Aldine Publishing Co., 1965).

Weakland, John. "Family Imagery in a Passage by Mao Tse-tung," *World Politics*, Vol. X (1958), pp. 387–407.

Whitson, William W., with Huang Chen-hsia. *The Chinese Communist High Command: A History of Military Politics, 1927–1969* (New York: Praeger, 1971).

Who's Who in Communist China (2 vols., Hong Kong: Union Research Institute, 1969–1970).

Whyte, Martin K. *Small Groups and Political Rituals in Communist China* (unpublished Ph.D. dissertation, Harvard University, 1970).

Wright, Mary C. "From Revolution to Restoration: The Transformation of Kuomintang Ideology," *Far Eastern Quarterly*, Vol. XIV, No. 4 (1955), pp. 515–532.

Zagoria, Donald S. *The Sino-Soviet Conflict, 1956–1961* (Princeton, N.J.: Princeton University Press, 1962).

―――. *Viet-Nam Triangle* (New York: Pegasus, 1967).

INDEX

Acheson, Dean, 161

Activist (*chi-chi fen-tzu*), activism, 561
emerges from the younger generation, 193, 525
as a political mobilizer, 198–200
as sign of subordination, 57
See also Mao Tse-tung: Political Attitudes, on activism

"Adventurism," 184–185

Aggression, emotions of
cause illness, 64n
childhood disciplining of, 67–70, 79, 559–560
controlled through ritual, 68, 79–80, 110, 124
expressed only to inferiors, 69, 79
and organizational unity, 238–239
overcome anxiety, 194–196
as political motivation, 6, 73n, 194–196, 204, 363, 364, 393, 439, 444, 499, 513–514, 522–523
and social change, 514, 522–523
suppression of, 70–73, 101, 559–560
turned against the self, 176, 192
See also: Eating, as aggression; Emotions

Agriculture, and economic development, 333ff.

Agricultural Producers' Cooperatives (APCs), 327, 334, 340, 348–349
amalgamated to form People's Communes, 327, 340, 358n, 360
transition from "primary stage" to "advanced stage," 353, 354–356, 357, 366

All-China Federation of Literary and Artistic Circles, 414, 450

All Men Are Brothers, 124

American culture, compared with Chinese, 4, 11, 40n, 67n, 118–120, 123, 125n, 138n, 559; *see also* Western culture, compared with Chinese

An Tzu-wen, Director CCP Organization Dept.

attacked in the Cultural Revolution, 448
disagrees with Mao on training successors, 462–463

Authority
ambivalence toward, 4, 60, 71, 104, 135, 150, 234, 501
anxiety in the face of, 5–6, 52, 57–58, 86, 112–116, 147, 192, 522
depersonalized, 179, 188, 257, 506
of group, 257
not to be criticized, 114–115, 316, 421–422
not internalized, 152, 517
personalized, 138, 144, 151
and security, 74–75, 104, 133–134, 139
sustained through deference rituals, 108
See also: Confucianism, filial piety; Communications, interpersonal

Autonomy, 52, 69, 86, 252, 522
as "selfishness," 4–5, 80, 254, 516

Balazs, Etienne, 116

Barnett, A. Doak, xviii

Bauer, Elizabeth K., xviii

Berris, Jan, xviii

Big character posters (*ta-tzu-pao*), 343–344, 490, 491, 498, 516, 572

"Blooming and contending." *See* Hundred Flowers Campaign

Bolshevik ["October"] Revolution (1917), 253
fortieth anniversary celebration of, 327, 379

Bureaucratic behavior, 116n, 120n, 148
Mao's opposition to, 173, 208–209, 263, 287, 292–293, 338–339, 342

Burmese culture, compared with Chinese, 51n

Calligraphy, 91n, 111

Campaigns (*yün-tung*), 256, 574; *see also:* Great Leap Forward; Hundred Flowers Campaign; Socialist Education Movement